ALSO BY DOUGLAS WALLER

*Disciples: The World War II Missions of the CIA
Directors Who Fought for Wild Bill Donovan*

*Wild Bill Donovan: The Spymaster Who Created the
OSS and Modern American Espionage*

*A Question of Loyalty: Gen. Billy Mitchell and the
Court-Martial That Gripped the Nation*

Big Red: The Three-Month Voyage of a Trident Nuclear Submarine

Air Warriors: The Inside Story of the Making of a Navy Pilot

The Commandos: The Inside Story of America's Secret Soldiers

THEIR

SECRET WAR

TO SAVE

A NATION

LINCOLN'S SPIES

DOUGLAS WALLER

SIMON & SCHUSTER

NEW YORK   LONDON   TORONTO   SYDNEY   NEW DELHI

Simon & Schuster
1230 Avenue of the Americas
New York, NY 10020

Copyright © 2019 by Douglas Waller

All rights reserved, including the right to reproduce this book or portions
thereof in any form whatsoever. For information, address Simon & Schuster Subsidiary
Rights Department, 1230 Avenue of the Americas, New York, NY 10020.

First Simon & Schuster hardcover edition August 2019

SIMON & SCHUSTER and colophon are registered
trademarks of Simon & Schuster, Inc.

For information about special discounts for bulk purchases,
please contact Simon & Schuster Special Sales at
1-866-506-1949 or business@simonandschuster.com.

The Simon & Schuster Speakers Bureau can bring authors to your live event.
For more information or to book an event, contact the Simon & Schuster Speakers
Bureau at 1-866-248-3049 or visit our website at www.simonspeakers.com.

Interior design by Ruth Lee-Mui
Maps by Paul J. Pugliese

Manufactured in the United States of America

10 9 8 7 6 5 4 3 2 1

Library of Congress Cataloging-in-Publication Data has been applied for.

ISBN 978-1-5011-2684-0
ISBN 978-1-5011-2687-1 (ebook)

To Cameron and Eva

CONTENTS

1861

1862

CAST OF CHARACTERS

Main Characters in Bold

UNION AGENTS

John Babcock. First hired by Allan Pinkerton, he became George Sharpe's top spy.

Joseph Stannard Baker. A cousin who worked for Lafayette Baker as an agent.

Lafayette Baker. A special provost marshal under War Secretary Edwin Stanton, he ran a secret service operation in Washington.

Luther Byron Baker. A cousin who worked for Lafayette Baker as an agent.

George Bangs. Chief of staff in the Pinkerton detective agency.

Charles Carter. A member of Elizabeth Van Lew's Union spy ring in Richmond.

Milton Cline. A spy in George Sharpe's Bureau of Military Information.

Everton Conger. An agent of Lafayette Baker's, who helped capture John Wilkes Booth.

Abby Green. An operative in Elizabeth Van Lew's Richmond spy ring.

Hattie Lawton. A Pinkerton agency employee, she worked undercover with Timothy Webster posing as his wife.

Pryce Lewis. A Welshman who spied for Pinkerton in Virginia.

Frederick Lohmann. A pro-Union operative in Elizabeth Van Lew's Richmond spy ring.

Joseph Maddox. A Union spy George Sharpe placed in Richmond.

John McEntee. Third-ranking spy in George Sharpe's Bureau of Military Information.

Allan Pinkerton. Head of a Chicago detective agency, he served as General George McClellan's intelligence chief.

Mary Richards (later Mary Bowser). One of Elizabeth Van Lew's African American servants who spied for her.

William Rowley. A pro-Union operative in Elizabeth Van Lew's Richmond spy ring.

Samuel Ruth. Superintendent of the Richmond, Fredericksburg and Potomac Railroad and spy for the Union.

John Scully. Pryce Lewis's partner on his trip to Richmond to find Timothy Webster.

George Sharpe. As head of the Bureau of Military Information, he served as intelligence chief for Generals Hooker, Meade, and Grant.

Isaac Silver. A spy in George Sharpe's Bureau of Military Information.

John Howard Skinker. A spy in George Sharpe's Bureau of Military Information.

Eliza Van Lew. Elizabeth Van Lew's mother.

Elizabeth Van Lew. The daughter of a wealthy merchant, she ran the Union spy ring in Richmond.

John Newton Van Lew. Elizabeth Van Lew's brother.

Kate Warne. The first female detective to work for Pinkerton's detective agency.

Timothy Webster. A detective from the Pinkerton agency, he was a top spy for Pinkerton when he served as McClellan's intelligence chief.

UNION OFFICIALS AND MILITARY LEADERS

Montgomery Blair. Lincoln's postmaster general.

Ambrose Burnside. Succeeded George McClellan as commander of the Army of the Potomac.

Benjamin Butler. The first Union general to receive intelligence from Elizabeth Van Lew.

Daniel Butterfield. Chief of staff for the Union's Army of the Potomac.

Salmon P. Chase. Lincoln's Treasury secretary.

Ulric Dahlgren. A Union cavalry officer killed in a raid on Richmond.

Edward Doherty. Led the cavalry detachment that helped capture John Wilkes Booth.

Ulysses S. Grant. A Union commander in the Western Theater who became general in chief of the Army.

Henry Halleck. First general in chief of the Union Army and later chief of staff under Ulysses S. Grant.

John Hay. A White House aide during the Lincoln administration.

Joseph "Fighting Joe" Hooker. Succeeded Ambrose Burnside as commander of the Union's Army of the Potomac.

Andrew Johnson. Lincoln's second vice president, who succeeded him after the assassination.

Abraham Lincoln. President of the United States.

Thaddeus Lowe. Head of the U.S. Army Balloon Corps.

George McClellan. The Union commander of the Army of the Potomac and general in chief.

Irvin McDowell. The general who commanded Union troops at the first Battle of Bull Run.

James McPhail. Union provost marshal in Baltimore.

George Meade. Succeeded Joseph Hooker as commander of the Union's Army of the Potomac.

John Nicolay. A White House aide during the Lincoln administration.

Marsena Patrick. Provost marshal general of the Union's Army of the Potomac.

Alfred Pleasonton. Union cavalry commander in the Army of the Potomac.

John Pope. The Union commander at the second Battle of Bull Run.

Winfield Scott. Commanding general of the Army when Lincoln became president.

William Seward. Lincoln's secretary of state.

Edwin Stanton. Lincoln's second war secretary.

Levi Turner. An Army major and special judge advocate.

Gideon Welles. Lincoln's Navy secretary.

William Wood. Superintendent of Old Capitol Prison.

CONFEDERATE AGENTS AND CONSPIRATORS

John Wilkes Booth. Lincoln's assassin.

Belle Boyd. Confederate spy supplying intelligence to Stonewall Jackson.

Rose O'Neal Greenhow. Ran a Confederate spy ring in Washington.

David Herold. One of the conspirators in the Lincoln assassination plot.

Thomas Jordan. A Confederate officer who oversaw Rose O'Neal Greenhow's spying in Washington.

CONFEDERATE OFFICIALS AND MILITARY LEADERS

Pierre G. T. Beauregard. Confederate general who commanded forces at Charleston for the attack on Fort Sumter, at the first Battle of Bull Run, and at Petersburg.

Jefferson Davis. President of the Confederate States of America.

Jubal Early. A Rebel division leader and then corps commander under Robert E. Lee.

Richard Ewell. One of Robert E. Lee's corps commanders.

A. P. Hill. One of Robert E. Lee's corps commanders.

Thomas "Stonewall" Jackson. One of Robert E. Lee's corps commanders, who died from wounds suffered at the Battle of Chancellorsville.

Joseph Johnston. Rebel general who commanded troops at the first Battle of Bull Run and was replaced by Robert E. Lee after being wounded at the Battle of Seven Pines.

Robert E. Lee. Commander of the Confederate Army of Northern Virginia.

James Longstreet. A Confederate corps commander under Lee.

George Pickett. A Confederate division commander under Lee.

James Ewell Brown "Jeb" Stuart. Robert E. Lee's cavalry commander.

John Winder. Confederate provost marshal general for Richmond.

THE WIVES

Jennie Baker. Lafayette Baker's wife.

Varina Davis. Jefferson Davis's wife.

Mary Lincoln. First lady.

Joan Pinkerton. Allan Pinkerton's wife.

Caroline "Carrie" Sharpe. George Sharpe's wife.

Mary Carter Van Lew. John Van Lew's wife and Elizabeth Van Lew's sister-in-law.

TIME LINE OF MAJOR EVENTS

February 23, 1861: Allan Pinkerton sneaks Abraham Lincoln through Baltimore

March 4, 1861: Lincoln's inauguration

April 13, 1861: Union surrender of Fort Sumter

May 1861: Pinkerton becomes George McClellan's spymaster

July 1861: Lafayette Baker begins spying for the Union and Elizabeth Van Lew begins helping Federal prisoners in Richmond

July 21, 1861: First Battle of Bull Run

July 26, 1861: McClellan arrives in Washington to take command of what became the Army of the Potomac

August 23, 1861: Pinkerton arrests Rebel spy Rose O'Neal Greenhow

October 1861: Timothy Webster begins spying in Richmond for Pinkerton

March–July, 1862: Peninsula campaign

April 29, 1862: Confederates execute Webster in Richmond for spying

July 11, 1862: Henry Halleck becomes general in chief of the Union Army

August 28–30, 1862: Second Battle of Bull Run

September 17, 1862: Battle of Antietam

November 1862: Ambrose Burnside replaces McClellan as commander of the Army of the Potomac and Pinkerton leaves with McClellan

December 11–15, 1862: Battle of Fredericksburg

January 26, 1863: Joseph Hooker replaces Burnside as commander of the Army of the Potomac

February 1863: George Sharpe becomes Hooker's spymaster, leading the Bureau of Military Information

April 30–May 6, 1863: Battle of Chancellorsville

June 28, 1863: George Meade replaces Hooker as commander of the Army of the Potomac

July 1–3, 1863: Battle of Gettysburg

January 1864: Van Lew and her spy ring begin working for Union general Benjamin Butler

February 28–March 2, 1864: Union general Hugh Judson Kilpatrick's failed raid on Richmond

March 9, 1864: Ulysses S. Grant given command of all the Union armies

May–June 1864: Overland Campaign

June 1864: Sharpe assumes oversight of Van Lew's Richmond spy operation

June 1864–April 1865: Richmond-Petersburg Campaign

November 8, 1864: Lincoln reelected to a second term

March 4, 1865: Lincoln's second inauguration

April 2, 1865: The Confederate government evacuates Richmond

April 3, 1865: Union troops occupy Richmond and Petersburg

April 9, 1865: Lee surrenders at Appomattox Court House

April 14, 1865: John Wilkes Booth assassinates Lincoln

April 26, 1865: Booth killed and his accomplice David Herold captured when Baker detectives and a cavalry detachment raid Garrett farm

July 3, 1868: Scorned in Washington, Baker dies in Philadelphia

July 1, 1884: Wealthy from his Chicago detective agency, Pinkerton dies

January 13, 1900: A prominent lawyer and public official postwar, Sharpe dies

September 25, 1900: Richmond's postmaster for a time after the war, Van Lew dies destitute.

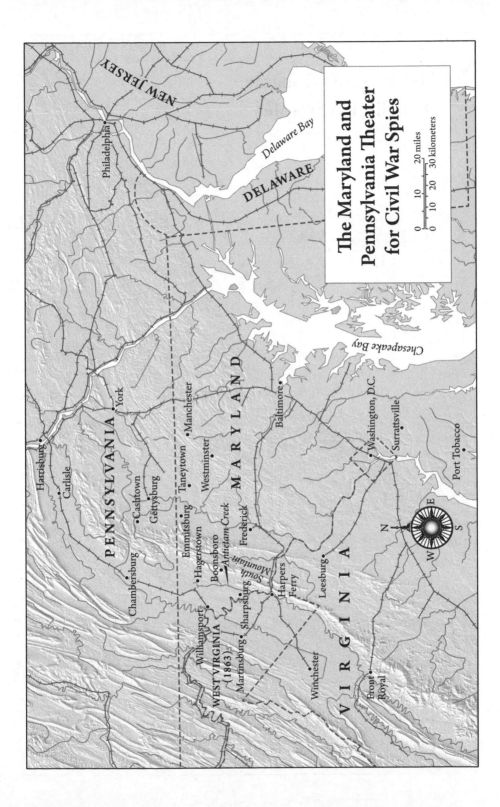

The Maryland and Pennsylvania Theater for Civil War Spies

NEW JERSEY

Delaware Bay

DELAWARE

Philadelphia

Chesapeake Bay

PENNSYLVANIA

Harrisburg

Carlisle

Cashtown

Gettysburg

York

Taneytown

Manchester

Westminster

MARYLAND

Chambersburg

Emmitsburg

Hagerstown

Boonsboro

Antietam Creek

Frederick

South Mountain

Baltimore

Williamsport

WEST VIRGINIA (1863)

Sharpsburg

Martinsburg

Harpers Ferry

Leesburg

Washington, D.C.

Surrattsville

Port Tobacco

Winchester

Front Royal

VIRGINIA

20 miles
10   20
0   10   20   30 kilometers

N E S W

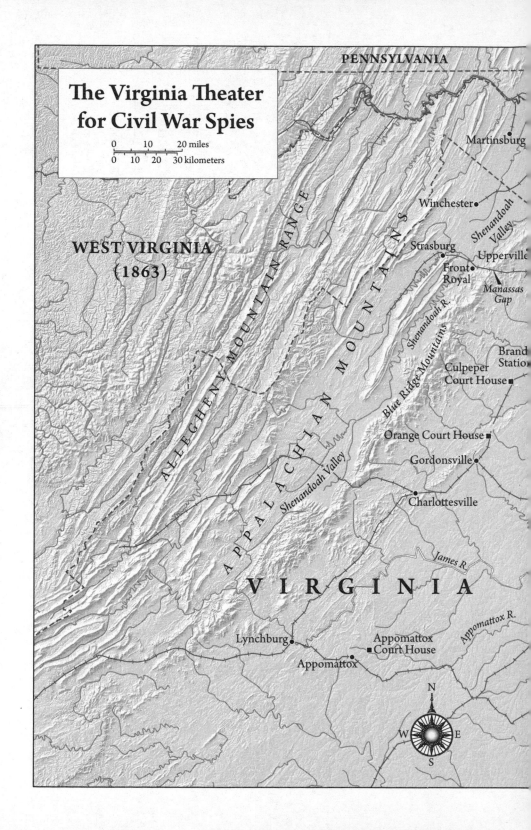

The Virginia Theater for Civil War Spies

0   10   20 miles
0   10   20   30 kilometers

PENNSYLVANIA

Martinsburg

Winchester

WEST VIRGINIA
(1863)

Shenandoah Valley

Strasburg

Upperville

Front Royal

Manassas Gap

ALLEGHENY MOUNTAIN RANGE

APPALACHIAN MOUNTAINS

Shenandoah R.

Blue Ridge Mountains

Brand Station

Culpeper Court House

Orange Court House

Gordonsville

Charlottesville

Shenandoah Valley

James R.

VIRGINIA

Appomattox R.

Lynchburg

Appomattox Court House

Appomattox

N
W   E
S

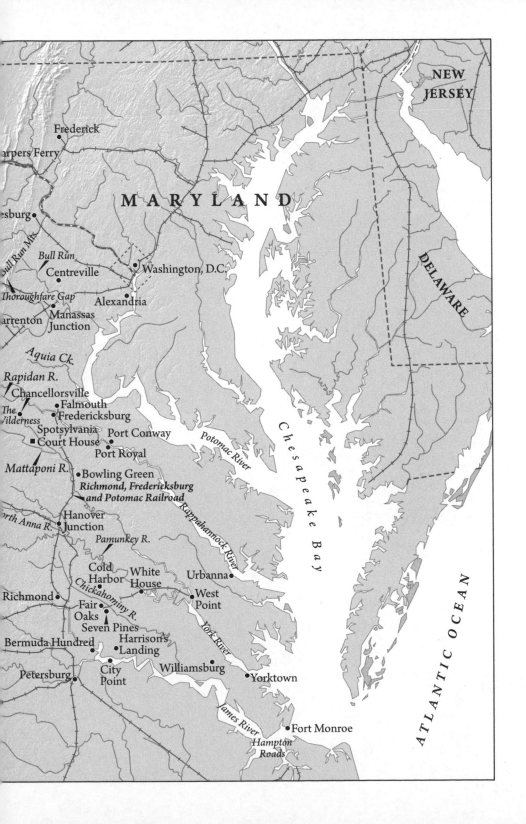

NEW JERSEY

Frederick

Harpers Ferry

MARYLAND

...esburg

Bull Run Mts.

Bull Run

Centreville

Washington, D.C.

DELAWARE

Thoroughfare Gap

Alexandria

...arrenton

Manassas
Junction

Aquia Ck.

Rapidan R.

Chancellorsville

The
Wilderness

Falmouth

Fredericksburg

Spotsylvania
Court House

Port Conway

Port Royal

Mattaponi R.

Bowling Green

Richmond, Fredericksburg
and Potomac Railroad

...rth Anna R.

Hanover
Junction

Pamunkey R.

Chesapeake Bay

Potomac River

Rappahannock River

Cold
Harbor

White
House

Urbanna

Richmond

Chickahominy R.

West
Point

Fair
Oaks

Seven Pines

Bermuda Hundred

Harrison's
Landing

York River

Petersburg

City
Point

Williamsburg

Yorktown

James River

Fort Monroe

Hampton
Roads

ATLANTIC OCEAN

NOTE TO READERS

Lincoln's Spies is the story of Allan Pinkerton, Lafayette Baker, George Sharpe, and Elizabeth Van Lew—important Union agents who operated mainly in the Civil War's Eastern Theater, which included Virginia, West Virginia, Maryland, Pennsylvania, and the District of Columbia. The U.S. government, of course, ran intelligence operations elsewhere—against Confederates in the Deep South and the western campaigns, for example, and to root out pro-Confederate subversives in the northeastern and northwestern states. To cover all the spying that went on in the Civil War would consume several volumes. This book focuses on the espionage and counterespionage of these four operatives in what became a crucial region for the war. The Eastern Theater, in which these agents fought in secret and the Union Army of the Potomac battled the Confederate Army of Northern Virginia in the open, included the capitals for the two belligerents, Washington and Richmond. On its fields and in its towns and cities were waged many of the largest, costliest, and most consequential battles, which helped determine the outcome of this tragic conflict and the fate of a nation.

Spies are a most important element in war.
—SUN TZU, *THE ART OF WAR*

Many intelligence reports in war are contradictory;
even more are false, and most are uncertain. . . .
In short, most intelligence is false.
—CARL VON CLAUSEWITZ, *ON WAR*

1861

ALLAN PINKERTON

hough they were still traveling through territory infested with secession sympathizers, the ride from Baltimore to Washington early the morning of February 23, 1861, proved uneventful. Allan Pinkerton finally relaxed. He joined Ward Hill Lamon in sipping from a liquor bottle. Pinkerton had not been particularly thrilled with Abraham Lincoln's hard-drinking Illinois law crony tagging along—the fewer people involved in this operation the better, he believed—but Mary Lincoln had insisted that the burly bodyguard accompany them as the detective escorted her husband on the dangerous trip to the nation's capital. The blustery Lamon, who sported a uniform he designed for himself, brought along two pistols, a large bowie knife, a pair of brass knuckles, and a thick hickory stick. Though Pinkerton usually abstained from alcohol (he told his son it made him grumpy), the detective could become a cigar-smoking whisky drinker if he needed to play one working a case.

Friends and associates believed Allan Pinkerton was gifted with courage and unusual powers of observation. As a young man he had been a labor agitator, falling under the spell of Scottish revolutionaries. He now hated slavery and had become a fanatical abolitionist. He thought his parents had been atheists and he considered himself one as well. He had honed a sixth sense to anticipate criminal activity before it happened. He was stubbornly persistent, refusing to be worn down by adversity. Yet he could be a tiresome prig, who harangued employees, friends, and relatives about the virtues of honesty, integrity, and courage. He was a tyrant at home, completely dominating his wife and children. He had dark, brooding eyes set deeply under a wide brow with a heavy beard that covered his face, save for his upper lip that he occasionally shaved. He was usually dour and humorless, only occasionally showing a sense of humor. He was a master publicist, skilled at promoting his business and shameless about air brushing his image. He was a disciple of phrenology, the pseudo-medicine that determines a person's character and intellect from measurements of the head's size and shape. A phrenologist examined him, writing that the detective's brain measured twenty-three inches ("very large," the professor reported) and concluding that he was blessed with "earnestness, enthusiasm, heartiness, whole-souledness, impetuosity and excitability."

The head of Pinkerton's National Detective Agency had reason to feel satisfied with himself that Saturday morning, February 23. His covert mission had begun a little more than a month earlier when Samuel Morse Felton, a kindly-looking Massachusetts man, hired him to investigate threats to Felton's Philadelphia, Wilmington and Baltimore Railroad from pro-secessionist saboteurs. The line was a vital rail link from the North to Washington, over which Federal troops and supplies would travel if war broke out with the South. Pinkerton, whose Chicago agency specialized in tracking and capturing train robbers, arrived in Baltimore on February 1 with a squad of his best detectives. Quickly his undercover operatives infiltrated Baltimore's secret societies and paramilitary organizations that supported southern secession from the Union. Each agent was identified on intelligence reports they delivered to him by code names or simply with their initials. Using the pseudonym John H. Hutchinson, Pinkerton posed as a chatty stockbroker from Charleston, South Carolina.

It soon became clear to him that the danger was far more serious than railroad vandalism. Practically from the day they arrived, Pinkerton and his detectives began picking up the stories swirling around Baltimore of plots to assassinate the president-elect when he passed through the city. Lincoln, who by tradition remained secluded during his successful 1860 presidential campaign while others stumped for him, had departed Springfield, Illinois, on February 11 for a twelve-day, 1,904-mile, roundabout trip to Washington, D.C., with frequent halts in key states he had won to greet the public and introduce himself to the country before his inauguration the next month as the sixteenth president of the United States. He was scheduled to arrive in Baltimore shortly after noon on February 23.

One of four loyal slave states, Maryland had 90,000 blacks in bondage and a determined minority that favored seceding from the Union. The state, which bordered Washington on three sides, had to be kept open to Union resupply for the nation's capital to survive. But Maryland was unstable. A tinderbox rife for assassination plotting, Baltimore, the South's largest and northernmost city, was a logical site to spring the trap. Visitors could reach Washington by train, steamship up the Potomac, or on one of six highways that ran through Virginia or Maryland. The Old Dominion state was far too dangerous to transit through for this president-elect. To reach Washington for his swearing-in, Lincoln had to pass through Maryland and more particularly Baltimore, the key center for railroads that were the most efficient means of moving northern troops in the future to the nation's capital. The best way for secessionists to nullify the election, perhaps to seize Confederate independence quickly, was to kill Lincoln in Baltimore. Pinkerton and his agents infiltrated the city's wealthy class, who they suspected would fund such an assassination plot, as well as its lower-class gangs likely to carry out the murder. They discovered what they believed was compelling evidence that when Lincoln changed trains in the city for the Baltimore & Ohio Railroad line that would take him to Washington, a dense and hostile crowd would surround him from which assassins would emerge to shoot or stab him. As near as Pinkerton could determine, the local police planned no escort or if they did have one it would be with disloyal officers sympathetic to the killers.

Pinkerton intercepted Lincoln at Philadelphia's luxurious Continental Hotel the night of February 21 and briefed him on the assassination threat he believed he had uncovered. Lincoln knew the detective and thought highly of his agency. Outwardly the president-elect refused to appear alarmed by personal threats. But there was evidence he was taking them more seriously than he let on. Lincoln began receiving death threats as early as October 1860, when his election victory seemed certain. After the vote, hate mail from all over the country piled up in Springfield. Warnings came that he would be poisoned. Several packages of tainted fruit arrived from the South. Newspapers were filled with stories of sinister forces that would prevent Lincoln from taking office. Washington was alive with rumors of assassination plots and conspiracies to burn down the city. One report out of New Orleans had a $40,000 bounty placed on his head. Lincoln's stepmother worried he never would return home alive from his presidency. So did Springfield friends.

It had been a logistical nightmare arranging the president-elect's travel. There was no direct rail line from Springfield to Washington. Instead, he had to chug along at thirty miles per hour over a hodgepodge of fifteen different lines, some of which were run by powerful railroad executives who sympathized with the South. His protection during the trip was woefully inadequate. There was no federal secret service to guard him. Lincoln refused to have an Army escort, believing it made him look like a warlord. No one traveling with him was even officially designated to be responsible for his security, so protection was handled by a makeshift detail of friends and military men aboard the train. In Baltimore, against a large angry crowd and hostile cops, the puny security detail would be easily overpowered.

Lincoln agreed to Pinkerton's complex plan to sneak him into Washington ahead of his announced travel schedule while his would-be Baltimore assassins slept. The evening of February 22, the president-elect, with only Lamon to guard him, quietly slipped away from his traveling party of more than a dozen in Harrisburg, where he had delivered an address to the state legislature, and boarded a special Pennsylvania Railroad train that Pinkerton had arranged to take him 110 miles east to Philadelphia. Pinkerton joined the pair in Philadelphia and took them in a carriage shortly after 10 p.m. to the station for Felton's Philadelphia, Wilmington and Baltimore Railroad on the south side of town, where they boarded the rear of a sleeping car.

Kate Warne, one of Pinkerton's female operatives, had reserved four double berths partitioned off from other passengers, which she told the conductor was for her sick brother.

At 3:30 a.m. on February 23, Lincoln, Pinkerton, and Lamon arrived in Baltimore, where the sleeping car was unhitched and pulled by a team of horses to the Baltimore & Ohio Railroad's Camden Street Station a mile away. As dawn was about to break, the B&O's Washington-bound train finally arrived, much to the relief of Pinkerton, who dreaded the thought of the president-elect stranded in a wide-awake Baltimore with just him and Lamon for protection. Lincoln's sleeper car was hooked up to it for the final thirty-eight-mile leg to Washington.

After his shot of whisky with Lamon, Pinkerton stretched out on the sleeping car's back platform. The cold wind buffeting his face, he watched as their southbound train sped by quiet hamlets and dingy farmhouses. Pinkerton was not a man given to deep introspection. But it was remarkable, if he ever stopped to think about it, that he had risen from roots as humble as Lincoln's to reach the point where he was now rescuing a future president.

Pinkerton could trace his line to seventeenth-century Gorbals, a Scottish burgh on the south bank of the River Clyde, annexed by Glasgow in 1661, which by the nineteenth century had become a bustling factory and workshop center for more than 35,000 people living in squalid thatched houses and multistory tenements along narrow streets.

William Pinkerton was a grim-faced muscular man, with a gloomy personality and a modest amount of schooling, who stood about six feet tall and was "straight built," according to his son Allan. He likely supplemented his falling income as a home handloom weaver by serving as a Glasgow city jail trustee, which gave him some standing in the community. Allan Pinkerton, who was prone to fabricating parts of his biography, claimed that his father died as a police sergeant battling rioters, but that story appears to have no basis in fact. William's first marriage was to Isabella Stevenson, who bore him seven children (five of whom lived beyond childhood) and who, according to family legend, died after delivering the last one in 1807. In his mid-forties, William married a thirty-three-year-old cotton mill worker named Isabella McQueen, who had Allan and another son, Robert, who survived to adulthood. Allan was born in 1819 in the couple's third-floor tenement apartment on Muirhead Street. The exact day is in dispute. Biographers have it variously as July 21, August 21, and August 25.

Little can be confirmed about Allan's childhood. Pinkerton's later accounts of it are riddled with inaccuracies. He claimed the household was "completely filled with the tensions of two families existing in a few rooms," but that may not have been the case. William was a stern father, but by the time Allan was five, the children of the first marriage had all left home and only Allan and his brother Robert remained in the apartment. Allan attended elementary school until age nine or ten, when his father died. With a firm grounding by then in reading, writing, and arithmetic he was considered adequately educated for that time. He later regretted not having any more formal schooling and thought he suffered because of it.

After several years of odd jobs for pennies a day, Pinkerton at age twelve decided to apprentice with William McCauley, a Gorbals barrel maker, to learn how to be a cooper. Six years later he had earned a journeyman's card. By then, he was five feet eight inches tall with powerful shoulders and arms from hours spent each day pounding iron barrel hoops with a ten-pound hammer. But he described himself as a "tramp cooper," roaming Scotland and northern England the next four years finding short-term work that ended each time with layoffs.

Industrial unrest swept Glasgow by the end of the 1830s, fueled by a downturn in the British economy, with cotton mill owners cutting wages, thousands of their workers striking, and union leaders being marched off to jail. In 1838, Pinkerton became a Chartist, named for a popular working-class movement whose six-point People's Charter called for democratic reforms and broader suffrage for men. Pinkerton, who became the Glasgow coopers' representative to the Chartist Convention in Birmingham, joined the grassroots revolt because "I was free in name, but a slave in fact," he recalled. He came to worship the frail yet charismatic George Julian Harney, a London communist among the Chartist leaders, and became Harney's strongman as he traveled through Scotland delivering fiery speeches. On

November 4, 1839, Pinkerton joined 5,000 men armed with mostly spears and clubs in the Newport, Wales, uprising to free Henry Vincent, an imprisoned Chartist orator. He escaped being among the twenty-two Chartists whom soldiers killed and the sixty-two whom police arrested after scattering the mob with a volley of musket fire.

In April 1841, while organizing a concert at O'Neil's Public House to raise money for striking spinners in Glasgow, Pinkerton couldn't take his eyes off fourteen-year-old Joan Carfrae, a bookbinder's apprentice who was singing soprano in the event. An Edinburgh orphan, Joan had been reared by her aunt, who educated her. She was a kind young girl, who sang in Glasgow's Unitarian Church on Center Street and was as committed as Pinkerton was to workers' rights. Allan courted her for almost a year before they married on March 13, 1842, when Joan was fifteen. She may have misled Pinkerton into believing she was eighteen. He was twenty-two.

The next month, Joan shared a filthy cabin with other women and Allan wedged into the crew's quarters aboard the merchant ship *Kent*, sailing for America and what the young couple hoped would be a better life. Pinkerton paid for their passage by working as the ship's cooper. Their first stop was to be Montreal, but storms blew the *Kent* far off course and she foundered 250 miles south on ice and reefs at Sable Island, southeast of Halifax, Nova Scotia. A lifeboat carried them to shore, where Indian raiders promptly robbed them of the few possessions they carried, including Joan's wedding ring. In May, they finally reached Montreal with only twenty-five pennies in Pinkerton's pocket. Allan and Joan found a room in a boardinghouse and Allan scratched out a living in Montreal making beef barrels until he was laid off several months later. Giving up on Canada, the couple planned to book a steamer south to Chicago, but they changed their minds and moved instead to the village of Warsaw, in western Illinois. Calamity struck once more— they were robbed of everything but the clothes on their back—so they decided to return to their original plan and move to Chicago.

Chicago in 1842 was a growing frontier town of 1,200 hardy people and some two dozen businesses, packed along muddy rutted streets with cattle herded on them to slaughterhouses and reeking gutters filled with garbage. Robbie Fergus, an old Glasgow friend who had settled there, let the couple stay in one of his rooms and helped Pinkerton find a job at Lill's Brewery, at the corner of Pine Street and Chicago Avenue, working for fifty cents a day making beer barrels as a cooper.

Fed up with how little money he took home after a year of slaving away at Lill's, Pinkerton moved thirty-eight miles northwest to Dundee, a settlement of some three hundred Scots and their dairy farms on the scenic Fox River in Kane County, Illinois. Dundee had a few country stores, a post office, several blacksmith shops, a mill, and two small taverns. Pinkerton built a one-story frame cabin at the edge of the village on a grassy knoll near a wooden bridge spanning the river and became the town's only cooper. Waking each morning at four thirty and laboring seven days a week, he built the business up with eight apprentices on his payroll by 1847, offering quality work at a lower cost for area farmers fed up with Chicago's high prices for barrels and churns. In 1846, Joan delivered their first child, William. Five would follow. Pinkerton named them all without consulting her.

A life-changing event occurred in June 1846. Always looking for ways to save money, Pinkerton poled his raft to a small island on Fox River a few miles above Dundee to cut wood for his barrel staves instead of buying them. He discovered hidden in the island's forest later that night what would turn out to be a band of counterfeiters hammering out coins around a roaring fire. Pinkerton hurried back to Dundee and told Luther Dearborn, Kane County's sheriff, who together with Pinkerton staked out the campsite for a night. Dearborn eventually brought in a posse and arrested the counterfeiters with their bag of bogus dimes.

Pinkerton became a local celebrity after the bust. Dearborn began dropping by to solicit his advice on cases. The next month, two Dundee merchants, Henry Hunt and Increase C. Bosworth, talked Pinkerton into trying to catch another counterfeiter. Wildcat bank currency was a problem in the rural Midwest. Laws regulating the national currency did not cover the growing number of states and independent institutions that issued banknotes backed by their gold reserves. Unreliable currency flooded the region and counterfeiters made the problem worse by printing phony versions of the bills these institutions issued. Little money circulated in Dundee—a barter system covered most transactions—but one institution that did issue high-quality currency in Kane County was George Smith's Wisconsin Marine and Fire Insurance Company, which had secured banking privileges in that state and had a branch in Chicago. His bills were nicknamed "George Smith's money." The Dundee merchants wanted Pinkerton to catch the scoundrel who had passed at least two phony ten-dollar bills of George Smith's money in Dundee. Pinkerton, who had never seen a bill as high as ten dollars, met and began ingratiating himself with the man the merchants suspected was the counterfeiter—John Craig, a tall, well-heeled, and swarthy-looking newcomer in his sixties who said he was from Vermont.

For a barefoot cooper in overalls, Pinkerton hatched an elaborate sting to try to catch Craig, eventually showing up with $125 of the merchants' silver as bait to buy fifty of Craig's bogus $10 bills. But the trap Pinkerton set ended up failing. The wily Craig, who always had surrogates do the dirty work so he could not be directly linked to the counterfeit money, eventually was arrested but he managed to escape from jail after bribing an officer. When Pinkerton visited the irascible George Smith in Milwaukee to be reimbursed at least for the time he spent running off Craig, the bank president griped but paid, warning that if the upstart cooper ever played detective again without his authorization, he wouldn't get a dime from George Smith. Pinkerton learned a hard lesson: always have a written contract before you take a case.

Pinkerton moved back to Chicago in 1848. He had become restless and Dundee had grown too conservative for his tastes. After chasing John Craig, he had taken a job on top of his cooper's business as a part-time Kane County deputy sheriff, but when he ran for sheriff on an abolitionist ticket in spring 1847 and the next year ran as a candidate on the Liberty Party ticket for the state's constitutional convention, Dundee's Baptist Church minister fiercely campaigned against him, accusing him of being a drunkard and an atheist. Pinkerton was not a drunkard but he was an atheist. He lost both elections.

In the five years Pinkerton had been away, Chicago had exploded to nearly 30,000 people, with new residential homes, business houses, hotels, and theaters being built, rail connections arriving, and ships lining up at the shores of Lake Michigan. Pinkerton, whose Dundee policing had made him well known around the state, became a deputy sheriff in Cook County, whose seat is Chicago. He built a two-room, clapboard frame house, painted white, on Adams Street near the lakeshore for his family. Pinkerton became the law enforcement agency's first detective, earning a reputation as a tough, fearless, and honest lawman, which in Chicago could be dangerous. While he walked up Clark Street one night to his home, a pistol-wielding thug he had likely once rousted shot him in the left arm.

Pinkerton remained on the force for about five years. He claimed he resigned because of "political interference," which may have been the case since the city's Democratic mayor did not take kindly to officers like Pinkerton who advocated the abolition of slavery. Pinkerton also may have left the Cook County position to pursue more lucrative detective work. The U.S. Post Office gave him a job as a mail agent to probe a rash of mail thefts plaguing the city. He posed as a mail clerk and found that the nephew of the Chicago postmaster, who had been given a sorter's job with the service, was stealing bank drafts and money orders from envelopes.

Needing more money for his growing family, Pinkerton around 1855, or perhaps earlier, formed with a lawyer named Edward Rucker the North-West Detective Agency and set up a tiny office at 89 Washington Street. Rucker, always a silent partner in the venture, dropped out of the arrangement the next year. Before resigning from official police work, Pinkerton had polled railroad executives on whether he should form a private detective firm. They thought it was an excellent idea. Crime plagued the region and no state or federal law enforcement agency existed. Local police forces often were filled with incompetent or corrupt officers their citizens considered no better than accomplices for the criminal class. Businessmen, who distrusted local cops even more, needed some type of protection and crime detection organization to guard their companies. The agency Pinkerton was forming would be the closest thing to a national investigative organization—his trademark soon becoming "We Never Sleep," under a drawing of an eye. He adopted the expression "private eye," which eventually became the nickname for detectives.

From his Chartist background, Pinkerton showed a genius for organizing and attention to detail—but often becoming an ironfisted micromanager and not delegating. He perfected policing and detection techniques sophisticated for the time, such as employing undercover disguises, exploiting the latest technology like the telegraph and photography, and compiling a vast picture gallery of criminals (Pinkerton's became the largest in the world). He paid his detectives $3 a day, a supervisor cost a client $8 a day, and Pinkerton charged $12 a day for his services. For the comfortable salaries they received, Pinkerton expected his operatives to abide by high ethical standards—an innovation at the time when the public considered most private detectives little different from the criminals they hunted. Pinkerton did not allow his employees to drink, smoke, play cards, or frequent "low dives." They had to wear "somber dress," could not cash in on their exploits with newspaper or magazine stories, and were forbidden from accepting rewards for the criminals they caught. That last prohibition helped Pinkerton maintain good relations with police forces throughout the Midwest.

The first man Pinkerton hired for his agency was the talented and patrician George Bangs, who had started out as a reporter and then drifted into police work before Pinkerton spotted him. A tall and handsome man with a commanding presence, Bangs was an efficient business manager as well as a skilled detective and quickly became Pinkerton's general superintendent. Other men were recruited, like Adam Roche (a pipe-smoking German who had worked on a lumber barge), John White (whom Pinkerton thought adept at catching con men because he looked like one), and John Fox (a talkative New Englander who had been a watchmaker).

Kate Warne, slender, brown-haired, and a widow at twenty-three, barged into Pinkerton's office one day and announced she wanted to be a detective, arguing that a woman could worm her way into situations males couldn't and glean valuable information. A startled Pinkerton had never considered a female for detective work, but after mulling it over for a day he decided to hire this graceful and self-assured woman. Warne proved to be a courageous and trusted operative. Men found her fascinating. She became expert at playing roles to entice suspects to divulge their secrets, posing once as a clairvoyant with costume and makeup to convince a superstitious woman to admit to poisoning her brother. Soon Warne headed Pinkerton's "Female Department," composed of several women. Some family members suspected that in later years Pinkerton and Warne had an affair.

He took all kinds of cases at the outset—except for divorce and infidelity investigations. He considered them undignified. But Pinkerton was not shy about unconventional methods, such as braying into the night like an angry ghost near the bed of a suspect to scare him into confessing. A Chicago newspaper questioned a $700 bill Pinkerton submitted to the city, which included $139 the paper considered a staggering amount for arresting what must have been a "multitude" of pickpockets. Within a short time Pinkerton had branch offices in neighboring states with agents investigating murders, counterfeiters, and mail thieves. He also started a uniformed guard service to protect Chicago meatpackers. As his reputation spread he began taking on more complicated interstate cases, infiltrating spies to protect companies from their enemies: robbers, thieving employees, and organized labor (he set aside the idealism of his Chartist days to become a well-paid tool of business interests).

A large part of his agency's income soon came from protecting railroads and the express companies that shipped freight, packages, and money on the trains. The vast railroad expansion of the mid-nineteenth century quickly exposed a serious security weakness for the industry; police could not protect the trains as they traveled from one jurisdiction to another. Six Midwest railroads paid Pinkerton $10,000 annually by 1855 to protect their lines. He signed security contracts with Wells Fargo, American Express Company, and Adams Express Company. His retainer for security work for one company, the Illinois Central Railroad, was drafted by its attorney, Abraham Lincoln, who was impressed with the work Pinkerton did for the company. Pinkerton never said anything about what he thought of the Illinois Central's lawyer. He became much closer to its vice president, George McClellan, whom he admired greatly.

Pinkerton's agency soon began attracting nationwide and even international attention. He chased train robbers and spied on conductors suspected of pocketing fares they collected from passengers. For Adams Express, his undercover agents set up an elaborate sting—which included Kate Warne posing as the wife of a shady businessman and John White pretending to be a big-city forger—to catch the Montgomery, Alabama, branch manager, who had stolen $40,000. Pinkerton changed the business's name to Pinkerton's National Detective Agency to reflect the fact that his Midwest company was evolving into a national one.

Pinkerton's aggressive tactics and incorruptibility made him hated by the criminal underworld. But it never cowed him. He found crooks, whom he studied intensely, generally to be an unimaginative lot with predictable patterns, who could not keep their mouths shut about the crimes they committed and who could easily be defeated, he said, by anyone with "a moderate amount of intelligence."

The champion lawman, however, was a lawbreaker in one respect. Pinkerton routinely aided runaway slaves, a violation of the Fugitive Slave Act that could have landed him in jail if he was caught. He allowed the attic and cellar of his house to be a way station for runaways coming up the Mississippi or Ohio Rivers to reach Canada, he became an emissary for John Brown, who visited his home with runaways, he met Frederick Douglass, and he raised money for the Underground Railroad. He found America's slaveholding class as repulsive as the "one against which I had rebelled across the ocean," he wrote. After Brown was captured in the abortive 1859 raid on the federal arsenal at Harpers Ferry, Pinkerton raised money for his legal defense fund.

As the sun rose on February 23, 1861, Pinkerton gave no thought to how Lincoln would be protected once he arrived in Washington. He should have. Remnants of prosecession paramilitary groups that had been openly drilling in Washington remained in the city. At 6 a.m. the B&O train pulled in to the dirty and cheerless Washington Depot with its tower and clock, which stood at New Jersey Avenue and C Street within sight of the Capitol. Buses and hacks lined up at the station's entrance, their drivers yelling at the top of their lungs to attract the attention of early-morning arrivals who needed rides. Lincoln stood up in the sleeper car, stretched his tall frame, gave a weary smile, and said to no one in particular: "Well boys, thank God this prayer meeting is over."

No one had slept during the nightlong train ride. It would have been difficult for Lincoln even if he had wanted to. The wooden beds in the rustic
sleeping car, partitioned by curtains, were too small for his six-foot-four-
inch frame. Most of the time he had sat on a padded bench and whispered
an occasional joke to Pinkerton and Lamon to break the silence. He routinely spun stories not only because he thought they were funny or to im-
part a broader message, but also as a defense mechanism to deflect criticism
or questions he did not want to answer. That night the stories may have
helped turn his mind off to the strategic catastrophe unfolding before him.
As Lincoln's train headed to Washington, seven southern states had already
seceded from the Union and four more would eventually follow. Jefferson
Davis had been inaugurated president of the Confederacy and had begun
establishing his government in Montgomery, Alabama, ahead of Lincoln
forming his in Washington. Lincoln would face 750,000 square miles of his
country cleaved away to form a rebel nation controlling most of the federal
government's military assets in that territory. The president-elect was left
with aging generals like Army commander Winfield Scott leading a pitifully
small force of 1,108 officers (one-third of them from the South) and 15,259
soldiers mostly scattered around the country in outposts watching Indians.

Lincoln was beginning his presidency with a sophisticated clandestine
operation—ironic, perhaps, considering he was one of the least experienced
men to enter that high office. The son of a poor Kentucky family who was
distant from his father, he had only the briefest of formal schooling, which
he never was proud of. He was largely a self-taught lawyer, who had served
only four terms in the Illinois state legislature and one term in Congress,
had failed twice in bids for the U.S. Senate, and had no administrative experience in a senior government position. He cultivated for political purposes
the image of a simple frontier "rail splitter," but disliked the nickname "Honest Abe" (preferring to be addressed as Mr. Lincoln); he was ambitious, and
he would assume the presidency not totally unfamiliar with the dark arts of
subterfuge and intrigue that Pinkerton practiced.

Lincoln had a slight brush with military service in the 1832 Black
Hawk War—no combat but it did give him a taste of leading men. (At one
point during that conflict he also spent three weeks in a unit called the

Independent Spy Company, which carried out reconnaissance operations.) Often writing political columns under aliases, in 1842 he used one of them to attack an Illinois state auditor in a newspaper. When the angry auditor learned it was Lincoln and challenged him to a duel, Lincoln found a way to back out and came away with a valuable lesson that black propaganda and publishing under a pseudonym could have unintended consequences. He paid close attention to the messaging and mechanics of his few political campaigns. He secretly bought a German-language weekly newspaper to print puff pieces on him for that important voting bloc in Illinois, and during the 1860 campaign for the presidency he had favorable stories about him planted in the press. At the Republican Party's nominating convention in Chicago, Lincoln's political team printed duplicate tickets to pack the Wigwam hall with his supporters in order to create the appearance of a groundswell for him. And during the race afterward he was a careful reader and evaluator of political intelligence.

Congressman Elihu Washburne, who had been alerted that Lincoln might arrive early, stood by a pillar on the platform, craning his neck to see if he was among the passengers climbing off the train. The Illinois Republican had funneled back-channel letters from Lincoln to Scott and had organized an informal "Public Safety Committee" to investigate threats to the future president. Washburne finally spotted Lincoln emerging from the rear sleeper car accompanied by two other men. He was wearing an old overcoat with a traveling shawl over his shoulders. To make himself less recognizable during the clandestine trip, Lincoln had left his signature stovepipe hat in Pennsylvania and wore instead a soft felt "Kossuth" hat a New York hatter had given him, which was popular then and looked like a flattened bowler with a wide brim. No one else around the station seemed to recognize the president-elect.

Washburne ran up waving his arm. "How are you, Lincoln!" he shouted. Pinkerton, thinking he was an attacker, jumped in front of the president-elect and delivered a sharp blow with his elbow to the congressman's chest, causing him to stagger backward. "Don't strike him, don't strike him—this is my friend Washburne!" Lincoln said, grabbing the detective by the shoulder. An embarrassed Pinkerton apologized for punching him.

The four men walked quickly out of the depot to the street, where Washburne had a carriage and driver waiting to take them to the Willard Hotel, a mile away. The Lincolns would stay there until the inauguration. The president-elect gazed out the carriage window as they rode over cobblestones, passing by the Capitol's unfinished steel dome surrounded with scaffolding and derricks, by street vendors setting up stands and shop owners opening their stores for the morning. A shabby stench hung over the city from the odorous B Street Canal and Tiber Creek, which ran through its center.

A block from the Willard, Pinkerton ordered the carriage driver to stop and climbed out with Washburne and Lincoln to walk the rest of the way. Lamon rode ahead with the driver to scout out the hotel's entrances for their arrival. When they reached the Willard, Lamon told them to take Lincoln through the less crowded ladies' entrance on the 14th Street side, where he had one of the Willard brothers standing to meet them. When Lincoln arrived in 1861, the Willard Hotel on Pennsylvania Avenue was considered more the center of Washington life than the Capitol or White House. Expanded three years earlier with a six-story addition built on the southwest corner of 14th and F Streets, the hotel had elegant gentlemen's and ladies' dining rooms serving as many as 2,500 customers a day, lavish parlors with pianos, sofas, and easy chairs, three large halls, and two broad oak staircases. Low-income clientele took the cheaper top-floor rooms while the well-heeled and foreign dignitaries occupied the better quarters of the lower floors. Now with escalating tensions, northern and southern guests stayed on different floors and were directed to separate exits to avoid clashes.

The hotel management had not expected Lincoln until the afternoon, and parlor number six, where he and his family would stay, was not yet ready, so he was ushered to a receiving room for the moment. Senator William Seward, whom Lincoln had picked to be his secretary of state, arrived shortly and the two men compared notes on the threat that may have existed in Baltimore. Word quickly spread through the hotel that Lincoln had arrived and guests from the drawing rooms began crowding halls to catch a glimpse of the future president. Exhausted, Lincoln retreated to the room the staff finally had ready for him.

Pinkerton also was worn out and checked in to a room, registering as E. J. Allen, for a hot bath and breakfast. Refreshed, he walked over to the telegraph office and sent coded messages that they had made it to Washington to Norman Judd, a Springfield lawyer with Lincoln's traveling party who had acted as a de facto chief of staff for the president-elect during the trip, and Edward Sanford, an American Telegraph Company executive who had helped with the operation in Pennsylvania. "Plums arrived here with Nuts this morning—all right," read the one to Sanford. "Plums" stood for Pinkerton. "Nuts" stood for Lincoln.

When he returned to the Willard, Pinkerton found an excited Lamon eager to tell the press about Lincoln's secret journey. Pinkerton angrily tried to talk him out of that bad idea. The detective still had operatives undercover in Baltimore, whose lives would be put at risk if the papers had the story. Pinkerton also suspected Lamon would spin the story to inflate his role and deflate Pinkerton's. Later, when the Baltimore operation was wrapped up, Pinkerton talked freely to reporters to make sure he had a prominent place in their accounts. Lamon, who was angling for a plum job in the new administration, wasn't about to keep quiet. Pinkerton later found him liquored up in the Willard's bar talking to a *New York Herald* reporter. He angrily confronted Lamon, reminding him that Lincoln had promised to keep quiet about the operation; he would go to the president-elect to make sure the blackout remained.

Lincoln broke free from a session with a congressional delegation to meet with Pinkerton about 2 p.m. and thank him. He agreed to keep Pinkerton's role secret. An hour later, Pinkerton climbed aboard the B&O train back to Baltimore to monitor the situation there with his agents until the inauguration, as he told Lincoln he would do. Three hours earlier, at 12:30 p.m., the train bearing Mary Lincoln, her two younger sons, and the rest of the traveling party left behind arrived in Baltimore, whose residents by then knew that her husband had slipped through the city and was safe in Washington. There were conflicting stories about how Baltimoreans reacted to Mary passing through their city. The *New York Times* reported that a rude and dangerous crowd of thousands greeted Mary at the station; aides kept her locked in a room as thugs, who thought reports of Lincoln already coming through a ruse, roamed through the cars looking for the president-elect. John Nicolay and John Hay, who would become Lincoln's closest White House aides and had been traveling with Mary, claimed the party encountered "no incivility" in Baltimore. But nobody disputed that the future first lady was still steaming over being left behind.

Pinkerton said Baltimore was "swearing mad" when he arrived about 5 p.m. as a cold rain pelted the city. Assassination conspirators he and his operatives had cultivated in the city were cursing over Lincoln's escape and vowing to hunt down the spies they thought had infiltrated their organization and tipped him off. Still keeping to his cover as a Charleston broker, Pinkerton pulled a ten-dollar bill out of his purse and gave it to one of the conspirators to help find the traitors.

One of Sanford's agents arrived from Philadelphia two days later with a copy of the *New York Herald*, which had run a story naming Pinkerton as part of a secret operation to spirit Lincoln through Baltimore. Furious, Pinkerton telegraphed Judd that Lamon had leaked the story and he needed to shut him up. But Pinkerton also became sloppy with security; he received letters at the Baltimore post office, some possibly from Chicago, with his real name on the envelope.

Pinkerton on March 19 sent Felton his bill. He charged the railroad man $10 a day for his time ($2 less than his usual fee) and $6 a day each for the work that five of his detectives did on the case (which was double what he paid them). It totaled up to $1,400 but he deducted $509.38 for expenses he decided not to charge Felton, bringing the final bill down to $890.62. Pinkerton continued to muscle for recognition, engaging in a long-running feud with New York City police chief John Kennedy, who had sent three undercover officers to Baltimore at the request of Seward to investigate the threat against the president-elect. Pinkerton accused Kennedy, who ran one of the best law enforcement agencies in the country, of trying to hog credit for the operation that took Lincoln through the city. But Pinkerton's larger problem became a growing political chorus that claimed he averted a threat that never existed.

Newspaper editorials excoriated Lincoln for the cowardly way he had sneaked into Washington. Baltimore police chief George Proctor Kane insisted his force would have provided ample protection. The *New York Times* reported that he had slipped through Baltimore wearing a Scotch plaid cap and long military cloak—a false story, but one that stuck when cartoonists drew "fugitive sketches" mocking him. Lincoln's presidency had taken a body blow before it had even begun, with all the hard work of his get-acquainted journey undone in one fell swoop. With just nine days before his inauguration, Lincoln, instead of preparing himself for a difficult presidency, was having to cope with a PR disaster—accused of coming "to the capital like a clown," as historian Bruce Catton put it, and further sowing misgivings among northern leaders that he was not up to the job.

Pinkerton came under fire as well. Lamon, hardly a fan of the detective, claimed Pinkerton's operatives swallowed a lot of harmless boasting by hotheads, which Pinkerton then used to concoct a conspiracy in order to drum up business for his agency. "How much longer will the people of this country be the dupes of these private detectives?" railed the *Chicago Democrat*. Lamon claimed that Lincoln later told him he regretted letting Pinkerton talk him into sneaking through Baltimore. The postwar memoirs of other members of his traveling party suggested that Lincoln realized he had been poorly advised in the matter. Tellingly, Lincoln, a serial storyteller, never told an anecdote or joke about his secret passage through Baltimore, perhaps because he considered it a sore subject. If a plot had existed, many twentieth-century historians have asked, why was no one ever arrested, tried, and punished for it? The known Baltimore plotters—like ringleader Cypriano Ferrandini, a Corsican barber in the city's Barnum's Hotel—were all easy to find and the Lincoln administration would soon demonstrate that it was not shy about throwing enemies of the government in jail.

Lamon later recanted somewhat, indicating in a memoir that the Baltimore plot may have been for real. Lincoln also sent mixed signals. Washburne said the Lincoln he picked up at the train station was neither "mortified" nor "chagrined" about how he got to Washington. Near the end of the Civil War, Lincoln told a congressman he thought a plot existed. The fact that Ferrandini and the others weren't tried does not necessarily mean they were innocent. Baltimore was in a turbulent state in early 1861. It was unlikely federal authorities would have pursued an investigation with war on the horizon and so many other urgent matters to attend to. It was also not a given that the conspirators would have been convicted if they had been arrested. The plotters would have had to have been tried in Baltimore, which would have alarmed its citizens at a time when Lincoln desperately wanted to keep Maryland in the Union. Lincoln also wanted to put the entire episode behind him—not eager for a trial that would bring him more political grief.

How close the alleged conspirators came to carrying out their plan can be argued, but what is not debatable is that the threat of them carrying it out was credible. For Pinkerton to have staged such an elaborate fabrication he would have had to have a lot of detectives in on the scheme, and none of them ever said it was a hoax. Moreover, Kennedy had independently uncovered evidence of the plot. Crowds in Baltimore erupted in anger when they discovered Lincoln had slipped through. Two months later riots, killings, and bridge burnings did occur in Baltimore when a Massachusetts regiment tried to make its way through the city and clashed with a mob. Besides, whether the evidence of a Baltimore plot ultimately proved true "was not the question," Nicolay and Hay wrote after the war. Lincoln had no right to ignore the danger Pinkerton uncovered. Not only his personal safety but "the fate of the government of the nation" hung in the balance. Lincoln had to take the threat seriously.

The fabrication charges deeply wounded Pinkerton, who until the day he died had no doubt that the Baltimore conspiracy was real and his operation averted a catastrophe. In the 1940s Pinkerton's family lobbied everyone from the *New York Times* to FBI director J. Edgar Hoover to recognize his role in preventing the assassination of Lincoln.

Two

GEORGE SHARPE

ore than 25,000 Washington residents and visitors to the capital turned out for the inauguration on a cloudy and gusty March 4, filling hotels and saloons to capacity, clogging muddy streets, some washing or urinating in public fountains. With the approval of both outgoing president James Buchanan and Lincoln, General Scott deployed some 2,000 troops to patrol the city. Guards were posted along the one-mile route that Lincoln's open carriage (surrounded by cavalrymen) traveled along Pennsylvania Avenue from the Willard to the Capitol. Sharpshooters were stationed from the windows of tall buildings and imported northern detectives watched for assassins, secessionists, rogues—anyone who might cause trouble. The show of force shocked Washingtonians, but Scott made no apologies for it. The District of Columbia, virtually undefended with a long history of organized and spontaneous mob violence, was primarily a southern, slave-owning city, many of whose residents were openly hostile to the new administration. Waves of political brawling had swept over D.C. since election day, Lincoln continued to receive threatening letters during his stay at the Willard, and a report circulated of a plot to blow up the inaugural platform at the Capitol as the new president took the oath. To the relief of Scott, Lincoln was sworn in without incident.

Along with stemming the cascade of states seceding from the Union, his immediate problem was holding on to federal property the seceding states were seizing within their borders. Among the most contentious of the few southern forts still in Union hands was Fort Sumter, an imposing, heavily bricked, big-gun compound still being built on a man-made granite island at the entrance of the Charleston, South Carolina, harbor, which veteran Major Robert Anderson commanded with eighty-five men. The new president was not averse to unconventional operations to hold on to federal assets. Starved for intelligence, he sent Lamon and two other emissaries to Charleston to collect information. Lincoln also considered a clandestine operation that Gustavus Vasa Fox, an adventurous former naval officer he admired, had hatched to secretly infiltrate reinforcements and supplies into Fort Sumter. Lincoln eventually abandoned the covert plan and simply notified South Carolina governor Francis Pickens that he intended just to resupply the fort. If the Confederates fired their guns to prevent it, Jefferson Davis, not Lincoln, would be starting the war. Davis took the bait. Before the federal relief fleet arrived, General Pierre G. T. Beauregard's forces unleashed their artillery on April 12, and after thirty-three hours of bombardment, Anderson's exhausted garrison surrendered on April 13.

The war was on. On April 15, Lincoln issued a proclamation calling on 75,000 state militiamen for ninety days of federal service. Galvanized by Fort Sumter's surrender, many northerners were euphoric at the outbreak of hostilities—none more so than the men and women of Kingston, a town on the west bank of the Hudson River in Ulster Country, ninety-one miles north of New York City. Antislavery sentiment ran strong in Kingston by 1855. Six militia companies had begun drilling and preparing for trouble, with the out-of-towners in their ranks filling up Kingston's four hotels or sleeping in encampments.

Within days after the Fort Sumter attack, a mass meeting was convened at Kingston's county courthouse, on the west side of Wall Street. One by one, the local congressmen and officers of the 20th New York State Militia, also called the "Ulster Guard," climbed onto a barrelhead at the top of the courthouse steps to deliver stirring speeches against the "traitor hands and traitor hearts" of the South. Among the officers caught up in the moment was Captain George Henry Sharpe, who took his turn atop the barrelhead to implore the young men in the crowd to volunteer for three months of duty. Within two days, young Captain Sharpe, who had hung a flag out of Kingston's old Brick Church to designate it as the recruiting station, had enlisted 248 men for his Company B. They were sent to the 20th Regiment's makeshift camps at Kingston and nearby Poughkeepsie, Rondout, and Athens.

Sharpe's superiors considered him a natural military leader, with a magnetic personality that made men want to follow him. He had a balding head, sad eyes, and a droopy mustache that gave him the look more of a city preacher than a combat commander. He was a learned man. In the breast pocket of his uniform coat he kept always a small, well-thumbed book of verses by his favorite poets, which he routinely read to his men. They never objected to his recitals. In Kingston, George Sharpe had found a life worth fighting for. In later years, he penned a lengthy newspaper article on the history of the town he so loved.

That history traced back to 1614, when explorers set up a trading post in the area. By 1653, as many as seventy Dutch men and women became the first settlers scattered about what was called the Esopus tract, named for the Esopus Indians the settlers began to drive out. Roving Indian bands launched savage reprisal raids until 1655, when an uneasy truce prevailed for the next three years. In 1661, Peter Stuyvesant, the director general of New Amsterdam, had selected a square-mile-shaped site for a village on high ground, enclosed with earthworks and named Wiltwyck. It was renamed Kingston in 1669, perhaps after Kingston-upon-Thames in England.

The farmers, tradesmen, and merchants who built stone homes in Kingston—many of them connected to one another by tunnels—were prudent and frugal people, rarely ostentatious, and practically all deeply religious. The Dutch among them, a strong cultural influence for the town, loved to dance and held regular socials at DeWall's Ballroom. General George Washington passed through during the Revolutionary War, enjoying himself at a party at the Benjamin Bogardus tavern. Kingston became the first capital of New York after independence was declared, with the state's Senate organizing there on September 10, 1777, in Abraham van Gaasbeek's modest stone house. A month later, the state legislators fled when British soldiers arrived and burned down most of the town's buildings along with its important granaries. The soldiers spared the old beer house, however, so they could enjoy the brew.

By the 1820s, Kingston had rebuilt the buildings the British torched and had developed into a regional trading center and departure point for steamers as well as sloops sailing old-money families down the Hudson to New York City. The town boasted its first hotel, a coffeehouse, tailor and halter shops, a saddle and harness maker, a watchmaker and jewelry shop, apple mill and distillery, candy shop and tobacco factory. The spire of the old Reformed Dutch Church now stood with so many spires from other Protestant churches that Kingston eventually became known as the "City of Churches." Henry Sharp, the son of a prosperous farmer, married Helen Hasbrouck, a member of one of Kingston's wealthiest French Huguenot families, all of whom lived in the town's finest stone houses. Sharp became a wealthy merchant in his own right, forming a partnership with his brother Peter and Francis C. Voorhees to operate a mercantile house on East Front Street. In due time, Henry set his family up in what one town history called a "striking Colonial residence" on Wall Street, surrounded by giant old elm trees.

George Henry Sharpe was born on February 26, 1828. He was Henry and Helen's only child. For some mysterious reason, the boy in later years attached an *e* to the end of his last name. Sharpe's mother lived until age ninety, but throughout her life she was tormented by a nauseous stomach that left her constantly vomiting. She treated her attacks of biliousness with homeopathy, which she believed worked best. George never knew his father. Henry died in 1830 after suffering two paralytic strokes at an asylum in New York, just before his son turned two years old. Sharpe's surrogate father—or at least the only father he felt he ever had—became Severyn Bruyn, a local banker who served as trustee of Henry Sharp's considerable

estate and doled out an allowance to George until he turned twenty-one
and was allowed to control his own finances.

Henry Sharp left behind enough money to give his son the finest education a young man could receive at the time. George attended Kingston
Academy, which he considered the best in New York. Before packing off to
college, he went to prep school at the elite Albany Academy. At age fifteen,
he entered Rutgers College in 1843 and graduated with honors at nineteen,
delivering his class's salutatory address in Latin. Sharpe next studied law at
Yale University, and within a year had begun apprenticing (for an annual
fee of one hundred dollars) in the New York City firm of Bidwell & Strong,
soon handling small-claims suits. He easily passed the New York state bar
exam at age twenty-one, writing Bruyn that it was not nearly as "rigid" as
the tests he took at Yale.

Before returning to Kingston, Sharpe sailed to Europe and spent the next
four years making his education more cosmopolitan. He studied French in
Paris just before Napoleon III organized his coup d'état in 1851, and he became so proficient in the language that Frenchmen thought he was a native.
He served as a secretary in the U.S. legation in Vienna, and then worked in
the legation in Rome, where he learned Italian.

Sharpe returned to Kingston in 1854, setting up an instantly prominent
law partnership on Main Street north from Green Street, first with a former
judge and after his death with a future congressman. He returned briefly to
his father's home on Wall Street and then found a place of his own on Albany
Court East. The law practice flourished. His professional reputation rising,
Sharpe took on important cases that the local newspaper began covering.
He became a full-fledged member of Kingston's and Ulster County's political and intellectual elite, enjoying wild-game hunting with clients, serving
as a delegate to political conventions, running for Kingston supervisor (he
lost that race), becoming a trustee of Kingston Academy, and delivering lec-
tures before the Plattekill Literary Association on subjects such as "Egypt
and the Nile." Sharpe also began dabbling in military affairs, appointed in
1858 as the legal officer for the New York State Militia's 3rd Division.

As his father had done, Sharpe in 1855 married into the wealthy

Hasbrouck family. He fell in love with Caroline Hone Hasbrouck, who was two years younger than he and whose father, Abraham Bruyn Hasbrouck, was an urbane and scholarly Kingston Academy and Yale graduate like Sharpe. Hasbrouck practiced law and for ten years was president of Rutgers College (Sharpe's alma mater). Sharpe always called his wife Carrie.

Sharpe and the other members of the 20th New York State Militia climbed aboard trains on April 23, 1861, and set off for Washington, departing Kingston with all the fanfare its proud citizens could offer. What had been a skeletal unit was now up to full strength. Even so, the Ulster Guard began its war poorly equipped. Abraham Hasbrouck organized Kingston's banks to advance the regiment $8,000 for uniforms and supplies, and an Ulster Military Relief Committee had been formed to collect small-dollar donations from citizens. But the money was only enough to buy old, worn-out uniforms and muskets that were antiques.

That they were marching off to war horribly prepared did not seem to bother Sharpe or the others. After all, their service was for just three months. With the North's vast natural resources, tremendous industrial capacity, and overwhelming advantage in railroad mileage—not to mention its 20 million inhabitants compared to the Confederacy's 9 million—senior administration officials like Seward thought ninety days would be enough to crush the rebellion. The men of the 20th did not know then that the war would last far longer. And George Sharpe did not realize he was marching off to become the Union Army's preeminent spymaster.

Three

ELIZABETH VAN LEW

A fter Fort Sumter's fall, Lincoln struggled to prevent any more secessions from the Union. He succeeded with the border states of Delaware, Maryland, Kentucky, and Missouri—although secessionist plotters remained active in Maryland throughout the war, Confederate guerrillas infested Missouri, and Kentucky was nearly evenly divided between northern and southern sympathizers. But four states did join the seven already rebelling—Arkansas, Tennessee, North Carolina, and the prize for the Confederacy, Virginia. In Richmond, joyous residents poured out of their homes and into the streets on April 14 when news reached the city by telegraph of the fort's capture. Cannon boomed out a hundred-gun salute, bonfires were lighted, girls at the Richmond Female Institute raised for the first time the Confederate flag. Women shunned men who refused now to put on the Rebel uniform.

Elizabeth Van Lew was disgusted by what she saw walking around Richmond three days later. Confederate banners hung from the windows of city buildings and a torchlight procession marched through the streets. A Virginia legislator Van Lew knew walked up to her and announced defiantly:

"The man who says slavery is wrong should be hung for murder." Another state senator confided that lawmakers who raised objections to a break from the Union now feared for their lives. "Jubilant" Richmond, Elizabeth wrote dejectedly in her diary, was becoming the "centre of treason"—so little moved by the "national outrage" of an American military facility being seized.

Elizabeth Van Lew was a short woman, who had been quite fetching in her youth. But now in her forties and unmarried, she was considered by Richmond society to be an old maid. She loved her state, always speaking of Virginians in her soft southern accent as "our people"—although that love would be tested sorely in the years to come. She wore her dark blond hair always in tight curls that hung along her cheeks and neck. She had a thin, nervous-looking face with high cheekbones, pointed nose, and sparkling blue eyes that bore into anyone facing her stare. She was almost always attired in the antebellum style with black silk dress and bonnet whose ribbons tied under her chin in the front. She was clever to the point of "almost unearthly brilliance," friends said, and decidedly feisty. She could be acid-tongued and scalding in her contempt for people whose social or political views clashed with her strong sense of right from wrong. She acknowledged it had made her life "intensely sad and earnest." Yet when she thought it would help her have her way, Elizabeth Van Lew could be gentle and flattering.

She came from energetic yet frugal Dutch stock, whose ancestors could be traced back to early-seventeenth-century Netherlands. Frederick Van Leeuwen, born in 1650, likely in Eindhoven, arrived in America when he was twenty and eventually settled in Jamaica on the western end of Long Island (now in the borough of Queens). One of his descendants was John Van Lew III, born in Jamaica in 1790 to parents who divorced when he was a teenager. John worked in a New York mercantile house until he was sixteen years old, when he moved south to Richmond and found a job with the Adams Hardware Company. He was an energetic employee, and by 1812 John Adams had made him a partner. Adams & Van Lew was the first hardware business in the city. The partnership failed, however, and Van Lew dutifully paid off his share of the massive $100,000 debt they had accumulated.

On January 10, 1818, John married Eliza Louise Baker at St. John's

Episcopal Church in the fashionable Church Hill neighborhood, where Patrick Henry, according to legend, delivered his "Give me liberty or give me death" speech. She was a woman as intellectual and tenderhearted as he was and who also came from the North—although Eliza, elegant and petite, with gray eyes and milky white skin, had adopted the manners of a true southern lady. Richmond newspapers announcing the union reported that they were now "both of this city." Eliza had been born in 1798 in Philadelphia, the daughter of German immigrant Hilarious Becker, who had anglicized his name to Hilary Baker. Baker fought in the Revolutionary War, had become one of the first members of the Pennsylvania Abolition Society, and had been elected three times as mayor of the city. But he died in office from a yellow fever epidemic that ravaged Philadelphia when Eliza was only three months old. After her mother died in 1808, the orphaned girl was sent to live with her older brother, Hilary Jr., in Richmond, where she eventually met John, by then considered a businessman on his way up.

Nine months after the wedding, Elizabeth arrived on October 15, 1818. A brother the parents named John Newton and a sister, Anna Paulina, followed. The three children were born into what was becoming a wealthy family in Richmond, which by the early 1800s was transitioning from a rustic port village on the James River into one of the region's leading manufacturing metropolises, powered, as other southern cities were, by slave labor. In 1823, thirty-three-year-old John Van Lew bought out Adams and soon joined Richmond's prosperous merchants. John partnered with other businessmen and by 1849 they operated out of several stores—one insured for $19,000 (more than $500,000 in today's dollars)—and advertised that they were "importers and dealers in hardware, cutlery, guns, saddlery and tools of every description." John Van Lew was the first in the city to set up a hardware-only store; previously those items were sold with dry goods or groceries. His new approach worked. Soon he had a small chain of five successful hardware stores in the Richmond area.

In 1828, John began renting the Church Hill mansion that Adams built in 1802 in the 2300 block of East Grace Street, which in its better days had entertained visiting luminaries like John Marshall and the Marquis de Lafayette. Eight years later, when Adams died and Van Lew was appointed administrator of his estate, he bought the run-down house and immediately began remodeling it. John put up a grand portico overlooking a picturesque falling yard, traveled to Italy for quality fixtures, installed inside blinds, and bought expensive mantels. He had enough left over after the renovations to also buy a small farm along the James River south of Richmond.

The three-and-a-half-story mansion, with its fourteen rooms and six long white columns rising to the roof supporting a large cornice in the front, became a showpiece. The land it rested on took up an entire city block atop one of the highest of Richmond's seven hills, cooled by tall oaks and magnolias, with a terraced garden in the back to the brow of the hill, giving the Van Lews a superb view of the James. Large doors at the entrance opened into an eighteen-foot-wide hall with a chandelier, carved mahogany benches, and Persian rugs over hardwood floors. The dining room off the kitchen, sitting room, drawing room, and library occupied the first floor, filled with expensive chairs, soft sofas, antique tables, candelabras, and priceless vases. The lower and upper chambers on the second and third floors had the family bedrooms and lounges. Basement and attic rooms housed the servants' quarters. Among treasured mementos—a purse believed to have belonged to George Washington. Elizabeth thought it was the world's most beautiful home.

The northern couple was spectacularly successful assimilating into southern society. The Church Hill neighborhood was a Whig enclave, its prominent members regulars at Van Lew parties. John gained a reputation as a public-spirited and benevolent citizen, often contributing secretly to charities. Celebrities visited the mansion, such as Edgar Allan Poe (who read "The Raven" in the drawing room) and Swedish opera soprano Jenny Lind (who sang on the back porch for a charity benefit). John and Eliza also corresponded with James Monroe, Daniel Webster, and Henry Clay.

For Elizabeth and her brother and sister, Church Hill became an intellectual hothouse. The library was stocked with almost 600 books, nearly 250 of which belonged to Eliza. Fifty dollars a year was allocated to increase the collection, which included two large volumes of William Shakespeare with steel plate engravings, Reverend Thomas Scott's six-volume Bible set, and theologian Thomas Burnet's *Sacred Theory of the Earth*. The parents, egalitarian in their marriage, made their children feel special, instilling deeply held values in them, which often ran counter to southern norms. Elizabeth, John, and Anna, as a result, developed a keen sense of loneliness and alienation, forced to play the role of outsider. Close to her mother, Elizabeth was the weakest physically, but the strongest willed.

She developed an early empathy for the slaves in her home and elsewhere. Their backbreaking work and the beatings she witnessed on city streets horrified her. On family vacations at western Virginia's Hot Springs, a resort to escape the summer heat, she became friends with a slave trader's daughter and was repelled by what she learned of the dreadful business. John Van Lew believed Richmond schools were inadequate, so he sent Elizabeth to Philadelphia and Eliza's family to be taught at one of the academies in the city's fashionable district. A governess in the home lectured her on the abolition of slavery and Van Lew's daughter returned to Richmond with an even fiercer hatred of human bondage. "Slave power," she said, "is arrogant, is jealous and intrusive, is cruel, is despotic, not only over the slave but over the community, the state."

Elizabeth returned to the South a beautiful, educated, and vivacious teenager from a wealthy family—an ideal match for many suitors who began to show up at the mansion. But they all discovered that her intellect and wit had an edge to it that was dangerous to trifle with. Elizabeth considered boys trespassers as much as love interests. She never married and many reasons were offered. Perhaps a failed romance broke her heart. Or that like her mother, Elizabeth's serious side turned off boys. Or she preferred the "homage of hundreds" rather than the "yoke" of one husband, as a Richmond newspaper later speculated. Family lore passed down over generations held that she had been engaged to the only man she loved but he died of yellow fever when she was twenty-three. Van Lew never confided with relatives or friends on the reason.

John Van Lew became seriously ill in 1838. What ailed him was never clear. His years soon "were passed in suffering and pain from a disease which baffled medical skill," a newspaper reported. The only treatment doctors could think of were the curative waters at western Virginia's White Sulphur Springs. John died on September 13, 1843. Hundreds of friends from

Richmond, Philadelphia, and New York attended his funeral at the mansion to pay tribute to a man "remembered alike for his useful and well-directed energies as a citizen, and for the goodness and charities of his heart," the *Richmond Compiler* eulogized.

But the legacy of her father that vexed Elizabeth was slavery. John owned fifteen slaves by 1840. An old-line Whig, he recognized the institution's evils and strived to treat his slaves well, but he understood that their forced labor was his ticket to Richmond's upper crust. Elizabeth had heated arguments with her father about slavery, begging him to free the blacks he had. John refused. It was likely the reason his will barred his wife from releasing the slaves after he died. Eliza wisely used her inheritance, which included the mansion and other real estate, to buy property in south Richmond and beyond, which at that moment was selling at deeply depressed prices. She sold many parcels in the 1850s when the city's economy revived, reaping a huge profit and guaranteeing that her family would remain wealthy. John left $10,000 (about $350,000 in today's dollars) to each of the children. Anna married a Philadelphia doctor in 1844 and moved to that city, but continued to keep close tabs on the family business. John, who had worked for his father in the hardware business, took over the stores and had them flourishing as the economy improved. John also showed his father's maverick intellectual streak, raising money for a Jewish school in Richmond at a time when anti-Semitism in the city was virulent and later writing a dry tome on matter and energy titled *Natural Force: A New View*. Elizabeth spent much of her inheritance circumventing the slavery provision in her father's will.

Instead of trying to openly free their slaves—a complicated legal exercise in Virginia even if John's will had not barred them from doing so—Eliza and Elizabeth made informal and secret arrangements with the African Americans to liberate them. Many of the blacks, given the option of fleeing north, decided to remain with Eliza and Elizabeth, whom they considered friends, working in the mansion or on their thirty-six-acre farm in Henrico County. She began paying the ones who remained under the table or hiring them out to other families and allowing them to keep the fees the families remitted to her. Van Lew also spent much of her inheritance buying slaves at Richmond's markets to keep their families from being broken up and then secretly freeing them. She bought nine this way. It was an expensive exercise. A slave named Louisa, whom Elizabeth purchased on January 1, 1863, cost her $1,000.

Mother and daughter took other small steps outside Richmond's social order. They sold a piece of real estate John had owned to two free black women. They hosted Swedish novelist and feminist Fredrika Bremer, who visited the United States to witness American slavery and found herself "immediately attracted to" Elizabeth as she showed her Richmond's seamier auction blocks. Elizabeth toured Europe and made regular trips to Philadelphia to be among ideological soul mates. Richmond friends caught her muttering incendiary statements like "The negroes have black faces but white hearts." On city streets among strangers occasionally, she impulsively engaged in arguments about slavery. Both women did little to hide their sorrow over John Brown's hanging. They had corresponded regularly with Brown and Frederick Douglass.

Yet they modulated their views to a degree. Eliza and Elizabeth were not overt abolitionists. They largely lived double lives—conforming outwardly to the South's social conventions, while privately taking steps to subvert them, like secretly freeing blacks. For better or worse, they were attached to Richmond's elite. Elizabeth remained devoted to the South. Northerners were just as complicit in maintaining the slave system, she felt; "these negro whips were made of the North cowhides," she once wrote. To flee Richmond just to be among those who agreed with her would abdicate the responsibility Elizabeth felt she had to improve the condition of blacks in her home and in her city. She could reconcile the deep moral qualms she had with living in slaveholding Richmond so long as she could continue chipping away at the system. Blacks in her household predicted to her that slavery would bring down this new Confederacy. Elizabeth agreed. Her private journal became her refuge to vent about the brutal treatment of blacks, "the poor creatures suffering punishment for any little thing."

Though they tried to maintain a veneer, gossip soon spread in Richmond society about the antislavery sentiments Eliza and Elizabeth displayed. Invitations to parties stopped coming. White men in the city who voiced such sentiments could find themselves being lynched. Women received more latitude. Even so, the blowback for the Van Lew ladies began to turn ugly. They found on the front steps of their mansion one morning a crudely written letter from the "White Caps," a predecessor to the Ku Klux Kan. "Old maid, is your house insured?" the threatening note read, with a drawing of a house on fire. "White Caps are around town. They are coming at night. Look out!"

Tensions boiled inside the Church Hill mansion as well. Elizabeth's brother, John, married Mary Carter West in January 1854. It was not a good match for either of them. Mary was a Virginia blue blood, whose father owned a plantation close to Malvern Hill near Richmond (where the July 1862 Battle of Malvern Hill would erupt practically in the family's front yard). John had first met Mary at the plantation's large blacksmith shop, which he visited frequently to buy materials for his stores. The West family, Mary included, were particularly devoted racists and secessionists—180 degrees opposite the Van Lews. John and Mary were able to paper over their differences until 1861, when the couple with their two daughters moved back into the Church Hill mansion. Soon Mary clashed openly with her mother- and sister-in-law.

Richmond and the rest of Virginia had been opposed to secession through much of 1860. But strident voices in the state's capital gained momentum. One city paper offered a hundred-dollar reward for Seward's head. The rise of the secessionists shocked Van Lew. After John Brown's Harpers Ferry raid, "our people were in a palpable state of war," she wrote in her diary. From the gallery in Mechanic's Hall, Van Lew watched the proceedings of the Virginia Secession Convention as the pendulum swung from moderates and Unionists to the "bold and more imprudently daring" (also her words) calling for a breakaway. Four days after Fort Sumter's capture, the state convention passed an ordinance of secession by a secret vote of 88 to 55. Van Lew was convinced many delegates had been coerced or even terrorized into voting to leave the Union. "One gentleman, who signed the ordinance of secession, told me he thought that if he had not done so, the streets of Richmond would have run with blood," she wrote. Democracy was under assault by the "full blast" of Rebel rule. "Madness was upon the people!"

Van Lew grew indignant at how quickly Richmond editors in their news-paper columns and preachers from their pulpits allowed the extremists to co-opt them. She held a special loathing for the "well dressed [southern] ladies of the highest education" so eager to hoist Confederate flags from their rooftops, sew fancy uniforms for their officers, and send their men off to war with brave words about killing "as many Yankees as you can for me" and returning with "Mr. Lincoln's head or a piece of his ear." Two days after Virginia's secession vote, word arrived of the bloody clash between Union troops and the Baltimore secessionists, resulting in the first casualties of the new war. On Richmond streets, Elizabeth saw joyful young women danc-ing and celebrating. She noticed that some of the young men's faces were "deadly pale."

Elizabeth walked home that night wiping tears from her eyes. Back at the mansion, she fell to her knees, clasped her hands, and prayed, "Father, forgive them for they know not what they do." She took down the American flag from the pole on the side of her chimney and hid pro-Union memo-rabilia that she had proudly displayed before in her home. She feared that would not be enough to protect her. She heard that mobs had been march-ing to the homes of suspected Unionists, threatening to hang them. "Loy-alty now was called treason and cursed," she wrote in her journal. Men and women who thought like her had to whisper their feelings in the privacy of their parlors. Some secessionists wanted all Unionists in the city driven to the streets and slaughtered. Worried for her safety, Van Lew paid a visit to Jefferson Davis. She could not get past the Confederate president's private secretary, who told her to take her case to Richmond mayor Joseph Mayo.

French visitors had called Richmond "Paris in miniature" with its ware-houses, tobacco factories, and flour mills crowding the James River bank, the city's commercial and residential center spread out on a long slope be-hind them to Council Chamber Hill, where at the city center the Capitol and its classical columns designed by Thomas Jefferson sat with other gov-ernment buildings. Gaslights illuminated streets as well as many homes and businesses. One hundred thousand tons of cargo reached Richmond's river port every year. "One seems to breathe tobacco, to see tobacco, and smell tobacco at every turn," a British visitor remarked. "The town is filthy with it."

Soon after the secession vote, the country around Richmond became one vast armed camp, the air filled all hours with the sounds of martial music, officers shouting commands, and soldiers tramping through city streets or being drilled at the Central Fair Grounds to the north. Drummers beat out reveille in the morning, buglers blew taps at night. Troops and officials from the new Confederate government poured into the city, which became the Rebel capital in May, soon tripling its population to about 100,000. Speculators, gamblers, prostitutes, and criminals (many disguised in Confederate uniforms) also arrived. Taxes had to be raised to provide extra city services for the influx, food prices surged from scarcities, and extortionists gouged customers. Van Lew refused to join the sewing societies Richmond women formed to make uniforms, roll bandages, and manufacture cartridges.

Shortly after John Brown's hanging at the end of 1859, Elizabeth had begun sending unsolicited letters to federal officials in Washington with her observations of economic conditions in Richmond and the growing secessionist sentiment there. By summer 1861, with her letters containing more information on Confederate troops moving about the city and the numbers she saw, Van Lew stopped using the mails and had trusted friends carry her notes to Washington. Though her criticism of slavery and refusal to sew shirts for soldiers became common knowledge around her neighborhood, Elizabeth still remained a member in good standing of Virginia's old-line aristocracy. No one could conceive of a woman from that class becoming a spy for the Union.

Four

LAFAYETTE BAKER

afayette Baker arrived in Washington to witness a city in panic after the first reliable reports arrived April 14 that Fort Sumter had fallen. Fears of a fifth-column uprising, so widespread before the inauguration, now became white hot. Cabinet members believed treason lurked in every corner of the city. A congressional investigation identified two hundred federal employees who were southern sympathizers—ideally suited for espionage. During the months before the war started, southern Army and Navy officers were allowed to pass freely through federal lines to join the Confederacy, taking secrets with them. A remarkable number of prosecession officers hung around Washington in the confusion of 1861. General Scott remained surrounded mainly by southern officers, whom Lincoln did not trust. With the war begun, Scott knew he had to set up some kind of intelligence collection service—and that he had to keep it secret from the officers closest to him. It may explain why the general was willing to meet with a poorly educated and aimless drifter who had been roaming the country for nearly two decades and who now had a vague notion of serving the Union cause as a spy.

Lafayette Curry Baker had taken a train from New York to Philadelphia and then had climbed onto a slate-gray mare to ride through the Maryland countryside and into Washington when news of Sumter's fall reached the city. In New York, talk of war had been "the all absorbing topic," he wrote his sister, with federal troops hurrying to board trains for Washington and crowds chanting "death to traitors." Baker said he felt the same "patriotic indignation" over the rebellion, even more so on the day Sumter surrendered. "That day sealed the doom of American slavery and Southern traitors," he wrote his sister. Baker had relocated to New York from California and had managed to get himself elected as a first lieutenant for a company of one hundred California expats in the city, who had decided to form a volunteer militia. He freely admitted that the only thing he knew about the military came from what he had picked up as a practically lawless vigilante in California. His vigilante days were also about the only work experience that qualified him for some type of espionage job in Washington.

Baker was a handsome man, with brown hair, a full red beard, and piercing gray eyes that were almost hypnotic. He stood five feet ten inches tall, a muscular 180 pounds, agile, almost catlike in his quick movements, always seemingly restless. He was a fine horseman, a crack shot. He did not swear or drink, priding himself on being a member of Sons of Temperance, a male brotherhood sworn against alcohol, which had started in New York City in 1842 and spread across the country. He was obsessed with Roman history. On his trip from California to New York, he devoured a book on a man who would become one of his role models: Eugène François Vidocq, the famed and, Baker acknowledged, unsavory French detective who helped create France's security police. Baker was as devious and manipulating as Vidocq, prone to lie about himself, with "the heart of a sneak thief," according to one profile of him. Patriotic fervor had not been all that compelled him to ride to Washington. The profit he hoped to turn from ventures in New York had not materialized—he blamed it on East Coast business being "almost entirely suspended," he wrote his sister—and Washington now looked like a good place to make money.

• • •

As a young boy, Baker loved to listen to family stories about his ancestors—"a migrating pioneering tribe," as one descendant described them. His lineage could be traced back to Alexander Baker, a thirty-two-year-old collar maker who emigrated from London to America in 1635, living in Gloucester, Massachusetts, for seven years and then moving to Boston, where he fathered a dozen children. One of Alexander's sons, Joshua Baker, born in 1642, moved when he was twenty-eight years old to New London, Connecticut, where he received a large tract of land from the chief of the Mohegan Indians. One of his grandsons, strangely named "Remember" when he was born in 1711, was given twenty acres of land to farm in Roxbury, Connecticut. Remember had a daughter and son before his life was cut short when a neighbor accidentally shot him in the head in 1737 while they were hunting.

His son, Remember Jr., who had been born eighteen days after his father's fatal accident, became an occasional soldier of fortune in the French and Indian War, meeting an end even more tragic than his father's. Over five years, the young man enlisted in militias several different times, joining the unsuccessful 1755 British and American expedition against Crown Point, on the narrows at the south end of Lake Champlain (where the French had built Fort Saint-Frédéric), and the attack on Fort Ticonderoga near there in 1758. Remember finally settled down with a family in 1760 and operated a sawmill the next six years in Arlington, Vermont, where he persuaded his three cousins—Ethan and Ira Allen and Seth Warner—to join him from Connecticut and seek their fortunes with the grants the New Hampshire colony gave Vermont settlers. But trouble soon followed Remember Jr., who was something of a hothead. New York colony speculators laid claim, likely fraudulently, to the Vermont land that New Hampshire was doling out to Remember Jr., his cousins, and others, and by 1770 the speculators were trying to sell this land to other settlers. The Vermonters mobilized to defend their property. Ethan Allen was chosen as colonel to lead the Green Mountain Boys to battle the New York interlopers, with Remember Jr. and Seth Warner serving under Allen as company captains. The fighting turned nasty at times; Captain Baker lost a thumb when a band of New Yorkers wounded and captured him briefly in 1772. During the Revolutionary War,

Captain Baker fought with the patriots, but in August 1775, Indians allied with the British attacked his scouting party near the Vermont border with Canada and killed him, chopping off his toes and sticking his severed head on a stake.

One of Captain Baker's grandsons, named Remember III after his warrior grandfather, also served in the cavalry along the Canadian frontier during the War of 1812, but he never took part in any heavy fighting. Remember III, who bought adjoining tracts of land with his brother, Luther, in Stafford, New York, halfway between Buffalo and Rochester, married Cynthia Stannard in 1807. The couple had eight children. Thirty years later, Remember III, growing restless, left his family behind for the moment and traveled west to central Michigan, where he cleared land in a dense forest near the village of Grand River City in Eaton County and built a log cabin before having his wife and children join him the next year. Life was hard in central Michigan. Remember was deeply religious, believing "that God will prepare me for all the events of his providence that await me," he wrote. He fell in love with central Michigan and dutifully served the Lord by helping build a seminary near the village.

But Remember III could be insufferable with his religious fervor. A stern Puritan, he ran his family like a military platoon. No one chafed under his authoritarian rule more than his second-youngest son, Lafayette, who had been born on October 13, 1825, and was thirteen when the family moved to Michigan. "Lafe," as he was nicknamed, rebelled against his father and wanted to run away as soon as he reached the state. Remember's endless preaching irritated Lafe so much he soon became an atheist.

The father left his children largely to educate themselves. Young Baker showed no interest in book learning, so he did little of it except to master the basics of reading and writing. He enjoyed instead fixing machinery, like farm equipment. He grew into a young man mostly uneducated—relying instead on his keen instinct and street smarts as guides. Lafe ran away from home in his late teens and became a wanderer drifting through a dozen states. He fled many cities after gunfights with other men. When his father died in 1847, Baker, then twenty-two, was working as a mechanic in Scranton, Pennsylvania. In 1848, he returned to New York for two years and then moved to Philadelphia, where he opened a dry goods store with money saved from his mechanic's jobs. Four years later he married Jennie Curry, a young Philadelphia woman who was somewhat plain looking, with a stolid disposition. The couple soon found they could not have children.

Jennie hoped her husband would settle down as a tradesman, but Baker became restless once more. His younger brother, Milo, wrote him from San Francisco, begging him to join him in California, where men were making fortunes mining gold. With his dry goods business foundering, Baker in 1853 set out for the West, leaving Jennie behind to move in with her parents in Philadelphia until he could send for her after striking it rich panning for gold.

Growing a bushy beard, Baker boarded a steamboat in New York bound for San Francisco by way of the southern route through Panama's isthmus. He reached San Francisco to find his brother prosperous enough to put him up for a week in an elegant city hotel until he started making money. San Francisco was a fast-growing city of more than 40,000, with gold hunters flooding in daily, inflated prices, jobs paying high wages because of a labor shortage, and gambling houses like the El Dorado open twenty-four hours a day. Baker, who brought his wife to California six months after he arrived there, found no gold and had to take odd jobs. He worked for a while making good money as a mechanic and as a bouncer in a Barbary Coast saloon. In 1856 he joined the 2,200 members of the San Francisco Vigilance Committee, each of whom was known only by his number. Baker's was 208. Since the 1849 gold rush and migration of some 300,000 fortune-seekers into California, San Francisco's crime rate had soared. The world's most ruthless criminals, many from Australia, had poured in, unchecked by the local government and its weak police force. A loose-knit criminal alliance called "the Hounds" soon began running the city, extorting workers and businesses, and launching nighttime rampages.

Fed up, San Franciscans decided to take the law into their own hands. A Committee of Vigilance was formed in 1851 with some seven hundred members and revived five years later with thousands more to fight crime. The uniformed, sword-carrying committeemen worked alongside the city government or in defiance of it, holding quick trials and hangings, becoming practically as lawless as the criminals they fought. Baker became a hardened vigilante, joining gangs of committee paramilitaries who terrorized citizens with night raids, beat up suspects under interrogation, framed evidence, lynched the ones deemed deserving of the death penalty, and recruited crooks, spies, and informers all in the name of law and order. He loved the work. It made him feel powerful, though he never rose higher in the committee than the rank of private.

After the group was dissolved, Baker took a job for a while with the city's regular police force. Next he became a license tax collector for several years, and finally he opened what he called a "mercantile agency," which was probably similar to his dry goods shop in Philadelphia. But he always considered vigilantism his true calling. For his Vigilance Committee crime busting San Francisco merchants gave him a $250 cane made of manzanita wood topped with polished gold quartz surrounded by nine oval stones. He treasured the souvenir of his days wielding unchecked power.

On New Year's Day 1861, Lafayette Baker boarded a fast clipper and sailed back to New York. He told Jennie he would return from the East with new business plans for making big money in San Francisco, but he never did. Instead, by mid-April he was in Washington City angling for a lucrative job in the new Lincoln administration.

Baker decided to apply with the highest-ranking officer in the U.S. Army. He would meet with Winfield Scott directly and talk him into giving him a job. But the general in chief was a busy man, inundated with callers and job seekers and hardly likely to allow strangers to just wander in for a chat. So Baker checked in to the Willard, believing the hotel would be the best spot for the networking he needed to do for an entrée to Scott. At the Willard, whose lobby during the war would serve as an unofficial Army headquarters with officers bearing field reports coming into and out of it at all hours of the day, Baker finally was able to buttonhole two men who had the connections to arrange an interview with Scott: Representative William Kelly of Philadelphia and Hiram Walbridge, a former New York congressman. Kelly ushered him into a suite of rooms at the hotel where the general in chief was ensconced.

Seventy-four-year-old Winfield Scott, a hero of the War of 1812 and the Mexican-American War, was now in decrepit shape. Years of consuming rich foods had made "Old Fuss and Feathers" (his nickname because he enjoyed military pomp) so fat at 350 pounds, he could not walk even short distances and had to be hoisted onto a strong horse to review his troops. Scott found stairs so painful to climb because of the gout he suffered that Lincoln walked down from his second-floor White House office to confer with the general. Yet Scott's mental acuity, as well as his ego, remained fit and trim. Scott justifiably considered himself an elder statesman as well as a military officer, which he felt accorded him the privilege of giving political advice to an administration, particularly this new one. To his credit, Scott was one of the few senior government officials at the moment mulling a coherent military strategy. Newspapers would dub it the "Anaconda Plan" to strangle the Confederacy with a blockade rather than pitched battle.

Baker later bragged in his memoirs that Scott instantly recognized him as a messiah, come to solve his intelligence collection woes. That account appears far-fetched, since Scott had never met this man. What can be verified is that Baker, wearing a new suit, did his best to butter up the old general. He told Scott his father had served under him during the War of 1812. And though he was largely uneducated, Baker was still a fast talker, skilled at ingratiating himself with superiors. He managed to spin enough of a tale about his vigilante experience to convince Scott that he could be a superb espionage agent.

Scott likely felt he had nothing to lose in hiring Baker. Signing him up on the spot was not that unusual. Even today, spy agencies accept walk-ins to fill a specific need, and after the Fort Sumter disaster, what Scott and the new administration desperately needed was intelligence on the Davis administration soon moving to Richmond. So Scott offered this stranger a job as a spy.

Baker never acknowledged it in his writings, but he may not have expected that he would get this far when he came to Washington and actually land a job with the Army's commanding general. Startled by his success, he hesitated. One account speculated that he wanted to shop around the federal capital to see if he could find a better position than the one Scott offered. Whatever the reason, Baker told the general that before he accepted the job he had to return to New York to clear up unfinished business. He claimed he left Scott "with the understanding that I should report to him as soon as circumstances would permit." The general in chief, who was swamped attending to other military matters, seemed content to let Baker drift away with no firm commitment on when, or if, he actually would show up for work.

Five

SECRET SERVICE

en days after the fall of Fort Sumter, Timothy Webster was ushered up to the second floor of the Executive Mansion, sometimes called the White House. Gas and water pipes had just been installed. Even so, the building was in shabby condition when the new first family arrived. Lincoln's large and austere office, which smelled musty from the tobacco smoke of previous presidents, doubled as a workspace for him—he toiled at an old mahogany desk in the corner with pigeonholes above it for files—and a meeting room for his cabinet, whose seven members sat around a heavy black walnut table in the center twice a week. A sofa and several upholstered armchairs lined the walls, which soon would have military maps tacked to them. Models of prototype weapons also would soon litter the office. Lincoln found the shell for a hand grenade useful as a paperweight.

Thirty-nine-year-old Webster, a strong and athletic British immigrant nicknamed "Big Tim," was a crack shot, fearless, and a talented actor, skilled at ingratiating himself in unfriendly environments during operations. Pinkerton had lured Webster away from the New York City Police

Department when the officer finally grew tired of political witch hunts of foreigners on the force. Webster, who had a wife and three children back in Illinois, quickly developed into a better undercover agent than Pinkerton. He sometimes used the code name "Peaches" when he sent messages to Pinkerton.

The president was buried in paperwork when Webster arrived. The thrusts and parries after Fort Sumter's fall had proved embarrassing for the new administration. On the night of April 18, Confederate raiders torched the armory at Harpers Ferry in western Virginia, destroying 15,000 muskets—a small but symbolically important victory for the South. Two days later, a Union captain abandoned the endangered Gosport Navy Yard near Norfolk, a setback for the U.S. sea service. Webster was at the White House as a courier of a bundle of about a dozen pieces of mail from businessmen and Lincoln political cronies in Chicago, who had important letters and reports that they asked Pinkerton to deliver to the chief executive. Webster also had an envelope for Lincoln with a special message from his boss. Regular mail and telegraphic service to Washington had been interrupted in April 1861 because violence in Baltimore had disrupted rail traffic and communications. Webster's journey through hostile parts of Maryland had been hazardous. Kate Warne had stitched the dozen dispatches between the linings of his coat and waistcoat to hide them from secessionists he might encounter.

Lincoln watched somewhat amused as Webster took off his coat and waistcoat, ripped open their linings, and handed him the letters, including the envelope from Pinkerton. "You have brought quite a mail with you, Mr. Webster," the president said, "more, perhaps, than it would be quite safe to attempt to carry another time."

"Yes, sir," Webster replied. "I don't think I would like to carry so much through Baltimore another time."

Lincoln had to prepare for a cabinet meeting and did not have time then to read carefully all the letters, as was his habit with paperwork. He told Webster to return the next morning at ten o'clock, after he had gone through the mail.

After perusing the notes from the Chicago businessmen and friends early the following morning, Lincoln tore open the envelope with Pinkerton's letter, which had "Confidential" printed at the top. "When I saw you last I said that if the time should ever come that I could be of service to you I was ready," the note began. "If that time has come I am on hand." Pinkerton had a force of up to eighteen employees, on "whose courage, skill and devotion to their country I can rely," which he now proposed to put at Lincoln's command to spy on traitors, courier sensitive White House letters, and perform "that class of secret service which is the most dangerous." "Secrecy is the great lever I propose to operate with," the detective wrote, the reason he had Webster hand-carry this message instead of trusting it to the telegraph wires. If Lincoln was interested, Webster had a four-page cipher key with word substitutions for him to use when he telegraphed back a message. "Whale oil" was used in the cipher for "Union." "Washington" became "Barley." Days of the week were different fowl like "turkey," "chicken," and "rooster."

With the federal capital sixty miles south of the Mason-Dixon Line, Lincoln did not have to be convinced. Confederate agents visited Washington so frequently, an employee at one hotel kept a room always reserved for them. With so many disloyal employees in the federal bureaucracy, Lincoln knew he could not rely on government agents to manage mundane defense contacts, much less a sensitive security service. Until northern forces arrived in April, Washington had felt dangerously isolated, with rumors—which panicked Mary Lincoln—spreading that Rebel batteries planted on the Virginia heights overlooking the city were ready to bombard it.

Webster showed up promptly at ten o'clock. Lincoln handed him two telegrams and asked him to send them out "when you have reached a point where communication is possible." One was to George McClellan in Columbus, Ohio, just made commanding general of the state's volunteer army. The other was for Pinkerton. Lincoln didn't bother with the cumbersome cipher; the message simply summoned Pinkerton to Washington, where his services were "greatly needed." Webster took the two pieces of paper, rolled them up tightly, and slipped them into the hollow of his walking cane. He screwed back on the cane's handle and left the Executive Mansion.

In late April, Pinkerton arrived in Washington. He found its streets packed "with soldiers, armed and eager for the fray," he later wrote, with officers and orderlies "galloping from place to place; the tramp of armed men was heard on every side, and strains of martial music filled the air." Washington, like Richmond, was becoming a city under arms. The federal capital's population had swelled to 200,000, the influx of soldiers taxing the antiquated water supply system pumping untreated water from the Potomac into homes, government buildings, and the White House. The Army's insatiable appetite for firewood eventually deforested the Virginia side of the Potomac River. Of Washington's 264 miles of streets, only Pennsylvania Avenue was smoothly paved and lighted; the rest were muddy, potholed brick or lumpy cobblestone roads with occasional lamps flickering. Stinking raw sewage accumulated near the White House. The British Foreign Office considered the city so uncivilized, it designated Washington a hardship post for its diplomats.

After several days in the city, Pinkerton finally secured a meeting with the president at eight in the evening of May 2. Even at that late hour, he found the Executive Mansion still "in a state of activity and bustle," he wrote later, with messengers running in and out of the building's entrance, clusters of Army officers huddled in serious conversations in the East Room on the first floor, and visitors lined up on staircases and along corridors to meet the new president and plead for a job in the administration. A doorkeeper took him up the steps to the second floor's south front, where Lincoln had summoned Seward to be with him in his office to hear out "our Chicago detective," as he told the secretary of state.

Navy secretary Gideon Welles thought Lincoln, though well-intentioned, was in over his head when it came to dealing with schemers and subterfuge. That quickly became not the case. Lincoln could be ruthless when he felt he had to be. Within months he would make clear to Congress that he considered prosecution of the war the chief executive's primary function, to be carried out with little meddling from the other branches of government and without allowing respect for civil liberties to interfere with national safety. The Constitution, in time of war, would restrain Congress more than it did Lincoln, who believed he had residual, even implied, powers to take any action he believed necessary to preserve the Union. Soon the president would suspend the writ of habeas corpus, allow the arbitrary arrest and jailing of thousands, shutter newspapers considered hostile to war aims, and even purge officials in Washington's city government deemed disloyal. Across the country he was prepared to disband popularly elected legislatures by force of arms if they tried to vote for secession.

Lincoln found subversion and propaganda useful tools to undermine the border states that had joined the Confederacy and to keep the ones that remained with the Union under his control. In Confederate Tennessee's eastern region, where Rebels were terrorizing and jailing pro-Union men, Lincoln in the summer would approve a fifth-column movement of federal loyalists in the region, secretly funded with $2,500 from Washington, to launch guerrilla attacks burning bridges and severing rail lines connecting Memphis and Nashville with Richmond. The plan eventually failed, but it did not dull Lincoln's willingness to launch fifth-column movements. In the critically important Union state of Kentucky, Lincoln could not use the hardball tactics he employed in Tennessee. He launched instead a propaganda campaign to woo the state, at the same time covertly arming pro-Unionists there, and had informants report regularly to him on whether the tactics were working.

Lincoln, whose Republican Party had its own paramilitary group called the "Wide Awakes" to protect campaign marchers from Democratic thugs, approved other unconventional schemes that crossed his desk. He was open to kidnapping Rebels to exchange for Union men the Confederates snatched. He was willing to let a U.S. Army officer venture out on an off-the-books operation the government would deny if he was caught. The Army colonel, who had been a Methodist minister before the war, would travel south undercover to entice Methodist Church members to defect. Lincoln had no doubt that Jefferson Davis would infiltrate subversives and spies into Union territory—which Davis would. The two men were alike in that respect.

Yet whatever enthusiasm Lincoln displayed early on for espionage and sabotage had to be tempered by the fact that he had no organization to carry it out. If that was what Pinkerton intended to propose as he settled into a chair across the cabinet table from the president and his secretary of state, he would be starting from scratch. Spying had remained largely dormant in the United States since the Revolutionary War. During the 1846–48 Mexican War, Scott employed a handful of Mexican bandits and Army engineers to collect intelligence.

Americans had an age-old resistance to the idea of standing armies with any kind of centralized spy service. When the Confederates shelled Fort Sumter, neither belligerent had made any preparations to collect military intelligence. It would not be until a year later that a Confederate Signal Bureau was officially organized to provide secure communications, intercept the enemy's signals, maintain courier lines to the North, and run espionage and counterespionage operations through a Secret Service Bureau.

The Rebels' intelligence operation would end up a poor match against what the Yankees eventually developed. But at the outset, the Union Army had no plan for organizing an intelligence staff or spy corps, and no official name for such an activity. Its officers did not even use the words commonly employed in the spy trade. Commanders gathered "information" rather than "intelligence" and sent out "scouts" or "guides" who were often spies. Organizations that came to be called secret services usually ended up being a hodgepodge of intelligence collection activities (the work of spies), counterintelligence (the job of spycatchers), and ordinary criminal investigations. Officers learned on the job how to gather intelligence, their secret agents tending to be volunteers—many were lawyers or actors—even more amateurish than rookie soldiers.

Fortunately for Lincoln, spying on the South would be relatively easy. Both sides shared the same nationality, language, and culture. Lincoln would not be dropping operatives into a foreign land. A Union spy with little practice could master a southern accent and learn local customs to blend in. The border now between North and South, stretching from the Virginia coast to Texas's border with the New Mexico territory, was long and porous—easy for spies to slip through. A sizable population of southerners opposed to secession could also be counted on to pass along intelligence and provide safe houses to hide Union agents.

Geography and familiarity helped the Confederates as well. Van Lew and friends who thought like her notwithstanding, Richmond did not have as large a population of disloyal residents eager to be spies as Washington had—although Confederate intelligence officers would soon find Washington's untrained and often uncontrollable civilian spies to be a mixed blessing. For the most part Confederate commanders would be operating on their home turf in the South, which they would always know better than their Union invaders.

Lincoln opened the discussion at the cabinet table. He had summoned the detective to Washington because he "had for some time entertained the idea of organizing a secret service department of the government, with the view of ascertaining the social, political and patriotic status of the numerous suspected persons in and around the city," Pinkerton recalled the president saying. Lincoln asked the detective how he would organize such a service. As concisely as he could, Pinkerton outlined the operation he could put together with his men and women to spy on subversives in the capital. His experience running a detective agency that collected intelligence for railroads and other business clients, the fact that he knew Lincoln along with other Washington political figures, and that he had already carried out a successful covert operation to smuggle the president through Baltimore made him a logical choice to head a government secret service. Lincoln thanked him for his time and said he would get back to him "in a few days."

Pinkerton hung around Washington for several days waiting for a decision. But none came. Just two months old, the administration was still organizing its government, as well as raising and equipping a large army. Pinkerton paid visits to the State and War Departments but found no one there to decide on his offer. Miffed, he boarded a train to return to Chicago and his business.

On a stopover in Philadelphia, he dashed off a letter to George McClellan, his old employer at the Illinois Central Railroad, who was in Columbus organizing his Ohio command. In his pocket Pinkerton had a letter he received from McClellan on April 26 asking him to come to the state. "I wish to see you with the least possible delay to make arrangements with you of an important nature," the note read. The detective could find him at the state capital or at his house on Ludlow Street in Cincinnati, which was serving for the moment as his headquarters. "Let no one know that you come to see me, and keep as quiet as possible," the general instructed.

Pinkerton had put off McClellan until he had an answer from Lincoln on his proposal for a secret service. But it was clear to him now the administration might never come to a decision, so Pinkerton was ready to go to Ohio. In Philadelphia, he wrote McClellan that he would be in Columbus no later than May 9.

Six

BULL RUN

*L*afayette Baker returned to Washington toward the end of June 1861. He met again with Scott to review the mission the general wanted him to take. Instead of Richmond, the intelligence target now was Manassas Junction, Virginia, little more than a railroad crossing thirty-five miles southwest of Washington. Lincoln had sent eight regiments across the Potomac River to the Virginia side on May 24 to seize Alexandria and Arlington Heights (where Rebel artillery batteries had been installed with a perfect view of Washington)—a move of more symbolic than strategic value, but nevertheless the first Union bridgehead on Rebel soil. Both sides spent the rest of June randomly, and aimlessly, skirmishing with each other. Lincoln decided on a bolder thrust with the 35,000 soldiers he had by then in Washington—an attack on the railroad junction at Manassas, which was important because as many as 22,000 Rebel soldiers were bivouacked near there under the command of Pierre Gustave Toutant Beauregard.

The dapperly uniformed victor at Fort Sumter, who applied liberal doses of black dye to keep the gray in his hair from showing, Beauregard had been twice wounded during the Mexican War as an engineering officer on Scott's staff and twice breveted for gallantry. Popular with the War Department, he was nevertheless relieved as superintendent of the U.S. Military Academy at West Point when it became clear he would follow his home state of Louisiana out of the Union. The army that General Beauregard now commanded near Manassas Junction had been a constant threat to Washington. Lincoln feared the southern commander would launch a counterattack to retake Alexandria just east of his position. With Union troops succeeding against small Confederate forces in western Virginia, Lincoln also was feeling political pressure to plow through Beauregard's larger army at Manassas and capture Richmond before the Rebel Congress convened there on July 20. "On to Richmond!" became the battle cry of the *New York Tribune*. Southern newspapers also clamored for an advance on Washington, which the aggressive Beauregard was eager to undertake.

The general who would lead the Union advance on Manassas was the energetic, imaginative, and Paris-educated Irvin McDowell, a teetotal and big-eating former staff officer for Scott who had no field command experience. McDowell realized his soldiers were terribly young, inexperienced, and poorly equipped. It worried him deeply. He asked for a delay to give his troops more training, but Lincoln argued that soldiers on both sides were green and ordered his general to expeditiously plan for a campaign. McDowell saluted and on June 29 presented to Lincoln and his cabinet a battle plan, which had no grand design for taking Richmond as the press wanted—just Manassas Junction. McDowell's army would cross a sluggish stream called Bull Run for a flank attack on Beauregard's force to the west of Manassas Junction. At the same time, 15,000 federal soldiers near Harpers Ferry, commanded by General Robert Patterson, a sixty-nine-year-old veteran of the War of 1812, would keep 11,000 Confederates in the Shenandoah Valley under the command of the cautious and fussy Joseph E. Johnston from rushing on a railroad line southeast toward Manassas to reinforce Beauregard's outnumbered army. McDowell had put together a workmanlike plan, but it was better suited to be carried out by experienced officers leading seasoned troops, which McDowell decidedly lacked.

McDowell also was short of good intelligence for the battlefield on

which his men would fight—missing simple but important bits of information like the best places for his soldiers to ford Bull Run. Unlike the Confederates, who had Washington spies and articles in unrestrained northern
newspapers tipping them off to federal plans and movements, McDowell
knew little about what Beauregard or Johnston planned to do. That was
where Lafayette Baker came in, Scott told him. The general had found it impossible to obtain accurate intelligence from Manassas Junction. He wanted
Baker to sneak into the area and vacuum up everything he could find there
about the enemy's strength and movements.

Baker proposed to infiltrate into Virginia pretending to be a photographer taking shots of high-ranking Confederate officers. Scott liked the idea,
but he told Baker he could pay him little. Baker said he would be fine with
just his expenses covered and the promise of a job when he returned. Scott
reached into his vest pocket, pulled out ten double eagle coins totaling two
hundred dollars, and handed them to his new spy. He wished him good luck
on his "excursion to Dixie."

Baker's first espionage mission ended up a comic fiasco. He adopted the
pseudonym "Samuel Munson," which happened to be the name of a Knoxville, Tennessee, man he had met in California. For his cover as a photographer, Baker said he visited a "Daguerrean establishment" in Washington and
bought an empty camera box for four dollars. The battered box slung across
his back with a leather strap, he set out for Manassas Junction the morning
of July 11, less than a week before McDowell would finally begin marching
his men southwest at a snail's pace. But almost immediately Maine sentries
posted at Alexandria four miles outside the city arrested Baker, believing
he was a spy, and sent him back to Washington for trial. Baker said Scott
did not tell Union sentries that he would be passing through their lines because he did not know whom to trust in his own army. "To let the Union
troops into the secret would be to send it to Richmond before I had reached
Manassas," Baker later wrote. But clearly neither Baker nor Scott did enough
planning in this slapdash operation for something as basic as conveying a
spy through his own lines. Instead of doing that, Scott had Baker freed and
simply told him, "well, try again."

Baker did so that night, this time slipping into what he thought was a disorganized line of troops marching into Arlington, Virginia, across Long Bridge. But an alert Union lieutenant grabbed him by the collar and had a guard take him back to Washington again. The next morning at dawn, Baker made try number three at launching his mission. He crossed another wooden bridge over the Potomac's eastern branch into Maryland's lower counties and walked thirty-five miles south, arriving late that night dirty, hungry, and tired at Port Tobacco, a village in Charles County infested with Confederate sympathizers.

The next day, Baker gave a black man one of Scott's twenty-dollar gold pieces to row him across the Potomac to its Virginia side and a spot just below Dumfries, off Quantico Creek. He then continued his walk on hot dusty roads northwest toward Manassas. But Baker made it only four miles from the Potomac when two Confederate soldiers, who were as suspicious of him as Union soldiers had been, nabbed him and began marching him to their camp eight miles away. The two Rebels turned out to be worse spy-catchers than Baker was a spy. Along the way, the captors and their prisoner came upon a roadside beer shop and stopped to down pints of ale Baker paid for with Scott's expense money. Soon the two drunken soldiers fell asleep on the stoop of the alehouse and Baker managed to slip away to resume his trek toward Manassas.

But not for long. He was seized once more, this time by four Confederate cavalrymen who popped out of the brush and marched him that night ten miles to a camp at Brentsville, south of Manassas, where he met Rebel brigadier general Milledge Bonham. Bonham interrogated Baker and suspected he was a spy, which did not take much detective work. Baker's cover story as a photographer was easy to unravel—his camera box was empty and he had none of the rest of a photographer's usual cumbersome equipment. Bonham had guards slap irons on Baker and take him to Beauregard at Manassas Junction, five miles north. Baker, who did his best after the fact to dress up his mission, claimed later that Beauregard personally interrogated him. It's questionable whether the busy general, just days away from fighting the biggest battle of his life, took valuable time to question a disreputable looking phony photographer. More likely, someone on Beauregard's staff quickly concluded, as Bonham had, that Baker was a spy and threw him into a stockade until they could decide when to hang him from a tree.

With Scott's expense money, Baker bought a warm breakfast from the stockade commander that came with a bottle of sour wine. He gave the wine to a guard and with another twenty-dollar gold piece as a bribe talked the stockade commander into letting him wander around Beauregard's head-quarters camp with the guard closely watching him. During his stroll, Baker counted units—the only useful intelligence he had so far collected in this sorry escapade if he had been able to get it back to Scott in time. As it was, after his walk Baker was put back into the stockade, where he suspected Confederate plants had been placed to strike up a conversation and trick him into revealing he was a spy. Within four days of being taken to Beau-regard's camp, or about the time McDowell's army began its march, Baker's mission turned from bad to even worse. Instead of being hung, he was carted to the Manassas Junction station and put in the freight car of a train headed to Richmond for authorities there to deal with him. At Richmond, guards locked him up in a comfortable third-floor room of a railroad engine house, where he stewed for about five days.

Baker later claimed he was hauled three times before Jefferson Davis, who grilled him to uncover his spying and extract information about Wash-ington's defenses. Baker said he stuck to his cover story of being Sam Mun-son, a photographer and Rebel sympathizer from Knoxville, and told Davis numbers on the Union force around Washington that he dreamed up in his head. Confederate leaders in Richmond kept their doors open for walk-ins. Davis was a micromanager willing to interview practically any visitor to the Capitol. But again, Baker, who was able miraculously to recount six years later detailed dialogues he allegedly had with Davis, appears to have been embellishing the story to portray himself as jousting with the highest lev-els of the Confederate government. It is doubtful that the president of the Confederate States of America, who was consumed as well by the battle at Manassas Junction and would travel there at one point to confer with his generals, would carve out any more time in his jammed schedule than Beau-regard had to interrogate a shady and low-level spy suspect. More likely, se-nior aides to Davis questioned Baker.

Baker's story gets better. He said he convinced Davis he really was Sam Munson and talked the Rebel president into issuing him a pass to roam around Richmond on the condition that he not leave the city. Baker claimed he used that opportunity to gather intelligence on military movements through the city. His head allegedly filled with secrets he anxiously wanted to share with Scott back in Washington, Baker claimed he next talked a Confederate provost marshal into writing out a pass for him to visit Fredericksburg, fifty-seven miles north of Richmond, where he planned to make his escape back to Washington.

Once at Fredericksburg, Baker said that after four unsuccessful tries he finally made it across the Rappahannock River, winding north and west of the city, with the help of a black man who rowed him in his boat. He began walking toward the Potomac River to the east but after just two miles was stopped by a Confederate officer and a soldier, who planned to haul him back to Fredericksburg. But Baker claimed he managed to slip away from the soldier guarding him (the man had fallen asleep), stealing his pistol and his horse. He next encountered two African Americans who fed him bread and milk for ten cents and hid him in their shack. Walking on the road the next evening, Baker finally came upon two Rebel soldiers of Dutch descent on the bank of the Potomac, who shared a fish dinner with him. Later that night, he stole their boat while they slept and, through a hail of bullets from the angry Dutchmen firing from the bank after they awoke, managed to row it to the Maryland side of the river.

Both sides routinely paroled the other's captured officers if they promised not to return to the fight. But it strains credulity to believe that security officials in the Davis administration would be so gullible they would set free a spy suspect, whose cover story had so many holes in it, so he could roam the capital of the Confederacy to observe whatever military activities he pleased. What likely happened was that Baker never did observe much military activity, being in Rebel custody or on the run most of the time. Somehow he managed to escape incarceration in Richmond and wandered around Virginia for weeks, living in shacks or the woods, and scrounging for food. He was detained again while passing through Fredericksburg on suspicion he was a spy, and escaped with the help of more people—including, by one account, a local prostitute.

Around July 30, Baker finally straggled into Washington looking like a homeless vagrant—which he had practically been the previous three weeks. He had returned too late. Washington was still in a state of shock, with wounded soldiers clogging its hospitals and hordes of the downcast, defeated, and unruly ones who could walk shambling about the city's streets, alleys, and bars. Setting out on July 16, McDowell had been painfully slow to advance toward Rebel defenses behind Bull Run, giving Beauregard the time to receive needed reinforcements from Johnston, whom Patterson had failed to pin down in the Shenandoah Valley. Curious civilians from Washington had ridden out in carriages with picnic lunches to witness what they thought would be a grand spectacle. What they saw instead was confusion on both sides in a battle of amateurs.

Lincoln went to Sunday services July 21 assured by Scott that their soldiers, though exhausted just marching to the front, would win the day's fight. Scott then took his afternoon nap. Within hours Confederates were routing federal troops, many of whom threw down their muskets and fled back to Washington along with terrified civilians like a panicky mob. When it ended that day, casualties for the Battle of Manassas (as the Confederates called it) or Bull Run (the Union name for it) had been small compared to later engagements—a total of about 3,500 killed or wounded—but the psychological impact for the North had been tremendous. The Union Army had been shamed. Washingtonians feared they would be invaded. Fortunately for the capital, Beauregard and Johnston, who scored a decisive tactical victory, decided their force was too weak and disorganized in the aftermath to pursue McDowell and capture the city.

Though McDowell's estimate of the Confederates' strength was reasonably accurate, on the whole, he and Patterson had inadequate or incorrect intelligence for this campaign. Armies in the field were difficult for spies to penetrate, particularly Beauregard's, which did not take kindly to visitors like Baker. His spy mission might have been of some value if he had escaped from Manassas and brought back to Washington last-minute information for McDowell from Beauregard's camp. Instead, Baker was hauled off to Richmond, where he and his intelligence languished for the entire battle. The information he provided Scott when he finally caught up with him in the study of his house on 18th Street was largely useless at that late date. Union files have no record of Scott ever submitting a report on what Baker told him.

But though he may have been a failed spy, Baker was a masterful storyteller. He spun for Scott a detailed and vivid yarn about his mission. If Scott had had an intelligence staff with trained agent handlers and analysts, they could have easily picked apart the discrepancies in Baker's report and would likely have sent him packing. Instead, Scott had only himself to evaluate Baker's intelligence and the former vigilante had little difficulty impressing the old general, whose military career would soon end after the Bull Run debacle. Baker filed a claim for $105 in expenses, beyond the $200 in gold pieces Scott advanced him. The commanding general approved the payment. Then he sent his spy to Lincoln's new secretary of war, who gave Baker a job.

An unsavory Pennsylvania party boss whom Lincoln made secretary of war as political payoff for his support during the campaign, Simon Cameron quickly discovered that running a department ramping up for a protracted conflict was too much for him. Disorganized and bewildered, he soon found his desk piled high with documents as well as charges of maladministration and contracting fraud. Baker's first job for Cameron came in August. The former vigilante turned out to be a better detective than spy. Sporting a slouch hat, linen duster, gray pantaloons, and two pistols, Baker took the train to Baltimore posing as a Confederate arms dealer and using his old cover name, Sam Munson, to catch two brothers suspected of smuggling critical northern goods such as small arms and ammunition to the Confederacy.

Baker convinced the brothers he was a secret Rebel buyer with cash to purchase northern goods. One of the brothers took him to Philadelphia to shop for the weapons. With the help of several canvas bags filled with fake gold coins, and Philadelphia's police chief—his name, of all things, was Benjamin Franklin and he hid under a bed in Baker's room at the American

House so he could listen in on the transaction—Baker set up an elaborate sting to capture the smugglers and break up their ring. The case brought him his first media attention. Franklin leaked the story of the sting to a New York newspaper, which hailed the police chief and an unnamed "celebrated Lincoln detective . . . a daring Californian, full of nerve," who pulled off the operation.

Elizabeth Van Lew watched largely in silence as Richmonders rejoiced over news of Beauregard's victory at Manassas Junction. Davis gave a glowing account of the battle to a large audience standing outside the Spotswood Hotel. Union handcuffs scavenged from the battlefield were exhibited in the hotel lobby, said to be intended for Davis and his officers. City residents and southerners elsewhere were convinced that northern leaders would wear the shackles, the Battle of Manassas would break the Union's backbone, and the war would be over by autumn's frost.

The city's exuberance was soon doused by the arrival in waves of Confederate casualties. First came the walking wounded, stumbling in as heavy rain drenched the city. Trains chugging into Richmond's rail station at 8th and Broad Streets carried the coffins of the second wave. Carriages took the ones bearing officers to the Capitol, a band following playing Handel's dreary "Dead March" from the oratorio *Saul*. The third wave soon followed—ambulance trains carrying the seriously wounded on stretchers. Van Lew and others stood at a mass meeting in Richmond's Capitol Square after the battle, as the mayor made arrangements for buildings to house the wounded and gave citizens their assignments to care for the men. The city was woefully unprepared for the influx of casualties.

Richmond also was not ready for Manassas's more than one thousand Union prisoners of war who poured in with the casualties. Government officials scrambled to set up camps and find empty buildings to house the captives. Van Lew quickly showed empathy for these poor inmates. The *Richmond Enquirer* disapprovingly noted her "assiduous attentions to the Yankee prisoners" and editorialized that the POWs were being treated better "than they deserve and have any right to expect."

Seven

THE OHIO DEPARTMENT

*P*inkerton had a trusted courier deliver his May 4 letter to McClellan telling him he was on his way to Ohio. McClellan wanted Pinkerton to be his spy. To whet his future boss's appetite for what the detective thought he could do for him, Pinkerton passed along in his May 4 letter the latest political intelligence he had collected during his Washington visit. General Scott considered McClellan an "able officer." Lincoln was impressed with a letter McClellan sent him outlining his ideas for the strategic direction of the war. From what he had learned from the president and other senior officials, Pinkerton was sure McClellan would command an area far larger than Ohio, which turned out to be correct. His territory would extend eventually to Indiana, Illinois, western Pennsylvania, western Virginia, and Missouri. Pinkerton added, a bit vainly, that McClellan might not know it but the detective was the man who got Lincoln safely through Baltimore to foil an assassination plot.

Pinkerton knew the political gossip he brought from Washington would massage McClellan's ego, which was massive. Trim and dapper with dark auburn hair, just a slight goatee, and a thick mustache, he was a handsome man to whom military appearance was important. With a pleasant smile and gray-blue eyes intently fixed on whomever he talked to, McClellan stirred remarkable affection among civilian friends, military subordinates, and strangers who had just met him. Only thirty-four and one of the most well-read men in the Army, he became a master at delivering inspiring proclamations. But he was a man "possessed by demons and delusions," wrote a biographer, obsessed with gathering more troops under his command, believing to the point of hallucination that the enemy always outnumbered him and hostile elements in the U.S. government plotted his destruction. Adulation went to his head. He developed a messiah complex, convinced he was the country's savior.

Born into upper Philadelphia society, McClellan had a superb education for military life, entering West Point at the young age of fifteen and a half years and graduating second in the class of 1846—angry because he thought he deserved the first position. Commissioned into the Engineer Corps, he went into the Mexican War attended to by a black servant and left with two brevet promotions for gallantry in battle, as well as a disdain for politicians to whom the military reported. After Mexico he took postgraduate courses on the art of war, learned German and French (as well as enough Russian to read its documents), and toured Europe for a year to study military strategy and the war in the Crimea (though it educated him more in how to train and administer armies than to lead them in battle). He resigned his commission at age thirty to work as a railroad executive—gaining a high regard for Pinkerton in that job, but not Lincoln, whose storytelling he found taxing. After Fort Sumter's fall, northern leaders dearly wanted George McClellan back in a Union uniform.

In April 1861, Ohio governor William Dennison, with the backing of Salmon P. Chase, the new Treasury secretary and past senator from that state, made McClellan a major general of volunteers in command of the newly formed Department of Ohio, headquartered in Cincinnati. The thriving city of more than 160,000 residents on the northern bank of the Ohio River would soon serve as a key western military hub for manufactured supplies from the East, but for now it was a city on edge fearing Confederates might target it for attack. McClellan hauled trainloads of lumber to build huts for Camp Dennison, seventeen miles northeast of Cincinnati off the Little Miami Railroad line. He was an energetic, hardworking, and popular commander, strutting about camp frequently atop a dark bay horse named Dan Webster to inspect the training and living conditions of his men. McClellan also showed a prickly side, soon feuding with General Scott over what he complained was the slow supply of muskets, heavy artillery, and gunboats for his force.

Pinkerton decided to meet McClellan at his Ludlow Street house in Cincinnati. He brought along his best operative, Timothy Webster. Taking seats in the parlor, Pinkerton recounted the runaround he experienced in Washington trying to set up a secret service. McClellan got right to the point, telling the detective he wanted him to set up that kind of agency for him. Pinkerton agreed to take the assignment, so McClellan cabled Scott to obtain his permission to have the detective work in Cincinnati rather than Washington, which the commanding general was happy to give. The Union Army expected its field generals to set up their own spy and counterspy services. Pinkerton rented a suite of rooms in a downtown office building and summoned eight detectives from his Chicago headquarters to join him and Webster in Cincinnati. He worked as a civilian, although he occasionally wore a uniform when he thought he needed to, and used his old pseudonym, E. J. Allen, in meetings with outsiders and for all his communications. Initially Pinkerton was not paid for his Ohio services. He had to draw a $1,500 advance from his Chicago office to cover expenses.

Four days after taking command, the ambitious McClellan had sent a hastily conceived grand plan to Scott for winning the war from his Ohio Department. He proposed to set up garrisons along the Ohio River frontier at key points to respond to rebel threats and then lead a huge army of 80,000 men either to cross quickly into western Virginia for a thrust on Richmond or to advance into more southern territory for a simultaneous attack on the Confederacy with eastern forces. Scott, who favored his Anaconda strategy of strangulation, thought McClellan's plan wildly impractical. Lincoln had a more immediate mission for his Ohio Department commander—Kentucky.

Desperate to keep the border state in the Union, the president feared

Kentucky would not stay that way for long with Confederate general Gideon Pillow's troops lurking nearby in Tennessee. Before Pinkerton arrived, McClellan had received numerous reports from loyalists alerting him to secessionist political activities and Rebel movements all over the region. He assured Scott he would gather all the intelligence he could on Kentucky. His first assignment for Pinkerton was to join in the collection of information, not only on the border states of Kentucky and Tennessee, but also deeper south into Mississippi. McClellan wanted a clear sense of whether Kentucky could become hostile. He prepared to move quickly if Tennessee's rebels intruded into that state. So finding out what Pillow had in mind for his force became an important intelligence objective.

Six hours after their first meeting on May 13 in McClellan's parlor, Webster, with two hundred dollars in his pocket for expenses and pretending to be a Baltimore secessionist, was on his way south, arriving in Louisville, Kentucky, that night. (Within days, Pinkerton sent out other scouts singly or in pairs.) From Louisville, Webster the next morning took the train to Bowling Green, Kentucky, quietly jotting down detailed notes on everything he saw along the way, as a good spy should, and using his affable personality to strike up friendly conversations with Kentuckians to gain a feel for the state's mood. After several days in Bowling Green, he took another train to Clarksville, Tennessee, just across the border. When he boarded the train there for Memphis, he noticed a swarthy-looking man following him, wearing civilian clothes, with long hair under a broad-brimmed hat. He learned later that the man was a Confederate counterespionage agent from a Tennessee unit called the "Safety Committee." Webster saw little of the agent during the remainder of the ride to Memphis, so he spent the time puffing on a cigar and taking mental notes on the Rebel soldiers, heavy guns, and carloads of ammunition he saw along the way from the car window, which suggested to him a buildup was under way at the border for some kind of offensive action.

The Memphis that Webster saw was a bustling commercial city of 30,000, with bales of cotton piled up at its long steamboat landing, carriages jamming its streets, and hotels crowded with visitors. Webster checked in to the Worsham House, ignoring the Confederate officer looking over his shoulder as he registered and the Safety Committee agent watching from the lobby. Soon he was in the hotel bar buying drinks for three Rebel officers who became freer with information as they got more lubricated. By the afternoon, he had three devoted friends, the lieutenant among them taking off his uniform hat and plopping it on Webster's head. "Henceforth you are now one of us," the officer proclaimed.

The next morning, Webster's military trio escorted him aboard a steamboat that took them up the Mississippi River a half-dozen miles to Camp Rector, where General Pillow had 3,700 men deployed. Webster spent a pleasant day as his pals showed off the camp's troops and artillery, his long-haired Safety Committee agent continuing to stalk him at a distance. At five o'clock the next morning, Webster checked out of the Worsham—he told his friends the night before that he was going to Chattanooga to look up a brother he had not seen in twelve years—and walked to the train depot. He looked carefully around but did not see his shadow, who he hoped was still asleep. Webster boarded the train crowded with soldiers for Chattanooga, again striking up conversations with officers on board. At the Grand Junction stop, he switched cars and took the northbound train to Jackson, Tennessee. Looking behind him after he settled into his seat, he spotted at the back of the car the long-haired agent with the broad-brimmed hat. The man apparently hadn't slept in. And he now had with him a companion, a hulk of a man who looked like he was the muscle for whatever they planned to do with Webster.

Webster summoned the conductor and, in a loud voice the pair in the back were sure to hear, asked him if he knew of a good hotel in Humboldt, the train's next stop north of Jackson, where he said he planned to stay for a couple days. The ruse worked. At Humboldt, Webster climbed off the car's front entrance and noticed with a smile that the two agents did the same at the other end. Pinkerton's operative walked to the pile of luggage workers off-loaded from the train. The two Rebel agents, assuming he would be picking up his bag and heading to the hotel, found a saloon for a drink before they planned to arrest their quarry at that establishment. As a heavy downpour drenched the village, Webster boarded an express train to Louisville.

By that night he was in Cincinnati, delivering a report to Pinkerton on his successful spy mission.

Webster made a second trip through Tennessee for two weeks in late July and early August, again cultivating Rebel officers along the way and collecting fairly accurate counts for troops and armaments in the state, which McClellan passed on to Scott. Confident, as he told McClellan, that Webster and his other agents were keeping him "well advised" on Kentucky and Tennessee, Pinkerton busied himself with other unconventional chores. He launched an investigation to catch bandits stealing supplies from Union Army warehouses in western Virginia. When he learned that a Georgian named T. Butler King was returning home from England with a well-known Confederate political agent named W. L. Yancey and would pass through northern states in disguise, he wrote Lincoln on July 19 proposing a scheme to nab the two men and use them as hostages to retaliate if Confederates harmed Union war prisoners. Lincoln never responded to the idea. A story leaked to the newspapers that Simon Bolivar Buckner, a military adviser to Kentucky's governor, said McClellan promised him he would not send troops to occupy the state, which caused an uproar in Washington, where the administration did not want to take that card off the table. Pinkerton took over damage control, telegraphing Lincoln that McClellan never made such a promise. Acting like a press secretary, the spy chief advised McClellan on a media strategy to knock down the story and contain the political damage done to him. Pinkerton, who now idolized McClellan, assured him in a memo that his Washington sources reported that while others in the capital might make trouble for him, the general was still "all right with the president and Secretary Cameron."

Shortly after Webster departed on May 13, Pinkerton, whom McClellan continued to badger for more intelligence from the South, decided to head out on a spy mission himself to Kentucky and Tennessee. He had spent time working cases there during the 1850s and considered himself an expert on the region. Even so, a spymaster should be at headquarters directing other agents and processing their reports. Pinkerton, who was well known and risked exposing himself and his operation, had no business going out in the field—particularly to the same territory he had just sent Webster to cover. There is no evidence that Pinkerton coordinated with Webster to make sure they did not bump into each other.

Pinkerton ended up collecting far less valuable intelligence than Webster did, spending as much time getting out of jams as he did uncovering secrets. Pretending to be a Georgia gentleman, his first stop was Louisville, where in conversations with the locals he found political turmoil and secessionists' energies focused on breaking Kentucky away from the Union or at least keeping it neutral. But "I decided then, from my own observations, that Kentucky would not cast her fortunes with the South," Pinkerton later wrote. He next took the train to Bowling Green, 116 miles south of Louisville, where he reported finding "very decided Union sentiment." Pinkerton bought a swift bay horse and rode another sixty-five miles south to Nashville, Tennessee, where he reported finding "profound" Union sentiment in some quarters but the disloyal elements "more united and outspoken." He claimed he uncovered one disturbing piece of intelligence in Nashville—a Confederate Army surgeon he met who was planning to send a commissary wagon full of strychnine-laced whisky to Union soldiers. Fortunately the poison plot was never carried out.

From Nashville, Pinkerton rode to Memphis 209 miles southwest, revolted by the sight of slave auctions in its market square. He studied the fortifications around the city, talked to Confederate soldiers (lucky to not run into Webster doing the same), and said he sipped brandy and water with General Pillow. Pinkerton found his most valuable sources were blacks forced to build earthworks and move arms and ammunition.

But then trouble started for him. On his third evening in Memphis, a black porter knocked softly on his hotel room door. When Pinkerton let him in, the porter warned that Confederate agents were onto the detective and would soon be coming to arrest him. Pinkerton quickly packed his bag, descended the stairs to the hotel's rear entrance, and fled on horseback to Jackson, Mississippi, two hundred miles south. He arrived in Jackson still pleased with his escapade—although the value of the intelligence he had picked up was never clear. But the next morning after breakfast, when he visited the hotel's barbershop for a shave, the German barber, who had once cut his hair in Chicago, recognized him. When Pinkerton couldn't convince the barber that he was not the famous detective, he pretended to be indignant, jumping out of the chair, jerking off the towel from around his neck, and shouting at the barber "I'll whip you on the spot!" if the man continued insisting he was the Yankee from Chicago. The poor barber stood silent and terrified. A crowd from the lobby soon gathered at the shop. Pinkerton eventually defused the tension, insisting he was a Georgian and buying the patrons a round of drinks at the hotel bar to placate them. He made his way back to Cincinnati.

McClellan's attention stretched to the east as well as south. To travel west from Washington, people, commerce, and military supplies had to take the Baltimore & Ohio Railroad line that ran through Maryland and western Virginia into the Ohio Valley. That artery, an important northern link to Ohio and the West, was subject to interruption, however, in Virginia's secessionist territory. But most of western Virginia's citizens were Unionists, who had not supported secession as eastern Virginians had and were ready to break from Richmond—presenting an opportunity for Abraham Lincoln and a problem for Jefferson Davis, who recognized full well the strategic value of the region as a link to the West. It was only a matter of time before western Virginia became a battleground.

Scott alerted McClellan that the Confederates were moving troops to Grafton, a key rail junction town on the B&O line near Maryland's border, and asked if he could "counteract" them. McClellan's intelligence sources already were warning him that secessionists were advancing from the Grafton junction northwest on the B&O's main line toward Wheeling and west on its branch to Parkersburg, a western Virginia transportation hub on the Ohio River, to destroy the railroad. McClellan received another report on May 26 that Confederates were burning bridges on the B&O line. His men also intercepted a circular distributed in western Virginia urging citizens to resist breaking away from the commonwealth and "being tacked on to the 'tail end' of Black Republican Despotism." But McClellan's intelligence reports told him these Richmond loyalists were in the minority. He advised Lincoln in a June 1 letter he believed "that very considerable numbers of volunteers can be raised in western Virginia as well as Kentucky" and asked for weapons to arm them.

McClellan now had two important objectives—first, to protect Unionists and the all-important rail line in western Virginia, and, second, to drive
a military force across the Alleghenies and into Tidewater Virginia by the
back door. He quickly put in motion his plan. His force rolled into Grafton
without firing a shot. Its few Confederates retreated eighteen miles south to
the town of Philippi and McClellan's men rebuilt the bridges they burned.
McClellan sent in reinforcements and on June 3 the Federals proceeded to
rout the Confederates at Philippi. Northern newspapers hailed what was a
minor skirmish as a major Union victory.

Alarmed by their defeat at Philippi, Robert E. Lee, who commanded
Virginia troops from Richmond, sent reinforcements. In addition to the
B&O rail route, there were two other east–west passages through the region's mountains—the Great Kanawha Valley and a turnpike connecting
Staunton in the Shenandoah Valley with Parkersburg. Lee sent his adjutant, Robert S. Garnett, to hold the turnpike from Staunton to Parkersburg. He dispatched Henry A. Wise, the crusty former Virginia governor
who had raised the Wise Legion, to operate in the Great Kanawha Valley.
McClellan with the bulk of the Union force took personal charge of the
campaign against Garnett. He sent Ohioan Jacob Cox, a low-key but politically ambitious general, to the Kanawha Valley with his brigade to fight
Wise.

McClellan reached Grafton on June 23 and spent the next two weeks supervising the deployment of his troops for the offensive—becoming an obsessive micromanager, convinced that little would be done correctly unless
he personally saw to it. The next day, Pinkerton sent him a message (one of
many updates) that he had a report, whose accuracy he was still trying to
verify, that 2,000 rebels from eastern Virginia had arrived in the Kanawha
Valley along with 200 cavalrymen. After his southern excursion, Pinkerton
had struck out once more, checking roads that intersected the Kanawha
Turnpike through the valley and hunting for Union loyalists. From his intelligence chief and other agents, McClellan had fairly detailed reports on the
topography of the valley and the Confederate defenses running through it.
But a more important spy mission into the valley began on June 27, four
days after McClellan reached Grafton. A Welshman carried it out.

Pryce Lewis was the epitome of an English gentleman—tall, manly, witty, debonair, a connoisseur of fine liquor and wine—the opposite of the short and dour Pinkerton. He had bushy side whiskers in the British style, dark brown eyes, and a deep resonant voice that was pleasant and invited people to like him. In private, however, Lewis was not easy for his family to live with—generous and honest, but a stickler for the truth, though he became expert at lying as a spy. He was born in the small town of Newtown in North Wales in 1831—although he may never have known the exact date— the charming and intelligent son of a wool sorter, who died when he was nineteen. Lewis emigrated to the United States and New York City when he was twenty-five, eventually marrying and having two children. Beginning in 1857 he sold books door-to-door in the Northeast for two years and then moved to Chicago, where he worked as a grocery clerk. In the spring of 1860, he became interested in hunting for gold in the Pikes Peak region of the southwestern Nebraska and western Kansas territories, and was packing for his trip when a friend talked him into being interviewed by George Bangs with the Pinkerton agency. Lewis laughed at the idea of becoming a detective, but Bangs saw potential in the Welshman and hired him.

Lewis found his early assignments shadowing suspects tiresome. But through that autumn, as he worked more substantial cases in the East, Midwest, and West he gradually began to like detective work. He found Pinkerton a bit of an eccentric. One autumn day walking with the boss on a New York City street, Pinkerton out of the blue told him to read Edward Bulwer-Lytton's melodramatic novel *Eugene Aram*, about the execution of a murderer—a request Lewis found odd. After Lewis finished the book, Pinkerton sent him to Jackson, Tennessee, in January 1861 to investigate the mysterious murder of a bank cashier. His mingling with southerners for six months became good training for later assignments. Lewis left Jackson on June 9, the day after Tennessee seceded. When he arrived in Chicago two days later, a telegram awaited him from Pinkerton, who wanted him to catch the first train to Cincinnati. When he arrived, Lewis filled his boss in on the military preparations he witnessed in the South, the report passed on to McClellan and then Cameron. Pinkerton wanted his sophisticated-looking Welshman to take another trip—this one into western Virginia.

Lewis carefully prepared for his mission, poring over maps of the region to select the best routes for his reconnaissance. He would pose as a British aristocrat touring the state to see sights like White Sulphur Springs, the Natural Bridge, and Hawk's Nest. Pinkerton fabricated a set of documents and letters introducing Lewis as the son of Lord Tracy, who had lived not far from his home in England—although Lewis, who thought the boss had too much of a flair for the dramatic, soon dropped the pseudonym and traveled under his real name. Lewis was outfitted with accoutrements that reeked of British upper class—a handsome cigar box with the English lion in ivory embossed on it, a case of champagne and another of expensive port, a fine carriage with spacious trunk and English army chest strapped to it, all pulled by a gray horse, and for his lordship a pricey suit of the latest European cut, a silk stovepipe hat, and a diamond ring for his finger. Acting as Lewis's footman and driver for the trip was Sam Bridgeman, a veteran Pinkerton detective in his early fifties and a native of Virginia. A Mexican War veteran and former New York City cop who had a shrewd and wary disposition, Bridgeman "handled the reins in a style worthy of a turnout in Pall Mall or Piccadilly," Lewis later wrote.

The preparations for their mission completed by the evening of June 27, Lewis and Bridgeman loaded their carriage and horse onto a freight boat that sailed them southeast down the winding Ohio River to the village of Guyandotte in western Virginia, where they stayed in the town's best hotel overnight on June 28. They checked out the next morning, driving off in their carriage through lush green Kanawha County to Charleston, farther east, where Pinkerton had reports that a thousand Rebel troops were bivouacked. Five o'clock that afternoon, five cavalry pickets from one of a number of Rebel patrols swarming the Kanawha Valley stopped them ten miles from Charleston and asked for their passes, which Lewis did not have. The pickets said they would escort the pair to their commandant's regimental headquarters in a farmhouse Lewis could see nearby. They were sure he would issue them the needed paperwork. This threw Lewis for a loop. Though his instructions for this mission were vague, he had planned to avoid Confederate soldiers as much as possible. But he made the best of it.

At the stately old farmhouse with a broad veranda and troop tents surrounding it for what was called Camp Tompkins, Lewis was introduced to Colonel George S. Patton, who had been a Charleston lawyer before organizing local farmers and merchants into the Kanawha Riflemen and whose grandson, General George S. Patton Jr., would gain fame in World War II. Just twenty-five years old, Colonel Patton turned out to be a pleasant fellow and a gracious host. Sitting in the farmhouse parlor, Lewis gave his cover story about being an upper-class British tourist, which impressed Patton, who signed a pass to Charleston for the pair. Patton told Lewis he could get a pass from Wise once he was there to go elsewhere. That scared Lewis, who had heard of the general's reputation for being difficult to deal with. The rest of the evening, Lewis and Patton sat on the veranda chatting. Lewis had Bridgeman fetch a bottle of champagne and two cigars for his host and acting like a haughty lord recounted his service in the Crimean War (Lewis knew enough about the conflict from books on the subject he had sold door-to-door) but pretended to be ignorant about this war the Americans were having.

Patton, who was responsible for guarding the forty miles of turnpike between Guyandotte and Charleston, bragged about his defenses. "I have fortifications here that with six hundred Confederate soldiers I can defend against ten thousand Yankees for ten years," he told Lewis.

"I have no doubt of it," Lewis replied, and ordered Bridgeman to retrieve more wine and cigars to keep the colonel talking. The fortifications Patton was talking about were at nearby Coal Mouth, the junction for the Coal and Kanawha Rivers west of Charleston, defending one of the main entrances into western Virginia.

Midday on June 30, Lewis and Bridgeman drove into Charleston, their carriage winding its way down the main drag, Summers Street, through crowds of Rebel soldiers and rough-looking mountaineers dressed in woolen shirts and overalls with revolvers tucked in their pockets. Lewis walked into the city's finest hotel, the Kanawha House, which was packed with Confederate officers because it happened to be the temporary headquarters for General Wise, who now commanded Patton's 600 men at Camp Tompkins and more than 2,000 other troops around Charleston.

After checking in and signing the hotel register as "Pryce Lewis and servant, London, England," the Welshman decided to take a stroll along the city's streets thronged with more soldiers than before. He overheard some of them talking loudly about "Old Wise" arresting "a lot of whining Unionists" that morning and throwing them in jail.

That evening, feeling he had entered the lion's den, Lewis, wearing a finely tailored jacket, walked into the hotel's dining room packed with Rebel officers and was ushered to the only free chair—at a large table across from the fearsome General Wise. Trying not to appear curious, Lewis sized up the fire-eater he had heard so much about. Wise, who had been Virginia's governor from 1856 to 1860 and signed the death warrant for John Brown, was thin and not particularly tall (Lewis guessed he was in his mid-fifties), with a clean-shaven face, stern mouth, and jaws somewhat cavernous. Lewis just ate his supper and listened as the officers around the table talked about the latest battles around the country. One remark chilled him. "There are spies all around us," an officer told a comrade.

After dinner, Lewis mingled in the crowded parlor until he found an opportunity to approach Wise. "I would like to speak to your excellency in private for a minute or two," he said.

"All right," Wise said gruffly, somewhat taken aback. "Come up to my office."

Lewis followed Wise up the stairs to his office, which was his bedroom and just across the hall from the room Lewis had rented. Wise sat down at a writing desk but did not offer Lewis a chair, so he took off his hat and remained standing. "What is your pleasure?" Wise asked coldly.

Lewis explained that he was a vacationing Englishman and that Colonel Patton had told him the general would have to issue him a pass to see Virginia's natural wonders.

"I can't give you a pass, sir!" Wise barked with a mean look on his face.

"Why?" Lewis asked, fearing he was risking his neck doing so.

"Don't you know there is a war in this country?" Wise answered, looking at him incredulously.

"No, I don't know it. I know there is some disturbance."

"I am surprised that any intelligent Englishman should come to this country without being fortified with passes before leaving London."

Lewis, pretending to be blasé about the entire matter, said he would go around Wise and apply for a pass with the British consul in Richmond. Wise looked like he was about to erupt. Lewis thought he would be joining the Unionists in jail. But the general only said gruffly: "Good day, sir."

Lewis found Bridgeman waiting anxiously at the foot of the stairs and recounted his run-in with Wise. Terrified, Bridgeman wanted to flee the city immediately. Lewis said no. He would write a letter to the British consul in Richmond, knowing the Confederates would likely open and read it, which Lewis wanted to have happen to preserve their cover. The time consumed with a letter reaching the consul (who Lewis didn't know was in England just then escaping Richmond's summer heat) would give both men time to collect intelligence for McClellan and plan their escape.

Bridgeman reluctantly mailed the letter on July 1. Lewis used the next couple days to roam about Charleston gathering details on its defenses. At one point he cultivated two Confederate officers over whisky and cigars in the Wilson House's billiards room. They invited him to their camp two miles outside of Charleston on its fairground, where he witnessed battalion drills and a regimental dress parade. "I thought the Confederates, considering the lack of uniformity in their dress, made a very creditable appearance," he wrote later. Lewis also learned that the commissary officer had issued 3,500 rations that day—important information because it gave him a fairly accurate count of the number of troops there.

Bridgeman also roamed the city's saloons collecting information from the soldiers in them. But he was also getting drunk in the bars. The Kanawha House's landlord complained to Lewis when Bridgeman staggered in one night and started insulting officers in the parlor. Lewis pulled Bridgeman aside and dressed him down, but his driver's binge drinking continued. Lewis knew his partner was a security threat. They needed to get away soon and take their intelligence back to McClellan.

Shortly past midnight on July 10, Lewis lay awake churning over in his head their escape plan when he heard a commotion from Wise's room across the hall. The next morning the landlord told him that Wise had taken all but two hundred of his troops to Parkersburg to meet the Yankees. Lewis found the colonel whom Wise left behind to command the two hundred

soldiers guarding Charleston's camps. He gave the Welshman permission
to travel to Richmond. After breakfast the morning of July 12, Lewis paid
their bill ($35.75 for nearly two weeks at the Kanawha House) and boarded
the carriage Bridgeman had brought around to the front. Continuing to
count Rebel forces along the way and fearful Wise would catch them, the
pair traveled east on the road to Richmond for about ten miles, but then
diverted southwest along a narrow bumpy trail that eventually took them
into friendly Kentucky, where they finally felt safe. From there they traveled
north as fast as they could to Ohio, arriving in Cincinnati the morning of
July 18.

Lewis hastily wrote his intelligence report. Pinkerton telegraphed its
highlights to McClellan, who was near Cheat Mountain, east of Charleston in western Virginia. Though he became overly cautious when battles
did not go according to plan, McClellan by then had succeeded in collaps-
ing the Confederate defense of the Parkersburg-to-Staunton turnpike, with
Rebel brigadier general Garnett mortally wounded leading a rearguard action. McClellan cabled Pinkerton to rush Lewis to Cox, the leader of his
Kanawha Valley campaign whose force had set up camp at Poca, a village
northwest of Charleston on the Kanawha River. Lewis arrived on a military
boat at the Poca headquarters in the early afternoon on July 21 and found
Cox aboard another vessel tied to the wharf, licking his wounds from the defeat of one of his regiments at Scary Creek, to the south. It had earned him a
stinging rebuke from McClellan, who thought the former Ohio lawyer was
moving too slowly in the valley.

Unreliable sources had reported to Cox that Wise had 60,000 soldiers,
which made the brigadier general understandably hesitant to attack. That
was nonsense, Lewis said. He told the astonished Cox that he had been
in Wise's camps and by his careful count the Rebel commander had only
5,500 troops. Lewis also had details on the location of those troops, their
equipment, and the artillery they had. Lewis then toured Cox's camp and afterward advised him that while his five regiments had fewer men than Wise's
force, the Union men were better armed and had far better artillery. With
Lewis's intelligence, Cox on July 24 attacked Wise's force five miles north
of Charleston and routed it. Setting up his headquarters in Charleston, Cox

two days later took off after Wise, who by August 1 had fled to Lewisburg, 112 miles southeast of the city. McClellan was jubilant. By September western Virginia would be completely in Union hands.

The North needed a battlefield hero after the Bull Run disaster and McClellan became it. He had separated strategically important western Virginia from the Confederacy—considered a major achievement earning him praise from Scott, Lincoln, and Congress. For their spying for the Ohio Department, Timothy Webster and Pryce Lewis became Pinkerton's stars.

Eight

WASHINGTON

Though the Battle of Bull Run had been a humiliating loss for the Union, Lincoln exuded not defeatism but renewed determination. He signed bills to bring troop strength up to one million men, fired inept generals, and summoned George McClellan to take command of the Division of the Potomac and Washington's defenses. McClellan was in the western Virginia town of Beverly when he received the orders the day after the Bull Run battle. He set out for Washington aboard a special train the next morning, cheered at refueling stops along the way. Pinkerton, who learned of McClellan's orders the day he got them, sent a courier to catch up with him in Wheeling and deliver a note that the detective would keep his spies in Kentucky, where they could be reached easily if McClellan needed them in Washington. Pinkerton enclosed a $3,000 bill for his agency's services. "The hopes of the nation now are upon you," he wrote at the end of his letter. "All say McClellan is the man."

McClellan wrote back that he did not know what to expect when he arrived in Washington. Be prepared for a summons for your services, he told Pinkerton. McClellan arrived at the capital the afternoon of July 26, proclaimed the conqueror of western Virginia and now the nation's savior, welcomed by the president and his cabinet, mobbed in the Senate chamber, and the center of attention at a state dinner. "I could become Dictator," he wrote his wife, Mary Ellen, his head swollen. On July 30, Pinkerton, who had continued to collect intelligence in Kentucky, Tennessee, and western Virginia, received a telegram from McClellan: "Join me in Washington as soon as possible. Come prepared to stay and bring with you two or three of your best men." Pinkerton quickly closed his Cincinnati office and took the train east.

When he reached Washington in early August, Pinkerton found McClellan, who was living in a large house on Jackson Place near the War Department and taking his meals at Wormley's restaurant just around the corner on I Street, busy rounding up stragglers in the city's bars and hotels, instilling discipline among his officers, reorganizing an unruly collection of 51,000 soldiers into a fighting force he renamed the Army of the Potomac, building fortifications around Washington, and drafting for Lincoln a breathtaking, and unrealistic, strategy to win the war with 273,000 troops. Before long, McClellan also was voicing the private opinion that Lincoln, who apparently never responded to the general's grand plan, was "an idiot" and Scott, who thought McClellan too young for such a large command, was either "a dotard or a traitor."

Washington up to that point had only a ragtag collection of largely unpaid informants mostly hunting Rebel spies for the city's military department. They were disbanded after Pinkerton set up his operation in a building he took over on I Street. Though McClellan promised him everything he needed for his secret service, Pinkerton found it as maddeningly slow in Washington as it had been in Ohio to get the federal government to pay his expenses. He had to wire Chicago for another $1,500 to tide him over the first month and operated on a shoestring budget, having desks he used in Cincinnati shipped to him and renting a carriage instead of owning one to ride around the city. However, when Washington did pay his bills, Pinkerton admitted later he "amassed considerable money" from the federal payments and the income from his Chicago business, which he continued to manage from the capital during his few free moments.

Though McClellan had summoned him, Pinkerton ended up working for three bosses. When the general took to the field with his army, Pinkerton served as his spy. When McClellan was in Washington, Pinkerton carried out operations for an assistant war secretary named Thomas Scott, a railroad man from Pennsylvania whom Pinkerton respected from the outset. He also worked in Washington under the city's Army provost marshal, Colonel Andrew Porter, whom McClellan liked for his high energy. (Provost marshals had wide-ranging military law enforcement duties, including suppressing political dissent and capturing enemy spies.) Pinkerton moved twenty of his employees from Cincinnati and Chicago to Washington, and began sending them into the field within days after they arrived. By the end of August he had racked up $3,936.08 in expenses and expected his payroll to quickly grow. He paid himself $300 to $310 a month, or $10 a day, which was $2 under his daily fee for commercial customers. His operatives made $114 to $186 a month plus expenses.

Pinkerton refused to divulge to Army finance officers the names of his operatives, listing them on expense reports by just their initials. He wanted his operation kept as secret as possible, believing Rebel spies infested the Army, federal government, and city police force like rats. He continued to use his E. J. Allen pseudonym, but after a year and a half that cover had grown thin and it was widely known around town that E. J. Allen was Allan Pinkerton. He was enraged after a Washington paper finally unmasked him and told readers the detective went by the two names.

Pinkerton believed a good detective could be a good spy. Kate Warne arrived to flit about as a southern socialite in Washington and Georgetown to glean secessionist secrets at fancy balls and cultivate southern ladies who spoke freely about husbands or boyfriends. At one party she met a visiting Shakespearean actor named John Wilkes Booth. George Bangs was directed to finish up company work in Philadelphia and join Pinkerton in Washington, where he was soon venturing across Rebel lines in disguise. Lewis and Bridgeman were sent to Baltimore for two weeks and then were brought to Washington. Lewis shadowed suspected spies and saboteurs. Pinkerton also had his fifteen-year-old son, William, come to the capital. He gave the quick-witted boy scouting assignments and other odd jobs. William's younger brother Robert joined them later.

The days became exhaustingly long for Pinkerton. He found an apartment at 404 E Street but spent little time there, becoming quickly bogged down with paperwork managing his agents and with roaming the streets himself all hours of the day and night on operations. He told Bangs he had never worked so hard in his life. Too busy to write Joan, who remained in Chicago, he had an agency detective check on her occasionally. He found Washington not as "pleasant" as Cincinnati, he wrote a friend. Many of his detectives felt the same and became homesick. Bangs was quickly worked to exhaustion. It was obvious to Pinkerton that the war would continue for some time. He was determined to stick it out with McClellan—or at least until the federal government paid him enough to recoup the money he had invested in this secret service operation.

For much of his early months, Pinkerton spent most of his time not spying on the enemy but instead hunting for enemy spies, people thought to be disloyal, or simply unscrupulous souls out to defraud the U.S government. He set up surveillance operations against treason suspects and their families, following them and searching their homes, compiling hundreds of dossiers on them. Operatives prowled the city's saloons. A doctor treated one of his agents for an ailment and aroused his patient's suspicion when he asked questions about troops in Memphis and eastern Virginia; that was enough to put the physician under watch to see if he might travel north to spy. Pinkerton alerted the War Department to a large and complicated fraud scheme that nine Chicago speculators and politicians tried to pull off to sell the Union Army poor-quality cattle at inflated prices. He also spied on the Lincoln administration, feeding gossip he learned to McClellan.

Pinkerton proved effective in applying his detective skills and those of his agents to uncover security threats. Within weeks of his arrival in Washington, he scored a counterintelligence triumph.

Many secessionists who fled south to join the Confederate Army or its civilian government left behind in Washington and border states like Maryland

wives or girlfriends who formed a corps of female southern sympathizers—
none more well connected than Rose O'Neal Greenhow, who lived in a
three-story brick house in Lafayette Square across from the White House. A
widow in her mid-forties when Pinkerton arrived in Washington, Greenhow,
whose husband had been a scholarly Virginian and former State Department official, had dark eyes and olive skin. She oozed sensuality, particularly
at night when she let her sleek black hair, with only a few gray strands in it,
fall down below her waist in her bedroom for one of her many lovers. She
enunciated words in an unnaturally distinct way and had manners "border-
ing on the theatrical," recalled a Union officer. Men found her captivating.
Even Pinkerton, who would become her nemesis, thought she was beautiful
and accomplished. Oddly adding to her allure, since March she had been
wearing nothing but black to grieve over her daughter Gertrude's death.

Rose set the template for generations of socially and politically ambitious Washington women to come. She loved the capital city—filled, as
she once wrote, with "great men and beautiful women who have showered
their wealth of loveliness upon the metropolis." With the help of influential
people opening doors for her, she thrilled at being able to mingle among the
"crème de la crème" of the city's political class. Washington's sophisticated
diplomatic corps dazzled her. She found White House receptions exciting.
Like a hunter targeting its prey, Rose spent practically every waking moment carefully courting to her advantage Washington's men of influence.

Invitations to soirees at her house were highly sought after. She became
close to Massachusetts senator Henry Wilson (chairman of the powerful Military Affairs Committee), Senator Joseph Lane of Oregon (also on
the military panel), Colonel Erasmus Keyes (General Scott's military secretary), and Charles Francis Adams (a future U.S. minister to Great Britain in the Lincoln administration). James Buchanan, whom she cultivated
through much of the 1850s, spent so many late-night tête-à-tête in her
house as president, gossip spread that the two had become lovers. Greenhow did little to dispel the rumors, which she knew inflamed her reputation
as a powerful woman.

By 1859, Rose was turning on her deep, alluring voice to argue more often the merits of human bondage at her dinner parties, making antislavery guests like Seward, who enjoyed her food and fine wine, increasingly wary. She viewed Lincoln as a force for evil, lamented the nation's rapid crumbling with his election, and condemned Unionists as traitors. But she continued to invite Seward to her dinner parties—though his abolitionist views got under her skin—and she refused to flee south and give up her power base in Washington. Greenhow continued to work her contacts among northerners and Unionists to gain favors from the new administration—like patronage jobs for friends and a promotion for her son-in-law, who was a Union Army captain. And Rose decided to become a Confederate spy.

In the spring of 1861, one of her lovers, Thomas Jordan, a handsome West Pointer and Union Army quartermaster captain, paid a visit to Greenhow's house to let her know he would leave in May to fight for his native Virginia. Well aware that Rose remained loyal to the South, Jordan asked her bluntly to help him organize an espionage ring in Washington. Greenhow readily agreed. Jordan, who had fought in the Seminole Indian and Mexican Wars, became a Confederate lieutenant colonel assigned as Beauregard's adjutant in Manassas, adopting the pseudonym Thomas John Rayford in his communications with Rose. He hastily put together a crude, twenty-six-symbol cipher key for her so she could write back to him in code. Jordan developed other spy rings in Washington, but he kept them compartmentalized so Greenhow never knew of the other networks. He did not completely trust the impetuous woman, or the agents in his other networks, for that matter.

Jordan's wariness with Greenhow was justified. Though she had valuable connections, she was not a skilled spy. She walked around town scribbling notes in a leather-bound journal on troops she saw, which if noticed by anyone would have easily given her away. She became indignant when military aides tried to screen her access to Union generals—sure to eventually raise suspicion about why she insisted on seeing them. And she continued to do little to hide her sympathy for the Confederate cause, like Van Lew receiving permission to aid war prisoners—in Greenhow's case, Confederates held in Washington. Greenhow, however, managed fairly quickly to organize a credible network of more than a dozen spies and couriers, many of them government clerks. Two of her reports from this network were sent less than a fortnight before the July 21 battle at Manassas.

At noon on July 10, Bettie Duval, a beautiful Marylander who lived in Washington and was one of Greenhow's couriers, arrived at General Bonham's advance post at Fairfax Court House, wearing a neat riding dress. She removed a tucking comb from her head to unravel out of her sleek black hair that had been braided a silk pouch with an enciphered message from Rose. Mid-nineteenth-century women dressed in hoop skirts and elaborately wound hairdos that offered many places for hiding documents. Greenhow the day before had written the brief message Duval carried, alerting Beauregard that McDowell's force intended to advance across the Potomac River and move on to Manassas Junction. Rose did not know the exact date for the Union launch because McDowell had yet to decide one himself. Her warning was rushed to Beauregard's headquarters. For weeks the Confederate commander had been receiving intelligence on the strength of McDowell's army and its general purpose. But he did not know what McDowell planned to do with that force and when he planned to do it. Greenhow supplied him a piece of that intelligence.

Five days later, on the night of July 16, a second Greenhow courier, a former government land surveyor named George Donellan, showed up at Beauregard's camp to let the general know that McDowell and 55,000 men (an inflated number in her report) had moved out toward Manassas Junction from Arlington Heights and Alexandria. Early the next morning, Beauregard relayed that message as well to Richmond and braced for battle.

Greenhow's intelligence was not as critically important as she and Beauregard later made it out to be. For weeks Washington had been awash with rumors that McDowell planned to attack. Beauregard would have had to have his head in the sand not to hear them and been incredibly stupid to ignore them. Greenhow likely picked up the information for her July 9 message from gossip she heard among well-informed political circles. Beauregard could also read stories in northern newspapers with detailed accounts of McDowell's plans. Greenhow's second report on July 16 that the Union Army was on the move likely came from her collaborators who earlier saw soldiers preparing to depart. By the time Beauregard had the note that night, his advanced pickets and scouts had already seen McDowell's lead units. Nevertheless, Rose's intelligence, though it hardly turned the tide of battle, did help Beauregard. No commander would rely just on news reports to shape his battle plans—particularly from the notoriously unreliable newspapers of that day. Greenhow's messages confirmed the rumors and energized Beauregard to prepare for the fight. Rose, who had been in New York during the July 21 battle, found a message when she returned home from Jordan passing along congratulations for her intelligence from Beauregard and Davis.

After Manassas, Greenhow served up at least nine ciphered messages for the Confederate command on arms stockpiles and troop movements in Washington that she and her agents observed, as well as lengthy reports with blueprints for defensive fortifications around the city. But Greenhow was an untrained spy—"not being a military man I can only trust to my untutored judgment as to what is of value," she wrote in one message to Jordan—her sources were weak, her information on the forts was sketchy, and her troop counts were inflated. She reported to Jordan that McClellan "is busy night and day" preparing for a simultaneous Rebel attack on Washington from Leesburg, Virginia, and from Baltimore. McClellan was busy, but not worrying about an assault that ambitious from the enemy.

Greenhow began to sense she was under suspicion. She developed an escape plan and began hiding copies of messages in her home and the clothing she wore. Her instincts proved correct. It became inevitable that federal officials would begin to take a hard look at the widow who still wore a black ruffled net over her face in August's oppressive heat. Reports of unusual activity at her house and rumors of her seducing federal officials soon reached Thomas Scott, the assistant war secretary. Colonel Porter's office had picked up leads as well.

Pinkerton had barely settled into his I Street headquarters in mid-August when Scott paid him a visit one afternoon. He ordered him to keep a "strict watch" on Greenhow's 16th Street house and report to him daily on what he saw. After the assistant war secretary left, Pinkerton summoned Lewis and Bridgeman and the three walked to Greenhow's neighborhood. The late afternoon had been dark and gloomy, a slight rain falling from threatening storm clouds as they left their headquarters. Pinkerton could see no signs of activity when he reached the Greenhow house, its window blinds all closed. He left Lewis and Bridgeman at a safe distance watching the home and returned to his headquarters to retrieve three more detectives for the surveillance. By the time he had returned, night had fallen and a furious thunderstorm burst over them.

Pinkerton posted the extra men around the house to observe it. The detective could see light peeking out from the windows of the first-floor parlor. He quietly crept up to the side of the house for a better look. The window was too high for him to see inside, so he signaled Lewis and Bridgeman to come. He took off his boots and in his socks climbed on their shoulders. Noiselessly he lifted up the sash and turned the slats of the blinds to look into the parlor. It was filled with luxurious furniture, valuable pictures hanging from the walls, and several pieces of statuary. But it was unoccupied.

"Shhh!" Lewis suddenly whispered. Someone was approaching. Drenched to the skin, they hid under the stoop to the front door as a tall Union Army captain in his forties walked up the steps, rang the bell, and was admitted. Pinkerton climbed back on Lewis's and Bridgeman's shoulders and saw the captain sitting ill at ease in Greenhow's parlor. Pinkerton recognized the infantry officer. He had met him several days earlier. The man commanded one of the city's provost marshal's stations. The detective never revealed his name, giving him later the pseudonym "Captain Ellison." His identity remains a mystery.

In a few moments, Greenhow entered the parlor and warmly greeted the officer, whose face lit up as he bowed from the waist. Pinkerton strained to listen as Greenhow and the man sat at a table talking in low voices. The officer pulled from the inner pocket of his coat what looked to Pinkerton like a map for fortifications and held it up to a gas lamp for Rose to see. The couple then left the parlor for an hour—Pinkerton assumed it was to make love—and returned arm in arm. The captain left about half past midnight, whispering good night and giving Rose what Pinkerton could hear was a kiss on the porch.

Pinkerton left Lewis, Bridgeman, and the others behind to watch the

Greenhow home and with one of his detectives, William Ascot, began following the captain in the rain still pouring down—Pinkerton scampering along in his stocking feet. But they followed the captain too closely to his garrison at Pennsylvania Avenue and 15th Street. Four guards with fixed bayonets there spotted the pair and arrested them.

A half hour later, Pinkerton stood dripping wet, muddy, and shivering before Captain Ellison, who toyed with a pair of revolvers on the table in front of him, apparently thinking that would intimidate his stalker.

"What is your name?" Ellison asked brusquely.

"E. J. Allen," Pinkerton answered.

"What is your business?"

"I have nothing further to say," Pinkerton replied.

"Very well," said the captain. "We will see what time will bring forth."

Ellison had guards throw him into a cold, dank jail cell filled with petty thieves and drunks rounded up that night. His detective, Ascot, sat in a corner, his teeth chattering. Pinkerton finally convinced a friendly guard to deliver a note from him to Scott.

About eight thirty the next morning, Ellison and four guards took Pinkerton to the home of the assistant war secretary, who had sent an order to the captain to bring his prisoner to him. Scott took Pinkerton into a room by himself and listened to the detective's account of what transpired the night before. He then tapped a bell on his table to have a servant bring in Ellison.

"Did you see anyone last evening who is inimical to the cause of the government?" the assistant secretary asked the officer.

"No, sir," the captain answered, his face flushed as he stole a quick glance at Pinkerton. "I have seen no person of that character."

"Are you quite sure of that?" Scott sternly inquired.

"I am, sir."

"In that case, Captain, you will please consider yourself under arrest."

Pinkerton's men searched Ellison's room and found enough evidence to convince them he had been feeding the enemy information through Greenhow. He was quickly packed off to Fort McHenry, which served as a military prison in Baltimore, to keep him from tipping off Rose. For about a week,

Pinkerton had a five-man detail watching Greenhow's home around the clock (recording who entered and left) and following her when she ventured out for walks. It did not take long for friends to warn her and for Greenhow herself to notice that brutish-looking men (who should have been more skilled in shadowing suspects) were lurking about her neighborhood and trailing her. Greenhow, who made a game of losing her tail, signaled to her operatives to be careful, but still had them courier her information south in coded letters.

Finally, Pinkerton, with Lewis and other detectives behind him, arrested Greenhow on her doorstep on August 23 as she returned home from a New York trip. Pinkerton identified himself as E. J. Allen. Greenhow, who was bigoted to the core, wrote later that the detective was an impertinent "German Jew," leading a pack of bloodhounds.

From a counterintelligence standpoint, the raid was a botched operation from the beginning. Greenhow should have been nabbed while she was away from her home so accomplices in the neighborhood would not be alerted that the spy ring had been breached and so agents could quietly and thoroughly search her house. As it was, everyone who knocked on the door while Pinkerton's men were inside was immediately arrested and Greenhow had time to destroy some evidence before the detectives could search the entire residence. While Pinkerton agents in Greenhow's parlor helped themselves to her rum and brandy, Rose managed to sneak into her library to hide a few documents. Lewis allowed her to go to her bedroom upstairs to change her clothes—another mistake. In her room with the door shut, Greenhow quickly began ripping up important papers like her cipher key. Lewis finally walked in as Rose was dressing. She reached for a revolver sitting on the mantel, which a careless agent had failed to find in the initial search, and pointed it at Lewis, ready to fire. Fortunately for him, Rose had forgotten to cock the pistol, giving another detective who had just walked in time to grab it out of her hand.

Greenhow's last-minute scramble to destroy documents could not hide the fact that she was a sloppy spy who failed to burn incriminating material beforehand in case the house was raided. It took a week, but Pinkerton's agents managed to haul away from her home a trove of papers that detailed fairly well her espionage network, its targets, and what she collected. They found hidden in her library and other rooms stacks of documents that Union officers appeared to have brought her (such as a printed copy of a May 4 War Department order detailing Lincoln's directions for increasing military strength) along with press clippings with military news (such as an August 19 report on Cameron issuing orders to governors for more soldiers). For documents she tried to shred, War Department clerks spent days piecing back together pages to uncover messages to Beauregard and others. Pinkerton detectives also had little difficulty breaking the crude cipher Jordan had given her and transcribing her intelligence reports into plain text.

The Greenhow haul revealed that while Rose may not have been the most knowledgeable agent, she raked up and sent a lot south. Reassembled letters, one addressed to "Mon Ami," dealt with Union regimental counts, federal troop movements into Virginia, New York affairs, McClellan's activities, and the location of forts around Washington. Fortunately for the administration, the intelligence reports revealed that Greenhow had not penetrated the White House or McClellan's inner command, as she later boasted to have done. Her chief sources turned out to be her collaborators she called "scouts," who walked around town vacuuming up rumors and noting troops on the march and fortresses being constructed. Pinkerton also would later exaggerate Greenhow's intelligence production as much as she did to make it appear that he had captured a master spy.

Separating just innocent friends who visited the Greenhow home from espionage collaborators became a major chore. Agents compiled a list of nine names at first suspected of being traitors but later deemed harmless. By the time Pinkerton finished, he had rolled up Rose's entire network. Its exposure, however, became an embarrassment for the Lincoln administration. Pinkerton had to huddle frequently with Cameron and Seward over separating public officials and Army officers who were merely Greenhow acquaintances from the ones who were love interests. Senator Henry Wilson was the most vexing problem. The powerful head of the Military Affairs Committee, Wilson was a florid and portly man who friends insisted was a prude devoted to his wife and whom the administration needed to keep on its good side. He routinely passed along to Greenhow military tidbits he had picked up at hearings, such as one on artillery emplacements—much of it harmless and only a fraction of what he knew as the committee chairman. But mixed in with those letters the agents confiscated were romantic notes telling Rose how much he longed to be with her. "You know that I do love you," the senator wrote in one. "Nothing . . . would soothe me so much as an hour with you." In other letters, Wilson and Greenhow appeared to be aware that their relationship was improper. Henry told her he had to be cautious visiting her, fearing spies were following him. Rose tied a batch of his letters together with ribbon, attaching a note that they should be burned in case of her "death or accident." Pinkerton thought the pair were having an affair, but no action was taken against the senator.

Lincoln thought Rose was a dangerous spy who had done considerable damage. She could have been tried and executed. But besides being loath to hang a woman, Lincoln feared that a Greenhow trial would reveal embarrassing secrets and ruin careers. Instead of the gallows, Rose and her eight-year-old daughter, "Little Rose," were put under house arrest at their 16th Street home, which newspapers soon dubbed "Fort Greenhow." Pinkerton hauled out furniture to make room and packed the place with guards plus other women suspected of spying for Rose, women who were just friends, women she didn't know and considered beneath her station, women who were prostitutes, and a few who were moles who informed on her. The widow and the detective soon were pitting wits. Greenhow bribed sympathetic guards or enticed friends allowed to visit her into sending out her notes to Jordan. Pinkerton intercepted many of the messages to follow their trail or plant disinformation in them. Jordan, who suspected that an enciphered letter he received from Greenhow in late October was actually written by Pinkerton, wrote his superiors that further "correspondence with her . . . is useless."

As the months passed, Greenhow's house confinement became a growing headache for Pinkerton, who considered her a sluttish diva. She still had powerful friends in Washington. Many of them, who feared alienating her because of what she knew about them, began lobbying for better treatment of her. Pinkerton resisted, worried that momentum would build for her to be released and exiled to the South. With newspapers publishing stories that she was still managing to sneak messages out of her house, Pinkerton and the administration began to reach the end of their rope with the thorny Rose. The last straw came when a November 17 letter she wrote to Seward complaining of her confinement ended up in the *Richmond Whig* newspaper the next month. Pinkerton confiscated her writing paper, ordered Fort Greenhow boarded up, and on January 18, 1862, had Lewis with several soldiers take the widow and her daughter to Old Capitol Prison at 1st and A Streets, where he imposed a blackout so she could send out no more letters. Rose told Lewis she felt like Marie Antoinette.

Put in a second-floor room with a straw bed, rough wood table, and rats skittering about, Greenhow became a demanding prisoner, alienating the guards, enjoying herself by pointing an unloaded pistol at them, sewing a Confederate flag to wave from her barred window, and complaining of the "stench from over 100 negroes" incarcerated near her. By spring of 1862, the U.S. government wanted to be rid of Greenhow. Over the objections of Pinkerton and McClellan, an armed escort on May 31 took the triumphant woman (a Confederate flag wrapped around her under her summer shawl) out of Old Capitol with Little Rose in tow and under orders from the War Department sent the two of them south to Richmond.

Pinkerton's shutdown of Greenhow's network ended much of the organized espionage by resident spies in Washington, but other intelligence pipelines that transient agents set up from Washington to the South remained throughout the war. Senior Union officers feared that Rebel spies had continual access to the highest levels of the U.S. government, reporting on Union war plans before they were even contemplated and sending Richmond accounts of discussions in cabinet meetings, but that was never the case. Confederate military leaders were almost always uncertain about federal plans and complained repeatedly about the lack of good espionage agents in Washington.

Greenhow proved to be a far better propaganda tool than spy. Richmond newspapers and Confederate officials hailed her as a brave and defiant agent who stole valuable secrets for the cause, which was far more credit than she deserved. Rose toured the South, writing Davis missives on what she heard and observed on the trips. The Rebel president sent her to Europe to lobby for diplomatic recognition of the Confederacy. On her return voyage aboard the British blockade runner *Condor*, the steamboat ran aground in rough Atlantic seas near the entrance to North Carolina's Cape Fear River on October 1, 1864. A high wave swamped the small rowboat taking Greenhow ashore. She drowned, weighed down by a chain around her neck attached to a bag with two thousand dollars' worth of gold from her book sales.

By late fall 1861, Allan Pinkerton had two dozen men and women on his payroll and a monthly budget of more than $6,500. Still his intelligence service, the first of its kind for an American army, was incomplete. McClellan had him collect information from Confederate prisoners, deserters, and refugees (black and white), as well as from the espionage agents he sent out. The detective also ran counterintelligence operations against the enemy. But McClellan kept other information pipelines, such as reports from his cavalry scouts and from his combat commanders' interrogations of prisoners and deserters, flowing directly to him and bypassing Pinkerton. The result: McClellan, who in addition to commanding the Army of the Potomac replaced Scott as general in chief in November, was flooded with lengthy reports not only from Pinkerton but also from his other pipelines and was too busy to make sense of it all. Pinkerton, who was a business contractor and neophyte when it came to intelligence the military needed, never had a complete picture of the enemy to present to McClellan in a concise, understandable way.

So he did his best with what he incorrectly thought was enough. Pinkerton found his most valuable interrogations were with Confederate deserters, especially Europeans and northerners who had been forced to join the Rebel service and had fled. So far, he found captured Confederate prisoners less cooperative. Pinkerton sent agents to the front lines to interview runaway slaves as they crossed into Union territory. All eager to talk, many of the runaways had little to offer because they had been enslaved on farms, isolated from the southern military. But others had seen Confederate deployments while traveling with their masters or had worked in Rebel camps as laborers, and Pinkerton found them to be careful observers with good memories. He ordered the runaways with some education or particularly good observation skills to be sent to him so he could evaluate whether they should become spies. McClellan at first disdained the idea of escaped blacks as spies, but soon he recognized their value.

By the time the Greenhow investigation had cooled down in November, Pinkerton had spies slipping into Richmond and roaming other parts of the South. Infiltrating the region proved fairly easy. Americans had become big travelers. A Pennsylvania man in New Orleans looking for a lost relative or an Atlantan on urgent business in New York did not arouse much suspicion. With the Confederacy short of war goods, black market commerce between North and South flourished, giving Pinkerton's agents a variety of covers as contraband smugglers. One operative, for example, roamed Rebel camps selling gilded embroideries that Confederate officers coveted for their uniforms.

The agents Pinkerton worked early into Richmond produced mixed results. Their operations moved slowly. Trips to the Confederate capital 106 miles south could take a week, conducting business in Richmond could last another week, and a return to Washington consumed a third week. An agent named E. H. Stein took a roundabout way of getting there, looping through Cincinnati and western Kentucky, where his wife, who was also on Pinkerton's payroll, joined him. His unconvincing cover made Rebel authorities immediately suspicious, he took few notes, and he returned to Washington with little of value to report to Pinkerton.

Pinkerton had better luck with Elizabeth H. Baker, who had worked in his Chicago office for years and before that had lived in Richmond. Her target became the Tredegar Iron Works, near the James River. The Richmond factory, its chimneys belching smoke day and night, was the South's most important iron manufacturing plant between the Potomac and the Rio Grande—the equivalent of the Krupp works of World War II Germany. Iron for Confederate guns, rails, and the armor for the scuttled USS *Merrimac* ship rebuilt and christened the CSS *Virginia* came from Tredegar's nine hundred workers. Pinkerton wanted to know what went on inside it. The day after Christmas in 1861, he interviewed a Baltimore machinist who had returned to Washington after spending three months working in Tredegar boring and rifling large cannon. The machinist gave the detective an idea of the plant's cannon production rate. Union Army private George F. Marshall, who escaped from a Richmond prison, had taken a tour of Tredegar and told Pinkerton the factory turned out twenty pieces of ordnance a week (mainly siege guns), and faced shortages of pig iron, brass, and copper.

Pinkerton picked Elizabeth Baker, a charming young widow with a convincing southern accent, to gather intelligence on a secret naval project in the plant. The Confederacy sorely wanted to break the Union blockade at the mouth of the James River emptying into the Chesapeake Bay so commercial trade could leave or enter Richmond. In the fall of 1861, the U.S. Navy had picked up rumors that the Rebels had found a solution to the blockade—a submarine that could detonate large torpedoes that its crew attached to enemy ships. The Union wanted a spy inside Tredegar, Pinkerton told Elizabeth, to report on the "infernal machines" being built.

Miss Baker arrived in Richmond on November 24 to visit Confederate captain Atwater and his wife, an upscale couple who were old family friends. Atwater was a Rebel ready to defect, so Elizabeth openly discussed with the couple her loyalty to the North. But she did not reveal the purpose of her trip. For a week, Atwater showed her around town and Pinkerton's spy unobtrusively took notes on Richmond's defenses.

One evening while they sipped tea, Elizabeth said casually that she would love to visit Tredegar.

"Why certainly," Atwater replied. "I will be most happy to go with you tomorrow."

"That will be delightful," Baker said enthusiastically.

"But stay a moment," the captain said. "I am afraid I will not be able to go tomorrow, as I have to go down the river to witness a test of a submarine battery."

"Why couldn't I go, too?" Elizabeth asked, pretending not to know what a submarine battery was. "I am sure I should enjoy it very much—that is, if there is no danger connected with it."

"Oh, there is no danger whatever," Atwater assured her, "and there will doubtless be a number of ladies present, and you can go if you wish."

The next day, Atwater, his wife, and Elizabeth took a carriage to the bank of the James about ten miles below the city, where a crowd had gathered to watch as a crew maneuvered a prototype vessel underwater to a large scow anchored in the middle of the river. The crew, swimming underwater, then attached to the scow's hull a magazine filled with projectiles and gunpowder, which they detonated by a long wire after their boat pulled away, sinking the scow. Peering through a looking glass, Elizabeth pretended to be clueless about what was happening so Atwater patiently explained how this contraption operated. That evening in her bedroom she wrote detailed notes on everything she had seen and heard, drew a sketch of the submarine, and hid the material in her bonnet.

The next day, arm in arm with the good captain, Elizabeth took a tour of Tredegar and inspected the formidable-looking boat being built, propped on heavy timbers. Plant officials let slip that they expected to have two of these vessels in the James River within a couple of months.

Baker rushed her information back to Washington, where Pinkerton said he passed it on to McClellan and Navy secretary Welles. The Union Navy rigged devices to defeat the sub—nets encircling their ships to catch divers trying to attach their torpedoes and a drag rope to snare the protruding air tubes and disable the boat.

One of Pinkerton's most skillful Richmond spies was Timothy Webster, who laid the groundwork for his espionage there while working undercover in Baltimore. With Hattie Lawton, a beautiful operative in her mid-twenties, pretending to be his wife, Webster had arrived in Maryland posing as a well-off southern arms buyer (with a carriage and team of fine horses Pinkerton provided) to root out secessionists smuggling weapons to the Confederacy. At one point he posed with another Pinkerton agent for a photograph at a studio holding a large Confederate flag.

The work, though, became dangerous. Webster had several close calls, often because of sloppy tradecraft on his part or Pinkerton's. While he sipped a drink in a Baltimore saloon with secessionist pals, a swaggering bully named Bill Zigler walked in and accosted him, shouting, "By God, I've been looking for you!" The surly man said he was sure he'd seen Webster in Washington talking to Pinkerton. Zigler probably had. Webster was not careful when he visited Pinkerton to brief him.

"You're a liar and a scoundrel!" Webster shouted back, pretending to be outraged. Zigler lunged for Webster but the operative punched him between the eyes. Zigler pulled out a knife, but Webster brandished a pistol, so the brute backed down.

Pinkerton had worked closely with Baltimore's provost marshal, James L. McPhail, who helped shadow and arrest suspects. But he never alerted McPhail that he had Webster posing as a southern sympathizer in Baltimore. McPhail soon picked up Webster's trail and had him arrested. Pinkerton helped Webster escape late one night from a carriage taking him to Fort McHenry's jail. What should have been just as damaging was the fact that a number of newspapers, like the *Baltimore American and Commercial Advertiser*, carried stories about Webster's arrest and escape. But ironically, Webster's run-ins with Zigler and McPhail ended up strengthening his cover. Baltimore secessionists became even more convinced these scrapes proved that Webster was one of them.

With a batch of letters that Baltimore's secessionists trusted him to take south to friends and relatives, Webster left the city for Richmond on October 14. It took him a fortnight to reach the Confederate capital, but Webster used the time wisely, vacuuming up military intelligence on the meandering route he rode. He finally reached the city the evening of October 28 and checked in to the five-story Spotswood Hotel, near Capitol Square, where many Confederate legislators stayed. Webster spent the next day delivering his letters from Baltimore. He wanted to visit Manassas and Winchester, Virginia, which had extensive Confederate deployment, but he was unable to obtain an appointment with the busy war secretary, Judah Benjamin, who approved passes civilians needed to travel anywhere in the state. So Webster pulled off a ploy he would use many times to secure travel clearances: he hooked up with a friendly Rebel sympathizer to give him cover and open doors for him.

His buddy this time was William Campbell, a Baltimore merchant in Richmond who befriended him. Campbell drove Webster around

Richmond to see its defenses and visit its Ordnance Department, where the spy counted 12,000 British-made Enfield muskets smuggled through the blockade. The next day, October 31, Campbell took Webster to the office of John B. Jones, the pass adjutant for Richmond's provost marshal. Jones issued them both the paperwork to travel to Manassas. Webster gave the clerk a flimsy story that he needed to go there to deliver one of his letters. A train the next morning took them to the town, where Webster counted enemy regiments, observed drills, and chatted with officers for hints about Rebel strategy. Webster found other sidekicks like Campbell to help him obtain passes to Warrenton and Centreville, where he collected the same type of intelligence.

On November 6, back with Campbell, Webster returned to Richmond and visited the War Department for a list of articles it needed that the two men might helpfully hunt for in the North—the aim being to have a sense of Confederate shortages. Department officials did not tell them much, except that they needed emery cloth for scouring metal equipment. Three days later, Webster began a five-day trek through the Virginia countryside back to Washington, again finding merchants along the way to help him obtain passes to towns with military camps. His written military information he largely reduced to numbers that would jog his excellent memory for the details of what he saw. Webster also brought with him a price list for consumer goods in Richmond so McClellan would have a sense of economic conditions in the city.

Pinkerton's spy finally reached Washington the evening of November 14 and spent all night writing his report. A skillful observer and interviewer, he returned from his one-month mission with valuable intelligence on the Confederate forces the Union Army would have to fight in many parts of Virginia. His count of enemy regiments was higher than what the Rebels actually had, but not far off the mark. Compared to Pinkerton's other agents', Webster's information was fairly accurate. The next day, however, Pinkerton overwhelmed McClellan with a forty-five-page report on the trip. Useful military intelligence was buried in pages of worthless travel trivia the poor general had to wade through.

Webster made a second trip to Richmond in late November with more mail to be delivered from Baltimore as his cover. He and the other Pinkerton agents using the mail courier scam brought hundreds of letters into and out of the Confederate capital—each one opened, read, and resealed by Pinkerton's staff before being passed on to their recipients—alerting Washington officials to subversives in Baltimore and giving them a sense of the mood among Richmonders. On this trip Webster collected impressive details about the Rebel ironclad CSS *Virginia* along with information on enemy defenses at Roanoke Island off the North Carolina coast, infantry regiments and artillery batteries in Norfolk, and Richmond's troop strength.

John Jones, the War Department clerk, refused to issue him any more travel passes, not because he suspected Webster was a spy but because he thought freelance mail carriers like him charged exorbitantly for deliveries. Webster had no trouble getting around Jones. Among the letters he carried from Baltimore was one from a doctor and southern sympathizer there to John Henry Winder, Richmond's powerful provost marshal, effusively vouching for Webster. The gullible general issued Webster a pass so he could take a personal message to Winder's son, who was serving in Washington as a Union Army captain. Webster did pass along the message when he returned to the federal capital, but not before alerting Union authorities that Winder wanted his son to defect to Richmond. Soon the captain was being watched closely for any suspicious activity. He was later transferred to California.

Webster had been back in Washington a little more than a week when he set off for Richmond a third time on Christmas Day. This trip did not go well. During the Potomac River crossing in a thunderstorm, the sailboat he rode in ran aground. Wading through waist-deep frigid water, Webster carried two southern women who had been passengers along with their three children to shore. His gallantry earned him an unexpected dividend. One of the women lost a packet of letters wrapped in oiled cloth that she planned to deliver to war secretary Benjamin. Webster never told the woman he retrieved the letter bag and stuck it inside his wet coat. He sent the mail back to Washington via a Union courier. The letters revealed that a federal provost marshal clerk was sending treasonous messages south.

The next morning, however, Webster woke up with his limbs aching from a painful attack of inflammatory rheumatism. After ten days in bed he recovered enough to make a tour (with Campbell and passes Benjamin this time signed) of Virginia, Tennessee, and Kentucky, taking copious notes on the number of Confederate troops he saw on trains, the earthwork defenses along the way, and at one stop the whorehouse that drunken Rebel soldiers frequented. When he returned to Pinkerton's office the morning of January 30, 1862, he wrote another voluminous report—cautioning that Confederate officers told him they often exaggerated their force number to bluff the Federals.

With his rheumatism appearing to have subsided, Webster set off once more for Richmond in early February. This time Hattie Lawton accompanied him, wearing one of Webster's overcoats and felt hats, which made her look like a man for the trip. Hattie likely went to take care of Webster if his rheumatism flared again. Pinkerton had egged him on, which he shouldn't have done. Webster was taking an incredible risk making one trip after another to Richmond—each one compounding his exposure in the field along with the chance of capture. Confederate authorities were hardly blind to the fact that Union spies were infiltrating into Virginia. Rebel general Joseph Johnston in northern Virginia sent a letter back to Richmond warning that his informant reported a suspicious traveler from Washington touring the Confederacy.

Then came the blackout. This was supposed to be a short trip. As weeks passed and Pinkerton heard nothing from Webster and Lawton, he began to worry. Something had gone wrong, he thought.

Nine

"ENEMIES OF THE STATE"

illiam Henry Seward was a well-educated, sophisticated diplomat with unruly hair, untidy clothes, an informal manner, and unbounded self-assurance despite battalions of detractors. (Mary Lincoln thought he was an "abolition sneak" who could not be trusted.) Though a private man, he had become a prominent Washington host for extravagant dinner parties in the well-appointed house he rented off Lafayette Square. He enjoyed a brandy and water before the meal and fine wines during and after it—though he took care never to indulge in alcohol to the extent of intoxication.

A child of privilege, first in his class at prestigious Union College, Seward had won New York's governorship in 1839 at age thirty-seven and a Senate seat ten years later, both with the help of powerful backers like Albany newspaper editor Thurlow Weed. A southern tour with his wife in 1836 left Seward profoundly shocked over slavery's depredations and a committed opponent of the institution. Seward assumed he would receive the Republican nomination for president in 1860 and was stunned and deeply hurt when he did not. But he campaigned vigorously for Lincoln and was rewarded with the position of secretary of state. Seward presumed he would be the real man in charge, vetoing cabinet nominees he considered rivals and becoming the administration's prime minister. Lincoln quickly let him know he would pick his own cabinet, run the government, and, when he chose to, overrule his secretary of state on foreign policy. Seward just as quickly came to accept Lincoln as president and formed a close bond with him. Operating out of a small, book-lined office in a modest brick building at the corner of 15th Street and Pennsylvania Avenue, Seward, with a staff of just thirty, ended up being the cabinet's most powerful officer. He became not only the administration's foreign policy spokesman; in July 1861, Lincoln also made him the czar of internal security to root out treasonous elements.

Seward set up a sweeping and ubiquitous operation. Subversives or persons suspected of subversion on the flimsiest of evidence were arrested, and because of Lincoln's suspension of the writ of habeas corpus they could be held indefinitely without charges or trial. Seward had U.S. marshals, friendly police chiefs, and political cronies in New York, Philadelphia, Boston, and other large cities recruit detectives and snitches for his security force. He paid them anywhere from five to ten dollars a day. Detectives often seized suspects at night, hauled them off to the nearest federal fort, stripped them of their valuables, and locked them in crowded cells for weeks and months. Postmaster General Montgomery Blair had his workers forward suspicious letters to the State Department to be opened and read, a federal judge whose ruling in a case angered the administration was put under surveillance, and an Ithaca, New York, publisher suspected of disloyalty was detained. Seward was reported to have boasted he could ring a little bell at his desk and have any man arrested. The secretary may not have said that and if he did he knew his authority was actually far from unfettered. From the outset, Lincoln was nervous about the arbitrary arrests, which prompted a storm of public protest, and Seward ended up releasing thousands taken in when the evidence against them appeared weak even to him or after they signed an oath pledging loyalty to the Union. But a large number—more than 13,000 during the entire war, by one count—were jailed for different periods of time.

Among the detectives Seward hired was Lafayette Baker, who left war secretary Cameron's office in late summer 1861 to join the State Department's treason bureau. Baker bragged that he instantly bonded with Seward and became his principal countersubversive agent. That was not the case. Seward stayed in far closer touch with New York police superintendent John Kennedy, who watched and arrested hundreds of suspects in that important state. But Baker built an aggressive operation in Washington, beginning with nine white detectives plus two black operatives and, considering how young and untested he was, drawing a hefty salary of $300 a month (the same as the more seasoned Pinkerton made). Baker claimed his large salary "is little enough," what with "the risk and responsibility I am compelled to assume." He also soon began racking up considerable expenses—in just one month $22.23 for a carriage and horse to cart him around town, $125 for his hotel bills, and $168 to pay informants. He told government auditors that because of the "peculiar nature" of his duties he "found it impossible to procure vouchers for" his expenses. The auditors accepted the excuse and paid him.

By the first week of September, Baker was expanding his operations north and west to cities like Baltimore, Philadelphia, New York, and Cincinnati. He spent so much time in New York, he set up a permanent office in lower Manhattan's Astor House, a luxury hotel at 12 Vesey Street. Seward ordered him to track correspondence running through Alexandria, Virginia, and sent him letters that State Department clerks had opened to track down and arrest their writers. Baker also set up surveillance to catch contraband smugglers. At a wharf near Washington's 7th Street he spotted a springy gangplank bow down unusually as a small, tastefully dressed woman walked up it to a steamboat. She had forty pounds of sewing silk hidden under her dress to take south. Seward kept Baker on a tight leash, demanding proof from him when suspects claimed they had been wrongly arrested and ordering him to release others he rounded up on thin evidence if they swore allegiance to the United States.

Baker moved his wife, Jennie, from Philadelphia to a comfortable Washington town house at 286 G Street. By the fall he was rarely at home, telegraphing her occasionally that he was on the road making "important arrests." As raw days of winter set in, Baker was spending much of his time in Maryland, which continued to bubble with talk of armed uprisings, particularly in the countryside, where the federal troop presence was thin. He joined Pinkerton in the Union's covert war there, attacking clandestine pipelines that carried mail and merchandise to the South. Baker's partner in cleaning out secessionists in southern Maryland soon became a dynamic division commander under McClellan named Joseph Hooker. In the region's five counties only a dozen people had voted for Lincoln and many of them had since been harassed into fleeing. Dangerously close to the federal capital, southern Maryland had become a smuggler's haven, with Rebel courier routes running through it and contraband ships launched from many spots along the Potomac River's eastern shore. Hooker lent Baker a detachment of three one hundred–man companies from his 3rd Indiana Cavalry Regiment, which since late October had been raiding suspect residences in the region with mixed results.

On November 20, Baker and his detectives launched their first joint operation with one hundred of Hooker's German American cavalrymen to clear out disloyal postmen relaying mail with intelligence to Richmond from southern Maryland's Charles, Prince George's, and Saint Mary's Counties. Anyone suspected of taking up arms against the U.S. government he was also ordered to arrest. Baker's first stop was the post office at Allens Fresh, Maryland, off the Wicomico River, where his men found fictitious letters that contained sealed notes inside them to well-known secessionists in Virginia. At the Newport post office, two miles from Allens Fresh, they found thirty-four letters with addresses for the North that had been written in Virginia and dropped at the post office by one person. At the Chaptico village post office, Baker confiscated a rough pine box with letters destined for the South; he shipped them to Washington. At the next stop, Leonardtown, one of the largest and most prosperous villages in southern Maryland that had sent a number of men south to fight with the Confederates, Baker's raiding party took over the weekly newspaper and forced its editor to print a pro-Union article one of Baker's men had written. At Great Mills, twelve miles away, he found a map he sent back to Seward with the contraband route that Rebels used from that village to Virginia. The southern Maryland sweep netted "four noted traitors and one rebel spy," Baker reported proudly to Hooker on November 25, as well as many documents "from which important results will flow."

Much of the confiscated mail, however, was not as important as Baker advertised. One harmless note, for example, was written by a Confederate soldier simply describing for northern friends the combat he had seen. But Baker was somewhat justified in writing Seward that southern Maryland was "wild and unsettled" and decidedly hostile to federal intruders. His cavalry raiders constantly had to deal with secessionists signaling quarries ahead of their detachment that the Federals were on their way to arrest them. After buying a meal at one southern Maryland home, his men fell violently ill. Baker suspected the homeowner tried to poison them.

Emboldened by his first foray, Baker talked Seward into approving two more cavalry raids into southern Maryland in mid-December and January. At a Potomac dock in Saint Mary's they discovered a forty-ton sloop, *Victory of Baltimore*, loaded with percussion caps, thread, brass buttons, and needles destined for the South. They captured near the Charles County village of Port Tobacco a planned shipment of Confederate uniforms down the Potomac and raided the White Horse tavern near Piscataway, Maryland, which Hooker suspected was helping deserters from his division escape.

Baker bragged that his sweep of southern Maryland had been a resounding success. Seward was delighted with the results. But the operation ended up doing little to disrupt secret Confederate mail and supply lines through the region. What Baker and his men did do was destroy boats, pillage houses, terrify southern sympathizers, threaten innocent citizens, and leave behind a population even more embittered toward the federal government. Hooker and his men ended up having deep misgivings over the ham-handed tactics Baker and his detectives employed, seizing schooners loyalists owned and arresting good Union men. One cavalry major complained in a December 21 memo to Hooker that the U.S. government would have been better served if the incompetent detectives assigned to his detachment had never shown up.

Baker also made incursions into foreign territory. The Confederates considered Canada, whose border stretching across the northern frontier of the United States was unguarded and whose citizens were administered by British representatives, a natural ally. Britain was officially neutral but along with many Canadians had set aside its antipathy toward southern slavery and supported or tolerated many Confederate policies. Canada provided a haven for Rebel prisoners escaping from northern camps. Its border geography made it attractive as a launching pad for Confederate operations against the United States. Confederate operatives were also posted in Canada to relay secret communications between Richmond and London. And by spring of 1862, Halifax, Nova Scotia, near Maine's coast, became a key departure point for British ships sailing with contraband to southern ports.

Seward had no qualms about playing hardball with foreigners or diplomats who consorted with the enemy. He sent agents, including Baker's, to stanch communications from the Confederacy to Canada and then to Great Britain as well as England's supply channel back to the South. In January 1862, Baker had four detectives, each being paid a hefty $154.69 a month, based in Canada. Baker also began traveling to the country himself to set up what he claimed was "a police system much needed in that section."

Whether Baker actually accomplished that is debatable. What is clear is that he went to Canada to play undercover operative. On an October 18, 1861, trip he set up a sting to capture Confederate congressmen just returned from Europe. Baker found a number of southern sympathizers checked in to the Clifton House at Niagara Falls on the Canadian side, their bags full of European correspondence to deliver south. Posing as Philip Herbert, a southern gentleman, and taking with him a black servant hired in Rochester to appear convincing, Baker booked a suite of rooms at Clifton House and soon was sitting at a table in the hotel bar playing cards with the southerners. He eventually enticed Confederate congressman S. W. Ashley, who intended to direct cross-border espionage operations, to take a walk with him on the Suspension Bridge over the Niagara River. When the two crossed to the American side, a federal agent arrested Ashley.

Edwin McMasters Stanton was "not handsome," according to one description of him, "but on the contrary, rather pig-faced." Twice a week, a clerk shaved only his upper lip in his office. Particular about his clothes, he wore always a formal frock coat and the tall hat of a gentleman. He has been described variously as vindictive, self-righteous, confrontational, hot-tempered, and easily irritated—a man who burned with ambition and thirsted for authority. Deeply insecure, he could be insincere, devious, dedicated to self-preservation—an expert at flattering bosses of any political stripe or jumping to any side of an issue in order to serve his own interests. Yet he was a devoted family man and a dedicated public servant of remarkable professional talents, able to absorb a tremendous amount of information. A nervous asthmatic, Stanton was an obsessive workaholic unable to relax or take a vacation. When work did overwhelm him, he often shut himself in his office and read British magazines or a Dickens novel to relax.

The son of a struggling Ohio doctor who died at age thirty-nine, Stanton early showed a love of books and a talent for the law. By 1836, he had a flourishing law practice in the state and by 1851 he was impressing Supreme Court justices in Washington with his oral arguments. In 1855, he was aghast at the idea of serving as co-counsel in a big patent infringement case with a hick lawyer from Illinois he was said to have described privately as a "long-armed ape." Whether Stanton actually said that about Abraham Lincoln and tried to have him dropped from the legal team is open to debate. There is evidence Lincoln did sense some hostility. In an eleventh-hour cabinet shuffle, President James Buchanan in December 1860 made Stanton, then a wealthy lawyer and confidential Justice Department consultant, his attorney general. Buchanan found that Stanton flattered him "ad nauseam," but he believed him to be an honest, skilled, and loyal attorney.

Loyal, Stanton was not. He quickly began leaking to reporters details of Buchanan cabinet meetings, which portrayed the president as weak and Stanton as the devoted Unionist stiffening his spine. Within a week of being made attorney general, Stanton had also set up a secret channel to Seward, delivering the nominee for secretary of state accounts of confidential discussions within Buchanan's inner circle. Stanton feared the U.S. government was riddled with secessionists intent on thwarting Lincoln's inauguration.

Realizing that Simon Cameron had no administrative ability and had proven to be blind to graft and inefficiency in the all-important War Department, Lincoln nudged him out of the position on January 13, 1862. Despite personal misgivings (an unsubstantiated rumor reached him earlier that Stanton had taken a bribe as attorney general), Lincoln replaced Cameron with the forty-seven-year-old lawyer, who was confirmed two days later.

Stanton began work on January 20 and in less than a month collapsed from exhaustion. Surrounding himself with aides as driven and passionate as he was—and treating them as a tyrant would—Stanton cleaned up graft and waste in the War Department and effectively managed what would become the largest army in the world. Within a year, Lincoln's attorney general, postmaster general, and Navy secretary would despise Stanton for his bullying tactics. Seward and, to a lesser degree, Treasury secretary Salmon Chase remained friendly with him. The only man who mattered to Stanton was Lincoln, who had concluded that his secretary's hard-driving and abrasive style was exactly what the War Department needed.

Before Stanton became war secretary, he had talked Lincoln into transferring the job of internal security enforcer from Seward to him. Protecting the North from espionage and internal subversion, as Stanton saw it, was as important as prosecuting the war in the South. On February 14, Lincoln signed Executive Order No. 1, making Stanton his internal security czar. Both deeply troubled by the human suffering arbitrary arrests and detentions had caused, Lincoln and Stanton promised a lighter hand. The president ordered hundreds of political prisoners released after they took oaths of loyalty to the U.S. government. But soon Stanton's policy on arrests and detentions tightened rather than relaxed. Federal jails were filled with even more political prisoners than Seward had packed in them.

Stanton turned to one of Seward's star players to ratchet up police state tactics. The day after Lincoln made his war secretary the security czar, Seward wrote Stanton a letter with a glowing recommendation for Lafayette Baker, who he said had "discharged his duties in a manner entirely acceptable." Seward still kept a few detectives on the State Department payroll after he transferred the internal security powers to Stanton. What Seward did with those agents and whether he told Stanton he had retained them is not recorded in the State Department's secret service records.

Lincoln was Baker's hero. The detective bragged that he was on intimate terms with the president, who admired his loyalty, was intrigued by stories of his secret adventures, and protected him from political enemies critical of his tactics. Baker also claimed he served as Lincoln's personal private eye, dispatched by the president on secret missions to investigate the brutal treatment of slaves in southern Maryland and to spy on Union generals suspected of being disloyal. There is no evidence that any of these claims is true. Baker had only a couple exchanges of correspondence with Lincoln. Instead he reported to Stanton and most of the time he did not report directly to the war secretary, which irritated him. Baker had wanted Stanton to promote him to the position of provost marshal general, to be the War Department's top security officer. He was angry and depressed when Stanton put him further down the ladder reporting to several bosses.

Army provost marshal general Andrew Porter decreed that he, and not Baker, had authority over all infractions of military regulations by soldiers and civilians in the city. Stanton also made Peter H. Watson, an old friend and the nation's leading patent attorney, his assistant secretary and Baker's immediate supervisor. Watson, however, only loosely supervised Baker, considering the man and his tactics a necessary evil. Keeping a tighter rein on Baker was the Judge Advocate General's Office, the Army's legal operation, headed by the controversial Joseph Holt, who prosecuted soldiers and civilians before courts-martial and military commissions. Under Holt was Major Levi C. Turner, a military lawyer Stanton had known who had the title "Special Judge Advocate." Turner issued arrest and detention orders to Baker, who he did not think was particularly bright.

Baker was left to invent a title for himself. At different times he called himself a "Special Provost Marshal" or "Chief of the National Detective Police Department" (the latter suggesting that he had a nationwide organization, which he did not). Baker liked his subordinates to address him as "Colonel," though at this point he held no military rank. Army officers simply called him "Mr. Baker." He was careful not to inflate his position in correspondence with them, signing his letters simply as an "Agent of the War Department."

By the time he joined Stanton's War Department, Baker had expanded his force to seventeen operatives. Pinkerton's budget was twice as large and he ended up commanding the larger salary. Baker had thought he would continue earning $300 a month, as Pinkerton did. But another assistant war secretary ordered that it be cut back to $200 a month, which irritated Baker. He set up his headquarters in an old two-story brick building at 217 Pennsylvania Avenue, near the Capitol. Its downstairs front offices were dingy with rough-looking men lounging about at all hours of the day and night waiting for orders. On one side of a wall stood a long rack filled with carbines. Pistols hung from other walls. Belts, cartridge boxes, heavy overcoats, and riding boots were stacked in spare rooms. Baker kept a private office upstairs. Rebel spies at different times were believed to have kept the building under surveillance from across the avenue.

Baker said his vision of an ideal operative was someone shrewd, self-reliant, smart, courageous, and "inapproachable by bribery." His men, many of them former California vigilantes skilled with knives, pistols, and killing without remorse, hardly lived up to that standard. A number of them over the course of the Civil War would be accused of being liars, exaggerators, or corrupt creatures without honor. Among his more reputable employees were two of his cousins from Lansing, Michigan, whom Baker literally summoned to his headquarters in the spring of 1862—Luther Byron Baker and his brother, Joseph Stannard Baker. Thirty-one-year-old Luther, who sometimes went by his middle name, Byron, wore a long beard like his cousin Lafayette but was more slightly built. Joseph, only twenty-two when he arrived in Washington, was a smart young man who interrupted college studies and teaching to fight in the war. He admitted he had a cold personality, intent on common sense always governing his emotions and actions.

For family, Luther and Joseph were treated to a frosty reception when they walked into cousin Lafayette's headquarters. For hours they sat in a front room waiting their turn to see Baker, who finally breezed by on his way out the front door and said only, "I will see you soon." Days passed and the brothers idly waited, catching only glimpses of their boss as he rushed in and out of his headquarters. Finally, Joseph approached Lafayette as he was about to climb into a carriage and told him he was anxious to start work. "You are on the payroll," Baker answered with a sneer. "What more do you want?" He drove off. Luther and Joseph immediately concluded that Cousin Lafayette was a devious and egotistical self-promoter, which was the case.

Baker became power hungry and intoxicated with the idea that the North could not win the war without him.

Joseph never knew exactly how many men worked in Baker's growing force, which he characterized charitably as "a miscellaneous lot." Some operated only during the day, others only at night. Frequently he would run into agents on the street he had never seen before. They would flash a silver badge Baker gave them to shoo away nosy police or military authorities. Baker had scores more snitches on his payroll, many of them prostitutes and barflies, whose exact number only he knew. His full-time agents included "Sargent" Brandt, a pompous man with a waxed mustache who rode around town as Baker's orderly sporting a black cape with red lining; Theodore Woodall, an illiterate house painter and then a brutish Baltimore cop before Baker hired him; Gilbert Lowe, whom Baker soon fired after catching him playing cards in a gambling den; and former California vigilante Tom Bowls, a bland, bald, but seasoned detective who looked at men with one eye when he talked to them. When he finally started working, Joseph ventured out on operations—typically a midnight raid on a Washington whorehouse or a Georgetown home to roust a Rebel sympathizer—with Baker's senior agent, John Odell, a short, corpulent man who had been a Cleveland police officer. Joseph soon preferred more honorable fieldwork with the Army over prowling the city's bars and brothels.

Baker's operation grew eventually to some thirty full-time detectives, who did more counterespionage and criminal investigations than actual intelligence collection. Simple crime was considered a national security threat as grave for the Union as espionage. The loyalty of Washington City police was doubtful and an efficient military police system had yet to be developed. The capital became an inviting target for corrupt northern and southern war profiteers bilking the Army. Secret service organizations like Baker's and Pinkerton's often spent more time chasing smugglers, horse thieves, draft dodgers, crooked contractors, and counterfeiters than they did on cloak-and-dagger work.

Baker bragged that he was building a national and even international secret service as fearsome as Vidocq's in France, but what he ended up with was a vigilante-style organization little different from San Francisco's, which terrorized southern and northern suspects. A plaque hung in his office proclaiming "Death to Traitors." And save for his New York bureau and the handful of agents he kept in Canada, he had only a scattering of operatives in other parts of the country.

Baker was not a big thinker. Instead of focusing on important tasks and delegating smaller jobs to subordinates, he wasted energy on minutiae, taking pleasure in shadowing suspects himself and setting up his own stings. He personally arrested a Union colonel trying to smuggle playing cards, tea, and coffee to the South for a $5,000 profit. He disguised himself in the oily overalls of an engineer of a tugboat that towed the *James Buchanan*, a schooner suspected of blockade running, out of Annapolis to a spot where the men he had aboard the tug could board the vessel and arrest the crew. He enjoyed interrogating suspects, tapping a woman's breasts to see if he heard the sound of tin being hit. It would indicate she concealed contraband drugs in the top of her corset.

Baker's arrests, along with those Pinkerton made, soon filled every square foot of space in Old Capitol Prison, which took in for different lengths of stay during the Civil War a total of 20,000 political prisoners, suspected spies, Rebel soldiers, and Union officers convicted of crimes. Inmates greeted new arrivals with shouts of "fresh fish!" Erected in 1800 as a tavern and boardinghouse and converted to a meeting place for both houses of Congress after the British burned the nearby U.S. Capitol during the War of 1812, the dilapidated three-story structure, which Washington residents always called "the Old Capitol building," was commandeered by the city's provost marshal in 1861 to house prisoners. Decaying walls and creaking stairways were repaired, iron bars replaced wooden slats in windows, extensions were added for kitchens plus more cells, and a row of houses on an adjoining block were connected to the main facility, the annex becoming known as Carroll Prison. All told, the complex had space for 1,500, although many more were soon crammed into it. The prison's first floor was taken up with guard quarters, rooms for interrogations, and a foul-smelling mess hall, where inmates ate meals on dented tin plates with their hands. Executions took place in a hundred-square-foot prison yard, partly paved and partly mud covered when it rained. The second and third floors had large rooms partitioned for prisoners and were infested with cockroaches, lice, bedbugs, and rats. No rules were written down, but strict discipline was enforced. Prisoners standing too close to windows risked being shot by guards patrolling outside.

William Wood was a short, ugly, and slovenly-looking man from Alexandria who had worked with Lincoln and Stanton on the patent case. Stanton rewarded him with a colonelcy and the superintendent's job at Old Capitol. Wood ruled the facility with an iron hand, though the prisoners considered him fair. The superintendent, who had a crafty side, knew their mood because he paid prison snitches to inform on cellmates. He once claimed to the *New York Times* that Old Capitol was orderly, clean, and comfortable—which it was not—and told his prisoners they were better cared for than the powers above him wanted them to be treated—which was likely the case. For the prisoners he put in Old Capitol, Pinkerton worked closely with Wood, though the detective considered him too crafty for his taste. Baker was at the facility so often, prisoners thought he was the de facto superintendent. Baker was not, but he and Wood worked closely interrogating prisoners in Room 19 of Old Capitol, sending the information they extracted to Stanton. Wood played the good cop. Baker tended to be brutal, often torturing prisoners to force them to talk. Baker also laced Old Capitol with informants to report to him on inmate conversations.

During the first two years of the Lincoln administration, Washington had two secret services operating side by side—Pinkerton's, who worked for McClellan, and Baker's, who reported to Stanton. The two did not coordinate, or even attempt to coordinate, their espionage and counterespionage activities. Though they never used the title during the war, each man claimed afterward that he had headed the nation's secret service. The only reason all-out bureaucratic warfare did not break out was that there was so much to do, neither man found much time to start a serious feud.

But it was inevitable the two men ended up clashing—and even spying on each other. Pinkerton investigated Baker agents suspected of wrongdoing. Baker did the same. In other instances, Baker and Pinkerton operations overlapped. On a trip to Richmond, Baker agent J. T. Kerby, an Englishman from Niagara Falls, Canada, struck up a conversation with Pinkerton operative E. H. Stein in front of the Confederate provost marshal's office. Both men pretended to be committed Rebels. Months later, Stein spotted Kerby in Washington and followed him to New York, where Pinkerton's men eventually arrested him and threw him into Old Capitol Prison. Baker had Kerby released.

Pinkerton developed a low opinion of Baker and considered himself the true head of the nation's first secret service. Pinkerton was always quick to point out that he was incorruptible. He could not say the same for his rival. Baker dismissed Pinkerton's intelligence service as a collection of useless amateurs. He thought the Chicago detective had bungled the Rose Greenhow case. He convinced Stanton that Pinkerton's methods were error-prone and that Pinkerton himself was too lenient with suspects. Stanton, who did not like the fact that Pinkerton reported to McClellan and not to him, needed no convincing. He fanned tensions between the secret service men. The war secretary would soon become a fierce critic of McClellan's and want Pinkerton fired along with the general. He egged on Baker to dig up damaging information about both McClellan and Pinkerton.

Soon reports and complaints began accumulating that Baker and his detectives were abusing their authority—more seriously, that they were making money raking in bribes, kickbacks, and war booty. Even Baker's own lawyer who defended him against some of the charges admitted he was an unsavory character "of little culture." Baker's agency became notorious for its snooping, its disregard for due process, its gathering of perjured testimony, its carelessness with the truth. His agents routinely seized suspects without warrants and held them for weeks. He was accused of blackmailing government officials into endorsing his espionage service. In a war that produced its share of shady characters, Baker became one of the worst, routinely referred to as the "czar of the underworld" and "the Devil's errand boy." A crusader against treason and government corruption—which Baker considered himself to be—would obviously attract enemies in Washington even if the crusader were on the up-and-up. Baker proved to be a dishonest and underhanded crusader. It earned him the distrust and disfavor of people in other government agencies fighting the same enemies.

Baker brooked no challenge to his methods. Lucius Chittenden, the register of the U.S. Treasury who never quite understood the authority under which Baker operated, wrote that if persons the detective falsely accused tried to publicly defend themselves, Baker, who "became a law unto himself," threw them into Old Capitol, "beyond the reach of the civil authorities," to silence them. When Baker arrested a New York cavalry officer who had a little too much to drink and spoke disrespectfully of Lincoln, Colonel William Doster, who succeeded Porter as the provost marshal of Washington, ordered the man released. The officer, Doster noted, had an otherwise exemplary record. Doster then became suspicious when people whom Baker arrested ended up mysteriously in Old Capitol with no paperwork on why they were placed there. When Doster questioned the incarcerations, "now began the reign of terror," he wrote in his memoirs. Baker brought trumped-up charges against the provost marshal, accusing him of misappropriating government funds, smuggling liquor, and sympathizing with traitors. Doster fought back and cleared his name.

Chittenden and others wondered how Baker, on a salary that amounted to only about seven dollars a day, maintained such a lavish lifestyle, staying in first-class hotels, a wad of money always in his pocket, riding about Washington dressed gaudily and on top of an expensive black stallion fit for a general. Even Baker's detectives noticed that he and his wife spent long stretches in the expensive Willard Hotel, which cost six dollars a day. By one estimate, Baker's accumulation of wealth amounted to eight to ten times his legitimate earnings for six years of government service.

He lived beyond his means by abusing his expense account from the secret funds Stanton provided and by ingeniously finding ways to shake the money tree on many of the raids and arrests he carried out. Chittenden noted how Civil War corruption seemed to spread when Baker's detectives were at work. Blockade runners who had been caught found they could soon be released after they paid Baker or one of his detectives a bribe. Government contractors who had paid off forage clerks were arrested for not greasing Baker's palm as well. Old Capitol became a cash cow. Dennis Mahoney, an Iowa editor and Lincoln opponent jailed there for three months, wrote in his diary that innocent men sometimes handed Baker sizable amounts so he wouldn't imprison them. Those who couldn't win their freedom found they could at least get a better room in the jail by bribing Baker. Peddlers sold liquor and food to inmates at inflated prices. The prisoners' complaints about the price gouging fell on deaf ears with Wood, Baker, and the guards, who were all skimming off the profits. After a man named Spahr was arrested in Washington, he suggested to a Baker detective that they grab a drink before he checked in to Old Capitol. Spahr claimed the detective took him to the back room of Baker's Pennsylvania Avenue headquarters, where a bar had been set up serving liquor. Baker had stocked it with booze his men had confiscated from saloons they raided. Tales of Baker's corruption from political prisoners, of course, had to be discounted some. Many of them hated Lincoln and everything about his administration. But the tales were too many to be ignored.

Augustus Green, a New York cavalry major posted at Fairfax Station, Virginia, became disgusted with Baker's men who roamed the area like "pirates" confiscating horses Union soldiers had captured from Confederates, then selling the animals and pocketing the profits. (Horses were a money-maker for the agents.) Green said one of Baker's men was in his tent as he negotiated with a local farmer named Sammy Jackson to provide forage for the four hundred horses in the major's unit. The well-meaning farmer was a southern sympathizer, but no spy. After Jackson left Green with the money and paperwork for the forage sale, Baker's men arrested him, seized his horse and wagon filled with produce, and threw him into Old Capitol. Green finally got Jackson released and his horse, wagon, and the produce in it returned. Afterward, the grateful farmer tipped off Green to Rebels threatening his camp.

Baker's roughshod tactics pleased Stanton but they infuriated the military and other members of Lincoln's cabinet. One Union general swore that if he caught "Baker's Brigands" in his camp he would shoot them on sight. Navy secretary Welles accused the detective of being "wholly unreliable" and a zealot. Postmaster General Montgomery Blair complained to

Lincoln that Baker was power mad after his detectives arrested the daughter of Blair's sister-in-law and two others near Fairfax Court House. Lincoln in this case did not intervene; the niece had 127 ounces of quinine laced inside her skirt, apparently destined for the South to treat malaria.

Reports on Baker's questionable operations made their way to Congress and into newspaper stories leaked by his enemies. Baker adamantly denied any wrongdoing, spinning elaborate but shaky justifications for his high-handed tactics. He argued in his memoirs that his bureau, though constitutionally unsuitable "in time of peace," was "indispensible in time of war" and thus allowed to cut corners. In a civil conflict as fearful as this one, "the unnatural condition of things calls for the detective service to watch and bring to justice the enemies of the State, who are plotting its ruin." He claimed that his service provided intelligence for "some of the most important army movements and battles" of the war (that was certainly not the case) and in the dirty shadow warfare he waged he did not have to give any authority or reason "for certain acts" (also not the case). Baker developed a martyr complex, claiming he was unfairly persecuted. Because his work was secret, he could not disclose details to defend himself.

He became a master buck passer. When public wrath over his tactics grew intense, he blamed Congress and cabinet members for forcing him to hire disreputable men. Baker claimed he caught only two employees with their hands in the till and he jailed them. He insisted that he accounted to Stanton for everything he confiscated and that both the war secretary and the president backed him up. Stanton did, but there was no evidence Lincoln knew enough about his work to react to it one way or the other. Eventually even Stanton appeared to become nervous that Baker's arbitrary arrests had gotten out of hand. On November 17, 1862, he ordered Turner to instruct Baker that he could not make any more arrests "without special authority." To counter all the criticism heaped on him, Baker liked to cite the gifts his devoted subordinates gave him—an elegant saber and China silk sash that cost $200, plus one of the finest saddles in the country costing $650. But it only begged the question: where did his men, who were paid the minimum wage of the day, get the money for such expensive presents?

Cousin Joseph recalled accompanying Baker in late fall 1862 to southern

Fairfax County, Virginia, to arrest a suspected enemy spy hiding there who had recently been prowling in Washington. The Rebel officer, who Joseph said was "a desperate character," resisted. Baker hacked the man to death with the Confederate's bowie knife. "The night ride back to Washington was a dreary one," Joseph later wrote. "My mind kept reverting shudderingly to that bloody corpse we had left in that lonely old Virginia house."

Newspapers in the South and North soon reported on the death, but never connected it to Baker. Several days later, Joseph walked into Baker's office holding a New York paper and pointed to a story about the slaying. Baker glanced at the article for a moment. He looked up at Joseph with his forefinger pressed against his lips, then returned to the letter he was writing. Joseph doubted that anyone else on the force ever knew about Baker's connection to the killing. The episode disgusted him.

1862

Ten

RICHMOND

"Oh how heavy was the air with horror!" Elizabeth Van Lew wrote in her journal. "Literally my breathing became labored. My heart seemed cramped! And the poor newly mustered young men! I could not look at them in the streets without tears coming to my eyes. Hundreds of times during the war, and after I learned to know them and their material, did I long to say to them, 'be not like dumb driven cattle.'"

As the new year of 1862 dawned, Van Lew could not escape the scene of young men marching off to war. Chilling rains and snow fell over Richmond that January, the shivering troops huddled by fires in the camps around the city, many racked by pneumonia, pleurisy, rheumatism, and catarrhal fevers. Hospital services had improved since Bull Run's influx of wounded, but medical care would soon be not much better than what was provided on battlefields, with dead bodies stacked up in hospital cellars awaiting burial and amputated arms and legs lying in backyards rotting. Civil servants, politicians, and military men crowded hotels and dining rooms. Demand outpaced supply, with inflation beginning to make food too costly for many. Beef had risen from 13 cents to 30 cents a pound. Yet a delusional gaiety, even frivolity, coursed through Richmond's polite society, with banquet tables still groaning with delicacies, perfumed ladies still attending evening military drills, and patriotic pride gushing everywhere. "Yankee" had become a derogatory word in Richmond, children using it to taunt others.

Jefferson Davis was inaugurated for a six-year term on a rainy February 22 and moved his family into the old Brockenbrough mansion at Clay and 12th Streets, which became the Confederate White House. Haggard and worn looking, Davis was afflicted with neuralgia, digestive disorders, venereal disease, and bronchial problems and had lost sight in one eye. A workaholic who buried himself in paperwork and did not budget his time wisely, Davis was inaccessible, haughty, and peevish—not suffering fools lightly and feuding with his generals. A week after his inaugural, the Rebel president declared martial law in Richmond. He had reason to do so. Crime was becoming a problem in the refugee-swollen city. Not all the citizens of the capital of the Confederacy—indeed the entire Confederacy, Davis quickly realized—could be counted on to be loyal to the cause. Van Lew was one of them.

Pro-Union sentiment had long existed in the South. The vote against secession averaged 20 percent in Mississippi, Florida, Alabama, Georgia, Louisiana, and Texas. Many in the South supported slavery and states' rights but not secession. Van Lew kept silent in crowds singing "Dixie," but she was not the only one silently humming Union songs. The political affiliations of Americans did not cleave neatly when the war started. Each side had long held commercial and familial bonds with the other that could not be instantly separated. Northern immigrants, a significant proportion of whom were Unionists, populated the South. Richmond had a large number of Scots, Huguenot French, Germans, and Portuguese still loyal to the United States. Secret organizations—with names like the Peace and Constitutional Society and Order of the Heroes of America—soon burrowed into southern cities with the aim of abolishing slavery, promoting peace, or gumming up the workings of local governments. In Richmond, pro-Union graffiti soon began appearing on building walls.

In the Confederate capital, the job of rooting out Union sympathizers, spies, and vandals chalking slogans on walls fell to Brigadier General John

Henry Winder, who within a year became quite busy at it. His tousled hair snowy white, Winder wore a gaudy general's uniform that made him look like a martinet, which many Richmonders thought he was. He was gruff, abrasive, vain, and profane, with a scar along one cheek that he earned in the Mexican War when another man's shattered skull slashed it. A Union war prisoner song had a stinging verse on Winder describing him as "like a Devil in Regions lost."

A West Point graduate who had served in U.S. Army posts all over the country, Winder reluctantly joined the Confederates in 1861 at age sixty-one, too old for a field command but bestowed a brigadier generalship from Davis, which he had long coveted in the federal army, where he had never been promoted past major. Winder was made inspector general of military camps around Richmond, with a multitude of duties, such as outfitting soldiers, overseeing training, and returning deserters. Five days after Davis's inauguration, Winder was also named provost marshal general for Richmond, tasked with enforcing the martial law Davis had declared—which meant hunting for criminals and subversives and supervising the prisons he sent them to.

Winder turned out to be not as aggressive at uncovering subversives as Pinkerton and Baker in Washington. Confederate general Joseph Johnston complained he was an abominable spycatcher and Richmond was riddled with Union agents. For all the duties he had, Winder commanded no more than 2,000 men, the most hated of whom were his civilian detectives. A native of Maryland, he recruited them from that state, many of them former cops and street thugs in Baltimore. Richmonders called them "alien plug uglies."

Winder tried to rule the city with an iron hand. His all-powerful security men, wearing shield-shaped silver badges with "C.S. Detective" stamped on them, rode around Richmond on horses arresting whomever they pleased. By mid-March, Winder had jailed twenty-eight men and two women for suspected disloyalty. Hotels were required to send his office a list of new arrivals each morning. Railroads had to report all passengers carried into the city. Believing desperate times demanded desperate action, Winder also tried unsuccessfully to combat inflation and public drunkenness by imposing price controls and boarding up saloons. He quickly became the most hated man in Richmond.

Jefferson Davis praised Winder as a kind and humane overseer of Richmond's prison system. The president's wife, Varina, claimed northern inmates in the South were fed as well as southerners held in the North. Perhaps in 1861 that was the case, when the relatively few Union prisoners captured posed little strain on the Confederacy and local commanders sometimes paroled or exchanged POWs with the other side. But conditions grew far worse when more federal captives from the big battles of 1862 poured into the South and inmate exchanges were halted by 1863. The more than 200,000 Union captives incarcerated in more than a hundred southern prisons and jails during the war lived in overcrowded, grime-covered, and disease-ridden facilities full of bugs and rats, with conditions for enlisted soldiers worse than for officers, and black Union soldiers treated far more harshly than the white ones. More than 30,000 Federals died in southern prisons, compared to the nearly 26,000 Rebels who perished in northern facilities.

Because of its proximity to enemy lines and the extensive rail and road network leading into it, Richmond became a receiving depot for federal prisoners, who usually arrived robbed of everything in their pockets by Rebel searches along the way. Soon overwhelmed, the Confederate government converted nearly a quarter of the city's tobacco warehouses into makeshift prisons. Some 3,000 political prisoners, Confederate deserters, black convicts, Union officers, and captured spies were packed into a complex of two tobacco factories and a warehouse on Cary Street, which went by the name Castle Thunder. It was a hellhole, whose sadistic commandant and brutal guards devised medieval tortures for prisoners, such as hanging them by their thumbs and branding them with hot irons. Ten thousand captured Union enlisted men would be confined on Belle Isle, an eighty-acre tract on the James River, where the lower fifteen acres of flat sandy land had been partitioned off for a makeshift tent prison with concentration camp–like conditions. During the winter, freezing prisoners without tents had to burrow into holes to keep warm at night.

More than 4,000 Union officers were eventually crowded into a three-story ship chandlery and grocery warehouse Winder commandeered on March 26, which had been owned by L. Libby & Son at the corner of Cary and 21st Streets. It soon went by the name of Libby Prison. Although the officers there fared better than the enlisted at Belle Isle, Libby Prison, whose rear faced the James River and Kanawha Canal, was still a squalid place to be locked up in, with scurvy common because of poor diet. Its commandant, Lieutenant Thomas Pratt Turner, hung a sign at the top of stairs leading to inmate rooms that read: "Abandon hope all who enter." As with other facilities, Libby had its share of thuggish overseers, like Erasmus Ross, a vicious clerk who strutted about with a pair of revolvers and a bowie knife, delighting in taunting and abusing prisoners. To keep up their spirits, the officers, many highly literate, penned diaries, carved napkins rings out of beef bones, set up foreign language classes, and formed the Libby Prison Minstrels, whose performances Richmond newspapers advertised for visitors to attend. Another important morale boost for the inmates at Libby and other Richmond prisons came from an upper-class Richmond woman who visited regularly—Elizabeth Van Lew.

She could see Libby Prison and Belle Isle from the porch of her Church Hill mansion. After the first wave of federal soldiers were marched into Richmond in July 1861, Union prisoners became Van Lew's cause. Aiding them was no easy task, however. Confederate authorities admired Richmond's women who brought cakes to Rebel camps. They did not think too kindly of the same hospitality extended to captured Union troops. Van Lew, who had seethed as she listened quietly to returning Confederate soldiers brag about desecrating the bodies of dead Federals, paid her first visit to the John L. Ligon & Sons tobacco factory on the banks of the James River at the corner of Main and 25th Streets. It had been converted into a prison to handle the first Bull Run captives and was commanded by Mary Lincoln's half brother, Lieutenant David Todd, one of the system's most brutal overseers, who was drunk and belligerent most of the time.

"How my heart beat," Van Lew recalled, as she walked into Todd's office and asked if she could be made a hospital nurse for the prisoners. "He took down my name, looked at me with surprise, and said I was the first and only lady that had made any such application," Van Lew recalled. Todd refused to let her see the inmates so Van Lew went to Confederate treasury secretary Christopher Memminger, whom she knew, to plead her case. Memminger also refused, but gave her a note of introduction to General John Winder.

Winder's office on Bank Street was crowded and frenetic. The busy general could carry on a conversation with three people at the same time while calmly signing papers. But Van Lew found Winder easy to manipulate. He had no qualms about his detectives harassing the city's lower class but he was respectful toward Richmond's elite, of which Van Lew was a part. "His personal vanity is so great," Van Lew wrote. She turned on the charm, going overboard to convince the old man that she was loyal to the cause and only wanted to be a good Christian with her help for the enemy. Van Lew actually thought Winder was "a kind hearted man," though "violent in his prejudices," she observed. She later had the general and his wife over for dinner to continue buttering him up. Winder allowed Van Lew and her mother to deliver not only medicine to the prisoners but also food, clothing, bedding, writing material, and books from her library.

To win over the brutal Lieutenant Todd at Ligon Prison, Van Lew plied him with ginger cakes and buttermilk. Another conquest was Erasmus Ross, the sadistic clerk at Libby Prison. Ross, who turned out to have an uncle who was a closet Unionist, secretly agreed to help Van Lew. When Union lieutenant colonel William Lounsbury was summoned to Ross's office for what he thought would be a torture session, the clerk surprised him with a Confederate uniform he told the federal officer to wear for his escape to Van Lew's house, where he was hidden until he could make it safely to Union lines. It was a ruse Ross pulled off with more prisoners.

Van Lew visited other facilities. At Howard's Factory next to Ligon, which was also converted to a prison, she befriended inmates like Massachusetts infantry major Paul J. Revere (grandson of the Revolutionary War patriot) with food and books. Revere's relatives never forgot the help. Winder had given her permission to deliver supplies to the prisoners, but she could not enter the jails or talk to the inmates. Van Lew found a way to work around the restriction. She talked surgeons into sending POWs to hospitals, where she could visit and feed them—and slip them money and messages hidden in a secret chamber in her custard dish. She was even allowed to bring to her home one prisoner stricken with typhoid fever to nurse him. Inmates she could not see in the jails soon found ways to secretly send her information on Confederate troop levels and movements—returning books she lent with words in them underlined or pinpricked for a makeshift code when strung together. Prisoners also sent her as mementos buttons from the bones they carved.

Van Lew could be tenacious in circumventing hurdles that Confederate authorities threw in front of her. When the prison system's chief surgeon blocked her in early 1862 from taking any more food to prison hospitals—inmates were being fed just fine without the help, he haughtily told her—Van Lew marched to the War Department with her delicious custard as a bribe. Winder eventually rescinded the surgeon's order.

Others helped Van Lew work the system. Her brother, John, joined a lobbying campaign to free a Unionist from Castle Thunder. Charles Palmer, a wealthy Richmond import-export merchant and an ardent Unionist, spent $30,000 of his own money to aid inmates at Castle Thunder and other prisons. (Palmer considered Confederate leaders to be traitors.) Abby Green, a Van Lew friend who became as outraged as her over the treatment of Union prisoners, began aiding sick inmates at Libby and slipping letters into the prison. (She eventually had to flee when Confederates discovered the letter smuggling.) William Rowley, a New Yorker who arrived in Richmond shortly before the war and was a man Van Lew considered the "bravest of the brave," worked with her to provide prison escapees safe houses, passes, disguises, and guides to make their way north. (Rowley used a wartime alias, "John Y. Phillips," to protect his identity and gave his fifteen-year-old son, Merritt, the pseudonym "Charles Phillips" to serve as a courier and spy for his father.)

Among the more important men in Van Lew's prison aid network was Frederick William Ernest Lohmann, a native of Prussia, who came to Richmond in the mid-1840s and became a saloonkeeper. Lohmann, who went by his middle name William, spent three years aiding the Union cause and eventually three months in Castle Thunder for doing so. In addition to helping prisoners escape, Lohmann distributed Confederate money from

Charles Palmer to the families of deserving Unionists in Richmond and later ventured out on spy missions all over Virginia.

Van Lew helped runaway slaves—and black servants on her staff like butler William Sewel and his family—make their way north. African Americans who remained in Richmond became key conduits for her aid to Union prisoners. Blacks who scrubbed jail floors carried messages. Robert Ford, a northern free black who had served as a teamster in the Union Army's quartermaster department before Confederates in the Shenandoah Valley captured him, worked as a hostler for the commandant at Libby Prison. Ford also helped Libby prisoners escape. Nearly every Sunday, Van Lew, dressed in the rough cotton clothes of a farm woman so as not to be noticed scouting prisons, walked by Libby and signaled prisoners watching from windows with an empty pitcher she held or a careless lifting of a handkerchief to her lips. Blacks working inside the prison alerted inmates to the ritual. Van Lew also posted black servants near Libby to help the ones escaping reach her house or the homes of others willing to harbor them until they made their way north.

At Church Hill, an old washstand blocked the view of a door to the large attic in her mansion, where Van Lew hid escapees in a secret chamber blocked off by a box and panel. Her niece Annie recalled tiptoeing quietly behind Van Lew one evening as she took a plate of food up the steps to the attic and seeing a man's head pop out from the chamber entrance when Van Lew moved the box and panel to serve him his meal.

Nosy neighbors soon noticed strange men peeping around columns at the mansion late at night. Rumors were whispered that she had hidden rooms in her house for Yankee prisoners, even wilder stories that she had a tunnel from her garden to Libby Prison. Despite several searches, Winder's detectives never discovered Van Lew's secret room in her attic, but neighbors remained convinced she was hiding men. Local ladies asked Elizabeth and her mother to make shirts for South Carolina troops encamped at Richmond's Old Fair Grounds. They were aghast when mother and daughter refused. The rumors and grumbling soon made their way into Richmond's rabidly pro-Confederate newspapers. On July 31, 1861, a fortnight after Van Lew had begun delivering supplies to Union prisoners, a threatening paragraph appeared in the Richmond *Daily Dispatch*. Elizabeth and her mother weren't named but *Dispatch* readers could easily guess. The paper warned that "females of Southern residence (and perhaps birth) but of decidedly Northern and Abolition proclivities" should halt their pro-Union activities while they can if they "do not wish to be exposed and dealt with as alien enemies." Other newspapers carried similar threats.

Van Lew had more to worry about than just bad press. On August 31, 1861, the Confederate Congress had escalated its campaign against suspected Unionists, passing the Sequestration Act to seize their property. Women were targeted as well as men. The day after Davis suspended the writ of habeas corpus, Winder arrested Palmer and two dozen other prominent Unionists. The import-export merchant and other detainees with powerful friends on the outside managed to win quick release and authorities were still hesitant to punish upper-class women. Even so, Van Lew began damage control. To demonstrate her loyalty and calm neighbors, she brought baskets of books and flowers to the South Carolina soldiers and began ministering to Rebels in their hospitals. At Church Hill she also took in as a boarder George Gibbs, who had replaced Todd as head of Ligon Prison, hoping the captain and his family would offer some protection against authorities raiding the house.

But Van Lew refused to be intimidated—even though Confederate officers continued to warn her that she was paying too much attention to federal prisoners. Her mother, Eliza, who at seventy-three had grown weaker as 1862 began, kept up the public front—offering refuge for hungry and wounded Rebel soldiers—while Elizabeth continued to work on behalf of the Union men. Ironically, her circle of dissidents grew after Winder's March arrests. As frightening as the security sweep was for all of them, the crackdown enabled Van Lew and other Unionists to identify one another and come together. They soon coalesced around Van Lew as their unofficial leader—their work becoming more than lessening the suffering of prisoners. The Union soldiers they helped escape provided northern newspapers with evidence of Confederate government repressiveness and the Unionist surfacing in the South.

• • •

As her network helped the prisoners, Van Lew also became a spymaster. The culture of the day gave her cover—at least at the outset. Though mid-nineteenth-century southern women had not progressed as far in the workforce as their northern sisters, one job opened new opportunities for them during the war—espionage. Women became effective spies because few expected them to engage in such unladylike behavior or to have the mental and physical capacity to succeed at the profession. Females were denied schooling in the military arts, men gave them little credit for knowing technical things, but they could read newspapers, which published long stories about army strength and movements, they could listen to men talking about battlefield victories and losses, and they could report what they heard to the other side. Northern and southern women often became spies because it was the only way to serve their cause besides nursing. Some females cross-dressed as male spies. Many were married and their husbands at the front did not know they were clandestine agents.

For generations after the war, stories persisted that Van Lew feigned mental illness as her cover for spying—dismissed as a harmless eccentric walking around town carelessly dressed and mumbling to herself. Even the CIA in an analytical report on the Civil War repeated the tale. The "crazy Bet" stories were a myth. Van Lew never acted crazy, she wore disguises only when the operation demanded it, and as the fear of arrest increased she never recklessly broadcast her Unionism in public. Neighbors considered her peculiar because of her sympathy for the northern cause and her "pernicious social equality doctrines," as one said, but not because she had a mental defect. What Elizabeth Van Lew did have was a talent nurtured since childhood for appearing to conform even though she did not—important for a spy. She had become expert in cultivating political enemies, endearing herself to them while working at the same time to subvert them. The cover succeeded.

Van Lew hated being known as a spy—she considered herself an honorable American patriot instead—and she was not a proficient intelligence collector in the beginning. Before the Bull Run battle she wrote as a private citizen to Lincoln and the War Department about what she saw happening in Richmond and what Union prisoners told her, not knowing who in

Washington was reading her mail. No one apparently was. By 1862, military intelligence from her ring was reaching the federal capital without Van Lew knowing it was getting there and without Pinkerton's secret service realizing that the information was helped along by her operatives. Take, for example, George F. Marshall, the Union private captured at Bull Run who provided Pinkerton with important intelligence on production at the Tredegar plant. After he bribed his way out of Libby Prison on Christmas Day 1861, Marshall went to the home of Burnham Wardwell, an ice dealer twice arrested for expressing pro-Union sentiments who was part of Van Lew's underground. Wardwell supplied Marshall with money and civilian clothes and introduced him to more than thirty other Unionists. One of them was Arnold B. Holmes, a foreman in a sewing machine factory and also part of Van Lew's network, who let Marshall stay at his house for three weeks, during which Holmes gave the Union private a tour of Tredegar. With passes the underground supplied, Marshall made his way back to Washington and Pinkerton, who appreciated his intelligence on the ironworks but strangely showed no curiosity about Wardwell, Holmes, or the dozens of other Unionists whom Marshall met. Pinkerton chose to send his own spies to the Confederate capital—with mixed results—instead of reaching out to the Unionists who lived there and might have been more effective agents.

Over time, Van Lew picked the members of her spy ring carefully. Many were established Richmond residents who had helped aid prisoners, like Abby Green, William Rowley, and Charles Palmer. To that core she added men like James Sharp, a Scotsman who emigrated to the United States in 1838 and worked for twenty years as a stonemason to save up enough money to buy an eighty-eight-acre farm in Charles City County, Virginia. Sharp helped relay packages of papers Van Lew sent north. Van Lew also developed her own sources inside the Confederate government—a clerk in the attorney general's office with access to troop strengths, as well as clerks in the War and Navy Departments.

Her brother, John, eventually joined in the espionage, carrying his secret papers in a velvet-lined leather dispatch box with "John Van Lew" handsomely engraved on it, which he hid in a leather satchel. But John's turbulent family life presented a security problem for his sister. His marriage to Mary was on the rocks. She started carousing with Confederate troops and leaving a sick child in Elizabeth's care. In September Mary ran away with their two daughters to her father's Malvern Hill plantation. John and a band of armed men rode to the farm and took back the children, whom Mary never saw again. From then on Mary plotted her revenge against John and the rest of the Van Lew family.

Mary had also been mean to Church Hill's servants, which Elizabeth Van Lew did not tolerate—not only on humanitarian grounds. Her servants and other African Americans in Richmond became an important part of her espionage operation. Though Robert E. Lee feared slaves were a security risk, most Confederate intelligence officers did not believe blacks were mentally capable of disclosing much military information; it was illegal, after all, to teach slaves to read and write. So even with a rigid pass system for blacks, they enjoyed the freedom, denied to most whites, to travel near military sites. Rebel pickets usually let African Americans pass without a search, considering them stupid and harmless.

Van Lew knew otherwise. Her slaves like Oliver Lewis and the brothers James and Peter Roane became couriers carrying messages to Union lines. She had a vegetable garden at her farm outside Richmond, which made a ready excuse for her servants to go in and out of the city. No one inspected the servants' muddy old brogans or the egg baskets they carried for messages Van Lew had hidden in them. Richmond's underground members also had the services of some of the city's more than 2,500 free blacks who were subject to restrictions like slaves and had to carry papers proving they were free. Sylvanus T. Brown, a free black who owned a small farm three miles from the Charles City Court House (and was forced to leave his property at times to work on Confederate fortifications), guided Union spies across Rebel lines into Richmond and took out prison escapees in his horse-drawn cart. William Brisby, free black wheelwright and blacksmith who owned fifty acres in New Kent County, Virginia, also helped evacuate Union escapees, along with runaway slaves. He usually brought a load of tobacco in the cart bearing his escapees to sell to Union soldiers, and passed along intelligence to their commanders that he had collected along the way.

Twice Brisby was put in Castle Thunder on suspicion of giving information to Yankees.

Mary Jane Richards knew she was born in Virginia—sometime between 1839 and 1841, she guessed—but not much else. She never knew her parents or how she got her last name Richards. On May 17, 1846, John Van Lew had her baptized in St. John's Church, which created a stir among its white members. Mary had been born into slavery in the Van Lew home but she remembered being taught early on by Elizabeth and her mother that she was not really a slave but instead would be brought up as an intelligent and educated young girl. They also told her she was destined to become a missionary in Africa. She was light-skinned, suggesting to others that she was a mulatto and her father was a member of the Van Lew family or extended family. A friend after the war recalled in a letter that Mary's mother was named Caroline, but no documents substantiate that. Mary said after the war that she felt "I had the advantage of most of my race both in blood and intelligence," indicating that Mary too believed her father was a Van Lew. She referred to Elizabeth as her "foster sister."

Mary demonstrated she was a bright child. It was clear Van Lew had a deep affection for her and felt responsible for her upbringing, affording her privileges and opportunities few white southern women of the day would give a black child—perhaps because Elizabeth suspected Mary was a blood relation is some way. Elizabeth sent her at age seven or eight to sister Anna's home in Philadelphia to be educated. In December 1854, when she was fifteen or younger, Mary set sail from New York aboard the three-masted ship *Lamartine* for Monrovia, Liberia. Elizabeth and her mother had arranged and paid for the trip through the American Colonization Society. Mary was to teach and be a missionary in Liberia as part of the colonization movement Van Lew and many whites, Lincoln included, considered as an alternative to emancipation and hostile coexistence of the races in the United States.

Mary admired Liberians, who fared better than blacks in America, she believed. The country's rich soil grew vegetables almost immediately, she found. But soon she began writing Van Lew, who corresponded with her almost daily, about how miserable she had become in the country's harsh jungle and hot humid weather. She begged Van Lew to bring her home, which Elizabeth finally did in the fall of 1859. "I do love that poor creature," Van Lew wrote Reverend Anthony Williams at the Colonization Society. She intended to "try to do the best I can by her."

Back in Richmond, Mary's health grew delicate. She was confined to a bed for a long time. Her situation became even more precarious when she recovered. While walking down the street on August 20, 1860, she was arrested for not having the proper papers. Under Virginia's complicated racial laws, a freed slave who had left the state was not allowed to return. Mary was jailed for several weeks and received five painful lashes during her incarceration. When she appeared before Richmond's Mayor's Court, she and Eliza convinced a judge that she had not violated the state's racial laws because she had never been freed in the first place. Mary claimed the Van Lews had sent her north to be educated, and then she sailed to Liberia. She had returned to the United States for a visit and had returned to Richmond at the Van Lew family's insistence. Eliza backed up her story, claiming Mary was still her slave. The judge fined Eliza ten dollars for letting Mary go to Liberia and returned her to her master. Mary ruefully told an audience years later that she was "finally sold into slavery," but returning to the Van Lews officially designated as their property kept her out of trouble.

During her arrest and court episode, Mary demonstrated a tradecraft talent. Likely trying to shield herself from scrutiny, she used two aliases, telling her captors at one point she was Mary Jane Henley and another time giving her name as Mary Jones. After her release from custody, Mary in fact became Mary Bowser. She met Wilson Bowser, a black man who worked at the Van Lew farm, likely when he brought produce to the mansion. On April 16, 1861, three days after the fall of Fort Sumter, Mary wed Wilson in St. John's Church—which the congregation again did not appreciate—and the couple moved into the mansion. John's wife, Mary, who would be out of the house in a little more than a year, was disgusted that the two "stupid niggers," as she called them, were allowed to live at Church Hill. She reserved a special venom for Mary Bowser.

When the war broke out, Mary became a courier and spy for Van Lew. It was perilous work. She often accompanied Van Lew on her walks near

Richmond prisons when she was disguised as a farm woman and sat in on secret meetings Van Lew held in the mansion with her ring members. By now in her twenties, Mary had grown into an attractive woman with her light skin and wide brown eyes. A reporter after the war wrote that she looked exactly like the beautiful abolitionist and feminist Anna Dickinson, with the same "fire and vim" the charismatic activist had. Mary was, in fact, assertive. She was described by whites as kindhearted and smart, with a sophisticated sense of humor that could turn sarcastic at times. Spying for Van Lew, she was not frightened easily by shadows. Her time in a Richmond prison had toughened her up. Since returning to the Confederate capital she had made a careful study of the psyche of Confederate soldiers and their officers. She thought she knew how to maneuver around those evil humans.

A second spy ring overlapped Van Lew's network for a couple years until the two more or less merged in 1864. Samuel Ruth led it. He was the superintendent of the Richmond, Fredericksburg and Potomac Railroad—enjoying "superior facilities," a postwar congressional committee concluded, "for obtaining information of value to the Union Army" on Rebel troop and supply movements. Van Lew could not match it.

A revolution in transportation occurred in America during the 1850s. The number of rail track lines ballooned. The speed at which goods could be hauled over these rails soared to thirty miles per hour. A horse could gallop that fast for only several miles. Railroads, which speeded up the transport of goods to market, also revolutionized the warfare Civil War commanders would fight. After Lincoln saw how a single track of the Baltimore & Ohio Railroad became a vital lifeline for troops and supplies to Washington, and after his generals realized Confederate reinforcements had been rushed by trains to the Manassas battlefield, protecting one's rail capability and attacking the enemy's became a major military objective. Key rail junctions like those in Atlanta and Chattanooga became strategically important. Union Army transportation officers studied closely how cavalrymen could quickly destroy enemy rail bridges and locomotive engines. Trains would revolutionize warfare as gunpowder had. The Civil War became a railroad war, with generals who knew the value of the tracks moving armies farther and faster to strategic points while preventing opponents from doing the same. The railroad, McClellan wrote within a week after taking command in Washington, "introduced a new and very important element into war."

Lee believed the same. The Confederacy, however, began and ended the war at a strategic disadvantage when it came to railroads. Of the 31,168 miles of track the nation had as of January 1861, only 8,783, or a quarter of it, lay in the South. Large swaths of the Confederacy were far removed from rail transportation, the lines that did exist were not always in the right places for moving forces to battlefields, and the important tracks running north–south had too many gaps in them or were separated into sections with different gauges. The South, moreover, proved painfully slow at building new track and manufacturing rolling stock, as well as making the best use of what it had. Rail owners were unwilling to sacrifice profit for the greater good and, unlike in the North, the states' rights–minded Confederate government was loath to enforce a unified transportation policy.

Situated beside the navigable James River, Richmond enjoyed the most extensive rail service of any city in the South, with five railroads converging on it. But the network had glaring weaknesses, such as the fact that passenger and freight trains could ride to Richmond but not through it. Track lines were not connected between terminals in the city, which Lee found maddening when he had to move divisions through the capital.

A Pennsylvanian by birth and a mechanic by training, Ruth settled in Richmond in 1839, finding a house for himself and his wife near his company's train depot at 8th and Broad Streets. A short man with a florid complexion and retiring demeanor, he claimed he had always been a Unionist, but that may not have been the case. Like Van Lew, Ruth was firmly rooted in Richmond society, but unlike her he was an opportunist who changed sides when he foresaw the Confederacy's inevitable defeat. As was the case with many railroad men, his allegiance was first to his company; politics concerned him little.

By 1853, Ruth had risen to the top rank of superintendent of transportation for the important Richmond, Fredericksburg and Potomac Railroad. He ended up supervising the fifty-five miles of RF&P track that ran from Richmond through Henrico, Hanover, and Caroline Counties, terminating at Hamilton's Crossing in Spotsylvania County. Hamilton's Crossing was about five miles south of the Rebel stronghold of Fredericksburg, which was halfway between the Confederate and federal capitals. The Union would control the remaining northern stretch of the RF&P track that ran to Aquia Creek Landing off the Potomac. Farther south, at Hanover Junction, Ruth's line also linked to the Virginia Central Railroad, which connected the Confederates at Fredericksburg to southern and western forces. For both the Union and Rebel armies, the single-track Richmond, Fredericksburg and Potomac Railroad line was a vital artery.

Disloyalty among Confederate railroad men was hard to uncover, particularly early in the war. Was an engine breakdown the result of sabotage or simply poor maintenance? Of the thirteen operating railroads in Virginia, only a few of their managers were ever suspected of being traitors, though many of them like Ruth had been born in the North. Ruth was not among the ones suspected, at least not in the beginning. His boss, RF&P president Peter V. Daniel Jr., was a rabid secessionist who kept Ruth in his job after the war started because he was good at what he did and likely because a majority of the line's stock was held by investors from Ruth's home state of Pennsylvania. Nearly all of the employees under Ruth became Union sympathizers, whom he dispatched for discreet sabotage jobs. (Daniel unwittingly helped him keep his cabal intact by convincing Confederate authorities to exempt the rail employees from military duty because they were needed to operate the line.) Ruth also eventually enlisted for espionage assignments Van Lew agents William Lohmann and Charles M. Carter, a Charles City County courier who spirited messages to the Union lines for both spymasters.

Van Lew soon would find Ruth to be a clever and diligent agent. Keenly aware of the railroad's importance for military operations, Ruth early on found ways to sabotage the RF&P line without the finger pointing at him, taking advantage of wartime conditions to create bottlenecks and inefficiencies in his operation. He regularly kept Union authorities posted on the condition of his fifty-five miles of track between Richmond and Hamilton's Crossing, reporting on damages to the rolling stock of his line and others, which he knew was information as important to the Federals as it was to the Confederates. Ruth even placed an ad in a Richmond paper detailing for the city's travelers the schedule of his trains traveling north over a bridge that had been rebuilt after the Federals destroyed it—so the Union would know to attack it again. During the next three years, he would find even more ways to help the northern cause.

As the months of 1862 passed, residents began to worry more about northern spies, saboteurs, and assassins infiltrating Richmond "to deliver the city into the hands of our enemies," as one put it. Government officials became just as paranoid. A city ordinance had been passed urging residents to inform on neighbors if they saw anything suspicious. Winder's agents did not feel they had enough evidence to arrest the socially prominent Van Lew women. But that didn't keep them from trying to find some. Hoping to trick her into revealing she was working for Washington, a Rebel operative approached Van Lew on the street one day pretending to be a Union courier ready to take any messages she had north. Van Lew didn't bite. She feigned outrage when a group of Confederate officers barged into the house to snoop, calling it "beneath the conduct of an officer and gentleman." The raids still turned up nothing.

On June 21, Captain Archibald Godwin, who ran the Castle Godwin Prison, dropped by to warn her that she had been reported once more to authorities for paying improper attention to federal prisoners. She responded again by entertaining young officers from the Richmond Howitzers. A young man knocked on her door one day asking to be boarded. Van Lew rented him a room, pretty much convinced he was a Confederate agent sent to spy on her. Better to have the snitch in her lair, she decided, where she could keep an eye on him. She wrote in her journal: "We have to be watchful and circumspect—wise as serpents—and harmless as doves, for truly the lions are seeking to devour us."

Eleven

"I HAVE THE HONOR
TO REPORT"

From the beginning of his presidency, Lincoln had been interested in new war-fighting technologies. He wanted his army to have the best equipment available and prodded its hidebound ordnance chief to develop new weapons and test new ideas—even the off-the-wall ones. Lincoln was always amused by inventors who visited his office; he'd hear them out and often point out the flaws he could see in their designs. He showed a strong interest in the mechanical arts, eagerly endorsing a design by a New Haven, Connecticut, businessman for an ironclad ship with revolving turret presented to him on September 13, 1861, and the next spring referring McClellan to an incendiary artillery shell a New York chemist developed, which Lincoln thought showed promise. He enjoyed seeing new gadgets demonstrated, firing a breech-loaded rifle (the wave of the future, he believed) at targets in a park south of the Executive Mansion and visiting a waste field nearby to watch the test of an experimental torpedo. Lincoln was also willing to put up government seed money for risky prototypes, shocking Navy secretary Welles with $150,000 to manufacture gunpowder that was safer and less likely to deteriorate over time.

Lincoln's instinct to push the edge of the technological envelope was correct. Although his generals did not realize it at first, new technology would transform not only how they fought battles, but also how they collected intelligence and protected secrets for those battles. The Union Army's one-year-old Signal Corps, an object of curiosity for many, eventually had its 300 officers and 2,500 soldiers perched atop tall trees, high mountains, church steeples, and two-hundred-foot towers to send messages wigwagging colored flags and to see return signals with telescopes. At night they waved torches, winked colored lights, fired off rockets, and even flipped window shades from lighted rooms. The telegraph, which since 1844 had linked cities and towns with rapid communication, would have the same profound effect on both armies connecting war departments, generals, and far-flung battlefields. Union forces alone would soon be transmitting 4,500 telegrams a day over the North's commercial network and some 15,000 miles of line its soldiers strung out.

Reading the other side's messages by flag or telegraph became a preoccupation as well. Sometimes in fast-moving maneuvers Union and Confederate troops had access to the same lines, or enemy telegraph stations were captured to intercept reports and send out false ones. Each side suspected the enemy was constantly wiretapping its lines, although the cases of successful interceptions were actually infrequent. To protect what did go over the wires or was waved from mountaintops, the North and South employed primitive codes or ciphers (where words, phrases, individual letters, or numbers were replaced with other words, letters, numbers, or symbols). Anson Stager, a former Western Union Telegraph Company superintendent, developed a simple word transposition cipher McClellan and Pinkerton used, which the Confederates were never able to break. Rebel commanders entrusted their important messages to the Vigenère substitution cipher, developed by a sixteenth-century French diplomat, which the Union soon broke because Confederate telegraphers often used it improperly. Southern leaders also had private codes they did not share with other states. On the Union side, when there was no time to encipher messages in emergencies, telegraph operators simply wrote words backward or garbled them with phonetic spellings.

America was fascinated with photography. Soldiers by the thousands posed stiffly for photos in their uniforms before marching off to war, and combat photographers would rivet the nation's attention with shots of battlefield dead. Pinkerton saw an intelligence value with the pictures. Alexander Gardner, the manager of Mathew Brady's studio in Washington, joined the detective's secret service to covertly photograph enemy troop encampments and future battlefields. Gardner's topographical photographs were also used to draw maps, which at the war's outset were notoriously unreliable.

On the afternoon of June 18, 1861, twenty-eight-year-old Thaddeus Sobleski Constantine Lowe ascended five hundred feet over Washington's Columbia Armory near the Capitol in a hydrogen-gas-filled balloon, tethered to the ground with a strong rope. Two nervous operators sat in its dangling wicker basket with Lowe, tapping out on a telegraph box a message transmitted on a wire strung from the balloon to Lincoln in the War Department. Lowe and everyone else watching were uncertain about this experiment succeeding. But it did. "I have pleasure in sending you this first dispatch ever telegraphed from an aerial station," Lowe's message to Lincoln read. The self-educated New Hampshire scientist and inventor had transformed what had been a novel contraption at county fairs into an aerial reconnaissance asset—and with a telegraph line attached to it an asset that could transmit intelligence in real time.

A month later, Lincoln, who had become a balloon enthusiast, summoned Lowe to his office, convinced that the Bull Run battle might have turned out different if an observer had been in the sky reporting the movements of Confederate forces. Prodded by Lincoln, a skeptical General Scott finally accepted Lowe in August 1861 and formed the U.S. Army Balloon Corps. McClellan became a balloon fan as well, making two aerial observations in them while in Washington. By the beginning of 1862, Professor T. S. C. Lowe, as he had come to be known, commanded a corps of seven balloons, with nine aeronauts to inflate and fly them. The Confederates were jealous of the Union's balloon capability but managed only to field a few of them, one of which was stitched together with silk from dress shops.

An Army engineer often accompanied Lowe's aeronauts on flights to

make the observations. A squad of soldiers escorted each balloon party and
held the rope to the craft. The balloons could rise as high as 1,000 feet but
200 to 500 feet was usually enough to scope out the battlefield ahead or direct artillery fire on a target. Balloonists communicated their observations
by shouting to the ground, using flag signals, or tapping messages over a
telegraph line. A Philadelphia inventor named Calvin Gardner proposed
combining photography with the balloon in what a century and a half later
would be called an aerial drone. A fifteen-pound, battery-operated camera
could be attached under a small balloon and sent a thousand feet up, Gardner wrote McClellan. The camera would be hooked by wire to a soldier on
the ground, who would send up an electrical charge to activate the camera's
shutter. There is no record that the Army ever followed up on Gardner's
suggestion with money for a prototype. A Union officer reviewing the idea
wrote that it was doubtful the balloon could keep the camera stable enough
to take a clear photograph.

Lowe's balloons had their disadvantages. The bulky machines used to
generate hydrogen gas did not travel well. Wooded terrain, fog, or battlefield smoke could hide targets and Confederates soon learned to camou-
flage encampments. The balloons had a tendency to spin, making the car's
occupants airsick, and even tethered the aircraft could be blown off course
by wind gusts. Lowe's aeronauts also had no military training, so they were
poor aerial observers. Experienced Army officers were often reluctant to go
up for good reason. Once one of Lowe's balloons had risen to the top of
trees, Confederate sharpshooters often opened up until it gained enough
altitude to be out of range.

Fighting a modern war with all these new technologies was an alien
exercise for U.S. officers at first. The overwhelming majority of the junior
ones were commissioned from civilian life, with hardly any military training. Those graduating from West Point had been taught little about strategic theory and even less on how intelligence could influence strategy.
West Point graduates were schooled in Napoleonic tactics, which called for
closed-rank formations of soldiers maneuvering in concert with frontal attacks and volleys of fire delivered at a range of no more than a few hundred
yards. But mass production of weapons and improvements, for example, in

rifled cannon and muskets, which resulted in the delivery of more accurate and deadly fire at longer ranges, made these tactics suicidal. Military leaders on both sides started choosing flank attacks over frontal assaults and loose-order tactics instead of tightly packed lines in order to win fights without incurring horrendous casualties. Commanders also discovered that with their new weapons and tactics they needed more accurate intelligence on where the enemy lurked and how strong it was. Confederate general Thomas "Stonewall" Jackson boiled it down to four things he wanted to know before he started a battle: the position of the enemy, the number of hostile troops and their movements, the generals in command on the other side, and, fourth, the location of the headquarters for the other commander. A Union general invading southern territory could find himself trapped if he didn't quickly know not only what lay ahead of him, but also the rebel forces that stood on his flanks or to his rear.

Superior intelligence on the enemy did not always guarantee a Civil War commander victory. He had to have the tactical skill and courage to act on what he knew. But intelligence certainly helped. A general who had bad information and lacked the will to fight was certain to fail—as Lincoln would soon discover with George McClellan.

By the beginning of 1862, McClellan's army had turned Washington into an armed camp. Quartermaster troops had built more than four hundred new structures, military tent cities surrounded the capital, 150 bakers baked 50,000 loaves of bread a day for the troops, and roads into and out of the city were clogged with marching infantrymen, galloping cavalrymen, and horses pulling wheeled artillery, ambulances, and commissary wagons. The city took on a rougher edge, with surly northern yeomen replacing distinguished-looking southern gentlemen, buildings appearing shabbier, government structures like the Washington monument remaining unfinished, and streets reeking with mud and manure.

McClellan throughout the fall and winter of 1861 had feared the Rebels in Manassas intended to cross the Potomac and attack him at any time. The Rebels feared just the opposite—that McClellan planned to attack them before 1861's winter set in. McClellan planned no such move. Indeed, complaints grew in Washington that he might not move at all. The general had posed for a formal photograph with his right hand thrust into the front of his uniform frock coat, a not-too-veiled effort to look like Napoleon, which succeeded, with the press soon calling him the "young Napoleon." McClellan certainly acted the part, riding into Washington from the field trailed by a gaudy entourage of one hundred matched horses, fifty attendants, twenty-five baggage wagons, and eventually three princes from France's House of Orléans who joined his staff. But McClellan, who believed God had selected him to save the Union, lacked Napoleon's will to fight. Fall 1861 dragged into early spring 1862 and the timid commanding general, whose confidence when he led the Ohio Department had disappeared, continued to train and parade his troops, making enemies of powerful cabinet officers like Seward and Stanton, who grew weary of his excuses for not moving.

Lincoln, who made many fruitless visits to McClellan's headquarters in a luxurious house on Lafayette Square to try to prod him forward, checked out books on military strategy from the Library of Congress and paced back and forth in his bedroom at night digesting them for a crash course in how to wage war. He had no military experience save for his brief fling in the Illinois militia and he could not critically inspect troops (particularly with commanders like McClellan hiding their quality behind dog-and-pony-show parades). But by 1862 Lincoln had learned on the job enough about military operations to dash off notes to McClellan and other generals, with astute suggestions on everything from troop movements to logistic trains that they would have done well to pay more attention to. Soon the War Department, a battered old brick building next to the White House, became the president's second home.

Pinkerton kept his ear close to the political war McClellan fought in Washington, blindly defending every last claim or complaint his general uttered. "Wily politicians," "jealous minded officers," and assorted other secret enemies, the detective wrote, were trying to "prejudice the mind" of Lincoln against McClellan, who throughout "pursued his course with unflinching courage." Pinkerton believed as the general did that the Union had suffered a humiliating defeat at Bull Run because McDowell had impetuously launched an attack before his troops were ready. McClellan would not repeat that mistake and Pinkerton was as convinced as the general was that critics who carped that he was too slow to put his army into action were just "scheming" ignoramuses. McClellan, Pinkerton insisted, comprehended "far better" than Washington's armchair warriors "the movements and intentions of the enemy." The detective knew for certain that this was the case because he briefed the general regularly on the Confederate force. But McClellan's enemies in Lincoln's cabinet, he charged, were "unfriendly" to Pinkerton's secret service and placed "little reliance" on the intelligence he had obtained. Pinkerton could not have been more wrong with his points—except for the one about the cabinet deeming his intelligence unreliable, which it did for good reason.

McClellan, who seemed always to be never quite ready to move his force, had convinced himself within a fortnight of coming to Washington that the Confederate Army of Joseph Johnston and P. G. T. Beauregard in the Manassas area numbered 100,000 men and was ready to pounce on his inferior force of about 55,000 at any time. The Confederates at Manassas actually had no more than 30,000 troops in August. McClellan came up with his 100,000 number not from Pinkerton, who had just arrived in Washington and had not had time to put together an intelligence-gathering operation, but instead from an assortment of generals under him, self-appointed amateur spies, and a Confederate deserter, with rumors and guesswork stirred into the mix. On September 8, McClellan raised the Rebel number to 130,000. Five days later he upped the enemy count once more to 170,000 compared to the 81,000 Federals he had. The Rebels by that time had 35,000 men at Manassas.

A cardinal rule for successful intelligence officers: they must be unbiased, scrupulous in assembling accurate information, and they must tell a superior what he needs to know, not what he wants to know. A spymaster must be willing to deliver uncomfortable truths. Pinkerton failed to do this. The poorly educated Chicago detective revered McClellan, who was considered one of the country's foremost military experts. Loyal to the point of sycophancy, Pinkerton never doubted the general's ability as a commander. Instead of serving his country or his president as a true intelligence officer, he made his friend happy.

Pinkerton and his detectives proved to be effective at the cloak-and-dagger work of catching Confederate spies and uncovering plots against the U.S. government. But neither he nor the men and women in his force had the military training or experience needed to effectively collect and evaluate intelligence on an enemy army. They were amateurs at war. Throughout the conflict, his secret service acted like a detective agency working for a business client. The result: practically every step in their collection and analysis of military intelligence was filled with error.

Pinkerton never understood the perishability of tactical military intelligence. He sent out agents with vague instructions for reporting what they found. Much of their information arrived too late to be of use. Instead of sending back intelligence by courier and staying in place to collect more, his operatives made time-consuming trips to Washington to deliver their reports, endangering themselves with their frequent journeys. His detectives were accustomed to slowly working cases until they had enough evidence to arrest a suspect and bring him to trial. Military intelligence collection had to move more quickly. Even if he had been skilled in army matters, Pinkerton was stretched too thin. In addition to collecting military intelligence, he was swamped by 1862 with other duties, such as chasing Confederate spies in Washington, hunting for Union deserters, catching corrupt contractors, investigating murders, seizing contraband goods headed south, and protecting Lincoln. It resulted in him not doing any of the jobs well.

On October 4, 1861, Pinkerton delivered his first of many estimates of Confederate troop strength. He always wrote them in the form of a letter and they began with a flowery opening officers of the day commonly used, such as "I have the honor to report . . ." This estimate, Pinkerton told McClellan, was based on files from his spies roaming Virginia and the interrogations he and his men conducted of runaway slaves, Rebel deserters, war prisoners, and refugees. "All agree remarkably well on the general features of the calculations I herewith furnish," he boasted to try to sell his findings.

Pinkerton claimed he was being conservative with his counts. "Generally speaking the Rebel Force is estimated much higher than my figures indicate," he asserted, which was not the case. He had seriously overestimated Confederate numbers, although not nearly as much as McClellan had. The detective reported that the Confederate forces under Johnston and Beauregard totaled 98,400 men—more than double their true number then of about 45,000. He had counts for the rest of Virginia as well, estimating that 11,000 Rebel soldiers were deployed in the western part of the state, 6,800 were garrisoned in Richmond, and Norfolk and Portsmouth had 10,400—for a total of 126,600. Pinkerton did allow that 15 percent of the men might be absent or sick, so he lowered the 126,600 number to 118,160.

Pinkerton was accurate in some respects. He noted that Confederate generals kept their troops moving about to create the impression that the force was larger than it was, which was the case. All his informants reported that the Rebels were short of ammunition, which was also true. And his interrogations had picked up evidence of discontent among Confederate soldiers over indecisive leaders, also true. But the report had enough fatally flawed assumptions, shady calculations, and even glaring math errors that an experienced intelligence analyst would have thrown it into the trash can.

Pinkerton claimed that 143 of Virginia's 184 regiments were deployed in front of McClellan around Manassas—a 64 percent overestimate. More serious, he assumed that the average strength of each Confederate regiment was 700 men, when in fact the regiments never totaled more than 500 or 600 at the most. Occasionally Pinkerton would get a Virginia deserter who told him his regimental number was far less—even as low as 100—but Pinkerton didn't believe them. The lower estimates, however, should have made him suspect that his 700 average was too high. McClellan would have had difficulty detecting many of these shortcomings. But he could have spotted one with what he learned in elementary school mathematics. Pinkerton stated that the 126,600 total should be discounted by 15 percent for Rebel soldiers absent or sick. But the clerk who wrote his report subtracted one-fifteenth, or 8,440, from the 126,600 instead of 15 percent, or 18,990, from the total. Because of the math error, Pinkerton reported the adjusted total as 118,160 instead of the mathematically correct number, 107,610.

Pinkerton admitted that he and McClellan had conspired to cook the books. In a later November 15 letter to the general, Pinkerton explained that his estimate of Confederate strength "was made large, as intimated to you at the time, so as to be sure to cover the entire number of the Enemy that our army was to meet." The controversial sentence appeared to show that before Pinkerton issued his October 4 report, he and McClellan agreed to deliberately inflate the Confederate numbers to be sure they included troops Pinkerton's agents might not know about. In other words, Pinkerton was padding the troop totals and McClellan knew he was padding them.

This was an astounding admission. Why did Pinkerton do it? Had he and McClellan rationalized that inflating the numbers in Confederate regiments and reporting more regiments than actually existed was justified to guard against their being surprised by unaccounted-for enemy? So they were prudently using worst-case numbers for safety's sake? Were they simply misinformed by their Confederate sources, who in turn had been fed inflated troop estimates by their commanders to make the Federals believe the South had a superior force? Or was this a case of two conspirators colluding to concoct higher Confederate troop estimates to bolster McClellan's stalling and his pleas for more soldiers?

It certainly had the look of a shady deal hatched in a back room. Obviously Pinkerton had not produced a professional product on October 4. His future reports would turn out to be even less scientific, with errors compounded, suggesting he was struggling to produce larger numbers for his boss. That should have bothered a well-educated professional soldier like McClellan. The fact that it didn't strongly suggests that the Army of the Potomac commander was looking not so much for information on the Confederates as he was a justification for more time and men.

Whatever understanding or motives the two men had, Pinkerton's inflated estimate of 98,400 troops under Johnston's command in the Manassas area still was not as inflated as McClellan wanted it to be. In a report to the Lincoln administration at the end of October, the general claimed the Confederates at Manassas totaled 150,000. (He arrived at a number three times what the Rebels had by cherry-picking higher but suspicious figures in Pinkerton's agent reports and creatively rounding up.) McClellan now wanted his army of 120,000 men increased to 208,000 before he attacked, demanding reinforcements from all over the country. He never sent the administration Pinkerton's October 4 report, either because he realized its obvious flaws or more likely because he knew Pinkerton's 98,400 number for the enemy around Manassas would make him look foolish. McClellan, who was drifting further away from reality working exhausting hours with little sleep, insisted he had his own accurate sources for his numbers and would tolerate no dissent from his conclusions. He wasn't the only Union general mistakenly convinced he was outnumbered, but he was the only one to stubbornly believe it for so long. McClellan had totally deceived himself.

A little more than a month after he made his October 4 estimate, Pinkerton, however, faced an embarrassing discrepancy. Timothy Webster, his best operative in the field, had returned to Washington in mid-November with a total count of 95,700 Rebel soldiers in 125 Virginia regiments. That was 30,900 men and 59 regiments less than Pinkerton's October 4 estimate of 126,600 Confederates in 184 regiments. To resolve the huge gap between his estimate and that of his top operative, Pinkerton in his November 15 memo to McClellan applied a little mathematical jujitsu to the numbers. First he updated his October estimates, adding 7,000 Rebel soldiers in Yorktown he had neglected to count before. That brought his new total to 133,600. Then he added 27,730 Confederates to Webster's estimate, claiming there were enemy encampments Webster had not seen and accounted for. (Pinkerton never explained how Webster missed 27,730 men; he always assumed there were phantom Confederate divisions out there none of his spies had found.) The new math, along with its parade of errors, conveniently shrank the difference between Pinkerton's estimate and Webster's to 10,170. That was a small enough difference, Pinkerton wrote McClellan, to make the two sets of numbers "approximate very nearly to accuracy."

McClellan kept Pinkerton's November 15 update to himself, likely for the same reasons he hadn't forwarded the detective's October 4 estimate to higher authorities. But Webster's and Pinkerton's lower estimates apparently did give him pause. On December 10 he wrote to Lincoln that intelligence he had just received "leads me to believe that the enemy could meet us in front with equal forces nearly." It was still an overestimate, but not as wild as the ones before.

There were senior officers in McClellan's army who did not believe the Confederate strength estimates he and Pinkerton peddled. Some, like James

Wadsworth, a New York brigadier general whose advance brigade faced the Rebels near Manassas and Centreville, were running their own intelligence operations that were turning up more accurate information. Wadsworth concluded from his scout reports and the interviews he conducted with refugees, war prisoners, and deserters that the Confederates ahead of him numbered 40,000 to 50,000, a far more accurate number than Pinkerton's. The enemy could easily be swept back, he said. McClellan ignored the report.

Instead, through December 1861 and into January and February 1862, Pinkerton peppered the Army of the Potomac commander with hundreds of pages of reports each week filled with raw intelligence—much of it unfiltered, unverified, unanalyzed, and inaccurate—mixed with mounds of useless trivia. He sent McClellan a dense twenty-six-page memo on an agent's trip to Richmond (revealing only at the end that the operative's information was just "reasonably reliable"), a lengthy statement by two Alexandria machinists (which he admitted was "founded upon hearsay"), and a report by a refugee that the South "is going to make a prodigious effort to put 700,000 men in the field" by spring of 1862 (the South would have no more than 450,000 under arms by the end of 1862). Rarely did Pinkerton include in his reports an evaluation of a source's reliability beyond a general impression he had of it. More often he left that to McClellan to judge for himself. Bogging himself down with the smallest of administrative details, the general took on the job of interpreting the mass of information Pinkerton shoveled to him.

At one point two of the French princes who joined McClellan's staff, Louis Philippe d' Orléans and his brother Robert, made a stab at serving as ad hoc intelligence analysts and tried to boil down the thousands of words from some Pinkerton reports into usable summaries. But the Orléans brothers did not have access to all the raw intelligence Pinkerton and others produced, so their summaries proved defective. McClellan still ended up hoarding the information and being his own intelligence analyst.

The delusional commanding general and his fawning intelligence officer became a toxic combination. As far as calculating enemy numbers was concerned, Pinkerton's secret service became practically worthless. McClellan would have done just as well without it. Even if Pinkerton had stood up to his boss and presented him with more accurate lower estimates, McClellan likely would have still ignored them.

The Army of the Potomac commander thought he could have his way with the backwoods president in the White House, who would not be expected to know how to spot errors in his intelligence findings. But Lincoln turned out to be no untrained dupe. He was forced to learn the craft of intelligence on the job as he had the art of war, and he proved to be a quick study. Early in his presidency, Lincoln had freelancers send him intelligence reports from different parts of the country. Less than a month after his inauguration he ordered Scott to send him daily intelligence reports, which Scott did. He made time in his busy schedule to interview correspondents on what they had seen during visits to the South and enjoyed pumping Army officers for information they picked up from the front. Lincoln saw good intelligence as the key to the Union winning battles. Knowledge of enemy movements, he wrote his western generals in early 1862, was "the most constantly present and the most difficult" of the military problems to be solved. Stanton feared that Lincoln was so kindhearted and open with friends that he would divulge sensitive national security information. The war secretary had his president pegged wrongly. Lincoln, who rarely told others his inner thoughts, knew how to keep a secret.

He had learned enough about intelligence by the winter of 1861 to be suspicious of the Confederate strength estimates McClellan gave him. Senior national security advisers like Seward, Stanton, and Welles doubted their credibility as well. But no one in the administration demanded that McClellan produce a written defense of his and Pinkerton's numbers— which would have quickly exposed the weakness of their evidence. They may not have wanted to pick a fight with the general and so calculated that it was easier just to live with his inflated figures and discount them when he pleaded for more troops. They also may not have wanted to challenge him because in the winter months of 1861 and 1862, McClellan's estimates were not considered outrageously out of bounds. The percentage of military-aged southern men put into their armed forces was much higher than the federal percentage. The Confederates also became adept in concentrating troops at danger points to give the appearance of a large army.

But that did not stop McClellan's exaggerating from becoming an inside joke in the administration. Lincoln reportedly once deadpanned to a visiting New England delegation that he knew the Confederates had a one-million-man army. Why? Because whenever his generals fought the Rebels they always told him they faced two-to-one odds. "Now I know we have a half million soldiers in the field," Lincoln said, "so I am bound to believe the rebels have twice that number."

Three months after the debacle at Bull Run, the Union Army had been embarrassed once more in a minor battle near the Rebel-held town of Leesburg, Virginia, thirty-five miles northwest of Washington. A small detachment under Brigadier General Charles Stone had crossed the Potomac to the Virginia side at Ball's Bluff to dislodge the Rebel force occupying the nearby town. Stone's detachment failed and suffered heavy casualties. McClellan had been partly at fault because of vaguely worded orders he issued for the attack, but congressional investigators pinned the blame on his brigadier general. Pinkerton helped McClellan collect dirt on Stone, gathering statements from refugees and war prisoners who alleged that he had become chummy with the Confederate general on the other side and wanted to avoid a big battle "where brother would fight against brother," according to one of the refugees interviewed. The hapless Stone was jailed for 189 days without charges. He was finally released but his military career was ruined.

Losing hope that McClellan would ever move his men, Lincoln at the beginning of December had proposed a workable plan to have half of the Army of the Potomac make a feint toward Centreville to hold the enemy in place. The other half would march or sail south along the Potomac River and then come up on the Confederate Army's rear to destroy the railroad supplying Johnston at Manassas and trap the enemy force. McClellan, who privately sniffed that the president did not understand the logistics of moving large armies (Lincoln did), opposed the maneuver—although just such an operation worried Johnston the most. McClellan told Lincoln he was hatching a plan far better and bolder than advancing on Manassas. But fearing leaks, the general would not share its details with his president, and Lincoln, still in his rookie year as commander in chief, did not think he had a right to know them. A quarantine then fell over McClellan's campaign plan when two days before Christmas he was stricken with typhoid and incapacitated for three weeks.

New Year's Day 1862 was gloomy for Lincoln. The Confederacy had embarrassed his administration with a string of high-profile victories and the Army of the Potomac was sitting still in winter quarters with its commander confined to his bed. There were bright spots beyond McClellan's army. Outside northern Virginia the war was not going particularly well for the South. Missouri and western Virginia had been lost. The Federals held much of Kentucky and threatened Tennessee. The Union Navy controlled key points along the Virginia and Carolinas coasts, beginning a blockade that soon would become punishing. And within months the Union Navy and Army would occupy strategically important New Orleans. But the Army of the Potomac was the war's center of attention. Rebel northern Virginia was within Lincoln's eyesight when he gazed at it from the roof of the Executive Mansion. Congress watched northern Virginia as well, as did reporters from the powerful Washington and New York papers—so did the entire nation, for that matter. With the transfer of the Confederate capital to Richmond, the 106 miles between it and Washington, D.C., became a focal point of the Civil War, where some of its most crucial battles would be fought.

No wonder Lincoln was at his wits' end. Northerners were impatient. Chase's Treasury Department was running out of money. "What shall I do?" Lincoln unburdened to his quartermaster general, Montgomery Meigs. "The bottom is out of the tub." Firing McClellan was not an option in Lincoln's mind. It might result in another Bull Run disaster but with no general like McClellan to pick up the pieces, or, even worse, it could destabilize the Union Army, breaking it up into rival factions.

Finally, on the night of January 10, Lincoln convened an informal war council in the White House with Seward, Chase, Assistant Secretary of War Thomas A. Scott, and two generals from the Army of the Potomac: Irvin McDowell, the Bull Run battle commander who now served under McClellan, and William B. Franklin, a division commander and McClellan confidant. The president told the attendees he had to do something and if McClellan, sick or well, did not plan to use his army right away, Lincoln would like to *borrow* it, "provided he could see how it could be made to do something," according to the notes McDowell took at the meeting. Lincoln sent McDowell and Franklin to quietly investigate the state of the Army of the Potomac and return with recommendations. McClellan learned of the conferences behind his back and, fearing their participants were conspiring against him (they clearly were), rose from his sickbed and attended a war council meeting on January 13. Though pale and feeble from the effects of typhoid, he managed to wrest control of his army from Lincoln. All the president could pry out of his sullen commanding general was a promise that he did have a plan and a time in mind for an advance. But McClellan refused to divulge the movement's details to Lincoln and his war council, believing they would leak them to the newspapers.

Lincoln said he was satisfied. But he was not. On January 27, he issued "President's General War Order, No. 1" setting February 22, George Washington's birthday, as the day for the "general movement" of the Army and Navy against the Confederacy. The order accomplished nothing. McClellan remained stationary—though the order did jolt him into realizing that his president would not tolerate him staying that way much longer.

Twelve

THE PENINSULA CAMPAIGN

he night after Timothy Webster reached Richmond with Hattie Lawton in February, his painful rheumatism flared once more. By the next morning he was bedridden in a hotel room, unable to move. Webster told Lawton not to leave Richmond with a message for Pinkerton. It would be too dangerous. Instead Lawton would play his devoted wife, nursing him back to health. Then they would leave.

Back in Washington, Pinkerton grew more alarmed by the day over what had happened to Webster and Lawton. Despite his large staff—he had twenty-seven operatives by the end of January—precious little intelligence was coming out of Richmond. Besides Webster and Lawton, who were silent, Pinkerton had just E. H. Stein and a man he identified only as "H. J. K." wandering around Virginia, and neither was sending back information. The agent drought could not have come at a worse time for Pinkerton, who was exhausted from near-twenty-four-hour days spent searching for intelligence on Virginia defenses.

On January 31, McClellan finally sent Stanton the campaign plan he had been incubating for months. Instead of attacking Johnston's force at

Manassas Junction and Centreville, the some 140,000 men of the Army of the Potomac would flank the Confederates by first marching northeast to Annapolis and the Chesapeake Bay. From there they would sail to Urbanna, a small tobacco port on the west bank of the lower Rappahannock, fifteen miles upriver from the Chesapeake Bay and fifty miles east of Richmond, and then march west to capture the Confederate capital. For the Urbanna strategy to succeed, Johnston must remain unsuspecting at Manassas and Centreville for as long as possible. McClellan calculated that if his movement were well under way before the Confederates detected it, he could cut off and isolate Johnston and capture Richmond before the Rebels could concentrate their troops there to save their capital. Johnston would be forced to fight on McClellan's terms.

As plans went, it wasn't a bad one. McClellan's thrust would be coordinated with an attack in the West. Lincoln, however, was cool to the Urbanna maneuver at first. Instead of the Federals marching south, the president would have to explain to an impatient public why the Army must move north to Annapolis, leaving Washington prey to Johnston menacing from Manassas. Arguing that the Confederate Army, not the capital, should be the objective, Lincoln preferred the overland maneuver he had suggested to capture Johnston. Washington defenses were adequate to keep Johnston at bay while he traveled to Urbanna, McClellan argued. Believing the roads too poor to permit a movement toward Centreville and then Manassas, he bought into Pinkerton's erroneous report that the Rebels had up to three hundred field artillery guns, as many as thirty siege guns, and a two-to-one troop advantage there. McClellan actually enjoyed the two-to-one advantage.

Pinkerton summoned Pryce Lewis to his headquarters office on I Street in early February. He had a serious look on his face, which worried Lewis.

"Have you any objections to going to Richmond?" Pinkerton asked.

"Yes," Lewis answered quickly and forcefully. "I have played the part of a spy for the last time. If my services are not wanted here in Washington, I will take a musket, join the Army, and go to the front."

"I don't want you to play the part of a spy," Pinkerton said.

"What do you want me to go for?"

"I simply want you to carry a letter to Tim Webster, who is in Richmond. I haven't heard from him in some time and I think he is sick."

"This looks very much like playing the spy."

"Well, I can't see it that way."

"There is no use in discussing it," Lewis said. "It would be folly for me to go to Richmond under any circumstance."

"Why?"

"I believe I am better known in Richmond as a detective, though I have never been there, than I am in Washington."

"How is that?"

"Good heavens, Mr. Pinkerton!" Lewis said, exasperated. "Think of the people I have assisted in arresting who have gone through the lines."

"Who are they?" Pinkerton asked.

Lewis rattled off a half dozen he could recall at the moment. They included Senator Jackson Morton's estranged wife, Elizabeth, who had remained in Washington with her four children after her philandering husband had fled south. Lewis had been part of a team that raided the Morton house a month ago and confiscated all her correspondence. Nothing incriminating had been found in the letters, so Mrs. Morton was allowed to leave Washington for Richmond with her four sons and daughters. Pinkerton brushed aside the names Lewis raised, claiming he had checked and all of them were elsewhere. The Morton family had gone on to Florida, he said.

"Are you sure of this?" Lewis asked skeptically.

Yes, Pinkerton insisted, although he was far from certain.

Lewis did not like this mission one bit, but finally he told Pinkerton he would undertake it if he could be assured he would not be recognized in Richmond. Pinkerton, who claimed in his memoirs that Lewis enthusiastically accepted the assignment, insisted that no one would know him in the Confederate capital. Lewis had a right to still be leery. An experienced spymaster would never send a counterespionage agent, as Lewis had become, on an espionage operation, because of the obvious danger of being identified by the people he had once pursued.

Lewis returned to Pinkerton's headquarters several days later to be briefed on the job. George Bangs was there this time. Spread out on a table in the parlor was a map of Virginia and a pile of gold coins for Lewis. Pinkerton also had two letters for him. One was "a mere blind and purports to be written by a good rebel" from Baltimore to Webster, warning him to be careful when he traveled north, Pinkerton said. Lewis could use it if Confederate authorities detained him and he needed to convince them he and Webster were loyal. The other was a letter of introduction to the editor of the *Richmond Dispatch*, who could tell Lewis where Webster was if he wasn't checked in to the Spotswood Hotel. Another Pinkerton agent sat at the table with Bangs—John Scully, who had been on the team with Lewis raiding the Morton house.

"I wish Mr. Scully to go with you," Pinkerton finally said.

"Then I will not go—positively," Lewis said.

"Why?'

Lewis wanted no more partners after his western Virginia foray with Sam Bridgeman, who had been a pain. "I don't want company that I must be responsible for," he now told Pinkerton. "It's dangerous, because one man can tell a story and stick to it. Two will be sure to differ."

Pinkerton insisted that Scully join him so he could come back with intelligence Webster had while Lewis continued southwest to Chattanooga to collect information on Confederate rails and defenses. This mission involved much more than delivering a letter, Lewis realized. But he reluctantly went along with it, agreeing with Pinkerton that McClellan was desperate for intelligence from Virginia. Lewis hardly knew Scully but he had nothing against the amiable Irishman, who was as tall as he and had a wife and two children. Scully was eager to please Pinkerton and good at following orders, but he was not particularly courageous. Lewis learned later that Scully was his partner only because Charles Rosch, another, more experienced agent, had refused to accept the dangerous mission unless Pinkerton provided for his family if he were killed, which Pinkerton would not do.

Lincoln finally approved McClellan's Urbanna plan on March 8. But the green light came with conditions. He ordered him to organize his army into four corps and told him who the corps commanders would be. McClellan and Pinkerton were outraged Lincoln had done this without consulting the general. Lincoln also ordered McClellan to leave behind enough of a force to protect Washington. McClellan also must move in ten days. No more delays.

Lincoln, in effect, was becoming McClellan's general in chief, with detailed orders for how he ran his force. The president also found military men to advise him—among them Brigadier General James Wadsworth, whom he appointed to defend Washington as military governor of the District of Columbia, with direct access to the White House. A wealthy New Yorker who had studied at Harvard and Yale, Wadsworth became a trusted military and political counselor, who like the president soon distrusted McClellan's leadership.

Lewis and Scully each bought new suits from a Washington haberdasher. They packed changes of clothes in large valises along with two six-shooters, the letters for Richmond, phony paperwork identifying them as southern blockade runners, and passes from the city's provost marshal to make it through Union lines.

The pair reached Richmond the morning of February 26. The Spotswood Hotel was fully booked so they found rooms at the pricier Exchange and Ballard Hotel, four blocks away. After lunch Lewis and Scully tracked down the Richmond editor, who told them they could find Webster laid up with rheumatism at the Monumental Hotel. Without scoping out the somewhat seedy establishment, partly hidden by linden trees, or first secretly communicating with Webster, Lewis and Scully that afternoon rashly rushed up to his room, which was long and narrow. Webster lay in a bed to the right of the door. Hattie Lawton sat in a chair at the foot of the bed while a Richmonder named P. B. Price, whom Webster had befriended at the Young Men's Christian Association, tended to the patient.

Webster was astonished to see the two men. Not knowing who this P. B. Price was, Lewis pretended to be a courier delivering the phony letter from Baltimore warning Webster not to travel north. Scully took Lawton and Price to the window out of earshot while Lewis leaned down beside Webster.

"Lewis, why in the hell did the old man send Scully here?" Webster asked in a low whisper.

"I don't know," Lewis replied. "I opposed it, but my objections were overruled."

Webster said he would arrange for mail Scully could deliver north to get him out of town quickly. Lewis told Webster he could give Scully any intelligence he had for McClellan, who was under considerable pressure to move his forces, and Lewis would head on to Chattanooga. Incapacitated by the rheumatism, Webster did not have much to give Scully.

They stayed making small talk and sipping coffee for about an hour. Webster told Price that Lewis and Scully were old friends from Baltimore. Then "we will go to the theater tonight!" Price announced. After supper he took Webster's two friends to a burlesque house, paying for their fifty-cent tickets, and to several saloons afterward for drinks.

The next morning before breakfast, Lewis asked Scully to come to his room. Before they set out that day, Lewis, somewhat on a whim, asked his partner if he was carrying anything on him that might be incriminating.

"No, I have nothing about me whatever," Scully said.

"Be sure," Lewis said, "feel in your pockets."

Scully did and found a letter from his wife in Chicago.

"Great God!" Lewis exclaimed. "Are you mad? [That's] enough to hang us both if we are arrested." The sooner he was rid of Scully, the better, Lewis decided.

Around three o'clock that afternoon, Lewis returned by himself to Webster's hotel room. This time he found Webster propped up in his bed talking to Captain Samuel McCubbin, a detective working for General John Winder, Richmond's provost marshal general. McCubbin seemed pleasant enough, telling Lewis that he rented the room next to Webster's and had struck up a friendship with him. Lewis admired Webster's nerve "ingratiating himself into the very citadel of the enemy," he later wrote. What Lewis did not know was that the reason McCubbin had become a neighbor was that Webster was now suspected of being a spy. Winder had posted his man there to gather evidence and keep watch if anyone approached the invalid and the woman who claimed to be his wife.

"I understand you and your friend came across the Potomac," McCubbin said nonchalantly.

"Yes," Lewis answered, fighting to remain calm.

"Have you reported to the military governor, General Winder?" McCubbin asked.

Lewis said he didn't know they needed to.

Oh, yes, McCubbin said. But it was just a formality, he assured them. Drop by his headquarters "at about four o'clock," the captain said. "I will meet you there and introduce you to the general."

Lewis rushed back to the Exchange and Ballard Hotel to make sure Scully had their cover story straight so there was no discrepancy if Winder's agents interrogated them separately. "I have forgotten all of it!" said Scully, who panicked.

"You are bound to hang us both!" Lewis nearly shouted, furious that Pinkerton had stuck him with a basket case. For a hurried few minutes Lewis drilled his partner on what they should both say and then the two of them walked quickly to Winder's busy headquarters, now on Main Street.

McCubbin ushered Lewis and Scully into Winder's office and then left. The general, who seemed to Lewis "very suave and gentlemanly," he recalled, could not have been more cordial. "I am very glad to meet any friends of Captain Webster's," Winder said. "He is a noble fellow, a most valuable man to us."

Lewis repeated his story that they came to Richmond to deliver a letter to him from Baltimore friends not to come north. "Webster must not go north again," Winder agreed. "We cannot afford to lose him."

The three chatted for a few minutes about politics and Washington. Lewis played the role of an Englishman, not tuned in to American affairs. Scully denounced Yankees so forcefully, Lewis said he tapped his partner's foot to make him stop, fearing he was overdoing it. Finally, Lewis broached the reason for their visit to Winder's office. "General, we are strangers here," he said, "and would like something from you to show that we have reported here and are all right, so to avoid interference from the guards."

"Oh, sir," said Winder, "you are all right. You require no pass or permit. If anyone interferes with you, just tell them you reported to me."

Lewis and Scully walked around town until suppertime, "feeling now perfectly secure," Lewis recalled. After a meal at the hotel, they went to Webster's room hoping he would have no more visitors so they could talk privately about Scully returning to Washington with whatever intelligence Webster had for McClellan while Lewis headed to Chattanooga.

Lewis, Scully, and Webster had been talking only about fifteen minutes when there was a knock at the door.

"Come in," Webster called.

George Clackner, one of Winder's star detectives, walked in with Chase Morton, the son of Senator Jackson Morton. Lewis and Scully immediately recognized him—the Morton family apparently had not gone to Florida as Pinkerton claimed—but Lewis pretended not to know the young man.

Scully did not wait to be introduced. He stood up and walked quickly out of the room—about the worst possible thing he could have done, Lewis thought. Lewis sat nervously as Chase eyed him, and Webster, not realizing the Morton connection, made small talk with Clackner, whom he knew. After about ten minutes, Lewis stood up and, trying to appear relaxed, told Webster good-bye and said he would return tomorrow.

Outside the room, Lewis found Scully waiting anxiously at the head of the stairs. "The dog is dead," Lewis told him quickly. They had to get out of there.

But at that moment, Clackner and Chase Morton walked out of Webster's room. At the bottom of the stairs stood McCubbin and four other Confederate detectives waiting to escort Lewis and Scully back to Winder's office.

The charm had vanished from the provost marshal's face when he walked into the room where Lewis and Scully had been placed. "How are you, Mr. Lewis, and how is Secretary Seward?" Winder asked accusingly.

"General, I don't understand you," Lewis replied. "I don't know what all this means. I never saw Secretary Seward in my life."

"Mr. Lewis," Winder said, tired of playing games, "there is no doubt you are a smart man. If you were not, they would not send you on this mission. But we are smart enough for you this time. I suspected you all along."

Lewis tried his best to convince Winder he and Scully were just innocent couriers, but the general wasn't buying their story. Winder finally asked
Chase if he was sure they were the two men who had raided the Morton
home in Washington. Chase was sure.

Detectives retrieved their valises at the Exchange and Ballard and
searched them, as well as every stitch of clothing Lewis and Scully wore.
The pair was then taken to the Henrico County Jail on the corner of 22nd
and Main Streets, but the jailer there had left with the keys, so Lewis and
Scully were locked up in a nearby guardhouse for the night.

The next morning, February 28, Clackner fetched Lewis and Scully at
the guardhouse to escort them to the Henrico Jail. But he first took them to
a saloon for a drink, which Lewis thought odd until he saw the man tending bar. He was Pinkerton's agent, E. H. Stein. Lewis guessed that Clackner
brought them to the saloon because Stein was under suspicion and the detective wanted to see if the men recognized each other. But his two prisoners' faces remained impassive and Stein pretended not to know them.

Later that day, McCubbin paid a visit to Webster's room at the Monumental. The detective told him of the arrests and politely but coolly questioned Webster about what he knew about Lewis and Scully. Webster
pleaded ignorance, claiming he had never met them before they arrived
with the letter from Baltimore. Hattie retrieved the note and gave it to
McCubbin, who tucked it into his coat pocket and left. Webster knew his
days were numbered. Hattie hoped for the best.

Sunday afternoon, March 9, the day after Lincoln had approved his maneuver to Urbanna, McClellan sat in his headquarters with the president and
Stanton when a telegram arrived from Pinkerton that blew apart the plan.
"I have reliable and corroborative information that the Rebels are evacuating Centreville and Manassas and falling back," the detective's message read.
Johnston, it turned out, had been more worried about Lincoln's proposal to
have McClellan's army outflank him just below the Occoquan River and cut
him off from Richmond than either Lincoln or McClellan realized. On February 19, the Confederate general, whose own intelligence reports warned

that the Federals far outnumbered him, had received Davis's very qualified permission to move his force back to a far more defensible position behind the Rappahannock River about thirty miles southwest of Manassas.

It took the Rebel commander nearly three weeks to finally start his force moving south on March 7, 8, and 9. For Pinkerton, it represented an intelligence failure as major as his inflation of Confederate troop counts. He had continued to inundate McClellan with hundreds of pages of statements from civilians, runaway slaves, Rebel deserters, and escaped Union prisoners. To get the general to pay attention to paragraphs he thought important, Pinkerton had begun drawing cartoonlike hands on the side pointing to them—a device newspapers of the day used. But though scores of runaways, refugees, train workers, and farmers around Centreville and Manassas had witnessed the large army move out by rail and on foot, none of them had made it to Pinkerton's interrogators ahead of time. Johnston had tightened his picket lines to curb deserters or prisoners from escaping to alert the Federals, but Pinkerton did not notice those sources drying up, which would be a tip-off.

In what amounted to an embarrassing postmortem, Pinkerton's agents interviewed runaways, refugees, and deserters to piece together a chronology of just how Johnston's army slipped out from under their noses. The interrogations revealed that the Rebels who retreated had been poorly fed, clothed, and shod, and their horses and mules were in sad condition from months of little forage. The interviews also turned up evidence of Confederate atrocities during the escape. Fifteen runaways reported that owners ordered slaves executed so they would not fall into the hands of the Yankees.

Within hours of receiving Pinkerton's telegram, McClellan ordered two cavalry regiments forward to probe what happened. The next day he led much of his army of 112,000 on what amounted to a rehearsal march to Centreville and Manassas to see for himself. What he and the reporters tagging along found proved to be even more embarrassing for the commanding general. Johnston's camp had deserted huts for only about half the men McClellan thought had been there. Several artillery redoubts had logs painted black to fool McClellan's scouts and Pinkerton's observers into thinking they were cannon. They came to be known as "Quaker guns" and the press had a field day with them—"proof-positive of the cowardice or inefficiency of General

McClellan," railed the *New York Times*. Three days later, Lafayette Baker arrived with his detectives to collect evidence that Johnston's force had been less than Pinkerton reported—and to browse around the Quaker guns, gloat over McClellan's folly, and arrest Union stragglers pocketing battlefield souvenirs, looting homes, and abusing the locals.

The successful escape was not only humiliating for McClellan. Johnston's retreat made the Urbanna plan a dead letter. Now back behind the Rappahannock, Johnston was within easy railroad distance of Richmond. Moreover, on the morning of March 9, Washington received the shocking news that the ironclad CSS *Virginia* had successfully attacked four Union ships the day before. McClellan worried that the *Virginia* might break out of Hampton Roads and assault the Union landing force on the Rappahannock, stranding his army in enemy territory. McClellan assumed that Johnston had moved back because the Union's Urbanna plan had been leaked to him. (It hadn't. Johnston feared Lincoln's plan. Neither he nor Davis knew ahead of time about the Urbanna option.) If the plan had leaked, McClellan feared, the Confederates would rush east and ambush his force before he could establish a beachhead at Urbanna.

To launch his attack on Richmond, McClellan now needed a safer base on the lower Virginia Peninsula, a bone-shaped body of land protruding out to Hampton Roads and the Chesapeake Bay between the York and James Rivers. He found it farther south of Urbanna at what had always been his fallback position—Fort Monroe, an enormous hexagonal stonework at the southern tip of the Peninsula in Hampton Roads bristling with heavy guns, which the Federals still occupied and which was seventy-five miles southeast of Richmond. By having the Union Navy transport his large army aboard an armada of ships from Washington down the Potomac River and Chesapeake Bay to Fort Monroe, McClellan would avoid the latticework of rivers, dense forests, and Rebel defenses crisscrossing the hundred-mile land path from Washington to Richmond, which could bog down and chew up an invading army. And when the Union ironclad *Monitor* held its own in a clash with the *Virginia* in Hampton Roads on March 9, McClellan knew he could bring his sea transports safely to Fort Monroe to continue his campaign.

On March 13, Stanton delivered to McClellan Lincoln's approval of the new Peninsula campaign, conditioned once more on Washington remaining secure and McClellan moving immediately. The Young Napoleon promised to leave 55,456 soldiers to protect the capital and started to move on March 17, one day ahead of Lincoln's deadline. But he left incensed over a slight from his president. Believing McClellan's plate was too full on the eve of a critical campaign, Lincoln stripped him of his general in chief position. For now, the president and his war secretary would take on that job. The general's demotion mattered little, since he still would lead the country's most important army. But it still rankled McClellan, who learned about it after reading a newspaper report. Pinkerton felt the same. "They had practically deposed him," he wrote later.

Pinkerton now scrambled to find out anything he could about Rebel defenses in the Peninsula and Richmond, but he was starting from a deep deficit. Intelligence on the lower Peninsula had not been a priority for him. Only Webster had set foot into the area in the course of his travels to and from Richmond. Pinkerton managed to produce three other reports on the region from interviews with a freed black, a Rebel deserter, and a Union prisoner who had escaped from Richmond. In the Confederate capital, he made no contact with the underground Van Lew led, whose agents could have helped. Instead, he hoped the operatives he had sent there would provide intelligence. But at the moment, all of them were either in bed, in jail, or incommunicado.

With a high wall surrounding two buildings built of granite and iron, the Henrico County Jail was considered escape-proof—no one had done it in 150 years—so guards were not kept around the facility. Inside, security was lax. Jailers frequently skipped out for a drink at a saloon, leaving the prisoners by themselves. Lewis and Scully were put in a second-floor room with six other inmates. They paid a jailer twenty-four dollars to bring them cots and blankets. Scully was downcast, but Lewis remained upbeat. On a stroll about the outer jail yard later, Lewis warned his partner to keep his mouth shut around other prisoners. There might be spies among them reporting to Winder's men what the two said. The second day, jailers came and took Scully away with his cot and blankets. Lewis did not see him again for weeks.

Almost immediately Lewis began plotting his escape with two other prisoners who had fashioned saws out of table knives to cut the bars on windows and jail doors. After two weeks, Lewis and now nine other prisoners had made enough progress with the sawing to escape on March 16. They scattered after the breakout, some managing to flee twenty miles outside the city, but soon most were hungry, wet, and miserable crossing swamps and streams in the countryside during the day and sleeping out in the stormy cold at night. Armed search parties captured all ten men by March 18. Considered the escape's ringleader, Lewis was thrown back into his jail cell and put in painful ankle shackles and wrist irons.

Some 126,000 soldiers, along with their artillery, animals, and equipment, boarded 389 steamers, schooners, and heavy barges at Alexandria for the voyage to Hampton Roads, which would take twenty days for a campaign that would end up being the largest of the war. Stowed aboard the ships was the best intelligence and communications technology available: three of Thaddeus Lowe's balloons with gas-generating machines, nearly two dozen U.S. Military Telegraph operators and their equipment to provide twenty-four-hour-a-day communications to Washington, and flag wavers to signal Navy ships. Fortunately for McClellan, Rebel intelligence failed to detect the massive Union movement.

Pinkerton had already proven himself to be a poor military intelligence analyst in Washington. He would be even more out of his element trying to run that operation in the field with divisions constantly moving and accurate reporting, almost hourly, of enemy strength and position critically important. He should have stayed in the capital chasing spies and dissidents. But Pinkerton was desperate to get to the front. He cleared out his cases of prisoners languishing at Old Capitol and pleaded with McClellan to allow him to join the Peninsula force. "I know I can be of great value to you," he wrote the general. Other officers in McClellan's command were not convinced and thought the detective should remain behind. Pinkerton accused them of failing to understand the importance of his work and asked McClellan to clear hurdles that the general's staff had placed in front of his coming.

McClellan did and allowed Pinkerton to join his field headquarters with George Bangs and a dozen other detectives. Pinkerton also brought along his fifteen-year-old son, William, who acted as a spy apprentice, taking a flight in Lowe's balloon and even coming under fire at one point. Eventually able to pitch a tent near McClellan's when they reached outside of Fort Monroe, Pinkerton also began looking for talent among the general's headquarters troops. He found John C. Babcock, a member of McClellan's bodyguard called the Sturgis Rifles, who proved adept at making much-needed battle maps.

Lafayette Baker was delighted to see Pinkerton go, believing it would allow him a free rein in Washington. That didn't happen. Pinkerton left behind detective William H. Scott and ten assistants to shadow suspected spies, hunt for crooked contractors, and roust malingerers from McClellan's army who still hung out in local hotels.

By the beginning of April, leaders from New York to Washington were optimistic. With Union gains in the West and McClellan's army poised at Fort Monroe to thrust up the Peninsula, the war would not last long, many northerners believed. Stanton, who strong-armed newspapers into printing positive stories, ordered on April 3 that all recruiting offices be closed, convinced there would be no need for more manpower. A refrain became popular that the federal Army would dine in Richmond by July 4.

Feelings ran the opposite in Richmond. The Confederate high command became greatly alarmed when it finally realized the vast army McClellan had amassed at Fort Monroe. Field fortifications around the city, grown dilapidated, were rebuilt. Johnston's army was called back to the capital. Richmond ladies began stitching together tens of thousands of sandbags. Flyers were distributed alerting citizens that large bodies of troops would be passing through the city and asking residents to cook food for them. In a fortnight, the Confederate Congress voted itself a pay raise and adjourned so its members could leave the threatened capital. Winder's office became crowded as well with residents seeking documents needed to flee the city.

Not all were panicked. Richmond's Unionists privately rejoiced. Van Lew, who by April 4 could hear the faint rumble of Union cannon to the south, began entertaining the notion that McClellan might soon be a guest in her home.

Late March, as McClellan's army sailed toward the Peninsula's tip, George Clackner walked into Lewis's jail cell with a blacksmith to cut off his restraints so Winder's detective could take him to the courthouse for his court-martial. In the nearly empty courtroom, Judge Advocate William W. Crump, the prosecuting attorney, told Lewis he had a right to legal representation. Scully, whose trial had taken place while Lewis was making his escape from the jail, had retained a man named Gilmer—"a first-rate lawyer," Crump assured him—so Lewis decided to use him as well. Gilmer, a middle-aged gentleman, then slipped his new client a note from Scully, who wrote that he had admitted working for the U.S. government but had become disgusted with the job and, since he was a foreigner, had decided to leave its service. Gilmer advised Lewis to offer the same defense. Lewis realized he had no choice but to do so, since the angry Morton family had identified them both as Pinkerton men.

Lewis was taken back not to the Henrico Jail, but to Castle Godwin, the old jail for African Americans on Lumpkin Alley that now held treason suspects. Guards soon moved him to the filthy and uncomfortable Condemned Cell after they caught him plotting an escape with other prisoners. The day after being sent to the Condemned Cell, Lewis was put on trial, which lasted a little more than three days. He was charged with being "an alien enemy in the employ of the Lincoln government," who had been collecting intelligence on Richmond's fortifications. Lewis had had no time to spy on the city's defenses, so he pleaded not guilty to all the charges. Winder, Clackner, McCubbin, and the Morton family members testified against him. Gilmer argued that Lewis had worked for the Lincoln government but had since renounced the job. "I had received a tolerably fair trial upon absurdly unfair charges," Lewis concluded afterward.

A couple of days later, he was escorted to a downstairs room at Castle Godwin and reunited with a tearful Scully, who lay on a cot and seemed to him physically and mentally ill. They compared notes on their trials and Lewis tried to cheer him up. They speculated on the chances of McClellan reaching Richmond and rescuing them before any sentence they faced was carried out.

That would not happen, they soon realized. On April 2, three Confederate officers visited the pair to inform them they had been found guilty and would be hanged in two days. Scully broke down from the news. Lewis, then just twenty-seven, was strong and calm, showing no fear of death. But he did start firing off letters to Catholic bishop McGill and the British consul in Richmond, begging them to intervene in their case. The Catholic Church came through with Father Augustine L. McMullen, a priest from St. Peter's Cathedral who showed up in their cells to minister to them the final two days. The clergyman probably was acting honorably, but Lewis did not trust him, convinced the good father was a Confederate plant. The morning of April 3, McMullen met with Scully and talked him into confessing what he knew about Webster. A Rebel officer took Lewis into another room so he would not hear what his partner told the priest. When Lewis was finally sent back to his cell, he found Scully there calm and "completely transformed," he said later.

Lewis hoped Richmond's British consul would at least secure a delay of the execution so Washington could arrange their release through a prisoner exchange. But Frederick John Cridland, the acting consul in Richmond, showed up at his cell on April 3 with not much to offer. George Moore, Richmond's consul who hated Americans no matter whether they were from the North or the South, had sailed to England to escape the onset of Richmond's summer heat. Cridland was a seasoned diplomat used to handling difficult cases, but in this instance there wasn't much the British government was willing to do for Lewis and Scully. Cridland was well aware that a British citizen who enlisted in a foreign military without royal approval forfeited his right to have Her Majesty's envoys bail him out. Lewis and Scully clearly had disobeyed British laws by working on behalf of the U.S. government, so neither was entitled now to British help. Before he visited Lewis, Cridland met with the Confederate officer presiding over the two men's cases and the evidence that officer showed him left no doubt in his mind that Lewis and Scully were Union spies.

Lewis admitted to Cridland that they were paid federal spies but they were still British subjects, he heatedly argued, and he begged the acting consul to save their lives. Cridland, who Lewis thought was "a fussy little man," reluctantly agreed to make a stab at intervening. The envoy met that same day with Davis and the Confederate secretaries of state and war, asking that the executions be postponed until British diplomats gathered evidence on behalf of both men. The Confederate government would make no promises.

After meeting with Cridland, Lewis learned from Scully he told Father McMullen that if General Winder would give him a pardon, he would tell what he knew about Webster. The news shocked Lewis. He next learned that Winder and Virginia attorney general John Randolph Tucker had extracted a confession out of Scully. Later that day he saw from his prison window Webster and Lawton being escorted into Castle Godwin, obviously under arrest. Lewis received a decent meal that evening but spent a fitful night before what he thought would be his last day alive. But the morning of April 4, the day set for their execution, Father McMullen arrived and informed the two men that Jefferson Davis had postponed their hanging for two weeks. It turned out that a few hours after Cridland's talks with senior Confederate officials the day before, Lewis and Scully's death sentence had been postponed, likely not to placate Cridland. Rebel authorities wanted time to use Lewis and Scully in building their case against Timothy Webster.

March optimism in Washington turned to April fury, particularly among congressional Republicans, as McClellan dawdled once more at the Peninsula's tip. On April 3, he finally issued an order for a force of 58,000 to begin moving out the next day from Fort Monroe to Yorktown, a key target twelve miles north he believed had about 15,000 Rebel defenders. It was an estimate reasonably close to the number actually there. McClellan expected to capture the colonial city in two days with a joint Army and Navy attack and then push farther north to West Point, Virginia, where the Pamunkey and Mattaponi Rivers joined to form the York River. West Point was a termi-nus for the important Richmond and York River Railroad line that ran to the Confederate capital thirty-nine miles west. The rail line would carry Union supplies as he advanced on Richmond. McClellan was furious, however, when the Navy would not cooperate in the bombardment of Yorktown.

Lincoln sabotaged his plan as well, McClellan believed. Tipped off by military aides that the Potomac Army commander had shorted him and left little more than 20,000 men behind to defend Washington instead of the some 55,000 he had promised, the president on April 3 ordered the 35,000 soldiers in General Irvin McDowell's 1st Corps, which had been destined to join McClellan on the Peninsula, held back to protect the city. Insisting that Washington was already adequately protected, McClellan and Pinkerton claimed the withdrawal of McDowell's corps wrecked the Peninsula cam-paign plan. It did not. The two men spun conspiracy theories in their heads that Stanton was behind Lincoln's order, to undercut McClellan so his army would be defeated on the Peninsula. More nonsense.

On April 5, McClellan halted his advance. He now believed he faced a line of heavily manned defenses in front of him that stretched like a moat behind the marshy and difficult-to-cross Warwick River from Yorktown on the eastern side of the Peninsula to the James River on the western side. Instead of the 15,000 Rebels he four days earlier thought were deployed there, McClellan now was convinced the enemy force totaled 100,000 or more. What the befuddled Union commander faced was actually a clever ruse created by John Bankhead Magruder, a tall, well-tailored Rebel general with a theatrical bent, who moved his soldiers back and forth along his line of infantry and artillery outposts behind the Warwick River to create the illusion, complete with sound effects, that he had more than the piddling 11,000-man army he actually led there. "Prince John" Magruder, as the crafty general was nicknamed, fooled McClellan, who knew woefully little about the natural or man-made obstacles he would face on the Peninsula; he fooled Pinkerton, who erroneously reported from a captured Alabama private he interrogated that Johnston was arriving with 100,000 soldiers; and he fooled Thaddeus Lowe, who did not detect the deception while hov-ering in a balloon near Yorktown.

With what he claimed was the unanimous agreement of his commanders and his staff, the timid McClellan, convinced that a battle of maneuver
to capture Yorktown would only waste lives, settled for a slow and safer siege
of the city. Pinkerton adamantly backed his boss's decision. The general had
been dealt "two serious disappointments," the detective later wrote—the
Navy refusing to cooperate and McDowell's corps yanked from his army.

The largest siege guns in the federal arsenal were slowly hauled up to the
Yorktown front, while McClellan engaged in a war of memos with Washington claiming that the loss of McDowell's corps plus other promised units
left him with just 85,000 men facing the Confederates' 100,000. Lincoln
and Stanton, however, now had other military sources feeding them the real
numbers that showed the Union force was far larger and the Confederate
defenders much smaller than McClellan reported. Lincoln fired back testy
notes that the general had more than enough men to quickly take Yorktown.
"You must act," the president implored. But McClellan did not. He spent a
month moving his big siege guns into place for the massive bombardment,
providing ample time for Joseph Johnston to shift his Rebel army to the Peninsula and for Prince John to substantially strengthen his lines at Yorktown.

The second week of April, Pinkerton made a trip back to Washington and
arranged a meeting with Lincoln. The detective wrote back on April 9 ad-
vising McClellan not to complain anymore about losing McDowell's corps
and to make the best use of the force he now had at his disposal. Pinkerton
believed from his White House meeting that Lincoln still had confidence
in his Army of the Potomac commander and was gratified "in the highest
degree" with him, he wrote. Pinkerton's only caution: "I can see that the
president thinks you are not sufficiently confident and it disturbs him."

Pinkerton had returned to Washington not just to scope out Lincoln's
sentiment toward his army commander. The detective was also at the White
House to deal with a crisis in Richmond.

On April 5, the day McClellan halted his advance on Yorktown, Pryce Lewis
paid a black jail trusty two dollars to slip a note to John Scully, who was
confined in another cell at Castle Godwin. "What have you told the authorities?" he asked his partner. Scully, who had practically a mental breakdown

after his trial and sentencing, sent notes back writing that he had "confessed everything." He urged Lewis, who was sure Father McMullen was behind this betrayal, to do the same. On April 8, the priest escorted Lewis down to the prison's Officers' Room, where Judge Advocate Crump and several others tried to convince him to talk. Lewis still wouldn't. But he was weakening. Since his confession, Scully had been placed in a comfortable cell while Lewis had been confined to a hovel, still clamped in irons. Finally, Lewis concluded, or rather rationalized, that Scully had not made a full confession and had withheld the fact that Webster was a spy. But he was sure Scully had told the Confederates that Lewis worked for Pinkerton. It was pointless to deny that now, he thought.

On April 10, Lewis sent a note to Crump that he wanted to see him. The judge advocate rushed to his cell that day. The Welshman spun for him a partial confession, claiming he worked for Pinkerton just "a few months" and during that time he had been in on the raid of the Morton home in Washington. Lewis claimed all he knew about Webster was that he was just supposed to deliver a letter to him (the bogus one the Confederates had already seized). Crump didn't believe he had gotten the whole truth out of him. Lewis learned later that he and Winder's men had suspected Lewis was also an emissary from Washington to whatever pro-Union underground existed in Richmond. If Lewis confessed fully, they thought, he would expose hundreds in that network. Lewis now waited, the clock still ticking on the two-week postponement of his death sentence.

Though what exactly Scully had confessed to was never revealed, most likely he gave pretty much the same story Lewis had. But combined with all the other evidence Winder's detectives had collected, the two men's statements were enough for Confederate authorities to conclude that Webster should be tried as a spy. Webster did himself no favors when he testified at Scully's trial that he had known the Irishman since April 1861 and that he was a friend of the South. The investigators knew from Lewis's and Scully's statements that Webster was lying, particularly about Scully being a southern loyalist. Also, Lewis's and Scully's disclosure that Pinkerton had asked them to deliver a letter to Webster clearly meant that Webster was part of the Pinkerton spy team. The revelations were embarrassing for the Confederate government. Webster had been a trusted mail courier between Richmond and Baltimore. He had been given sensitive letters and documents to carry between the two cities. The Rebel leadership was now out for blood.

Webster's trial lasted several days. Scully disclosed even more than what Lewis had earlier assumed—that Webster had been a Pinkerton employee and that Scully had come to Richmond to collect information from Webster and take it back to Washington. Lewis, who hardly recognized Webster because he looked so pale and gaunt, tried to stick to the story he gave Crump. He told the court that he did not really know Webster, that he had heard that Webster had carried Confederate mail but had never seen him do it, and that he came to Richmond only to deliver to Webster a letter, whose content he hadn't read.

While McClellan prepared to lay his siege, Richmond newspapers reached Pinkerton at the Army of the Potomac's headquarters south of Yorktown with stories that Lewis and Scully had been sentenced to die for spying but had been spared after they fingered Webster. (Richmond's papers arrived at the detective's tent almost as fast as they landed on the doorsteps of the city's residents, which irritated Confederate officials no end.) Stunned, Pinkerton went to McClellan and begged him to send emissaries under a flag of truce to Richmond to bargain for the release of the three men. McClellan refused, fearing such a move would acknowledge the three were spies and hasten their walk to the hangman. Pinkerton had pleaded the case for Lewis, Scully, and Webster when he met with Lincoln and during follow-up conferences with Stanton and other cabinet members.

Throughout the Civil War, the Union and Confederate armies followed the unofficial rule that if an agent was caught behind enemy lines wearing a uniform, he was not considered a spy and was treated as a war prisoner. If he was disguised in civilian clothes or traveling under false pretenses, he was deemed a spy and could be hung. Many spies were arrested but only a handful were executed. Most escaped jail, bribed their way out, or were exchanged for enemy prisoners. In numerous cases, Lincoln disapproved or commuted the death sentences for spies and ordered many of them released if they swore an oath of allegiance to the Union. Lincoln's cabinet decided to send a message to Richmond pointing out that Washington had been lenient with captured Confederate spies. If Lewis, Scully, and Webster were executed, the Federals might change that policy and start hanging Confederate agents, the message warned. Pinkerton then waited for a response.

It came on April 25 as McClellan still maneuvered his siege guns into place. Lewis and Scully had been spared the gallows, but the court in Richmond delivered its guilty verdict that day in Webster's case and ordered him to be hanged on April 29. Hattie Lawton was allowed daily visits to comfort Webster, who was still racked with rheumatism. She appealed to Davis's wife to spare her "husband." Varina Davis refused to become involved in the case. Webster asked Winder if he could be executed honorably by a firing squad instead of being "hanged like a common felon." The provost marshal refused.

With Lawton crumpled on the floor wailing, guards dragged Webster, who could barely walk, out of his cell as dawn broke on April 29. A carriage escorted by a cavalry company took him to the old Richmond fairgrounds, which was now Camp Lee. Soldiers and curious spectators crowded around a wooden scaffold erected on the north side of the parade grounds. A jailer and one of Winder's detectives lifted the condemned spy up the steps to hangman John Caphart, who bound his hands behind his back and his feet together with ropes and placed a black cloth bag over his head. But Caphart fit the rope around Webster's neck too loosely. The trapdoor was sprung and with a sickening thud Webster fell from the gibbet to the ground below, where he lay dazed and confused. His head had slipped through the noose. The jailer and detective lifted him up the steps once more. "I suffer a double death," Webster said with one of his last breaths.

The trapdoor was reset. Caphart this time fit the noose so tightly around Webster's neck, it choked him. The execution succeeded when the trapdoor was sprung once more. Webster's body was left to hang for a half hour. A Richmond paper reported that the rope used to kill him was then cut up into pieces and handed out to Winder's detectives as souvenirs. Lawton, who would be imprisoned in Richmond for another year, had bought a metal coffin for Webster, likely with money Pinkerton slipped to her.

Elizabeth Van Lew called Webster's execution a "heartless murder." Afterward she visited Hattie in prison to comfort her. Webster, who had served the U.S. government for just twelve months, was buried in an unmarked pauper's grave. Totally distraught, Pinkerton tried to retrieve his body, but Winder refused to ship it north. Pinkerton vowed to one day find his agent's remains and move them back to Illinois.

On May 3, Pinkerton delivered an intelligence report to McClellan, who planned to fire off his massive cannonade from his heavy batteries against the rebel defenses at Yorktown in two days. The Rebel army there numbered as many as 120,000 men—a figure he arrived at based on spy dispatches, interviews with intelligence sources, and a report he had received from a captured Confederate commissary worker that 119,000 rations were being issued to their defenders daily. Even that 120,000 number was likely an underestimate, Pinkerton cautioned. Rebel general Joe Johnston, who was more clearheaded about McClellan's army than McClellan was about his, knew the opposite was the case. Calculating the Union Army's number by having his scouts count the vessels sailing to Fort Monroe and estimating the troop-carrying capacity of each ship, Johnston by the end of April believed McClellan outnumbered him by five to two. He overestimated federal manpower by 20 percent. But Pinkerton overestimated the Confederate advantage by 112 percent.

Johnston decided he would not let McClellan pulverize his weaker force with the Union siege guns. The night of May 3 and into the early-morning hours of May 4, the Rebel army slipped away from its Yorktown defenses and began a retreat toward Richmond. Evacuating nearly 56,000 men along with three dozen artillery batteries in secret was almost impossible. Early on, Federal Signal Corps officers, and even a Philadelphia reporter embedded with the Union force, had picked up hints that a move was afoot. Fortunately for Johnston, bottlenecks in the Union Army's reporting chain kept that information from reaching McClellan promptly. On a nocturnal balloon flight at midnight on May 3, Lowe discovered that Yorktown's fortifications were being emptied. Early morning on May 4, General Samuel Heintzelman, McClellan's 3rd Corps commander who enjoyed playing aeronaut, went up in the balloon *Intrepid* with Lowe and confirmed the Rebels were leaving.

McClellan ordered his army to chase Johnston. But it ended up being a cautious pursuit. On May 5, the Rebels fought a rearguard battle with Union forces at Williamsburg, the Virginia commonwealth's colonial capital, eleven miles northwest, then continued their march to a new defensive line west of the Chickahominy River, a sluggish, water moccasin–infested stream surrounded by swampland and tangled forest twenty miles from Richmond. McClellan telegraphed Stanton that he had taken Yorktown, exulting that "every hour proves our victory more complete." He glossed over the fact that Johnston had given him the slip, which infuriated Lincoln when he found out about it.

With Stanton and Chase in tow, Lincoln arrived at Fort Monroe on May 6 aboard the Treasury Department's new revenue cutter, *Miami*, wanting to confer with McClellan and the president's Navy commanders on the course of the campaign. McClellan claimed he was too busy to ride back to the fort to meet his commander in chief. It wasn't the first or last time the general ignored Lincoln and missed an opportunity to improve relations with a president who was losing confidence in him. Pinkerton, who remained in awe of Lincoln, always offered his tent during these surprise presidential visits to the field as a place where the chief executive could relax by himself. McClellan knew it and when he didn't want to be bothered by Lincoln was content to let Pinkerton entertain him.

Muddy and exhausted Rebel stragglers and skulkers from the battles fought so far began trickling into Richmond. Winder was ordered to round them up and send them back to the front. Panicked civilians began evacuating the city in wagons full of furniture. George Randolph, who had succeeded Judah Benjamin as Confederate war secretary, ordered the department's records boxed up in case they needed to be shipped out quickly. The Treasury Department did the same for gold reserves loaded onto a special train. Residents on the city's eastern edge could see from their rooftops Union balloons lurking at a distance in the sky. Ladies gathered regularly at St. Paul's Church to prepare hospital bedding. At the slightest suspicion of danger to the city, bells on the tower at Capitol Square would sound an alarm. Those bells now clanged often.

Richmond's underground felt different. Van Lew tidied up her guest room for what she thought would be McClellan's appearance any day now. Samuel Ruth began dragging his feet repairing important bridges destroyed by Union or Confederate soldiers. He also began sending couriers through federal lines with reports for McClellan on conditions inside Richmond and the evacuation under way.

For his final advance on Richmond, McClellan by mid-May had set up his enormous operational base and supply depot twenty-three miles east of the city, at White House Landing, which sat along the Richmond and York River Railroad line just across the Pamunkey River and whose White House plantation had been where George Washington had courted Martha Custis. Still commanding more than two dozen operatives there and in Washington, Pinkerton was overworked running intelligence collection operations from the base camp, supervising his Washington agents from afar, drafting maps, and recruiting guides to help McClellan's corps commanders travel west to Richmond.

By the time he arrived at White House Landing, Pinkerton had solved McClellan's problem of groping his way blindly across Virginia's countryside because of unreliable maps. John Babcock, whom the detective had added to his force in March, had proven a godsend at making accurate maps, as well as sketches of enemy fortifications. To draw them, Babcock did his own scouting—on foot, by horse, and eventually aboard balloons. The cartography work became exceedingly dangerous, but the result was a series of two hundred maps covering the route to Richmond. McClellan was delighted and Pinkerton proudly sent copies to Lincoln, Stanton, and Seward to show them off.

At White House Landing, McClellan, primed by inaccurate informant reports Pinkerton's team provided, began firing off telegrams to Washington warning that Johnston's "well disciplined" force of between 140,000 and 160,00 men intended to ferociously fight the Union Army, which he claimed was half that number. Lincoln didn't believe the numbers; nevertheless, he approved marching McDowell's corps south to link up with the right wing of McClellan's army north of Richmond. But the move again came with a condition: McDowell's corps, while it moved south, must always remain between the Confederate capital and the Union capital so it would be in a position to protect Washington. Lincoln's fear of a defenseless Washington remained unabated.

Robert E. Lee, now serving as Davis's principal military counselor, devised a plan to stoke that fear in order to halt reinforcements coming to McClellan. The Shenandoah Valley, then one of the world's most beautiful and agriculturally productive regions, stretched southwest to northeast through western Virginia, bordered by the Blue Ridge Mountains on the east and the Allegheny Range on the west. The strategically important valley afforded the Confederate Army not only a vast granary to feed its soldiers but also a shielded corridor for invading Maryland, Pennsylvania, and the back door of Washington, D.C. As McClellan moved up the Peninsula, the Lincoln administration worried about the whereabouts and intentions of Confederate Major General Thomas Jonathan "Stonewall" Jackson, a humorless, secretive disciplinarian, almost fanatically religious, who earned his nickname in the Manassas battle. Early in May, Lee ordered Jackson, who had been on guard in the Shenandoah against Union general Nathaniel P. Banks, to move on Banks in order to make Lincoln believe that the Confederates planned to attack Washington.

Jackson's Shenandoah campaign was a masterpiece in diversion. For a month and a half his reinforced army of 17,000 men outmaneuvered three separate Union forces that totaled 33,000, at one point reaching near the Potomac at Harpers Ferry. Alarm bells sounded in Washington. Recruiting stations reopened. Lincoln, camped in the War Department's telegraph office moving units about, suspended McDowell's move south on May 24 and ordered his 20,000 men to join western forces in protecting Washington and crushing Jackson in the valley. McClellan, incensed once more, argued that Jackson had no intention of striking Washington and, as a result of baseless fear for the city's safety, Lincoln withheld regiments he needed to defeat Johnston. Pinkerton felt the same. Lincoln's diversion of McDowell's corps to chase Jackson indeed was a strategic blunder. The ponderous-moving Union forces never bagged the fleet-footed Confederate commander.

· · ·

By early June, Pinkerton was physically ill. It was never recorded in the records what afflicted him. It could have been exhaustion from work, or he could have been stricken by the multitude of diseases that ravaged both sides during the war. (Twice as many Union and Confederate soldiers died from disease as did from enemy weapons.) Whatever the malady, it laid up Pinkerton for all of June and into early July. George Bangs took over sending information to McClellan and managing the secret service in Washington. Pinkerton still dictated letters from his cot in the field and later a bed in Washington. He telegraphed Bangs on July 6 from the capital that he was still "very sick," but hoped to rejoin Bangs in two to three days. Pinkerton did reach his deputy in a few days, appearing feeble with some kind of ailment that Bangs said looked like "malarious fever."

What Pinkerton rejoined the second week of July was not a victorious force dining in Richmond as many had predicted but instead a demoralized army languishing some twenty-five miles south of the Confederate capital at Harrison's Landing on the James River.

McClellan's backpedaling began on the morning of May 31, when Johnston launched his reinforced army of 75,000 against the Union commander, who was bed-ridden with dysentery. McClellan's force of more than 100,000 at that point was within five miles of Richmond and divided by the rain-swollen Chickahominy. The spires of the Confederate capital's churches could be seen and their bells could be clearly heard from the battle lines. Richmonders rode out in carriages to Johnston's eastern lines to watch the spectacle like theatergoers.

McClellan's intelligence apparatus served him poorly once more. The attack caught his corps commanders by surprise. High winds grounded two balloons until the afternoon of May 31 and when they did ascend their observers could see little through the wooded countryside. In what became variously known as the two-day Battle of Seven Pines (named for the seven large pines that stood at the crossroads village) or Fair Oaks (as the Yankees called it for the rail station there), McClellan eventually succeeded in uniting his divided army to contain Johnston's onslaught in a confused battle over muddy roads and swampy countryside, which Confederate leaders managed poorly. Casualties were high—5,031 for the Union and 6,134 for the Confederates. Rebel dead piled in wagons and wounded crammed into ambulances were caravanned back to Richmond. "Death had a carnival in our city," one resident wrote. Among the seriously injured was Joe Johnston. A runaway slave later reported to Pinkerton's agents that the general had been "dreadfully wounded" in the right shoulder and chest and was taken to a house in Richmond that was cordoned off with a chain so wagons could not drive by to disturb him.

Van Lew's hopes that McClellan would use her mansion as his personal quarters were dashed when word filtered back from the front that the two armies had essentially fought to a draw and the Union commander was stalled once more. The horrors of the battle's two days had indeed wrecked the self-confidence of McClellan. Pale and physically weak from dysentery, he made no move for another three weeks. He would be shaken even more by Robert E. Lee, a gray-haired, somewhat inscrutable general who replaced Johnston on the afternoon of June 1 as commander of the Army of Northern Virginia and would stretch the national conflict far longer than anyone at that point could imagine.

Lee was an old-school general, who believed wars should be fought in the field by uniformed soldiers, not in the shadows by spooks. As a rule, he distrusted spies, wanting no part of their dirty work. He was wary of the telegraph for sending sensitive information. Female agents tended to be unreliable, he believed, "not apt to take a calm and dispassionate view of events attending the war," he wrote. For the intelligence he did need, Lee preferred that it be collected by experienced scouts or espionage agents, not civilian amateurs—although Union officers were later shocked by reports from Van Lew's ring that he used little boys as spies. He was critical of unreliable scout reports, complaining they often inflated enemy numbers by an order of six or even twelve times. Unlike McClellan, Lee wanted his scouts to properly evaluate the intelligence they raked up and not waste his time with baseless information. "Exalted statements do much harm," he lectured them.

The Army of Northern Virginia ran its own agents and kept its distance from the secret services the Confederate War and State Departments ran.

Lee developed an impressive scouting capability under James Ewell Brown "Jeb" Stuart, a cavalry brigade commander always decked out in a gold-braided jacket, yellow sash, cape, and plumed hat, as well as an irregular warfare force that operated behind Union lines under leaders like John Singleton Mosby, an aggressive former Bristol, Virginia, lawyer eventually nicknamed the "Gray Ghost." But Lee never matched the interrogation services Pinkerton and other Union intelligence officers developed. When a well-informed Union prisoner or deserter came along, Lee's men often could not evaluate or fit his information into the larger picture. Lee served mostly as his own intelligence chief, delegating only some of the duties to Stuart and a handful of staff officers. Above all, he operated more on instinct and experience than on the evidence his agents brought him. Lee's maps were no better—and often worse—than the ones the Federals used, but he already knew northern Virginia well and could fill in the details his cartographers failed to provide. He had a talent for realizing what was really happening in any tactical situation and proved superb at coming to weighty battlefield decisions based on very little information, or none at all.

McClellan wrote Lincoln he preferred fighting Lee over Johnston, opining that though the new Army of Northern Virginia commander was brave, he lacked "moral firmness." Southerners had their doubts as well about the soft-spoken Lee, who had not been viewed as a dynamic leader in the western Virginia battles he managed. His skeptics could not have been more wrong. Lee, whose primary mission for the rest of the war basically became defending Richmond, developed an innovative defensive and offensive strategy—building up the Confederate capital's fortifications with 25,000 men to shield it and blowing up McClellan's plan to lay siege to the city by launching a bold attack to destroy the Union legions with practically everything he had left. Reading McClellan's leaks in northern papers that he was outnumbered and correctly sizing him up as easily frightened, Lee undertook a wide-ranging deception campaign to convince the Union commander he was outnumbered. McClellan took the bait. So did the Pinkerton team at his headquarters, believing as their commander did that the Army of the Potomac now faced 200,000 rebels—more than double the actual number Lee eventually had. Demanding reinforcements from Washington,

McClellan wasted much of June—and the significant numerical advantage he enjoyed at that point over Lee—laboriously preparing for a slow-moving defensive campaign against what he thought was a superior enemy.

To reconnoiter Union positions and strength before he sprang his offensive, Lee on June 12 sent Stuart's 1,200-man cavalry on a three-day ride around McClellan's entire army. The cavalry chief captured enough Union prisoners to determine the identity of the Federal units he passed, but the 150-mile circumnavigation accomplished little else in the way of useful intelligence. McClellan was unfazed. But the Rebel jaunt made for superb psychological warfare. Bangs's agents failed to detect it. White House aides thought Stuart had made a fool of the Union commander.

By the third week of June, Lee had assembled the largest army he would ever command—as many as 94,000 combat-ready men—coming the closest he ever would to matching McClellan's force of about 115,000. Jefferson Davis was confident of success. "A total defeat of McClellan," he wrote his wife on June 21, "will relieve the Confederacy of its embarrassments in the East."

From his sickbed, Pinkerton continued to grieve over Webster's death. After the execution the *Richmond Dispatch* mocked Lewis and Scully, claiming they were to blame for the spy's execution because "they let the cat out of the bag on him after their conviction." Pinkerton blamed neither Scully for breaking first and implicating Webster nor Lewis for opening "his mouth" afterward, the detective later wrote. Lewis, who along with his partner was transferred to the dreaded Castle Thunder prison on August 18, also was not angry at Scully, whom he considered young, inexperienced, and not particularly bright.

But a burning resentment simmered in Lewis against Pinkerton, who should have never sent them to Richmond, he believed. Lewis was outraged to read a story in the *Richmond Whig* on June 18 that Paul Dennis, a Pinkerton agent involved in the arrest of Rose Greenhow, had been spotted in the Exchange and Ballard Hotel's parlor by Greenhow's daughter, who ran to tell her mother whom she saw. Pinkerton had foolishly sent Dennis to Richmond to collect information on Lewis and Scully. Fortunately for the

Union agent, he recognized the little girl at the same time she discovered him. Dennis fled north.

Elizabeth Van Lew asked Confederate authorities if they would allow Hattie Lawton to move to the Church Hill mansion. The authorities denied her request. During Van Lew's prison visits, Lawton maintained her cover that she was Webster's wife and never revealed she was a Pinkerton agent. Van Lew likewise never confided to Lawton that she was part of Richmond's Union underground. Webster's case, which Van Lew had followed closely in the newspapers, worried her. The jolting discovery of a Pinkerton espionage ring in Richmond made Winder and the city's citizens even more paranoid about spies in their midst, fueling more rumors about reputable ladies in the capital supporting the Union. Confederate authorities had passed a sweeping conscription act, compelling all white men ages eighteen to thirty-five to join the military. Richmond conscription agents began to target suspected Unionists. A group of fifteen refugees from Richmond, many of them Irish born, crossed into Union lines to the east and told Pinkerton's men they feared the Rebels planned to require everyone to take an oath of allegiance or be banished from the city.

For Van Lew, Webster's death brought home the dangers of her secret war. It was more important than ever for her to maintain her façade of loyalty to the Confederacy to preserve her freedom, she knew. If she were exposed as a Union agent she would be imprisoned like Lawton, perhaps executed like Webster, she feared.

Two days before what would be the largest battle of the Civil War up to that point, Pinkerton's team delivered to McClellan's field headquarters a report on their interrogation of a black man named Henry Marshal, who provided them an incredibly detailed description of the country the Federals would be fighting over on their front from the Richmond and York River Railroad to the James River in the south. Marshal, who had a photographic memory, painted the topography of the area farm by farm, acre by acre, and house by house. But before McClellan could use this valuable information to launch his attack on Richmond, Robert E. Lee—the man he had judged too cautious—tore into the Union Army on June 25.

Lee began what became known as the Seven Days Battles because of the time it lasted. The campaign, which was poorly executed by both sides, would decide Richmond's fate. From June 25 to July 1—in savage fighting, sometimes hand to hand, at Oak Grove, Mechanicsville, Gaines's Mill, Garnett's Farm, Savage's Station, Glendale, and Malvern Hill—Lee forced McClellan's army to retreat south down the Peninsula to the Berkeley Plantation at Harrison's Landing on the James River, where U.S. Navy gunboats could protect and supply him.

Van Lew and two friends had ridden in a carriage out the Mechanicsville Turnpike on the oppressively hot day of June 26 to visit Unionist John Minor Botts. He had a farm in Hanover County near the crossroads village of Mechanicsville, six miles north of the capital, where Lee's army was attacking McClellan's force. Richmonders had streamed out and perched themselves on nearby hilltops to watch the spectacle. A Confederate picket waved Van Lew's party on after she showed them her travel pass—the roar of the guns growing louder as they rode north. "The excitement on the Mechanicsville Turnpike was more thrilling than I could conceive," she later wrote in her diary. "Men riding and leading horses at full speed; the rattling of their gear, their canteens and arms; the rush of the poor beasts into and out of the pond at which they were watered. The dust, the cannons on the crop roads and fields, the ambulances, the long line of infantry awaiting orders. We enquired the news of the picket who stopped us. He told us that we were whipping the Federals right, left and in the centre." Van Lew dearly hoped that was not the case.

McClellan's casualties for the Seven Days Battles totaled 15,849—the combat deaths alone greater than what all the Union armies combined had suffered so far. Lee, whose gentle demeanor masked a commander willing to launch costly operations, racked up 20,614 in casualties. Richmond's fifty hospitals filled so quickly, to make room for new patients, stretcher-bearers carted to graveyards the wounded who were expected to die before they actually expired while soldiers walked the streets with amputations only three days old. With practically every house mourning a dead relative or caring for a wounded one, Richmond ladies abandoned extravagant gowns and wore plainer mended dresses. Van Lew noted that most of the city's women, of whom she could not have been more contemptuous, cared only for the Confederate wounded who poured in. Van Lew and her mother tried to tend to the injured Union prisoners who arrived as well, but that became more dangerous as security authorities squeezed off access to them.

Though he succeeded in saving Richmond, Lee ended up deeply frustrated that he could not finish off McClellan. Elements of his force, like Stonewall Jackson's corps, had been slow moving at critical junctures. A rookie at managing complicated battles and exhausted by the end of the fight, Lee had given imprecise orders and at times had failed to launch coordinated attacks. The seven days were even more humiliating for McClellan. Less than halfway through the weeklong battle, he lost his will to fight. Mentally exhausted and panicked, he ordered a premature retreat. By June 28, the Young Napoleon became practically unhinged, writing a hysterical letter to Stanton, blaming the loss on the war secretary and others in Washington, who "have done your best to sacrifice this army." Pinkerton agreed that McClellan had been "pushed beyond all control by the foolish, unfriendly and unjust course of those at Washington." Lincoln tried to calm down his general. "Save your army, at all events," the president telegraphed. "Will send reinforcements as fast as we can."

Still feeble from what ailed him, Pinkerton found a wretched crowded encampment when he arrived at Harrison's Landing in early July. Temperatures soared past 100 degrees and swarming flies from the James River bottomland drove soldier and beast mad. McClellan's men lived in filth and drank polluted water. By the end of the month more than 42,000 of them would be on sick call. McClellan set up his headquarters at the Harrison Mansion on Berkeley Plantation, where soldiers strung telegraph lines and a signal station was perched on the roof to communicate by flags to Navy ships on the river. Though harboring private delusions and bitter resentments, McClellan retained his showman's flare, staging grand reviews at Harrison's Landing, firing off gun salutes with the band playing, and putting out propaganda for the public that he had scored a victory over superior forces. Swallowing the line, newspapers like the Washington *Evening Star* published glowing accounts of the campaign or like the *New York Herald* excoriated Stanton for not supporting the general.

To resume the campaign, McClellan messaged Washington that he now had only 50,000 men and needed 100,000 more. Lincoln found the request absurd and cabled back that it could not be done. Fed with alarming prisoner reports by Pinkerton's team, the Union commander feared the entire Confederate Army would now attack him, which was not the case. Lowe's balloons made regular ascents but detected no Rebel activity. Lee, it turned out, was receiving intelligence reports on McClellan as exaggerated as the reports McClellan was receiving on Lee. Confederate spies tracked Union steamers sailing in and out of Harrison's Landing with troops aboard, Lee wrote Davis, concluding that the Yankees had been reinforced and were planning "further operations." Chastened by the spy reports and his own battlefield setbacks, Lee decided to leave McClellan alone.

At Harrison's Landing, Pinkerton and McClellan showed their vindictive side to a clerk in the detective's service named Thad Seybold, who took down the statements of war prisoners. Seybold was thrown into a filthy jail for sending letters to Seward critical of the general and his spy chief. Pinkerton accused the clerk of leaking secrets to the Rebels and McClellan ordered him held in isolation. A later investigation by Levi Turner, the Army's special judge advocate, concluded the charge was false. Seybold was an honest clerk brutally and unfairly persecuted for leaking to Seward the poor state of McClellan's command and Pinkerton's intelligence service.

Lincoln sailed up the James River aboard the *Ariel* on July 8 to confer with McClellan and his corps commanders and assess for himself the condition of the Union Army. McClellan's suspicious strength reports now had 45,000 men missing beyond the casualties that could be accounted for. Lincoln did not have enough time in the three hours he walked and rode among the soldiers to count the number of troops McClellan actually had, but he did find morale among the rank and file far better than he expected. McClellan remained as uncommunicative as ever about his plans for renewing the campaign. Sitting on the deck of the *Ariel*, he did hand Lincoln what amounted to a political memo he drafted for how the president should run the war and the country—remarkable chutzpah for a general who had lost so many battles. There has been unconfirmed speculation that Pinkerton helped McClellan compose the letter. Lincoln read the note quickly, thanked McClellan, and pocketed it without saying another word.

The first thing the president did when he returned to Washington on July 11 was make Henry Halleck the general in chief of the Army. A balding, potbellied, and scholarly officer who had excelled at West Point, authored books on strategic theory, and was called "Old Brains" behind his back, Halleck had been summoned to the federal capital from his command of the Mississippi River theater. He had rather circumscribed rules for espionage, which helps explain why he fumbled valuable intelligence he received as a western commander. A general, Halleck once wrote, could rightfully buy information or accept the services a spy offered. But a general could not seduce a person to commit an act of treachery toward an enemy, such as espionage, which would make that person a felon and subject to a felon's death. Even information a spy freely volunteered was likely of little value, Halleck believed. Such information was "unreliable," he said, and most spies sold to both sides.

McClellan resented Halleck's appointment, but Lincoln hoped it would relieve McClellan of onerous duties supervising the Army and Halleck would be the key to victory. McClellan, Lincoln concluded, would never fight; he would just keep asking for reinforcements. The president told Halleck he could keep or fire the Army of the Potomac commander as he saw fit. Halleck, however, proved to be slow to move and aggressive only in his writings. As general in chief, he had more authority than he had the courage to use. Any important decision, he believed, must be cleared first with Lincoln (who had sacked other commanders for ignoring his wishes), which made it impossible for Halleck to act at all and meant that Lincoln was forced to remain as de facto general in chief.

On July 25, Halleck visited McClellan's headquarters to discuss the future of his army. McClellan's count of the number of Rebel troops he now faced made Halleck's head spin. The Army of the Potomac commander

had earlier estimated that casualties from the Seven Days Battles had reduced the effective strength of Lee's army to 150,000. By the time Halleck
arrived at Harrison's Landing, McClellan had raised the enemy number to
200,000—an even wilder overestimate that presumed Halleck to be gullible enough to believe that in just weeks Lee had miraculously increased his
force by 50,000 men.

After some haggling, McClellan agreed to advance up the north bank
of the James River and attack Richmond if Washington gave him 30,000
more men to add to the 90,000 he now claimed he had at Harrison's Landing. Halleck, who concluded after his meeting with McClellan that the man
"does not understand strategy and should never plan a campaign," would
provide only 20,000 Union troops. And that offer came with an ultimatum:
McClellan must advance on Richmond with the 110,000 he would now
have or abandon the Peninsula campaign entirely and bring his army back
north. McClellan agreed. His campaign was saved—but only for twenty-
four hours.

Halleck soon suffered a near nervous breakdown from dealing with
multiple crises. Hemorrhoids and McClellan added to his agitation. On
the day Halleck returned to Washington from his Harrison's Landing trip,
McClellan telegraphed that he now needed 55,000 more troops. From interviews Pinkerton's men had with sick or wounded Yankees the Confederates
had paroled to Union lines, McClellan deduced that Rebel reinforcements
poured into Richmond from the South and the West. Halleck knew that if
he agreed to the 55,000, McClellan would just come back and ask for more.
The general in chief ordered his Potomac Army commander on August 3 to
begin evacuating his force from the Peninsula.

Then a bizarre twist in McClellan's numbers game arrived—fueled
partly by Pinkerton's tabulations. On August 12, McClellan, desperate to
have Halleck's order rescinded, wrote him that Lee's army, which a little
more than a fortnight earlier he had insisted totaled 200,000 men, now numbered just 36,000. What happened to the other 164,000 soldiers? McClellan pumped up the casualties the Confederates suffered during the Seven
Days Battles and claimed that Jackson had left Richmond with a large chunk
of the force. Pinkerton also reported that Lee's army had shrunk, but only to

80,000 by his calculations. McClellan dropped Pinkerton's total even more, to 36,000, in order to bolster his case for remaining in the Peninsula to attack Richmond.

Ironically, McClellan's new 36,000 estimate was one of the few times he approached the truth; it was only about 25 percent lower than the number Lee actually had. But already feeling flimflammed, Lincoln and Halleck weren't buying McClellan's latest epiphany or about-face or duplicity or whatever it was. The withdrawal order stood.

Thirteen

SECOND BULL RUN

*I*t was about midnight on August 27 and George Sharpe, a newly minted colonel, hurried to unload the men of his 120th New York Infantry Regiment from trains that had pulled into Washington's depot. Sharpe was recovering from a severe lung infection, likely pneumonia, which he contracted in the spring. He was exhausted, still running a high fever and suffering bouts of diarrhea.

The 120th was even newer to action than Sharpe. The regiment arrived in Washington with precious little training and hardly any weapons. In the darkness at the train station, Army ordnance officers quickly passed out muskets and cartridge boxes to his men. No time to inspect or test fire the small arms. At 10 a.m. the next day Sharpe received orders to march his unit across the Potomac on Long Bridge south of Washington to Arlington Heights and camp on Virginia soil—in sight of Robert E. Lee's former home.

Sharpe's 120th Regiment was the offspring of the 20th Regiment he had briefly served in earlier as a captain. After the Rebel attack on Fort Sumter, the 20th Regiment, with Sharpe leading its B Company, had been sent to

New York City on April 29, 1861, and from there to Washington, where it had been assigned to guard a rail line from Annapolis to Washington and Baltimore. Sharpe was popular with his men but not adored. In June 1861, he lost an election the soldiers held for who should lead the entire regiment. He and his men were obligated to serve only a three-month enlistment, the conventional wisdom then being that the war would be short. In September 1861, Company B disbanded.

Sharpe took a break from the military to dabble in politics. He attended the fall Republican state convention, speaking out on behalf of harmonious relations with War Democrats who backed the Union. In response to Lincoln's July 1862 call-up of 300,000 troops for three-year duty, New York's 10th Senatorial District Committee for Ulster and neighboring Greene Counties was appointed to raise a regiment. New York's governor made Sharpe the regiment's commander with the rank of colonel.

Speaking daily at town hall meetings throughout Ulster, Green, and Dutchess Counties, Sharpe energetically began recruiting soldiers. He became a zealous salesman. When one village proved indifferent to contributing men, Sharpe, in a show of bravado, offered to return his colonel's commission to the governor and enlist as a private from the village to help meet its obligation. The village soon offered up seven men. The spring lung infection dogging him, Sharpe drove himself to near physical exhaustion organizing his regiment. But he made steady progress. As volunteers enlisted, he sent them to Camp Samson for training. In a little more than three weeks Sharpe had recruited 906 men. The ladies of Kingston and nearby Ellenville presented the unit with a silk regimental flag they had sewn for them to carry into battle. A speechless Sharpe was overcome with emotion from the gift. He knew the pain his men felt leaving loved ones—some perhaps for good.

Early Sunday morning, August 24, Sharpe marched his regiment to Rondout on the Hudson River, where the steamer *Manhattan* carried the men down to New York City. At City Hall Park some of the soldiers received old muskets from Army stores, but no other equipment. A ferry took them to Jersey City that afternoon, where they boarded boxcars for an uncomfortable train ride to Philadelphia. The next morning they were crammed into the boxcars once more for the ride to Baltimore and finally to Washington on August 27, where they bivouacked on the street near the train station for the rest of the night.

The Washington that Sharpe passed through the next morning to reach Arlington Heights was gloomy over the war's progress and steaming from the usual August heat (that month and September always bringing on the most disease). Everything seemed to be going wrong for the president—his hope of bringing the conflict to a speedy end dashed.

In the days after the Peninsula campaign, Washington had been flooded with dead or wounded soldiers. The federal government converted hotels, churches, schools, and homes into military hospitals. Union officers killed in battle were packed in charcoal, shipped to the capital first, and then sent home in coffins by train. As in Richmond, Washington fell short in giving fallen soldiers honorable burials. Coffins were often poorly sealed, funeral trains were delayed. Embalming parlors multiplied—the practice becoming an environmental hazard from the chemicals used in these "stench factories," as newspapers called them.

Sharpe was already gaining a reputation as a capable officer, clear-eyed about soon leading his men into combat. He would need the levelheadedness that morning of August 28. The battle, which soon would be called Second Manassas or Second Bull Run, was beginning.

John Pope was the handsome, articulate, and energetic son of a Lincoln associate in Illinois. He was also a boastful man, a Union general from the Western Theater scornful of eastern commanders like McClellan. While the Army of the Potomac slogged through the Seven Days Battles, Lincoln had made Pope one of his informal military advisers. Likely prodded by retired general Winfield Scott, the president on June 26 formed the Army of Virginia out of the three corps McDowell, Banks, and John C. Frémont led plus units from Washington and western Virginia. Pope was given command of the 47,000 men. He had multiple missions—to protect Washington, keep the Confederates clear of the Shenandoah Valley, and draw the enemy away from McClellan. The appointment of the blustery Army of

Virginia commander was controversial. Frémont, who outranked Pope and had created political headaches for Lincoln in the western department, refused to serve under him, so Lincoln had Major General Franz Sigel (a hero among German American soldiers) take over Frémont's corps. Unlike Halleck, Pope was enthusiastic about espionage and delivered stern orders to his commanders to have spies and cavalry detachments collect information on the Rebels.

A chess match began after Pope assumed command. Lee by mid-July 1862 realized he was in not too promising a position, what with McClellan's army at Harrison's Landing just twenty-five miles from the Confederate capital, Pope moving to the upper Rappahannock River, and General Ambrose Burnside bringing 12,000 Union soldiers up from North Carolina. All told, Lee could soon be facing a federal force double the army he could assemble. He decided to put Pope out of action before he could concentrate his force against the Confederates along the Rappahannock and threaten Richmond. Lee calculated that McClellan would remain inactive and pose little danger for the moment.

Lee again had McClellan correctly pegged. Halleck had ordered him on August 3 to move his force one hundred miles north to Aquia Creek, off the Potomac River east of Rappahannock Station, so his army could unite under Pope's army. If the two men had worked together they could have defeated Lee. But that proved impossible for McClellan and Pope, who detested each other. McClellan dragged his feet and did not even begin to slowly redeploy his force until August 14. Lee shifted his chess pieces faster, riding with James Longstreet's corps of 25,000, which a day earlier had moved out to join the some 30,000 men Stonewall Jackson now had in order to bring the full weight of the Rebel Army of Northern Virginia against John Pope's force, which was increasing to 55,000.

As outraged as McClellan over Halleck's order that the Army of the Potomac must aid Pope, Pinkerton on August 10 delivered an intelligence report to his general's headquarters designed more to stroke McClellan's huge ego than to provide him any useful information. The detective reported that a captured private from a Virginia cavalry regiment had told him that Rebel troops were denigrating Pope and praising McClellan "as a gentleman only officer and a good soldier," who they believed could bring "reconciliation between the North and the South." How a lowly private would be privy to this kind of sweeping political intelligence is anybody's guess. It sounded like Pinkerton had made up the report or, at best, was being fed disinformation by southern agents.

Through much of August, Lee's and Pope's armies, each numbering about 55,000, fought a series of battles at Cedar Mountain (a hill west of Fredericksburg, Virginia) and near the Rapidan and Rappahannock Rivers. Pope pleaded with Washington for speedier help from the Army of the Potomac, but McClellan, who did not sail for Aquia Landing until August 23 and did not set up his new base at Alexandria until August 26, ignored Halleck's demand to stop dawdling. McClellan was in no hurry to rush his forces to Pope.

Both Pope and Lee ran aggressive intelligence operations against each other during the month of August. The Richmond underground was at work as well. Samuel Ruth enlisted the aid of William Rowley's teen-aged son, Merritt, to sabotage a Rebel ammunition train Lee desperately needed. Ruth supplied Merritt with a bottle of sulfuric acid that the boy poured into the train's locomotive tender, causing it to break down after a couple of miles. The chief of McClellan's secret service also launched an espionage operation—not at the Confederates, but instead against his own government.

The third week of August, McClellan sent Pinkerton to Washington to spy on the Lincoln administration and the general's rivals in the military. George Bangs, who was hobbled with diarrhea, remained with McClellan to forward to him the secret letters Pinkerton sent. Bangs and Pinkerton agreed that a trusted "special messenger" would deliver the spy chief's sensitive reports to McClellan's headquarters. "If any of these letters were to get lost," Pinkerton warned Bangs, "they would raise the Devil." McClellan anxiously waited for each report Pinkerton sent.

Pinkerton snooped throughout the White House and War Department, shaking down aides to Lincoln, Halleck, Stanton, and other cabinet members for intelligence on sentiments toward McClellan. The spying on his own government was highly unethical, but Pinkerton, a fiercely loyal member of McClellan's inner circle, approached this mission with the diligence and energy he would a Chicago crime case. He left no stone unturned.

In a sealed letter to McClellan on August 25, Pinkerton reported that Pope, who by then was fighting Lee fiercely southwest of Washington, was already out of favor with Lincoln because of battlefield reverses the previous four days. Whether that was really the case at that point was open to question. Nevertheless, Pinkerton assured McClellan that "Pope is declining and unless some other military genius appears soon they cannot do otherwise than to appoint you to the command." Halleck would oppose McClellan usurping Pope, Pinkerton wrote. The general in chief had become Lincoln's lapdog. "The president is several times every day at Halleck's house or headquarters and from all I can learn Halleck lays all his plans before him for approval," wrote the detective. Pinkerton said he discovered that Pope, meanwhile, was feeding derogatory information about McClellan to Lincoln. A cabinet source also told him that McClellan's "conduct of the war affects financial markets," but this source had not heard Treasury secretary Chase "say anything against you" for the last few weeks. Pinkerton turned out to be as poor at collecting political intelligence as he was military secrets. Chase by now was plotting to have McClellan ousted.

Fortunately for George Sharpe and his hastily trained men, the 120th Regiment was not called on to take part in the heavy combat at the Manassas battlefield where Confederate and Union troops had fought thirteen months earlier. Camped at Arlington on August 28, Sharpe could hear the booming of cannon to the southwest. Early the next morning, his soldiers were rousted from their tents, hastily supplied with rations, and ordered to move out in fifteen minutes. They marched ten miles up to Fort Ethan Allen, one of the earthwork fortifications that protected Washington on its west side. Sharpe had found what he thought was a competent Army surgeon to treat his lung infection. Only occasionally would he be incapacitated with a high fever and diarrhea the next couple of months.

The 120th Regiment was one of a number of detachments sent from the capital to guard against Lee's troops swinging around behind Pope's army to get between him and Washington. Lee never did. But in three days Sharpe and his men watched as divisions of Pope's men, their uniforms torn and mud splattered, retreated through Fort Ethan Allen and other Washington defenses—demoralized by defeat.

After three weeks of sparring over the countryside some thirty miles west of Washington, Lee, who was quickly becoming a master at beating elements of the Union Army before they could combine to defeat him, confronted Pope on the old Manassas battlefield at the end of August. Hoping to lure the Union Army into battle, Jackson on August 28 ordered an attack on a federal column passing across his front on the Warrenton Turnpike, running southwest from Washington, but the several hours of fighting at the Brawner family farm off the road ended in a stalemate. Convinced he had Jackson trapped, Pope on August 29 launched a series of imperfectly organized attacks against the Rebel commander along an unfinished railroad line just south of Sudley Springs, where Catharpin Creek branched off from Bull Run. Jackson beat back the Union assault, with both sides taking heavy casualties. Longstreet's corps of 30,000 rebels, meanwhile, slipped through the Thoroughfare Gap of the Bull Run Mountains west of Manassas Junction and assembled on Jackson's right flank at noon that day.

Pope renewed his offensive on August 30, unaware that Longstreet had arrived on the scene to strengthen significantly the Confederate force. When a massive Rebel artillery barrage devastated General Fitz John Porter's 5th Corps assault, Longstreet's 30,000 men counterattacked, crushing Pope's left wing and driving his entire army to Bull Run. That night and through the next day, Pope retreated along the Warrenton Turnpike northeast to Centreville and finally halted the Rebels from sweeping around to block the highway between that town and Washington. The Union Army then limped back behind Washington's defenses—and Lee turned his sights toward Maryland.

Pope, who had committed his share of blunders the previous two days, had repeatedly called for reinforcements from the Army of the Potomac. Halleck had wanted 25,000 men from two of McClellan's corps sent immediately to help Pope, but McClellan stalled, so they arrived too late to be of any use in the battle. Pope later complained of "unsoldierly and dangerous conduct" among McClellan's brigade and division commanders who did reach him. Incensed by McClellan's advice to him to "leave Pope to get out of his scrape," Lincoln strongly suspected the Potomac Army commander wanted his rival to fail. Pinkerton gloated that Pope's defeat at Manassas was due to the "culpable folly of" the cowardly Halleck "ignoring the genius and bravery of McClellan."

As the Union's East Coast armies stalled during the summer and fall of 1862, Lafayette Baker was preoccupied with mundane detective work. His agents seized a schooner with contraband cargo on the Rappahannock River and investigated a superintendent for Samuel Felton's Philadelphia, Wilmington and Baltimore Railroad line, accused of working with secessionists to destroy the line's bridges—a northern version of the headaches Richmond authorities had with Samuel Ruth. A cavalry major asked Baker's men to shadow a man posing as a *New York Times* correspondent who was suspected of spying for the South. Major Levi Turner, the special judge advocate, gave Baker many of his assignments, such as ordering him to track down a thief selling Army blankets and shirts stolen from the government.

A teetotaler, Baker went on a prohibition campaign in the Army that enraged officers who became his targets. Captains to generals inundated Turner and Stanton with angry letters griping that Baker agents had illegally seized boxes of liquor they bought or had friends ship to them. Army regulations allowed officers to keep private stocks of spirits in the field and soldiers occasionally were ladled out whisky after intense combat or to fight off the cold while on picket duty. Complaints began piling up at the War Department that sticky-fingered detectives were seizing not only thousands of dollars' worth of liquor but also pocketing cash they found with the booze. Turner ordered the cash returned and the Army's Quartermaster General's Office began requiring Baker to submit detailed inventories of the property his agents seized.

Turner found himself often having to clean up after botched raids Baker's men conducted. A Georgetown druggist hauled in on charges of selling quinine to the South was released after Union officers reported the medicine was actually being sent to the U.S. government. The judge advocate also had to repair a diplomatic breach Baker created. Lord Lyons, the British minister to Washington, complained to Seward that Baker's agents had arrested three British citizens and threatened to throw them into Old Capitol Prison unless they took an oath of allegiance to the United States. In a condescending note to Baker, Turner reminded his detective "that the oath of allegiance to the United States is not and cannot be required of a man who is really a British subject."

Baker had an equally spotty record with women accused of being subversives. That fall, his cousin Joseph Stannard Baker and a dozen detectives riding south to raid blockade runners at Port Tobacco in Maryland stopped at the Surratt Tavern along the way. Its owner, Mary Surratt, who Joseph said was a sour-faced, middle-aged woman "overbearing in her manner," gave the detectives a frosty reception along with their meal. Baker and his cousin claimed they knew Mary's tavern was a haven for plotters against the government, but they did not have enough evidence to arrest her so they kept her under watch. Their story doesn't ring true. Baker jailed suspects on far less evidence and if his men did keep Surratt under surveillance, they did a poor job of it. Mary, who was hung for her part in the conspiracy to assassinate Lincoln, freely moved about unmolested.

At the end of July, the famous Belle Boyd climbed off the train to the platform of the Washington station with Pinkerton agent Alfred Cridge keeping a firm grasp of her arm. Standing on the platform waiting for Boyd was Lafayette Baker, who manhandled the woman away from Cridge and hauled her off in a carriage to Old Capitol Prison. It infuriated Pinkerton, whose men had done all the work to bring her to Washington.

Belle Boyd turned out to be more a media star than an espionage heroine. Reared in the bustling western Virginia town of Martinsburg in the Shenandoah Valley, Belle became a horse-riding tomboy, attended an elite boarding school in Baltimore, and led a generally unhappy life growing up under her merchant father, who joined Jackson's army in the Shenandoah Valley when war broke out. At seventeen, she was having her way with men, considered "disturbingly attractive" by one contemporary account, with a good figure, though she had a horseface, as some described it, with a long nose and buckteeth. Belle also had a temper. On July 4, 1861, she shot and killed a drunken Union soldier who had pushed his way into her house and insulted her mother. The soldier's commander, determining the man had been belligerent, did not arrest Boyd and have her hanged, as other officers demanded.

The shooting began Boyd's career as a spy. Martinsburg, which had a major depot along the Baltimore & Ohio Railroad, turned out to be an espionage haven and Boyd shocked friends by flirting with soldiers from both sides. She began with low-level work for the southern cause, nursing Rebels in field hospitals, carrying their mail, and eavesdropping on the conversation of Union officers for information that could be passed on to the Confederates. After the first Battle of Bull Run, Boyd became a courier for messages to Jackson and Beauregard. As a spy, she was more amateurish than most of her day. The reports she delivered to the Confederates on federal troop strength and movements were written on paper and not in code. Union officers intercepted one of her plain-text letters to Jeb Stuart and arrested her at the end of 1861. They soon let her go, but kept her under watch. Boyd then began spying at Front Royal, Virginia, southwest of Martinsburg.

Her fifteen minutes of fame came during Jackson's maneuvers through the Shenandoah Valley in May 1862 to convince the Lincoln administration that the Confederates planned to attack Washington. Boyd, two weeks past her eighteenth birthday, became one of a number of valley residents who alerted Jackson to federal troop whereabouts. On May 23, Union general Nathaniel Banks, who had been jousting with Jackson in the Valley, had most of his 10,000-man force that day at Strasburg, twelve miles northwest of Front Royal. But Banks had left a holding force of 1,060 soldiers at Front Royal.

Banks thought Jackson was at Harrisonburg sixty-four miles south. The Rebel general actually was a mile and a half from Front Royal on May 23 and about to issue orders for his next move when Boyd, wearing a flowing white dress, ran out of the town, across hills, and over a field to Jackson's party. Breathlessly she informed the general's aides that only a "very small" Federal unit occupied Front Royal. He should attack quickly. Jackson did and suffered only fifty casualties to the Union's nine hundred. Jackson, who had never heard of Boyd before her scamper to his command post, sent her a thank-you note and later bestowed on her the title of honorary aide-de-camp. But he was being overly generous. The information Boyd provided only confirmed what Jackson already knew about the weak Union force at Front Royal. No matter. Word quickly spread through Front Royal and across the nation over news wires of the southern heroine who ran out to alert Stonewall Jackson. The Civil War's most overrated spy became a newspaper darling overnight.

It was impossible for Allan Pinkerton not to arrest Belle Boyd. The headstrong young woman had become more a public relations headache than a counterintelligence problem for Washington. Boyd, meanwhile, did her best to blow what little spy cover she ever had. Newspapers trumpeted her as the "Secesh Cleopatra." The Associated Press also reported the rumor that she was "an accomplished prostitute," which Boyd resented.

Jackson left Front Royal for Richmond in June and the Yankees returned to occupy the town. Boyd again flirted with Union soldiers, visiting the federal commander there on June 22 to inquire about Rebel prisoners. Three days later Pinkerton delivered Stanton a report from three of his informants at Front Royal, who advised that Boyd continued to traipse around town acting like a not-so-secret agent. A little more than a week later, Boyd approached what she thought was a Confederate prisoner on parole and asked if he would take a message to Jackson. The soldier was actually a Union spy from a local division.

By the third week of July, Pinkerton had three men working the Belle Boyd case. A federal surgeon in Front Royal wrote Stanton to pass along gossip that Boyd either had fallen in love with the medical director for the Union's 1st Corps or she was seducing the doctor for espionage purposes. The Front Royal surgeon suggested that Union authorities might want to exploit the liaison to feed the Confederates disinformation. But Stanton by then had decided not to play any more games with Belle. Pinkerton operative Alfred Cridge had been dispatched to Front Royal to find and arrest her. Twelve days later, Cridge returned to Washington with Boyd in custody.

Despite having his high-profile prisoner rudely snatched at the Washington depot on July 30, Pinkerton the next day sent one of his detectives to Old Capitol to interview Boyd. She liked Wood, Old Capitol's superintendent, who treated her like a celebrity, promising her a comfortable room and letting one of her servants attend to her as long as she behaved. Boyd didn't hold the same opinion of Baker, who walked into her cell at eight o'clock the first night and tried to browbeat her into confessing and swearing an oath of allegiance to the Union. Boyd thought Baker was an oafish country bumpkin and refused. "If it is a crime to love the South, its cause and its president, then I am a criminal," she told him defiantly. Prisoners nearby could hear their angry argument and cheered. "Well, if this is your resolution, you'll have to lay here and die!" Baker shouted back and stalked out.

Like Rose Greenhow, Boyd was a lively inmate early on, bragging that she could remain in Old Capitol longer than Stanton could afford to keep her there. Her spirits quickly sagged, however, and she began to complain about being held without charges. On August 28, federal authorities finally packed Belle off in a prisoner-exchange boat to Richmond, where she received a hero's welcome as Greenhow had. In the spring of 1863, she slipped back into Martinsburg to continue trying to be a spy but failed again. Baker's detectives arrested her once more, sent her to Carroll Prison for a little more than three months, and then delivered her for the second time to Richmond.

Confusion gripped Washington as Pope's defeated army streamed into the city. "We are whipped again," Lincoln muttered forlornly to an aide. Newspapers reported it was now a distinct possibility that Lee's army would follow Pope's and conquer the capital. Stanton and Chase had circulated a letter for their cabinet colleagues to sign demanding that McClellan be fired and hinting that they would resign if he wasn't. Lincoln preempted the move, however, announcing that he was putting Pope's army and Washington's defenses under McClellan's command. Pope would be exiled to Minnesota. The decision stunned the cabinet but Lincoln felt he had no choice. His East Coast army was in deep disarray. Lincoln feared mutiny if he kept Pope in command and cashiered McClellan, who was still popular among the troops and expert in organizing and training armies—even if he wouldn't fight with them.

McClellan arrived in Washington on September 1 with Pinkerton at his side and after being told by Lincoln the next day that Pope's army would be folded into his, he immediately set about doing what he did best—restoring administrative order, reorganizing the forces, and stage-managing grand reviews with soldiers cheering him. In less than a week McClellan's army of 85,000 then moved out at a leisurely pace to intercept Lee, who was marching not into Washington but instead to Maryland. Sharpe's 120th Regiment was left behind and put on picket duty at different points around Washington.

Pinkerton, who joined McClellan at his new field headquarters in Rockville, Maryland, claimed after the war that his men had learned that Lee planned an advance into that state, but there's no hard evidence they did. A Union Signal Corps lookout station atop Sugar Loaf Mountain, the highest point in Maryland, just north of the Potomac River and south of Frederick, is credited with spotting the Confederate movement north and alerting Washington. Pinkerton also does not appear to have supplied McClellan with any more lengthy Confederate strength reports as he had before and during the Peninsula campaign. At this point, it would likely have mattered little if he had. Though McClellan left Washington again with a two-to-one advantage over his enemy, in his mind it was set in stone that the Confederates outnumbered him as they had before. The Union commander would move cautiously in Maryland, as he had in Virginia.

Fourteen

ANTIETAM

ee saw many advantages in taking the battle into the North. His army would feed off Maryland and Pennsylvania farms and draw the Yankees away from war-ravaged Virginia during its harvest season, a Rebel victory might induce European powers like England and France to finally recognize the Confederacy as a nation, peace Democrats might gain seats in the upcoming midterm elections, and Lincoln might be forced to sue for peace. So on September 4, Lee started his army of 55,000 across the Potomac and toward Frederick, Maryland, forty miles northwest of Washington, with no solid intelligence on how McClellan would react, just gut instinct that the Union Army was demoralized and its ever-cautious commander would not feel prepared to take the offensive for three or four weeks. That gave the Rebels a window to make their thrust into the North.

McClellan moved faster than Lee expected, but with an intelligence operation diminished from what he had during the Peninsula campaign. Deprived of Army wagons and horses to transport their equipment, Professor Lowe's balloons languished in Washington. Pinkerton's traveling party included Bangs, Babcock, and eleven other operatives he rushed to send behind enemy lines. He found more than a dozen civilians along the way to serve as guides or messengers. Though McClellan's army enjoyed a far friendlier population in Maryland than in Virginia, spy networks took months to set up and Maryland's countryside was virgin territory for Pinkerton. His agents had to work on the fly.

As a result, Pinkerton contributed little to the intelligence gathering in Maryland and what he did provide made not much of an impression on his boss. McClellan instead relied on a grab bag of questionable sources that he admitted to Washington gave him only a vague picture of the enemy. A telegraph operator in Hanover, Pennsylvania, reported that more than 100,000 Confederates were near Frederick, double their actual strength. Brigadier General Alfred Pleasonton, McClellan's new cavalry commander, sent out patrols in a widening arc ahead of the Potomac Army to probe for information. McClellan was high on Pleasonton, but he proved to be inept at gathering intelligence and gullible in evaluating what he collected. The cavalry chief also reported that Lee had 100,000 men at Frederick. His source for this "most reliable information," as he put it, turned out to be secondhand: a Maryland Unionist eavesdropping on the conversation of a Rebel officer who had too much to drink. The most fanciful reports came from Pennsylvania governor Andrew Curtin, who was terrified the Confederates would occupy his state and had assembled his own makeshift spy operation. Curtin delivered to McClellan and Lincoln second- and even thirdhand information from his constituents—whom he also vouched for as "reliable and truthful"—that Lee had as many as 200,000 men ready to march on the state capital at Harrisburg and that the Rebels had another 250,000 concentrated in Virginia to menace Washington.

Convinced from all these reports that he faced 120,000 Rebels, McClellan, whose army by September 10 was less than twenty miles from Frederick, dared not move quickly or strike boldly for fear of losing again. He finally put his force in motion on September 12 to hunt for Lee, telegraphing to Halleck that he believed the Confederates had marched out of Frederick. McClellan had no idea why the Rebels had done this. He would find out the next day with one of the greatest intelligence coups ever dropped into a general's lap. The windfall came not from Pinkerton or any other federal spy but instead from a Union Army corporal sitting in a meadow near Frederick warming himself in the sun.

Though Lee expected his forty threadbare brigades to live largely off the land, he needed to open a minimal supply line south through the Shenandoah Valley, at least to bring up ammunition. Without that avenue open he would be isolated and cut off as he moved north. But standing in the way of his Valley supply line like a roadblock were the Union garrisons of some 12,000 men at Harpers Ferry and Martinsburg. Lee decided to detach two-thirds of his army to capture Harpers Ferry. Dividing his force, which was already half the size of McClellan's, was risky, but Lee calculated he could seize the garrison and reunite his army before the slow-moving McClellan reacted. With his supply base to the south secured and stocks at Harpers Ferry replenishing his army, Lee could continue north into Pennsylvania unchallenged and, with McClellan in the dark about his movements and intentions, threaten Philadelphia, Baltimore, and Washington. Then the other dominoes would fall—European recognition of the Confederacy, peace Democrats winning the House, Lincoln forced into an armistice.

Tuesday morning, September 9, Lee drafted Special Orders No. 191 to put his audacious plan into motion the next day. Without warning a half-dozen divisions would converge quickly on Harpers Ferry from three directions, trapping the garrison's defenders. Lee's order directed General John Walker's small division to recross the Potomac back into Virginia and come upon Loudoun Heights, just south of Harpers Ferry. Lafayette McLaws would take two divisions and cross the South Mountain range, which was the long extension of the Blue Ridge running northeast from Harpers Ferry into Pennsylvania, and seize the commanding Maryland Heights just north of the town. Stonewall Jackson's three divisions had a longer trek. They would take the National Road leading northwest out of Frederick, cross the South Mountain range at Turner's Gap, then turn west after passing Boonsboro in Maryland, cross the Potomac into the Shenandoah Valley, capture the Union garrison northwest of Harpers Ferry at Martinsburg, and then move to Bolivar Heights west of Harpers Ferry to seal the town off from that direction. The trap would be sprung on September 12. The rest of Lee's army, meanwhile, would move across South Mountain and park at Boonsboro. After Harpers Ferry was taken, all the divisions would reunite at Boonsboro or Hagerstown, Maryland.

As he had done before with McClellan, Lee would undertake the unexpected, dividing his army into four parts, with twenty-six of his forty brigades swooping in on Harpers Ferry to make Union resistance there hopeless. But the risks were tremendous. The remaining fourteen brigades would be dangerously isolated. Jackson could not come to their rescue. The plan depended on speed. It counted on McClellan moving blindly and cautiously.

Lee's adjutant made ten copies of the order to send out to each commander involved in this complicated maneuver. Curiously, no extra precautions were taken with the distribution of this highly sensitive document. The regular couriers detailed to headquarters mounted horses to deliver the copies to the generals. Longstreet carefully read his copy and chewed it like tobacco. Walker pinned his order to the inside of his field jacket. Jackson read his version and transcribed another copy to deliver to General D. H. Hill, who he thought was still under his command and now led a division assigned rearguard duty. Then Jackson burned his copy. Lee, however, had already sent a copy to Hill—but Hill said he never got it.

Saturday morning, September 13, Union sergeant John Bloss and Corporal Barton Mitchell plunked themselves down in a grassy meadow near Frederick's city limits, where their 27th Indiana Regiment had been ordered to set up camp. Mitchell spotted a large envelope nearby and opening it up found three fine cigars with what appeared to be a military document wrapped around them. Curious, Mitchell and Bloss read the piece of paper. It was Lee's Special Orders No. 191. The two enlisted men took their find to their company commander, who rushed the document up the chain of command. How a copy of Orders 191 went missing remains a mystery. Most likely the one Lee sent to Hill, which Hill said he never received, was lost by the careless courier who took it or by Hill's clerk who received it.

Midmorning that day, McClellan, who had ridden into Frederick with his headquarters staff to a tumultuous greeting from the town, was meeting with a delegation of local citizens to discuss the Army's stay there when the copy of Orders 191 was handed to him. McClellan broke off his meeting with the citizens' group to read the document. After he finished, he threw up his hands and exclaimed: "Now I know what to do!"

McClellan realized instantly the importance of what came to be called "the lost dispatch." Not for a minute did he think the paper was a ruse. "I have all the plans of the rebels," he telegraphed Lincoln, "and will catch them in their own trap. . . . Will send you trophies."

Security screening at McClellan's Frederick headquarters—which Pinkerton should have overseen—was lax. Among the citizens in the delegation meeting McClellan was a Confederate sympathizer from the city. There is no evidence McClellan or his aides divulged to the man or anyone else in the delegation that they had received Lee's order. But the sympathizer could clearly see that McClellan's headquarters was suddenly bustling with activity and the man could guess that it was because of some piece of important intelligence the general left their meeting to review. The Marylander located Jeb Stuart near Turner's Gap and explained what he had seen—that the Federals appeared to be embarking on some kind of offensive operation. Stuart passed the tip to Lee in Hagerstown. But Lee was clueless over why McClellan was stirring. Not until the spring of 1863 would he learn that McClellan had a copy of his order when he read stories about it in northern papers.

From Orders 191, McClellan knew that beyond South Mountain, Lee had split his army four ways—and at least two of the Rebel elements were vulnerable to being isolated and beaten. Disparate bits of confusing intelligence that had trickled into his headquarters now made sense. McClellan realized that Jackson was not retreating into Virginia, but instead falling on Harpers Ferry from the west. The Rebels his scouts had reported seeing on National Road beyond South Mountain were Longstreet's. The column informants spotted on Harpers Ferry Road was McLaws's division headed for Maryland Heights. It was all spelled out in the order, which included a timetable. The document's loss was disastrous for Lee, a godsend for McClellan, who could now divide and conquer.

McClellan was even luckier than he realized. Too optimistic with his timetable for capturing Harpers Ferry, Lee by September 13 was falling behind schedule, which only prolonged the dangerous fragmentation of his army. McClellan wired Lincoln that "no time shall be lost" in exploiting this opportunity. But waste time is exactly what McClellan did. Eighteen precious hours passed before his army began marching in response to Orders 191. Still convinced by intelligence from Pinkerton and others that Lee outnumbered him, McClellan intended to inch forward cautiously— even with Lee's playbook in his hands. Aggressiveness simply was not in his DNA. As a result, he gave Lee an additional eighteen hours to recover from a massive security failure.

Late on the night of September 13, McClellan finally ordered Ambrose Burnside's 9th Corps and William Franklin's 6th Corps to march west across Catoctin Creek toward two gaps in the South Mountain range where a Union Army could pass through to reach Lee's forces. Burnside was to proceed to Turner's Gap south of Boonsboro. Franklin's corps was to move to Crampton's Gap, six miles farther south near Rohrersville.

At his Hagerstown headquarters Lee spent much of September 13 out of touch with rapidly unfolding events. He became increasingly concerned as nightfall approached. His operation against Harpers Ferry was now a day behind schedule. Intelligence came trickling in from Stuart's cavalry scouts that the Federals were launching some kind of offensive. To buy time for his divisions to capture Harpers Ferry, Lee quickly shifted forces to block the South Mountain passes through Turner's Gap, Fox's Gap, and Crampton's Gap.

McClellan sent his army forward into battle on September 14. His two corps eventually broke through Confederate defenses at the gaps. If he and his commanders had been more aggressive, they could have saved the Harpers Ferry garrison, crushed different fragments of Lee's army, and perhaps won the war before September ended. But they were glacially slow in moving. McClellan never alerted his senior generals to the secrets revealed in Orders 191. A New York Tribune correspondent at his headquarters reported that the Potomac Army commander "had a singular air of detachment— almost that of a disinterested spectator." McClellan ended up winning the Battle of South Mountain but Rebel commanders held off his corps at two gaps long enough for Jackson to capture Harpers Ferry on September 15 (along with the garrison's 13,000 small arms) and for Lee to begin concentrating his army at a Maryland village close to the Potomac River called Sharpsburg, which was situated just west of the windy Antietam Creek.

Sharpsburg north of Harpers Ferry was a quiet town founded almost a century earlier, whose 1,300 residents lived and worked in stone, brick, and frame structures, and was surrounded by farms, many of which German Americans owned. Antietam Creek snaked east of the town and was as wide as twenty-five yards in spots, with three stone bridges over the stream near Sharpsburg that Union troops could use to cross. By September 15, Lee had Longstreet's and Hill's 18,000 men near the town with guns on the high ground that overlooked the creek. He waited anxiously for Jackson and the rest of the Rebel army, along with the arsenal seized from Harpers Ferry, to join him.

McClellan arrived at the east bank of Antietam Creek that afternoon with an enormous army train that stretched over fifty miles of road. He saw no need to hurry. Setting up his headquarters at a farm in Keedysville, northeast of Sharpsburg, McClellan spent the rest of the day and all of September 16 tending to paperwork, scouting the lower Antietam, and laboriously laying out his men and guns on the east side of the creek to attack Lee on his high ground. The delay gave Lee the opportunity to bring his force at Sharpsburg up to 40,000 men—still less than half the number McClellan was assembling—for the battle the next day.

McClellan made only a halfhearted effort to reconnoiter Lee's positions before sending his marching orders the night of September 16 for the next day's battle. Pinkerton had joined one cavalry party that rode across Antietam Creek and discovered only several Confederate artillery batteries being shifted. As he rode back across the creek, hidden Rebel cannon opened fire, wounding several of the cavalrymen and killing the sorrel Pinkerton had been riding. "I narrowly escaped with my life," he later wrote.

Lafayette Baker sent John Odell, his chubby former Cleveland cop, to Sharpsburg to snoop around McClellan's camp in civilian clothes. It was later claimed that Lincoln had asked for Odell to be his eyes there, but there was no evidence that was the case. Baker on his own seemed to have ordered this spy mission, which accomplished nothing.

• • •

In a bloody cornfield north of Sharpsburg, at a corpse-clogged sunken road southeast of Dunker Church, past one of the stone bridges across Antietam Creek, McClellan and Lee on September 17 threw division after division against each other in some of the hardest fighting of the war. Men exchanged murderous musket volleys standing up just 250 yards apart. Chaos and confusion took charge. Shouted commands went unheard in the cacophony of fire. Battle smoke became so thick, nothing could be seen save for waving regimental flags. Rebel yells were met by Indian war whoops from Yankees. Soldiers fought at times like madmen, led by some officers grown drunk swilling whisky for courage.

McClellan, who slept through the first dawn attacks he ordered, sent his forces off in driblets uncoordinated. Unsettled by the morning wave of slaughter, he ultimately held back a large portion of his available force from the fight. Lee, who sat atop Traveller but had an aide lead his horse by the reins because the general's two hands were splinted and bandaged from earlier accidents, scrambled throughout the day rushing what few reinforcements he had to patch holes in punctured lines.

"The whole landscape for an instant turned slightly red," recalled a New York private. By nightfall the two sides had fought to a draw, ending up pretty much holding the same ground they held at dawn. Cries of men in agony then replaced the boom of cannon. Civilians returned to property littered with corpses. Nearly 6,000 were dead or dying, and another 17,000 fell wounded for a total casualty count of about 23,000—the highest for any one day of the war. It took soldiers ten days to bury the bodies. Among the slightly wounded was Pinkerton's son Willie struck in the knee by shrapnel from an exploding artillery shell.

McClellan awoke Thursday morning, September 18, believing he had "fought the battle splendidly" the day before, as he wrote his wife. With a force now of 62,000 Federals who had survived Antietam or had not fought in the battle at all, McClellan was in an ideal position to continue the attack on Lee's seriously wounded army, which had been reduced to about 36,000 exhausted and hungry men. But McClellan, who still would not risk winning for fear of losing, did not intend to be the first to move on September 18, continuing to believe Lee outnumbered his weakened army. Pinkerton, whose operatives began counting Confederate casualties and prisoners, also still thought the Federals were outnumbered and McClellan's decision to stand down that Thursday was sound. Antietam had been a "brilliant and decisive victory," he later wrote. Critics who faulted McClellan for not moving September 18 were people who fought the battle "on paper."

Lee, who had accomplished none of his strategic goals, defiantly stood his ground Thursday and even mulled continuing his campaign after a short halt to replenish his army. It soon became clear to him, however, that his crippled force could be driven no further. That night Lee began moving his troops back across the Potomac River toward the Shenandoah Valley for the trip south. McClellan made a feeble stab at chasing after the Rebels, but gave it up a day later—content that he had won just by driving Lee out of Maryland. The Army of the Potomac commander now convinced himself that his military reputation had been restored, he should replace Halleck as general in chief, and that Stanton should be fired. His mood grew dark as it quickly became clear that Stanton was going nowhere and Halleck continued sending him telegrams with what he thought were nitpicking complaints.

Shortly after the Rebels slipped away, McClellan sent Pinkerton to Washington once more to spy on the Lincoln administration. On September 22, the detective wandered into the White House and began casually sounding out John Hay in his second-floor corner office, which sat across the waiting room from Lincoln's with a view of Lafayette Square. Hay, one of two aides Lincoln brought with him from Illinois, was always good for political intelligence, Pinkerton found. On the spur of the moment—or at least Pinkerton thought it was the spur of the moment—Hay walked him over to Lincoln's office for a chat with the president. Hay, a twenty-three-year-old Brown University graduate and former journalist, more likely calculated that Pinkerton was a man the president needed to work over.

Lincoln had a lot on his plate that day. Earlier in July he had informed his cabinet he intended to issue an Emancipation Proclamation, which he advertised as "a war measure" rather than "a measure of morality." They advised him to wait until the Army had a military victory. Lincoln, who thought African Americans were entitled to the rights in the Declaration of

Independence but did not believe they were socially equal to whites, agreed to postpone the announcement. Antietam's outcome was not the resounding victory he had hoped for, but he believed it gave him enough political cover to issue a preliminary Emancipation Proclamation on September 22 declaring that if the rebellious states did not return to the Union by January 1, their slaves would be "forever free." An ardent abolitionist, Pinkerton remained silent about the proclamation, likely because his boss, McClellan, was not happy with it. Lafayette Baker, who condemned cruelty to blacks and had freed them from slave catchers, cheered the measure. One of the few letters Baker wrote to Lincoln was about African Americans he found being shamelessly abused in Maryland and the District of Columbia. He asked for instructions to protect "the helpless victims." There is no record of Lincoln responding. Elizabeth Van Lew was overjoyed as well with Lincoln's announcement, although she had to keep her elation secret. Virginia's legislature approved a measure giving Confederate citizens the right to hunt down and kill antislavery Unionists.

Pinkerton, who had had his fill of armchair generals he encountered in Washington this time second-guessing McClellan, settled into a faded green horsehair chair in Lincoln's cluttered office intent on shaking down the president for information useful for the Potomac Army commander. When he worked in his office, Lincoln always wore a loose-fitting, black broadcloth suit whose cuffs were frayed and shabby-looking carpet slippers on his feet. He slumped into his worn leather chair when he met visitors like Pinkerton and casually draped a long leg over one of its arms. Critics still sneered that he was an uncouth country lawyer unfit for the White House, but Lincoln had developed into a cunning administrator who knew how to get what he wanted. And what Lincoln wanted now was to turn the tables on Pinkerton, milk him for information, and send him back to McClellan with a message from the commander in chief.

Lincoln had grown particularly anxious when barroom talk among military officers about a coup reached the White House. He would later fire an Army major with loose lips. Burnside, whom Halleck had brought with him to interview McClellan at Harrison's Landing in July, had picked up rumblings then among the general's officers about marching to Washington and overthrowing the government. After Antietam, Lincoln moved delicately to determine if McClellan was involved in this coup talk the White House kept hearing.

Pinkerton was now being played for a gullible patsy. Lincoln, as friendly as he could be, told the detective he wanted to learn everything he could about the movements of McClellan's army. He wasn't being critical of McClellan over what he might have done or not done, Lincoln assured Pinkerton. He just wanted to find out what the detective knew. The battles at South Mountain and Antietam were hard-fought victories "of the greatest value to the nation," Lincoln said, and McClellan had succeeded in pushing the Rebels out of Maryland and relieving the danger to Washington. Lincoln said he owed "a deep debt of gratitude" to the general for taking command of the army in a time of great peril.

Pinkerton relaxed.

But there were some things Lincoln said he wanted to know that perhaps Pinkerton could enlighten him on.

The detective agreed that McClellan did not burden the White House with a lot of minor details. What did the president want to know?

Had everything been done to hold on to Harpers Ferry? Lincoln asked.

Pinkerton assured him it had.

What kind of condition were the two armies in when they met at Antietam?

The Rebel force numbered 140,000, Pinkerton claimed, and McClellan had only about 90,000. Lincoln said he thought McClellan had about 100,000, but he added quickly that he agreed with Pinkerton's count for the Rebels. (Lincoln was lying on that last point, likely to flatter the detective; he knew the 140,000 estimate was wildly inflated.)

Why didn't the Army of the Potomac fight on September 18? Lincoln continued. Why was it slow to move in the days that followed?

The dead and wounded needed to be cleared, ammunition was short, and McClellan had to be careful because he faced a superior enemy force, Pinkerton explained. In the days that followed, the Union Army "had to move cautiously in order to do so successfully."

"I must say, General," Pinkerton wrote later in his report to McClellan, "that I never saw a man feel better than he did with these explanations. He expressed himself as highly pleased and gratified with all you had done." Pinkerton could not have been more wrong. Lincoln was becoming increasingly fed up with McClellan, but he knew Pinkerton would carry back to the general that the president was in his corner.

With practically no notice, Lincoln arrived at McClellan's camp along Antietam Creek on October 1 to review his troops and privately prod the general to start moving. Pinkerton squired the president around the battlefield and posed for a photograph with him in front of the detective's tent. Lincoln took a train back to Washington on October 4, believing he had McClellan's promise to pursue Lee's army into Virginia. Pinkerton hopped aboard to continue his spying on the president. "There is no doubt in my mind but that he now appreciates your worth," Pinkerton wrote McClellan. Lincoln "feels disposed to give you all you want." Again it was faulty political intelligence and Pinkerton could have known he was being played for a sucker if he had read the newspapers carefully. The day after the train trip, John Hay had penned an anonymous article in a Midwest paper (likely cleared by Lincoln since it reflected his sentiments) that stated sarcastically that if McClellan had a million men, he would claim he could not act unless he had "just another regiment."

Finally, on October 26, after almost six weeks of stalling at Antietam, McClellan's army of 100,000 began crossing the Potomac, which took nine long days. He spent the time trading angry letters with Washington (blaming the administration for failing to support his army) and continuing to keep the White House in the dark over what he planned to do with his force besides move it slowly south. He appeared to Lincoln to be wandering aimlessly, with no clear idea where the enemy was or of its plans—which was pretty close to being the case. McClellan's snail's pace gave Lee plenty of time to place Longstreet's corps between Richmond and the Yankees, while Jackson's corps remained in the Shenandoah Valley on the Union flank. Lincoln had enough. On November 5, after midterm elections left Republicans still in control of Congress, he ordered Halleck to fire McClellan.

Fearing McClellan might launch a military uprising, Stanton carefully engineered the transition to the new Army of the Potomac commander,

Ambrose E. Burnside, the head of McClellan's 9th Corps who had impressed Lincoln with his North Carolina operations before joining McClellan and whose bushy muttonchops supposedly fathered the term *sideburns*. McClellan, however, accepted the dismissal gracefully, basking in the rousing cheers thousands of his men gave him when he departed. For several weeks Stanton still remained suspicious that the general might lead a coup. McClellan believed government agents were following him and opening his mail so he began sending telegrams to friends in code. The *New York Herald* reported that the agents shadowing McClellan were Pinkerton's men. McClellan wrote the detective that he knew the story was false. "I have never doubted your friendship for me," the general said.

Pinkerton did not have McClellan under surveillance because, after the general's firing, his spymaster followed him out the door. Disgusted with how McClellan had been treated, and unwilling to work for Burnside, whom he didn't trust and thought was incompetent, Pinkerton resigned. He claimed Stanton tried to talk him into staying as the Army of the Potomac's spy chief, but that does not ring true. Stanton knew that Pinkerton had fed McClellan's delusions of being outnumbered by the enemy and Burnside was happy to be rid of the detective.

Pinkerton had George Bangs buy from the Army the latest gray mare he had been riding and ship her to him. He continued haggling with the Treasury Department into the winter of 1865 over unpaid bills dating back to his spy work for McClellan in the Ohio Department. He also ordered his detectives who had worked for the Army of the Potomac to return to his company headquarters and he boxed up all his military records (including the spy reports) and shipped them to Chicago. Burnside was left with practically empty intelligence files when he took command.

With Pinkerton out of the picture, Stanton allowed Lafayette Baker to expand his force from two dozen operatives in October to about thirty in November and become Washington's only secret service chief hunting southern subversives. He proved to be even less competent in military intelligence and counterintelligence than Pinkerton.

Pinkerton quit being a spy, but he continued as a federal contractor, having his detectives investigate fraud in New York's Disbursing and Mustering

Office and illegal contraband trade in the cotton-buying operations Union forces supervised in the Deep South territory they occupied. This was work far more suited to his detective skills than espionage. Pinkerton also continued to share with McClellan gossip he picked up on the Army of the Potomac commanders who succeeded the general. When military officers later asked for his records—particularly his estimates of Confederate capabilities—Pinkerton balked. Only McClellan could have access to those files in preparing his lengthy after-action report on his campaigns. "I have always considered the service in which I was engaged by you as personal to you," he wrote the general to explain why he would not cooperate. That was true and was why he had failed as a military intelligence officer.

FREDERICKSBURG

ith an expensive new carbine strapped to his back that he bought for twenty-five dollars, George Sharpe marched his 120th Regiment on October 17 from Upton's Hill in the western end of what was later designated Arlington County, Virginia, to the Fairfax Seminary, farther west. He still felt the effects of his old lung ailment, fighting off fatigue as he walked with his troops. On November 1, his men, with their shelter tents strapped to their knapsacks, joined Colonel George B. Hall's 2nd (Excelsior) Brigade. Hall's brigade was part of Brigadier General Daniel Sickles's 2nd Division in the Army of the Potomac, which Burnside now commanded. Lincoln and members of his cabinet reviewed the former New York congressman's division that day. Sharpe thought there would be no campaigning during the cold snowy months. Burnside's army would simply shelter into winter quarters. But if they did fight, "it will be in one of the southern states," Sharpe wrote his uncle, Jansen Hasbrouck.

It was soon not too difficult for Sharpe to surmise that the 120th would not be resting in winter quarters. For four weeks his regiment and the others in the Army of the Potomac slogged slowly over muddy, rain-soaked roads and swollen rivers until November 28, when they were encamped within a couple miles of Falmouth, a small port town on the north side of the Rappahannock River. Falmouth was just opposite Fredericksburg, their military objective just off the river's south side. The boyhood home of George Washington, old Fredericksburg, with its 5,000 residents and stately brick buildings, had become a key commercial and transportation center halfway between Washington and Richmond. The Rappahannock twisted northwest from Chesapeake Bay, looping around Fredericksburg on its east and north sides, with its main tributary, the Rapidan River, feeding into it just west of the city.

Ambrose Burnside did not consider himself qualified to lead the Army of the Potomac, which soon proved to be the case. He started out well enough. Instead of marching straight south against Longstreet's corps and depending on the single-track Orange and Alexandria Railroad line to supply his force, the general, with Lincoln's consent, moved his cumbersome 120,000-man army fairly quickly southeast to Falmouth, where he would have a safer supply line from the Potomac River just north. From Falmouth, he planned to rapidly cross the Rappahannock, capture Fredericksburg, and use it as his base for moving fifty-six miles farther south and attacking Lee at Richmond. The first elements of Burnside's army began arriving at Falmouth on November 17, but the pontoon bridges his forces would use to cross the deep Rappahannock and capture Fredericksburg were late in coming, giving Lee time to rush Longstreet's and Jackson's corps to the city to block the Union advance. The first pontoon bridges finally showed up on November 25, but by the time Burnside's engineers had finished laying all of them across the river more than two weeks later, Longstreet and Jackson had their troops firmly dug in on the south side of the Rappahannock and were waiting for the Union Army.

Burnside turned out to be inept at managing a large force. He also misunderstood his enemy across the river. It wasn't so much that he had bad intelligence on the enemy, which was the case with McClellan. Burnside's problem was that he had little intelligence, good or bad. And he had nobody to blame but himself. His front had been pretty much stable for almost a month, giving him plenty of time to reconnoiter the Rebels on the other side with his cavalry and spies. Pinkerton had abandoned the Army of the Potomac, but he left behind one capable operative to take his place—John Babcock.

A handsome and dapper man sporting a black vest studded with shiny brass buttons and wearing a hat always cocked jauntily to the side, Babcock had moved to Chicago in 1855, working first as an apprentice draftsman in an architectural firm. Showing a talent as a sketch artist, he later set up his own business as an architect. He became a fitness enthusiast as well, visiting a gymnasium often and joining a local rowing team. When Pinkerton left, Babcock was technically still in the Army's Sturgis Rifles, where the detective had discovered him and his mapmaking talent. Babcock was ordered to report to Burnside, who wanted him to assume Pinkerton's secret service duties and report to him as a confidential agent. Babcock knew Burnside well. He had done architectural work for him in Chicago. He liked the general—although he said McClellan's military ability was "superior." Pinkerton's "unceremonious departure" had left the secret service department "in a rather disorderly condition," Babcock told Burnside, but he said he would take the job with conditions. He wanted to work as a civilian and be paid $250 a month. Anxious to set up a spy bureau, Burnside agreed. To partly solve the problem of Pinkerton's absconding with all the intelligence reports, Babcock rode to Washington and copied the ones filed there.

Babcock soon soured on his new job, however. He quickly came to resent Burnside's staff, which he claimed was a "worthless and inefficient" bunch. The Army commander's aides viewed Babcock as a holdover from Pinkerton's operation, which they had distrusted. When Burnside's chief of staff one day made a disparaging remark about Pinkerton, Babcock undiplomatically let him know he resented it. Burnside's spy chief got the silent treatment after that. Babcock identified a double agent who had worked for Pinkerton and spotted him lurking around their Falmouth headquarters. But otherwise Burnside and his senior aides ignored his small operation. Babcock's men weren't allowed to interrogate runaway slaves, refugees, and prisoners brought in. The interrogation summaries he saw from others were useless, he thought. Nor was he able to investigate shady civilians and hucksters who infested their camp.

Burnside paid dearly for not using the intelligence capability he had at hand. The general failed to detect that Lee did not have Jackson's force at Fredericksburg until November 30. The Potomac Army commander could have attacked across the river before then, when Lee had only half his army there with Longstreet's corps. When Lee's army was finally assembled in front of him, Burnside—who did not use his cavalry to gather information, who had left Unionists around Fredericksburg untapped for information, and who did not send up his balloons until the last minute—mistakenly believed that the bulk of the Confederate force was arranged ten to fifteen miles downriver of Fredericksburg and that the Rebel position on Lee's left flank behind the town was relatively weak. Just the opposite was the case. The Marye's Heights ridge behind Fredericksburg was far more heavily defended by the Rebels than the less formidable ground on the Confederate right south of the town.

Burnside's 120,000 crossed the Rappahannock in icy, dense fog on December 12 and the next morning attacked Lee's army of 85,000 entrenched on higher ground. Union general William B. Franklin's left wing was to attack Jackson's Confederates on the right, while the Union right flank was to probe Longstreet's corps on the left, dug in at Marye's Heights west of Fredericksburg. If Franklin rolled up Jackson, the Union right was to mount a real attack. But Burnside issued confusing orders and Franklin failed to push forward with his 50,000 men. Meanwhile, the probes from the Union's right flank turned into a series of suicidal brigade attacks as waves of Federal soldiers streamed uphill out of Fredericksburg only to be mowed down by ranks of dug-in Rebel defenders from the Marye's Heights high ground pouring down volleys of fire. More than 12,500 Union men were killed, wounded, or went missing, most of them at Marye's Heights.

Sharpe's regiment mercifully escaped the slaughter that decimated so many others at Fredericksburg. Since December 4 most of the 120th had been detached to an engineering outfit to help build corduroy roads about sixteen miles south of the Rappahannock. It was not until the afternoon of December 13 that his men reached Sickles's 2nd Division, which was across the river with Franklin's left wing and taking heavy cannon fire from Jackson's corps. Sharpe's regiment was immediately ordered to the front line within easy musket range of Rebel soldiers. He put out eighty skirmishers who found cover in a ditch within two dozen yards of the Confederates and throughout the rest of the afternoon and evening rotated soldiers in and out of that dangerous spot with shells shrieking over their heads. This was their first time in combat. Several were wounded. Although their fighting was not intense December 13, Sharpe felt his men kept their cool under fire. Likewise, Sickles was pleased with the performance of the rookie regiment and its commander.

Sharpe had an opportunity to demonstrate his linguistic skills that day. Near the 120th was a New York City regiment composed almost entirely of French immigrants who did not speak English. The colonel commanding them did not speak their language, so the Frenchmen could not understand his commands. Confusion resulted, threatening a serious break in the lines until Sharpe, who was fluent in French, intervened to put the regiment in its proper position.

Confederate artillery fire on the 120th and other regiments in Sickles's division did not end until dusk. The Confederates advanced no farther and the two sides settled into their positions for the night. Sharpe's regiment was ordered forward thirty paces to relieve another regiment at the crest of a hill, his men having to walk over dead bodies and moaning soldiers near death along the way. Sharpe then advanced a company of skirmishers to a ditch just ahead of them. When morning dawned December 14, the forward skirmishers found themselves under brisk fire from Rebel sharpshooters, so Sharpe ordered them back to his more sheltered position briefly, then sent them back out to repel a Confederate advance of skirmishers. The rest of the regiment hunkered down to endure occasional enemy artillery rounds plopping on their position. Otherwise, combat virtually ceased on December 14. During that night, as the sound of Confederates chopping trees and hammering out barricades could be heard from afar, Sharpe bedded down his men, ordering a squad from each company to remain on alert while the other exhausted soldiers slept clutching their muskets.

Burnside wanted to personally lead another charge against Confederate defenses on December 14, but his generals talked him out of it. By 2 p.m. on December 15, firing had ceased and the field in front of Sharpe's regiment had grown silent. Under a flag of truce, both sides' stretcher-bearers roamed the battlefield to collect their dead and wounded. About midnight, with a bitter-cold storm raging, Sharpe's regiment marched back across the Rappahannock over the pontoon bridges to a position the 2nd Division occupied a half mile from the river's north bank. The next day they moved back to the camp they had occupied before the battle. Burnside took the blame for the debacle at Fredericksburg, but it was Lincoln and his administration that bore the brunt of the criticism over another failed campaign. Fredericksburg became the symbol for all that was wrong with the war being waged. "If there is a worse place than Hell," Lincoln lamented, "I am in it."

Fredericksburg's residents thought the winter had been quite mild, but for the southern and northern soldiers camped there it seemed severe. Frigid rains pelted the men, left to burrow into makeshift shelters as best they could. By January the snow reached one foot deep. Typhoid fever, diarrhea, and scurvy (medical officers attributed it to lack of fresh vegetables) ravaged the Army of the Potomac. Sharpe's regiment suffered its share of sickness and death. By January he had fit for duty only 400 of the 906 men he started out with from Kingston four months earlier.

Just before the Fredericksburg battle, Hattie Lawton was finally released from Castle Thunder, along with a Union cavalry colonel, as part of a prisoner exchange. The Pennsylvania colonel, who had become friends with Pryce Lewis at Castle Thunder, secretly carried a note from the agent to Pinkerton. Lawton went immediately to Washington to brief federal authorities on what had happened to Timothy Webster.

Pinkerton had a subordinate write a letter back to Lewis, which reached him on New Year's Eve. The former spy chief "regrets your arrest, your sufferings, your long confinement, and that his efforts thus far, have not proved successful in your liberation," the letter read. Everyone at the Pinkerton agency "desire[s] to express the wish and hope of your early deliverance."

Van Lew and other Richmonders could hear the muffled rumble of artillery fire from the Fredericksburg battle to the north. The Confederate capital had become infested with pickpockets, prostitutes, burglars, and thugs. Van

Lew and other ladies felt threatened on city streets. Rapes increased. Castle Godwin became packed with criminals. Winder's corrupt detectives raided brothels and gambling houses with little effect. Burglars even struck the home of the provost marshal general, who was already in an ill mood after he learned he would not be promoted to major general.

The wealthy began feeling the economic pinch. Slaves slipped away and headed north, taking with them clothing, bedding, and any other articles they could carry from mansions. Confederate currency became deeply depreciated. Citizens were at the mercy of speculators. With food and fuel becoming scarcer because of the Union naval blockade taking hold, the city's young elite organized what they called the "Starvation Club," with spartan supplies for weekly parties. Van Lew had the resources to get through the shortages, but conditions became more serious for the working class. Bread riots later erupted among hungry and angry women, which Jeff Davis had to personally defuse. To compound Richmond's woes, a smallpox epidemic broke out in poor sections of the city, which had to be quarantined.

Van Lew had to be even more careful now in aiding Union war prisoners. Looking out their windows, Richmonders were outraged to see Rebel soldiers from Fredericksburg walking through the streets barefoot in the snow. They became even more hostile to the Union men crammed in their jails, whom they saw as the perpetrators of this evil visited upon them. One lady kept a pile of Federals' bones at her pump to enjoy the view. Another woman hunted for a Yankee skull to hold toilet trinkets.

Lee's army began to feel the effects of subversion by one of Van Lew's Unionists. For the Battle of Fredericksburg and afterward, Lee had endless trouble feeding and equipping his army. Part of his problem could be blamed on the chronic incompetence of the head of the Confederate Commissary Service, charged with supplying his force. But the other part of the problem at Fredericksburg had been transportation. To get food and equipment to his troops there, Lee had depended on the single-track Richmond, Fredericksburg and Potomac Railroad, whose superintendent was Samuel Ruth.

Ruth slowed the rail shipments to Lee's army at Fredericksburg. He had work crews take their time repairing track and bridges. Loyal employees also sent him intelligence they picked up on their trips to Fredericksburg. Ruth had to be clever in masking his activities. His boss, Peter Daniel, would never tolerate him openly subverting Lee. Fortunately for Ruth, other lines in the system were notoriously slow and inefficient, so problems with the Richmond, Fredericksburg and Potomac Railroad did not stand out as unusual. And Ruth, who was a seasoned railroad man, always had a reasonable excuse for the bottlenecks. Even if he had been a loyal Confederate, his line still would have underperformed. The track, rolling stock, and employees were too overworked to quickly transport the crushing load of supplies Lee's army needed. Daniel was constantly writing Richmond authorities pleading for more crossties, firewood, and slaves for his track and Richmond kept turning him down.

Lee was a professional engineer and knew a thing or two about rail mechanics. He strongly suspected Ruth was more than just a lackadaisical superintendent. He thought the man was a traitor. On December 8, five days before the Fredericksburg battle, Lee wrote a confidential dispatch to Davis complaining about Ruth's lack of energy in hauling supplies to his troops. It was making his stand at Fredericksburg untenable. Daniel tried to smooth things over with Lee but the general wouldn't be placated. After the battle, Lee fired off a second letter to Davis on January 23, again describing the severe supply shortage his men faced and suggesting that Captain Thomas R. Sharp, a quartermaster officer from North Carolina experienced in rail operations, replace Ruth. A hard-driving and no-nonsense officer, Sharp would not have tolerated delays as Ruth had, and military transport on the line would likely have improved.

Davis refused to oust Ruth. He had worked for the Richmond, Fredericksburg and Potomac Railroad for twenty-five years and compiled a spotless safety record. Ruth also had powerful Confederate friends who defended him. He was allowed to continue his clandestine work against Lee.

Sharpe's men moved out on January 20, 1863, for another attack. But the 120th trudged slowly along poor roads, making only a mile and a half of progress before it stopped for the evening as a winter nor'easter blew in, which continued through the next day. Burnside wanted to march his army up along the Rappahannock and cross the river to attack and turn Lee's left flank above Fredericksburg. The heavy rains that came, however, made muddy roads impassable. Wagons and artillery sank to their axles in the deep, sticky muck. "I saw often sixteen horses endeavoring to move a single caisson without success," Sharpe recalled. Burnside gave up a day later and his army returned to camp. The embarrassing foray became known as the "Mud March." On the other side of the river, Confederate soldiers watching Burnside's troops become hopelessly stuck jeered and held up signs to taunt them. Babcock thought Burnside deserved to be hooted. Sharpe noticed the Rebels had painted on one of their signs details on how the Federals had planned to carry out the march, which apparently were not a secret to anyone.

About the only silver lining Sharpe found after the disastrous Mud March: an Army paymaster arrived at his regiment and paid his men. But they were shorted in the amount they were supposed to receive. The paymaster had only enough money to give them what they were due up to October 31 and their fees to the sutlers who followed the army and sold them provisions ate up a good deal of what was left. Sharpe had $5,994 of the soldiers' pay he planned to take back to Washington in a few days to wire back to their families.

Fed up with his bungling, Lincoln fired Burnside and replaced him with Major General Joseph "Fighting Joe" Hooker, one of the Potomac Army's corps commanders who had been critical of his superior. Sharpe would serve under Hooker, not as a regimental commander but instead as the general's spy chief.

1863

Sixteen

"THE GREAT GAME"

George Sharpe was in Washington on February 3 depositing his regiment's pay and wiring a money draft to his uncle Jansen to be put in a New York bank for his men. Sharpe had other things on his mind that day. He wrote his uncle that he might be joining General Hooker's staff. "I have the offer if I choose to accept it," he said. But he kept quiet about what exactly this staff work entailed, hinting only to Uncle Jansen that it was now keeping him extremely busy in Washington. Sharpe had just returned to the capital at 11 p.m. on February 7 from a side trip to Baltimore the day before. "This is confidential," he warned his uncle. "Don't tell anyone about the Baltimore trip. I hope to be able to see you soon, and then you will know more of it." Sharpe's wife, Carrie, would visit him at the end of February and he would have an opportunity then to confide in her.

Sharpe had good reason to be closemouthed. He had not yet accepted Hooker's offer, but he agreed to do a favor for the general, which was why he traveled to Baltimore. There he met at Barnum's Hotel Colonel Daniel Van Buren, a fellow lawyer from Kingston and now an adjutant at Fort Monroe.

The two men discussed how the Potomac Army could put spies behind Confederate lines posing as Union deserters or contraband smugglers.

Of all things, it was Sharpe's fluency in French that had brought him to the attention of Hooker. When the general took command of the Army of the Potomac on January 26, he had apparently heard the story about one of his officers who had put the French regiment on the correct line in the Fredericksburg battle. Hooker summoned that officer. He asked Sharpe how fast he could translate French. About as fast as he could read it, the colonel responded. Hooker handed Sharpe a book written in French describing the organization of that country's secret service and asked Sharpe to translate it. Sharpe did and then asked to be returned to his regiment. But Hooker, impressed with the colonel's language skills, instead asked him to submit a plan for organizing a secret service. Sharpe again complied.

Impressed once more, Hooker asked Sharpe if he would head up the Army of the Potomac's spy bureau. Sharpe wanted to stay with his regiment, but he told the general he would give the offer some thought. Perhaps it was as a tryout or an assignment to whet his appetite that Hooker had sent Sharpe to Baltimore to brainstorm infiltrating agents. Whatever the reason, after he returned from Baltimore, Sharpe agreed to join Hooker's staff as his spymaster.

He had no experience in espionage matters. He had sent one brief intelligence report to Burnside a month earlier on Confederate forces moving through the Shenandoah Valley, based on his regiment's interrogation of Rebel deserters who seemed intelligent to him. But Sharpe took to the secret world almost immediately. A general order announcing his move to Hooker's staff did not appear until more than a month later and the title the order conferred upon him—deputy provost marshal general—revealed little of the true work he would do. The spy service he was ordered to lead was given a bland name—the Bureau of Military Information—which obscured its true intent. Like Pinkerton, Sharpe began using a code name in some of his correspondence with agents—"Colonel Streight"—and many of his informants never knew they were working for an espionage agency. But unlike Pinkerton, Sharpe was a military man, with some combat experience. He understood the intelligence a commander needed and the value of speeding information to him quickly.

It would have been difficult for Sharpe to turn down the Potomac Army's new leader. The hard-charging Joe Hooker was extremely popular with his troops. He was not as beloved by fellow generals who thought he was an egotistical ladder climber with a big mouth. Lincoln knew he was taking a chance naming him chief of the North's most important army. A tall, handsome soldier, clean-shaven with light auburn hair tossed back, Hooker was far too vocal with his opinions, insubordinate at times, and an intriguer. He gambled and drank but disliked the nickname "Fighting Joe," which reporters had given him, because he thought it made him look like a hothead. The prostitutes who followed his camp did not get their slang name "hookers" from him, as conventional wisdom has it, but whores did tag along with his wink and nod. Navy secretary Welles thought he was too fond of whisky and had other bad habits. A staff officer described Hooker as "little better than a drunken West Point military adventurer." But Fighting Joe understood how to command the Army of the Potomac better than the two generals before him.

A career soldier, Hooker had compiled a commendable record leading from the front as a brigade, division, and corps commander. Shot in the foot at Antietam, he was convinced he could run the Potomac Army far better than McClellan or Burnside. The northern press hailed his replacing Burnside, but both Halleck, who had a long-running feud with Hooker, and Stanton strenuously opposed the move. Lincoln coupled the appointment with a frank letter to Hooker admonishing him for his naked ambition. Lee was surprised when he heard the news, but it came with no great respect for Hooker's ability to handle such a large command. Hooker had an equally low opinion of Lee, considering him a subpar officer.

The army bequeathed to Fighting Joe was not as bad as Burnside's detractors made it out to be, but it needed repair. Morale was back in the dumps, divisions were poorly policed, and medical services were substandard. Hooker found desertions running at two hundred a day, with relatives sending soldiers packages of civilian clothes to help them flee. Hooker ordered his commissary officers to issue troops vegetables and bread twice a week and upgraded field hospitals. He passed out medals and had the men sew on shoulder patches designating their corps to instill martial spirit and unit pride. Morale improved, sick list numbers and desertions dropped. But feuding generals under Hooker still grumbled behind his back and Halleck grew irritated when he bypassed him to deal directly with Lincoln, who continued to worry that his new army commander was too cocky.

Hooker also re-formed his army's intelligence-gathering operation. As a division commander he had chafed at the dearth of information he received from higher headquarters on the enemy and had eagerly employed his own spies, many of them escaped slaves. He had no qualms about working with Lafayette Baker and the seamy covert tactics he employed. When McClellan headed the Army of the Potomac, Hooker had one of Lowe's balloons assigned to him and flew in it. When he took over the Army of the Potomac, he found no intelligence documents on Confederate forces in his headquarters. Recalled his chief of staff, Daniel Butterfield: "We were almost as ignorant of the enemy in our immediate front as if they had been in China."

Hooker issued strict orders to his commanders to speed up delivery of deserters, war prisoners, escaped slaves, refugees, and southern newspapers to his headquarters so Sharpe could exploit them for information. He vowed to court-martial officers who sent in incorrect or inflated reports on the enemy from their pickets. Stanton cleared bureaucratic hurdles so Hooker had unfettered access to Lowe's balloons. Sharpe's new Bureau of Military Information was ordered to send out spies, rake in all the intelligence coming from Hooker's commanders and balloons, analyze this flood of information, and quickly produce for him useful reports on the enemy. The New York lawyer turned regimental commander became an energetic pioneer of what spy agencies today call "all-source intelligence."

Sharpe's spy reports went to Hooker through his chief of staff and alter ego, Major General Daniel "Little Dan" Butterfield, a short and frail former businessman with sad eyes and a walrus mustache, who had led a division under Hooker when he commanded a corps. A skilled administrator,

Butterfield (who designed the shoulder patches) shared his boss's enthusiasm for all-source intelligence and worked closely with Sharpe to provide it.

Butterfield, however, was not Sharpe's immediate boss. He and his Bureau of Military Information were put under the administrative control of Marsena Patrick, the Army of the Potomac's provost marshal general. Patrick had early misgivings about this new information bureau, questioning how it could be organized with "so little good material" to work with, as he put it. Butterfield's endorsement of Sharpe didn't mean much to him; Patrick despised the chief of staff, whose mission in life, it seemed to him, was to generate more paperwork for everybody. But after Patrick interviewed Sharpe for the job on February 10, he found the colonel's civilian education and amicable demeanor far more impressive than his thin army record. "I think he would be a pleasant man to be associated with," Patrick recorded in his diary.

For the stern provost marshal general, that was high praise. Patrick was a slender man, bald on the top with a fringe of hair on the sides of his head sticking out like cat ears and a bushy gray beard covering his face. He looked like "he could bite the head off a tenpenny nail," he was so mean, according to a private who worked under him. Others shared that opinion until the day he died. Patrick once dressed down an officer so harshly the thirty-five-year-old man wept like a child. Patrick knew he was not popular with the units he commanded but he thought his soldiers at least respected his ironfisted rule. He acted like a martinet with his wife and children as well.

Patrick suffered chronic intestinal disorders, hemorrhoids, and shoulder pains. (The shoulder was made worse, he admitted, after he knocked down a subordinate for being insolent.) He tried electric treatments for the bad shoulder and swallowed an iodine preparation for his stomach ailments. Combat, however, had made Patrick more religious and he did have a gentle side when he cared to show it. He enjoyed feminine company and considered himself a lady charmer, particularly with Virginia women from whom he wanted information. He also sympathized with war victims on both sides, posting guards to protect southern homes and chastising soldiers who marauded noncombatants.

Patrick ran away from home and a domineering mother when he was ten years old. At West Point, he ranked only forty-eight out of a class of fifty-six. He served in the Mexican War but later resigned from the Army and became a successful farmer, organizing an agricultural college. At the Civil War's outbreak, Patrick was inspector general of New York's volunteer army. At the Antietam battle, he accumulated a solid, although not brilliant, combat record as a brigade commander. Afterward, McClellan made Patrick his provost marshal general for the Army of the Potomac because of his reputation for unflinching honesty. Also, Patrick had not been a particularly outstanding field commander, so he was channeled into staff work.

As provost marshal general, Patrick had a wide range of policing duties— enforcing camp discipline, battling vice, arresting criminals, carrying out court-martial sentences, rounding up deserters and stragglers. By the end of January he had 2,830 men under him to carry out these assignments. During his first months on the job, Patrick also spent more and more time on another function he was ordered to oversee—intelligence collection. He set up a system of guards and passes for security against Rebel agents. In southern territory the Union controlled, Patrick also fancied himself a seductive sleuth, playing cat-and-mouse for information with the wives of husbands who were off to war. When Hooker took over, he told Patrick to continue his intelligence oversight. Patrick had served with Hooker under Burnside and was not impressed with the man. He had an equally low opinion of Stanton, who found Patrick suspect because he backed the Democratic Party. But though the two were often at odds over travel passes, the treatment of slaves, and arrests of civilians, Stanton did not interfere with Patrick's promotion to brigadier general.

Sharpe quickly put together what became the war's most highly developed intelligence activity. He used many of the same sources Pinkerton tapped, interviewing hundreds of prisoners, deserters, and war refugees and sending out operatives to troll for information. He found southern soldiers on leave to homes in territory the Union now controlled to be particularly open with his agents. He continued Pinkerton's use of blacks and other minorities, like southern Virginia's Pamunkey Indians, eventually employing five African Americans and paying them the same as what his white spies received. By the end of February, Sharpe also had a large letter-opening operation under way as Pinkerton had. Bags full of confiscated Confederate mail, mostly intended for Maryland, were captured in Virginia's Northern Neck, giving him early hints about Rebel troop numbers and movements around Fredericksburg as well as tidbits on Confederate generals, the condition of their forces, and the problems they were having with soldiers slipping away from their camps.

Sharpe took his intelligence operation an important step further than his predecessor. Pinkerton had compiled his reports based only on his interrogations and what his espionage agents discovered. The rest—cavalry scout dispatches, balloon reports, and all the other bits of information that found their way to headquarters—bypassed Pinkerton and went directly to McClellan, who sorted through the jumble to come up with his own foggy picture of the enemy. Sharpe now had access to everything that came to Hooker's headquarters—the reports from cavalry reconnaissance missions, Signal Corps stations, and balloons in the sky, the interceptions of Confederate flag messages, the newspapers from Richmond, the intelligence telegraphed from neighboring commands. Sharpe's bureau then sorted, synthesized, and analyzed all the information to present to Hooker the clearest, most comprehensive picture of the enemy a Union commander had ever had. The Bureau of Military Information was a major innovation, decades ahead of its time.

Sharpe eventually had seventy agents. They worked seven days a week—no time off. He called them "guides" or "scouts"—never "spies." They infiltrated into enemy territory with no Confederate credentials or sometimes with false passes for identities they wanted to assume. Occasionally agents wore Rebel uniforms but more often they dressed in civilian clothes. Their expenses in the field were high. Bribes had to be paid for information. Patrick delivered monthly to Sharpe southern currency confiscated from prisoners. In April, for example, 1,751 Confederate dollars were turned over to the information bureau. Intelligence now moved quickly to the Potomac Army headquarters. His agents who crossed Rebel lines returned frequently, delivering their reports most of the time from memory rather than risking being caught with documents on them. Resident spies who lived in Rebel territory, on the other hand, sent written reports conveyed by a cadre of couriers Sharpe employed—some of them women. Occasionally the information was enciphered in tiny script on slips of paper. Sharpe had crude invisible ink on hand, but it was rarely used.

His top aide was Pinkerton's skilled mapmaker, John Babcock. While Sharpe was still mulling whether to take the spy job, Babcock sent a memo to Hooker outlining how a "secret service department" should be set up. The report served as a blueprint for the bureau Sharpe organized. With seven operatives he brought with him from the old organization, Babcock became Sharpe's chief interrogator and a human storehouse of facts and figures about Lee's army. A newspaper after the war reported that Babcock's work became so damaging to the southern cause, the Confederates wanted to kidnap and execute him. Every day a long line of runaways, refugees, and Rebel soldiers waiting to be interviewed stretched out from his tent.

In just the month of February, Babcock and his team questioned prisoners and deserters from two dozen enemy infantry regiments and artillery batteries. Babcock's clerks kept extensive files on the statements of each Rebel interrogated along with maps they drew for the interviewer on unit locations. Sharpe devised an incentive that helped separate fact from fiction in these interviews. A Confederate who made a full and accurate statement about what he knew was recommended for release to work in the North rather than being returned to a dreaded prison camp. The bureau's interrogators became more adept than Pinkerton's at spotting phony deserters Lee dispatched to plant misinformation. If Sharpe and Babcock doubted a deserter's authenticity, they were willing to use torture to extract the truth.

Third-ranking in the spy bureau was Captain John McEntee, a Kingston neighbor who had operated a flour and feed business with his father and had done business with Sharpe before the war. Tall and gaunt-looking with dark, brooding eyes under thick brows, McEntee rose to the rank of company commander in the 20th New York State Militia, in which Sharpe had first served. He moved to the information bureau just before he turned twenty-eight because it seemed to him less structured than an infantry regiment and a place where he could operate with more independence, which proved to be the case. Sharpe had McEntee lead far-flung intelligence expeditions behind enemy lines. He also became expert in the makeup of the Confederate Army facing Hooker. Babcock nicknamed him "McAnty."

Sharpe's bureau became an unconventional organization, attracting freethinkers who proved well suited to gathering and analyzing intelligence under wartime pressure. Men mostly on the lower social scale performed the actual spying for him. Sharpe had military officers direct the espionage activities, but with the exception of Babcock, McEntee, and himself on occasion, the officers were not personally engaged in the snooping. This setup ensured that every spy mission had a manager over it. Sharpe found that the agents he dispatched rarely returned with important smoking-gun intelligence. No Civil War spy did. Neither side had moles in high government circles. The spies' best contacts usually were low-level officials. Agents depended a good bit on camp gossip. Inside information from command circles was rare—as were accurate estimates by any one agent on enemy strength. It may explain why Sharpe tended to be lenient with poor performers who were sent out. Penetrating armies in the field could be extremely difficult. But within a month, Sharpe had set up an espionage network to spy on the Confederate Army that was unprecedented. Practically all of Lee's major units had been pinpointed.

In rapid fire, Sharpe began sending out his spies. Hooker's appetite for anything the agents produced was insatiable. The new intelligence chief telegraphed McEntee, who spent much of his time in the field collecting, that the commanding general wanted any information he considered reliable sent to him immediately "no matter whether you think anybody else has forwarded it or not." Ernest Yager, a hardworking German American with a thick accent who had been an Army scout, was one of the first agents Sharpe ordered behind Confederate lines on February 17. For eight days, Yager made a wide-ranging tour of northeast Virginia that took in Dumfries, Brentsville, Catlett's Station, Warrenton, Culpeper Court House, and Richmond. He reported finding the railroad at Catlett's Station in good order, elements of Lee's infantry and cavalry crossing a bridge at the Rappahannock, and "four formidable ironclads . . . nearly ready in Richmond." Unlike Pinkerton, who did not appreciate the perishability of military intelligence,

Sharpe set deadlines and demanded fast turnarounds. The day after Yager returned, Babcock sent him out once more to track Confederate regiments near Manassas and Aldie, west of Washington, and almost immediately after that trip Sharpe dispatched him to learn the names of Rebel generals commanding Confederates between Kelly's Ford, across the Rappahannock, and Culpeper Court House, northwest of Fredericksburg—and to scout the changes they were making in their positions. "And then come back here as soon as you can," Sharpe instructed, "telegraphing first if possible."

Milton W. Cline, a veteran sergeant from the 3rd Indiana Cavalry Regiment, became one of Sharpe's most capable spies. A week after he launched Yager's mission, Sharpe dispatched Cline to penetrate the remote fringes of Lee's army on Virginia's Northern Neck, bounded by the Potomac on the north and Rappahannock on the south. Wearing a Confederate uniform, Cline crossed the Rappahannock three miles below Port Royal southeast of Fredericksburg, striking up conversations with Confederate soldiers along the way, counting their numbers, the rifle pits they manned, and the gun emplacements they occupied. He hooked up with a Rebel company for a while, spent a day with a Confederate ordnance officer, and then made his way back to Fredericksburg. With quite a haul Cline rode to Sharpe on March 5—on a horse he stole after a poker game. Covering 250 miles in ten days, he identified sixty-four major enemy installations, twenty-four camps, a dozen artillery batteries, twenty-five fortifications, and five wagon and ambulance parks. He wrote his detailed observations in one long sentence without punctuation.

More spies went out. Babcock sent John Howard Skinker, who owned a farm on Poplar Road north of the Rappahannock, to check out a report from a black woman who spied for the Union in Fredericksburg. The woman used a clothesline code to deliver messages. One piece of clothing hanging from the wash line was the signal that Confederate forces around Fredericksburg were on the move, two pieces hanging from the line signaled that the Rebel force there was the same as it had been since the battle, three pieces meant the Confederates were being reinforced, and no clothing on the line meant that all the Rebel forces had gone away. Skinker reported that he saw one piece of clothing on the line March 11; the Rebels were on the move.

For risky missions south of the Rappahannock, Sharpe also sent out a former source of Burnside's named Isaac Silver, whose farm inside Confederate lines on the Plank Road was three miles east of the important crossroads at Chancellorsville and seven miles west of Fredericksburg, right in the middle of the left wing of Lee's army. Silver, who had been born in New Jersey and was fifty-two years old, was called "the Old Man" in intelligence documents. His first report was couriered March 13 to headquarters by Ebenezer McGee, another Burnside spy whom Sharpe put on his payroll because he knew his way around the area. Silver's spelling was poor, some of the troop numbers were too high, and a few unit placements were slightly off, but he managed to deliver a fairly complete report on the strength and location of Lee's divisions. Hooker sent a copy of the Old Man's memo to Stanton—with the spelling corrected.

Patrick and Sharpe were intent on keeping meddling Washington officials away from their lines. It sparked a major feud with one of the city's most cutthroat bureaucrats—Lafayette Baker. The detective had men prowling up and down the East Coast—staging stings to catch blockade runners, following innocent northern Jews he now suspected of trading with the enemy, working fraud cases in Philadelphia and New York, and confiscating so much contraband clothing, shoes, liquor, wine, and playing cards he asked Stanton if he could stage an auction to sell it off. Baker considered the territory the Army of the Potomac occupied his territory as well. He began sending detectives inside the Army's lines to hunt for subversives and had his men board ships that carried supplies from Washington to Hooker's base camp at Aquia Creek in order to investigate illegal trading in contraband goods. Battling hostile agents and any kind of criminal activity in the Army of the Potomac's operating area was Patrick's responsibility and he fiercely resisted Baker bigfooting him. The two men waged a war against each other that lasted almost the entire Civil War.

Burnside and then Hooker had issued orders that Baker's men be kept out of the Potomac Army's lines unless Patrick approved their presence. But Patrick fumed that the two generals never enforced the orders and he knew why. Baker had supplied Burnside with a prostitute he kept at Falmouth and

Baker's detectives, who had all Washington gambling houses under surveillance, caught Hooker one time sneaking into one to bet away his paycheck. So Patrick took matters into his own hands. When he found Baker's detectives on boats at Aquia Creek or caught them snooping around the Army's camps in the field, he had soldiers arrest the men and throw them into the cells of a prison ship. The arrests infuriated Baker, who suspected Patrick was turning a blind eye to black marketing among his officers and even issuing permits for contraband goods to be sent south. He protested to Stanton, who intervened each time and ordered that Baker's men be released.

Baker's operatives did uncover legitimate fraud cases inside the Army of the Potomac. His detectives arrested one captain there for illegally selling flour from commissary stores. Even Patrick thought the captain was guilty. Army quartermaster officers also thought Baker's men were more skilled than Patrick's soldiers at catching smugglers and black marketers. Patrick, however, thought Baker had more in mind than law enforcement. He had evidence that Baker was trying to burrow his agents into the Potomac Army's postal operation to read soldiers' mail and he suspected Baker had spies wandering around the camps looking for derogatory information to telegraph back to Washington. Patrick had reason to be wary. Baker did have an informant who wormed his way into Patrick's department to keep him posted on what the provost marshal and his deputy, George Sharpe, were up to.

The Baker-Patrick feud became particularly volatile over liquor and women. Baker was outraged over the whisky, prostitutes, and pornography pouring into Hooker's camps, which in fact were gaining a reputation for being places no self-respecting man or woman could visit. Stanton worried as well that the vice problem had gotten out of hand. So did Patrick. Out riding one day, he dressed down a group of soldiers imbibing at eleven o'clock in the morning. He launched a campaign to punish officers abusing their liquor privilege, rounded up whores and sent them packing, and hauled away boxes of dirty books being sold to troops. Patrick also suspected that Hooker was involved in some of the liquor and sex trafficking.

But the provost marshal bitterly fought Baker's swooping in to clean up the problem. Convinced that sutlers were bribing Army officers to allow liquor to be illegally ferried in government ships to Aquia Creek Landing and that Patrick had been giving passes to prostitutes to visit the camps, Baker set out to stop the flow. He posted detectives at the Washington wharfs, aboard the ships, and at Aquia Creek Landing to seize suspicious packages. He rode out at one point to Washington's 6th Street wharf to oversee the seizures himself. Complaints poured into Patrick's department from angry Potomac Army officers who complained that Baker's detectives had stolen not only liquor and wine legally shipped to them, but also a trove of other items, such as blankets, chewing tobacco, clothing, and, in one instance, a bushel of oysters with crockery. The seizures were causing "a good deal of ill feeling throughout this army," Patrick warned Washington.

He strongly suspected, as others did, that Baker and his men were selling the liquor and other items they confiscated and pocketing the cash. One letter in the surviving Baker records hints that his detectives might have set up bars in the boats sailing from Aquia Creek Landing to Washington and sold whisky to soldiers returning from the front. On January 29, Patrick penned a blistering memo to Butterfield, Hooker's chief of staff, accusing Baker of being little better than a crime boss. His detectives "have systematically robbed the officers and men of this Army of clothing, subsistence, mess and other stores and necessaries," Patrick wrote. No one could trace where the goods Baker's men took had ended up, he charged, implying that Baker was fencing them. Patrick accused Baker of "making any statement however false, and of committing any act, however criminal and damaging the public service, to gratify his own passions." The incendiary memo soon reached Washington. Baker, who was stricken at the time with a serious illness, climbed out of a sickbed to angrily demand that Patrick prove his charges. Patrick had no proof and was forced to retract his accusation that Baker was a criminal. But Patrick—and he believed everyone else in the Army of the Potomac's headquarters—believed the man was a crook.

Was he? No evidence exists in Baker's government files that proves he enriched himself from the huge amount of goods seized. But there is little in the files showing what exactly happened to all the property Baker confiscated. One spreadsheet in his records states that for the month of June 1863, Baker's men seized $32,261 worth of weapons, horses, saddles, camp equipment, clothing, and liquor (about $636,000 in today's dollars). The sheet states only that all the weapons and equipment went to a "store house" and the animals were taken to a "government corral." Cryptic letters also remain hinting that Baker and his older brother Calvin were trading in government horses, to which Baker had access.

Baker also seemed to have an inordinate interest in federal property— even if he had not seized it. Shortly after Patrick fired off his accusatory memo, Baker wrote to the Quartermaster General's Office proposing that private contractors collect abandoned tents, wagon covers, sacks, rags, blankets, and uniforms. Salvage disposal was a subject far afield for a secret service chief. The Quartermaster General's Office rejected the idea, fearing such a practice would be open to abuse.

Baker extracted payback for Patrick maligning his reputation. His detectives reported finding large quantities of salt sent to Richmond with a permit from the provost marshal. Baker also accused Patrick of shipping to the North plunder taken from the Fredericksburg battle. Patrick dismissed the charges as a smear and they did not stick. His allies in Washington knew he was incorruptible and had fought pillaging.

Another case Baker assembled against Patrick, however, proved embarrassing. His detectives arrested James L. Green, whom Patrick had given passes to take his family from Falmouth to New York. Baker had evidence that Green was a Rebel officer and spy. His men discovered the Falmouth man trying to ship contraband goods and confiscated not only the passes Patrick had signed but also an unusually chummy letter he had written to Green's wife. Patrick, who seemed enamored with the woman, claimed he never found evidence that her husband was working for the South. But some of Patrick's headquarters colleagues considered Green a dangerous agent. An Army judge advocate general officer who investigated the case reported to Stanton the evidence was strong that Green was in fact a spy. Patrick was naïve in issuing him the passes, the JAG officer concluded, and he had acted improperly in fraternizing with Green's wife.

The commander of Sharpe's old brigade wanted him back leading the 120th Regiment. A month earlier, Sharpe would have been amenable to it. But by the second week of March, he had become totally consumed with spying and had made too much progress with his young bureau to give it up. Sharpe, who wrote his uncle that he had become "one of the hardest working men in the Army," even ventured out on his own scouting mission. On March 13, he rode to the Rappahannock to personally reconnoiter fords that Union columns could use to cross the river at points where there was little Confederate resistance.

When he returned from his foray, Sharpe sat down in his tent that same day, pulled out paper and pen, and took stock of the intelligence his Bureau of Military Information had accumulated so far. On two sheets he wrote down extracts of the various reports he had received on the positions of the Rebel army along the Rappahannock and around Fredericksburg. It was a summary of where every major Confederate unit was as of March 13 and Sharpe used it as an outline to draft his first monthly report, which he delivered to Butterfield two days later on what his spy agency had accomplished.

It had been a lot. Sharpe summarized the first thirty days of spying in a remarkably well-organized, concise, and largely accurate report, which ran six pages long and detailed the location and strength of Lee's infantry. The March 15 memo also came with seven pages of extracts from the sources Sharpe considered reliable, as well as an addendum describing the five brigades of Lee's cavalry commanded by Jeb Stuart. Sharpe's agents had penetrated enemy lines numerous times, he reported to Butterfield, multiple prisoner and deserter interrogations had been conducted, and Union Signal Corps officers had broken the code Confederate flagmen used so "their messages are read daily . . . whenever they can be observed from our stations." In a pointed reference to Pinkerton, Sharpe told Butterfield that accurate intelligence on the Rebel force "has never before been obtained [by] this army until it was too late to use it."

Hooker's new spymaster succinctly spelled out how Lee arranged his chess pieces. Longstreet had gone south with three divisions, Sharpe reported. Lee and Jackson "are now opposite us," with six infantry divisions around Fredericksburg plus a division of cavalry Stuart commanded. Sharpe calculated that the twenty-five Rebel brigades in those six infantry divisions facing Hooker had at the most 1,700 men in each of them—or about 378 per regiment. That would bring the total strength of Lee's army to 42,500. But Sharpe considered that estimate too high. He had evidence from agent reports and interrogations that many of the Rebel regiments numbered only about 350, so using that as the average, Lee had only 39,375 infantrymen in his army. But Sharpe was suspicious of even that number. Some Confederate regiments, he found, were actually no larger than a battalion. So using that lower count, Lee's total strength was only about 32,500 infantrymen.

Sharpe's report had its errors. Lee's infantrymen actually numbered 49,000. Sharpe and Babcock believed the Rebel commander had twenty-five infantry brigades. Lee had twenty-eight. They also underestimated the troop numbers per brigade. But their errors on the low side were a breath of fresh air for Hooker, who believed all along that the Rebels were less powerful than McClellan's imagination had conjured them up to be. Babcock surely told Sharpe about the problems with Pinkerton's math and inflated estimates. Avoiding those faults became second nature for these two men. Though it had been operating for only a month, Sharpe's bureau had produced the best intelligence report a Potomac Army commander had ever seen up to that point. Professionals were now in charge of military spying. Sharpe felt the full weight of the shadow war falling on his shoulders. "In the great game that is now being played," he later told a potential source, "everything in the way of advantage depends on which side gets the best information."

Seventeen

CHANCELLORSVILLE

ooker had put Sharpe and his staff to work learning all they could about the area around Chancellorsville. The hamlet itself was not that important, consisting of little more than a two-and-a-half-story redbrick building with white pillars erected in 1816 to be a tavern for weary travelers at the junction of the Orange Turnpike and Ely's Ford Road west of Fredericksburg. The imposing house with its outbuildings was now the home of the Chancellor family, which consisted of the widow Fannie Pound Chancellor, her young son, and six unmarried, and unusually attractive, daughters. Of more concern to Sharpe was the vast seventy square miles of woodland stretching from the Rappahannock and Rapidan Rivers to several miles south of Chancellorsville and some fifteen miles east to Fredericksburg, with its irregular ravines, low hills, and dense thicket of dwarf pine, cedar, hickory, and scrub oak, which made it nearly impossible for infantry, artillery, and cavalry to shoot, move, and communicate through it in anything resembling well-ordered formations. The maze was aptly called "the Wilderness." With the help of county maps they could find, Sharpe's agents joined topographical engineers in charting the network of roads and trails running around and through the Wilderness, as well as the best crossing points over the Rappahannock and Rapidan Rivers just north. The intelligence was critically important for Hooker. Chancellorsville, the Wilderness, and the Rappahannock and Rapidan to the north would be the battleground for his fight with Robert E. Lee.

As armies do when they ready for a campaign, Hooker by late March was tightening security around his. He had good reason to obsess with secrecy. Rebel scouts continued to roam in the rear of his force. Agent Skinker for one grew anxious over information leakage. After one foray he reported to Sharpe that Union pickets appeared more intent on stopping him than the enemy. Skinker sent his intelligence chief the names of nine suspect citizens in the area who should be rounded up. Hooker ordered Patrick to restrict civilian traffic through Union lines, halt the trade of northern for southern newspapers along picket lines, and clamp down on reporters publishing militarily sensitive information (expelling or jailing the ones who did not comply). Hooker also kept secret, even from his senior commanders, the plans churning in his mind for attacking Lee.

Patrick and Sharpe moved aggressively, ordering that land not be cleared of timber a mile and half around the Army base at Aquia Creek Landing, giving enemy agents a clear view from commanding hills. When he learned that Union pickets were talking across the Rappahannock to their inquisitive Rebel counterparts, Patrick ordered officers to stand watch with the men to shut off the chatter. Lee felt the pinch, writing to Davis on April 2 that Hooker's "lines are so closely guarded that it is difficult to penetrate them." For the first time on Virginia soil the Federals knew more about what was happening on Lee's side than he did on theirs.

Sharpe moved energetically to gather the puzzle pieces of information Hooker needed for an attack. Skinker sent in intelligence collected above Falmouth and reported on the shortage of grain and hay for Rebel cavalry and artillery horses at Culpeper Court House, to the west. Other scouts identified fords across the Rappahannock where the Confederate forces guarding them were strong or weak. No detail was too small for Sharpe to vacuum. He tasked the provost marshal at Aquia Creek with asking an Alabama deserter just brought in if Lee "has any negroes under arms, or doing picket duty along the river"; they could be enticed to desert with information.

On March 21, Sharpe delivered to Hooker a startling conclusion reached from scores of interviews with his spies and prisoners: the supply system feeding Lee's army "seems to be nearing the point of total failure." Although Sharpe did not know it at the time, Samuel Ruth exacerbated Lee's problems by sabotaging the rail portion of his supply line to the Chancellorsville area. Each Confederate soldier received a measly pint of flour and quarter pound of bacon or pork daily, Sharpe reported, with commissary stores having long run out of basic articles like candles for the men. Lee's brigades were made up of "ragged and beggarly fellows," Sharpe told Hooker, attaching a Richmond newspaper clipping showing that inflated food prices made conditions in the Confederate capital not much better.

On April 1, Sharpe's effort to set up a secret listening post inside Richmond appeared to him to be bearing fruit. That same day he received word from James L. McPhail, the Union provost marshal in Baltimore, that Joseph H. Maddox had arrived in the Confederate capital. Sharpe fired off a telegram to McPhail the next day. Hooker wanted Maddox back quickly with a report on the organization of Confederate forces around Richmond and farther south, along with the numbers for Lee's army at Fredericksburg. "The general is very much interested in this matter," his spy chief wrote.

Sharpe had begun Project Maddox almost from the very day he joined Hooker's headquarters. He had visited Baltimore a second time in early February to meet with McPhail on an important mission Hooker wanted launched. The Baltimore provost marshal had compiled a colorful record rooting out Maryland secessionists and arresting contraband merchants at the city's ports for Lafayette Baker. The Army of the Potomac needed intelligence they so far "had not been able to get" out of Richmond, Sharpe told McPhail. Could he find them "a man of intelligence" to infiltrate the Confederate capital? Several weeks later, McPhail produced Maddox, a wealthy Carroll County, Maryland, merchant who had made a fortune in the Confederacy as a commodity speculator. Maddox lobbied for the assignment, claiming that the other agents McPhail was considering for the job would surely be caught by the Confederate secret service.

Red flags were soon raised about Maddox working for the U.S. government. Stanton and Baker received anonymous letters warning he was a Confederate sympathizer and had made his money in illegal contraband trade with the South. During his December 1861 visit to Richmond, Timothy Webster told Pinkerton he saw Maddox there and the man had confided that he was working out an arrangement with a Rebel captain to set up a signal system from Maddox's Maryland home to warn Confederates of the movement of Union troops near him. Pinkerton quickly reported to McClellan and later to Stanton that it was clear Maddox was a Rebel spy and "should be arrested at once."

Maddox insisted he had always been a loyal Unionist. Sharpe had nothing but praise for the Maryland businessman, insisting he was a valuable operative. But the intelligence chief likely had a blind spot with this agent. After the war, federal investigators rooting through captured Confederate documents found a letter Maddox had sent to the war secretary in Richmond offering to raise a Rebel cavalry regiment in the southern Maryland counties. The chairman of the federal government's Committee on Claims, who had read every document in the Maddox case, concluded that he had spied for "both sides."

On March 21, Maddox visited the Army of the Potomac's headquarters at Aquia Creek Landing. Sharpe handed him a dozen details Hooker wanted him to find out during his Richmond mission, such as how many troops might have been added to Lee's force at Fredericksburg and what units the Rebel commander might have sent south. Maddox agreed to work without pay as long as he could bring along items to sell from his trading business. Sharpe believed that made for a plausible cover. Unfazed by ugly rumors swirling around Maddox, the spymaster wrote McPhail that day: "I think he understands our position and expectations." Sharpe's expectations might have been too high. When he arrived in Richmond, Maddox made no contact with Van Lew and other Unionists, who could have provided him information Hooker would certainly have found useful. Maddox exuded self-confidence. But it was far from certain he would discover much on his own.

Tension between Patrick and Sharpe began to grow. The night of

March 17, Sharpe joined other headquarters officers in hoisting a potent punch to celebrate St. Patrick's Day. He had other things to cheer besides the Irish celebration. Union general William Averell's 3,100 horsemen and artillerymen that day had performed admirably in an isolated clash at Kelly's Ford with Brigadier General Fitzhugh Lee's cavalry brigade, thanks in part to intelligence Sharpe's men had provided Averell on the Rebels' location. Patrick, who could suck the joy out of any festive occasion, became irritated that his deputy joined the other officers in drinking too much that night.

Different work cultures divided them. Patrick enforced Army rules—zealously so. Sharpe's mission was to convince people on the other side to break rules and betray their cause. Sharpe was the subtle intelligence officer who dealt in bits of information and nuances that told larger stories, proved or disproved facts, and helped him understand fluid situations. Patrick was a cut-and-dried Army disciplinarian, who saw everything as either black or white. By St. Patrick's Day he was beginning to have his doubts about the man he once thought was his kind of pleasant fellow.

The rift between the two men was widened as well by other Union officers who were jealous of Sharpe's access to Hooker. They trashed the intelligence chief behind his back in whispered conversations with Patrick. The provost marshal began scribbling more gripes about his deputy in his diary. He disapproved of Sharpe having his wife visit the headquarters camp, as other officers occasionally did. He considered it unseemly that Sharpe collected political gossip during trips to Washington on intelligence business—although Patrick did not mind his sharing with him the latest he picked up on feuding among top generals. Sharpe, Patrick concluded, was too fun-loving and "very irregular in all his ways." Of course, the characteristics Patrick found objectionable in Sharpe—his refusal to be chained to routine or regimen, his willingness to bend rules, and even his sense of play—were the very traits that made Sharpe an excellent spymaster.

On April 8, Lincoln sailed down the Potomac to the wharf at Aquia Creek Landing, where he boarded a bunting-draped railcar to take him to the headquarters of the commander about whom he still harbored doubts. With bands playing, Hooker staged an impressive review and Lincoln could clearly see from the long straight lines he inspected and the soldiers he chatted with that morale had improved. But he had learned from bitter experience that a well-drilled army was not necessarily a fighting army and Hooker's boasts about what he would do *after* he took Richmond worried Lincoln. "May God have mercy on General Lee, for I will have none," the Potomac Army's latest commander had earlier bragged. The parting advice Lincoln conveyed: "In your next fight, put in all your men." McClellan had not done that. Patrick was repulsed by the show staged for Lincoln. Hooker had to order him to attend a reception headquarters officers hosted for the president. Patrick also fretted over security for Lincoln's visit. A Confederate observer outside the camp perimeter might spot the presidential entourage, he feared, and drop "a shell amongst us."

Four days later, Butterfield sat alone with Lincoln in the White House on Sunday as the president read a secret document. It spelled out Hooker's battle plan for destroying Lee's army of about 60,000, hunkered down in fortified defenses along the south bank of the Rappahannock River at Fredericksburg. Lee had sent Longstreet with the divisions commanded by George Pickett and John Bell Hood to the Virginia and North Carolina coast to guard against a Union move there, so Hooker's better-equipped and reinvigorated army was double the size of Lee's force at Fredericksburg. The intelligence Sharpe had provided helped shape the Union battle plan. The March 21 information bureau report that Lee's army was poorly fed led Hooker to believe that at least for now, the Rebel commander would have to remain on the defensive because of his supply problems. Union brigadier general George Stoneman's 12,000-man cavalry, minus a brigade, would shortly cross the Rappahannock far upstream above Brandy Station, make a wide sweep west over the Rapidan River around Lee's left flank, and then speed south to the Richmond, Fredericksburg and Potomac Railroad line to cut off at Hanover Junction Lee's critical supply artery from the Rebel capital.

Meanwhile, three of Hooker's infantry corps would march thirty miles upstream to cross the Rappahannock at Kelly's Ford. Skinker had provided intelligence on the Rebel defenses Hooker could expect at that crossing. After traversing Kelly's Ford the three corps would move downriver and capture the Confederate fortifications at U.S. Ford and Banks's Ford to the southeast. The capture of U.S. Ford would enable Hooker to send two additional corps across it to reinforce the marching column so together they could move directly against the rear of Lee's lines at Fredericksburg. A farmer's spy report to Sharpe revealed weaknesses in the Confederates' left flank as well as a gap that opened directly onto the rear of their main force. Two Union corps would pretend to launch a full attack at Fredericksburg to freeze Lee's right flank, but they had orders to pursue the Rebels vigorously if they appeared to be falling back. Lee would be trapped in a crushing pincer on his left and right flanks.

He would then have two choices, equally distasteful, Hooker believed—either come out of his Fredericksburg fortifications and fight in the open or retreat to Richmond. Hooker made his calculation on the option Lee would pick once more with Sharpe's March 21 report in mind. With no stockpiles for his poorly fed and equipped army, Hooker reasoned, Lee would be forced to react immediately to Stoneman's cutting his railroad lifeline and to retreat south. When he did, Stoneman's cavalry, which Hooker called his "Dragoon force," would plant itself to hold him in check while Hooker's infantry attacked the rear of the Rebel army to destroy it.

Then Richmond would be open to the Army of the Potomac. Two days before his White House briefing, Butterfield received a report from Sharpe and Babcock on their interrogation of James Craig, a Scotsman and refugee from Richmond who had crossed into Union lines. Craig, who observed the movement of troops through the Rebel capital, knew of no Confederate soldiers returning to Lee's army in Fredericksburg after Pickett's and Hood's divisions "went away." Sharpe was still awaiting a report from the spy he placed in Richmond—Joseph Maddox.

Hooker's plan to maneuver Lee out of impregnable Fredericksburg looked like a strategic masterpiece that would win the war. He was supremely confident. The operation, he wrote Lincoln, would start April 13. After reading the secret letter, Lincoln scribbled his endorsement on the document. But he reminded Hooker that his primary objective was Lee's army in front of him—not Richmond.

As Butterfield wrapped up his White House briefing, Stoneman received detailed orders from Hooker for his grand sweep around Lee's left flank. The cavalry general would be helped by an intelligence windfall from his Signal Corps, which Butterfield carefully crafted into a successful deception operation. Earlier in April, Hooker's signalmen, who had already broken the Rebel communications code, learned that the Confederates had done the same with theirs and could read Union flag signals being sent in a simple alphabet code. The Yankees quickly changed to a cipher the Rebels could not break, but they camouflaged the change by sending deceptive transmissions in the old code to make the Confederates believe their breakthrough had not been discovered. Butterfield tucked away this important ploy in his head for future use.

To mislead the enemy about his real objective, Stoneman on April 12 was ordered to spread the word that his cavalry was heading to the Shenandoah Valley to chase Rebels there. The next day, Butterfield had his signalmen send the same message about Stoneman's Shenandoah mission by flag using the old code. Rebel signalmen intercepted and decoded the Union message, and alerted Lee. The Rebel commander took the bait, reporting to Davis that he believed Hooker's cavalry was heading to the valley. Jeb Stuart, Lee's cavalry commander, remained suspicious that some sort of feint was in the works here, but he nevertheless moved his horsemen far west to intercept Stoneman in the Shenandoah. That move created a twenty-mile gap between Lee's infantry and Stuart's cavalry, where there were no Confederates to spot Stoneman's real path.

On April 13, Stoneman's large cavalry force began to move out. To help preserve secrecy, Hooker had the Washington postmaster hold up mail from the Rappahannock area for twenty-four hours. A violent rainstorm on April 15, however, swelled the Rappahannock, forcing Stoneman's cavalry back to the north side of the river. When Hooker notified him of the delay, Lincoln telegraphed back: "I greatly fear it is another failure."

Undeterred, Hooker abruptly altered his plans, again thanks to intelligence Sharpe provided. Between Fredericksburg and the point where the Rapidan River emptied into the Rappahannock northwest of the town, there were two feasible crossing points—at U.S Ford, just south of where the Rapidan fed into the Rappahannock, and at Banks's Ford, farther south. It would be difficult for Hooker to lay pontoon bridges at either site if the Confederates put up a fight there, which he was sure Lee would do. So rather than trying to battle his way across those two fords, Hooker decided on a maneuver. John Babcock, Sharpe's walking enemy-order-of-battle calculator, had already charted the makeup and strength of Lee's force all along the Rappahannock. It was critically important now for Hooker to receive any updates on the whereabouts and strength of Lee's units. Sharpe's information bureau supplied him with that intelligence.

Thaddeus Lowe's balloons and Yankee observation stations atop towers and trees could easily see the position of Stonewall Jackson's troops from Fredericksburg eastward. But the two divisions of Longstreet's 1st Corps that Richard Anderson and Lafayette McLaws commanded west and south of Fredericksburg were in the heavy woods of the Wilderness and difficult for the Federals to observe. The location of those two divisions was important for Hooker as he rejiggered his battle plan.

On April 15, Isaac Silver came to the rescue. His farm on Orange Plank Road just east of Chancellorsville was in the middle of the Confederate position most difficult for the Federals to observe. Ebenezer McGee that day couriered to Sharpe Silver's important report on the units within the Anderson and McLaws divisions. Sharpe immediately passed it on to Hooker. Cadmus Wilcox's Confederate brigade was nearby to back up Rebel pickets at Banks's Ford, Silver reported. To the west at U.S. Ford sat Carnot Posey's Rebel brigade with two artillery batteries, but they "are very much scattered" from that ford on the Rappahannock to Ely's Ford on the Rapidan farther west, Silver noted. The Old Man counted 2,500 Rebels close to each ford, with another 1,000 to 1,200 Confederates south of U.S. Ford. These were all soldiers from Anderson's division. There were "no other standing troops" eastward for five miles, Silver reported. The next troop concentration he spotted was along Telegraph Road south of Fredericksburg and those men appeared to him to be poorly equipped. Hooker already knew from previous intelligence reports Sharpe's agents had provided that Chancellorsville west of Banks's Ford was now left unguarded. From Silver's April 15 observation it appeared that Lee's farthest defenses upriver from Fredericksburg were light rather than heavy and concentrated at Banks's Ford and U.S. Ford. Otherwise, the left flank and rear of Lee's army were open.

Hooker decided to let Stoneman go on his grand sweep south to cut the Richmond, Fredericksburg and Potomac Railroad line as planned. But his main army now would dash behind Confederate lines. Infantry rather than cavalry would immediately threaten Lee's supply lifeline, forcing him to battle in the open on Hooker's terms. It was a bold and innovative plan. At its heart would be a grand turning movement by his infantry. Hooker would march three corps of 45,000 men secretly upriver along the Rappahannock's north bank. They would overrun Rebel pickets at Kelly's Ford to the northwest, lay down a pontoon bridge to cross the Rappahannock, do the same at the Rapidan River fords, and then march back down to Chancellorsville to sneak up on the rear of Lee's army. To distract Lee, Hooker would still have two corps cross the Rappahannock just below Fredericksburg. The beauty of Hooker's new plan "was its promise of stealing a long march on Robert E. Lee," writes military historian Stephen W. Sears. Butterfield's signal ruse still kept the Rebel cavalry out of the action far to the west and the twenty-mile gap still open, with the Kelly's Ford crossing guarded by only several dozen Confederate pickets. And Silver had found the road to Lee's rear clear of significant opposition. Hooker set near the end of April for the launch of this daring operation.

Still obsessed with secrecy, Hooker kept many of his corps commanders in the dark about the entire plan until the last minute. On April 17, however, a leak in Washington jolted the elaborate security measures Sharpe, Patrick, and Butterfield had put in place and rattled Hooker. That day's edition of the *Washington Morning Chronicle* reprinted correspondence from the Army of the Potomac's medical director on his sick call numbers and the ratio of that count to the number of healthy soldiers. It enabled anyone with simple arithmetic to put the size of Hooker's army at 159,329. Sharpe "would have willingly paid $1,000 for such information," Hooker fumed in a letter to Stanton. Fortunately for the Potomac Army commander, Lee received a secondhand account of the article late and believed the extrapolated number was an exaggeration.

Sharpe's bureau became a madhouse of activity. Hooker's headquarters seemed electrified with anticipation of impending attack. Deserters poured in from all elements of Lee's army, filling in blanks that Silver's April 15 report had not answered. Sharpe briefed Stoneman on the opposition he might face during his sweep south and provided him Ernest Yager to scout the enemy ahead of him. The evening of April 24, Sharpe wrote Butterfield that his bureau's POW interrogations since the previous night had turned up no evidence of Rebel reinforcements arriving from Richmond. That remained the case in a memo Sharpe wrote five days later. Skinker, just returned from Kelly's Ford, reported on April 28 that it was still lightly defended. Sharpe forwarded the information to Hooker. John McEntee returned that same day to report the condition of roads on which Union forces would have to travel west of Fredericksburg. Even Patrick hopped on a horse and rode out to interview citizens who had observed Confederate troop movements—and to uncover Union pickets along the river still having unauthorized conversations with Confederate pickets.

On April 28, Sharpe also delivered to Hooker Babcock's final update before the battle on the organization of Lee's forces and their numbers. It was all summarized neatly on one sheet of paper—the six divisions Lee and Jackson had on their side of the Rappahannock, with their strength and commanders listed down to the brigade level, plus the count for Stuart's cavalry division. The numbers totaled up to 61,800 men—only one-quarter of 1 percent off from the actual number Lee had.

"So far the rebels have not the slightest idea what we are about today," Patrick wrote in his diary on April 28. "Even the pickets know nothing." Hooker, on the other hand, now knew everything he needed to know about Lee's army in order to defeat it. What Hooker could not fathom was how Lee would react to his audacious plan. He did not know that the Rebel commander had no intention of letting himself be trapped by the Union Army.

Sharpe wrote his uncle Jansen at the end of April that the Army of the Potomac at last had a commander "who means to fight to win—and when the blow is struck, it will be one of the heaviest ever felt on this continent." Sharpe stayed close to Hooker, who kept on the move while his forces maneuvered. Babcock remained with Butterfield at their Falmouth headquarters to manage the flood of intelligence expected from prisoners, deserters, signal stations, and balloons. Sharpe had reason to feel confident. His intelligence triumph had put Hooker in the position to annihilate Lee's army. The spymaster did not know, however, that his information would not be enough to save Hooker and his commanders from their battlefield mistakes.

By April 30, Hooker's forces had crossed the Rappahannock both at Kelly's Ford and at a point south of Fredericksburg. The complex maneuvers caught Lee napping. Hooker, whose gamble had given him Chancellorsville at virtually no cost and a head start against Lee, boasted to reporters riding with him that "the rebel army is now the legitimate property of the Army of the Potomac." Patrick, who had less confidence in the commanders serving under Hooker, wasn't so sure.

Butterfield ordered Colonel Sharpe and Professor Lowe "to be vigilant and watchful; to get all information possible." Hooker wanted to know every move Lee made in response to his moves. Sharpe rode his horse at a gallop to the Union position south of Fredericksburg to help with the interrogation of prisoners for any hint that Longstreet's two divisions in southern Virginia and North Carolina might be reinforcing Lee. If those two divisions stirred, Hooker wanted to know it. The prisoners said no more troops had arrived. Lowe's three balloons ascended as frequently as weather permitted to watch Rebel forces across the Rappahannock from U.S Ford to south of Fredericksburg. Hooker wanted the balloons up practically every daylight hour to observe Confederate movements and sometimes into the night ("to see where the enemy's camp-fires are," the general's aide told Lowe). Hooker demanded that their reports be sent to him immediately.

The confident Potomac Army commander moved his headquarters to the widow Chancellor's mansion at Chancellorsville, expecting—or more likely, hoping—that Lee would not fight in the face of five Union Army corps there or near there. But on May 1, after dense fog in early morning gave way to a beautiful spring day with a soft breeze, Lee, who faced his toughest opponent so far in Hooker, kept a skeletal force of about 12,400 soldiers to hold off the 47,000 Yankees south of Fredericksburg and attacked the advancing Union force east of Chancellorsville with the remaining 36,300 infantrymen he had there. Fighting Joe, who had about 50,000 men confronting Lee with 22,000 more on the way, grew too cautious too soon. Losing his nerve, he ceded the initiative to the Confederate commander and ordered his men to fall back to Chancellorsville and what he considered a better defensive position. Why became a subject of hot debate after the battle. Hooker lacked moral stamina, some concluded—a man bold when leading a division or corps but timid with an entire army. Perhaps fatigue conquered him. Perhaps he had been drinking. Or sober when he needed a shot of whisky to stiffen his spine.

But did intelligence, or in some instances the lack of it, also play a role in Hooker's much-criticized decision to pull back? Sharpe's spies like Silver were not suited for reporting on fast-moving tactics as a battle got under way. Southern troops, in fact, had surrounded Silver's immediate neighborhood, rendering him immobile for the moment. Lowe's balloons and the Signal Corps' observation stations had missed Confederate movements from Fredericksburg the night of April 30 and were little help early the next morning because of the fog off the Rappahannock. As a battle unfolded, cavalrymen were a commander's best eyes and ears. But Stoneman took most of that force south. Hooker had only 1,300 mounted men with him—not enough for reconnoitering the enemy approaching from Fredericksburg.

The intelligence that did come to Hooker on May 1 from Sharpe, Butterfield, and Lowe's balloons gave him reason to believe that the enemy directly in front of him was more formidable than he had previously realized. Lowe's balloons ascended after early-morning fog cleared and, along with Signal Corps observers from their posts, reported a heavy force of Confederate infantry and artillery moving west from Fredericksburg toward Chancellorsville and Hooker's army. It numbered as many as 15,000 men, Butterfield telegraphed Hooker. How many more had moved when fog obscured the view, the chief of staff couldn't tell. But Hooker could do the math. The dense columns of Rebel troops Lowe's aeronauts saw marching toward him had to be Jackson's corps, which Babcock's April 28 report had told him numbered 35,100 soldiers. Combine them with Anderson's and McLaws's divisions already in front of him, which Babcock said numbered 14,700, and Hooker now faced 49,800 Rebels if Jackson's entire corps was marching west or slightly less if Jackson had left a blocking force south of Fredericksburg.

Hooker had a far larger army than Jackson's 49,800 soldiers. But on the morning of May 1, he had sent out to march east no more than 30,000 men in three columns. He feared those soldiers would be chewed up by Jackson's larger force before he could get reinforcements to them. What's more, Butterfield also messaged that two deserters just interrogated after they crossed Union lines south of Fredericksburg claimed reinforcements had arrived from Richmond. Babcock and Sharpe discounted the deserter reports; Confederates may have planted the men along with others to spread disinformation. But Butterfield believed these two Rebels, which only stoked Hooker's paranoia that Longstreet's divisions would arrive soon from southern Virginia and North Carolina. If the enemy was now larger than Hooker had projected, falling back to a defensive position made sense. A defensive battle was a better bet to win than an attack, which Lee appeared to be launching. Hooker believed he would succeed in his stronger position farther back at Chancellorsville. But his withdrawal would cost him his mastery of the battlefield.

The evening of May 1, Joseph Maddox's report from Richmond finally arrived with a description of the Confederate Army and how its elements might be moved. Butterfield rushed it to Hooker shortly after 7 p.m. Maddox reported that 59,000 daily rations had been issued to Lee's infantry, exclusive of those issued to the cavalry, which he estimated at 8,000 to 12,000 horsemen. Maddox's count was slightly higher than Babcock's estimate. He speculated that Longstreet's two divisions in southern Virginia and North Carolina, along with several thousand soldiers elsewhere, were available to reinforce Lee. Up to 10,000 Confederates were posted at or near Richmond, Maddox said, to defend the southern capital—Hooker's target after he defeated Lee at Chancellorsville. Sharpe, who along with Babcock spent the rest of the night of May 1 interrogating deserters and prisoners from the day's fighting, was delighted with Maddox's report. But his agent's intelligence on the Richmond defenses the Federals faced would not be needed for now. Hooker never took back the advantage he gave up on May 1. Darius

Couch, Hooker's 2nd Corps leader who protested the retreat, concluded that "my commanding general was a whipped man."

Sunrise on May 2, Robert E. Lee seized the initiative with a risky maneuver. While feisty Jubal Early and his division of 12,400 Rebels held in check timid John Sedgwick and his Union corps south of Fredericksburg and while about 15,000 Rebels confronted Hooker's main force at Chancellorsville, Lee sent Stonewall Jackson and 30,000 men on a circuitous twelve-mile route through the Wilderness's thick woods to swing around west and attack Hooker on his right. Hooker discovered the maneuver. Buffeted by stiff winds, Lowe's aeronauts in balloons had difficulty viewing any of Jackson's flanking march, but Federal lookouts, peering through telescopes from treetops at the edge of a clearing called Hazel Grove, a mile southwest of Chancellorsville, spotted Confederates marching across an opening in the woods to the south. Hooker warned General Oliver Otis Howard on his extreme right to be prepared for a flank attack on his 11th Corps. But then Hooker had a second thought—which proved disastrous. He assumed Jackson's movement meant Lee was fleeing south and he failed to prepare for the blow about to hammer him. Lee was not retreating. Late afternoon that day, Jackson's three divisions, with bugles blaring and men screaming Rebel yells at the top of their lungs, stormed into the 11th Corps on Hooker's right sending "Uh-Oh Howard" (as he came to be called afterward) and the Federals reeling east toward a defensive line near Chancellorsville. It was a brilliant gambit for Lee, marred only by a strategically critical case of friendly fire that night. Jackson was accidentally shot in the right hand, left forearm, and upper left arm by his own men. His left arm had to be amputated just below the shoulder and he died eight days later of pneumonia complications from the wounds. Lee lamented that he had lost his "right arm."

Meanwhile, the question of whether Hood's and Pickett's divisions had been ordered back to Fredericksburg continued to haunt Butterfield, Sharpe, and Babcock. Some Rebel deserters rounded up on May 2 and the next day said they could arrive at any time. Other intelligence contradicted the claim. Sharpe peppered Babcock with requests for any information he had on the two divisions, but Babcock could offer back only a muddled picture. By May 3, his interrogation team had interviewed 824 Rebel prisoners or deserters and found that not a single one of them belonged to Hood's or Pickett's division.

While the inept Sedgwick was kept at bay west of Fredericksburg, Hooker scrunched his force on May 3 into a semicircle around Chancellorsville and allowed himself to be attacked by Confederates from two sides—in a pincer he had once envisioned putting on Lee. Sharpe and Babcock fed him intelligence updates throughout the day pinpointing Rebel divisions in front of him at Chancellorsville and the weaker enemy force facing Sedgwick at Fredericksburg. Stoneman, meanwhile, was at least two days behind schedule in striking the Richmond, Fredericksburg and Potomac Railroad. When he finally attacked the line on May 3, he did so weakly and in the wrong place—even though Sharpe's bureau had carefully plotted the target for him. Sharpe had intelligence that the Rebels had always been worried about being cut off from Richmond. He saw that concern now put into action. Track crews repaired the line and had it up and running in less than forty-eight hours.

At about nine thirty that Sunday morning, a twelve-pound Confederate cannonball fired from Hazel Grove sailed in knocking a tall porch pillar Hooker was leaning against at Chancellor House. Wood and splinters slammed into the commanding general's head and side. Carried into the house, Hooker, who ended up black-and-blue on that side of his body, was dazed, confused, and temporarily unable to command. Revived with a shot of brandy but still in intense pain, he recovered enough to order a retreat to north of Chancellorsville. For Lee, the triumph was the greatest of his military career. Victory that day had cost him 8,962 casualties. Hooker lost 8,623, a third of whom had been taken prisoner.

In Richmond, Van Lew that Sunday morning heard church bells ringing not for the call to worship but to sound the alarm for the feared Yankees thought to be arriving. Women packed trunks to be ready for evacuation while militiamen gathered at City Hall to mobilize for the capital's defense. A hundred miles north in the federal capital, Lincoln, camped out in the War Department's telegraph office, fired off a terse note to Butterfield at four thirty that afternoon, which summed up his dismay: "Where is Gen. Hooker? Where is Sedgwick? Where is Stoneman?"

The answers he received the next two days hardly satisfied him. The Battle of Chancellorsville continued May 4. Sedgwick withdrew his force back across the Rappahannock during the night. A majority of Hooker's corps commanders wanted to counterattack. Rebel prisoners and deserters continued to insist that reinforcements from Longstreet had arrived. Butterfield believed they had and Babcock was now willing to concede that perhaps some of Pickett's division had shown up. If so, Hooker should strike immediately while he still enjoyed a hefty numerical advantage, Babcock thought. He scribbled a short message to Sharpe: "The Rebel camps are fatigued and hungry and should be pressed hard before they get a fresh supply of provisions." But Hooker, who likely had not fully recovered from his concussion and who certainly had lost his will to fight on, pulled back his force to the north bank of the Rappahannock. In the Battle of Chancellorsville he had used only about half his army—exactly what Lincoln had told him not to do.

At 10 a.m. on May 5, Babcock reported to Sharpe that he was now certain no reinforcements from Longstreet had arrived. The intelligence had no effect on the grim retreat under way across the Rappahannock. Dark clouds poured down a cold and steady rain, deluging roads and flooding rifle pits. Soldiers were astonished and downcast by the retreat order. Through the evening and into the chilly night, horses and mules strained to pull artillery and supply wagons through the slippery mud as officers, some of them drunk, berated troops who lagged.

The fallback continued the morning of May 6. Hooker, returning to his old bluster, issued a general order to his men congratulating them on their successful campaign. It disgusted Patrick. He and the other generals had been "perfectly astonished at the retrograde movement," he wrote in his diary on May 6. "No confidence is felt in Hooker." Sharpe was dismayed as well. " 'Fighting Joe' Hooker, for inexplicable reasons, failed to fight his army," the spymaster said after the war. After he received Butterfield's grim report, Lincoln walked up and down a floor of the White House practically wailing: "My God! My God! What will the country say?" Patrick assigned Sharpe the duty of negotiating with the Confederates for the burial of Union dead and the evacuation of some 4,000 wounded left behind on the south side of the Rappahannock—a job that took him nine days to complete.

Hooker had been ill served by incompetent subordinates. Slow-moving George Stoneman had failed to sever Lee's railroad supply line in a timely manner. "Uh-Oh" Howard had been shamefully unprepared for an attack by Jackson. Dilatory John Sedgwick failed to break through Confederate lines at Fredericksburg despite outnumbering his enemy. But Hooker made serious mistakes of his own, such as giving up the initiative to Lee early in the campaign and retreating when his army still had plenty of fight left. Malicious gossip persisted that he had been drunk during the campaign. Butterfield said he never saw Hooker intoxicated. Sharpe, who was with the Army commander much of the time, said anyone who claimed the general was inebriated "lies in his throat."

Lincoln, who visited Hooker's Falmouth headquarters after the Chancellorsville debacle, decided to retain his Potomac Army commander—despite the fact that most of Hooker's corps commanders let the president know directly or through intermediaries that they blamed him for the defeat. Hooker blamed others. He also began sending Lincoln telegrams claiming, with no evidence from Sharpe to back it up, that the enemy had outnumbered him.

Sharpe's bureau, meanwhile, continued cranking out high-quality products. From interrogations of deserters and Richmond refugees he was able to confirm that Longstreet, with Hood's and Pickett's divisions, had finally joined Lee. Babcock produced leather-bound, fourteen-page booklets Hooker and his commanders could carry with accurate information on regiments, brigades, and divisions in Lee's Army of Northern Virginia. Sharpe also sent Butterfield a topographical study of the fifteen fords stretching across the Rappahannock and the fourteen fords over the Rapidan, which either side might use in a follow-up attack. It would all be important intelligence the Army of the Potomac would need to deal with Robert E. Lee's next incursion—this time into Pennsylvania.

Eighteen

GETTYSBURG

After Chancellorsville, Sharpe nursed a mordant view of the Army of the Potomac. It was, he later recalled, "an army that was criticized for not moving enough, but never for not dying enough." It would be tested once more. On May 15, Robert E. Lee, in poor health with the first signs of angina but buoyed by victories in five major battles, unveiled his dazzling plan before Jefferson Davis to defeat the North in its backyard by invading Pennsylvania. A demoralized Hooker, Lee believed, would have to follow his army as it moved. The Union threat from the Rappahannock would be removed and the war would be moved to Maryland and Pennsylvania, where Lee could replenish his army on northern soil, force Lincoln to think about protecting Washington instead of capturing Richmond, and push him to the negotiating table. When he eventually realized Lee's intent, Sharpe believed the bold plan was born of desperation. Sharpe could see that the Union Army was wearing down the Confederates. "A great diversion was required," he concluded.

From mid-May until mid-June, Lee reorganized his army, adding 18,000 men from two divisions under the stern and aloof James Longstreet, the

"Old War Horse," as the Georgian became known. For the Pennsylvania invasion, the Army of Northern Virginia totaled 75,000 men, in three infantry corps and six cavalry brigades. The Rebel reorganization became a headache for Babcock, who was trying to pin down the changes and the new commanders for brigades.

Lee's army had to reach Pennsylvania before Hooker realized what he was doing. The Rebel commander set the assembly point for his northern invasion at Culpeper, Virginia, which was about thirty miles northwest of Fredericksburg, twelve miles south of the Rappahannock, and beyond the right flank of Hooker's army. He intended to shift two-thirds of his force northwest and past Hooker's flank, while A. P. Hill's 3rd Corps remained at Fredericksburg to observe the Union commander and hopefully keep him in place long enough for the rest of Lee's army to get ahead of the Federals. From Culpeper to Maryland and Pennsylvania, Jeb Stuart's cavalry would screen the Rebel march. Stuart could be a savvy covert warrior. He sometimes infiltrated his scouts behind enemy lines dressed in Union uniforms, built campfires before leaving an area to make the enemy think he wasn't moving, or had his horsemen raise dust columns to deceive the Federals on the strength of the force they faced. Lee also employed what today is called information warfare—instructing his corps commanders to tell citizens along the way that his advances were headed in one direction when he intended to march in another and planting coached deserters and refugees behind Union lines with disinformation.

During the Chancellorsville battle, an aide asked Lee what he believed Hooker's next move would be and the cocky commander answered that it did not matter; all that mattered was that he could get to the Yankees to fight them. Lee was being overly boastful. It did matter to him what Hooker would do—particularly now. Stuart's other mission for the northern campaign, equally as important as screening Lee's movement from northern eyes, was to use his cavalry scouts and guerrilla units, such as Mosby's Rangers, to gather information on Hooker's whereabouts during the Rebel march north.

Lee worried about intelligence leaking from slaves. He didn't realize how much information also hemorrhaged from Rebel prisoners, deserters, and

white civilians. Before launching his Pennsylvania invasion, Lee ordered officers to stop feeding southern reporters information on the number of men
being taken into battle and the casualties being suffered. Their stories, he
knew, enabled the Union to determine the size of his force. Lee's success in
mining northern newspapers for information may have led him to believe
that the Union Army also relied on southern papers for its intelligence. He
did not know that a skilled spy service was operating against him and that
Sharpe's men were now busy unraveling exactly what he was up to.

MAY 17, 1863

Where was Lee's army? How big was it? How was it now organized? What
was the significance of Rebel movements Union scouts detected? Hooker
ordered his cavalry, along with Sharpe's spies, to find him answers. At the
same time he was intent on keeping Lee in the dark about his plans. He
dispatched that day a five-hundred-man cavalry detachment, joined by
Sharpe's agents, for a sweep in Virginia's Northern Neck, which was southeast of his Falmouth base camp above Fredericksburg. They were to gather
intelligence on enemy activity, seize mail, and interdict Rebel supply lines.
Rumors and speculation ran rampant that Lee planned just a cavalry raid
into the North. The stories masked the far larger operation he intended.
Hooker's mounted force soon would prove of little value in uncovering the
truth. The job fell to Sharpe and his spies.

Where were Hooker's forces located? What did the Union general intend to do with them? Would he launch an attack that would derail Lee's
plans? Would he cross the Rappahannock and strike Lee's rear as he moved
north or would he move against Richmond when Lee slipped away? The
Confederate commander heard from citizens and spies north of the river
that Hooker contemplated a change of base to the James River area west
and south of Richmond. Lee began showing signs of stress from the pressure of finding answers to his questions.

MAY 24

Rumors were picked up everywhere that Lee was headed north. Major General Erasmus Keyes, who commanded the Yorktown District, telegraphed Hooker he kept hearing "that an invasion of Maryland and Pennsylvania is soon to be made." A Baltimore man wrote Stanton on May 20 that a relative of his who was a Rebel told him the Confederates intended to invade Maryland and capture Baltimore and Washington. The war secretary took the rumors seriously, querying Halleck on May 23 about the measures he intended to defend Baltimore, Washington, and Alexandria. Halleck responded the same day with details. Sharpe noticed in the May 22 edition of the *Richmond Examiner* a story hinting that Lee planned some kind of march north. The item squared with reports he had received from his spies and a Rebel deserter.

On May 24, Sharpe penned a four-page memo to Butterfield with a digest of the military-related stories recently in Richmond papers. He also wrote that one of his spies had learned Lee issued a general order, read to his men five days ago, congratulating them on the Chancellorsville battle and "informing them that they were about to enter upon a campaign of long marches and hard fighting in a part of the country where they would find no railroad communications." From other scouts, Sharpe learned that "a whole division of the enemy is at or near Culpeper," just beyond Hooker's right flank.

MAY 26

Intelligence with more pieces to the puzzle trickled in. One of Lowe's aeronauts reported that during a balloon ascension he made that morning he was able to spot a dozen Rebel encampments around Fredericksburg. The aeronaut thought Sharpe should be able to identify the units from the descriptions he gave him. (The Confederates became increasingly sensitive to Lowe's men watching their movements north and tried to skirt their forces out of eyesight of the aerial observers.) Stanton received a letter from Michael Graham, a railroad entrepreneur who also spied for Major General

Robert Milroy, a division commander in Winchester, Virginia. Graham warned that the Shenandoah Valley (Lee's invasion corridor) could not be held unless 15,000 Federal infantrymen and 5,000 cavalrymen were rushed to it. Graham also believed a large force of Rebel cavalry and infantry would attack Milroy's outpost "in less than ten days." (The attack would actually come in nineteen days.)

Hooker sent an order to all his military commanders directing them to help John McEntee and any operatives Sharpe's top agent might have in his scouting party with supplies. The commanding general made McEntee's spying a priority. The day before, Hooker had been to the White House with the intelligence he had so far from Sharpe and tried to convince Lincoln and Stanton that he needed reinforcements. No decision came out of the meeting. Lincoln was still not convinced that Hooker had regained the confidence of his subordinates after Chancellorsville. Soon he began quietly looking for a new Potomac Army commander.

MAY 27

After analyzing raw reports collected so far, Sharpe delivered an intelligence summary to Hooker as professional as any modern-day version. The Confederate line now in front of the Army of the Potomac stretched from Banks's Ford west of Fredericksburg to near Moss Neck, seventeen miles to the east, he reported. Sharpe pinpointed the locations for the six Rebel divisions commanded by Richard Anderson, Lafayette McLaws, Jubal Early, Isaac Trimble, Robert Rodes, and A. P. Hill. George Pickett's division had arrived from Suffolk, Virginia, and John Bell Hood's division was on its way from Suffolk. Meanwhile, 4,700 Rebel cavalrymen in three brigades were three miles from Culpeper Court House. "The Confederate Army is under marching orders," Sharpe concluded. "All the deserters say that the idea is very prevalent in the ranks that they are about to move forward upon or above our right flank," the spymaster wrote, and apparently head north through the Shenandoah Valley. Hooker forwarded Sharpe's memo to Halleck in Washington with the notation that he had "a good deal of confidence" in its findings that "the enemy will soon be in motion."

But to what purpose? Hooker wrote Lincoln the same day that all he had were rumors "that important changes are being made" by the Confederates. He still didn't know what those changes amounted to. A report from the cavalry scouts that Brigadier General Alfred Pleasonton commanded clouded the picture for him. Pleasonton's men detected the same concentration of Rebel horsemen around Culpeper but concluded that it meant Stuart was planning a big cavalry raid—a possibility Sharpe could not discount.

Sharpe's excellent all-source intelligence report ended up being wasted in Washington. Because of a clerical snafu in delivery, his memo did not actually reach the capital until June 8. By then its information was outdated.

MAY 29

Pressure mounted on Sharpe to deliver results and deliver them quickly on exactly what Lee planned. Hooker wrote Stanton the day before that he could not provide any new insights on the direction the Rebels might be heading. Lee might be attempting another move into Maryland "however desperate it may appear," said the general. Sharpe sent Joseph Maddox back to Richmond, anxious for him to provide more intelligence from the Confederate government, but Maddox was arrested when he arrived at the capital. Friends eventually secured his release on parole, but he remained detained in Richmond for the next ten months, providing no intelligence reports.

Sharpe began dispatching spies in all directions to learn more about the movements of Lee's divisions. Skinker sneaked across the Rappahannock. McEntee led a half-dozen spies to Bealeton Station along the Orange and Alexandria Railroad line northwest of Fredericksburg on a risky mission to enter enemy territory past the river. Confederate pickets blocked some of his men from crossing the Rappahannock. But under pressure from Sharpe to produce, some managed to slip past the Rebels' cavalry screen and hand out Confederate currency to buy information. Two days later they sent back reports on Lee's northwest units—some written with invisible ink.

Lee, meanwhile, fared worse in determining what Hooker was up to. Scouts at one point warned him the Union general planned to freeze the

Rebel army at its position around Fredericksburg while federal troops on the York River to the south tried to capture Richmond. But the intelligence was contradictory. Hooker's cavalry had improved its capability to screen the Union Army's moves, and the general, with Sharpe's help, had imposed strict security measures. Lee had to be sure that Richmond remained safe while his army moved north. (He did not know that a request he sent out by flag signal for information on Yankee movements ended up in Hooker's headquarters tent because a Union signal station intercepted the message.) Lee had no intelligence staff and his espionage operation had become hit-and-miss. Longstreet requisitioned gold coins from Richmond and gave them to Henry Thomas Harrison, a Confederate scout, to pay for his infiltrating the federal government in Washington and sending back intelligence to the Army while it moved north. Otherwise, Jeb Stuart had to be Lee's eyes and ears.

JUNE 1

As June began, McEntee began clashing regularly with Hooker's cavalry commander, Alfred Pleasonton. A dandy who sported a waxed mustache and straw hat in the field, Pleasonton showed a pattern of failing to follow orders. He presumptuously offered McClellan strategic advice rather than sticking to his job of scouting. A shameless self-promoter, at Chancellorsville he made outlandish claims about his saving the Union Army from defeat. Hooker, nevertheless, rewarded him with command of his cavalry corps, which soon grew to 11,500 horsemen. Such a unit served as the primary information gatherer while an army was on the move, but Pleasonton, whose men were prone to pass along inaccurate, unsubstantiated, or misleading intelligence, failed to detect Lee's invasion north until it was well under way. He never took seriously the valuable resource he had in Sharpe's information bureau, treating its spies not as collaborators but as competitors to be ignored.

Pleasonton made life miserable for McEntee, whose team operated with the general's cavalry somewhat independently but still needed its cooperation. Despite Hooker and Butterfield ordering them to do so, Pleasonton's men refused to send McEntee the prisoners, deserters, and civilians they rounded up so they could be properly interrogated by his agents. The result: misinformation or little information was extracted from the interviews Pleasonton's soldiers conducted. McEntee was at his wits' end and routinely complained to Sharpe about Pleasonton shutting him out. Patrick thought Pleasonton was arrogant and stupid. Butterfield became frustrated, and even Hooker, who personally liked his cavalry commander, grew angry.

JUNE 3

Two-thirds of Lee's army began moving westward from Fredericksburg. He left the other third at the city temporarily as cover. Lee planned to march west to Culpeper Court House and then turn right to head north through the Shenandoah Valley. The Rappahannock, which separated his force from Hooker's, plus the Wilderness west of Fredericksburg, helped conceal his opening moves from Sharpe's agents. Confederate picketing also tightened to help keep the march secret and prevented McEntee's men from penetrating Confederate lines. Few Rebels deserted, which meant Babcock vacuumed up less information—but it also made him suspicious that Lee was likely on the move. Numerous reports came from balloonists, Signal Corps observers, and pickets who saw dust clouds from columns in motion or heard the clanking of rolling wagon trains. The reports worried Hooker. No trend or pattern was apparent to him from them.

Rebel deserters who did reach Babcock that day claimed Lee's army would try to attack across the Rappahannock the next morning. They may have been plants from Lee to divert the Federals' attention away from his movement north. Skinker arrived at Sharpe's tent to report that Confederate cavalry were concentrating at Culpeper Court House. With no hard evidence, just pure deduction, Skinker predicted the Confederates planned a large cavalry raid on Pennsylvania while the rest of Lee's army moved southward. The report only confused the picture more for Sharpe and Hooker.

That night, Hooker ordered his army to be ready the next morning for any orders he issued to move. But the Army commander did not know to where he would be moving. Fortunately for Sharpe, Lee would pause when he reached Culpeper in order to receive reinforcements and supplies. It gave the spymaster more time to discover what was happening.

JUNE 4

Clues trickled in for the picture Sharpe was painting of what Lee intended. It was a cool and pleasant summer day, ideal for Lowe's balloonists, who reported that west of Fredericksburg two Rebel camps had cleared out at Banks's Ford, several artillery batteries were moving, a line of dust could be seen from a column near Salem Church also west of Fredericksburg, and thirty wagons were rolling north on Telegraph Road below the city. Sharpe kept badgering McEntee for intelligence. The frustrated agent tried to set his boss straight on the problems he was having in the field. Pleasonton continued to be of no help. McEntee tried to slip agents past the Confederates' tight security line along the upper Rappahannock, but it wasn't easy and the agents' horses were beginning to wear out. On top of that, he suspected that one of his spies, a prosperous Virginian named George Smith, who owned a home in Culpeper County, was a double agent working for the Rebels. Sharpe messaged back not to give Smith any sensitive information but still use him to gather intelligence. Just keep trying, the spymaster ordered.

McEntee did come up with one useful bit of information that day. He learned that Confederate brigadier general William "Grumble" Jones's 1,600 cavalrymen from the Shenandoah Valley and two North Carolina cavalry regiments had joined Jeb Stuart, whose reinforced division of 9,500 horsemen roamed between Culpeper and Brandy Station just northeast— more evidence that some kind of heavy cavalry expedition was in the works. Sharpe ordered McEntee to keep him posted on Stuart's movements.

The spy chief turned his attention back to Fredericksburg, from which there was "considerable movement of the enemy," he reported to Hooker. Rebel infantry camps were "disappearing at some points." Where were the infantrymen going? Sharpe didn't know. Butterfield speculated that Lee might be moving his entire army northwest from Fredericksburg to Culpeper Court House, but it was only speculation. Hooker, though, reacted quickly. He ordered John Sedgwick on his left flank to send a division from his 6th Corps across the Rappahannock downstream of Fredericksburg and probe for what the enemy was doing.

The next day, June 5, brought more conflicting intelligence for Sharpe to untangle. A report arrived from a Connecticut man now living in the Shenandoah Valley, who said his brother in Aldie, Virginia, west of Washington, told him that the entire Rebel Army around Richmond was in motion, some forces were arriving from North Carolina, and Lee would strike somewhere soon. One of the strangest reports Sharpe ever had to evaluate came from a mulatto boy who claimed he had been one of General A. P. Hill's servants and had overheard his master talking about Lee's plan to invade Pennsylvania. But the youngster described an invasion route that seemed improbable to Sharpe. Could the boy have been another disinformation agent?

Hooker, becoming increasingly apprehensive, wrote Lincoln late that morning what he thought was happening based on the shards of intelligence Sharpe and the general's other sources had sent him. Lee has been greatly reinforced, Hooker told the president in a long letter, and he intended either to cross the upper Potomac River and invade Maryland or to throw his army between the Union force and Washington. In either case, the Confederate Army would be spread out from Fredericksburg to Culpeper and Hooker wanted to strike the rear of Lee's column at Fredericksburg. It was a sound plan. An attack on Lee's rear would almost surely have halted his invasion. Halleck, however, nixed the idea, fearing as Lincoln did that Hooker could become bogged down at Fredericksburg. Instead, Halleck telegraphed Hooker that the Potomac Army should stay on Lee's right flank if he headed north to cut him in two and protect Washington at the same time.

On June 6, Sedgwick found from his division's reconnaissance in force an escaped slave who reported that Lee and Longstreet were nearby to personally scout out whether Hooker's army would cross the river and attack him. This was important information. Lee, in fact, was checking things out for himself rather than relying on reports from subordinates. The maneuver he was planning could not have been more risky—crossing the Blue Ridge Mountains and then moving north into Maryland and Pennsylvania with Richard Ewell's corps leading the way and Longstreet's corps following, while Stuart's cavalry screened the infantry's movements and Hill's lone corps remained at Fredericksburg to keep the Yankees occupied until the march was well under way. But Lee could not allow a large part of his army to leave the area if a major threat of a Union attack remained. So he took time to investigate the situation personally. After he did, he wired Jeff Davis that he was satisfied no major threat existed.

Hooker did not know the calculations Lee made at this point. But he did know from intelligence Sharpe had pieced together that it was time to do something about Stuart's cavalry on his right flank at Culpeper. McEntee sent an enciphered message to Sharpe on June 6 that Stuart had staged a "grand review" of his cavalry the day before near Culpeper Court House—an appalling security breach for the Rebel commander. Convinced that Stuart planned a large raid, Hooker decided to send Pleasonton with 8,000 horsemen and 3,000 infantrymen west to break up the Rebel cavalry around Culpeper three days later.

JUNE 7

Sharpe sat down and wrote Butterfield a four-page memo summarizing the intelligence he had on what the Confederates were doing at Culpeper. He estimated that Stuart's cavalry force there and at nearby Brandy Station totaled 12,900 horsemen, but cautioned that the number might be as high as 15,000. That was an overestimate. But Sharpe's report had an even bigger error. From all the evidence McEntee had provided, the 12,900 to 15,000 Stuart had gathered there suggested that they "are on the eve of making the most important expedition ever attempted in this country," the spy chief wrote Butterfield. And when Stuart departed for his raid, "there are strong indications that the enemy's entire infantry will fall back upon Richmond and thence reinforce their armies in the west." Sharpe had been duped by Lee's disinformation campaign. The Rebel army was not falling back to Richmond. As Sharpe was finishing his report, all three of Ewell's divisions and two of Longstreet's divisions (more than 37,000 men total) had arrived at Culpeper. Lee had successfully screened their movement. Three of McEntee's spies reported the next day that Rebel infantry at Fredericksburg had changed camps for sanitary reasons. The infantrymen had moved, but not for the sake of hygiene.

All that was left at Fredericksburg was Hill's corps of 22,000 successfully keeping Hooker's 78,000 distracted and in place.

On the misty early morning of June 9, with McEntee and George Smith serving as guides, Pleasonton's mounted men quietly crossed the Rappahannock at Beverly Ford north of Stuart's position and swooped down on his surprised units bivouacked out front at Brandy Station—to prevent a raid Stuart never planned to carry out. It was the largest cavalry battle of the war, with 18,000 men fighting what turned out to be a confused sixteen-hour clash. Pleasonton later bragged that he seized Stuart's headquarters documents, which tipped him off to Lee's northern invasion plans. It was a lie. Pleasonton found only a few unimportant papers. Moreover, he had not discovered Lee's infantrymen, who had been kept out of sight nearby. By nightfall Lee was content to let Pleasonton's cavalry recross the Rappahannock unmolested while the lead element of his army, Ewell's brigades, began marching stealthily into the Shenandoah Valley the next day.

As the cavalry commander battled Stuart on June 9, Sharpe penned another memo to Hooker with updated intelligence that corrected the erroneous information he reported two days earlier. Sharpe now began to detect Lee's true plans. Hill's corps was in front of Hamilton's Crossing south of Fredericksburg but the rest of Lee's army was stretched out much farther west than Sharpe had realized. His spies now reported that Ewell's and Longstreet's corps had moved to near Kelly's Ford on the Rappahannock and Brandy Station. Sharpe no longer believed Lee's army would head south to Richmond. The spy chief hoped to locate Ewell and Longstreet more definitely, "but it is difficult to fix positioning, or penetrate designs, at the outset of a movement, which has as yet had no opportunity to develop," he pointed out. Indeed it was difficult. Spying on a stationary army was hard enough; gathering intelligence on Lee's forces while they moved was straining Sharpe, McEntee, and the other agents to their limit.

The next day, Pleasonton's men found two runaway slaves at Brandy Station, who had been servants to Confederate officers. They told the cavalry soldiers that Lee, Longstreet, A. P. Hill, and Ewell had been at Culpeper Court House on June 8 attending another of Stuart's grand cavalry reviews. No foot soldiers joined in the review, but the runaways insisted that five or six Rebel infantry divisions were nearby. They added that the cavalrymen were told they would be issued three days' rations and after that "they were to ration themselves up in Pennsylvania," Pleasonton reported to Hooker. It was a startling piece of intelligence. If Pleasonton had followed up on it and patrolled the region leading to the Blue Ridge Mountains, he would have discovered Ewell's men marching toward the Shenandoah and could have cut them off or called for infantry reinforcements to disrupt or even foil Lee's invasion plans. But Pleasonton instead wasted the day resting his troops, reorganizing his force, and staging his own cavalry review to celebrate what he considered his Brandy Station victory.

JUNE 13

In the lazy days of summer, all seemed to be going well for Lee. He enjoyed the initiative and believed the enemy had been "mystified" by his movements. He underestimated the flow of intelligence into Sharpe's bureau, but for now he benefited from the Allegheny and Blue Ridge mountain ranges concealing his army in the Shenandoah Valley corridor, from Stuart screening their movement north, and from Pleasonton's ineptness in pinpointing the enemy's location. Meanwhile, lethargy overtook Hooker's camp, which irritated Patrick, with soldiers and officers granted leaves, even corps commanders taking vacations.

Sharpe and McEntee had no time off, working nearly around the clock in search of the enemy. McEntee tricked a captured cavalry lieutenant into revealing the location of one of Stuart's brigades. A wily Union cavalry private named Martin Hogan arrived at McEntee's tent and volunteered to sneak into Lee's camp dressed as a Rebel soldier. He returned with information on Rebel soldiers marching toward the Blue Ridge. A young African American man named Charley Wright, another servant in Lee's army who closely watched its moves and had an excellent memory, confirmed to Sharpe on June 12 that Ewell's corps had set off for the Shenandoah Valley with Longstreet's corps following. By the next afternoon, Hooker had enough intelligence from Sharpe to fairly conclude that Ewell's and Longstreet's corps had moved on toward the valley. By June 14, the Union general had started his army in pursuit of Lee. Within a day, all further doubt that the Confederates intended a northern invasion had been erased; Hill's corps vacated Fredericksburg to join the rest of Lee's army, and Ewell's lead corps captured Winchester and Martinsburg to the northwest in Virginia, clearing the enemy facing Lee in the valley and opening a passage to the Potomac River and Maryland.

Hoping to hide his intentions from Lee, Hooker asked Stanton on June 16 to plant a story in northern papers that his army would be moving south to the James River. Lee wasn't sure of Hooker's intentions but his cavalry scouts had no trouble seeing the Yankees depart. It infuriated Patrick that when the men pulled out they followed the same routine, burning all the trash and camp shacks, which sent plumes of smoke alerting anyone nearby that the Army of the Potomac was on the move. One thing not torched this time—a cache of pornography at Hooker's Falmouth headquarters, which a Richmond reporter found later.

Hooker slowly marched his soldiers north from Falmouth. He moved parallel to Lee's army on the Union commander's left with the Blue Ridge mountain range separating them, trying to keep his federal force always between the Rebels and Washington. The hapless Pleasonton continued to fail in accurately tracking the northern march of the Confederates and to make it difficult for McEntee to do so. At one point while McEntee visited Sharpe at Hooker's headquarters, Pleasonton commandeered all his men to be guides and couriers, leaving McEntee with no way to operate. McEntee was ready to quit but Sharpe ordered him to remain with the horsemen. Instead of coming down hard on Pleasonton, Hooker asked Halleck to promote him to major general.

Balloons no longer helped. Lowe had been relieved of duty in a squabble with his superiors. As Hooker marched north, the professor was in Washington writing a report to answer fraud charges Lafayette Baker had been investigating. An informant later told one of Baker's detectives that Lowe was hiding in his home balloon equipment he reported missing in the Peninsula campaign. The experiment of balloons providing aerial surveillance came to an end. Ground commanders by then did not believe balloons were worth the hassle of transporting the unwieldy contraptions from place to place. The burden of determining the strength and location of Lee's army continued to fall on Sharpe's bureau.

JUNE 19

The days grew warmer as Lee and Hooker moved their large armies side by side northward, each largely blind to where the other was. It frustrated both men. "The reports from north of the Potomac are uncertain and unreliable," Butterfield wrote. "Nobody has been able to count over 1,500 of the enemy." Patrick worriedly wrote in his diary that Hooker might "catch a blow in the wrong place" moving this way in the dark. His troops stretched all over Virginia, Hooker on June 17 brought them nearly to a halt until he could locate the enemy and divine his intentions. The Army of the Potomac, Butterfield said, "cannot go boggling around until we know what we are going after." Hooker ordered his signal officers to set up observation stations above Harpers Ferry at Crampton's Gap and South Mountain, "where they can see the whole country north of the Potomac and telegraph movements of any column." Sharpe, meanwhile, organized four espionage expeditions whose targets spanned Fredericksburg in the rear to the area north of the Potomac.

The spymaster was coming under increasing fire from the Army high command. Ignoring how skillfully Stuart's cavalry had screened Lee's movement, particularly from Pleasonton, Halleck questioned how Sharpe's vaunted information bureau could not track tens of thousands of Confederates marching to its left. Sharpe, who was now sleeping in the same tent with Hooker and Butterfield, was finding the commanding general more hostile. Since Chancellorsville, Hooker had become increasingly disrespectful of the colonel. He appeared to have lost confidence in his intelligence chief, even though Sharpe's operation had been a resounding success.

By June 19, the tension had become toxic for Patrick, who believed Halleck was now the Potomac Army's de facto commander, with a stream of orders telegraphed from Washington to micromanage it. "We get accurate information, but Hooker will not use it and insults all who differ from him in opinion," the provost marshal wrote in his diary that night. "He has declared the enemy are over 100,000 strong. It is his only salvation to make it appear that the enemy's forces are larger than his own, which is all false and he knows it. He knows that Lee is his master and is afraid to meet him in a fair battle." Patrick wanted out. He began lobbying for a division command. But Hooker needed him as provost marshal and would not consider a transfer until the next battle was fought.

With the summer heat becoming oppressive and another battle possibly looming near Washington, Sharpe sent Carrie, who had remained in the capital with the children after visiting him at his camp, to cooler and safer Kingston. Fed up with Pleasonton and frustrated with Hooker's cold shoulder, Sharpe also applied for a transfer back to his old 120th Regiment. If Hooker indeed had lost confidence in him, Sharpe believed he would approve the transfer.

Hooker then had to decide whether to remain in his present defensive crouch around Washington south of the Potomac or cross the river and move into Maryland to keep up with Lee's army. Sharpe wrote his uncle Jansen that he was constrained in what he could tell him because he was "near the throne" and privy to top decisions, but he did divulge that if Lee planned to move north across the Potomac, Hooker wanted to overtake him in a battle. Lee "must whip us before he goes in force into Maryland or Pennsylvania," Sharpe wrote cryptically. "If he doesn't, we propose to let him go, and when we get behind him, we would like to know how many men he will take back." But to act quickly, Hooker still needed accurate intelligence on where his enemy was. He ordered Sharpe that day to send Babcock to Frederick, Maryland, northwest of Washington. Sharpe's number two man was to set up a spy station, recruiting citizen scouts and having them search for Lee in the northern end of the Shenandoah Valley as well as the Cumberland Valley in Maryland.

Babcock set out early that morning, stopping at the War Department in Washington along the way to draw funds for his operation. He was familiar with Frederick. He had worked in the crossroads city before for Pinkerton during the Antietam battle. This was a risky assignment. Loyalties in Frederick and the western Maryland country around it were divided. Hooker's army was some forty-four miles south below the Potomac—too far away to come to the rescue.

Babcock arrived in the city at midmorning on June 19 and immediately realized he might soon be in trouble. He rushed a telegram to Sharpe back at Hooker's headquarters. Confederates were expected in Frederick at any moment, he wrote the colonel. Babcock said he would flee to Hagerstown twenty-five miles northwest if he could. But if Sharpe wanted him to accomplish anything, he had better send him Milton Cline, the daring and resourceful cavalry sergeant working for the information bureau, as well as more Confederate currency to buy information from Rebel deserters. Babcock set up his spy station in the Frederick Female Academy, whose principal, Hiram Winchester, was one of three volunteer spies he found eager to serve the Union. The other two men, who had worked for him before and had just fled the Rebels invading Martinsburg, were James Greenwood and Isaac Moore.

The next day, June 20, Babcock telegraphed Sharpe "all I can learn at present"—that 6,000 Rebel infantrymen had so far crossed the Potomac into Maryland and a vanguard of 2,000 Confederate cavalrymen had ridden farther to Chambersburg, in south central Pennsylvania. Babcock also discovered a Rebel detachment showed up in Boonsboro, some fifteen miles northwest of Frederick, and had returned again to Hagerstown after stealing a few horses. "They may make a raid here at any moment," Babcock wrote Sharpe, "and I am not anxious to be . . ." At this point in the letter he drew a stick figure of a man being hung.

As if Babcock didn't know well enough the gravity of his mission, Hooker personally telegraphed him on June 20 with precise instructions for his spying. Send your citizen agents to the top of South Mountain "to overlook the valley beyond and see if the enemy have camps there," the general ordered. Confederate cavalry had blocked the Signal Corps observers from getting there. Use spies who "can look upon a body of armed men without being frightened out of their senses," Hooker continued. "If they take a position in the forest they can even count them as they pass on the road with impunity." Hooker wanted only "authentic" information. No rumors or false reports. "It is necessary for me to know if the enemy has any considerable number of his forces on the north side of the Potomac." That would be an important sign that Lee intended to invade Maryland or Pennsylvania and not attack Washington. "Be vigilant and active," Hooker lectured. Pass out money liberally for information "and it shall be returned to you." Babcock telegraphed back quickly that he was already on the case. He had sent Greenwood and Moore to South Mountain with a telescope. He hoped to report back to Hooker soon with "reliable information."

Tracking Lee's army over this vast an area with just a handful of volunteer spies was no easy task, but by late afternoon Babcock had important news he quickly telegraphed to Hooker. He had just interviewed a doctor from Williamsport, a village west of Frederick and just north of the Potomac, who reported that as many as 5,000 infantrymen from Ewell's corps had crossed the river there with 1,200 cavalrymen and were moving into Maryland. Babcock added that he had an unconfirmed report of other Rebel units crossing the river into Maryland farther south at Shepherdstown. Actually more Confederates had traversed the Potomac by that point, but Babcock's telegraph offered confirmation for Hooker that Lee's army would not attack Washington. Instead it appeared to be moving into Maryland and likely Pennsylvania, whose border lay just a dozen miles north.

Babcock had no time to send more reports from Frederick. At about five o'clock that afternoon a detachment of some twenty-five Confederate cavalrymen rushed into the city. Secessionists there had already identified him as a federal spy. He would surely be strung up if the raiders found him. Quickly Babcock hid his bags and papers and burned incriminating documents he couldn't conceal. He commandeered a railroad handcar and fled on a track—a step ahead of Rebels who chased him.

Babcock returned the next day to Monocacy Junction, a village just below Frederick, to try to piece back together his operation. But he knew that the Rebels had overrun most of the Union signal stations and he worried that they had captured Greenwood and Moore on South Mountain.

JUNE 22

More than a dozen intelligence-gathering efforts besides Sharpe's were now under way in northwest Virginia, Maryland, and Pennsylvania. Some were Washington units sent out to scout; others were launched by local commanders, railroad men, or state officials worried about Lee's hordes descending upon them. Hooker would soon be flooded with intelligence reports from these disparate groups. Among the Washington freelancers roaming the area and producing little of value for the general was Lafayette Baker and a battalion of cavalrymen Stanton had allowed him to organize.

Baker had been spending much of his time that summer as a glorified errand boy, fielding orders from Levi Turner, the special judge advocate, to arrest military officers and civilians accused of spying for the Confederates, shipping contraband goods south, or defrauding the U.S government. Baker's counterintelligence operation, meanwhile, had an embarrassing failure he never realized as Lee's army moved north.

Thomas Nelson Conrad, a native of Virginia and a graduate of Dickinson College in Pennsylvania, became one of the most elusive spies the Confederates had in Washington. A master of disguises, Conrad started out as a Georgetown boys' school headmaster, helping some students sneak away to join the Rebels and instructing others on how to pass messages to Confederates across the Potomac by flipping the shades in their dormitory room windows. Federal authorities sent him to Old Capitol Prison several times on suspicion of being an enemy agent, but Conrad always denied the charges and managed to talk his way out of jail and be put on parole. Once free, Conrad variously plotted an assassination of Winfield Scott (Confederate officials rejected it), fed the Rebels intelligence on McClellan's troop strength during the Peninsula campaign, and sent information to Richmond before the second Battle of Bull Run.

In mid-June, Stuart, who had made Conrad a cavalry chaplain as cover for his spying, sent the agent to Washington to keep him posted on federal movements there while Lee's army marched into Pennsylvania. Conrad used the Van Ness mansion, owned by a Confederate loyalist two blocks from the War Department, as his safe house. He worked his contacts among the city's remaining secessionists and plumbed informants buried in the War Department. Baker's men finally picked up Conrad's trail and began to close in on him. But Baker did not know that among Conrad's many snitches was a mole in the secret service chief's organization—a man named Edward Norton (although that may have been a pseudonym). Norton tipped off Conrad that Baker's detectives were about to raid the Van Ness house. Conrad vanished. But he had Norton deliver to Baker a lengthy report on the Rebel's spying to make Baker think Norton had been investigating Conrad and was a valuable agent. The mole continued to work in Baker's office.

Baker by then was preoccupied with a scheme he had been brainstorming for months to expand his organization, as well as his prestige. On May 6, Stanton signed an order the detective had lobbied for authorizing him to organize the 1st District of Columbia Cavalry Battalion. Baker claimed the unit was set up as a praetorian guard to root out subversives in Washington and protect the capital from Confederate raiders—a dubious mission considering that cavalrymen were hardly ideal counterespionage agents and the city was already heavily defended against an attack Lee had shown little interest in making. More likely, Baker wanted the battalion as military muscle for his raids, which the Army increasingly balked at providing. Baker also would receive the colonel's commission he desperately wanted by commanding the battalion, which Stanton a little more than a month later expanded to a full regiment of some 1,200 horsemen. Halleck and other senior generals opposed the cavalry unit and derisively called it "Baker's Rangers," a name the vain secret service chief actually liked.

He set up what he called "Camp Baker" near Capitol Hill to train his men. He bought his enlisted soldiers the finest repeating rifles, along with shiny new sabers and top-of-the-line Colt revolvers for his officers, and traveled to Philadelphia to find the best horses on the market. For himself, he purchased a tailored colonel's uniform with gaudy epaulettes and a sash to prance about on his horse like a peacock. Baker bragged that he wanted to be relieved of all his detective duties in Washington so he could lead his men into battle. But he turned out to be only an occasional commander. His cousin, Joseph Stannard Baker, who was made a company captain, resented the fact that Baker came to the cavalry camp no more than once a week, dressed in his fancy military costume, "always with much flourish" for ceremonial functions. He would order the men to "fall in" and stand at attention, Joseph recalled, "while he made a little speech to them in short, nervous sentences, all quite unimportant."

Stanton issued a press release to publicize Baker's Rangers. The *New*

York Times ran a story May 11, reporting that "honesty, sobriety and intelligence are conditions of service" in Baker's unit, which wasn't necessarily the case. Baker claimed thousands of applications poured in from soldiers who wanted to join the elite unit, also not entirely true. He did have some officers interested in signing up, but he had to hustle to fill the rest of the ranks. Baker lobbied New York's governor to let him recruit from the western part of that state, insisting he wanted only high-quality soldiers for his force. Critics complained Baker also settled for thugs and criminals. When Stanton later expanded his force to a regiment, Baker talked Maine's governor into turning over eight companies with eight hundred men from his state. The Maine soldiers expected to have easy duty parading around Washington in their finery. They grumbled when Baker sent them to the front to battle Confederates. Army generals, who considered Baker's Rangers little more than a glorified pack of spies and detectives, also grumbled when they showed up at their battlefields.

It did not take long before Baker was defending his cavalry as he had his detectives from charges they were a lawless bunch of vigilantes illegally confiscating property. "No military authority has achieved such power in Washington and the surrounding country as the cavalry force under the command of Colonel Baker," read one newspaper item. "Many . . . complaints have been made of the abuse of this power in the arbitrary arrests." A poison-pen letter arrived at Stanton's office from a Nevada territory man who had read the article and suggested the war secretary have one of his aides write the San Francisco Police Department for the record it had on Baker. "He is a most untrustworthy man and an unmitigated liar, and much worse than that could be proven against him," the Nevada resident wrote. Stanton kept the letter but there is no evidence in his files that he ever investigated allegations about Baker's past.

As Lee's force moved into Maryland and Pennsylvania, Baker's 1st D.C. Cavalry, many of whose members had not yet been fully trained, roamed Fairfax, Loudoun, and Fauquier Counties west of Washington hunting intelligence for Hooker and chasing Baker's obsession—Rebel guerrilla commander John Mosby. The intelligence his men uncovered proved paltry. A Rebel deserter reported widespread dissatisfaction among the South's poor and working class for the Confederate cause—hardly breaking news for Sharpe. Baker vowed his rangers would capture Mosby, but his rookies were no match for this seasoned unconventional warrior. Joseph thought the excursion was a waste of time.

After Lee's Pennsylvania campaign, Baker lost interest in leading what ended up being aimless forays to skirmish with the Rebels. He never took command of the 1st D.C. Cavalry again, letting subordinates like Joseph supervise it in the field. The War Department, seeing no value to the regiment being with the detectives, eventually reassigned it to the regular Army for combat operations in Virginia. But Baker got to keep his colonel's rank.

JUNE 24

The Rebel raid at Frederick cost Babcock two valuable days of spying. Greenwood and Moore, who had been sent to South Mountain, had not been heard from. They might have gone to Harpers Ferry, he telegraphed Sharpe, or they might have been captured—a blow for Hooker, who wanted them replaced with other mountaintop observers.

Babcock recovered quickly with the help of more men Sharpe rushed to him at Monocacy Junction. The station chief now kept the advancing Confederates under continual observation, his agents moving with Lee's forces as they approached the Potomac and crossed it. A steady stream of intelligence now flowed to Sharpe. Cline had been out for a week, disguised with others in his party as Confederate irregulars to mix with Lee's troops. The sergeant returned June 22 with valuable information on Ewell's corps drawing supplies from Maryland and Pennsylvania, on the position of Hood's and Pickett's divisions in Longstreet's corps, and on the location of Hill's corps. But it would be erroneous intelligence from Babcock that finally propelled Hooker across the Potomac to get a jump on Lee.

The Union commander as of June 23 remained uncertain whether Lee's objective was Pennsylvania (despite the large Rebel force that appeared to be headed there), or Baltimore or still Washington. So he continued to hold his army south of the Potomac River, deployed from Manassas to Leesburg, Virginia, to protect the federal capital. Babcock's cables on June 24 settled the question. Tapping a number of sources—including lookouts on South Mountain and student refugees from St. James College, near Hagerstown, who spotted Ewell's corps with seventy artillery pieces passing through their town—he told Hooker that Lee's *entire* army "beyond a doubt" had crossed the Potomac into Maryland, with thousands already in Pennsylvania. Babcock's report, along with others Hooker had received, finally convinced him that Lee was heading north and Washington was no longer threatened.

Hooker sent orders to his seven corps commanders that night and the next morning to cross the Potomac and move into Maryland. By June 27 all his infantry as well as his cavalry were north of the river. It was a forthright move for a commander who had been slow-moving up to that point. But it turned out the move was based on erroneous information Babcock had provided. The rear of Lee's army was not across the Potomac, as the operative reported, but instead was two days' march short of that. The reason for Babcock's error was a simple switch he and his agents had not detected.

For a long time, Hill's corps, which had been the last to leave Fredericksburg, had been Lee's rear element far behind Longstreet's corps. But the two Rebel corps had since changed positions. James Longstreet now trailed behind A. P. Hill. But Babcock and the Union signal officers observing the Confederate movement didn't realize a switch had occurred. When they saw Hill's corps cross the Potomac, they assumed it was still following Longstreet's corps and thus all of Lee's army was on the north side of the river and in Maryland. In fact, Longstreet's corps on June 24 was still in Virginia some forty-five miles south of where it would cross the Potomac. Longstreet wouldn't get his men over the river until two days later. A disinformation campaign Lee had waged to deceive Hooker on the location of his different corps added to the confusion. Babcock's bad intelligence, however, ended up having a good result. Hooker's army crossed the Potomac hours ahead of Lee's, and, unknown to the Rebel commander, got a jump on him in what turned out to be a race for crucial position at the point where the two would clash—Gettysburg.

Two more days passed before Lee learned that Hooker had stolen a march on him and was no longer in Virginia. On June 25, the Confederate commander had imprudently allowed Stuart to take much of his cavalry on a wide sweep east around the entire Potomac Army to keep Lee informed on enemy movements. For a week, however, Lee heard not a word from his valuable cavalry chief. Stuart left behind two cavalry brigades under an incompetent brigadier general named Beverly H. Robertson, who failed abysmally at the outset to screen Lee's movements or to detect Hooker's crossing the Potomac.

When Lee and his headquarters element forded the river at Williamsport and then crossed the Mason-Dixon Line into Pennsylvania, it was as if he had entered a dark room with no candlelight. The countryside was rich to feed his army but Pennsylvanians were not friendly. Away from his Virginia base, Lee had no access to his spy networks. Stuart was absent and in the week to come Robertson did not get any better at collecting intelligence. Lee faced an information blackout.

For Sharpe the intelligence game changed radically. He was now on friendly northern soil in Pennsylvania. Stretched through both Maryland and Pennsylvania, Lee did not have enough pickets, nor Stuart's skills in screening, to keep curious citizens and their prying eyes from passing through his lines. Anticipating a bumper crop of information, Sharpe moved quickly, dashing off a telegram to McEntee before he splashed across the Potomac with Hooker's headquarters staff to "send out everybody immediately to learn what the enemy movements are." The windfall came soon. A few hours after Sharpe rode into Frederick with Hooker's staff, the spymaster had a pretty clear picture from interviews with local citizens on where many of the Rebel corps and divisions were positioned in Pennsylvania. Hagerstown blacksmith Thomas McCammon gave him a detailed record on Confederate units that marched through the city toward the Pennsylvania line. A mailman the Rebels captured on his delivery route managed to escape and pass along information on a cavalry column and the seven artillery pieces accompanying it. County official William Logan and another resident, William Protzman, provided the most accurate count of the invaders' number—80,000 soldiers and 275 artillery guns—plus what they observed of the physical condition of the soldiers.

During the next week more than one hundred substantial reports on the movement and strength of Lee's army—from Sharpe's spies and from numerous citizen scouts—poured into his headquarters tent. Three-quarters of the reports were substantially correct. Sharpe was able to churn out in rapid fire enemy situation summaries with only a few errors in them, which were couriered or telegraphed quickly to Hooker, his subordinate generals, the War Department in Washington, and to panicky state officials at Pennsylvania's capital, in Harrisburg. Yet despite the flood of intelligence pouring in to him—which indicated that Lee's formidable legions were probably overextended—the Army of the Potomac commander on June 27 did not appear to be optimistic, or resolute.

JUNE 28

Lincoln fired Hooker. The weeks after the Chancellorsville debacle had been miserable for the president with war protests in the North escalating and Democrats in Congress attacking him. Lincoln saw Lee's incursion into Pennsylvania as an ideal opportunity to destroy the Rebel commander's army far from its base. But his confidence had evaporated that the Union commander who could accomplish this was Fighting Joe, who in telegram exchanges with the White House appeared to have become more and more like McClellan, complaining that he did not have enough troops and finding excuses for not moving. Other senior officials in Washington had lost confidence in Hooker as well. So had key subordinates under him, including Patrick and Sharpe.

After a squabble with Halleck over whether a 10,000-man garrison should remain at Harpers Ferry—Hooker wanted it removed while Halleck wanted it to stay in place—Hooker in a huff tendered his resignation, not expecting it would be accepted on the eve of such an important battle. But Lincoln quickly did. At 3 a.m. on June 28, Stanton's Army aide tapped on George Gordon Meade's tent pole at the Frederick headquarters for his 5th Corps to wake him. The groggy general at first thought he was being rousted from bed to be arrested. The aide lit a candle and told Meade he now commanded the Potomac Army.

A tall and wiry man with a sallow face, thinning brown hair flecked with gray, and dark eyes behind spectacles he often wore perched on his beak nose, Meade had never been popular among officers who served under him—"irritable, petulant and dyspeptic," as one aide said. "A damned old goggle-eyed snapping turtle," according to another soldier. Meade was nothing if not single-minded, always deadly earnest and harsh with skulkers. Short-tempered, he struck a man cowering behind a tree at the Antietam battle with the flat of his saber for not falling into ranks. He rarely acknowledged the cheers of his troops as he rode by them on his white horse. Born in Spain to American parents who reared him in Philadelphia, Meade had ranked only in the lower half of his West Point class but served during his early military years in the topographical engineers. He preferred to be hands-on with intelligence. During the Mexican War he rode out himself to scout targets, question pickets near enemy lines, and check the ground before a looming fight. As a division and corps commander, Meade frequently interrogated deserters for information. Taking command of the Army of the Potomac, he quickly let his staff know that he preferred receiving raw intelligence rather than processed reports.

Meade was not particularly friendly with Butterfield but decided to keep him for the moment as his chief of staff. Meade already knew that Pleasonton liked to fight Confederates rather than gain information from them, but he decided to keep him as his cavalry commander, albeit on a short leash, with explicit orders to collect intelligence. As for Sharpe, Meade had always been deferential to him in the past, but he knew little about the information bureau the colonel ran and did not know what use he could make of the outfit as he sat in his tent in the dark early-morning hours of June 28 collecting his thoughts.

As dawn broke, Meade also knew little about where the enemy was and even where his own forces were. The secretive Hooker had not shared with him or the other corps commanders the intelligence collected or the plans he had for the Union Army. Butterfield and Sharpe spent the rest of the day bringing the new commander up to speed on the positions of the federal corps and the considerable amount of information they had accumulated so far on Lee's forces. Meade quickly realized the armies were not that far apart. His seven corps with 90,000 men were clustered around Frederick. Lee's force of some 75,000 was feeding off the land in a wide arc northwest and northeast around a small Pennsylvania town near the Maryland border called Gettysburg. Longstreet's and Hill's corps sat near Chambersburg, Pennsylvania, west of Gettysburg. Two divisions from Ewell's corps were north of Carlisle, Pennsylvania, and preparing to capture Harrisburg to the east while his third division, commanded by Jubal Early, stood farthest east near York, Pennsylvania, threatening a railroad bridge over the Susquehanna River. As for catching and defeating Lee, Meade concluded that his predecessor had no plan in the works. It seemed to him that Hooker was content to let Lee dictate events as he had at Chancellorsville.

Meade was not. With less than twenty-four hours of Potomac Army command under his belt but feeling confident in the intelligence Sharpe placed in his hands, Meade that night issued marching orders to his corps commanders. Beginning at 4 a.m. the next day, his force would move northeastward, fanning out toward the Pennsylvania state line with its left flank headed for Emmitsburg, Maryland, and its right flank going to Westminster, Maryland.

Robert E. Lee saw a far more obscured picture for most of June 28 than Meade. It cleared considerably that night when dirty and ragged-looking Henry Thomas Harrison, the spy Longstreet sent to Washington, reached Lee's headquarters with startling news that the entire Potomac Army was across the Potomac River moving northward and it was now led by George Meade. After he got over his irritation at being unaware of Hooker's river crossing for three days, Lee realized he was in a vulnerable position with his force scattered in a forty-five- to sixty-mile crescent through southern Pennsylvania and the Union Army packed tightly nearby. Meade, whom Lee thought perfectly capable of taking advantage of any blunder the Rebels made, could chew up his force piece by piece. The Rebel commander abandoned his plan for Ewell to capture Harrisburg and sent out midnight orders to him, Longstreet, and Hill to converge their corps quickly above Gettysburg.

JUNE 29

It turned into a hot day as Meade's seven corps, flanked by cavalry and trailed by artillery, marched north with drums beating and bands playing.

Soon soldiers stripped to their underwear to cool off. Sunstroke felled some. Already showing signs of stress from practically no sleep since he was made Potomac Army commander, Meade changed his plans. Instead of attacking Lee, he would set up a defensive line. The strongest one, as he saw it, lay behind a stream called Pipe Creek, in northern Maryland southeast of Gettysburg. Sharpe now had twenty-one scouts and spies in his mobile information bureau, along with civilian volunteers, sending him information, plus Pleasonton's cavalrymen under orders to cooperate. To learn more about Lee's forces and how he planned to use them, an anxious Meade instructed Sharpe's agents to scout ahead in Pennsylvania that night. Teams hurried to Hanover, Greencastle, Chambersburg, Jefferson, and to what both sides were beginning to see was the critically important town of Gettysburg. "Get as much information as you can of the numbers, position, and force of the enemy, with their movements," Butterfield told Sharpe.

Eighty-year-old Gettysburg lay in a basin surrounded by ridges, with its 2,400 residents living and working in brick buildings, many as blacksmiths or carriage makers. The town also boasted a small college and a Lutheran seminary. Meade knew nothing about the sleepy village, its surrounding countryside, and more important, whether it was best suited for offense or defense. The only thing he could determine so far was that Lee might be coming there, although he didn't know if he would be fighting the Rebel commander at that very spot. Looking at his map, Lee could see as well that Gettysburg was an important hub in south-central Pennsylvania for ten roads, most of which ran through the mountains to the west or led southeast toward Baltimore and Washington. It would be an important intersection for either army.

Gettysburg increasingly became the target of Meade's spies. When Major General John Reynolds, who commanded the Union 1st Corps and Meade's left wing, arrived in Emmitsburg that day, Edwin Hopkins, one of Sharpe's agents who had just been to Gettysburg, rushed to him on his galloping horse with a report on Confederate movements in that area. Reynolds immediately couriered a message with Hopkins's information to Butterfield at Hooker's headquarters. One of McEntee's best spies, Hopkins was part of a three-man team Sharpe called his "soda water scouts," because they got that nickname when they shared a tent in an artillery battery. Hopkins quickly set up a pipeline from Sharpe to what became a makeshift civilian spy network in Gettysburg, led by a lawyer there named David McConaughy. The attorney began sending Sharpe intelligence on Rebel forces north of the town, which Sharpe found startlingly valuable because of its minute detail. He rushed the information to Meade, who was delighted with the reports.

At seven o'clock that evening, Sharpe scribbled a note and had a courier hurry it to McConaughy in Gettysburg. Deliver us more intelligence and we'll deliver you a victory, he told the lawyer, and urged him to recruit as many of the town's residents as he could to collect information. The names of Confederate generals and the number of troops they commanded in their units "are very important to us," Sharpe wrote. "The General begs, if in your power, that you make such arrangements with intelligent friends in the country beyond you to this effect, and that you continue your attention to us, as much as convenience will permit." McConaughy's reports, more than any others, focused like a laser beam the Union sights on Gettysburg. Sharpe hoped that one day after whatever happened in this clash of two great armies he could see coming he would be able to find McConaughy and shake his hand.

JUNE 30

At times like these, the information needs of both armies shifted from broad strategic intelligence to finer-grain tactical information on the strength of smaller enemy units and their precise movements, provided best by cavalry. At this point with Lee still missing Stuart, Meade enjoyed the cavalry advantage, with the better part of a corps of horsemen at his disposal. Pleasonton was a subpar spy but one of his division commanders, Brigadier General John Buford, an unassuming yet reliable officer, was not. Among the last orders Hooker had issued before relinquishing command was to send this skilled intelligence gatherer to Gettysburg to reconnoiter. Midmorning on June 30, Buford rode into the town with two brigades.

When he made his way to the western end of Gettysburg, Buford came under fire from Rebel skirmishers. They were from a North Carolina brigade in Henry Heth's division commanded by Brigadier General J. Johnston Pettigrew, who had planned to enter the town to forage for supplies. Pettigrew backed off and alerted Heth back at Cashtown, just to the northwest. Heth, a headstrong major general, decided he would take his division into Gettysburg the next day to clear out the federal horsemen. Buford, meanwhile, decided that he and his 2,950 troopers would stay put and not surrender the town without a fight.

By the end of June 30, Buford had collected a considerable amount of information. Excited townsfolk eagerly told him about Confederate units they had seen. McConaughy's network alerted him to A. P. Hill's corps northwest of the city. From their reports and those of scouting parties he dispatched with McEntee's agents in all directions, Buford had assembled a clearer picture of a potentially heavy Confederate force assembling northwest of Gettysburg. Buford also determined that the high ground around Gettysburg, particularly east and south of the town, might afford Union soldiers a strong defensive position. At midnight, the cavalry leader sent a courier with a dispatch detailing the valuable intelligence he had collected to Major General John Reynolds, Meade's corps commander on the left wing, who was closest to Buford at Emmitsburg, Maryland, just below the Pennsylvania line. But Buford's information wouldn't reach Meade until the next morning.

With Butterfield and Sharpe close by, Meade moved his headquarters to Taneytown, a Maryland hamlet below the Pennsylvania line now clogged with Union troop and supply trains. He could not tell yet where his battle with Lee might be, so he told his corps commanders to be ready to fight anywhere. All day on June 30 Meade had digested report after report from Sharpe and Pleasonton's cavalrymen, drafting plans to move his army in one direction and then changing his mind and drafting plans to move in another direction. He was not befuddled or vacillating. From intelligence reports he clearly knew the Confederate Army had been strung out over southern Pennsylvania. Lee now appeared to be shifting his forces to concentrate them around Gettysburg, but keeping track of all the moving parts on this very fluid day proved more difficult for Sharpe. Meade had alerted his corps commanders that Confederates in large numbers were advancing toward Gettysburg. But somewhat uneasy, he had decided to hold his force in place north and south of the Mason-Dixon Line until Confederate plans, he said, "have been more fully developed." Gettysburg was a possible battle site in Meade's mind, but not the only one, and Sharpe was sure from his conversations with the general that Gettysburg was not the place he wanted to fight Lee.

While Meade sorted through a steady flow of intelligence coming into his headquarters, Lee faced the opposite problem—little information reaching him, with his trusted intelligence gatherer, Jeb Stuart, seriously behind schedule in reuniting with his army. On June 30, the southern commander had only a vague idea of his enemy's whereabouts. So Lee, who had envisioned a bold maneuver campaign, marked time while he continued to concentrate his three corps that night to within a twenty-five-mile radius of Gettysburg—a convenient gathering place but not necessarily the spot he envisioned fighting a major battle. Rebel scouts arrived with erroneous reports placing much of Meade's army further south of Gettysburg than it actually was. But then a surprising and somewhat disturbing report reached his headquarters that Pettigrew's brigade had clashed with an unidentified federal force occupying Gettysburg.

JULY 1

Sharpe was struck by the moonlit night when he rode out with Meade and his senior staff from their Taneytown headquarters. They spurred their horses to a fast trot up Taneytown Road and made the fourteen-mile trip to the south of Gettysburg quickly. Shortly before midnight, their party stopped at Little Round Top, on Meade's left, which was three miles south of the town. He inspected the rocky knoll that rose into the dark night and then galloped on, wearily entering the Evergreen graveyard south of the city on hundred-foot-high Cemetery Hill. This was where he had ordered his troops to concentrate. The general, Sharpe, and the other aides rode past broken tombstones and dismounted at the gatekeeper's lodge. With the light of the full moon, Sharpe could see the Confederate infantrymen camped just north of the hill.

Meade had not acted hastily when he received news of the Confederate advance on Gettysburg, but he had begun hurrying the rear of his army to join its forward area south of the town. Sharpe recalled distinctly the solemnity of the conversation now at the gatekeeper's lodge, brought on by everyone's realization that an enormous confrontation loomed. Three of Meade's corps commanders—Oliver Otis Howard, Henry Slocum, and Daniel Sickles—met him at the lodge as Union troops continued to move that night into the high ground to the left and right of Cemetery Hill.

"Is this the place to fight the battle?" Meade asked after the generals finished greeting one another. The three corps commanders were satisfied with it, they told the army commander. The high-ground position the Confederate forces had pushed the Potomac Army back to the day of July 1—a long arc from Culp's Hill southeast of Gettysburg, around Cemetery Hill, and two miles south down Cemetery Ridge to Little Round Top—was a powerful defensive location, which Meade could hold and launch from to take the offensive if he chose to. "I'm glad to hear you say so," Meade answered grimly, "for it is too late to leave now." He began giving directions on the placement of his forces.

Sharpe's intelligence could no longer influence the time and place of battle. But he could still contribute a great deal to the outcome. About seven hundred Rebels had been captured that day. Babcock, McEntee, and a small information bureau team had ridden to Gettysburg with an advanced detachment and had begun interrogating as many captives as they could. The rest were hustled to a depot Patrick set up at Taneytown, where operatives left behind in Sharpe's bureau questioned them before they were moved to prison pens in Washington or Baltimore. From the interviews, Sharpe knew the Federals would have a tough fight the next day. Lee and his lieutenants might be worried, but the Confederate rank and file thought they could demolish the Yankee army at Gettysburg. They had whipped McClellan, Burnside, and Hooker and would do the same now with Meade. "Every nerve had been strained to convert the Army of Northern Virginia into the most powerful weapon the Confederacy could forge," Sharpe recalled. Lee's "three great infantry corps," each larger than a Union corps, averaged 25,000 men apiece, Sharpe calculated. Lee's three corps commanders—Longstreet, Hill, and Ewell—and the nine division commanders under them were West Point graduates, now seasoned war veterans, and for the most part the Confederacy's best, Sharpe determined. "They were already hailed with the prophecy of victory," he said.

Chafing as all commanders do on the eve of battle, Meade had remained at his busy Taneytown headquarters until Gettysburg more or less had been selected for him and Lee on July 1. That morning had begun with A. P. Hill sending General Heth to the town to check out what kind of Union force was there. When Harry Heth clashed with John Buford's brigade at 7:30 a.m., he did not know it was not two local Yankee militia companies, as he had anticipated, but instead two advanced cavalry brigades for the entire Army of the Potomac. With less than half his men in the vicinity, Lee was not ready for a general engagement and expected July 1 to be a peaceful day. Instead of pulling back as the Rebel army commander wanted, Heth, with no orders telling him to do so, fought on and soon realized he was in for more than he and Hill had bargained for. Certain that Hill's corps was advancing on him from the west and Ewell's corps was driving in from the north, Buford put up a spirited defense to buy time. He dispatched a courier to summon reinforcements. Heth did the same with Hill. General Reynolds, Meade's left-wing commander who was eager to fight, had quickly marched his 1st Corps and Howard's 11th Corps forward to back up the two cavalry brigades. He took Babcock and McEntee with him.

Meade that morning was no more prepared or anxious to fight at Gettysburg than Lee. His chosen ground for a battle with the Rebels was what he considered a better defensive position behind Pipe Creek, just below the Pennsylvania–Maryland line. He wanted the 1st and 11th Corps under Reynolds to lure the Rebels into following them as they fell back to Meade's army at the creek. But Meade's hopes for his Pipe Creek plan faded when he received a morning report from Reynolds that he was trying to beat the Confederates to the high ground at Gettysburg "and keep them back as long as possible," fighting them street by street through the town if he had to. Meade surmised that there had been a mix-up and Reynolds had not received his circular outlining his Pipe Creek plan or his instructions for the left-wing commander simply to evaluate what was happening at Gettysburg.

After an hour of fighting, Reynolds was killed from an enemy Minié ball that struck him in the back of the neck. Meade got the sad news at 1 p.m. and a half hour later dispatched Major General Winfield Scott Hancock, his 2nd Corps commander, to Gettysburg to decide if the army should fight there or at Pipe Creek. By then Lee was riding toward the town to take command at a battlefield he had not picked or wanted at this point, but at which two of his corps, Hill's and Ewell's, were now engaged. Although he still did not know how much of Meade's army he might be facing that afternoon, Lee quickly seized the opportunity and authorized Hill and Ewell to attack. Their two corps, enjoying a numerical advantage at this point, drove the Union 1st and 11th Corps south through Gettysburg's streets, in what at times became chaotic hand-to-hand fighting, to Cemetery Hill and Cemetery Ridge.

Around 4 p.m., Hancock arrived on Cemetery Hill as the battered 1st and 11th Corps showed up. He took command of them and with Howard rallied the Union force, posting soldiers and artillery defensively to stem the Rebel advance. The highly capable Hancock also decided that Gettysburg should be the Potomac Army's battlefield and messaged Meade an hour later that they could fight from advantageous ground at Cemetery Hill and Cemetery Ridge. Sharpe was lying on the ground in a corner of Meade's tent at Taneytown when Hancock's dispatch arrived. He eavesdropped as the general read it out loud. High ground wasn't the only reason for moving the Union force north, Sharpe thought. It would cripple the soldiers' morale, he believed, if they vacated what they had fought so hard for that day at the town and moved down to Pipe Creek, "giving the impression of a retreat." For the rest of the afternoon and into the silent night, Meade carefully but swiftly brought the rest of his army north to Gettysburg.

By the evening, Robert E. Lee was not his usual calm self but instead excited, uneasy, anxious, and still seething over Stuart's continued absence, over Heth's jumping the gun, and over Hill's letting that happen. He determined nevertheless that he must keep up the initiative gained from chasing the Yankees out of Gettysburg and have his 3rd Corps, commanded by Longstreet, join the other two for the next day's battle.

JULY 2

The day brought more than 16,000 casualties for both sides. From his vantage point at the little white-frame farmhouse that the widow Lydia Leister owned on the east slope of Cemetery Ridge south of Cemetery Hill, and which Meade had picked for his field headquarters, Sharpe saw the entire conflict unfold. Stricken with diarrhea, Lee wanted Longstreet as early as possible to attack Cemetery Ridge, which rose about forty feet from the surrounding land and stretched two miles down Meade's left flank. But Longstreet, grumpy and unenthusiastic about Lee's plan, did not put his men in position to strike until 4 p.m. When his brigades started to move forward, Union riflemen and artillery pointing down at them from along Cemetery Ridge's higher ground threw them back until the decimated ranks gave up at nightfall. Stuart, who had been away from the Confederate Army since June 25, finally arrived at Lee's headquarters in the afternoon—to a frosty reception from his commander. On Meade's right flank at steep and heavily wooded Culp's Hill, Ewell turned what was supposed to be a demonstration of force to divert federal attention from Longstreet's assault into a full-scale attack that the Yankees succeeded in driving off as darkness fell.

Throughout the day, the Confederate offensive became uncoordinated, improvised, and lacked the good generalship Lee had displayed so far. Waves of attacks and counterattacks flowed across the fields of battle, with Lee's men having to fall back each time their assault was on the cusp of success. Pale and careworn, with dark lines under his eyes from another night of little sleep, Meade spent practically the entire day in the saddle riding from one point to another on adrenaline, coolly, skillfully, and decisively moving troops to the right spots to plug holes or reinforce weakened defenses. Unlike McClellan, who kept to his rear headquarters, Meade fearlessly ventured close enough to the fighting that his horse, Old Baldy, was wounded at one point. His troops, too busy to cheer him when he passed by, for the most part held firm their lines. The fighting—in places given macabre names like Devil's Den and the Slaughter Pen—at times became so intense Union artillerymen fended off Rebel advances "using handspikes, rammers, pistols, and even stones," Meade recalled in his memoirs. The savagery reminded Sharpe of a line from Wellington at Waterloo: "Hard pounding, this, gentlemen; but we will pound the longest."

Sharpe, Babcock, and McEntee began the day expecting that being so close to the enemy would enable them to fill in all the blank spots in their records on Lee's army. Recently added regiments would be identified, their assignments to brigades verified. This was more than a bookkeeping exercise. If they could identify an enemy regiment at a particular front, Sharpe's team could identify the division (even the entire corps) the Union soldiers faced. That was important information for Meade as he darted from one position to another that day—especially when it was combined with the reports Signal Corps observers posted around the battlefield messaged to headquarters on enemy movements.

At 8 a.m., Sharpe scribbled a short note to Butterfield with the latest count of prisoners picked up that morning, along with their regiments identified. The interrogations also produced a significant piece of intelligence that would become even more important as the day wore on. "All prisoners now agree that their whole army is here," Sharpe informed Butterfield, "that A. P. Hill and Longstreet forces were badly hurt yesterday and that several general officers are injured." Lee's army was wounded and there were no reinforcements to rescue him. The fighting that day brought 1,360 Rebel prisoners to the Yankee stockades Patrick had erected east of the Leister House. From that huge pool, Babcock discovered POWs from one hundred different Confederate regiments and from every brigade in Lee's army— except for the four brigades of Pickett's division. This was more important information for Meade. In the two days of fighting at Gettysburg, Lee had used almost his entire infantry—but not Pickett's division, the smallest in his army. It was bringing up Lee's rear and represented the only reinforcement of fresh troops he had for the battle. Babcock labored to write his important report, which was forwarded to Butterfield. The task was made more difficult by the fact that Sharpe's deputy had been slightly wounded during the day.

June 2 ended with an ear-splitting artillery duel between the two sides. Meade and his staff rode along the lines at Cemetery Ridge, finally stopping in an open field for a limp celebration when they learned their men had successfully beaten back all the Rebel attacks and punished the enemy severely for launching them. Meade would say only, "It is all right now." For how long, he did not know.

By nightfall the two sides stood bloodied and exhausted at much the same positions they had started from in the morning, along the arc from Culp's Hill to Little Round Top. The guns fell silent. Bobbing lights from the lanterns of stretcher-bearers collecting the dead and wounded added to the illumination of the near-full moon. Each side's pickets left the stretcher-bearers alone to accomplish their grim work. A dozen generals rode up to the Leister House, tied their horses to a white picket fence along its front, and tromped inside for a war council Meade had called. The hot, cramped house, which had only a bed, a table, and a few chairs in its front room, reeked of cigar smoke and body odor from men too long without baths now crammed inside it.

Unsure his army could take another brutal day like the one that just ended, Meade had summoned Sharpe to his headquarters before the war council convened. He asked his spymaster for any more details he might have on Babcock's important report that the only reserve Lee had was Pickett's small division. Sharpe left and quickly found Babcock, who said the report still stood, except for minor updates, which the colonel scribbled on notepaper. A small Confederate cavalry unit still had not been used and Pickett's division had now arrived. It was bivouacked and ready to go into action tomorrow morning.

Sharpe rushed back to the Leister House clutching a sheaf of reports. He found Meade at the small table, which had a burning candle, a plate of crackers, and a half-pint flask of whisky on it. Hancock and Slocum were stretched out on the rough cot in the corner. Other generals stood or sat around the Potomac Army commander. For all the horror its members had witnessed that day and could expect to see the next, the war council had the air of a routine business meeting. Butterfield read out loud the roster reports. The generals listed the condition of each U.S. corps. The Yankees had inflicted tremendous casualties on the enemy and had stood off Long-street's ferocious onslaught at Cemetery Ridge without having to tap the considerable strength of the 6th Corps. What's more, large parts of the 5th and 12th Corps had not been used much in the day's battle. Butterfield estimated Meade had 58,000 troops fit for duty.

Meade then called on Sharpe, who recited Babcock's report to the war council with the update he had just received. The only fresh men Lee had for his worn-out army were from Pickett's division, "which has come up and is now in bivouac," Sharpe said assertively. The generals in the room did the math quickly in their heads. With Lee's exhausted force depleted and a hefty chunk of Meade's force still unused, the Army of the Potomac could count on having a six-to-one advantage in fresh troops for July 3. Hancock looked up and said with a smile: "We have got them nicked!" He added, glancing at the spymaster with the same smile, that Sharpe deserved a whisky and cracker for the intelligence he provided. Sharpe, who was famished, would have reached for the snack in front of Meade if he'd had a higher rank than colonel.

Meade put the options they now had to a vote among his war council. Should they retire to Pipe Creek, nearer their supply base, or remain at Gettysburg to fight? The generals voted to remain at Gettysburg. The Potomac Army had retreated too much and Sharpe's intelligence told them the odds were with them if they remained where they were. Meade's second question: should the army attack at Gettysburg or await the Rebel attack? Remain on the defensive on the high ground, the generals answered; let the Rebels waste lives charging uphill.

After the war council meeting broke up, Captain Ulric Dahlgren, a dashing young cavalry officer whose father was a top Navy admiral, rode into Meade's headquarters camp with intelligence that backed up Babcock's report. Dahlgren had been leading a scouting party, which included Sharpe's agent Milton Cline, in the enemy's rear in the Cumberland Valley thirty miles west. They had captured in the town square of Greencastle, Pennsylvania, near the border, twenty-two Confederate soldiers, one of whom had a saddle valise with dispatches for Lee from Jefferson Davis and his adjutant general, Samuel Cooper. The letters, which Davis had foolishly neglected to put in code, informed Lee that Rebel armies in other theaters were hard-pressed and Richmond had barely enough troops for its protection, so no reinforcements were available for the Pennsylvania campaign. Lee would have to continue fighting with the men he had there. Dahlgren was promoted to colonel as reward for his find. Lee did not pick up hints that the enemy knew he would receive no reinforcements until a week later, when he read northern newspaper accounts of Dahlgren intercepting the dispatches.

JULY 3

The day began bright and clear. Looking haggard from no sleep and little food, Meade rode along the Union line from Culp's Hill to Little Round Top with Sharpe and other aides in tow, ensuring that his flanks were secure and his center along Cemetery Ridge was reinforced for what he expected to be the brunt of the Rebel attack if Lee made one. Meade had quick and nervous movements, likely symptoms of extreme fatigue. But he read the southern commander's mind well. Lee was stubbornly undaunted by the federal defense wall his northern campaign had run into the day before. He stuck to his plan and ordered Ewell to charge his corps up Culp's Hill on the Union right and Longstreet to launch a frontal attack on the Union center at Cemetery Ridge. Ewell and Longstreet thought straight-ahead assaults were insane but Lee would not be talked out of them. Sharpe and his spies also believed the Confederates would attack the Union center. That day's battle would be grisly, they thought.

Meade had a good picture of the threat he faced on his right flank. Babcock had confirmed the previous day's information that Ewell's entire corps of 21,200 was in place there. After hours of bloody fighting, the Union force regained lost ground at Culp's Hill and by 11 a.m. Ewell was defeated. The Rebels began their Cemetery Ridge attack with a massive 150-gun artillery barrage at 1 p.m., which could be heard 140 miles away. Yankee soldiers hugged the ground behind stone walls and breastworks, but fortunately for the front line, the poor ammunition the Confederates used overshot. It resulted in Meade's headquarters, with Sharpe's bureau there, being shelled by the high rounds. Shrapnel punctured Butterfield's neck. Meade, Sharpe, and the other aides were forced to move temporarily farther back to a barn near Baltimore Pike and then to Powers Hill. Not satisfied, Meade soon returned to his old headquarters at the more exposed Leister House.

After the two-hour bombardment ended, Pickett's spearhead division, joined by two other divisions, charged up slanting open field to Cemetery Ridge. Backed by federal artillery, 9,000 veteran Union soldiers crowded shoulder to shoulder like an angry mob behind fortified positions on the ridge to take their best shots—with frustrated troopers behind them throwing rocks to get in their licks and plenty of reserves even farther behind to mow down any enemy not torn to pieces by the front line. Pickett's charge and those of the other divisions ended in disaster. Of the some 14,000 Rebels who marched forward, barely half returned. Pickett, a proud Virginian and Mexican War hero, retreated in tears.

Exhausted, unaccustomed to losing, and depressed, Lee lamented: "All this has been my fault." And it had been. Lee fought that day appallingly uninformed about the enemy he faced—far different than Meade, who had good intelligence on his foe from Sharpe's bureau. When told at the crest of Cemetery Ridge that the Confederate assault had been thoroughly repulsed, Meade said quietly, "Thank God."

Meade still had large numbers of fresh troops to continue the fight. Their morale was high. Lee's army was used up, about a third of it destroyed by the end of the day. The Rebel commander expected a counterattack. So did many of the Union commander's subordinates. Butterfield and Hancock (who had been wounded in the thigh during Pickett's charge) were among those who urged Meade to take the offensive. But Meade felt unsure about how badly he had hurt the enemy. Even though Sharpe had provided him reliable reports at the beginning of the Gettysburg battle that he outnumbered Lee's army of 75,000, Meade still believed the Confederate force remained as strong as his—perhaps stronger—even after suffering huge losses. He had enough reports coming in from his commanders and his information bureau to guess that Lee had suffered casualties as grievous as his. At the end of the day's battle, Sharpe scratched off a short note to Butterfield with his best count of Confederates they captured: 3,202. Babcock recovered enough from his injury to compile a list of ten senior Rebel officers killed or wounded. But Meade had a healthy respect for Lee and could scarcely believe he had beaten him. The Potomac Army commander did not want to jeopardize the hard-fought victory he had achieved that day by attacking a strong position Lee might still command. "We have done well enough," Meade told his officers. Later that night he moved his headquarters to a grove near the Leister House, which had become a crowded field hospital. Near a boulder, Meade, Sharpe, and the other headquarters aides slept miserably in a thunderstorm.

JULY 4 TO 14

Celebrations broke out in sweltering-hot Washington when news arrived on Independence Day that Lee had been defeated at Gettysburg and was retreating. Newspapers hailed the Union commander as a hero. Word arrived several days later that Confederate forces at strategically important Vicksburg, Mississippi, had surrendered to Ulysses S. Grant, a western general gaining more attention in the capital. Lee would win further victories in a war that dragged on for two more years, but Gettysburg, coupled with Vicksburg's loss, became an important turning point for the rebellion. Never again would a Rebel army be able to take the fight to northern soil. Sharpe also guessed that Confederate hopes for European recognition had now been extinguished, which proved to be the case.

Meade had a falling-out with Sharpe after the Gettysburg battle. In telegrams to Halleck as he tentatively followed Lee's army to the Potomac River, Meade complained he was having "great difficulty in getting reliable information," as he wrote in one note. In a letter to his wife he vented: "I . . . have to grope my way in the dark." But that was hardly the case. Sharpe, whose spies were barely mentioned in Gettysburg after-action reports, provided a steady stream of intelligence reports to Meade on the location, strength, and intentions of Lee's army as it retreated south. Meade also continued to pepper Sharpe with requests for information. But he disregarded much of the intelligence he received.

He also did away with the all-source intelligence system Sharpe and Hooker had pioneered. From now on, Sharpe would send him only the information he had gleaned from his agents and interrogations. Meade wanted no more analytical summaries drawn from Sharpe's spying and reports from cavalrymen and signal officers. Meade took on the job of analyzing the intelligence himself. He believed he was more skilled at doing this than McClellan, which in fact he was. Tellingly, when Meade held another war council on July 12 to discuss among his generals whether they should quickly attack Lee's army as it stood on the Maryland shore of the Potomac, he did not invite Sharpe to the meeting, as he had ten days earlier at Gettysburg. Meade was now his own spymaster. For his generals, he would be the one to interpret the intelligence coming in, not Sharpe. And Meade's interpretation of the intelligence now was clouded by the great caution gripping him as he pursued Lee after Gettysburg. He feared committing a tactical blunder that would result in extreme casualties and tarnish his triumph at Gettysburg. So he dithered instead of lunging boldly.

Lincoln pressed his commander to deliver one more blow to crush Lee's army and likely end the rebellion. But Meade on July 14 let the battered Confederate force slip across the Potomac unmolested at Williamsport, Maryland, to the safety of Virginia. Lincoln was furious. He wrote the general a scathing letter, but decided not to send it. Meade, who quickly learned of the White House displeasure, offered to resign, but Lincoln decided he could not fire the man the press and public proclaimed the victor at Gettysburg. He also didn't have another general with whom he could replace Meade.

After crossing the Potomac, Lee moved slowly back into Virginia, arriving at Culpeper Court House, where he started his northern march six weeks earlier, by July 24. Meade, who had the confidence of Lincoln restored by then, followed Lee south slowly—too slowly, Sharpe thought. Just crossing the Potomac beginning July 17 took its toll on many of Meade's men in the oppressive summer heat. "We must stop soon, as horses and mules are dropping dead every day and the men are nearly exhausted," Sharpe wrote his uncle Jansen. Through the rest of the summer, fall, and winter the two commanders maneuvered and fought minor engagements against each other—Lee keeping his force south of the Rapidan while Meade's army stayed north of the river—but they accomplished little. Neither army was in much shape for a major battle until it rebuilt.

Sharpe had spies on the move throughout the rest of the year and considered himself the best-informed officer in Meade's army on Lee's movements—although Meade continued to carp in letters to Halleck that he had "no reliable intelligence." Citizen agents from Sharpe's old Virginia network like Isaac Silver fed him intelligence from Orange County, where Lee had his operating base. Richmond refugees reported to him on the movement of Confederate units through the capital. An observant runaway slave who had waited on Stuart's staff had details on the cavalry general's headquarters at one point at William Bradford's house near Culpeper Court House. For what he called an "intelligence diary," Sharpe collected a stack of valuable Richmond newspapers, whose stories Confederate authorities obviously had not censored, which contained the transcript of Lee's after-action report for the Maryland and Pennsylvania campaign, unit dispatches on different engagements, and strength summaries for the Army of Northern Virginia as of August 11.

Not all Sharpe's agents delivered accurate intelligence. Michael Graham, the former spy for General Milroy in Winchester who now fed Sharpe information and believed a vast Jewish conspiracy plotted against the Union, reported in October that Lee had rebuilt his force into the "largest and finest army he has ever had" and would soon invade Maryland to capture Baltimore and Washington. Sharpe suspected Graham had been duped by southern agents and grilled him on his sources. Sharpe also occasionally interrogated Rebel deserters with similar disinformation that Lee's army had been fortified to 100,000. He and Babcock knew from their interviews with hundreds of other bedraggled prisoners and deserters that Lee's army by early November still numbered about 52,000 largely dispirited souls and if anything was moving farther south, "living from hand to mouth" because of supply shortages, as he wrote in a September memo. Sharpe could plainly see from the Rebels crossing into Union lines that Lee was plagued by desertions. From Richmonders he interviewed it was also clear that friction had grown between their star general and the Confederate cabinet over the failed Pennsylvania campaign.

Meade may have been disenchanted with his spymaster, but Sharpe's reputation for being a skilled intelligence collector spread to other commands. Western generals telegraphed him for information he gathered that might help them in their theaters. But Meade's hostility drove Sharpe's morale to rock bottom. His health suffered once more, this time from the brutal August heat. By December, Sharpe took the complaints he and other aides had about Meade to Patrick. The general, Sharpe told the provost marshal, "had been so snappish and cross that no one dared speak to him." Sharpe still wanted to be transferred to his old regiment. If Meade approved it, the colonel intended to have the unit assigned to Washington. The 120th, which had suffered heavy casualties during the Gettysburg battle, had done enough fighting and dying for this war, he thought. Assignment to Washington also would put him closer to Carrie in New York. He worried she was also in poor health and managed to obtain a leave to visit her in Kingston.

Patrick also asked Meade for a transfer to command a combat division. He took a leave of absence in mid-August to deal with a serious family illness. It was his first time home since the war started. He returned to Meade's headquarters still thoroughly disgusted with Meade's lack of aggressiveness, his indifference to the morale of his foot soldiers, his remoteness from his staff. Discipline throughout the Potomac Army was "horrible," with "depredations of all kinds," he wrote in his diary. "Commanders of every rank cover up the rascality of their troops." "Meade's head is tolerably clear, generally," the provost marshal continued, "but when he gets 'Lee on the Brain' he errs through timidity."

Neither man would get his transfer. Meade talked Patrick out of moving to a division. He never acted on Sharpe's request to take over the 120th Regiment. Curiously, Meade would grow impatient whenever Sharpe was gone too long from headquarters, demanding that he return quickly—perhaps because the colonel was a better spymaster than his commander would openly acknowledge.

1864

MUCKRAKER

aker lost interest in cavalry combat likely because other high-profile investigations in Washington occupied more of his time. He now expended as much effort attacking contractor fraud, ferreting out corruption in the Army Quartermaster Corps, and hunting for deserters as he did chasing spies. He became an international celebrity for those cases, compared in European newspapers to Joseph Fouché, Napoleon's ferocious police minister. The newly minted colonel now hungered to be promoted to general.

Complaints about his abuses reached the president. A cavalry captain wrote Lincoln offering to fill him in on the detective's questionable tactics. A justice of the peace in Charles County, Maryland, complained that Baker's men had launched a campaign of "systematic" looting there; they would "raise some frivolous charge, arrest the individual and then plunder his home." Lincoln sent the letters to Stanton, but there is nothing in the War Department records that shows the secretary ever investigated the charges or that Lincoln ever followed up on them. Baker insisted sinister officials were trying to impede his operation by discrediting him and his anticorruption campaign, which he said saved the U.S. Treasury hundreds of thousands of dollars. Cousins Joseph Stannard and Luther Byron questioned their boss's claims of success, fearing that many of the detectives on his payroll were barely a step above common criminals.

By the end of the year, Baker had plunged into what became a controversial investigation even further afield of his secret service duties. Three days before Christmas 1863, he sat in the spacious Treasury office of Salmon Portland Chase, taking in its gray velvet carpet, black walnut desk, and carved window-cornices. The secretary, who had no detectives to investigate corruption in his department, had reluctantly asked Stanton to lend him one of his. Baker decided to take this assignment himself.

A seasoned lawyer who had risen in Ohio politics and had been one of Lincoln's rivals for the presidency, Chase was an imposing and unsociable man of six foot two, who unlike Lincoln never joked and generally took a dark view of his boss—and, for that matter, the rest of the world. His home soon became a refuge for Lincoln critics, and just as soon Chase began plotting to deny the president a second term so he could replace him in the White House. Upon Chase's broad shoulders rested the crushing responsibility to fund the Union's warmaking capability through various combinations of taxes, fees, and bank and public loans that would keep coffers in the antiquated Treasury Department he inherited from hitting empty. To accomplish this huge assignment, the bureaucracy under Chase exploded to more than 2,000 employees, making him a patronage king in the federal government. No one accused Chase of being personally corrupt. For the most part his department operated efficiently. But he proved to be a poor judge of men, highly susceptible to flattery, hiring a good many sycophants who turned out to be incompetent or corrupt.

Baker was sitting in Chase's office because of one bad apple. Charles Cornwall, whose job was to burn canceled Treasury notes, was caught embezzling up to $32,000 of them and returning the notes to circulation. Alarmed, as well as worried about mud splattering on his own political ambitions, Chase wanted Baker to probe the extent of fraudulent activity in the department. The detective soon arrested a warrant clerk by the name of G. A. Henderson who worked in Chase's inner office and was suspected of taking gifts in exchange for giving priority to Treasury warrants for payment. Treasury officers complained that Baker botched the investigation of the case and prosecutors were forced to free Henderson for lack of evidence. But Chase did have him fired.

Baker kept digging on his own and soon uncovered what he claimed was a major scandal in the way U.S. currency was printed. Until August 1862, all of it along with financial notes the Treasury Department issued were printed by three New York banknote firms: the American, National, and Continental companies. These businesses shipped the printed sheets for securities such as money, government bonds, and postage currency to the Treasury Department, where the time of a lot of employees was consumed cutting and trimming the paper by hand. The entire process was expensive. Chase was convinced there had to be a cheaper way to print the nation's currency notes. That August he made Spencer Clark in the disbursing office head of the department's printing bureau. Clark, a Vermont businessman and engineer before joining the department in 1856, worked quickly. He had a machine built to cut and trim currency sheets and another device constructed to affix the Treasury seal on the notes—all of which saved the department a good deal of money.

But considerably more tax dollars could be saved, Clark realized, if the department did its own printing. It made no sense leaving valuable plates, dyes, and paper far away in New York City in the hands of three private companies, which enjoyed a monopoly and could dictate printing prices to the U.S. government. Clark began bringing in printing machines, installing them in the basement and north wing attic of the Treasury building next to the White House, to gradually start taking over the printing operation from the New York companies. He began with roller machines to make the impressions on paper. In the summer of 1863, Clark added new machines developed by Stuart Gwynn, a middle-aged New York consulting engineer, chemist, and inventor who used hydraulic pressure rather than rollers, plus a different type of paper, to produce the currency sheets.

Gwynn believed hydraulic presses could print faster than the old roller machines and Clark agreed. But Gwynn's new technology still had bugs to be worked out and by the end of 1863 few of his machines were operating yet. It would take until late spring 1864 before mechanics had fixed the problems and Gwynn's machines began outperforming the roller versions. The presses Clark did have running soon were saving the Treasury Department millions of dollars in printing costs. The New York companies charged, for example, $59 per 1,000 impressions for fractional currencies (paper money for amounts less than a dollar). Clark's machines did the work for almost a third of that amount.

Faced with losing millions in rich patronage, the three New York companies mounted a fierce lobbying campaign to convince Chase and Clark to give up in-house printing. When both men refused, the companies played dirty. A banknote executive first offered Clark a $50,000 bribe to quit the department. When that didn't work, company executives tried a smear campaign to convince Chase that his printing chief was an immoral charlatan who should be fired. Chase stood by Clark.

Baker inspected Gwynn's machines, most of which were not working at that point, and on January 6, 1864, without authority from any Treasury Department official, he arrested the New York inventor and seized his private papers. Baker reported to the department's solicitor, Edward Jordan, that Gwynn had perpetrated a massive fraud against the U.S. government, so Jordan approved having the man committed to Old Capitol Prison until the detective could prepare a report on him.

Gwynn had committed no crime. He was guilty only of installing printing machines that needed more work before they could be fully operational. But the poor fellow stewed in a jail cell for three months, adamantly denying any fraud to Jordan, who visited him, while Baker prepared his report. The voluminous document the detective finally sent to Chase contained no evidence of any crime on Gwynn's part or illegal money he had received from the project. Instead, Baker's report recited in intricate detail all the problems he saw in Gwynn's hydraulic press technology and all the delays it had experienced becoming operational. Baker concluded that Gwynn and Clark had colluded to induce the Treasury Department to spend a huge amount of money for the troubled machines, hoping to reap a personal fortune from the contract. But Baker never explained how the two men would make their money from this endeavor. Gwynn was soon released from prison.

Carefully reading Baker's long report, Clark noticed something fishy about it. Baker knew nothing about complex printing technology before he began his investigation a little more than three months earlier. But his detailed report showed a surprising grasp of the intricacies of hydraulic printing compared to the roller method. Clark also found that some of the phrasing Baker used was strikingly similar to what the banknote companies had written in reports critical of Clark's machines. Treasury employees, furthermore, told Clark they spotted the banknote company presidents walking into and out of Baker's headquarters. Congressional investigators later concluded that the detective had colluded with the firms, whose executives had written the bulk of his report. The congressmen suspected the companies paid off Baker to investigate Gwynn and produce the damaging report to shut down Clark's operation. Baker denied it.

Fighting mad, Gwynn filed three lawsuits against Baker after he got out of prison, accusing him of libel, false arrest, and an illegal seizure of papers from his home and office. Baker went to Jordan and asked him if the Treasury Department would defend him against Gwynn's suits, which if upheld by a court might put the detective in danger of being charged criminally. Jordan demurred. It would depend on whether Baker had been justified in arresting Gwynn and jailing him for three months, the solicitor told the detective. Angry with that answer, Baker warned that if Treasury did not defend him, he would expose more corruption in the department. It amounted to blackmail, and when Jordan refused to play along, Baker carried out his threat.

His targets became Clark, which delighted the New York banknote companies, and the three hundred female employees Chase had reluctantly hired at Treasury for clerical work. The women were easy prey. Washington's labor force had been all male, with the city's females expected to remain at home cleaning, cooking, and rearing children. A federal job was not considered proper for a lady to have. Chase's hires, however, became the first of thousands of "government girls." The pro-Democratic *New York*

Herald, which loved to skewer "Conjurer Chase," as the paper called him for allegedly printing money on a whim, railed against his hiring women. His department, the *Herald* claimed, had become an "asylum" for the girlfriends of congressmen. Reports soon circulated that the government girls had become too much of a temptation for male coworkers and that the Treasury Department now sheltered a whorehouse. They were cruel rumors. A majority of the women at Treasury were wives or sisters of soldiers who had fallen in battle. They wanted only to serve their country as well as eke out a living.

No matter. After Jordan turned him down, Baker scrambled to dig up dirt on the women. He hired Ada Thompson, a local burlesque queen and occasional prostitute, to help him. Thompson had befriended two Treasury employees, Ella Jackson and Jenny Germon, who lived next to her on the fourth floor of an apartment house at No. 276 Pennsylvania Avenue. While the two women were away, Baker and Thompson broke into their room, taking away private papers, diaries, and letters to document whatever indiscretions Baker could find. When Ella Jackson returned to the room, Baker arrested her and, lying, told her that her roommate had confessed to various intrigues and immoralities at Treasury. There was nothing left for Ella to do but make the same confession or be thrown into the dreaded Old Capitol Prison. Pretending to be her friend, Thompson urged Ella to cooperate and left her alone with Baker and the horror of being jailed. Terrified, Ella signed a statement Baker had written for her, in which she admitted she and her roommate went to the seedy Central Hotel on Pennsylvania Avenue and slept with Spencer Clark and G. A. Henderson. (Only later did she admit to Clark that Baker had coerced her into making the statement.) When Ella's roommate, Jenny, returned home, Baker went through the same drill and forced the young woman to sign a similar confession he wrote for her.

Baker then took his evidence to a friendly Democratic representative, James Brooks of New York, who had been energetically collecting rumors about Treasury shenanigans to embarrass Chase and the Republican administration. After reading the two confessions Baker produced, a pious Brooks publicly denounced the Treasury Department as "a house of orgies and bacchanals" and demanded a congressional investigation. The *New York Herald*, which closely covered the congressional probe, concluded that "females should be excluded from all government occupations in which they are brought into too frequent contact with or are subject to the immediate control of the other sex."

Baker raced to find other damaging evidence on Clark—a happily married man who adamantly denied ever having affairs with any of his female employees—but none of it held up to the bright light of scrutiny. The detective claimed that Clark had sent Catherine Dodson, a black doorkeeper at Treasury, to another employee, Bettie Weedon, with offers of $100 and $500 to have sex with him. But Dodson denied ever running the errand. Baker claimed a witness saw Clark's principal assistant and a female employee having sex in the department's bonnet room. But all the witness, a fourteen-year-old girl, actually saw was a young man walking out of the room and the woman remaining there. The confessions Baker had coerced out of Ella Jackson and Jenny Germon held up poorly as well. The corroborating evidence he produced to prove that Clark and Henderson had taken the two women to the Center Hotel was full of contradictions. Baker also claimed Clark and Henderson took the two women, dressed as men, to one of Washington's burlesque houses and to a Philadelphia hotel for sex. Again, the evidence he produced to back it up was flimsy at best.

Baker became a zealot in helping Brooks collect damaging testimony. In one instance—"with a barbarity rarely surpassed," according to a congressional report—Baker rode up and halted the funeral procession carrying the body of Treasury employee Laura Duvall. He was convinced the woman had died from a botched abortion after having sex at the department. With the Duvall family looking on in horror, Baker seized the coffin and had a doctor perform an autopsy on the corpse. The woman was a virgin, the physician determined; she died of tuberculosis.

A House select committee, chaired by James Garfield, an Ohio Republican who had fought in the war and later was elected president, convened in May 1864 to investigate the allegations. In a 418-page report, Garfield's committee concluded that the charges against Clark and Gwynn had been trumped up on behalf of the banknote companies and that Baker was likely a part of that conspiracy. Baker and Brooks claimed Garfield's two-month investigation was a whitewash to protect Chase and the Lincoln administration.

Among the detectives joining Baker's secret service the month the Treasury report was released was Pryce Lewis. How the Pinkerton agent became a Baker operative was a story with twists and turns.

By the beginning of 1863, life was slowly ebbing from Lewis, who along with John Scully had been rotting in fetid Castle Thunder, living off maggot-infested soup and suffering bouts of dysentery. Lewis's hair had turned gray and he looked haggard and nervous. Pinkerton wrote him occasionally, managed to have cash sent to him to buy food and clothing, and kept in touch with the families of both men. In his letters, Pinkerton assured Lewis he didn't blame him for what happened to Webster and that he was doing all he could to free the two men in a prisoner exchange. Pinkerton did lobby strenuously to have Lewis and Scully included in one of the exchanges, pleading with Lincoln at one point to intervene, but each time he thought he had a deal struck, it had fallen through. Finally, on September 29, 1863, Lewis and Scully left Richmond in an exchange that freed 150 Union prisoners.

The two were first taken to City Point, Virginia, and then transported on a flag-of-truce boat to Annapolis with only the clothes on their backs and their pockets empty. They received hardly a hero's welcome. At Annapolis, a surly Army major refused them further transportation unless they paid for it. Lewis sold his tattered coat to buy two train tickets. He and Scully arrived in Washington at 9 p.m. on September 30, twenty months and eight days since they had left the capital.

They did not know where to go once they arrived. Pinkerton was long gone. Lewis finally decided they should pay a visit to William Wood, superintendent at Old Capitol. After a little prodding by Lewis, Wood recognized the two bedraggled men. He fed them, gave them a place to sleep in the prison, and wired Pinkerton, who was in Philadelphia at the time. Pinkerton quickly wired back instructing the superintendent to buy the pair train tickets to Philadelphia. Pinkerton would pay their fare. "Tell them to avoid all publicity of their affairs until they see me," he instructed in his telegram.

The Philadelphia reunion on October 2 was not a joyous one. Nearly two years of resentment boiled inside Lewis. He blasted Pinkerton for what he considered his criminal "carelessness in getting us into enemy hands," as Lewis recalled later. Taken aback, Pinkerton angrily accused the two men of selling out Webster. Lewis, he thought, was also an ingrate, considering all he had done for both of them while imprisoned. Scully went to work for Pinkerton. Lewis never saw his old boss again, although he did remain friendly with Pinkerton's son William.

Stanton absolved Lewis of blame and gave the Englishman a job at Old Capitol as a bailiff and detective. Lewis transported prisoners, investigated guards bribed by inmates, and arranged for the incarcerated with cash to buy food, clothing, and whisky. He also enjoyed fraternizing with the females behind bars. Among the high-profile prisoners Lewis transported was Belle Boyd, who was sent to Richmond again after a second stay at Old Capitol. Before packing her off, Lewis took Boyd to Mathew Brady's shop, where she was photographed on Stanton's orders. The war secretary may have wanted a shot taken of the woman so she could be recognized if she tried to slip back into Washington. Lewis had Brady's photographer take his picture, too.

On June 20, Baker made Lewis one of his detectives. Lewis arrested deserters, chased blockade runners, and did other odd jobs. But he quit working there a little more than two months later, fed up with the corruption and bribe taking he witnessed in Baker's service. He moved to Chicago in August.

Twenty

THE RICHMOND RING

ews of Lee's defeat at Gettysburg overwhelmed Richmonders, who took comfort only in follow-up reports that Meade allowed their demoralized army to escape. Nearly half the area once in the Confederacy was now under Union control. The Confederacy would never recover the territory it lost and as autumn gave way to winter in 1863, the southern way of life was in danger. Richmond was growing rusty, dilapidated, war-torn. In the four months after Gettysburg, prices in the South shot up 70 percent. Jefferson Davis designated days for fasting and urged patriotic citizens to observe them. In defiance "we always tried to have a little better dinner" on those days, Van Lew wrote.

Lee ordered horses in Richmond confiscated for the cavalry. Soldiers stopped ladies riding carriages, cut the reins, and led away the animals. Van Lew needed her mount for spying. When she heard that troops were on their way to seize it, she hid the horse first in her smokehouse and later in her mansion's study, spreading straw on the floor to muffle the sound of clomping hoofs. The dire economic conditions crimped her espionage. She was running out of money to pay for spy work and inflation ate away at what she had left to spread around for operations. She sold the family cow to raise cash.

As 1864 began, Joseph Maddox continued to be Sharpe's resident spy in Richmond. He earlier messaged that Lee had about 40,000 men, only 2,500 of whom were scattered about the Confederate capital. A couple thousand Union cavalrymen could raid the vulnerable city and seize Davis, he reported. "Now is the time to capture Richmond." Maddox was being wildly optimistic in predicting how easy a coup de main by a small force would be. Sharpe did not know at this point that Van Lew had a ring far more skilled than Maddox in gauging Richmond's defenses. Another Union officer discovered her espionage network before him.

With his cockeye and mane of curly hair flowing off the back of his bald head, Benjamin F. Butler was the Union general most hated by southerners. They nicknamed him "Beast Butler." Lee's wife, Mary Custis, called him "scum." Jefferson Davis branded him an outlaw who deserved to be hanged if the Rebels captured him. Even many federal officers had a low opinion of Butler, who was a cantankerous political general from Massachusetts, not a true military man, and a favored presidential candidate for many Radical Republicans.

As commander of the Department of Virginia, he led an expedition out of Fort Monroe on June 10, 1861, to strike the Confederates at Big Bethel on the Virginia Peninsula, in what was the first true land battle of the war. The attack failed miserably. Ten months later, a combined Army-Navy force led by Butler and sea captain David Farragut seized New Orleans. Butler became the city's military governor, enraging citizens with his thieving Union troops and vindictive set of restrictions. Davis put a bounty on his head after the general declared that local women who continued to insult federal soldiers and dump the contents of chamber pots on them from their windows would be treated as whores. Seward eventually convinced Lincoln to recall Butler at the end of 1862. On November 2, 1863, he was made commander of the Department of Virginia and North Carolina, which put him in charge of Union-occupied eastern Virginia with his headquarters at Fort Monroe on the Peninsula's tip. A little more than a month later, Beast Butler, who recruited escaped slaves to be spies and would spend $11,250 on espionage operations at the fort, discovered Elizabeth Van Lew.

She came to Butler's attention through two escapees from Libby Prison. John A. McCullough, a Wisconsin soldier and an assistant surgeon working as a steward in Libby's hospital, had been visited by fifteen-year-old Josephine Holmes, a member of Van Lew's underground, who brought him a bag of tobacco to smoke. On the night of December 8, 1863, McCullough pretended to be deceased in the hospital's morgue, called the "dead house." A Union captain who went by the alias "Harry Howard" (his real name was Harry Catlin and he had been a scout in Butler's army) carted McCullough out with other corpses for burial. The two men ditched the wagon when they had gotten far enough away from Libby, and Josephine took them to the Henrico County home of William Rowley, one of Van Lew's most trusted operatives. Miss Holmes and the other women sewed clothes for Howard and McCullough out of Confederate blankets. Rowley hid the men in his house for ten days and then with the help of Samuel Ruth bought them passes so they could flee north. A Richmond paper republished a story in the Washington press of their unusual escape—a serious security breach that put the Richmond underground in danger.

Howard and McCullough reported back to Butler on what appeared to them to be a highly effective underground in the Confederate capital headed by Van Lew. Butler was intrigued. But before he risked sending Howard back to Richmond to recruit the woman, he confidentially wrote one of her old friends, Commander Charles Boutelle of the Coast Guard Survey Office in Washington, to ask if he could vouch for her. Boutelle did.

January 1864, Howard returned to Rowley's home with Butler's material for secretly corresponding with Van Lew. Their communication would be simple and in the open. They would use the regular mail. Richmonders could trade correspondence with northerners by flag-of-truce exchanges through the post office in the Confederate capital. Butler and Van Lew would pretend to be relatives in their letters. Butler would sign his notes as "James Ap. Jones," Van Lew's affectionate uncle. Van Lew would sign hers as

"Eliza A. Jones." Between the lines of innocuous family news in their letters they would write in invisible ink the messages they wanted to convey.

Van Lew visited Rowley's house and Howard showed her how the invisible ink, which was a clear liquid in a bottle, worked. The captain then handed her a January 18 letter from Butler and showed her how she could read the message in invisible ink by applying a mild acid and heat to the paper. Van Lew tried it and could read Butler's instructions on how she could write him through the flag-of-truce mail system. Butler wrote that he understood Van Lew was willing to send him intelligence and he was delighted she could help. For messages not written in invisible ink, Howard also gave Van Lew a simple cipher key, which was a small square sheet of paper with a chart to convert letters into a number code. She folded the key tightly and tucked it into her watch case.

Van Lew's new espionage arrangement was threatened, however, within days of its launch. Howard wrapped up his business and set off for Butler's headquarters. Though the general did not pay Van Lew, Howard did promise Rowley a hundred dollars a month for his services and provided him with a thousand Confederate dollars for bribes. But not long into his trip back to Fort Monroe, Howard was nabbed once more by Rebel soldiers and sent to Castle Thunder. Fortunately for Van Lew, the Union officer kept silent and after about two weeks in jail managed to escape once more with another inmate in early February. Rowley again let him hide out at his home and with Ruth's assistance helped him reach Union lines.

After a year and a half of informally sending information north, with no one recognizing its value or that of the people delivering it, Van Lew and her fellow Unionists were now formally enlisted in the U.S. government's secret service. She became the ring's spymaster, her mansion the underground's base station, where she deployed loyal operatives like Rowley all over the city to collect information. Butler and other circumspect Union officials rarely mentioned Van Lew by her real name. She often went by the code name "Babcock" or was referred to in government documents as "a lady in Richmond" and her ring as "our friends in Richmond."

Van Lew had to step up security as well. A Richmond grand jury at one point issued arrest warrants for her and her mother, accusing them of dealing in Union currency. The charge could never be proved, but investigators continued to probe. A woman from Winder's office tried to trick Van Lew into revealing that she was a spy. Van Lew didn't take the bait. Butler also sent highly risky assignments, dispatching her at one point into the lion's den to take a message to Captain Philip Cashmeyer, Winder's chief detective. A German immigrant, Cashmeyer had been a "plug ugly" cop in Baltimore before the war and Butler believed he was vulnerable to recruitment. Van Lew walked into Cashmeyer's office, pulled a letter out from the inside of her blouse, and handed it to him. The note from Butler stated that he wanted to see the detective "as soon as possible" at New Kent Court House, southeast of Richmond, or anywhere else the captain considered safe for a rendezvous. Cashmeyer "turned deadly pale" as he read the letter, Van Lew recalled. He begged her never to enter his office again. "He would come to see me," Van Lew recounted. The detective, who never betrayed Van Lew to Winder, paid her secret visits from time to time, but she never divulged if he passed along information.

Keeping a detailed journal of her espionage activity was too risky, Van Lew decided. If the authorities raided her mansion, she would be sent to prison if they found such a diary. At night she placed sensitive papers, such as agents' reports and her own intelligence notes, at her bedside table to destroy quickly if she had to or to quickly hide in other places in the mansion like the library. Documents there could be stored in the pilasters of the library's iron fireplace that reached part of the way up to its mantel. Two bronze couchant lions, with secret cavities in them, sat atop the pilasters, making for an ideal hiding place. Van Lew quickly mastered the tedious process of encoding messages to Butler with the cipher Howard provided. She often tore the ciphered note into several pieces and sent each by different couriers on different routes directly to the general instead of using the post office. Family servants who acted as couriers sometimes put messages in scraped-out eggshells hidden in baskets of real eggs or among the paper patterns seamstresses carried. The Van Lew family's vegetable farm near the Richmond–Henrico County line below the city became the first of five stops along the James River where couriers could drop off or pick up messages to pass along to Fort Monroe.

Allan Pinkerton with his wife, Joan, emigrated from Scotland to the United States in 1842, with little more than a pocketful of change, and ended up in Chicago making beer barrels as a cooper. Around 1855 he formed a successful private detective agency, which soon became national in scope.

A political cartoon lampoons Abraham Lincoln. In February 1861, he secretly left Pennsylvania by train with Pinkerton, who sneaked him through Baltimore, where it was feared secessionists wanted to assassinate the president-elect to keep him from reaching Washington. Pinkerton was accused of making up the threat.

Pinkerton, pictured here at the Battle of Antietam in the fall of 1862, became General George McClellan's spy chief. Untrained in the collection and analysis of military intelligence, Pinkerton routinely overestimated the strength of Confederate forces.

4

5

A poorly educated and aimless drifter as a young man, Lafayette Baker ended up in San Francisco in the early 1850s, where he joined a vigilante group rousting criminals. He arrived in Washington in April 1861, after the fall of Fort Sumter, and talked his way into a spy job with the Union Army.

The beautiful daughter of a wealthy Richmond merchant, Elizabeth Van Lew was educated in Philadelphia, where she became steeped in the movement to abolish slavery. She returned to Virginia with a fierce hatred for human bondage, and soon became part of the Unionist underground.

6

The Van Lew mansion at Church Hill was one of Richmond's finest, with a well-stocked library, many parties for the southern elite, and celebrity guests like Edgar Allan Poe visitng. During the war, Church Hill became the operating base for Elizabeth's espionage ring spying on the Confederacy.

Despite his "Honest Abe" image, Lincoln entered the White House well versed in political intrigue. As president he appreciated the importance of accurate information on the enemy, demanded regular intelligence briefings from the Army, and was not shy about using subversion or propaganda to achieve his war aims.

Secretary of State William Seward became Lincoln's first internal security czar, hiring Lafayette Baker and other detectives to root out treasonous elements in a wide-ranging operation. Seward was reported to have boasted that he could ring a little bell at his desk and have any man arrested.

Edwin Stanton took over the War Department in January 1862. A workaholic and ruthless administrator, Stanton assumed the internal security function from Seward and turned to Lafayette Baker to ratchet up police state tactics as the department's chief detective.

Lafayette Baker, who rose to the
rank of brigadier general, mounted
counterintelligence operations
to uncover Rebel spies as well as
anticorruption campaigns to combat
contractor fraud, illegal contraband
trade, and enlistment irregularities. But
corruption charges dogged Baker and
his men, who were accused of raking
off money and goods from their raids.

An erudite New York lawyer, Colonel
George Sharpe became the Army of
the Potomac's spymaster in early 1863,
proving to be far more successful at the
job than Pinkerton. Sharpe pioneered
all-source intelligence collection
and accurate analysis, which gave
Union commanders a clear picture
of the Rebel forces they faced.

Unmarried and in her early forties when
war broke out, Elizabeth Van Lew was
deemed by Richmond security officers
to be a harmless wealthy spinster just
a bit too free with her abolitionist
sentiments. They never uncovered the
ring she set up to aid Union soldiers
in Richmond's prisons and to spy
on the Confederate government.

Rose O'Neal Greenhow, shown here with her daughter in the federal Old Capitol Prison, led an early Rebel espionage operation in Washington that had been moderately successful. In August 1861, Pinkerton arrested Greenhow, who was not particularly skilled as a secret agent, and broke up her ring.

In July 1861, Greenhow couriered warnings to General Pierre Beauregard that federal troops were preparing to attack his army at Manassas Junction. Greenhow's intelligence, however, was not as critically important in the Battle of Bull Run as she and Beauregard later made it out to be.

Belle Boyd, whom Pinkerton's men arrested, turned out to be more a media star than an espionage heroine. Boyd alerted Confederate general Stonewall Jackson in May 1862 that Front Royal, Virginia, was lightly defended, which only confirmed what Jackson already knew about the weak Union force there.

16

Winfield Scott, the Army's aging commanding general, hired Lafayette Baker (knowing nothing about him) to collect intelligence around Manassas Junction before the July 1861 battle. Though he failed in his mission, Baker, a fast talker, managed to convince Scott he was a skilled spy.

17

General George McClellan (posing here with his wife, Mary Ellen) developed a messiah complex, convinced he was the country's savior. Believing the enemy always outnumbered him, McClellan took Pinkerton's inflated estimates of Confederate strength and dialed them up even more.

18

Benjamin Butler was the Union commander most hated by southerners, who nicknamed him "Beast Butler" because of his harsh occupation of Rebel territory. Butler was the first Union general to reach out to Elizabeth Van Lew, supplying her with invisible ink and a cipher key to send him coded messages with intelligence from Richmond.

20

Timothy Webster was a top spy for Allan Pinkerton, collecting surprisingly accurate intelligence on Rebel forces in Virginia. But he made one too many trips to Richmond, where authorities eventually arrested and hanged him.

Born in Wales, Pryce Lewis was a skilled clandestine operative, using the cover of an English gentleman on vacation to collect intelligence for Pinkerton in Rebel territory. But Pinkerton unwisely sent Lewis to Richmond to investigate what had happened to Webster.

21

The dapper John Babcock began making much-needed battle maps for Pinkerton. By the time Ulysses Grant took over the Army, Babcock had assembled highly accurate intelligence on every major unit in the Confederate force facing Grant.

Pinkerton is seated right, with his operatives at the Antietam battle. The agents include John Babcock (*standing in the middle*) and George Bangs (*standing to the left*) who was a manager in Pinkerton's detective agency. Pinkerton used many of his detectives as military spies, with mixed results.

When Lincoln visited McClellan's field headquarters, McClellan often was content to let Pinkerton tend to the President so the Army commander wouldn't have to be bothered with him. Major General John A. McClernand stands to the right.

The Union balloon *Intrepid* is being inflated for the Battle of Fair Oaks in May 1862. Yankee balloons ascended to observe battlefields. These important aerial reconnaissance platforms, however, were done away with by June 1863. Commanders considered the equipment needed to transport and put the balloons in the air too cumbersome.

Elizabeth Van Lew and her operatives did their best to supply Richmond's notorious Libby Prison, which held Union officers, with food and medical care. Her ring also helped inmates escape and sheltered them in safe houses after they broke out.

26

In February 1864, Van Lew alerted General Butler that Federal prisoners at the squalid Belle Isle prison camp on the James River, as well as inmates at other POW facilities in Richmond, would be moved to the prison camp in Andersonville, Georgia. The intelligence prompted two Union attempts to rescue the prisoners.

Allan Pinkerton and Lafayette Baker dumped many of the people they arrested into Old Capitol Prison in Washington, D.C. Baker often harshly interrogated inmates and put informants in the facility to report to him on what prisoners said.

Made general-in-chief of the Army, the scholarly Henry Halleck was skeptical about spies and favored strict rules for their use. He quickly grew leery of the inflated Confederate strength estimates McClellan peddled.

General Joseph "Fighting Joe" Hooker reformed the Army of the Potomac's intelligence gathering operation, making George Sharpe head of its successful Bureau of Military Information. But the timid Hooker failed to exploit Sharpe's intelligence, giving up the initiative to the enemy.

General George Meade, who replaced Hooker as commander of the Army of the Potomac, did not appreciate Sharpe's intelligence collection or analysis operation. Meade denigrated Sharpe and his spy bureau.

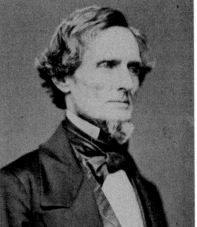

31

When Confederate President Jefferson Davis caught a black servant of Elizabeth Van Lew's snooping in his Richmond office he simply shooed her away, never thinking for a moment that an African American had the intelligence to be a spy.

32

An old-school general, Robert E. Lee believed wars should be fought in the field by soldiers, not in the shadows by spooks. But though he distrusted spies, Lee did deploy them. Some were young boys.

John Winder (shown here as a U.S. Army officer before defecting to the South) became Richmond's powerful provost marshal, charged with rooting out pro-Union subversives in the Rebel capital. But Winder never uncovered the ring headed by Elizabeth Van Lew, who succeeded in manipulating the gullible general.

33

34

35

Soon after taking over the Union Army in March 1864, Ulysses S. Grant brought George Sharpe and his information bureau into his headquarters and gave the spymaster wider authority to collect and evaluate intelligence.

General Marsena Patrick, the prickly provost marshal for the Army of the Potomac, oversaw Sharpe and his information bureau. A stern taskmaster, Patrick thought Sharpe was too fun-loving. He also had a bitter feud with Lafayette Baker, who tried to invade his turf.

36

George Sharpe (*left*) sits with John Babcock (*beside him*), who became his top deputy; an unidentified soldier; and John McEntee (*far right*), who was third-ranking in the spy bureau. Sharpe's intelligence collection quickly outpaced the Confederate effort.

38

Treasury secretary Salmon P. Chase asked Lafayette Baker to investigate fraudulent activity in his department, a decision he came to regret. Botching the initial probe, Baker on his own then uncovered what he thought was a major scandal in the way U.S. currency was printed. But there was no scandal.

Baker was supposed to uncover threats to Abraham Lincoln. But John Wilkes Booth and his conspirators roamed Washington freely under the secret service chief's nose. It was a spectacular intelligence failure on Baker's part.

39

War secretary Edwin Stanton offered a $50,000 reward for the capture of Booth and $25,000 each for the capture of two of his conspirators: David Herold and John Surratt Jr. It sparked a frenzy among Baker and other manhunters hoping to strike it rich.

On April 24, 1865, Lafayette Baker huddled over a map with aides Luther Byron Baker (*left*) and Everton Conger (*right*), and pointed to an area near Virginia's Rappahannock River where he wanted them to hunt for Booth and Herold. A rival claimed Baker stole his lead on where the fugitives were. Baker denied it.

To throw them off the scent so souvenir hunters would not scavenge the corpse, Lafayette Baker fed reporters a false story that he buried Booth's body at sea. Baker actually had Booth buried in an unmarked grave at the Old Arsenal Penitentiary (now Fort McNair).

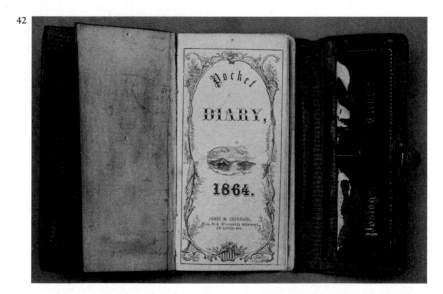

After Booth was captured and killed, Everton Conger and Luther Byron Baker found a pocket diary on him. Lafayette Baker later accused war secretary Stanton of tearing some eighteen pages out of it, which presumably contained evidence linking Stanton and Vice President Andrew Johnson to Lincoln's assassination. There was no evidence to support this sensational charge.

As the years passed and his health deteriorated, Pinkerton turned his successful detective agency over to his two sons to run. His end came in 1884 from a freak accident. Tripping on a sidewalk he bit deeply into his tongue and died after gangrene set in.

President Andrew Johnson was outraged when Lafayette Baker detained a woman obtaining postwar pardons from the White House for Confederate and Union soldiers, accusing him of meddling in Administration business. Baker was put on trial for false imprisonment and extortion in the incident.

Pryce Lewis, who never forgave Pinkerton for sending him on the ill-fated mission to Richmond, worked as a detective after the war. Eventually destitute and despondent, Lewis in 1911 took an elevator and stairs to the top of New York's World Building and jumped, falling 365 feet to his death.

One of the riskiest operations Elizabeth Van Lew's ring carried out was exhuming the body of Union colonel Ulric Dahlgren, who was killed in a raid to free federal prisoners in Richmond and dumped in an unmarked grave. The ring reburied the body at a nearby farm to keep it safe for Dahlgren's father to eventually retrieve.

With a servant attending them, Van Lew enjoys an outdoor lunch on the mansion grounds with her nieces and her brother John, who helped in her espionage. After the war, neighbors in Richmond shunned her for her northern sympathies.

Though she landed the lucrative job of Richmond postmaster during President Grant's administration, in her final years Van Lew was broke, with no income and mounting debts. She depended on the charity of northern friends and died in 1900 at age eighty-one.

Within six months, Van Lew was running more than a dozen agents and couriers in addition to Mary Bowser and her other African American servants. She had at her disposal a devoted group of friends, like Rowley, Josephine, F. W. E. Lohmann, Charles Palmer, and Abby Green. Many, like Lohmann, already had run-ins with Confederate authorities and risked long prison terms or even hanging if they were caught. Her reports to Butler paid more attention to living conditions in Richmond than to military matters. But her military information was not insignificant. Butler, who sent Rowley 50,000 Confederate dollars for the ring's expenses and promised more if needed, was insatiable, writing Van Lew in invisible ink with intelligence he wanted, such as updates on "Rebel rams" (boats built to slam into Union shipping) and enemy strategy for North Carolina. Van Lew messaged him developments at the Richmond Navy Yard and everything her ring col- lected on Confederate moves in the Tar Heel State. Her agents also man- aged to unearth intelligence that contributed to two daring operations the Federals launched early that year.

On February 4, a boy Van Lew used as a messenger sat in Butler's office at Fort Monroe clutching a carved peach seed each of her ring members carried to identify one another. The boy had a message he had memorized from the spymaster, plus a January 30 letter she had written in invisible ink. The general applied the acid and warmed the letter over a candle so it would reveal Van Lew's message. He read it carefully. The note contained updates on Rebel troop movements, but its most disturbing piece of news was Van Lew's alert that the Confederates intended to send Richmond's federal prisoners "to Georgia very soon." If Butler was thinking about rescuing the prisoners, he should not attempt it with fewer than 30,000 cavalrymen and 15,000 infantrymen, she warned. "Do not underestimate their strength and desperation." The Confederates could assemble as many as 25,000 soldiers in the city within five to ten days to fight the rescuers.

Butler laid down the note. "Well, boy, where did you get that letter from?" the general asked.

"Miss Van Lew gave it to me," the boy nervously answered. "Miss Lizzie told me what to tell you."

"Well, what did she tell you to say? You need have no fear here."

The young messenger ticked off the Rebel units moving around and through the capital. "Richmond could be taken easier now than at any time since war began," the boy said. He passed along the advice from "Quaker" (likely the code name for Rowley) that if the Federals intended to rescue the prisoners they should "make a feint on Petersburg" and then attack Richmond from the west.

Jefferson Davis tried to lowball the death rate at Confederate prisons but it was high and growing higher. Richmond prisons overflowed. The entire surface of the Belle Isle camp was covered in human and animal excrement, with a quarter of the inmates seriously sick. Winter had been brutal for Libby inmates, subsisting on vile corn bread and just an ounce of meat daily. With illnesses becoming epidemic, dead bodies piled up in a cellar, some eaten by dogs at night. The Georgia prison Van Lew noted in her letter was the Andersonville camp, where nearly 13,000 federal inmates eventually perished.

The day after the boy's visit, Butler rushed a memo to Stanton with Van Lew's letter and a transcript of the conversation he had with her messenger. Richmond appeared to be lightly defended, he told the war secretary, so "now is the time to strike." Butler proposed to "make a dash" into the city with 6,000 men to free the Union prisoners before they were moved to Georgia. Stanton and Lincoln knew the Confederates were building a new prison there. Confederate officials had not been too secretive about the project. Northern outrage had been building over Confederate treatment of federal prisoners, with newspapers calling for retribution to be exacted on Rebel prisoners the Union held. Stanton and Lincoln approved the rescue attempt.

Butler scrambled to quickly put together the operation, finding city maps of Richmond to help his raiders locate its prisons and scouring the Army for cavalry that could be rushed to Fort Monroe. Stanton agreed to lend him the 1st D.C. Cavalry, but Baker coughed up only a portion of his regiment, which irritated Butler, and he was slow to send that portion. For the field commander of this critically important operation, Butler chose Brigadier General Isaac J. Wistar, a Philadelphia lawyer wounded at Antietam.

Believing speed and surprise were keys to success, Butler gave Wistar three ambitious assignments. His 6,000-man cavalry and infantry force were to rush into Richmond to free the Union prisoners, who would then join Wistar's raiders to burn down public buildings, arsenals, the Tredegar Iron Works, supply depots, rail equipment, and commissary stocks. The raiders were also ordered to capture Jefferson Davis and other top Rebel leaders. Wistar was sent one of Davis's gardeners who had deserted to the Union Army and could direct a team to the president's mansion. Wistar would then hunker down with his men until Butler reached him with a larger force from Fort Monroe to occupy the city.

Wistar's raid flopped almost from the beginning. He sent two linemen out ahead of time to cut telegraph wires connecting Richmond to other Rebel forces. At 11 a.m. on February 6, General John Sedgwick, who was standing in as acting commander of the Army of the Potomac because Meade was sick in bed, began an artillery barrage to stage a demonstration against Lee's army on the Rapidan River, which Wistar hoped would keep him distracted so he wouldn't send units to Richmond. Wistar had moved his men out two hours earlier, hoping to attack the capital by 5 a.m. the next day. But when he and his cavalry reached Bottom's Bridge, which spanned the Chickahominy River twelve miles east of Richmond, at about 2:30 a.m. on February 7, he discovered the crossing point not guarded by two dozen Rebel pickets, as had been the case the previous two months. Instead Bottom's Bridge had been knocked out and what was left standing was being guarded by as many as three Confederate regiments of infantry and cavalry plus four artillery batteries, entrenched in earthworks, with felled trees lying across the road to block Wistar's cavalry.

It turned out that what Butler had planned as a surprise was no surprise to the Confederates. Richmond newspapers had been speculating about potential prison uprisings since last November. Guards had been increased at the facilities. Three days before Wistar moved out, Davis announced his government had received information about plots to free Richmond prisoners. Rebel spies had been snooping around for evidence. A key piece of intelligence came from a New York cavalry soldier named William Boyle, who had been sentenced to death for killing another man. Boyle had deserted from Wistar's command and fled to Richmond, where he tipped off Confederate authorities to the planned raid.

When the sun rose on February 7, Wistar made a stab at a cavalry charge, but it failed. His infantry showed up at noon, but by then Wistar could see more Rebel troops arriving and that all hope of a surprise raid had evaporated. He decided to limp back with his detachment to Fort Monroe. Butler sent a message across the lines to the Confederate government offering any Rebel soldier the Union had in its prisons for Boyle, whom the general now dearly wanted to hang. He never blamed himself for failing to heed Van Lew's warning not to attempt the raid with fewer than 45,000 troops.

Van Lew was disappointed but not discouraged. While Butler was planning his raid, her spy ring had been working with Union officers inside Libby, who were plotting their escape from the detestable prison. Using as an intermediary Robert Ford, a captured black Union Army teamster who took care of the warden's horses, Abby Green since the previous spring had been feeding the inmates valuable intelligence on the number of Libby guards, the arms stockpiles on the outside that the escapees could raid for weapons, and the strength of Richmond fortifications that might hinder their flight north. When the prisoners told her in early February that they were nearly finished digging a tunnel through a cellar and under a vacant lot outside the facility to a tobacco shed, Green sent them directions to safe houses they could hide in until arrangements could be made for their passage out of the city. Van Lew's money bankrolled this communications line between the prisoners and the outside world. Alerted by Green that a breakout would soon happen, the spymaster prepared a room in her mansion to harbor Libby escapees.

Two days after the failed Wistar raid, Libby prisoners on the night of February 9 began crawling through the cramped and suffocating tunnel. By the next morning, 109 inmates had escaped. When guards discovered the breakout, Confederate soldiers immediately began a manhunt. Within a few days, fifty-two escapees had been captured. Others found refuge among the white and black members of Richmond's underground.

A handful showed up at the Church Hill mansion. But not knowing that

February 9 was the night for the breakout, Van Lew happened to be away from home helping her brother, John, evade Confederate authorities who wanted to put him back in the Rebel army. He had been having a running battle with the authorities in trying to evade mandatory service, claiming at one point to be physically unfit. A doctor ruled that though John was frail he could serve in the military so he was ordered to report for duty. His sister Elizabeth, venturing out in disguise, was at a friend's house where John was now hiding. He eventually escaped north to federal lines and swore an oath of allegiance to the Union.

Not knowing of the Libby escape, Mary Bowser and the other Van Lew servants turned away the Union men who knocked on the door that night. Van Lew was distraught when she learned her hiding place would not be used. Her servants, however, had reason to be cautious. After Van Lew returned, Mary said six men showed up at the mansion's front steps claiming they were escapees and they understood that Van Lew and her mother were Unionists. "No, no," Van Lew answered, becoming suspicious. "No Unionists here." The six men were Rebel detectives disguised as federal prisoners.

One of the officers who escaped and evaded capture was Colonel Abel D. Streight, a large Indiana man who feared he might not fit through the narrow tunnel. Streight, who had led a destructive mounted infantry raid into Alabama and impudently stood up to his jailers after he was captured, was both hated and feared by the Confederates. They desperately wanted him back. The colonel and three other officers followed Abby Green's directions and ran to a house near the prison, which was owned by a black woman who led them to a rendezvous with Green. She then took the men to the home of John Quarles, a Van Lew ring member who lived near Davis's mansion. Lucy Rice, another underground member Van Lew often supplied with money, arrived at the Quarles house and began cooking and caring for the starved fugitives. Six days later, Rice took Van Lew to meet Streight and the other escapees at her humble house, where the men had been taken to on the eastern outskirts of the city. The colonel had asked to meet the woman whom Libby's prisoners considered their savior.

Settling into a chair in the parlor, Van Lew recalled that she could barely speak for a moment because she was so "overcome with terror" over the safety of these four men. Two of the officers looked sick and feeble but Streight seemed to Van Lew to be in good condition. She told the colonel the Confederates loathed him because they said he had commanded a black regiment.

"I did not," Streight answered, "but would have had no objection" to doing so.

Streight asked her what she thought caused this war. "I tried to say, Democracy," Van Lew recalled, "though in my heart I thought it was slavery."

It was "a very pleasant visit," she wrote later in her journal. "How my heart ached all the while for their peril!" One of the officers showed her the chisel he used to dig the tunnel, a treasured memento he intended to keep. "We had a little laughing and talking and then I said good bye, with the most fervent, 'God help you,' in my heart towards all of them."

Streight and his comrades managed to escape to Union lines. Richmond newspapers excoriated Winder for allowing the Libby breakout to happen. In what some Confederate officials admitted was an overreaction, the security chief ordered prison officials to pour two hundred pounds of gunpowder into Libby's cellar, to be a giant land mine that guards warned prisoners they would detonate to kill them all if they attempted another escape.

Richmond was in a state of high anxiety after the Libby breakout. Soldiers searched the houses of practically every suspected Union sympathizer, including Van Lew's. She managed to convince Confederate authorities she played no part in the escape. They allowed her to visit the perimeter of the Belle Isle camp on February 27. But they kept a close watch on her when she did to make sure nothing got exchanged during the visit. Guards had begun moving the first of the Belle Isle prisoners to Andersonville two days earlier. Van Lew was shocked by the "wretchedness and squalid filth" she said she saw. The spymaster did not know that the next day the Union Army would launch another raid to free the inmates at Belle Isle and Richmond's other prisons.

The operation was hatched by Brigadier General Hugh Judson Kilpatrick, a twenty-eight-year-old, wiry West Pointer always decked out in a stylish cutaway Union coat with a cocked hat and bushy ginger-colored sideburns. Other Union generals dismissed Kilpatrick, who had soared through promotions, as a fool. The 3rd Cavalry Division commander had been nicknamed "Kill-cavalry" because of the reckless way he led his mounted soldiers into battles that resulted in many of them killed to satisfy his thirst for personal glory. Everything about Kilpatrick seemed seamy. A womanizer, at the front he kept a prostitute disguised as a male soldier he called "Charley." A world-class braggart, he disgusted fellow officers with the fraudulent battle reports that always inflated his role. But Kilpatrick had influential friends in Washington. He hoped the special operation he now planned would get him promoted to major general if it succeeded and one day propel him to the presidency.

Kilpatrick made an end run around Pleasonton and Meade, and went directly to Lincoln with his idea for a second attempt to rescue Union prisoners in Richmond. Pleasonton thought Kilpatrick's plan would fail as Butler's had, but the young general sold Lincoln, who was still desperate to free the inmates before any more were shipped off to Andersonville. The president approved the mission. He also wanted Kilpatrick's men to spread copies of his Emancipation Proclamation among Richmonders. Meade, who had been kept in the dark about the plan presented to Lincoln, hated the upstart cavalry general but reluctantly went along with the mission. Perhaps Kilpatrick might succeed in rescuing the 15,000 prisoners in Richmond, he thought. Sharpe still received reports from Maddox that the Rebel capital continued to be lightly defended, and Meade believed them.

On February 28, Kilpatrick, with some 4,000 cavalrymen and six artillery pieces, crossed the Rapidan River and headed south to Richmond. Sedgwick's corps and 2,000 cavalrymen under Brigadier General George Custer launched diversionary moves, once more hoping to distract Lee so he would not send reinforcements to the capital. Sharpe kept close tabs on the operation, messaging Meade and Pleasonton updates from his spies who accompanied the cavalrymen. When they arrived north of Richmond, Kilpatrick sent about 500 of his horsemen under Colonel Ulric Dahlgren to attack the city from the south while the rest of the force charged into the capital from the north. At twenty-one, Dahlgren was the Union's youngest colonel and already considered a brash war hero for his capture of the important dispatches from Davis to Lee at Gettysburg. Dahlgren was wounded a few days after that battle and had to have his right leg amputated above the knee. Ulric's father, Admiral John Dahlgren, was also a favorite of Lincoln, who enjoyed hearing his sea stories.

Sharpe sent McEntee to join Kilpatrick's raid along with a group of agents (including Milton Cline) to serve as guides. The agents brought along Confederate uniforms to disguise themselves. A spy team went with Dahlgren, who was wary about having them. But Sharpe vouched for their trustworthiness.

Kill-cavalry turned out to be not as daring as he made himself out to be. When he reached enemy fortifications a mile from Richmond's city limits on March 1, Rebel infantry and artillery opened up on him. A number of sources had warned Confederate authorities that the Union Army was launching a second raid to free the prisoners. Throughout the morning, Van Lew could see citizens called out to man barricades. After a brief skirmish, Kilpatrick lost his nerve and scurried to Williamsburg and the safety of Butler's lines, leaving Dahlgren stranded.

Meanwhile, on the left bank of the Mattaponi River near King and Queen Court House, northeast of Richmond, Ulric Dahlgren and about ninety of his men who had become separated from the rest of his detachment were ambushed on March 2 by a hastily gathered Richmond militia force. Dahlgren was killed and the ambushers captured many of his soldiers, plus all but one of McEntee's agents, who made it back slightly wounded. McEntee considered the Kilpatrick operation botched from beginning to end. Meade agreed and launched an investigation. In a confidential afteraction report McEntee sent to Sharpe, he also did not have kind words for how his agents had performed. He accused Cline, one of Sharpe's better spies, of disobeying orders, which McEntee thought resulted in a lot of his agents being captured.

The debacle did not end with Kilpatrick's retreat and Dahlgren's death. Davis insisted that the Confederates treated the young Union colonel's body with respect, but that was hardly the case. Someone cut off one of Dahlgren's fingers to steal a ring. His artificial leg was removed and sent to

Davis, who inspected it with his cabinet members. The wooden leg was then displayed in a store window. But it was the documents accompanying the artificial limb that set off Davis and senior Confederate officials.

After the ambush, thirteen-year-old William Littlepage found Dahlgren's body in a ditch with his one foot propped up against a tree. Hunting through the corpse's pockets, the boy discovered a memo box with several sheets of paper in it. They appeared to be a text of a speech Dahlgren had delivered to his men, explaining that their mission was not only to rescue Union prisoners but also to burn down Richmond (one rumor had it that the Federals carried incendiary devices for the job) and to kill Jefferson Davis and his cabinet. The explosive documents were rushed to Davis along with the wooden leg.

The Confederate president and generals like Lee realized they had been handed a propaganda windfall and leaked copies of the Dahlgren papers to the Richmond press, as well as to friendly contacts in Europe. Public outrage predictably erupted. Confederate war secretary James Seddon believed the documents justified hanging Dahlgren's captured men as assassins. That would be a bad idea, Lee counseled. But vengeful southerners, who blamed Lincoln personally for the death and destruction visited on them, began calling more openly for the president of the United States to be felled from an assassin's bullet he wished on the president of the Confederacy.

In the North, federal officials insisted the documents did not reflect U.S. government policy and questioned their authenticity. The *New York Times* claimed they were forgeries. So did Admiral Dahlgren, who eventually saw a photographic copy of the papers and pointed out that the handwriting wasn't his son's and that the signature at the end of one document had his name misspelled.

Behind the scenes, however, Meade launched an intensive investigation to determine if that was really the case. He ordered Dahlgren's personal effects left behind at his base camp packed up and rushed to his headquarters so they could be thoroughly searched for incriminating evidence. He had Pleasonton and Patrick scour their files for all instructions the young colonel received. Meade also grilled Kilpatrick on what orders he gave Dahlgren and on whether his subordinate delivered instructions to his men to torch Richmond and kill its top officials. Kilpatrick adamantly insisted he and Dahlgren never issued such orders.

On April 1, Lee delivered to Meade a letter with photocopies of the Dahlgren documents enclosed, asking if the U.S. government had authorized this mission. Meade wrote back on April 17, denying that Washington, Kilpatrick, or he himself had ever ordered the burning of Richmond and the assassination of its leaders. In private, however, Meade wondered if Dahlgren had been involved in a plot approved by higher-ups. Meade had not been in the meeting Kilpatrick had with Lincoln, where the operation was discussed. No document linked Lincoln to any wider plot. But the president had approved Butler's earlier raid and the general's instructions to Wistar included destroying buildings and capturing Davis and other senior officials. Patrick was convinced the Dahlgren papers were genuine. So was McEntee, who had been with Kilpatrick on the mission and who told Patrick the papers "correspond with what D[ahlgren] told *him*," the provost marshal wrote in his diary. Whatever the truth in this "pretty ugly piece of business," Meade was "determined," he wrote his wife, that "my skirts should be clear."

Van Lew adamantly believed Confederates had fabricated the Dahlgren papers to "inflame the southern people," she said. After all, these were the same officials who filled Libby Prison with dynamite to commit mass murder. She read the March 8 issue of the *Richmond Examiner*, which described the ghoulish treatment of Dahlgren's remains. Not only had someone chopped his finger off to filch his ring, the *Examiner* and other papers proudly reported, but Dahlgren's body had been stripped naked, dumped in a shallow muddy hole near where he had been killed, and covered with dirt. The body was later dug up and taken to the York River Railroad depot for a ghastly public viewing before being hauled off to a hidden grave for a "dog's burial." Van Lew visited the train station to view the desecrated body and the artificial leg on display. It sickened her. "The heart of every loyal person was stirred to its depths," she wrote. She and other members of her ring, like Lohmann and Rowley, began talking about what they should do to right this terrible wrong. They decided to find Dahlgren's grave, exhume the body, and give it a proper burial.

Van Lew ran a well-oiled machine by that time, which could easily take on a grave-robbing job. Even so, she and her ring members were putting this finely tuned network at extreme risk to move a dead person—a risk that could land them in jail if they were caught and destroy all they had yet to accomplish for the Union they loved. Why did they do it? Why take on an operation that so violated sound tradecraft? Van Lew biographer Elizabeth Varon has the best explanation. It lies in the psyche of these spies and in the way men and women of their era coped with all too frequent deaths. That piece of mid-nineteenth-century American culture—almost mystical in nature—strove for a person's "good death"—an honorable and serene end to send one along to the afterlife. Tossed into a muddy hole, displayed like a slab of meat at a train depot, and dumped in a hidden grave, Ulric Dahlgren had not enjoyed a good death. As if they were the family of this young man, Van Lew and her agents felt compelled to intervene and make things right—regardless of the danger.

Finding Dahlgren's body was no easy task for Lohmann and other ring members. Under orders from Davis to put the corpse in a secret grave, Lieutenant Colonel John Atkinson selected a secluded spot just below Oakwood Cemetery, on Richmond's eastern edge. Atkinson's burial team, which included another officer and several soldiers to dig the hole, tried to clear away all cemetery employees from the graveyard to conceal the internment. Even so, the burial spot was noted by a black gravedigger who hid behind a tree nearby at midnight. Lohmann and his comrades had to move cautiously, making quiet inquiries to guess where the body might have been taken to after its public display. Fortunately they had the services of Martin Lipscomb, a bricklayer who once ran for mayor of Richmond and who now oversaw the burial of all federal soldiers who died in the city. Lipscomb narrowed down Dahlgren's likely resting place to near the Oakwood Cemetery. Lohmann then found the black worker who witnessed the burial.

On the dark, stormy night of April 6, Lohmann, his brother John, and Lipscomb sneaked into the cemetery and the black worker directed them to Dahlgren's grave nearby. With pickaxes and shovels they quickly dug up an ordinary-looking pine box, pried open its top, and examined the body carefully to confirm it was Dahlgren's. It was. The right leg was missing. The colonel had been dressed in just a coarse cotton shirt and his uniform pants. The only wound Lohmann and the others could see from the waist up was one to the young man's temple, which they guessed was the fatal shot. Lohmann was impressed that the body was "in a perfect state of preservation," as he wrote later. Dahlgren's features, his hair and flesh looked quite natural. Lohmann guessed the cold temperatures of early spring had chilled the soil enough to help preserve the corpse.

Quickly they loaded the wooden coffin onto a mule-drawn spring wagon, filled the empty hole with the dirt they had dug out, and drove the remains to Rowley's farm not far from Richmond, arriving there at 11 p.m. The men hid the pine box in an outbuilding that night until Lohmann could bring a better metal coffin and the remains could be transferred to another, more secure site for a proper burial. Like a sentry, Rowley watched over the body for the rest of the night. Finding a metal coffin the next day was not easy. The high-end varieties were scarce and expensive. Lohmann had to pay a lot for one of them.

The morning of April 7, Elizabeth Van Lew and other ring members visited the Rowley farm to view the remains and hold what amounted to a wake for Ulric Dahlgren. With their eyes and hands they examined the body carefully, as if reading it. They cut a lock of the colonel's hair to send to his father. "The comeliness of the young face was gone," Van Lew recalled, "yet the features seemed regular and there was a wonderful look, firmness or energy stamped upon them."

Early the next afternoon, Rowley and Lohmann gently lifted the body, wrapped in a blue military blanket, out of the pine box and put it in the metal coffin, which they loaded onto Rowley's wagon. He covered it with young peach trees to conceal it from Confederate pickets at posts, and with the Lohmann brothers riding ahead to scout for trouble, he drove it some ten miles from the city to the farm of a Scotsman named Robert Orrock, who had agreed to bury the coffin on his property. Lohmann applied a concoction of chalk and oil to seal the casket and the men lowered it into a hole Orrock had dug. A peach tree was planted over the grave to mark the place where the body would remain for one year and two days.

It ended up being unfortunate that Van Lew's ring stole Dahlgren's body for safekeeping. Davis, it turned out, eventually was ready to deliver the remains to the colonel's father. The admiral had made four trips to Fort Monroe trying to arrange the transfer. He wrote Davis a personal letter begging for his son and enclosed a hundred dollars in gold coins to pay for transportation expenses. General Butler, under pressure from Lincoln to retrieve the body, challenged Rebel authorities to produce it to prove it had not been submitted to "indignity and outrage." Butler knew it had and that evidence of a mutilated corpse would be a propaganda antidote to the advantage the Confederates had enjoyed so far.

Butler finally extracted a promise from Davis that the body would be returned. But when Atkinson went to the grave site to retrieve the remains, he found it empty, which greatly embarrassed Davis. Confederate authorities notified Butler and insisted they had launched an intensive search for the corpse. Butler passed the news on to the heartbroken admiral on April 17. Three days later he wrote John Dahlgren that he had just received a message from "Union friends" in Richmond; they had taken the body and buried it in a safe place "beyond the reach of the rebel authorities." (A Van Lew courier later slipped into Washington, knocked on the door of the admiral's house, and handed him the lock of the colonel's hair.) Butler asked the elder Dahlgren to keep quiet about the message they received. He did not want to expose the Van Lew ring.

Aftershocks from the grave robbery continued to reverberate. The affair demonstrated to Butler that Van Lew's operatives were intensely loyal and cunningly skillful. For Van Lew's inner circle, as well as for Union sympathizers throughout the city, the special operation was a tremendous morale boost. The body theft, coming on the heels of the Libby breakout, also rattled Richmonders and their government. The *Richmond Examiner* speculated whether Dahlgren had "been resurrected." Confederate officials realized they had a formidable fifth column in their midst, able to spy and make bodies disappear. Davis ordered Winder to hunt down the grave robbers but the baffled security chief turned up no clues.

Twenty-One

ULYSSES S. GRANT

G rant slipped into Washington unnoticed as dusk fell on March 8. He checked in with his son Fred at the Willard and after freshening up took the teenager to the hotel dining room for dinner. Soon other guests realized the famous general was in their midst and began cheering and banging fists on their tables until he stood up, embarrassed somewhat and fumbling with his napkin, to take a bow. After sending Fred to bed, Grant walked by himself to the White House, where a crowd had gathered by nine thirty for the president's weekly reception. Beaming, Lincoln practically bounded up to the general when he spotted him and grabbed his hand. "Well, this is a great pleasure!" he said and led the small, stoop-shouldered officer (eight inches shorter than he) around the Blue Room to meet others.

Ulysses S. Grant was a soft-spoken introvert, who enjoyed a short and mediocre military career after graduating in the bottom half of his West Point class and then a string of unsuccessful civilian jobs before the Civil War. He suffered from chronic migraines and reports persisted that he was a binge drinker. Stanton had his doubts about the man, as did Halleck, but in the war's Western Theater, much of it fought along rivers in amphibious operations requiring cooperation between the Army and Navy, Grant proved adept. With campaigns at Paducah on the Ohio River, at Belmont in Missouri, at Fort Henry and Fort Donelson on the Tennessee and Cumberland Rivers, at Shiloh in Tennessee, at Vicksburg in Mississippi, and at Chattanooga also in Tennessee, Grant had demonstrated he would take risks, seize the initiative, absorb Confederate counterattacks, and not panic. He had his leadership faults, failing at times to appreciate that his enemy might try the unexpected. He came under fire from political enemies for heavy casualties accompanying many of his victories (such as at Shiloh) and over rumors he was intoxicated for some fights. But like Lee, Grant showed talent for taking advantage of enemy mistakes. Lack of information did not paralyze him on the battlefield. He arrived in Washington convinced that victories lie in holding the initiative, forcing his opponents to react to his moves instead of the reverse.

When calls grew to dismiss the controversial Grant, Lincoln reportedly responded: "I can't spare this man—he fights." A ruthless determination consumed the president. With their defeat at Gettysburg, their east coast blockaded, and their western domain shrinking, it became evident that the Rebels could not win the war. But they were not ready to lose it. The bloody conflict had gone on too long, Lincoln believed. It was time to force it to a close, but he saw little evidence that Meade, who seemed to be engaged in endless feints and maneuvers with Lee, shared his sense of urgency. The day after Grant arrived in Washington, Lincoln presided over a White House ceremony to present him his commission as a lieutenant general, replacing Halleck as general in chief of the Army. Halleck remained as Grant's Washington chief of staff, implementing his orders and tending to paperwork his new boss did not want to be bothered with.

Though not disposed to do so at first, Grant decided to keep Meade as commander of the Army of the Potomac. But Grant would call the shots on where and when that army fought. The West's three best generals now took over the war against the Confederacy. William Tecumseh Sherman, made brigadier general after impressing Lincoln in the first Bull Run battle and by leading a corps at Vicksburg, succeeded Grant as commander of the western armies. Philip Henry Sheridan, a rough-edged general sporting always a porkpie hat and not averse to scorched-earth tactics, came east to replace Pleasonton as leader of the cavalry. The day after his commissioning ceremony, Grant took the train in a blinding rainstorm to Meade's headquarters at Brandy Station, north of the Rapidan, where he remained through the night discussing past and future campaigns with the Potomac Army commander. Sharpe sat in the background with other staffers as the two generals talked, impressed, he wrote his uncle Jansen, with how "very unostentatious" the new general in chief appeared. Grant declined a special train to come down to Meade's headquarters, boarding instead the regular run. He also did not want a grand review of the troops and "kicked over everyone's preparations to fete him and left unexpectedly the next morning," Sharpe added in his letter. It was clear to the spymaster from the meetings he sat in on that Grant "means to run the machine."

Meade was outwardly cordial, professing to be glad to see Grant and offering to relinquish his command if he wanted him to. Grant did not, which pleased Meade. But he was not happy when he learned that Grant intended to remain in the field and set up his headquarters just six miles west of Meade's at Culpeper Court House. Sherman had advised Grant to stay as far away from Washington's bureaucratic snake pit as he could. Grant took the advice to heart but he had a far more important reason for parking his headquarters with the Army of the Potomac. Virginia was the last nexus for the conflict, the state where the fate of the Union and the Confederacy finally would be decided. Lee's army defending Richmond was the enemy's strongest, most seasoned, best equipped, and best led. Union victories elsewhere would not end the war as long as Lee's force stood.

Intending to crush the rebellion and end the war before the November elections, Grant devised a battle plan, which Lincoln had been urging, for heavy coordinated blows to fall on the Confederacy in many places. Meade's army, with Grant watching it closely, would march south to chase Lee. Sherman would move south from Chattanooga to break up Johnston's army and invade the southern interior, with Georgia as the ultimate aim. As for the three political generals he couldn't replace, Grant ordered Nathaniel Banks's

Army of the Gulf in Louisiana to capture Mobile and push north against the Rebels in Alabama. Benjamin Butler's Army of the James was to advance up that river on the Peninsula, cut the Petersburg-to-Richmond rail connection, and threaten the Rebel capital. Franz Sigel's force in West Virginia and the Shenandoah was ordered to move up the valley to pin down its defenders and sever Lee's links to that vital region.

Sharpe noted—approvingly—that Grant sent three horses to Meade's headquarters, which to the intelligence chief meant that the Army chief "means to move with us." Knowing the prickly Meade, Sharpe predicted to his uncle that "the fur will fly" when Grant returned. Meade would come to admire Grant and work tolerably well with him. But he could not help but feel demoted, commanding an army now with the boss literally looking over his shoulder. Cocky staff officers Grant brought with him did not hide that they thought the Potomac Army would now fight to its potential with western men in charge. Soon reporters began referring to the force in their articles as "Grant's army," which rankled Meade.

Carrie and the children had returned to Washington and Sharpe located a private house for them, which he thought was better than any affordable, but miserable, hotel he could find in the city. General Sickles, Sharpe's old division commander, had asked that the spymaster accompany him on a western trip, but Meade objected and "said I couldn't be spared from here," Sharpe wrote his uncle. It was ironic, he added, what with all the derogatory comments the Potomac Army commander had made about the Bureau of Military Information, "Meade is afraid I will get away from him entirely." Sharpe was willing to endure another campaign, but after that he wanted to resign from the Army. He was tired of this war and George Meade.

Sharpe soon discovered a new mentor, however. Grant found the Army of the Potomac in better shape than he expected. He also was impressed with the spy chief Meade had on his staff. The past three years Grant had learned a lot about how to gather and use intelligence in battles. His headquarters, wherever he set it up, was an information clearinghouse, with reports streaming in from a variety of sources. Grant became a seasoned, and wary, intelligence customer. He had learned that information from scouts and spies always had to be evaluated carefully because it was not always correct. He was leery of reports from local citizens who walked into his camp. The Confederate sympathizers among them rarely told the truth, he found, and even the Unionists kept silent at times or were forced to lie by Rebels in their midst. He also did not place much stock in information from deserters; they rarely knew what was happening at the corps or army level.

Sharpe's force of more than two dozen agents, operating out of a couple of ramshackle huts at Meade's Brandy Station headquarters, had suffered under Meade's indifference. The information bureau rejuvenated quickly when Grant arrived. Patrick quietly worked out an arrangement where Sharpe began spending a good deal of time at Grant's Culpeper Court House headquarters. The general in chief's aides soon considered this eastern officer a valuable member of their staff. Though he remained Meade's intelligence officer, Sharpe began overseeing a much wider spy operation for Grant's entire command. He sent one of his lieutenants, Frederick Manning, to Butler's Army of the James. For Sigel's army in the Shenandoah Valley, Sharpe dispatched one of his best officers, Captain John McEntee.

Soon Manning and another lieutenant on Butler's staff, John Davenport, were managing the general's correspondence with Van Lew. McEntee, however, became disenchanted with his assignment. Setting up his spy base at Harpers Ferry, he quickly concluded that Sharpe had banished him to a miserable and lonely outpost. He assembled nearly two dozen agents to work for him and discovered what he told Sharpe was a "Union League" of forty more men in Loudoun County, Virginia, who were willing to supply him intelligence on Confederates around them and to venture into the Shenandoah Valley to spy. McEntee's Union League, made up mostly of farmers, also agreed to work for free.

But McEntee was soon homesick for the Army of the Potomac. He was one of Sharpe's top performers, but it took more than a month before he gained Sigel's confidence and the obtuse general would finally tell him where his men were deployed, let him in on his plans for using them, and allow him to supervise his army's secret service operation. Sending reports back to Sharpe proved difficult, with couriers always in danger of being captured by Rebel patrols. Even McEntee narrowly missed being nabbed by one and suffered a minor shrapnel wound when a shell exploded near him. Communication from Sharpe likewise was spotty, which frustrated McEntee. And he was always going "dead broke," he complained, when funds did not arrive on time for him and his agents. His Harpers Ferry landlord nearly evicted him because he had no money for the room rent.

Sigel finally came to appreciate the information McEntee supplied him. The intelligence officer, though he considered Sigel a brave fellow, soon concluded the general was an inept commander. McEntee began sending Sharpe as many reports on Sigel's movements (or lack of them) as he did on moves by Confederates in the valley.

Quickly settling into his Culpeper Court House headquarters, Grant began preparing Meade's army to cross the Rapidan River and attack Lee on the other side in a showdown battle south of the Wilderness, whose thick pines and scrub oak had bedeviled Hooker a year earlier. For the Army of the Potomac to succeed, though, Grant needed to be able to track the movement of Rebel forces south of the Rapidan. That became no easy job for Sharpe. Through March and April he had constant headaches pinpointing exactly where all Lee's army was, particularly the two divisions in Longstreet's corps, which Sharpe knew had left Tennessee and had headed east. He messaged McEntee in early March to vent his frustration at being unable to track Lee as he had in the past. "There is considerable movement of the enemy," he wrote. "Their camps are disappearing at some points. . . . You must be very active in the employment of everybody and everything. Telegraph me three times a day if there is the least thing to say."

Instead of clarity, interrogations of Confederate prisoners and deserters, as well as citizens in the area, were producing a panoply of conflicting evidence. Reports from McEntee and others that Lee's army was not on the move were followed by reports that he was moving. Fixing Longstreet's location became particularly vexing for Sharpe. There were camp rumors that his corps had been joined by Pickett's division when in fact Pickett was actually in the Richmond area. Another rumor arrived that a portion of Longstreet's corps had already reached Richmond when it had not. Numerous sources, including McEntee in the Shenandoah Valley and Isaac Silver near Chancellorsville (still referred to as the "Old Man" in intelligence memos), reported to Sharpe that Longstreet himself had joined Lee at his Orange

Court House headquarters on the turnpike west of Fredericksburg by late April. Longstreet's corps, however, was reported to be everywhere—from Charlottesville in western Virginia to Sperryville northwest of Culpeper. Finally on April 29, McEntee telegraphed Sharpe that a reliable citizen reported that Longstreet's force "was in the neighborhood of Gordonsville in easy supporting distance of Lee." The citizen report turned out to be the accurate one. Longstreet's two divisions were in fact around Gordonsville, Virginia, on the Orange and Alexandria Railroad line southwest of Lee's Orange Court House headquarters.

Though Sharpe's picture of the position of Lee's forces was murky, it appeared clear to the Union spymaster that as Grant prepared to move against Lee, so too was Lee readying a move on Grant. The Confederate commander had orders read to his soldiers at a dress parade that if they were captured they should not divulge the brigade or division to which they belonged, nor reveal where these units were located or moving to. But the scores of Rebel deserters Sharpe interviewed were only too happy to talk. From their interviews, the clues of an impending enemy attack, which Sharpe quickly forwarded to Grant and Meade, were unmistakable. The deserters claimed Lee's army was under marching orders and had been directed to keep cooked rations constantly on hand. Teamsters who had returned from Lee's headquarters at Orange Court House revealed that Rebel troops were arriving there by trains on the Orange and Alexandria Railroad line. McEntee sent Sharpe a rumor he picked up from one of the Confederate camps in the Shenandoah that Lee had taken all his artillery to the front. Agents like Isaac Silver reported that the Rebel leader's 15,000-man cavalry was riding from Hamilton's Crossing, south of Fredericksburg, to the headquarters as well.

Sharpe found gossip spreading through the Rebel camps that Lee had said: "The Army of the Potomac had lain around Culpeper long enough and he would shortly make it travel." Captured Confederate officers even boasted that they hoped Lee again would march into Pennsylvania and they believed he would do just that. Sharpe sent out citizen spies he used during the Chancellorsville campaign and who still lived in Fredericksburg or along the Rappahannock. They found places for the Federals to ford the

Rapidan, but reported being blocked from getting within six and a half miles of Lee's headquarters at Orange Court House. Mail service to Fredericksburg had been cut off and its citizens were not allowed to leave their homes. So Sharpe's spies improvised. They pretended to be on business when Rebel pickets halted them, striking up conversations with the soldiers encountered and even stealing their mail to find out what their units were up to. Sharpe didn't always have to resort to thievery to read enemy correspondence. He kept a file of southern newspapers that imprudently printed letters Confederate troops wrote home.

Meanwhile, Joseph Maddox, whom Sharpe continued to trust while others still doubted his loyalty, reported that Lee had enough rations at Gordonsville to feed his army for eighty days, though meat was in short supply, so cornmeal and molasses appeared to be the standard fare. Maddox also learned that a Frenchman had developed new conical-shaped torpedoes for the Confederates and had placed the formidable mines in the Rappahannock below Tappahannock, Virginia, southeast of Fredericksburg. Isaac Silver had sent Sharpe the same report from his sources.

On May 4, Grant and the Army of the Potomac crossed the Rapidan River at Germanna and Ely's Fords and began moving south. He hoped to steal a march on Lee, proceeding quickly through the dense thicket of the Wilderness, and then turn Lee's right flank on the east to force him into a fight out in the open, where the numerical advantage of Grant's 118,000 soldiers and 316 artillery pieces would make the difference. Sharpe had already estimated from his intelligence sources that Lee's army numbered about 70,000 soldiers, which was about 5,000 under the total Lee actually had. In this highly fluid situation, Sharpe's spies had only limited intelligence on the area south of the Rapidan, but they provided what they could of Confederate movements that day and the next. Grant still did not know exactly where all of Lee's forces were.

Grant's force plunged into the Wilderness nonetheless, hoping to beat Lee in a race to more maneuverable ground outside it. In Grant's mind the only important information he needed was that Lee's army would face him south of the Rapidan. The Union commander, who let Meade make the tactical decisions, did not believe he needed to know much more for the broader decisions he would make. Unlike McClellan, Grant did not intend to dawdle until he had every scrap of intelligence in hand and lose the initiative.

Lee allowed Grant to cross the Rapidan unmolested but then rushed his army east to meet him May 5 inside the heart of the Wilderness, where the Union advantage in troop numbers and artillery was negated by the tangled woods and poor visibility. For two days they fought viciously in a confused and frenzied battle that amounted to a bloody draw. Musket shots and exploding shells touched off wildfires that burned to death some of the wounded lying on the ground. Grant suffered about 18,000 casualties, compared to some 11,000 for Lee—whose wounded included Longstreet with a bullet in his shoulder. But unlike Hooker the year before, Grant did not let the slaughter scare him back across the Rapidan in retreat. He remained on the offensive, moving once more with little knowledge of what Lee had in store for him. He ordered his staff to stop fretting about the Rebel commander. "Some of you always seem to think he is suddenly going to turn a double somersault, and land in your rear and on both of our flanks at the same time," he lectured his officers. "Go back to your command, and try to think what we are going to do ourselves, instead of what Lee is going to do." Putting himself closer to Richmond, Grant marched his army twelve miles southeast for nearly two more weeks of heavy fighting with Lee, some of it hand to hand, at the crossroads hamlet of Spotsylvania Court House. It resulted in another 30,000 casualties for both sides.

Throughout the Wilderness and Spotsylvania battles, Sharpe's team, as it had at Gettysburg, interrogated hundreds of prisoners in assembly-line fashion to funnel reports to Meade on Confederate brigades and divisions shifting about, along with losses they had endured (particularly among senior officers) and the depleted rations they were having to fight on. Working in a combat zone became dangerous for Sharpe's men. Cline at one point ran out of ammunition in a shoot-out he was forced to have with Rebel cavalry scouts. Meade added to the unpleasantness. With Grant a constant presence, the Potomac Army commander became "cross as a bear," Patrick wrote in his diary.

On the bright side, the provost marshal noted with delight in his journal that among the three thousand prisoners rounded up were two Rebel generals, who became "very much disgusted" when Patrick rattled off details about their units from information Sharpe had provided. Sharpe scored a counterintelligence coup as well in mid-May. A team of his operatives monitoring railroad trains supplying Lee's army captured one of Jeb Stuart's signal officers, who revealed that he and his comrades had spies posted at the mouth of the Potomac Creek tributary northeast of Fredericksburg to observe Union steamers sailing up and down the Potomac River. "They are perfectly familiar with everything we have lately done in that direction," Sharpe warned Meade.

Northerners cheered Grant's advance in what became known as the Overland Campaign but were shocked by its price in carnage. In Washington alone the Army was burying six hundred soldiers a month. Embalming surgeons like Doctor W. J. Bunnell, growing wealthy making thousands of corpses presentable for grieving families, advertised in a flyer that he traveled with the Potomac Army and had a new preservation procedure "invariably giving the best satisfaction." Among the living, McEntee messaged Sharpe he caught Union deserters from the Wilderness battle's horrors roaming near his Harpers Ferry base pretending to be Rebel deserters.

Meanwhile, Grant's three political generals who were supposed to squeeze the Confederacy in unison with Meade failed in the missions he gave them. Banks was never able to capture Mobile and push north against the Rebels in Alabama. In the Shenandoah Valley, Confederate forces routed Sigel at New Market, Virginia. Butler managed to successfully steam up the James River with his 39,000 men to a spot north of Petersburg between the James and Appomattox Rivers known as Bermuda Hundred. From there he had an ideal opportunity to cut the railroad line running between the two cities and capture Richmond, which along with Petersburg had fewer than 10,000 soldiers and militiamen defending them both. But instead of striking quickly with his overwhelming force, Butler slowly and cautiously sent detachments forward, giving General Beauregard time to bring in reinforcements from the Carolinas to bottle him up. Grant, however, remained a bulldog. He messaged Washington that there would be no turning back: "I propose to fight it out on this line if it takes all summer." Lincoln found the general's drive refreshing.

A war-weary Van Lew did not feel the early excitement Richmonders did when first reports claimed Lee had bested Grant in the Wilderness. "It seems we have suffered past all excitement," she wrote in her diary. "Nothing elates me. I have calm hope. But there is much heart sadness with it." Cannon fire from the Spotsylvania battle awakened her the morning of May 14. She sent Mary Bowser and other servants out to hunt for news from the front while she climbed to the rooftop of her mansion and spent much of the day squinting to view the white smoke of battle drifting to the city from the north. Stores were closed and streets were mostly empty. Van Lew's spies had delivered Butler intelligence that most of Richmond's troops had been sent to help Lee and the lightly garrisoned city was ripe for attack. She later managed to secure a pass from Richmond authorities to visit a friend's farm outside the city if she promised not to reveal to anyone anything she saw on the visit that might harm Rebel military activities. Van Lew had no intention of keeping that promise. She, meanwhile, grew depressed when news arrived that Beauregard had Butler penned up at Bermuda Hundred. Richmond's liberation was still far off, she realized.

But Grant's "determination is immense," Sharpe wrote his uncle Jansen, "and I begin to think him as considerable of a man. We have certainly not been whipped." With the Confederates refusing to budge from Spotsylvania, Grant sidled east and south for twenty-five miles to try to swing around Lee's flank at Hanover Junction's rail crossing, near the North Anna River. Lee spotted Grant's move and rushed his army behind the North Anna before the Union force arrived. So Grant moved down another twenty miles to make another try at outflanking Lee at Cold Harbor, a dusty crossroads ten miles northeast of Richmond. As Virginia's dogwoods still bloomed and rain showers cooled sweltering hot days, the two replenished armies— some 109,000 under Grant and 59,000 under Lee—arrived at Cold Harbor late on June 1 and through the next two days fought another brutal battle. Casualties again became heavy. By early afternoon on June 3, Grant called off further attacks. He resumed trench warfare, and another gruesome stalemate, for the next ten days.

Meade became more irritated that Grant dominated press coverage after

the battles. "The papers are giving Grant all the credit of what they call successes," he groused in a letter to his wife. "I hope they will remember this
if anything goes wrong." Though he remained outwardly disdainful of his
information bureau, Meade during the trek south nervously demanded that
anything Sharpe found be rushed to his command post. He even summoned
McEntee and his team at one point to appear before him at his headquarters
with their report.

From Spotsylvania to Cold Harbor, Sharpe spent most of his time tracking the movements and defenses of Lee's divisions to Grant's right and
providing his commanders with topographical reports on the land ahead
of them. Senior officers were keeping close watch on Rebel prisoners passing through the lines, suspecting Lee had salted them with spies. But Sharpe
took pity on a pregnant mother and her fourteen-year-old daughter, whom
Union troops had taken from their home near Cold Harbor. The two had
told Confederate soldiers who stayed in the house what they had seen of
federal men marching in the area. The "simple minded" women, Sharpe
wrote, would likely have told him what they had seen of Confederate troops
if he had met them first. "I think they had no idea that they were doing any
harm." Patrick agreed that they should be returned to their home.

The information Sharpe received from deserters, civilians, and his own
spies painted a collective portrait of a southern army deeply shaken by the
Wilderness and Spotsylvania slaughter and nearly breaking apart. A German man who fled Richmond said the city was in a chaotic state, with refugees pouring in and supplies from Petersburg cut off by the Union force. A
deserter from the Confederate Signal Corps told Sharpe that all the capital's
businesses and government departments had been closed so male employees could be rushed to the front. But Grant painfully discovered at Cold
Harbor that Lee still refused to be beaten.

Grant had brought the Union Army the closest to Richmond that it
had been in two years. When the general made his next sidle east and then
south—to the gates of Petersburg below the James River—Sharpe took
over the Van Lew spy ring, which would be needed for the final drive on

Richmond. Intelligence from her network and from Samuel Ruth's operatives actually had been trickling in to him and Grant since the general
took over the Army. In mid-March, Lohmann had sent Sharpe warnings
that Rebels planned a raid on the Orange and Alexandria Railroad and
were preparing an attack on Norfolk. The next month Butler forwarded to
Grant's chief of staff a report a Van Lew courier brought and vouched for
"Miss Eliza's" reliability. And throughout the Wilderness, Spotsylvania, and
Cold Harbor campaigns much of the Richmond intelligence Butler sent
to Sharpe originated from Van Lew. Finally on June 11, as Grant prepared
to move the Potomac Army to Petersburg and take over the attack on that
city and Richmond from the hapless Butler, John Van Lew, who had been
on the run from Confederate authorities wanting to put him back in their
army, arrived at Meade's headquarters. He explained to Sharpe's team how
his sister's well-organized ring in Richmond could provide them with valuable information. Sharpe had the Van Lew account moved to his hut so he
could personally supervise the network and its female spymaster, whom he
soon came to admire.

Van Lew quickly discovered that her new boss was far better than Butler. Sharpe sent crisp requests for specific information, and her communications with him became frequent, as well as more secure than they had
been with Butler, she thought. Her underground began focusing less on
Richmond's prisoners and more on answering Sharpe's questions about the
Confederate military. Van Lew also now became more a manager than a spy.
Instead of walking the streets to gather information, she spent more time in
her mansion fielding Sharpe's queries, deploying her agents to gather the
intelligence, and then analyzing what the spies brought back and drafting
reports for the Union command. Sharpe soon had a squad of different Van
Lew couriers showing up at his hut with her dispatches. Many were farmers,
storekeepers, and factory workers she recruited. Others were black servants
who worked for her or other ring members. The couriers carried their messages along the windy route south from Richmond to the new field headquarters Grant set up northeast of Petersburg at the tiny town of City Point,
where the Appomattox and James Rivers met.

Within months, Van Lew's network was churning out an average of three intelligence reports a week for Sharpe. They covered Richmond's defenses, troop movements between the capital and the Shenandoah Valley, economic conditions in the city, and the morale of its residents. Sharpe soon boasted that whatever Grant wanted in the way of information from the capital, Van Lew's ring could provide it. "She represented," the colonel later wrote, "all that was left of the power of the U.S. government in the city of Richmond."

Twenty-Two

THE RICHMOND– PETERSBURG CAMPAIGN

ichmond, which had lured Union legions to defeat, now immobilized Lee's army, which had to defend it. The city was extensively fortified on its north and east sides. Its soft underbelly lay with the southern and western defenses. So to the south side, where Butler had been ordered to attack from below the James River, Grant had decided to take his army. The general in chief had conceived an audacious plan to cut Lee's important supply lines and flush him out of his trenches and fortifications to fight in the open field, where the Union's advantage in numbers mattered. He fired the timid Sigel and ordered Major General David Hunter to take that force into the Shenandoah Valley to sever its railroads, capture Staunton, cross the Blue Ridge to destroy the vital Confederate supply depot at Lynchburg, Virginia, and then move east toward Richmond. From the other end, Sheridan was ordered to take two cavalry divisions westward also to raid railroads and link up with Hunter's force in the Shenandoah. Meanwhile, Grant in the evening of June 12 and early-morning hours of the next day quietly disengaged from the Cold Harbor front and sneaked his large force east and then south once more in a complex and risky fifty-mile move to seize Petersburg's vitally important rail hub, linking Richmond and its army to supplies from southern states.

Grant, Hunter, and Sheridan carried out the first part of their plans splendidly. Outgeneraling Lee, Grant succeeded in sneaking into his rear, crossing the James with his army beginning on June 14. Before Lee knew what was happening, Grant the next day had two corps approaching Petersburg, which Beauregard defended with only about 2,500 men. But after that, Lee, who could be fooled only for so long, responded forcefully. Many of Grant's subordinate commanders, in whom he had placed too much faith, lost their nerve and the three-pronged attack soon unraveled. Hunter proved to be no match for the enemy and ended up retreating from the Shenandoah Valley into West Virginia. Sheridan's expedition fared only slightly better, but Lee's cavalry headed off his men near Trevilian Station, sixty miles northwest of Richmond, in a bloody fight. Sheridan managed to tear up a railroad but abandoned his plan to link up with Hunter. Meanwhile, Grant's corps commanders at Petersburg, fearing Lee had arrived with reinforcements, moved too cautiously the next three days, failing to break through Beauregard's defense and giving Lee time to show up with backup to defend the city.

By June 18, Grant's Overland Campaign had consumed forty-six days of moving and fighting—with 65,000 northern casualties—and Lee remained undefeated. Many Union enlistments were about to expire and the Army of the Potomac was worn out. Both sides started construction of massive fortifications stretching from below Petersburg north across the James River and toward Richmond—to begin ten months of complicated trench warfare. For George Sharpe, the Overland Campaign ended with a major intelligence failure. He lost track of an entire Confederate corps.

Seeing that Grant had dispatched Hunter and Sheridan to the Shenandoah, Lee decided he had to risk weakening Richmond's defenses so he could save the valley's rich harvest, desperately needed to feed his army. He rushed Major General Wade Hampton's cavalry division to intercept Sheridan. He also ordered the men of the 2nd Corps, now commanded by Jubal Early, to depart for Lynchburg to take care of Hunter and reclaim the valley's grain fields and supplies. Stoop-shouldered from rheumatism, the forty-seven-year-old Early was a grizzled lieutenant general shot through the shoulder by a musket bullet two years earlier. After securing the valley supplies, Lee told Early, he could cross the Potomac and threaten Washington if his force wasn't needed back in Richmond. It would certainly distract Grant and perhaps force him to loosen his grip on Richmond. From this gambit, Lee wrote Davis, "I anticipate good results."

Grant had not anticipated this move by Lee. The Union commander, who before the war had met many of the men now leading the Confederate Army and who said often that he knew exactly how each general would react in combat, thought Lee had no choice but to concentrate his troops at Petersburg and Richmond to save the capital—not divert forces to the Shenandoah (though he understood the valley was the breadbasket for Lee's army and his corridor to the North). Grant plainly underestimated Lee's boldness when the odds were long. Sharpe's bureau did not detect the departure of Early's corps, not because Lee succeeded in masking its movement. Instead, a confluence of coincidence enabled the Confederate commander to slip away unnoticed.

Early's 8,000 men, who had been positioned at Cold Harbor behind A. P. Hill's corps and out of immediate view of Union scouts, began their trek west late on June 12—around the time Grant began his secret move to the James River and Lee's rear. (Major General John C. Breckinridge's brigade of 4,000 already in the valley joined Early, increasing his force to about 12,000.) Each side had tighter picket lines, which cut back on deserters and spies who might sneak through to tip off the other on movements. More important, each side was preoccupied with its own getaway. Grant's crossing the James helped cloak Early's departure better than Lee could have. The two generals, in effect, had stolen marches on each other.

As Grant moved to the James, Sharpe's intelligence operation practically ground to a halt, disrupted as it always was by all the activity involved when this massive army changed operating bases. Moreover, Sharpe had been tied up with policing chores Patrick assigned him to round up stragglers, arrest looters, and prevent destruction of private property. Spy duties had been left to John Babcock to oversee. The burden of finding Early should have fallen to McEntee, Sharpe's agent in the Shenandoah. But McEntee, who faced all kinds of problems gathering information when Sigel was in command, experienced the same headaches with Sigel's successor, Hunter, who proved indifferent to intelligence collection, assigning McEntee "thieves and loafers" for his scouts. Not until June 17, when Early had already passed Charlottesville and was on his way to Lynchburg, did Sharpe issue his first intelligence summary for Meade since they had left Cold Harbor. But that report focused on the strength of Petersburg's Rebel garrison and on whether Lee had detected the federal move. Sharpe assumed that Early remained with Lee in the Richmond defenses.

It was not until June 20 that Rebel prisoners brought in that day and the next two began alerting Sharpe to the fact that Early's corps might not be with Lee. But the prisoners had heard only rumors that Early had marched west toward the Shenandoah. Sharpe remained unsure of his whereabouts for the next two weeks. His misplacing this corps turned out to have serious consequences for Grant.

Early's men had reached Charlottesville on June 16. The Rebel general learned that Hunter's force was within twenty miles of Lynchburg to the southwest. Early beat Hunter to the town and routed his force on June 18. McEntee estimated Early's corps numbered about 20,000 and guessed that they probably had returned to Richmond by now. Sharpe and Grant agreed. Lee needed all his men to defend the capital. Grant, Sharpe, and McEntee could not have been more wrong. On June 28, Early had reached Mount Sidney on his way northeast down the valley.

Within days, alarm bells began sounding in Washington. Halleck telegraphed Grant on July 1 that he had received conflicting reports about a large Rebel force in the Shenandoah Valley. It made sense, the chief of staff worried. While Hunter's soldiers were out of the valley, the Confederates could raid Maryland and Pennsylvania. But Grant was still convinced, based on what Sharpe fed him, that Early's corps had returned to Richmond. The next day, rumors poured into Washington from the Union's valley outposts at Strasburg, Martinsburg, Harpers Ferry, and other points of a large

Confederate force advancing in their direction. Lincoln, Stanton, and Halleck queried Grant at City Point. The general in chief continued to assure them that Early's corps was at Richmond.

On July 3, Halleck telegraphed Grant that he now had reports that Early's corps was marching toward the Potomac River. Grant continued to discount them—but he was not as sure as he once was. He scoured again the intelligence that had come in from Sharpe and peppered Meade with questions. "Is it not certain that Early has returned to your front?"

Meade was not certain and Grant was becoming less so. Deserters from other commands had reported that Early had returned to Richmond five or six days ago, but curiously no deserters had been captured from his corps since it was reported to be back in the capital. Independence Day brought another troubling report. A Rebel deserter told Sharpe a camp rumor that Early's corps was already at Arlington Heights, Virginia, just southwest of Washington on the other side of the Potomac and that the Rebels expected to seize the federal capital soon. Grant rushed Sharpe's report to Halleck. It was from a deserter, he cautioned, and Grant could produce reports from other deserters who still claimed Early was in Richmond. The fact was, Sharpe didn't know where the hell Jubal Early was. Grant nevertheless advised Halleck to bring into the city all the forces he could find around Washington.

Panic now gripped the District of Columbia. While the two main Union armies seemed bogged down in front of Richmond and Atlanta, the federal capital was in danger of being seized. Lincoln's two senior aides, John Nicolay and John Hay, judged a raid on Washington not as far-fetched as it later seemed—what with a ragtag force of not more than 20,000 undisciplined soldiers and militiamen by their estimate defending the seat of government against what they heard were well-seasoned Confederate shock troops. Even if the Rebels had half the 20,000 to 30,000 some accounts placed them at, Halleck worried they would overwhelm the city. Other administration officials feared Rebel spies already had infiltrated the capital to inform the raiders about Washington's fortifications. Lincoln remained calm although he and Stanton had no confidence in Halleck and the gaggle of generals in the city taking firm command of its defense. Without the president's knowledge, the Navy had a vessel readied to whisk the first family away on the Potomac if Early did succeed in capturing Washington.

On July 6, twenty-four days after Early departed Cold Harbor, Grant finally acknowledged that his corps was near the Potomac, although Sharpe wasn't sure of its exact location or strength. Grant scrambled to get Meade's 6th Corps to Washington, while Hunter returned to the valley to overtake Early from behind. The general in chief cabled Halleck that if Lincoln thought it advisable, he would return to Washington himself to lead the force he was sending.

Grant did not have to go north. While the 6th Corps rushed to Washington, Union general Lew Wallace in Maryland posted his 6,000 troops along the Monocacy River near Frederick, to where two roads, one leading to Baltimore and the other to Washington, crossed the river. Late on July 9, Early's corps overwhelmed Wallace and sent him hobbled back to Baltimore, but with dusk at hand the Confederate commander was forced to halt for the night. Wallace had succeeded in delaying Early long enough to allow the remaining divisions of Grant's 6th Corps to reach the capital.

Early made it to Washington's northern suburbs by July 11 and probed its defenses through the next day. But by then the Union 19th Corps had joined the 6th Corps in the city, along with 3,000 government clerks hastily organized into militia companies. Lincoln mounted a parapet at Fort Stevens, north of the city, for a peek at the fighting. When he stood up wearing his stovepipe hat to look out over the parapet, soldiers shouted at him: "Get down!" Early realized he could not attack Washington with Grant's reinforcements there and retreated. By July 14 he was back in Virginia, with Lincoln predictably furious that he had been allowed to slip away.

Sharpe got permission from Meade to travel to Washington. He arrived there on July 12, the second day of Early's probe, to see Carrie before she left for New York. "My coming was well timed to allay her fears about an invasion," he later wrote his uncle Jansen. Sharpe also found himself soon surrounded by administration officials and Union officers looking for any information he had on Early's force. Sharpe was proud he could recite every regiment in the corps, along with their numbers. He avoided mentioning that he had not known where these men had been the past three weeks.

Washington had been in little danger from the raid. A thirty-seven-mile ring of fortifications, with sixty-eight forts and ninety-three artillery positions, surrounded the city so a small number of soldiers could hold off invaders at any point until reinforcements arrived. Early's pure military gains had been insignificant. But his expedition dealt the North a major psychological blow—"our national humiliation," as Navy secretary Welles put it in his diary. For Grant, the raid had been a huge embarrassment. For Sharpe, it was a humiliating intelligence failure.

Instead of returning to Richmond, Jubal Early continued to be a headache for Grant in the Shenandoah, reaping the fall harvest and continuing to threaten Baltimore and Washington. In August the Union Army chief dispatched Sheridan to the valley to root out Early and lay waste to Lee's supply source there. To sever Lee from the Shenandoah without jeopardizing Union operations against Richmond, Grant needed accurate intelligence from Sharpe on Confederate troop movements between the Rebel capital and the valley. With that kind of information, Grant could coordinate Union movements in both regions to isolate Lee from Early and make it difficult for one to come to the other's rescue. But first Grant had to deal with the problem of an entire corps slipping from under his nose and marching to Washington's perimeter without him knowing it. Another raid like Early's could jeopardize Grant's Virginia campaign, already a target of critics for little progress, as well as Lincoln's reelection chances in November. Could it happen again? Grant moved to make sure it didn't. Quickly he re-formed his command structure in the Shenandoah region. He also renovated his intelligence service.

Before Early's raid on Washington, Sharpe had already been spending a lot of time at Grant's City Point headquarters. But Meade still jealously guarded Sharpe's intelligence operation so that all his reports went first through the Potomac Army commander before being forwarded to Grant. The first week of July, Grant took direct control of Sharpe's information bureau, making Patrick provost marshal of his command (now designated the Armies Operating Against Richmond) and having Sharpe as Patrick's deputy join him in the move. Grant also lifted Meade's restrictions that hamstrung Sharpe and restored his access to the cavalry scout and signal intelligence he had under Hooker. McEntee was moved from the valley back to the Richmond front. Instead of shrinking Sharpe's portfolio, as Meade would have done after the Early episode, Grant expanded it so the colonel now oversaw the intelligence collection of other elements of Grant's command, such as Butler's army and Hunter's force. Sharpe was now Grant's spymaster.

An enraged Meade protested. He vented to Patrick that he wanted "no partnership with Grant" and lashed out that Sharpe's bureau "was good for nothing." Patrick and Sharpe were only too happy to be out from under Meade's thumb. As the summer days grew hotter, a bitter feud had erupted between Meade and his provost marshal, who claimed that Meade was only angry over the move because he knew most of his staff would also flee his oppressive command if given the chance. Meade, who could be tyrannical with subordinates, routinely sent Patrick messages the provost marshal considered insulting and continued to blow up at Sharpe when he believed the intelligence officer had done something wrong.

In fairness to Meade, Patrick was a prickly staff officer to have around—his sour mood exacerbated by the pain in his shoulder that the electric shocks he had been receiving did not seem to be relieving. He could be cold with people even when they tried to be nice to him. When enlisted men brought him a handsome sword as a thank-you, the provost marshal refused to accept the gift until Grant ordered him to take it. Continuing to believe that Sharpe was a political intriguer, Patrick became so paranoid his deputy was trying to undermine his authority that when he took a leave he arranged for Sharpe to be away at the same time so his deputy would not be in camp plotting against him during his absence.

To smooth Meade's ruffled feathers Grant held off making any formal announcement of the transfer for five months and agreed to allow Patrick to remain at Meade's command post along with Sharpe for the time being. But soon Sharpe was spending all his time at Grant's headquarters at City Point, which became a formidable military base built on a bluff overlooking the junction of the Appomattox and James Rivers, with a harbor for U.S. Navy vessels, a rail track carrying supplies from the docks to Union entrenchments, and a telegraph line linking the general in chief to Washington.

At night Sharpe and other staff officers sat on rough seats around a roaring fire in front of Grant's wall tent to puff cigars and discuss the war and the intelligence Sharpe had received from Richmond. The campfire chat usually wore on until 3 or 4 a.m., when Grant finally went to bed. Unknown to the general in chief, Sharpe and the other aides drew lots to have one of them stay awake through the rest of the night to guard the tent while he slept. The officers worried Rebel agents might try to sneak into City Point to kidnap their commander. It was not an unfounded fear. Shortly before noon on August 9, as Grant sat in front of his tent with Sharpe and other staff officers discussing the danger of enemy agents infiltrating their camp, a huge explosion showered bullets, shell fragments, and splinters everywhere, some of the splinters hitting Grant and Sharpe. A boat filled with ordnance stores at the nearby James River wharf had blown up, killing 43 and injuring 126. Later it was determined that Virginia saboteurs had placed a time bomb on the vessel.

Sharpe could clearly see a long siege ahead. If Grant tried to assault Lee in this sweltering heat, "I think we would be whipped beyond a [doubt]," he wrote Uncle Jansen. "Fifty odd days of fighting and marching have reduced the effective force of both armies to incredible extent." The one advantage Sharpe saw for the North: it could replenish its army with more men. "But the enemy," he wrote his uncle, "have their last man in the field." Grant agreed. Mutually assured attrition worked in the Union's favor. Sharpe had struck up a conversation with a captured Confederate colonel who candidly admitted to him that "100,000 [Union] men could now march anywhere on the continent, except within ten miles of Richmond or Atlanta." They were the two enclaves the Confederates fiercely retained. Sharpe had gotten to practice his French with an artillery officer Emperor Louis-Napoléon had sent to observe Grant's army. The Frenchman told Sharpe he did not see how the Rebels could stand this war much longer. "I don't, either," Sharpe replied. "But they stand a good deal." So both sides hunkered down in their trenches, waiting and shelling and sniping at each other.

Frustrated at one point by the stalemate at Petersburg, Grant and Meade approved an operation Ambrose Burnside (now the 9th Corps commander) enthusiastically pushed to dig a long tunnel under a Rebel redoubt, pack it with explosives, and blow open a crater that Union soldiers could pour through to breach the Confederate defense. Babcock provided Burnside's coal miners digging the tunnel with intelligence on the Petersburg defenses. He also alerted Meade that the Confederates suspected Union mines were being placed under their defenses. But when Grant on June 26 and 27 had forces stage a demonstration attack on Richmond to divert the Rebels, Babcock and Van Lew's ring confirmed that Lee took the lure and depleted his Petersburg defenses to send units to the capital. On July 30, the Federals detonated the explosives and created a huge gap in the Confederate line. But what followed in the Battle of the Crater, as it came to be called, was a "miserable failure," Grant concluded. Poorly led Yankees failed to fight their way through the Confederates' ruptured line and all Grant was left with was a big hole and some 4,000 casualties.

McEntee reported afterward that about 250 black Union prisoners were forced to exhume the dead in the crater. They found it ghastly work pulling out mangled bodies. Sharpe also turned up evidence the Confederates were digging mines at Petersburg as well. A black refugee arrived on August 16, saying he had toiled in a Richmond shop making fans to ventilate underground shafts dug in Petersburg. A gang of forty slaves were sent there to work in mines, the refugee added.

Lincoln visited Grant several times at City Point to review the dreary siege-like campaign. Assistant war secretary Charles Dana had been placed in the headquarters earlier to keep watch on the general and report back to Washington on his operations. Sharpe came to revere Grant and to increasingly resent the president's meddling. "I have a strong liking for [Grant's] entire simplicity and truthfulness of character united to a great firmness and decision," he wrote his uncle. He wished the general were the Republican Party's presidential nominee in the next election instead of Lincoln. A Kingston resident paid Sharpe a visit at City Point and told him New York political circles had also "prominently" mentioned the intelligence chief as a possible candidate for Congress after the war. Sharpe was intrigued with the idea.

The Petersburg and Richmond campaign made Sharpe's spy job far easier. The space between the two opposing lines narrowed to as little as forty yards in some places—a shorter distance for Rebel deserters who were now crossing at a rate of eighty to one hundred a day. Lincoln had issued an order offering as much as eight dollars (about $130 in today's money) to each Confederate soldier who fled with his weapon. Lieutenant Manning, Sharpe's intelligence officer with Butler, devised an aerial propaganda drop to publicize the president's offer. He flew a kite over Rebel lines, which dumped clumps of paper slips with the order printed on them. Confederates clutching the paper and their arms ventured across.

The close quarters made commuting to work easier for spies like Milton Cline, who slipped through the lines regularly at Petersburg to scout weak points in the defenses, pinpoint the position of divisions, and chat with blacks in the city. Lee also shifted his units in full view of federal signalmen peering through telescopes atop seventy observation stations along the front. The watchers could also read the flag signal messages that Confederates waved on the roof of the customs house in Petersburg. Grant was delighted, bragging to anyone who would listen that the flood of intelligence enabled him now to locate every brigade and division in Lee's army. Location information was crucial. Grant wanted to keep Lee's army pinned down in Richmond and Petersburg, so it was important that he know of any detachments slipping away to, say, the Shenandoah or Atlanta.

Sharpe finally got McEntee to find him a servant from Meade's headquarters named William to wait on him as he settled into a routine at City Point, interrupted practically every week by at least one surprise. A scout reported on October 20 that the Confederates were drafting twelve-year-olds to man fortifications. Among the refugees McEntee sent to his hut to be interviewed one day was a little boy even younger, holding a gun almost bigger than he was. Sharpe didn't know what in the world to do with the child. Four deserters arrived claiming that Rebel authorities had offered $20,000 for the assassination of Beast Butler, and a hit team with sharpshooters and "telescopic rifles" had been assembled for the job. Sharpe kept Patrick posted on the political gossip he picked up from his military sources in Washington—among several tidbits making the rounds were that Butler would replace Stanton as war secretary (that would never happen) and McClellan would be given a military command (also never to happen). He also found time to slip away from City Point and visit his old 120th

Regiment, entrenched along the Petersburg line, to share a Sunday religious service with them.

Reports from fleeing refugees, Van Lew's ring, and Sharpe's agents described chaotic conditions inside Richmond and Petersburg. Confederate soldiers were eating half rations and grumbling about it. Seven deserters from a Georgia regiment claimed morale in their unit had plummeted and nearly all of its conscripts, who had been forced into the army against their will, would flee if they had a chance. Petersburg residents were reported to be trying to escape or moving valuables out of the city or digging caves if they couldn't get out to survive an expected Union artillery bombardment. Sharpe alerted Grant to a particularly troubling piece of intelligence. One of his agents just returned from Richmond said he saw wagon trains being readied "to send out of the enemy's lines and throw on our hands large numbers of women, children and decrepit persons, said to be the families of persons who had fled to our lines or avoided Confederate service."

It wasn't the only bizarre report Sharpe received. Late in July, Butler delivered to him a Confederate deserter from Wilmington, North Carolina, named Thomas J. Powell, who had a story Sharpe found "incredible," as he later reported to Washington. Powell claimed the Confederates had launched an expedition of three steamers with 1,600 marines and 30,000 weapons to sail north along the East Coast to the grimly deplorable Union war prison at Point Lookout, on the sandy tip of the Virginia Peninsula where the Potomac River joined the Chesapeake Bay. They planned to free its 15,000 inmates. Powell said he acquired some of his information by pickpocketing documents describing the mission from a Confederate detective he had been walking with along a Wilmington street. Sharpe had heard a lot of tall tales from deserters trying to inflate the value of their information and he suspected this was one of them. But he thought there might be a kernel of truth in Powell's account so he alerted Patrick, Grant, and Washington.

Powell did, in fact, have some of the story right. His numbers, however, were wrong—800 volunteers with 20,000 weapons on five boats planned to sail from Wilmington to Point Lookout—and the prison raid never came off. While Early marched north to Washington, Lee got Davis to approve adding another mission for his expedition: as he approached Washington a cavalry force would break off and ride to Point Lookout to link up with the Wilmington contingent and free the prisoners. But Early's detachment never made it to Point Lookout, and Davis, fearing word had leaked of the plan, called back the Wilmington group on July 11.

Sharpe's spy operation had its dirty aspects as well. At the end of August, McEntee turned over to him two deserters who had been tortured to no avail. John Boyle arrived claiming he had fled a Virginia regiment. McEntee thought he was lying and had him tied by his thumbs all day—a common punishment during the war that prisoners found painful when applied for long periods. But "he still sticks to his story," McEntee told Sharpe. "I turn him over to you for treatment." Which meant another torture technique to force him to confess he was a Confederate plant. The other man was George McKay, who claimed to be a Canadian forced into the Rebel Army. McEntee concluded McKay was "totally deranged." An aide "had him tortured here," he told Sharpe, "and it made a perfect lunatic of him for twenty-four hours."

As summer stretched to autumn, Sharpe put together a system to detect the all-important movement of Confederate soldiers between Lee's army defending Richmond and Petersburg and Early's force preserving Lee's supply lifeline from the Shenandoah. Sharpe, Babcock, and McEntee exchanged memos constantly, with updates on regiments moving between Richmond and the Shenandoah, which were drawn from daily interrogations, reports of their agents behind the lines, and coded messages Elizabeth Van Lew and Samuel Ruth delivered from their networks. Judson Knight, whom Sharpe had sent out from Grant's headquarters on regular trips behind the lines, picked out buildings in the City Point compound to house a dozen of Sharpe's best men and set up a regular communications line with Van Lew's underground. One of the operatives whom Sharpe sent to Knight for the infiltrations was a Richmond man who had been a clerk for John Van Lew. Meanwhile, Sharpe ordered Babcock to Washington in early August to devise a clandestine system to monitor Early's main rail links with Richmond. Three Unionists Babcock used before who lived near the depots for the three major Richmond-to-Shenandoah railroads—Isaac Silver, James Cammack, and Ebenezer McGee—visited the stations regularly to question passengers and rail employees about traffic and to watch specifically for troop trains chugging to the valley. Within a month, Babcock had reports from the watchers coming in several times a week.

For the regular flow of messages from Van Lew, a steam launch landed a Sharpe scout—usually a man named Kearney—on the north bank of the James early in the night. Before daylight the next day, Kearney met with Van Lew's courier and returned to the Union side of the river with her messages. Other times Van Lew had Ruth and his employees carried messages on trains riding the rails south out of Richmond. The rendezvous with the Van Lew couriers could be dangerous for Sharpe's men. Rebel scouts nearly captured one of them when he met Van Lew's messenger on another route near the Chickahominy River. Before the Confederates rode up to him, Van Lew's courier managed to swallow the slips of paper with her report. Fortunately for Sharpe's man, the courier remembered some of the information the papers contained.

Along with her messages, Grant received editions of the Richmond papers from Van Lew, plus a rose picked from her garden for each delivery. Grant, who began referring to Van Lew's intelligence as coming from "a lady in Richmond," thought the rose for his breakfast table was a nice touch and he devoured the Richmond papers for news on Lee's army before telegraphing summaries to Washington, where Stanton and Halleck eagerly waited to read them. The several dozen operatives vacuuming up information for Van Lew now included a clerk in the adjutant general's office (with access to "returns showing the strength of rebel regiments, brigades, divisions and corps, their movements and where they were stationed," according to one of Grant's headquarters officers) and an agent in the engineering department (who made "beautifully accurate plans of the Rebel defenses around Richmond and Petersburg, which were promptly forwarded to Grant," the officer said). Van Lew funneled to the Union commander information on the condition of Lee's army, the strength of Richmond defenses girding the city, the serious lack of food and consumer goods, and the deterioration of the residents' morale. Grant was deeply interested in her insights on whether the grinding away strategy was working.

Her ring also delivered a steady stream of intelligence to Sharpe on the

whereabouts and condition of Early's army in the Shenandoah Valley—
important information for Grant's war of attrition. When Sharpe received
reports from Van Lew and others that Lee had sent reinforcements to Early,
Grant battered Lee's Richmond defenses to make him pay a price for sending troops away. When reports from Van Lew's ring and Sheridan's own
spies came in that Early had sent detachments back to Richmond, the
Union cavalry leader pounced on him in the Shenandoah, leaving his army
reeling. By March 1865, Sheridan had destroyed Early's force and rendered
the Shenandoah a wasteland, burning down seventy mills and 2,000 barns,
seizing or destroying 435,800 bushels of wheat, 3,800 horses, 10,900 cows,
12,000 sheep, 77,000 bushels of corn, 12,000 pounds of bacon, and 20,400
tons of hay. Van Lew kept Grant posted on the hardship for Richmonders
because of the loss of the Shenandoah.

John Van Lew, who had relocated to Philadelphia, did what he could to
help, having trusted couriers smuggle food and letters with checks in them
to his sister. He used the alias "Emma G. Plane" for the address on the envelope. Sharpe also sent in Confederate money to help defray Van Lew's
expenses. Among the items she requested for her spying—a pair of shoes,
gunpowder tea, and stylish muffs as the days grew colder. McEntee urged
Sharpe to provide the supplies—including the muffs, which seemed a bit
extravagant. "The people are worth it," he said.

Van Lew's servant Mary Bowser, with her photographic memory and
talent for adopting different aliases, became a valued agent. In the morning
Van Lew often woke up asking Mary for the latest news in the city. She always had an answer. Van Lew sent her on discreet and often risky missions.
She traveled to Fredericksburg to help Union authorities capture two Rebel
officers and a large amount of tobacco. She sneaked into a stationery closet
for the Confederate Senate while it was holding a secret session to consider
a conscription bill. Rebel lawmakers had been intensely debating whether
to enlist slaves to fight for the South. Bowser reported back to the ring what
she heard. In August 1864, with Van Lew's network scouring the city for
information on Lee's plans for maneuvering against Grant and what Jefferson Davis might know of the plans, Mary walked up to the Davis mansion
pretending to be there to collect the wash.

Situated on the brow of a high hill at the corner of Twelfth and Clay Streets, the Confederate White House was a gray Federal-style mansion with four pairs of tall columns in front. Unpopular with Richmonders, Varina Davis had trouble keeping servants in the home. Her husband blamed the frequent runaways, some with gold and silverware filched from the estate, on bribes the Federals offered for them to flee. While inside the mansion, Bowser said later, a clerk ushered her into Davis's private office. Davis was not in the room. The clerk left. Mary began snooping around, opening doors to a cabinet that might have documents important for the spy ring.

Suddenly Davis walked in on her. He asked what she was doing. Bowser played the dumb slave. Davis, who thought blacks were almost subhuman and could not conceive of one being smart enough to spy in his office, let Mary go. She quickly left the mansion, thankful she had not been hauled off to jail again.*

---

* Spy histories are perennial prey to exaggeration. Over the years, Mary Bowser's one foray into the Davis mansion, which is all she acknowledged in a postwar talk about her espionage, has been blown up into a major infiltration operation Van Lew supposedly had at the Confederate White House. According to family lore, speculative news reports, and history books that embellished the story with every retelling, Van Lew allegedly offered Bowser's services to Varina Davis, who needed servants when she arrived in Richmond. While waiting on the first family, Mary, so the story has developed, soaked up information from sensitive conversations Jefferson Davis had with Confederate officials and his family, and brought accounts of them back to Van Lew.

There is no documentary evidence in the Van Lew papers or Union and Confederate files to support this fantastic tale. The sole source for the yarn was Van Lew's niece, Annie Hall, who told a magazine writer nearly fifty years after the fact that she recalled as a little girl in Van Lew's home hearing that Bowser had worked in the Davis household. Friends questioned how a nine-year-old girl would know about such a spy operation—not to mention how fifty years later she could recall such details from her early childhood. Varina Davis later adamantly denied that she ever took in a black servant from Van Lew. And it strains credulity to believe that Mrs. Davis would accept from a vocal Unionist as Van Lew was known to be an African American servant who had lived in the North and who had been arrested by Richmond authorities when she returned from Liberia.

Nevertheless, the story, which has always been too good to check out, lives on and gets better with every new version of it. The CIA swallowed the tale that Van Lew planted a slave in the mansion. So did today's U.S. Army's Military Intelligence Corps, which inducted Mary Bowser into its Hall of Fame in 1995.

Sharpe's other important "friends" in Richmond were rail superintendent Samuel Ruth and operatives who worked for him and occasionally Van Lew, like F. W. E. Lohmann and Charles Carter. Railroad information became highly prized by Grant. Lee desperately needed supplies over the rails the Confederacy still controlled. Working with Lohmann and Carter, Ruth sent Sharpe intelligence on Rebel strength guarding bridges, along with assessments of the supply shortages caused by Union destruction of tracks and rolling stock. It enabled the intelligence officer to deliver to Grant's headquarters on September 3 the status of all railroads north of Richmond—the ones operating, under repair, or knocked out. To the east, Ruth and his agents explained to Sharpe how the rail lines cooperated with blockade runners to sneak in supplies, how company employees devised workarounds for tracks Union soldiers had cut. Sharpe paid Ruth and Carter $500 each for their services and Lohmann $200 for his work. The spy chief considered it a bargain. So did Grant.

As summer ended, Abraham Lincoln did not believe he would be reelected and, indeed, prospects for a second term appeared dim. Northerners were weary of stalemate in the war, no incumbent had been renominated since 1840 or reelected since 1832, Treasury secretary Chase schemed to replace Lincoln on the Republican ticket, and Democrats picked as their candidate the still-popular George McClellan, who they hoped would bring the war to a speedy end. Pinkerton was among the disgruntled Republicans attending the Democrats' August nominating convention in Chicago and jubilantly predicted his old commander would be the next president. The detective had kept up a friendly exchange of letters with McClellan since both left the Army—making sure his secret service was mentioned in McClellan's historical report on his wartime service, trading gossip on the Potomac Army's battles that year, and sending the general a bundle of grouse for his dinner table.

Pinkerton shared with McClellan political intelligence he picked up in the Midwest. He warned him of peace Democrats trying to lure him to their wing of the party. He also rallied influential friends in the railroad and utility industries to back his candidacy. Two weeks before the election, Pinkerton also came to the general with an extraordinary report. The Lincoln administration, he said, had information about a conspiracy by "friends of McClellan" to assassinate the president and those McClellan associates were now being closely watched by government agents. McClellan had not lost his wartime paranoia—he believed Stanton had detectives following him during the campaign—but he correctly dismissed this story as nonsense.

Lincoln, who had struck a bond with rank-and-file soldiers during his many visits to the front, correctly guessed that the Army that McClellan left behind supported the incumbent president over the Young Napoleon. To ensure a favorable turnout from the 850,000 northern men in uniform, Republican-controlled states set up ballot boxes in military camps. At Stanton's behest, Dana sent a stern note to Patrick, known to be a Democrat, that the War Department had learned he was cooperating with agents that New York Democratic governor Horatio Seymour sent to Grant's army to drum up support for McClellan. The department ordered him to halt any help he was giving election agents and remain neutral. It turned out that Lafayette Baker—Patrick's old nemesis—was behind the warning. Baker had alerted Dana that Seymour had hired "an old California ballot box stuffer" to roam the Army of the Potomac and round up votes legally or illegally.

Through the summer and autumn months, Baker continued to prowl among the criminal and greedy-minded of the war's underbelly. In July, he busted up a counterfeiting ring in St. Louis. During the fall, he uncovered a scheme by New York politicians, corrupt government officials, and a group of Army officers to illegally trade food and supplies for smuggled cotton from the South, which fetched hundreds of thousands of dollars in profits or bribes for everyone involved.

Also in the fall, Mathew Brady, who had become a celebrity for his wartime photographs, lobbied Grant and his wife to allow him to embed with the Army of the Potomac to take shots. Grant eventually agreed and sent his wife photos Brady had taken that she could view on her stereoscope, which created a three-dimensional effect. Baker, however, alerted Dana that Brady was doing more than just recording Grant's army on glass plates. The photographer hatched an insider information scheme with Wall Street speculators to telegraph them coded messages with advance notice of successes or defeats Grant's army had with military movements around Petersburg and Richmond before a press blackout was lifted and newspapers could report them. The speculators used that intelligence to cash in at the stock and gold markets, whose prices fluctuated depending on news from the front. There is no record of any response from Grant, who was flattered by the photos Brady took of him.

Baker also chased reports of seditious plots. In late October he went to Dana with what he insisted was ironclad evidence that disgraced Major General Fitz John Porter, who had been court-martialed for his failures during the second Battle of Bull Run two years earlier, was leading a cabal of Army of the Potomac officers who were selling arms and ammunition to western states for an insurrection to prevent Lincoln's inauguration if he was reelected. There are no documents in the Army files that indicate Dana ever took this report seriously or that such a conspiracy ever occurred or was even contemplated.

Lincoln skillfully had surrogates crush the covert campaign Chase waged to secure the Republican nomination. McClellan's election chances were dashed two days after the Democrats nominated him. On September 2, Sherman captured Atlanta. Public opinion turned for Lincoln, who was now viewed as a victorious leader. Grant ordered a gun salute to honor Sherman's success. Lincoln won the popular vote by more than 400,000 and routed McClellan in the Electoral College with ten times as many votes. Pinkerton, despondent, returned to rebuilding his business in Chicago.

Van Lew had couriers deliver messages to Sharpe on Richmond's mood and condition after Lincoln's victory. It was grim on all fronts. The president's reelection signaled the North was prepared to exhaust the South into surrender. As Grant's 120,000 soldiers tightened the noose around Petersburg and Richmond during the fall and into the winter and Lee's army of 55,000 shrank daily from desertions, fear and panic gripped civilians who could plainly see final defeat looming.

Sharpe and McEntee reported from their interviews of refugees that Petersburg was nearly deserted. Most of the residents who remained had fled to the upper part of the city or the woods above it and were living in tents. A battalion of government workers from Richmond was ordered south to Petersburg for its defenses. One of Sharpe's agents returned from the Rebel capital on September 22 and reported that business activity in the city had been suspended and the few Union deserters who crossed into Confederate lines had been put to work at the Tredegar plant, whose regular employees had been sent to the front. Van Lew also passed along a tip to Sharpe that small boats bearing loads of tin, brass, and copper to repair railroad engines at the plant were slipping into Petersburg from the nearby Blackwater River. But there didn't appear to be much good the contraband could do at this point. With the Richmond papers and her rose for Grant, Van Lew on September 26 delivered to Sharpe the latest quotes for skyrocketing gold and silver prices in the city, along with persistent rumors her ring members heard that Richmond would have to be evacuated.

Van Lew continued to live under constant danger of having her spying exposed and Confederate authorities showing up at her door to lock her up. One time a botched operation Sharpe launched threatened her. Lemuel E. Babcock, originally from St. Albans, Vermont, had settled on a thirty-five-acre farm with a lumber business in Charles City County, southeast of Richmond. Constantly harassed by Confederate authorities for his opposition to slavery, Babcock was finally arrested in 1862, accused of reading abolitionist material to blacks, but eventually was released for lack of evidence. He joined the Confederate home guard, hoping it would divert suspicion about his loyalty, but began doing odd jobs for Van Lew's network. When Grant's force neared Richmond, the elderly Lemuel began working more for Sharpe, infiltrating into Richmond on seven occasions to collect intelligence and bring back messages from Van Lew. Considering his past run-ins with Confederate authorities, this was dangerous work.

Mission failure occurred when Sharpe sent Lemuel back into Richmond with an Englishman named R. W. Pole, whom Lemuel was supposed to pass off to Rebel officials as a Union deserter. Pole was then to make sketches of Richmond fortifications and bring them back to Grant. But unknown to Sharpe, Pole was a Confederate loyalist who intended all along to betray Lemuel Babcock when the two arrived in Richmond. Pole did just that, informing the provost marshal that his escort was a Union agent. Lemuel was thrown into a cramped, dirty cell at Castle Thunder, where he languished, finally escaping execution when Union forces entered the city in April 1865. Van Lew was terrified her operative might have revealed her network to the traitor Pole, but he apparently never had, or if he did, Pole never passed the information on to Rebel authorities. As a precaution, Van Lew changed her code name from "Babcock" to "Romona."

Van Lew had ample reason to be paranoid just then. That summer the Confederate government launched a full investigation of her. It was begun by Richmond's new provost marshal, Thomas Doswell, who wanted to build a case against Elizabeth and her mother by collecting damaging testimony from friends and acquaintances. Van Lew was defiant when she got wind of the probe. She truly did not consider herself a disloyal spy but instead a true patriot resisting the oppression and "reign of terror" by her enemies. Doswell's investigation, she believed, was an example of Confederate depravity. She worried that it would kill her feeble mother.

The inquisition dragged on for months. L. M. Bullifont, who knew the family well, testified before investigators that Van Lew and Eliza once told him "the Yankees would certainly whip the Confederates and take Richmond." When Bullifont told them he thought the Rebels were winning, the two women replied that they hoped it was not the case. A. B. Montcastle, who delivered wagonloads of oats to the mansion, said that on one occasion, Van Lew and her mother asked him why he did not pledge allegiance to the United States. The deliveryman paid no attention to the remark, regarding them simply as misguided Yankees. George Mott and his wife, who lived across the street from the Church Hill mansion and occasionally dined with the women, had concluded the two "were disloyal to extremity." Mott's wife found their views "obnoxious" and "offensive."

Potentially the most damaging testimony came from Mary Carter Van Lew, John's estranged wife, who returned to Richmond in August. She held a long-standing grudge against her sister- and mother-in-law, who considered her an unfit mother for her two daughters and had assumed the care of them. Mary did not want the two girls taken north if a tribunal banished Elizabeth and Eliza there. Mary's testimony, however, turned out to be less damaging than investigators had hoped. She knew nothing of the Van Lew spy ring. Mary testified that she had lived in the mansion from 1854 to 1857 and had visited it frequently after that. But all she could divulge about Elizabeth and Eliza were that "they are strong abolitionists," that they sent a black woman north to be educated, that she heard them express an ardent desire for the victory of the Federal army, and that her husband, John, had gone north "on account of his preference for that government."

Rebel authorities concluded they did not have enough evidence to throw Van Lew and her mother in jail or expel them from the Confederacy. After reviewing the file, Charles Blackford with the Adjutant General's Office ruled in October that Van Lew was certainly "very unfriendly in her statements toward the South and has expressed her desire for the success of the Federal armies." The woman was opinionated but it did not appear to him that she had done anything "to infirm" the Confederate cause. "Like most of her sex, she seems to have talked freely," Blackford believed, "and in the presence of her female friends who have informed on her."

The Rebel investigators found no evidence of espionage because Van Lew, even though she voiced her views freely at times when she shouldn't have, kept that part of her life carefully hidden from the government. She became even more cautious now. When she walked by Libby Prison, she dared not look up at its barred windows, worried Confederate detectives followed and watched her every move. Van Lew was also saved by southern class prejudice and sexism. The investigators were too biased to believe that a Richmond spinster of high birth and wealth could actually sabotage the Confederate cause. They never realized that even in the middle of their probe, Van Lew continued to send messages to Sharpe.

As November's chill set in, Grant, Sharpe, and the other staff officers at City Point moved from their tents into wooden cabins. Babcock telegraphed Sharpe a report from a deserter that Confederate soldiers were "suffering considerable for want of clothing." Grant knew from Van Lew's reports that Union soldiers in Richmond's prisons were freezing. On Christmas Eve he delivered a letter to the Confederate agent his army dealt with for prisoner exchanges to ask if he could send blankets to them. Van Lew's ring reported that Jefferson Davis, who suffered a number of maladies during his presidency, was once more "very sick." Another report from her arrived on December 19 relaying a wild rumor that Davis was so depressed by the news that Sherman's army was about to capture Savannah off Georgia's Atlantic coast that he tried to poison himself.

Sharpe tested a new cipher that inventor Oliver Cox had devised for his far-flung intelligence operation and found it useful. But by mid-December his information bureau was running out of money. He got Grant's supply chief, Major General Rufus Ingalls, to approve a draw from a $150,000 Army account with the Treasury Department. He urged Patrick to have a messenger rush the money to him, "as I am forced to admit that some of our failures here have been owing to want of funds," he said.

Sharpe was in no mood for penny-pinching at this point. In fact, he was fed up with pretty much everything to do with the U.S. Army. The previous month he had taken a military steamboat to Washington and enjoyed a hot bath and a soft bed at the Willard. He was in the capital for what he considered serious business. Sharpe was furious that Meade had not put his name up for promotion to brigadier general. He was in town to lobby Stanton and other generals for it. To let them know he was serious, Sharpe had submitted a resignation letter if he was to remain stuck as a colonel.

He returned to City Point with his superiors acting neither on his promotion nor his resignation letter and shared a Thanksgiving turkey dinner with Patrick. Sharpe downed a strong "Bishop" drink, which was a potent sweet punch, while Patrick sipped his milder claret. The high command, however, got the message. Sharpe was promoted to brevet brigadier general in February 1865, which meant he would not yet receive the rank's higher pay. Sharpe enlisted his congressman to have the brevet made a full brigadier's rank with the extra money. He remained bitter that he had to grovel for this.

1865

RICHMOND'S FALL

*S*harpe's new brigadier general's rank entitled him to a seat in the Senate gallery on the somber and drizzly morning of March 4. Men with mud-splattered boots and women in fine dresses spoiled by the cold drench settled into the seats around him as they watched Andrew Johnson walk into the chamber at noon arm in arm with Hannibal Hamlin, whom he was replacing as vice president. Sharpe was disgusted by what he saw. The Tennessee senator, his face flushed and his words slurred as he delivered a somewhat incoherent acceptance speech, appeared to Sharpe to be drunk, which he was. To brace himself for the ceremony, Johnson, who was not feeling well, had downed a tall glass of whisky in the Vice President's Room and with the Senate chamber now hot and clammy, he was intoxicated. Sharpe wrote later he had "never been present at such an official disgrace before."

After Johnson finished taking the oath and new senators were sworn in, the procession walked outside to the inauguration platform erected on the east front of the Capitol, where some 50,000 shivering and soaked citizens stood to hear Abraham Lincoln deliver his second inaugural speech. That ceremony Sharpe was proud to witness. "The simple dignity and earnest-ness of Mr. Lincoln went far to relieve the previous vice-presidential fiasco," he wrote. As sunshine finally burst through, he stood silent, as the rest of the crowd did, to hear the president deliver the noble words: "With malice toward none, with charity for all, with firmness in the right as God gives us to see the right, let us strive on to finish the work we are in."

Lincoln was exhausted and after the ceremony climbed into bed for sev-eral days of rest. Mary worried about his health, urging him to work less and take in the theater more to relax. The president liked Shakespeare's plays and would watch the famed thespian Edwin Booth perform *Hamlet* in a few weeks.

Halleck worried about Lincoln's exposure during the open inaugura-tion. Pickets had been placed at roads and bridges leading into Washington, at all the street corners from the White House to the Capitol squads of cav-alrymen had been posted to watch crowds straining for a peek at Lincoln in his carriage, riflemen leaned out open windows from the Capitol, and police in plain clothes mixed in with the audience. John Wilkes Booth, also an actor but not nearly as talented as his older brother Edwin, stood on a balcony behind the inaugural stands watching the ceremony. When Lincoln walked out of the Rotunda's east door to the platform, police seized an ex-cited young man trying to break through the line they had set up to keep the crowd out. An officer later testified that Booth looked like the man who had been briefly detained in the scuffle.

As head of the secret service in Washington, Lafayette Baker's job was, or should have been, to collect intelligence on threats to the president. With newspapers and administration officials speculating about danger to Lin-coln, one would expect Baker to be in the city inauguration day to keep watch for trouble. But that was not the case. He was away in New York in-vestigating what had become rampant corruption in the way young men were put into the U.S. Army and Navy.

The Union needed massive numbers of troops by the winter of 1862 and 1863. With the system that enticed volunteers for service breaking down, Congress passed the Enrollment Act in March 1863. Americans for the most part hated what became the country's first national draft law. The legislation had loopholes so a well-off draftee could escape service by paying a substitute to take his place. Resistance among the poor quickly became widespread with draft riots erupting in New York City four months after the law was passed. To avoid the distasteful job of forcing the unwilling into service, communities around the country, each of which had enlistment quotas to meet, began offering men cash rewards called "bounties" to lure them into volunteering for the military.

Corruption blossomed from the bounties. Communities competed with their offers that could run $300 or higher for each man. Potential recruits roamed different towns looking for the highest bounty districts. Some men, who became known as "bounty jumpers," grew wealthy enlisting, deserting, and then enlisting again dozens of times. The system also produced a corps of unscrupulous entrepreneurs called "bounty brokers," who interposed themselves between the recruits and the bounties they collected for volunteering. The draft law did not require that communities employ bounty brokers to find men to fill their quotas or that recruits use these intermediaries to assist them in enlisting and collecting their money. But local officials faced with quota deadlines soon became convinced they needed bounty brokers to find them bodies quickly. And bounty brokers soon swarmed around federal enlistment centers cultivating the recruiting officers inside them and convincing the recruits who walked up—many of whom were poorly educated, uninformed about the draft law, or just gullible—that they could not enlist and collect their bounty without the help of a broker. As a fee for his services, the broker then took a portion of each cash reward. Ruthless bounty brokers became rich fabricating paperwork for phantom recruits, organizing bounty jumping, and viciously exploiting young men they rounded up for the Army or Navy.

Alarmed that abuses in the bounties, as well as in the system for finding substitutes, had gotten out of hand—only a quarter of the men being enlisted were actually reaching the front as soldiers—the War Department on January 16 ordered Baker to investigate the mess and start making arrests. He decided to take aim first at New York City, which he correctly concluded had become the nation's center, he said, for "gamblers in recruiting." Baker and a handful of detectives who came with him had little trouble uncovering the infestation. The buying and selling of bounties and draft exemptions had become big business there, with brokers openly advertising their services in newspapers. A. Lyons & Company, a "Volunteer & Substitute Agency" at No. 243 Broadway, boasted to community representatives visiting the city to look for men that its recruits and substitutes were "furnished promptly at low prices. County and town quotas contracted for and promptly furnished."

After the *New York Herald* ran a story that Baker was in town investigating bounty swindling, letters and affidavits poured in from victims who had been cheated. Baker discovered brokers routinely made off with two-thirds or more of a recruit's bounty. Some of the brokers were alluring women, who got recruits, many as young as sixteen, drunk or drugged and hauled them to enlistment centers to sign forms and then give up most of their reward. If the brokers didn't have time for whisky or drugs to take effect, they simply threatened, beat up, or kidnapped recruits. One letter to Baker recounted how a broker lured two sixteen-year-old boys from their Brooklyn home, threw them into a locked carriage, and drove them to Boston, where the terrified youths were forced to enlist and give up their bounties. European diplomats began complaining that their citizens were being recruited in their home countries to cross the Atlantic and cash in on rich bounties for joining the Army—only to find the broker at the dock when they arrived to steal their reward and force them into the military.

One of the first meetings Baker had after checking in to the Astor House was with a broker named Theodore Allen, who agreed to be a snitch and explained how the recruiting frauds were usually carried out. Allen also provided the detective with the names and addresses of the city's most notorious brokers—no doubt wanting to clear some of his competitors from the field. As he had done in many previous cases, Baker hatched a sting. He posed as an upstate New York supervisor visiting the city to fill his enlistment quota.

Two bounty brokers, James Devlin and James Cabron, showed up at his hotel room with sixteen sets of naval enlistment papers they were selling for $525 apiece. Baker paid the men with a wad of cash the War Department supplied him for the sting. He then promptly arrested Devlin and

Cabron and squeezed out of them a story even the seasoned secret service chief found astounding. All around New York, phony enlistments by the thousands were being processed. The town of Delhi to the north, for example, had filled its quota of 223 men with forged enlistment papers "and not a single man enlisted," Baker reported in a memo to the War Department. "Forged papers are . . . daily sold in public saloons. . . . They can be bought any day at the Merchants' Hotel on Cortlandt Street." Devlin and Cabron confessed that their scam had roped in numerous recruiting officers and clerks being paid off at the Brooklyn Navy Yard enlistment center. The center's commander, an old cripple easily manipulated, had his duties practically taken over by the con men.

An elaborate shell game was staged to fool out-of-town enlistment officials desperate to fill quotas, Devlin and Cabron explained. Two clerks in charge of the books at the naval enlistment center copied the names of all recruits legitimately enlisted each day and sent them to the two brokers, who wrote them on blank enlistment forms. The brokers then took the forms to a notary on their payroll, who certified that the recruit named on the form had appeared before him and had been properly sworn in. Devlin and Cabron then sold the seemingly legitimate enlistment forms to unsuspecting officials with quotas to fill. If the out-of-towner wanted to check that the enlistments had been properly recorded before he paid for them, Devlin and Cabron had a ruse to take care of that. The brokers took their mark to the naval center, where the recruits' names had already been enrolled and, unbeknown to the out-of-towner, were credited to another district. To fool their official, Devlin and Cabron took him to a booking clerk they had bribed who had a flysheet identical to the originals that was inserted into the book's pages with the recruits' names the out-of-towner had paid for written in as being credited to his district. After the brokers were paid by their satisfied customer, the clerk removed the flysheet from the book and threw it away.

Baker locked up Devlin and Cabron and lured to the Astor House nine more brokers selling phony enlistments to other centers. He arrested them along with mustering officers, clerks, and doctors on the take at the facilities. Estimating that New York City alone had about 10,000 professional bounty jumpers Baker had one of his detectives infiltrate a gang of them that a broker organized. He also tried his hand at posing as a bounty jumper—although as a spy manager he had no business doing so. Dressed in grubby clothes, he walked into a recruiting office near the Astor House, where a broker quickly corralled him. Over the course of the day, Baker enlisted himself three times at different centers, taking a small cut of the bounty the broker collected each time. He pretended to swallow an alcohol concoction laced with a drug that the broker gave him at a saloon to make him more malleable for the scheme. Tipped off that Hoboken, New Jersey, was a bounty-jumping haven, Baker set up a phony enlistment center at the Odd Fellows Hall there. When word spread that the center allowed enlistees to escape, bounty jumpers flocked to the hall. Baker managed to capture 183 of them to take to jail. Always the showman, he wanted to parade his prisoners down Broadway in chains. The War Department vetoed the idea.

As was the case with his other operations, allegations of impropriety dogged Baker and his detectives during their crackdown. He was sued forty times for false arrest and along with his detectives accused of taking bribes and raking off bounty money from the brokers and jumpers they nabbed. None of the lawsuits succeeded and Baker denied he had enriched himself. A War Department official, however, admonished him that he didn't have sufficient evidence for some of his arrests. Suspicion was further fueled over $5,000 that had been raised for a testimonial fund to reward Baker for his efforts to clean up military recruiting. It turned out that several bounty brokers had donated most of the money to the fund. When the questionable source became public, Baker refused to accept the reward.

He ended up jailing sixty-six brokers, enlistment paper forgers, and recruiting officials. The War Department was delighted. Baker had disrupted a number of broker operations, although many swindlers escaped his dragnet. Yet with the war clearly nearing a finale and the Union's need for recruits tapering off, even Baker admitted that his corruption crusade in New York had become less important by the end of March. By then he clearly could have found better things to do with his time back in Washington.

• • •

For Sharpe, Grant, and senior officials in Washington the signs poured in during the early months of 1865 that the rebellion was nearing collapse. Southern railroads were broken down; Confederate deserters roamed aimlessly about the countryside. The Van Lew ring reported that the Richmond government had thrown "nearly $4 million of paper into the market," sparking hyperinflation. The Rebels had collected all the lead they could find in the city—about nine hundred pounds' worth—to make bullets, but gunpowder was growing short to fire the rounds. Meanwhile, the ring reported to Sharpe, Lee was pleading with farmers to sell or loan cornmeal and molasses—whatever they could afford—to his army, which was running out of food. A deserter told Babcock that Lee had addressed three divisions that repeatedly refused orders to charge. The general "wept like a child," the deserter claimed. Other line crossers reported that officers in Pickett's division were holding meetings with their men on whether they should continue fighting or accept Union surrender terms.

Reports also arrived at City Point that the Confederate government was melting away in Richmond. Van Lew's ring passed along a rumor that Davis had sold furniture in the mansion, which turned out not to be true, but the Rebel War Department did pack up its archives to send off. Rumors, some of which Van Lew sent Sharpe, also spread that Davis and other senior officials had their horses saddled and ready to flee, or that they had a steamer docked along the North Carolina coast waiting to take them to Nassau, Bahamas. The hated "plug ugly" detectives Winder had hired from Baltimore also had made arrangements to sneak out of the city "to save themselves," Van Lew reported.

Always worried that Lee would slip from his grasp, Grant ordered Sharpe to scour his networks for indications the military commander was preparing to evacuate Richmond to continue the fight elsewhere. Van Lew's spies reported that Lee was sending munitions south, Longstreet's corps was also being readied for a move south, and that cotton, tobacco, guns, and ammunition were being moved west to Lynchburg—all strong signs that an evacuation was in the works. Sharpe asked Ruth to plumb his sources with the Richmond and Danville Railroad Company for evidence Lee's army

was preparing to ride that line southwest to Danville on the North Carolina border. Ruth chatted with the line's employees, who told him they had
been instructed to "get everything ready" for an evacuation. The company
was running eight trains daily even though a third of its forty-five engines
were out of commission. Ruth passed that important information along to
Sharpe. The spy chief also clipped an article out of a Richmond newspaper that reported that Lee was planning a move that would "astonish the
world"—relocating his force to Danville, which the paper speculated was far
more defensible than Richmond.

But Sharpe remained skeptical that an evacuation was near—based
largely on cautions Van Lew sent. The Rebel commander still had a lot of
fight left in him "and he will die on the field, with the reputation of being
one of the ablest soldiers the world has ever seen," Sharpe predicted in a
letter to Uncle Jansen. In a lengthy intelligence analysis he sent Grant on
February 23, Sharpe said the Van Lew ring, which he considered the best
informed of his sources, reported that the machinery and workshops that
had been removed from Richmond "have simply been steps of prudence
and not preparation" to take flight. Van Lew insisted Richmond "will not be
evacuated because it is the capital of the Confederacy," Sharpe wrote Grant,
"and so long as they can retain their capital, they are as much a country as
they have ever been." Based on reports from Van Lew's network, Sharpe
postulated to Grant that Lee was intent on "holding four or five points,"
which included Danville southwest of Richmond, Lynchburg west of Richmond, the Confederate capital itself, and a point north of Richmond, perhaps Gordonsville. Within that western swath, which held large grain fields,
Lee's army—made up mostly of better-fighting Virginians and North Caro-
linians, Sharpe believed—could hold out for a long time.

Sharpe's intelligence analysis included another wild card that worried
Grant. The Confederate Congress had decided to arm blacks for the southern cause. Sharpe had reports that the Rebels hoped to draft 200,000 slaves.
One of his agents said wealthy Richmonders had been buying thousands of
slaves and in patriotic zeal turning them over to Rebel enrollment officers to
be processed into the army. Sharpe proposed a covert operation to disrupt
this plan. Grant should print an order promising rewards to Confederate

Army blacks who deserted with their weapons. Black Union soldiers would be infiltrated into the Rebels' African American ranks to spread the news of Grant's order and foment mass revolt. Revealing his own prejudices, Sharpe predicted to Grant that blacks would spread word of the order quickly, "as negroes are fond of doing" with any rumor. Nothing much came of the Rebel black army. A Confederate War Department clerk dismissed the parade of a few black companies in Richmond on March 23 as a "ridiculous affair."

Steadily Grant extended his lines around Petersburg to try to cut the last remaining supply routes into Richmond. Meanwhile, Sherman marched north through South Carolina to join the Army commander. Lee, whom Davis had made general in chief for all Confederate forces, continued to hold off Grant at Richmond, but Rebels farther south could not stop Sherman or large Union expeditions elsewhere. Van Lew's Church Hill mansion and Sharpe's City Point bureau became frenetic centers for spying and processing intelligence. Together they "laid bare" the insides of the crumbling Confederacy, Sharpe later recalled. With the intelligence that Van Lew's ring and his other agents provided, Sharpe kept a constantly updated roster in his office of troop numbers and position for each regiment, brigade, and division in Lee's army. Grant forwarded the more important Van Lew reports to the White House for Lincoln to read—identifying them only as coming from "our Richmond friends."

Swamped with work, Sharpe brought in a captain from the 5th New York Volunteer Regiment named Paul Oliver, who knew nothing about intelligence gathering but became a quick study. A squad of clerks at City Point labored day and night to decipher coded messages Van Lew and Sharpe's other agents poured in. In her haste, Van Lew sometimes dispensed with the time-consuming cipher and had couriers convey messages orally. Or she wrote them out in plain text in her hard-to-read handwriting, addressing them to "my friend" and signing them with her code name Romona. One letter Van Lew rushed to Sharpe January 20 in her scrawl reported that "General Lee is strengthening his right wing" and revealed that Alabama and Mississippi soldiers forced into one depleted regiment had mutinied. Van Lew also became a fact-checker for Sharpe. When a report came to

him from up North that Confederates had booby-trapped Richmond buildings with mines to blow up when Union troops entered them, he ran it by
Van Lew, who knocked down the story. There were no mines in Richmond
buildings, she messaged back, except for the gunpowder piled under Libby
Prison.

Confederate authorities tried in vain to stanch the flood of information
they could plainly see escaping the city. "There is an entire prohibition of all
news, to such extent that people are not allowed even to talk upon the streets
about what is happening," Van Lew wrote Sharpe, adding in another note
that with city residents gripped by such "extraordinary excitement," it was
becoming more difficult for her ring members "to distinguish truth from
falsehood in the rumors." But Van Lew kept the intelligence flowing along
with Richmond newspapers most every day. Her ring was "wide awake,"
Sharpe told Meade. "They promise us continually abundant information."
Grant asked Stanton for $20,000 to $50,000 in Confederate money to help
defray her expenses and those of Sharpe's other agents. Washington scraped
up $10,000 to send.

Samuel Ruth suggested that Union authorities run newspaper advertise-
ments offering southern railworkers higher salaries if they defected. Federal
officials took up the suggestion and slipped northern papers with the ads
across the lines into the South. It worked. Large numbers of southern rail
employees defected, and panicked Rebel authorities scrambled to halt the
outflow. But operations like these soon took their toll on Ruth. Tipped off
that members of his network had been helping refugees flee north, Confederate detectives arrested Lohmann and seven other spy ring members on
January 20. Three days later, agents stormed Ruth's railroad office at 8th and
Broad Streets and arrested him. All the men were thrown into Castle Thunder, where Lohmann languished until April 2. Ruth, however, had social and
political standing in Richmond. He worked these contacts hard and, along
with 2,500 Confederate dollars for legal fees and perhaps bribes, managed
to win his release on February 1. His friends, and Richmond newspapers,
could not believe that such an upstanding member of the community would
be a spy.

Ruth immediately went back to work for Sharpe. Two weeks after his release, he tipped off Captain Oliver to an exchange of 400,000 pounds of tobacco for northern bacon and other foods. A Rebel captain had appeared in Ruth's office to inform him that the Confederate government planned to ship the manufactured tobacco in 4,000 boxes on Ruth's railroad line to the train depot at Hamilton's Crossing, where they would be off-loaded to wagons that would be driven north to Fredericksburg and from there on to the Potomac, where the exchange for bacon would be made.

Oliver alerted Grant, who organized a raid with 2,100 cavalrymen, infantrymen, and guides whom Sharpe supplied to seize the tobacco at Fredericksburg. The operation was a spectacular success. On March 5, Navy gunboats ferried the expedition on the Rappahannock River from Fort Monroe to Fredericksburg, where the Federals seized without a fight freight cars and wagons loaded with the tobacco plus corn and vegetables. The detachment commander estimated that the tobacco, along with the other stores and barrels of liquor they seized, were worth $700,000. The Federals burned a railroad bridge, a train depot, a telegraph office, and all but 45,100 pounds of the tobacco, which along with eighty bushels of grain and forty-six muskets were hauled back to Fort Monroe.

But there was a postscript to this story. Joseph Maddox, Sharpe's spy in Richmond who received no pay for his espionage services, had maintained a trading business in the Confederate capital exchanging goods with the North that were approved by the Lincoln administration. His trading business conveniently provided him a cover and an income. Maddox, it turned out, had legally obtained a Treasury Department permit to buy 400,000 pounds of tobacco and barter it with the U.S. government for bacon and other food. Union authorities arrested Maddox after the raid but released him about two months later when it was clear he had violated no laws. After the war, Maddox petitioned Washington to reimburse him for the money lost in the deal or at the very least to deliver him the tobacco Grant's men hadn't burned. The U.S. government rejected Maddox's claim and Grant told Washington he had delivered the seized tobacco to black troops to smoke.

• • •

For Van Lew, all signs now pointed to the Rebel army soon abandoning the capital. On March 2, she rushed a note to Sharpe that Lee had met with Davis to discuss the final disposition of Richmond's and Petersburg's cotton and tobacco. It would be destroyed if the army evacuated, they decided. Her ring followed up with another report: kindling was being packed into warehouses storing cotton and tobacco to set them ablaze quickly if an evacuation was ordered. On March 14, Grant's "lady in Richmond" reported citizens were being organized "to prevent plundering" when the army left. Fear of famine swept the isolated city. "May God bless you and bring you soon to deliver us," Van Lew wrote Sharpe on March 22. "We are all in an awful situation here. There is great want of food." Nine days later she reported to Sharpe that the Post Office and State Department were leaving Richmond and that Varina Davis and the families of other cabinet officers had been sent south.

Tensions mounted at City Point, with officers under tremendous strain from a campaign soon to reach its climax. Overworked staffers in Sharpe's operation snapped at each other more. Sharpe complained to Manning, one of his aides in the Army of the James, that scouts the officer sent to Richmond to meet Van Lew's agents had acted belligerently toward them, which upset Van Lew. Sharpe wanted it stopped. Patrick was surlier than usual. He found fault more in little things Sharpe did. The provost marshal celebrated his fifty-fourth birthday on March 15 by dressing down his deputy "for meddling in matters that do not belong at all to him," he wrote in his diary, not explaining what those matters were.

As the end of March drew near, Lee was convinced he would soon have to abandon his Petersburg lines to keep his shrinking army of 50,000 from being encircled by Grant's more than 120,000. Richmond also could not be held much longer, with the Federals cutting railroads and starving the city. As a last gasp the Rebel commander launched a surprise assault on March 25 on Fort Stedman, which the Union held just outside his defenses to the east of Petersburg, to try to punch through Union lines and join General Joe Johnston to the south. The attack turned out to be less than a complete surprise for Grant. Ruth had warned him that Lee planned such a breakout, although the railroad man did not know the precise date the lunge would occur. Lee's last gamble failed. Rebels succeeded in swarming into Fort Stedman but Grant quickly counterattacked, recapturing the lost ground and driving Lee back to his previous lines with 4,000 casualties and his defenses dangerously thinned.

Showing signs of severe strain, Lincoln sailed to City Point aboard the USS *River Queen* with Mary, his son Tad, and a security officer to rejuvenate himself inspecting troops and to confer with Grant, Sherman, and Rear Admiral David Dixon Porter aboard the ship on the war's end. Lincoln also wanted to be in on what he expected to be the fall of Richmond.

Grant did not intend to wait for Lee's next move after his failed Fort Stedman attack. Quickly he moved on March 29 to crush Lee so he could not join his army with Johnston's. A Union infantry corps, plus Sheridan's cavalry, recently back from the Shenandoah, swung south and west of Petersburg, severing railroad connections with North Carolina and finally pushing through Pickett's lines at an obscure crossroads named Five Forks on April 1 to threaten the Confederate rear. After learning of Pickett's collapse, Grant launched a massive attack with heavy artillery bombardment and infantry assaults all along the front early the next day. Sharpe stood at Grant's side watching as he put the final squeeze on Lee's thinned lines. At about 11 a.m. that balmy Sunday, a War Department courier interrupted Jefferson Davis's prayers at St. Paul's Church on 9th Street to deliver a telegram from Lee. His army, which he now estimated had dwindled to no more than 33,000 men, must evacuate from Richmond and Petersburg to save it from destruction by the Federals, Lee told his president.

Through the rest of Sunday and into early Monday morning, chaos overtook Richmond as Lee's ragged army fled west, hoping to resupply and then march south to join Joe Johnston's force and keep fighting. Davis and the cabinet fled the city to Danville, taking a special train carrying gold remaining in the treasury and boxes of documents not burned. Richmond's citizens were left to take care of themselves. Soldiers torched public buildings, tobacco warehouses, and commissary stores, their fires spreading to other parts of the city. Libby Prison and Castle Thunder inmates were evacuated. Criminals were set free. Depositors rushed to banks to collect their gold. Others buried millions in Confederate paper money at Capitol Square. Crowds sacked liquor stores and emptied casks they couldn't drink up. Whisky flowed in the streets and so the city smelled of smoke and alcohol. Roads soon filled with troops and affluent white civilians fleeing the city—as blacks stood on the side silent. The night was quickly ruled by drunken looters, thieves, and pillaging mobs.

Thunderous explosions from powder magazines detonating through the night and into the next day jarred Van Lew as she watched out the window of her mansion. "The bursting shells rent the air and lighted the darkness," she wrote in her journal. Van Lew did what she could to help confused neighbors who came to her doorstep in despair, lending some her wheelbarrows to save their belongings, accepting treasured items from others to keep safe in her house. She took in Unionist refugees who arrived, as well as two Castle Thunder escapees (among hundreds wandering the city, many with their heads shaved). "Word was sent to us that our house was to be burned," she recalled. "Some soldiers had said so." Earlier Van Lew had arranged for Butler to smuggle to her in a package a nine-by-twenty-foot American flag with thirty-four stars, which proved to be no easy task for the general. The morning of April 3, Van Lew climbed to the rooftop of her mansion and proudly hoisted the flag up the pole by her chimney so that when Union soldiers entered through the eastern end of the city they would see it fluttering as they marched up Main Street.

Seeing the Stars and Stripes flying above Church Hill that morning, an angry crowd stormed Van Lew's front yard, vowing to burn down her home. Her eyes blazing, the spinster defiantly stood her ground. "Lower that flag or hurt one bit of this property," she screamed, pointing to several men she recognized in the crowd, "and I'll see that General Butler pays you back in kind—every one of you!" The threat of Beast Butler razing their houses proved enough. The mob dispersed.

Then, for one of her last war missions, Van Lew rushed to the deserted state capitol and hunted among the ashes for Confederate documents that could be salvaged for the Union Army. Stanton wanted the Rebel papers preserved so they could be used to prosecute Confederates for war crimes. Eighty-one boxes weighing ten tons were eventually salvaged. Among the documents Van Lew took away for safekeeping were John Brown's papers that Virginia authorities had seized.

Godfrey Weitzel, a German American major general, led the first contingent of Union soldiers, half of whom were black troops, into Richmond the morning of April 3. They began putting out fires, restoring order, and freeing federal inmates who remained in prisons. U.S. Army bands eventually struck up martial music and blacks cheered their liberators while sullen and dirty-looking whites watched silently. Lincoln joined Grant on April 3 to tour Petersburg with him. Grant then rode west with his army to chase Lee, while Lincoln, accompanied by about a dozen armed marines that Porter provided, visited Richmond on the morning of April 4. Mobs of jubilant black laborers surrounded him as he strolled down streets. Whites stayed in their homes with windows shuttered. Stanton and Seward were horrified that the president had exposed himself to the threat of assassination in a hostile city still filled with what they considered treacherous Rebel supporters, but Lincoln shrugged off the danger. He wandered into the Confederate White House, which Weitzel had made his headquarters, sat in the chair behind Davis's desk, enjoyed a lunch, and received visitors in the mansion's Georgia Room.

On Grant's orders, a detail of Union troops led by Colonel Ely Parker quickly arrived at Van Lew's house to protect it. Parker was also under orders to ensure that "all Van Lew's wants [were] supplied," according to another Grant aide. Butler made arrangements for her brother, John, to return home. During the next several weeks the Church Hill mansion was filled with Sharpe, Patrick, and other Union officers come to pay their respects, along with Unionists who feared retaliation from city residents. Sharpe also later tracked down Lohmann, who had been freed from Castle Thunder, and Ruth. He became friends with the two men, who impressed him greatly.

Lafayette Baker sent detectives to Richmond to retrieve Ulric Dahlgren's corpse, along with his wooden leg, and return them to his father. Stanton, who wanted the remains recovered quickly, had already been alerted by Sharpe, who had checked with Van Lew, that Dahlgren had been buried near Robert Orrock's house. Lohmann said he took a Union surgeon to the Orrock farm to exhume the body.

Sharpe remained with Grant on his chase west to bag Lee. The Union commander now suffered painful migraines that hot water and mustard plaster applied to his feet, wrists, and neck did not relieve. Along the way, Sharpe interviewed refugees who had spotted Davis and his cabinet in Danville. The spy chief's intelligence report was forwarded to the White House.

About ninety miles southwest of Richmond, near Appomattox Court House, Grant finally trapped Lee on the morning of April 9. The Confederate commander tried one last surge that Palm Sunday at Sheridan's horsemen, pushing them back briefly, but Union infantry soon arrived behind their cavalry and closed in on Lee's rear. Practically surrounded by a force nearly six times larger than his, Lee sent a note to Grant to discuss surrender terms.

Sharpe checked his watch. It was shortly before 3 p.m. that day when he and other staff officers filed down the narrow center hall of the McLean house—one of those old-fashioned Virginia double homes perched on a knoll, he observed, with a large piazza that ran along the full length of it—and turned to the left into a little parlor, bare save for a table and two or three chairs. Sharpe took a moment to sketch on a piece of paper where everyone stood or sat in the room. Grant and Lee sat at the table with their aides-de-camp beside them to take notes and reduce to writing terms of the surrender for the Army of Northern Virginia to the Army of the Potomac. Crowded in the opposite corner with Grant's other aides, Sharpe craned his neck to see and hear what he said was "one of the most remarkable transactions of this nineteenth century." Lee's hair, he observed, "was white as driven snow. There was not a speck upon his coat; not a spot upon those gauntlets that he wore, which were as bright and fair as a lady's glove." Grant, by stark contrast, Sharpe believed, wore boots "nearly covered with mud; one button of his coat . . . had clearly gone astray."

The two men struggled to make small talk—Grant apologizing for not wearing a sword as Lee did and asking what had become of the white horse the Rebel commander rode when they both served in Mexico. Lee responded with stiff bows, few words, and a "coldness of manner," Sharpe recalled, that was "almost haughtiness."

The surrender took the form of correspondence the two men signed, which arranged for its terms. They were generous: Lee's officers and enlisted men would be given paroles guaranteeing them immunity from prosecution for treason if they promised not to take up arms against the U.S. government, and the soldiers would be allowed to return home with their horses to put in the spring crops. Then "there was a whispered conversation between Grant and Lee, which nobody in the room heard," Sharpe recalled. Their business finished, Lee stood up "and bowed to every person in the room on our side," he said.

After the Rebel leader left, Grant gathered Sharpe and the other staff officers around him to tell them what the whispered conversation had been about. "General Lee's army is on the point of starvation," he said. Grant ordered his commissaries, quartermasters, and soldiers of each corps to donate food. Lee had admitted to him he had no idea how many troops he had left after their scramble to Appomattox. Grant, who received a daily enemy strength estimate from Sharpe, offered rations for 25,000 men, which turned out to be fairly close to the number Lee had.

After Grant left, Union officers descended on the brick house to buy souvenirs from what they all realized was a historic meeting. Sharpe paid the McLean family ten dollars for a pair of brass candlesticks. He also remained at Appomattox to implement one part of the surrender terms. Grant put him in charge of compiling lists of Confederate officers and enlisted men and giving them paroles. Sharpe had not planned to issue Lee a parole but the Rebel commander asked to be given one as well, so Sharpe penned one for him and six members of his staff. Lee and his senior officers, the spymaster wrote, surrendered to the Union Army and swore they "will not hereafter serve in the armies of the Confederate States, or in any military capacity whatever, against the United States of America." Lee and his aides would not be disturbed by U.S. authorities "so long as they observe their parole."

The Rebel commander's parole request might be interpreted as a noble gesture to be treated just like his men. More likely, Lee wanted to save his skin. Grant had been magnanimous at the McLean house but others did not feel so kindly toward the Rebel commander. His generalship was admired by both sides but it had led tens of thousands of young men—Union and Confederate—to their deaths defending a repulsive slave system. Many Radical Republicans and northern newspapers wanted him arrested. Navy secretary Welles considered Lee a traitor to his country, who might lead a guerrilla movement after the war. Davis was roundly denounced in northern papers as an "arch traitor" who should be hung. Lee was considered no different.

Some Grant aides thought Lee was criminally derelict when he fled Richmond with his army, leaving its miserable wretches in burning chaos, and they were not impressed with the duplicity they thought Lee showed the day before his surrender when he toyed with Grant about giving up and then continued fighting for another day. When Lee finally agreed to capitulate on April 9, Sheridan still believed it might be a ruse so the southern commander could escape once more. Weeks later, senior Union officers remained nervous that Lee and his staff continued to hang around Richmond. The Federals wanted them dispersed so they would be less able to stir up discontent among southerners who did not want the war to end.

Lee found the parole Sharpe signed for him particularly valuable in June when a grand jury in Norfolk indicted him for treason. He waved the paper, arguing that it protected him from prosecution. Grant agreed and got the indictment quashed.

With Captain Oliver and a squad of information bureau officers and clerks to help, Sharpe labored day and night for nearly a week at Appomattox Court House, compiling personnel lists and processing paroles for Lee's army, which they estimated totaled more than 26,000. It became a difficult job, he discovered. Lee's force had become so disorganized in the final days of the war, his officers did not have a clear picture of who was in their ranks. Adding to the confusion, many Rebels who had deserted the battlefield began showing up when they heard about the benefits offered by the parole. Sharpe also became quickly disgusted by some of Lee's commanders who pocketed their paroles and rode home "leaving their men and subordinate officers without advice or assistance," he wrote. Many in the rank and file came to appreciate Sharpe and his officers, who took care of them better than their supposedly chivalrous generals who deserted them.

After he finished, Sharpe packed the stacks of parole records into a wagon and with Oliver rode back to City Point. Lee had signed passes for them to travel through Confederate ranks unmolested. A Rebel colonel Sharpe had paroled joined them on the ride back. Sharpe enjoyed his company. When they arrived at Grant's sprawling headquarters off the James River with American flags fluttering over a number of tents, tears welled up in the Rebel's eyes. "After all, General Sharpe, there is only one flag," the colonel said.

At City Point, Sharpe and Oliver transferred the boxes of records to a steamer and sailed back to Washington. On the voyage, Sharpe still longed to return to his old unit. He had been offered a more prestigious brigade command but turned it down. Though he had reached Grant's inner circle, Sharpe told his uncle he did not intend "to remain permanently away from the regiment."

Elizabeth Van Lew was overjoyed by the hundred-gun salute she heard Union troops fire off to celebrate Lee's surrender at Appomattox Court House. Her neighbors did not feel the same, the die-hards among them grumbling that Lee would never have capitulated if Davis had been present to stiffen his spine. As it was, nearly two months passed before all the remaining Rebel forces in the South finally laid down their arms.

In Richmond, Marsena Patrick was named provost marshal general of the Department of Virginia and given the job of managing its capital. His superiors considered his "purity of character," familiarity with Virginia culture, and his business experience ideal qualifications for running the city. Mary Bowser, Van Lew's loyal servant, did not share that warm feeling about the provost marshal. She was appalled when Patrick humiliated a black man who had defended his wife from an attack by a Union soldier. Patrick wanted the husband executed.

Washingtonians awoke April 10 to news in their papers that Lee had surrendered and a ground-shaking five-hundred-gun salute hailing victory at last. Soon "the streets were shockingly muddy, but were all alive with people singing and cheering, carrying flags, and saluting everybody," said journalist

Noah Brooks. The next night an upstairs window was opened and Lincoln leaned out to address an immense throng with bands and banners that had poured into the semicircular avenue in front of the White House. "We meet this evening not in sorrow, but in gladness of heart," he began in a speech longer than anyone anticipated, which outlined his thoughts for reconstruction. In the boisterous crowd below him stood John Wilkes Booth, a narcissistic attention grabber who had developed into a rabid southern sympathizer. "That is the last speech he will ever make," the actor said under his breath to a companion.

Booth had become a frequent caller at Mary Surratt's boardinghouse on H Street, just nine blocks from Lafayette Baker's headquarters. (The Maryland widow, who gave Baker's men a frosty reception at her Surrattsville tavern in 1862, had moved to Washington in 1864.) Other rough-edged men in the makeshift gang Booth had assembled were regular boarders at the house, which had become a rendezvous for Confederate spies, smugglers, and couriers. Baker bragged there was no hostile agent in Washington that he or his men didn't know about, but that was clearly not the case—at least not with John Wilkes Booth and the conspirators meeting under Baker's nose at the Surratt house.

Grant worried about Lincoln's personal safety after Lee's surrender, but Baker did not have any particular concern. He had returned to Washington on April 9, checking in to the Willard and toasting Lee's surrender with his detectives the next day. Wearing his gaudy colonel's uniform, he also made the rounds at the War Department lobbying for his promotion to brigadier general. The morning of April 13, Baker took the train to New York and checked back in to the Astor House. There were loose ends to tie up in his recruiting investigation—although its importance now was practically nil.

Twenty-Four

ASSASSINATION

*L*incoln, who earlier told an aide he had dreamed of visiting his own funeral after his assassination, attended Ford's Theatre with Mary on a blustery cold Good Friday evening April 14 to see the popular comedy *Our American Cousin*. Major Henry Rathbone and his fiancée, Clara Harris, joined them. Lincoln's guard for the evening, an inept Washington Metropolitan policeman named John Parker, had left his post in the passageway to the theater box to sip a drink at a saloon next door and then watch the rest of the show from the gallery. Sitting in the vestibule, White House footman Charles Forbes let Booth into the presidential box after he showed him his card. Booth then calmly pulled out a derringer, pumped a bullet into the back of the president's head, knifed Rathbone when he tried to seize the actor, and vaulted over the box's balustrade to the stage twelve feet below, melodramatically shouting "Sic semper tyrannis!" ("Thus always to tyrants") after he landed.

Booth had planned a triple assassination to decapitate the U.S. government. Conspirators Lewis Powell, a muscular and brutish ex–Confederate soldier, and David Herold, a small and stooped young man with protruding teeth, went to Seward's Lafayette Square residence. While Herold waited outside, Powell barged into the home and with a bowie knife stabbed the secretary of state, who was bedridden from a carriage accident, nearly killing him. George Atzerodt, meanwhile, was supposed to murder Vice President Johnson in his room at the Kirkwood Hotel, but the short and thickset German American lost his nerve fifteen minutes before he was supposed to strike and fled the hotel for Georgetown.

Booth escaped Ford's Theatre on horseback, riding at a gallop southeast through the capital and crossing the 11th Street Bridge over the Potomac's Eastern Branch (now known as the Anacostia River) into Maryland. Herold, who had abandoned Powell at Seward's house, joined the assassin about eight miles from Washington in Maryland.

John Jones, a former Rebel War Department clerk in Richmond, cautioned friends to show "no feeling" about the assassination when they walked around town; it might spark a backlash from their Union occupiers. Seventeen Confederate generals signed a letter to Grant denying any involvement in the killing. The federal commander and other senior U.S. officials weren't yet ready to believe their former enemy's protestations of innocence.

Elizabeth Van Lew sat down and penned a heartfelt letter a Union officer could not convince any Richmond paper to publish. "Oh, how can we welcome you our deliverers?" she wrote. "Was ever so glorious a cause entrusted to an army—to any people! Justice, truth, humanity vindicated—this our glorious army has wrought for us. . . . I had written this poor tribute when the stunning news came of the death—the assassination of our Beloved President. Words cannot express the grief—the sympathy of the little band of firm unionists in our midst."

A messenger knocked on the door of Lafayette Baker's Astor House room early Saturday morning, April 15, and gave him the news that Lincoln had been assassinated. He was shocked and truly grief-stricken. Later that afternoon, Baker, who knew nothing about this assassin named Booth, received a telegram from Stanton. "Come here immediately and see if you can find the murderers of the president," it read. Baker had visions he would take personal command of the manhunt. That would hardly be the case. Since the night before, Stanton, who had taken over running the government for the moment, had been summoning everybody he could think of to join in the search. About two hours before messaging Baker, Stanton had telegraphed New York police chief John Kennedy asking for three or four of his best detectives to come to Washington and investigate the assassination.

Baker wasn't able to book a train back to Washington until Sunday morning. On the ride down, he admitted later, he felt a tinge of guilt. Baker should have felt guilty. Throughout Lincoln's presidency the specter of assassination was hardly a state secret. Certainly it came as no surprise to Stanton, who along with others continually warned that the president faced danger. Considering all the attempts and threatened attempts on his life, it was a miracle this highly controversial president, hated and feared by so many embittered southerners and disaffected northerners, had lived for as long as he did. Security for Lincoln began notoriously lax and improved only marginally over the years, with a cavalry detail and not particularly well-trained police officers assigned to guard him. Lincoln hated the protection, complaining it made him seem like an emperor remote from his people.

Before he joined McClellan in the field, Allan Pinkerton considered guarding Lincoln one of his duties in Washington—although it's questionable how much presidential protection the detective actually did. Baker's critics claimed that as Pinkerton's successor heading Washington's secret service, he was responsible for guarding the president—and he failed at that job. Baker insisted the Army had taken over protecting Lincoln and that it was Halleck and the generals under him who failed.

Yet if guarding the president of the United States was not specifically Baker's responsibility, uncovering threats to him certainly was. Baker was well aware of the many stories circulating of plots to kill or kidnap Lincoln. He could read about them in the newspapers and he had a number of files on southern sympathizers who had threatened the president. He claimed in his memoirs that he personally warned Lincoln about the danger. If that was really the case—Baker fabricated many of the conversations he said he had with the president—why did he not act on the intelligence he collected? Baker and his detectives poked into practically every corner of Washington, arresting suspected enemies of the government on the slightest suspicion. Yet Booth, Herold, Atzerodt, Powell, and a handful of other conspirators— none of them particularly skilled at subterfuge—freely roamed the nation's capital, sometimes using Mary Surratt's H Street boardinghouse as an operating base to plot and carry out the greatest subversive operation of the Civil War. It was a spectacular intelligence failure on Baker's part.

Through Friday night and into Saturday, Booth and Herold rode southeast across open Maryland country, stopping at Surrattsville to pick up a loaded Spencer repeating carbine and field glasses at the tavern Mary Surratt now had a renter operate and then proceeding to the Charles County farm of Samuel A. Mudd, a helpful doctor Booth knew. Mudd, who never had a particularly thriving medical practice, improvised a splint for the left fibula Booth fractured jumping to the Ford's Theatre stage and let the assassin and his companion rest in one of his rooms until evening. From Mudd's farm, Booth and Herold traveled southeast and then southwest along a windy route the Rebel underground used during the war, stopping at the farms of friendly southern sympathizers along the way and dodging federal soldiers, cavalrymen, and detectives who had begun scouring the area, until they reached Dent's Meadow, along the banks of the Potomac, on April 20. It took three more days before the pair was finally able to row across the river in a flat-bottomed skiff and land near Mathias Point on the Virginia side the morning of April 23.

With the willing and, in one case, unwilling help of Virginians along the way, Booth and Herold by the next day reached Port Conway, a small town north of the Rappahannock. There they met three ragged-looking ex–Confederate soldiers—Mortimer Ruggles and Absalom Bainbridge from John Mosby's old command, and William Jett from the 9th Virginia Cavalry—who took the fugitives under their wing and crossed the river with them in a ferryboat to the old tobacco trading town of Port Royal on the south side of the Rappahannock. From Port Royal, the Confederates escorted Booth and Herold farther southwest to the five-hundred-acre Locust Hill farm of Richard Garrett, whose family quickly grew uneasy about having these two suspicious characters on their property.

• • •

The April 17 edition of the *New York Herald* announced Baker's arrival in Washington, predicting that with the secret service chief on the case, Booth would be caught in twenty-four hours. Baker claimed he found little had been done to track down the conspirators. That was not true. With the new president, his government, and the public stunned by the assassination, Stanton had launched the most wide-ranging manhunt in U.S. history by the time his chief detective reached the capital. Baker was just one cog in that massive operation.

Working first out of the Petersen House across the street from Ford's Theatre, where the stricken president had been taken on Friday night, the war secretary alerted Grant and directed units under Major General Christopher Augur, commander of the military district of Washington, to fan out to protect other cabinet members, beef up the city's defenses, and hunt for the assassins. Grant ordered Washington's postmaster to halt mail to Richmond and open and read the letters addressed to the old Confederate capital that were currently in the post office to look for anything suspicious. Telegraph wires crackled with messages from Army field commanders to Stanton assuring him they were searching everywhere for Booth—from Virginia to Baltimore to New York City. By 2 a.m. on April 15, Augur had identified in addition to Booth the conspirators Herold, Atzerodt, and Mary Surratt's son, John, a slender man with a boyish face and receding eyes who had carried messages for the Confederate secret service. On Stanton's orders, Augur announced the morning of April 15 that a $10,000 reward was being offered for the arrest of the assassins.

Meanwhile, soldiers and detectives had raided Booth's room at Washington's National Hotel, discovering important clues among his effects, like a Confederate secret service cipher key and a letter that indicated a larger conspiracy. They stormed Mary Surratt's boardinghouse to begin questioning her and her tenants. A military policeman working for Washington's provost marshal, Major James O'Beirne, broke down the door to the room Atzerodt had rented at the Kirkwood Hotel and found it filled with weapons, a Virginia map, and a Montreal bankbook with a credit entered for Booth. And while Booth slept at Dr. Mudd's farmhouse the afternoon of April 15, federal cavalrymen who had ridden south from Washington roamed several miles away.

Baker, who had a well-deserved reputation in Washington for being a publicity hog and a bureaucratic bigfoot, found other investigators like Augur, Kennedy's New York detectives, and Washington police chief Almarin Richards not eager to share leads they had developed the past two days hunting for conspirators. So Baker planted moles in his competitors' operations to discover what they had found. Then he set out to search for Booth on his own. Because a number of his detectives remained in New York wrapping up the recruiting fraud case, Baker had only eight men in Washington when he arrived on April 16. He quickly borrowed a half-dozen cops from the Washington and Philadelphia forces.

Immediately Baker filled one obvious void in the investigation. No one had found photographs of the conspirators to circulate among the public along with physical descriptions. By the end of Sunday, April 16, he had rounded up photos of Booth, Herold, and John Surratt Jr. and printed handbills along with descriptions of the three men and the $10,000 reward Augur had been authorized to offer. The next evening he sent two of his men on fast horses to Maryland to circulate handbills and mailed out more of them to detectives in other parts of the country. Baker also soon printed posters offering a $30,000 reward for the capture of Booth—although he had no authority to do so and no money to pay anyone who produced the assassin.

Baker again resorted to methods that had served him in other cases with mixed results. He interviewed a Booth acquaintance (the man said he had talked to the actor only about theatrical matters) and Booth's niece, Blanche (she had not seen her uncle for nearly two years and he had given no indication then that he intended an assassination). Baker also hauled in for rough interrogations men and women whom informants had fingered as disloyal. Booth sightings poured into his office as they did to other investigators. Newspapers reported the actor in a dozen northern cities. Stanton received reports Booth was heading toward the Mississippi River or was holed up in a Chicago whorehouse disguised as a prostitute. An informant telegraphed Baker he had "no doubt" that the assassin was in Burlington, Vermont, preparing to cross the Canadian border. (Baker later sent two Washington policemen to Canada to hunt for John Surratt, who had, in fact, fled to that country.) A prankster even sent a note to Augur claiming to be Booth and writing: "I'm still in your midst. I will remain in the city. God willed that I should do it. I defy detection."

But from information his moles had purloined from Augur, O'Beirne, and other investigators, Baker knew that Booth and Herold had escaped south into Maryland and had traveled as far as Prince George's and then Charles Counties. On April 18, he dispatched a half-dozen detectives to southern Maryland and the Eastern Shore to distribute handbills with photos and hunt for the fugitives. They turned up nothing and returned to Washington five days later. By then Powell, Atzerodt, Mary Surratt, and three other members of Booth's gang had been arrested. But none of the investigators—Baker included—knew where Booth and Herold were. The two men had been tracked as far as the farm of Samuel Mudd, who was also soon arrested. But from there the trail had gone cold.

On April 20, the day after Lincoln's grim funeral in Washington, Stanton announced that a $50,000 reward would be offered for the capture of Booth, $25,000 for the capture of Herold, and $25,000 for the capture of John Surratt. The $100,000 up for grabs (about $1.5 million in today's dollars) sparked a frenzy among Union officers, soldiers, policemen, would-be sleuths, and particularly Lafayette Baker—all hoping to strike it rich.

News of Lincoln's assassination reached Pinkerton at the Army's headquarters in New Orleans, where he was still investigating government contract frauds. On April 19 he telegraphed Stanton (with his old flair for the dramatic, he enciphered the message and signed it with his pseudonym E. J. Allen) to remind the war secretary that he had saved Lincoln from assassination in Baltimore four years earlier. "How I regret that I had not been near him previous to this final act," Pinkerton wrote. "I might have been the means to arrest it." This was a self-serving condolence, to be sure, but until his dying day Pinkerton believed that if he had been in charge of Lincoln's security, Booth would never have gotten near him.

Pinkerton offered his services in hunting down the assassins. Stanton telegraphed back on April 25, telling the detective that a number of conspirators had been arrested but Booth, Herold, and Surratt were still at large. The actor "may have made his way West with a view of getting to Texas or Mexico," Stanton wrote, which demonstrated that he had no idea where Booth was at that point. The war secretary told Pinkerton "to watch the western rivers and you may get him."

Midmorning on April 24, Baker happened to be in the War Department telegraph office when a message arrived from O'Beirne, who was searching with his detectives along the Maryland side of the Potomac downstream from Port Tobacco. The Washington provost marshal reported that a local resident told one of his detectives he had seen two men (O'Beirne was sure they were Booth and Herold) crossing the Potomac from Swan Point on the Maryland side to White Point on the Virginia side the morning of April 16. It turned out that O'Beirne had the wrong date for when Booth and Herold actually crossed the river, and the Swan Point–White Point route he was told they took was far south of where the fugitives actually sailed. The two men O'Beirne's source said he saw were not Booth and Herold. No matter. Baker grabbed the telegram and rushed back to his office, believing he had the vital clue that put the fugitives in Virginia.

Baker later hotly denied that he had stolen O'Beirne's lead. He claimed that an old black man had told him on April 24 that he saw two men who looked like Booth and Herold crossing the Potomac into Virginia the night of April 22. Senior Army officers found that story suspect. Baker never revealed who this black man was and no African American ever came forward to claim a share of the large reward, which surely would have happened if this informant were real. Most likely O'Beirne's telegraph, as flawed as it was, sparked a hunch on Baker's part that Booth and Herold were now in Virginia. From his previous investigations Baker knew enough about the underground routes Confederate spies and couriers used in Virginia's Northern Neck to make an educated guess that these two fugitives might be somewhere between the Potomac and the Rappahannock.

Back at his headquarters by noon on April 24, Baker quickly summoned his cousin Luther Byron Baker and Everton J. Conger. A hard-bitten, pipe-puffing lieutenant colonel, Conger had been shot through the hip fighting with Baker's Rangers and still limped when he walked. Baker spread out a map on a small table before his two assistants. "I have information that Booth crossed the river here," he said, pointing to Mathias Point on the Virginia side with his pencil.

"He is right in there," Baker said, drawing a circle around the Rappahannock at Port Conway on the north bank and Port Royal on the south bank. "I want you to go to this place, search the country thoroughly, and get Booth." Baker told Conger and his cousin he would provide them cavalry for the mission. "Don't come back without" Booth and Herold, he ordered the two men, "for they are certainly in that vicinity."

With an eye toward capturing the reward money, Baker had a photographer come in and take a publicity shot of him pointing on the map with his pencil and Luther and Conger standing over him.

With Stanton's approval, Baker delivered an order to the division commander at Winchester to send him twenty-five cavalrymen for the mission. Two hours later, Lieutenant Edward Doherty, a twenty-five-year-old Canadian who had worked in a Boston dry goods store before the war and had seen his share of intense combat since, arrived with twenty-six horsemen from the 16th New York Cavalry Regiment. Baker showed Doherty the circles on the map where he believed the fugitives were, handed him photos of Booth, and introduced him to Luther Baker and Conger, who would join him on the expedition.

The lieutenant was immediately suspicious of Lafayette Baker's cousin being assigned to this mission. It smelled to the cavalryman of rank nepotism—a way for the Baker family to garner most of the reward money. It was also curious that Lafayette Baker did not lead the manhunt himself, considering that he often hopped on his horse to chase suspects in far more trivial cases. Perhaps he was not so sure about Booth's whereabouts as he made himself out to be before his cousin and Conger, and he didn't want to waste his time on what might be a wild-goose chase.

Luther Baker, Everton Conger, Edward Doherty's cavalry detachment, and their horses boarded the steamship *John S. Ide* out of Washington late afternoon on April 24 and sailed for four hours down the Potomac. They docked about 10 p.m. at Belle Plain, a Union supply base on Potomac Creek jutting a mile and a half from the main river on the Virginia side west of Mathias Point. Doherty ordered the *Ide* captain to wait at the dock for two days before returning to Washington.

The detectives and their cavalry traveled southeast toward Port Conway on the Rappahannock but did so separately. Baker and Conger went ahead, pretending when they stopped at houses along the way to be former blockade runners chased by the Yankees and looking for two friends. They asked residents whom they might have seen crossing the Rappahannock. Doherty followed with the cavalrymen, questioning anyone they met and looking for doctors besides Mudd who might have treated a man with a broken leg. Neither party turned up any leads in the Northern Neck that night and into the morning of April 25.

After about twelve hours of knocking on doors separately, the weary detectives and cavalrymen converged on Port Conway around 4 p.m. Baker approached William Rollins, a local fisherman and farmer sitting on the front steps of his hut, and got the best lead of the expedition. Two men, one with a broken leg, plus three ex–Confederate soldiers, crossed the Rappahannock the day before, Rollins said. Baker showed him two photographs. Rollins identified Booth and Herold. He also said one of the Confederates was Willie Jett. Rollins's wife added another important morsel. Jett, according to the rumor she heard, could be found in Bowling Green southwest of Port Royal, where he courted the daughter of a hotel owner. Rollins agreed to guide the party after they crossed the river to Bowling Green, which, although they didn't know it at that point, was about five miles from the Garrett farm.

Shortly after 11 p.m., the cavalry party trotted into the small town of Bowling Green and raided the Star Hotel. They found Jett sleeping on a mattress in a second-floor room.

"Is your name Jett?" Conger shouted with a growl.

"Yes, sir," the startled man stammered as he was about to climb out of bed.

"Get up! I want you," Conger demanded as Jett struggled with his pants. Jett was manhandled down the stairs, where with a revolver pointed to his head it didn't take him long to confess that Booth and Herold were holed up at the Garrett house. With their Rebel prisoner forced to serve as their guide, Baker, Conger, and Doherty's cavalry galloped to the farm. Jett was left at the outer gate to the property and the raiders raced to the farmhouse. It was about 2 a.m.

Doherty's cavalrymen rushed through an inner gate and fanned out around the two-story, white-frame farmhouse while the lieutenant, Conger, and Baker bounded up the front porch steps and with dogs barking outside pounded on the door. Richard Garrett answered in his nightclothes. "Where are the two men who stopped here?" Conger demanded. Garrett talked in circles as if he were trying to buy time. Fed up, Conger threatened to hang the old man if he didn't tell them immediately where Booth and Herold were. Garrett's son, John, who had been sleeping in a nearby corn crib, intervened on the porch and took the detectives to the tobacco barn on the left, where the fugitives had been sleeping. The Garrett boys had become suspicious of the visitors and insisted they sleep in the barn, whose door they locked from the outside to make sure the pair didn't slip away with the family's horses.

Doherty quickly ordered his men to surround the barn, which stored corn fodder and old furniture. Conger and Baker then took over, which the lieutenant did not like. Baker shouted to Booth and Herold that they had fifteen minutes to surrender or "I will burn this barn down!" Conger and Baker were seasoned detectives by this time. But their negotiations with Booth to convince him to give up were amateurish and clumsy. Booth remained defiant. "Well, my brave boys, you can prepare a stretcher for me!" the actor answered back dramatically. After a furious argument with Booth, Herold soon fled the barn to surrender and soldiers tied him to a tree.

It was extremely important to Stanton that Booth be captured alive so federal investigators could interrogate him to unravel the extent of the conspiracy and determine how it might link to Jefferson Davis and his government. Baker and Conger, however, botched the operation. Instead of slowly turning up the pressure and waiting out Booth, who was outnumbered nearly thirty to one, Conger lost his cool and his patience. After the fifteen-minute deadline had passed and Booth appeared to him to be stalling,

Conger wanted to end the standoff. So did Baker. Doherty wanted to wait until daylight but the two detectives overruled him.

Conger struck a match and lit a pile of pine needles and hay at one corner of the barn to force the actor out. Quickly flames shot up the structure's weathered boards and timbers. Baker had unlocked the barn door at the opposite end and stood near the entrance to look inside. As the fire spread inside, Booth, clutching a pistol and carbine with a crutch under one arm, hobbled to the center of the barn.

Sergeant Thomas "Boston" Corbett was an eccentric religious fanatic who emigrated from England and castrated himself so he would not be tempted by immoral women. Peering through a space in the barn siding, the trigger-happy Union soldier had kept his Colt revolver trained on Booth. When the actor began taking steps toward the barn door where Baker stood, Corbett fired his weapon. He claimed he squeezed off a shot because he thought Booth was about to shoot Baker and that he aimed for the actor's shoulder. But the round struck Booth high in the back of his neck—a mortal wound.

Corbett said "providence" directed him to pull the trigger. Conger was furious with the sergeant, realizing that his rash act killed the chances for having Booth reveal any larger conspiracy. The assassin was dragged from the burning barn and placed first under an apple tree, then carried to the veranda of the farmhouse, where he was put on a mattress. Conger sent a soldier to Port Royal to find a doctor and with Baker hovered over the actor as he lay dying. When Baker opened Booth's collar he found where the bullet had struck him.

After trying to swallow water and then whisky from a glass, Booth attempted to speak but did so only in gasps and faint whispers. "Kill me," he mumbled several times. He was paralyzed from the neck down. Conger put his ear close to Booth's mouth to listen. "Tell my mother I die for my country," he heard the actor mutter. The two detectives could get him to say nothing of value.

Conger and Baker rifled through Booth's pockets to collect his personal effects, including what appeared to be a pocket diary. Conger wrapped it all in a handkerchief. They also took what little Herold had on him, which included a small piece of a map. And just to confirm that the man lying in front of them was Booth, the detectives pulled out their photos of the actor and held them close to his face.

A doctor from Port Royal finally arrived but said there was nothing he could do. While Booth lay dying, Conger and Corbett climbed onto their horses and rode quickly back to the Belle Plain landing. Conger wanted to rush back to Washington with the news on Booth and Herold, along with the weapons and personal effects found on the two men. It would also give him a head start putting together his story to claim the reward. The others would follow later with Booth, Herold, Jett, and the two Garrett brothers. At Belle Plain, Conger left Corbett at the wharf to wait for them and boarded the steamer *Keyport*, which took him to the capital.

Luther Baker and the cavalrymen watched Booth die shortly after 7 a.m. on April 26. They wrapped his body in a coarse army blanket with "U.S." stamped on it, one of the Garrett girls stitched it up with thread and needle, and the cavalrymen loaded the corpse onto a wagon for the ride back to Belle Plain and the steamer *John S. Ide*. Luther sat nervously in the wagon's front seat during the trip. Blood oozed out of the blanketed form lying in the back. He was riding through what was still considered Confederate country. He could only imagine what might happen to them if hostile residents discovered they were carrying the now-martyred assassin of the president they so hated.

Conger walked into Lafayette Baker's office about 5 p.m. and told him Booth had been killed and Herold had been captured. He then laid on a table Booth's diary along with the weapons and other items found on the two men. Baker was ecstatic. He glanced through the diary quickly (it appeared to him to be a travelogue of Booth's time on the run) and then dashed off a short message to the War Department telegraph office that he would be at the dock at Alexandria to take custody of Herold and Booth's body when the *John S. Ide* docked. With Conger in tow he climbed into a carriage and rode quickly to Stanton's house.

"We have got Booth," Baker said excitedly and spread out the diary and other items taken on a center table in the war secretary's parlor. Stanton put his hands on his eyes and lay on his couch for a moment without saying a word, overcome with emotion. Conger then briefly recounted the mission. He left the diary and Booth's personal effects with Stanton.

Baker, who had not changed clothes since he arrived back in Washington ten days earlier, met the *John S. Ide* at the Alexandria dock at 10:40 p.m. and rode with the vessel to the Navy Yard, where it was moored next to the ironclad gunboat *Montauk*. Sailors took Herold, in double irons, down into the hold of the *Montauk*, where he was locked up with other prisoners believed to have been part of the conspiracy. Booth's body was carried to the gunboat's deck and surrounded by a Marine guard. Stanton wanted to be absolutely sure the body was Booth's. A half dozen of the actor's acquaintances had been quickly rounded up and, with Baker looking on, each proceeded up to the corpse and vouched that it was Booth. So did a Washington physician who had removed a benign tumor from the actor's neck and spotted the scar. Dr. Joseph K. Barnes, the Army's surgeon general, then performed a quick autopsy with an assistant, carving out two inches of spinal column from the assassin's neck, through which the bullet had passed.

The body was beginning to smell and Baker was furious to find people scavenging it for souvenirs. He grabbed one lady who snipped a lock of Booth's hair and seized her treasure. Stanton wanted the assassin dumped into a secret grave, where no one would find the remains to strip it of more relics to sell. So Baker and cousin Luther piled the body into a boat after midnight and rowed it several miles down the Potomac to near Giesboro Point, where old government horses were brought to be slaughtered. Baker told the press later Booth had been buried at sea. That was a lie. He and Luther off-loaded the corpse at the nearby Old Arsenal penitentiary (now Fort McNair), where prison workers packed it into a musket crate, threw it into a deep hole in one of the facility's cells, covered it with dirt, and replaced the stone slab from the cell floor.

Baker spent the rest of April and all of May joining other investigators in collecting evidence for the prosecutors who tried the eight assassination conspirators. On a blazing hot July 7, the secret service chief and four of his detectives stood in the prison yard of the Old Arsenal as part of a large audience watching four of the conspirators—Herold, Powell, Atzerodt, and

Mary Surratt—hanged from a scaffold. Baker then preoccupied himself with what became an obsession—the reward money.

He had become a national celebrity after the capture of Booth and Herold, hailed by some as a supersleuth for tracking down the assassins so quickly. Stanton promoted him to brigadier general—although he did so without public fanfare for fear of arousing Baker's many fierce enemies in Washington. Believing the war secretary was in his corner, the secret service chief thought he had the inside track to receive the lion's share of the $25,000 reward for Herold's capture and the $50,000 prize for Booth. To grease the skids he sent a five-page memo to Stanton on the manhunt and fed the *New York Times* an account that portrayed him as the mastermind behind it.

But Baker had competitors who proved as greedy as he was. Conger considered himself the leader of the cavalry expedition that actually found Booth and Herold. He thought he deserved a large chunk of the reward—as did cousin Luther. Lieutenant Doherty thought he and his men deserved most of the $75,000 and also launched an intensive lobbying and publicity campaign. Doherty claimed he was the true leader of the expedition—Conger and cousin Luther just came along for the ride—and that he and his men did all the hard work tracking down the fugitives and capturing them at the Garrett farm. Stanton was soon besieged with hundreds of claimants, not only for the Booth and Herold rewards but also for the money offered for other captured conspirators and for Jefferson Davis, who was finally nabbed in Georgia on May 10.

The war secretary wisely turned over the thorny question of who got what to a military claims court to resolve, which angered Baker. The court's officers, who were suspicious of Baker's account of the manhunt, decided to apply the rule the U.S. Navy used to apportion money for the war prizes its men captured at sea. The commanding officer of a fleet or squadron—that was Baker in this case, the claims officers decided—received under the Navy rule one-twentieth of the prize money awarded to vessels under his command. So Baker should receive $3,750 of the $75,000 reward. As the cavalry detachment's military commander, Doherty was considered like a ship's captain and by the Navy rule he should receive one-tenth of the prize money—or $7,500 in this case. The claims officers decided that Luther Baker and Everton Conger should get $4,000 each and the rest of the Booth-Herold reward should be divided up among Doherty's twenty-six cavalrymen.

Congress eventually approved this apportionment and Baker received a $3,750 check. He was livid over this measly amount, blaming Stanton for cheating him out of what he thought should have been a much higher share of the prize. It left the war secretary's top spy in a mood to get even.

Twenty-Five

PEACE

The capital city spent two days at the end of May hosting a farewell for the troops who had fought so valiantly and for so long to save the Union. More than 150,000 soldiers, led in many units by young generals on horseback, marched with bands playing in a grand review through the city, passing by the White House, where stands had been erected on both sides of Pennsylvania Avenue for President Johnson, his cabinet, congressmen, and senior officers like Grant, Meade, and Sherman. The skies were bright and clear. "People came from every part of the United States to look upon the passing pageant," recorded journalist Noah Brooks. "Never in the history of Washington had there been such an enormous influx of visitors."

The price had been staggering. The Civil War lasted 1,512 days, resulted in 1,882 general engagements, battles, or major skirmishes, and cost more than 750,000 dead soldiers. By numbers, victory should never have been in doubt for the North, which enjoyed a two-to-one manpower advantage on the battlefield and clear superiority in economic resources, military logistics, and naval power. The South had the strategic advantage of defending home territory from an invading army that had to muster a larger force to conquer hostile country. In the early stages of the war, the Confederacy fielded better generals like Beauregard, Jackson, and Lee. It took longer for aggressive northern generals such as Grant, Sherman, and Sheridan to rise to the top for the Union. But as the war of attrition ground on, the South's economy deteriorated, and its civilian and soldier morale collapsed. Only for so long could the region endure this kind of pounding.

What role did intelligence play in this conflict? More than was acknowledged at the time. Northern and southern civilian leaders largely neglected the gathering of political and economic intelligence because they knew the other's politics, geography, and economic wherewithal. Each side's generals had been classmates in the same military academies and had fought together. They often showed disinterest in strategic and tactical intelligence, believing they could already foresee how an adversary they had known for years would react on the battlefield. But the work of Lincoln's spies—even his inept ones like Pinkerton, his corrupt ones like Baker, and particularly his best ones like Sharpe and Van Lew—made a difference.

The North had its failures, including Pinkerton's faulty reports before and during the Peninsula campaign. Confederate cavalry reconnaissance always outran the Union's. But over the four years of war, federal intelligence gathering proved more successful, in battles like Gettysburg's, than that of the Confederates. The Union's ability to track changes in enemy numbers and organization, even Pinkerton's flawed operation, always outpaced the Rebel capability. The Federals proved better at protecting their communications and intercepting the enemy's. They had more balloons.

Lafayette Baker put many innocent people in jail and pocketed some of the graft he discovered, and he failed miserably in uncovering threats to Lincoln, but he also locked up the guilty and uncovered fraud. His counterintelligence operation in Washington was far ahead of John Winder's in Richmond. The South had its showy celebrity spies, like Rose Greenhow and Belle Boyd, whose espionage turned out to be of marginal value. The North had the courageous workhorse Elizabeth Van Lew, who operated quietly in the shadows, providing intelligence crucial for Grant's drive on Richmond. The quiet and unassuming George Sharpe pioneered what today is called all-source intelligence—merging espionage, cavalry reconnaissance, and signal intercepts with prisoner, deserter, and refugee interrogations to produce reports on Confederate strength and movement. The phone tapping, human collection, and aerial snooping today's U.S. spy community engages in can be traced to the Civil War. It's no wonder that the CIA tasked analysts to study the era's tradecraft for lessons learned.

Allan Pinkerton lamented the fact that he had lost valuable publicity during the war years because he used his pseudonym E. J. Allen. He was bitter that Lafayette Baker became a celebrity after the capture of Booth and Herold. He felt he had not received the recognition he deserved for protecting Lincoln's life in Baltimore, while Baker was promoted to brigadier general and escaped blame for the president's assassination. Still, the Civil War was profitable for Pinkerton. He earned $38,567 as McClellan's spy chief and made money after that investigating contract fraud in New Orleans.

Pinkerton returned to Chicago and resumed directing his detective agency, which subordinates like George Bangs had been managing in his absence. His sons William and Robert joined the firm. The mushrooming of factories, telegraphs, railroads, and banks in the nineteenth century's second half brought in a huge amount of business for Pinkerton's National Detective Agency, which hired out guards and spies for strikebreaking robber barons, caught pilfering employees, and hunted bandits preying on companies. With lawlessness rampant across the Midwest, Southwest, and Wild West, his detectives became penny-press celebrities chasing notorious train and bank robbers such as the Reno brothers, the Rube Barrow ring, and the Jesse James–Cole Younger gang. New York officials offered the forty-eight-year-old Pinkerton the job of superintendent for the city's police force, but he was making far too much money as a private detective to consider it seriously. By 1868, he had a million-dollar-a-year business with branches in New York, Philadelphia, and Boston. Until the Justice Department began the Bureau of Investigation (forerunner of today's FBI) in 1908, Pinkerton's agency was the country's only national police force to speak of, boasting voluminous files and photos on criminals, scores of operatives roaming the country, and even liaisons with police departments in Europe to trade tips on international culprits.

Pinkerton never forgot his Civil War comrades. He sent Bangs to Richmond to locate Timothy Webster's grave and ship his remains to Illinois for "burial in the soil of a loyal state." On a slab of marble in the Onarga Cemetery south of Chicago was chiseled: "Timothy Webster—I died for my country." New Year's Day in 1868, Pinkerton sat at Kate Warne's bedside when she died in her sleep at age thirty-five after a long illness. He kept up regular correspondence with McClellan (who was elected governor of New Jersey in 1878), Chase (whom Lincoln eased out as Treasury secretary and then appointed Chief Justice of the Supreme Court), and Seward (who retired to Auburn, New York, in 1869).

A workaholic and micromanager, Pinkerton often saddled up his horse to ride after suspects himself and as the years passed he became increasingly demanding of his employees, writing Bangs and even his sons scathing letters when they did not meet his expectations. He remained tyrannical at home as well, accusing his daughter Joan of betrayal when she fell in love with William Chalmers, the brother of one of her college classmates, whom Pinkerton was convinced would never amount to much. Joan stood up to her father and married Chalmers, who became a multimillionaire industrialist.

Pinkerton's exhausting pace took its toll. He endured blinding headaches because of overwork and on May 5, 1869, suffered a debilitating stroke that left him paralyzed on his right side. Pinkerton rushed to New York to consult with the best doctor he could find. In December he heard about a "magnetic well" at the central Michigan town of St. Louis, which boasted a spring so rich in minerals it magnetized steel. Pinkerton sent one of his detectives to investigate and the agent reported back that the well, discovered in July, appeared to help paralysis victims. His doctor thought the mineral springs might be better for his patient than sailing to Europe for treatment. So Pinkerton took the train to Michigan and reported to Seward afterward that the waters miraculously cured him. A year after his stroke, he said, he could use his right side "very well" and raise his right arm. His mental faculties also returned and he could speak.

The Great Chicago Fire of October 1871 destroyed the Pinkerton agency's downtown building and four hundred gigantic volumes with records for his detective cases. More important for history's sake, the blaze consumed Civil War records the detective took with him when he left McClellan's service. Pinkerton was getting ready to sell them back to the U.S. government. He believed he could fetch $50,000 for the documents—which technically belonged to the Army.

During the 1870s and early 1880s, with his health somewhat restored and the agency's administration left more in the hands of his sons, Pinkerton with the help of seven writers produced eighteen books (totaling some three million words) on his most famous cases and the techniques he had perfected for catching criminals. He fancied himself an accomplished author, bragging that he was well-read and that Charles Dickens was a fan. But he overwrote and suffered from a flowery style, though many of his books became bestsellers and a few garnered respectable reviews. More important for his business, the volumes provided valuable publicity. One of his books, *The Spy of the Rebellion*, was devoted to his intelligence operations during the Civil War. Larded with exaggerations and fabrications, the 688-page memoir burnished his role in that conflict.

Pryce Lewis was outraged that Pinkerton's book accused Scully and him of selling out Timothy Webster in Richmond. Lewis disputed his version of the operation. In 1906, William Pinkerton, who continued friendly correspondence with Lewis, published a pamphlet on the Richmond mission, writing that Scully had implicated Webster but Lewis "did not confess."

Lewis married, had a daughter and son, and set up a detective agency in New Jersey and later in New York, which prospered for thirty years until client numbers eventually dropped. He contracted with a ghostwriter to write his account of working under Pinkerton, but they found no publisher. Lewis was denied a war pension because he remained a British citizen, so he did odd jobs for a New York lawyer and eventually relied on the charity of friends. By the turn of the century, he was gaunt and stoop-shouldered, living alone in a small attic room at 83 Jefferson Avenue in Jersey City that he rented for six dollars a month. His wife and son had died. He was estranged from his daughter.

Despondent over the denial of his war pension and barely able to feed himself, eighty-year-old Pryce Lewis on December 6, 1911, scribbled out a suicide note and boarded a train and then a streetcar to Joseph Pulitzer's World Building on Park Row in New York City. He took the elevator to the building's sixteenth floor, calmly climbed a flight of stairs to the observation platform on the top of its dome, and jumped, landing on the hood of a gray touring car.

During his convalescence from the stroke, Pinkerton built a grand country villa he called "The Larches" on 254 acres of land he had bought eleven years earlier near the village of Onarga, south of Chicago. The expansive square structure, just one story, was surrounded by a pillared porch and topped by a square cupola with a flagstaff. A large hall lit by four crystal chandeliers cut down its middle with bedrooms on one side and on the other three rooms for entertaining (one thoroughly soundproofed). A wine cellar linked by a tunnel to the main house; a cider cellar and root house were built nearby. Pinkerton kept it guarded like a fortress, staffing the estate with liveried footmen, gardeners, and groomsmen for the stables. He used Larches to house a small fortune in the paintings he bought and to entertain lavishly VIP guests like Grant and Chase.

By the early 1880s, with his health deteriorating, Pinkerton showed up at the office less often. He spent time during the summer of 1883 at a hot springs in the South, which seemed to revive him some. By spring 1884 it was clear he was near the end of his life, though he still managed to step out of his Chicago home on Monroe Street for morning walks. It was on one of those walks in early June that a freak accident felled him. He tripped off a sidewalk and bit deeply into his tongue. His tongue became infected. Gangrene set in. His family was at his bedside when he died at 3:05 p.m. on July 1.

Chicago papers covered his death with long stories about his Civil War service and career fighting crime. So did the *New York Times*, New York *World*, and *New York Herald*. At his funeral, a friend eulogized that "Allan Pinkerton was shaped to a larger model than most men. . . . His willpower was wonderful. His judgment once formed and conclusion reached, they could not be altered. His determination was made of iron." He left behind

$500,000, most of which went to his wife, Joan, who died several months later. To William and Robert he left his detective agency. The brothers chased Butch Cassidy and the Sundance Kid, battled the mafia from New York to New Orleans, and expanded the company's protection services for businesses. Today Pinkerton Consulting and Investigations Inc., headquartered in Ann Arbor, Michigan, is a global security and risk management company with offices all over the world.

In September 1865, Lafayette Baker asked one of Jennie's Philadelphia friends to rush to Washington because his wife was "dangerously sick." A month later he moved her to Philadelphia to recover. He continued his secret service work in Washington for the new administration. Andrew Johnson, who could be obstinate and testy, was unqualified in temperament and political skills to lead a nation emerging from its greatest war. He soon clashed with Stanton over Reconstruction policy and tried to oust the war secretary, who enlisted congressional allies to protect his job and at one point barricaded himself in his office. Johnson, who made clear he would not be bullied by Congress, became a bitter enemy of its Radical Republicans, with rumors spread that he was somehow involved in Lincoln's assassination and talk of impeachment growing.

Baker was not close to Johnson, who after Lincoln's assassination received derogatory reports on the secret service chief from Baker's political enemies. Johnson sent him to Alabama and Georgia to retrieve documents from senior aides to Jefferson Davis. He ordered Baker to put under surveillance a Tennessee Rebel who had denounced him in 1861 when Johnson was stumping his state as a Union backer. The man was now in Washington begging for a pardon, which Johnson refused.

On December 1, 1865, Baker delivered a lengthy report to Stanton boasting that his secret service during the war arrested 1,254 persons and recovered a little over $1 million in defrauded government money—all for just $170,920 that his bureau incurred in expenses. There was no way for Stanton to verify these numbers, at least one of which was suspect. Baker later testified before Congress that his secret service spent over $400,000 during the war, more than double the amount he reported to Stanton.

Baker's enemies in Congress and the military spread rumors he pocketed $200,000 during the war through extortion and the sale of seized war booty. Washington's *National Republican*, a pro-Lincoln newspaper, called for Baker's spy unit to be abolished. Baker ignored the charges believing Johnson would protect him. That would not be the case.

Baker claimed Johnson asked him to provide presidential protection so he set up a shield around the chief. There was some question whether Johnson asked Baker for the guards and whether Baker had another reason for assigning detectives to the White House. He later said he sent his men to the Executive Mansion to spy on Johnson at the request of Stanton. It was that spying, along with the heavy-handed tactics Baker had used during the war, that finally landed him in serious trouble.

The pardon broker business was out of control in Washington. Scores of shady operators set up shop in the capital, preying on gullible ex-Confederates, whose cases did not fall under the general amnesty the U.S. Army granted, as well as Unionists seeking relief for past offenses, convincing them that for a hefty fee they could get President Johnson to grant a pardon. In reality, the new president would have given the pardon much more readily if the applicants brought their requests directly to him. His anterooms at the White House were jammed with people seeking favors and, like Lincoln, he believed he must see all who called on him. He had a soft spot for pardon brokers, said a journalist who covered him, and he was liberal with his pardons. Baker reported that of the 123 people he arrested during his time with the new administration, 93 were pardoned by the president.

One of his detectives guarding the White House reported to Baker that disreputable brokers, many of them females, swarmed outside and inside the building day and night clutching pardon papers for the president to sign. Baker discovered these brokers prowled the city's hotels and bars advertising they could procure a pardon within twelve hours for anyone willing to pay a fee—which could be as much as $1,000. He also picked up gossip that Johnson's son Robert, who was an alcoholic, had become an easy mark for the pardon brokers, who occasionally paid him off to obtain his father's signature. Convinced he needed to protect Johnson from this unscrupulous lot, Baker decided to target one of the pardon brokers with a sting operation.

Mrs. Lucy Livingston Cobb was twenty-six years old, uneducated, and considered low-class in Washington. After her brother died in the Battle of Gettysburg, she opened a cigar store on Pennsylvania Avenue and briefly served as a nurse in one of the city's hospitals. She married Joseph Cobb, a Treasury Department auditor who had an inflated sense of his importance and wrote Johnson numerous letters he labeled "Sub Rosa," identifying men he thought were administration enemies. Lucy had the right attributes for a scam artist. She was a beautiful and voluptuous woman with dark eyes, who knew how to turn on the charm. On Capitol Hill, congressmen, pages, and policemen were friendly to her. She became a favorite as well at the White House among secretaries, doorkeepers, the president's son Robert, and even Johnson. In the winter of 1863, Baker evicted the couple when a landlord complained they hadn't paid their rent. The next year, Baker arrested Joseph, who then worked as an assistant Navy paymaster, on a minor offense and jailed him briefly in Old Capitol Prison.

Baker had Lieutenant Henry Hine, a former Colorado cavalryman he hired, approach Lucy on November 5, 1865, posing as Clarence Howell, an ex–Confederate spy seeking a pardon. According to Hine, Lucy told him that for $300 she could secure him a presidential pardon within twelve hours. Hine said that Lucy claimed she had obtained many pardons in the past and must charge a high amount because she had to split her fee with various government clerks on the take. Hine paid Mrs. Cobb $100 Baker gave him to serve as a retainer and got a contract and receipt that he turned over to his boss.

By November 8, Lucy had all the signatures needed for the pardon, including the president's, and told Hine that all he had to do was swear an oath of allegiance to the United States the next day and he would be officially pardoned. Hine paid Lucy the remaining $200.

At six o'clock that evening, Lucy and Joseph Cobb heard a rap on the door of their room at the Avenue House. Baker stood there with another detective. He ordered the couple to grab their hats and coats and come with him downstairs to a carriage that would take them to his headquarters. Once there, Baker parked Joseph in a chair on the ground floor and took his wife upstairs to his office. He told Lucy he intended to break up the pardon broker operation in Washington and demanded the $200 Hine had given her. Mrs. Cobb refused to surrender the cash, saying she had a friend in the White House. Johnson had signed these pardons. "This will cost you your commission," she said. "I shall see the president tomorrow and have you mustered out of the service!" Baker threatened to slap handcuffs on her and search her himself. Lucy turned over the four $50 bills Hine had given her.

Baker summoned a clerk to watch her while he took all the evidence to the White House. At the Executive Mansion, he laid out all of Lucy's documents on a table before the president, expecting to be praised for the action he took. Johnson instead was furious. He summoned Robert, who confirmed his father had signed the pardon. Johnson accused Baker of meddling in White House affairs. "What business have you to interfere here?" he said. Johnson ordered Baker to return the next evening after he talked to Mrs. Cobb.

Baker returned to his office about 11 p.m. He told Lucy and Joseph they were free to go. Baker claimed Johnson had been angry when he learned of the pardon broker scheme and banned her from setting foot in the White House. If she did he would arrest her. Lucy guessed that Baker was lying. When one of his detectives barred her from entering the White House the next day, she went around to a back door and slipped in, giving Johnson an earful about her clash with Baker and his detective who had just blocked her entry.

That evening, Johnson flew into a tirade when Baker showed up. The president of the United States decides who visits the White House, not a government detective, Johnson shouted at Baker. Those guards who had been posted around the Executive Mansion were nothing more than goons the Radical Republicans had sent to keep watch on him, Johnson charged. He ordered them and Baker out of his sight. He refused to take any action against Mrs. Cobb, whom he considered a virtuous woman.

Lucy marched into the office of Washington's district attorney to file a complaint against Baker. The district attorney was only too happy to have a grand jury indict Baker for false imprisonment and extortion for taking the $200 from her.

The seven-day trial, which began January 24, 1866, became a media extravaganza, with spectators jamming the courtroom and reporters for Washington's dailies covering the proceedings gavel to gavel. Lucy portrayed herself as a humble, hardworking girl just trying to scratch out a living in an honest profession, helping clients secure the pardons they deserved as she did with the man who identified himself as Clarence Howell. She testified that Baker arrested her and her husband without a warrant, held them against their will for five hours at his headquarters, browbeat her with foul language, and then stole $200 from her. She also claimed that when Baker returned from the White House that night, he told her he would pay her off with a bribe if she did not say anything about this episode to anyone. Lucy said she refused. Baker's case wasn't helped when prosecutors disclosed that Hine had been convicted of false imprisonment and fraud while serving as a provost marshal and that Baker had rescued the lieutenant from a two-year prison sentence by hiring him.

Baker's lawyers portrayed Lucy "as a woman of notorious bad character," as one of them put it. Baker gave an account of what transpired November 8 when he knocked on Lucy's door that was 180 degrees different from hers. The detective denied he ever arrested the couple or illegally detained them, claiming he simply asked the pair to come to his headquarters for a friendly chat about the pardon broker business and they willingly complied.

The defense attorneys punched a hole in the extortion charge, pointing out that Baker could not be found guilty of stealing the $200 from Lucy because that money was already his. The lawyers revealed that Baker had a detective mark the four $50 bills before he gave them to Hine, putting two pinholes on the U and S for the "United States" printed on each one. Baker had those marked bills with him to show the court.

After deliberating just an hour and twenty minutes, the jury of twelve men came back with a verdict of not guilty on the extortion charge, but guilty on the charge of false imprisonment. They did not believe Baker's rosy account of November 8. The judge considered Lucy's five hours with Baker a technical violation of the false imprisonment law. He fined Baker one dollar and ordered him to pay court costs, which amounted to about thirty dollars.

After the trial some newspapers defended Baker, but others, like the

New York *Daily News* and *New York Herald*, hailed the verdict as long over-due for the disreputable character who had preyed upon the public for so long; they called for him to be fired and his operation disbanded. That is what happened. Nine days before the trial started Baker was mustered out of the Army, and after the verdict the president ordered his headquarters at 217 Pennsylvania Avenue shuttered.

Baker departed Washington with the conviction that a vast conspiracy of disloyalists and citizens he had arrested sabotaged him during the trial. He also left with a deep hatred of Andrew Johnson, whom he blamed for the guilty verdict, and Edwin Stanton, who he thought had stiffed him on the Booth reward money and did nothing to keep him from being mustered out. Baker moved to Lansing, Michigan, where he invested the money he made in Washington into a hotel venture, which soon failed, wiping out his savings.

Hoping to replenish his finances, Lafayette Baker hired a ghostwriter to compile his memoirs. When he left Washington, he took with him, as Pinkerton had, stacks of government documents and correspondence, which he dumped on the writer to assemble a 704-page tome titled *History of the United States Secret Service*. His memoir outdid Pinkerton's in exaggerating his wartime service.* Among the documents Baker had hoped to add to the pile he gave the ghostwriter was the diary Conger took from Booth, which Baker had turned over to Stanton. Baker claimed Stanton promised him the diary for his book but had reneged.

On February 6, 1867, the House Judiciary Committee began hearing witnesses in its investigation of the impeachment of Andrew Johnson, which would gain momentum by his move to oust Stanton. The committee held the sessions behind closed doors. Johnson enlisted the help of Allan Pinkerton, who had a female agent sweet-talk one of the panel's male stenographers into slipping her daily transcripts of the hearings, which were passed to the White House. Johnson could not have liked what he read in the transcript for the first day.

---

*The title is also misleading because his agency was not the forerunner of today's U.S. Secret Service.

Lafayette Baker was the opening witness. On February 6 and over the course of six more appearances before the Judiciary Committee, Baker dropped bombshell after bombshell. He testified that in the fall of 1865 he obtained a letter Johnson had written to Jefferson Davis in early 1864 when he was military governor of Tennessee, which indicated that the two had been secretly corresponding. Baker claimed that in the letter he read, Johnson offered policy and military advice to Davis and disclosed to the Confederate president the number of troops defending Washington. In September 1865, Baker testified, a Nashville telegraph operator told him Johnson had sent "very scandalous" telegrams to that city about a conspiracy to overrun the loyalist government in Tennessee. Baker claimed Johnson sent the message from the War Department telegraph office using a secret cipher Stanton did not know about. He told the congressmen that the Executive Branch, led by Seward, tried to suppress the tell-all book he was writing exposing the pardon broker affair and other scandals in the Johnson administration. For good measure, he alleged that Johnson was having an affair with the notorious Lucy Cobb.

On the hearing's second day, the committee chairman showed Baker Booth's diary, which Conger had taken from the actor's pocket. Baker inspected it at the witness table and dropped his final bombshell.

Not much larger than a wallet, it was not a diary per se but rather an appointment book for 1864, in which Booth began writing entries shortly before the assassination. Baker told the committee the diary was missing as many as eighteen pages that had been torn out. Baker said he was certain no pages were missing when he handed it to Stanton at his home. The implication of Baker's testimony was that Stanton had torn out the pages when he read the diary. Some newspapers had reported on the actor's journal in April 1865, but its existence was quickly forgotten by the press. Prosecutors never introduced the diary as evidence during the trial for the assassination conspirators.

Baker's allegations were earthshaking. He was accusing Johnson, an avowed Unionist, of secretly conspiring with the president of the Confederacy during the war. Radical Republicans took Baker's story further, suggesting that Johnson's collaboration with Davis was more sinister—that he joined in the plot to assassinate Lincoln so he could assume the presidency. The Radicals conjectured that Stanton tore out the pages as Baker alleged because they contained writing that connected the war secretary and President Johnson to the assassination plot. Stanton, according to one story later unspooled, headed a group of fifty northern politicians and military men who wanted Lincoln removed. Baker's testimony helped spawn wild theories that Stanton and Johnson participated in the plot to assassinate Lincoln. Ironically, conspiracy peddlers later speculated that Baker was a Johnson and Stanton accomplice in the plot. The detective had found Booth so quickly because he knew of his assassination plan and escape route. Baker's men then killed the actor to shut him up.

In 1977, the FBI examined Booth's pocket diary for any signs or invisible writing that might tie Johnson, Stanton, or others to the assassination. The bureau's lab found nothing.

Baker's explosive congressional testimony was a tapestry of lies the committee members had little difficulty unraveling with follow-up questions and interrogations of other witnesses. Baker admitted he did not have the letter Johnson allegedly wrote Davis. As for the scandalous telegrams Johnson supposedly sent to Nashville, Baker admitted he never actually saw them. Brigadier General Thomas Eckert, who ran the military telegraph office, testified that the story was false. Johnson never sent a message in a secret cipher from that office. Seward hotly denied before the committee that he ever tried to interfere with the publication of Baker's book.

Baker finally admitted that he never carefully read the Booth diary the brief time he saw it. What's more, everybody who came in contact with the journal—including Baker's own men—contradicted his account of the missing pages. Conger, for example, testified that he had a chance to read the diary carefully on his long boat trip back to Washington with Booth's possessions and noticed that pages had been torn out. Joseph Holt, the chief prosecutor for the assassination conspiracy trial, said he didn't introduce the diary as evidence because there was nothing in it incriminating to anyone except Booth, and Booth was dead. Writing in pencil, the actor recounted on its pages proudly shooting Lincoln at Ford's Theatre and "being hunted like a dog" afterward.

The most plausible explanation for the missing pages is that Booth ripped them out to use as writing paper for notes he sent. Military historian David Eicher summarizes it best: Civil War "literature abounds with hypotheses about conspiracies involving everyone from the Confederate government to Stanton to Catholics to Jefferson Davis to foreign governments. The simple facts, extensively analyzed at a microscopic level, support the case that Booth and his cohorts were loosely connected with Confederate authorities but pulled off the final version of their attacks essentially on their own, impelled by the collapse of the Confederacy."

The five-member Republican majority on the Judiciary Committee never mentioned Baker's charges in their final report recommending Johnson's impeachment, signaling that they did not think much of the allegations he made. Two Democrats were scathing in their minority report: "It is doubtful whether [Baker] has in any one thing told the truth, even by accident." The Democratic committeemen found it appalling "that this miserable wretch for years held, as it were, in the hollow of his hand, the liberties of the American people."

Baker moved back to Philadelphia with Jennie. His book did not sell well. Stripped of his power, disgraced and dejected, he became a recluse in his house at 1738 Coates Street. In the spring of 1868 he contracted typhoid fever and lost the will to live. He died in his home, with Jennie at his side, in the early morning on July 3. He was forty-two years old. His death certificate listed the cause as spinal meningitis, which can sometimes be a complication of typhoid fever. Conspiracy enthusiasts were convinced that Stanton's agents poisoned him to keep him from spilling more secrets on the Lincoln assassination.

Newspapers speculated that Baker died with hundreds of thousands of dollars socked away from his graft. That was not true. He was not destitute when he passed, but he was hardly wealthy. In his will he left $605 to his six brothers and sisters and directed that whatever remained go to his wife, Jennie.

The New York *Evening Post* published an editorial after his death, which aptly encapsulated Baker's life. "He was an adventurer, keen and unscrupulous and active. His services were probably thought necessary during the war, when Washington was filled with spies." The paper concluded that Baker was ruthlessly efficient at suppressing insurrection, but "very often deceived by the rogues who it was his business to entrap; and kept in profound ignorance of really important plots, while he was excited by false reports. It will always be thus with the head of what is called a 'Secret Police' whose operations are likely to be secret to all honest people but very transparent to the rogues."

Patrick had work piled up for George Sharpe and his information bureau when his deputy finished processing parole records in Washington and returned to occupied Richmond in May 1865. Scores of legal matters had to be settled to rent spaces for Union troops and to find rightful owners for abandoned goods and real estate in the city. Police detectives had to be organized to hunt war criminals and common criminals. Sharpe brought Patrick the latest political news as he always did from the capital. It was depressing. Washington was in a "muddle," Sharpe told his boss. Political intrigue gripped the city after Lincoln's death. General Butler, Sharpe said, was now trying to capitalize on the assassination and drive Stanton out of office so he could replace him as war secretary.

Patrick cleared out Confederate soldiers in Union prison pens and sent them home to plant summer crops. He was besieged by northern sightseers come to gawk at the captured city. Meanwhile, Babcock headed up a squad of about a dozen detectives, which included former Richmond underground operatives like F. W. E. Lohmann, who chased escaped convicts.

Patrick sympathized with ex-Confederates trying to pick up the pieces of their lives after the war. He took long walks with Robert E. Lee to talk about the future and he kept in regular touch with the Rebel commander's son and daughter. "Troubles are to come" for the South, Patrick wrote after one of his lengthy conversations with Lee, which "made me feel very sad." He had far less sympathy for former slaves. He called the Freedmen's Bureau, which Lincoln established to aid destitute black families, the "Nigger Bureau." "I never can love these people very strongly, who are so bitter against the South," he wrote in his diary.

Patrick called on Van Lew occasionally to see how she was faring.

Elizabeth visited his office occasionally—to dress him down for what she thought were his "secession proclivities." Van Lew found his cozying up to "Rebel society" disgusting. Grant felt the same and on July 7 he removed Patrick from his provost marshal post.

Sharpe did not stick around long in Richmond. On June 3 he finally secured his relief from Grant's headquarters as Patrick's deputy and joined his old 120th Regiment on its return home. He mustered out of the Army shortly after that, having been made a major general of the volunteers.

The steamer *Thomas Cornell* landed at the Hudson River dock for Rondout on June 9. A large crowd, many with tears in their eyes, cheered and threw bouquets as the 120th troops disembarked. The regiment marched through a massive arch in the upper part of the town erected with evergreens and flowers topped by a live eagle, and continued to Kingston, finally halting at the Academy green, where another large crowd had assembled to hear politicians speak, listen to schoolchildren sing "Victory at Last," and watch Sharpe present an elegant sword as a gift to the colonel then commanding the 120th. Sharpe was also given a sword engraved with the names of the Civil War battles he had fought in. Family legend later had it that he tied a black crepe ribbon to the sword's hilt that was a piece of Lincoln's bier Sharpe took as a memento when he was detailed to the funeral.

Sharpe helped organize a 120th regimental alumni group, which met annually each winter to reminisce and hear speeches from retired Union generals and each summer to picnic. In 1888 he chaired a committee to erect a monument for the 120th at Gettysburg. At its dedication that June, a special train took him and other 120th members to the battlefield. A superb orator with a sonorous and powerful voice, Sharpe delivered an eloquent dedication speech, borrowing from Lincoln in his phrasing:

> Here the greatest deeds have been wrought, and here the most eloquent words have been spoken; for here on these heights of Gettysburg, contemporaneously with Vicksburg, were the crucial hours of the stupendous conflict, when it was settled, not for a day, but for all time, that the government of the people, for the people and by the people should not perish from the earth.

It brought tears to the eyes of many of the men listening. They had reason to be emotional. The regiment left Kingston with 906 soldiers; in less than three years 394 had been wounded in action and 297 killed by hostile fire, disease, or as prisoners.

In all the speeches he gave on the war years at 120th reunions and before civic groups, Sharpe almost never talked about the spy organization he led. The one exception was a lecture he gave in 1876 at the Harlem Congregational Church, where he touched on the intelligence his information bureau provided and praised "the lady" in Richmond, Elizabeth Van Lew. Likewise, Patrick, when he reminisced about the war, preferred to recall his days as a brigade commander in combat rather than the intelligence collection he oversaw as provost marshal. Unlike Pinkerton and Baker, Sharpe never wrote a postwar memoir about his spy organization. Neither did Babcock. Henry, one of Sharpe's sons who became a major general in the Army, tried to convince his father to write a history of his espionage work. Sharpe had brought home a number of important intelligence documents. Henry wanted to get in touch with Van Lew, about whom his father had told him so much, to see if there was anything in her papers that might be useful in assembling an account of the Bureau of Military Information, but he never did. And his father never wrote a history.

Sharpe settled into a comfortable family residence in Kingston, aptly called "the Orchard" because the acreage around it was devoted to fruit trees. He hosted a number of prominent visitors to his home, such as Grant, Hooker, Sherman, and future president (as well as close friend) Chester A. Arthur. The spymaster maintained his literary flair, writing a lengthy article, for example, on the Revolutionary War history of Kingston for its 1877 centennial celebration. Invitations to the elegant dinner parties Carrie staged with her European gourmet became prized among Kingston society.

Sharpe did not stay planted at home with his law practice. In January 1867, he sailed for Europe on a spy mission. Seward dispatched him to hunt for American citizens abroad who might have been involved in the Lincoln murder conspiracy and, in particular, who might have helped John Surratt Jr. Suspected of plotting with Booth to kidnap Lincoln and then of being part of the assassination plan, Mary Surratt's son had remained hidden in Canada while she was tried and hanged. With the help of former Rebel agents, he sailed to Liverpool and eventually made his way to the Papal States, which were territories on the Italian peninsula then under the rule of the pope. He enlisted in the pope's army, the Papal Zouaves, and hid out using the alias "John Watson" until an acquaintance recognized him and tipped off the U.S. minister in Rome. Surratt was arrested but managed to escape to Alexandria, Egypt, where he was arrested once more by U.S. officials and sent back to Washington in early 1867 for trial.

For six months, Sharpe roamed Liverpool, London, Paris, Brussels, and Rome—often covertly so he wouldn't arouse suspicion among possible Surratt cohorts or local authorities—to retrace the fugitive's steps and hunt for Americans who might have helped him along the way. He had a grand time touring Europe, "enjoying it hugely," he said. He attended a formal dinner at the French ambassador's residence in Rome and discussed European geopolitics with everyone along the way. Sharpe found American prestige had risen "one monstrous stride" because of the Union victory, he wrote his uncle—though Europeans were perplexed over how magnanimous the North had been to the South after the war. Sharpe also ran across Europeans "who hate us because we have succeeded."

He returned to Washington in July and reported to Seward that he had found no proof of Americans in Europe helping Surratt that was strong enough for the U.S. government to demand their extradition. The next year, Seward sent Sharpe on another fact-finding trip—this time to Vermont to investigate plans by the Fenians, a radical Irish group, to invade Canada. After his two trips, a newspaper touted him as a good candidate for a diplomatic posting.

No position overseas came his way. Back home, Sharpe became a proud member of what was called "the Grant family of generals"—subordinates from the war who revered the Army commander and remained at his beck and call. Sharpe, who had become a family friend, campaigned for Grant during the 1868 presidential election and afterward performed political favors for the White House.

Patrick was not a family member. Disgusted with Radical Republicans, he remained a loyal Democrat and ran for New York State treasurer. He was defeated and turned his attention to his first love, tending his cropland near

Manlius, New York, and speaking around the state to agricultural societies on the virtues of scientific farming.

Grant rewarded his intelligence chief when he became president, appointing him U.S. marshal for the Southern District of New York in 1870, where William M. "Boss" Tweed's political machine ruled. One of Sharpe's first jobs was taking the census and battling Tweed and city authorities, who had rigged the count in the past to favor Democrats. At one point, Tweed followers threatened Sharpe's life. Two Tweed men, one a Democratic central committee member, eventually were convicted and Sharpe was praised for finally imposing an accurate count.

In 1873, Grant made Sharpe surveyor of the Port of New York, a position he held for the next five years. He also chaired a commission promoting commercial relations between the United States and Central and South America and was given the rank of envoy extraordinary and minister plenipotentiary. Sharpe tried his hand at elective office in 1878, winning a seat in the New York Assembly as a Republican. Two years later he was made the legislature's speaker, often showing an irascible streak that angered fellow lawmakers and party bigwigs. In 1890, he left his position as president of the National Bank of Rondout for one more government post as a member of the seven-person Board of U.S. General Appraisers, which decided appeals cases on the duties for imported goods. It was a prestigious job that paid more than a federal judgeship. He stayed on the board until just after he turned seventy-one in 1899.

Sharpe then returned to Kingston to begin a lonely retirement. Suffering from rheumatic gout, Carrie had died, which devastated him and weakened his resolve to live. He presented to the First Reformed Church in Kingston a four-foot-high bronze statue of an angel in memory of her.

After his wife died in 1880, Marsena Patrick, afflicted with rheumatism, moved to Dayton, Ohio, where he became governor of the Central Branch National Home for Disabled Volunteer Soldiers. As he had in the Army, Patrick quickly earned a reputation as a strict disciplinarian running the home, which angered some in Congress. He died eight years later.

Historians occasionally wrote to John Babcock after the war for his estimates on the number of soldiers in Lee's army. Babcock's intelligence was still considered a reliable source. He tried to retrieve his records from the Sturgis Rifles in Illinois and at one point to obtain an appointment as a civil service clerk so he could write a history of the information bureau. He exchanged regular letters with Sharpe's son Henry to pursue the idea. But nothing came of the effort and Babcock eventually settled in Mount Vernon, New York, where he set up a practice as an architect.

Still an avid sculler, Babcock helped create the National Association of Amateur Oarsmen, which later became the U.S. Rowing Association. He invented the sliding seat used in sculling boats. With two other men, he also helped found the New York Athletic Club in 1868 and was elected its first vice president. His health began to decline by 1905. He found bicycle riding improved it some. He died of a stroke in 1908.

Shortly before Christmas in 1899, Sharpe took the train to New York City to spend the holidays with his daughter and her husband at their town house on East 39th Street. He fell seriously ill just after New Year's Day. Sharpe, who was overweight, underwent surgery but because of his advanced age he did not survive. He died the night of January 13, 1900, with his daughter and two sons at his bedside.

A large crowd, many of them old soldiers, assembled for his funeral on January 16 at the Sharpe family home on Albany Avenue in Kingston. The battle-scarred flag of the 120th Regiment covered his casket. Uptown schools were let out early so teachers could attend the service. The American flag flew at half-staff at all the schools. Reverend Dr. J. G. Van Slyke delivered the eulogy. "The homage which the world is waiting to pay is due in part to the superior compass of his intelligence," Van Slyke said of Sharpe, "in part to the embellishments of culture which draped his native vigor and in part to the astounding generosity of his heart."

Sharpe was buried in the family plot at Wiltwyck Cemetery. A spot at Kingston's Academy green on the corner of Albany Avenue and Maiden Lane was later selected for a memorial to be erected honoring the spymaster, but it was never built. At the 120th annual reunion in 1912, Sharpe's son Severyn and his little daughter passed out bronze medals with a bas-relief of the general to the eighty-eight members of the regiment still alive.

· · ·

Months after Richmond's surrender, Grant and his wife, Julia, paid a visit to Church Hill to thank Elizabeth Van Lew for her wartime service. General Butler, her first handler, wrote her an effusive note. "There is no lady I would rather meet than yourself," he said, and promised to help her whenever he could.

The city was not as friendly. Richmond neighbors continued to despise Van Lew for her northern sympathies. They shunned her "as if I were plague-stricken," she wrote, insulting the spinster when she walked the streets, refusing to grant her access to nearby summer resorts, all of which pained Elizabeth greatly. Angry whites were further revolted by her outspoken support of civil rights for blacks after the war. Virginia's former governor Henry Wise was outraged when he learned that Elizabeth's mother—"the traitorous old Mrs. Van Lew," a correspondent wrote—danced at a party with Union major general Alfred H. Terry, who was assistant commissioner of the Freedmen's Bureau in the state. When Elizabeth puttered outside in her garden (she now refused to pick the flowers regarding it as vandalism against nature's beauty) children walking by screamed: "Witch, witch!"

Van Lew grew just as angry at her city. The men charting Virginia's future under the Johnson administration were the same violent secessionists who brought the state to ruin, she believed. Richmond's racial caste system she had fought so long did not change after the war, Van Lew lamented. Blacks and Unionists were still persecuted. Ex-Confederates still ruled. Every year, when taxes were due, she refused to pay, or if she did she filed a written protest with her return, which she published in the newspapers, complaining that it was "taxation without representation," because as a woman she was barred from voting. Her unpaid tax bill soon totaled $5,000.

Church Hill remained her haven. Inside the mansion she frequently entertained "cultured people," as a nephew put it, who believed as she did and who often came just to meet the famous spy. Suffragette Susan B. Anthony spent several days as a houseguest. Van Lew had a wide range of literary friends, she read Alexander Pope, Joseph Addison, and Victor Hugo avidly, and she corresponded with Frederick Douglass, *New York Tribune* editor Horace Greeley, and future Supreme Court associate justice Oliver Wendell Holmes Jr.

Van Lew remained a kindly woman, always deeply touched by the condition of the poor—white and black—and always eager to help anyone she considered oppressed. She visited city jails to improve conditions for prisoners. When a friend's home burned down, she let him stay in the house on her farm outside Richmond for two years rent-free. She also helped an Army investigator assemble a case against a traitorous Union lieutenant the Rebels placed in Libby Prison to spy on federal inmates.

Van Lew asked the War Department in Washington to send her all her intelligence reports as well as other documents kept on file about her Richmond operation. She wanted them to build a case for the payment claim she planned to submit for her wartime service—and to ensure that none of the material about her spying was made public. Northern newspapers soon began publishing stories about her heroism and that of her underground in aiding Union prisoners. But there was no mention of her espionage. She wanted to keep it that way. She confided with no one outside the ring about her spy work, not even close friends, never trusting them to keep it a secret. Any revelation of the full extent of her intelligence network would invite severe retaliation from Richmonders, she knew. The War Department sent her the files and after she extracted what she needed for her compensation claim, she burned them.

Mary Bowser spoke little after the war about her spying, knowing that southern retribution for a black woman would be even more severe. Her marriage to Wilson Bowser ended before the Confederate surrender and she reverted to her maiden name, Mary Richards. For more than a year she traveled around Virginia and Florida, intent on putting the education Van Lew gave her to good use by teaching blacks to read and write. She complained to Patrick when he was Richmond's provost marshal about the hostility whites showed toward the school she set up in the city for 180 African American students.

By February 1867, Mary was teaching at a Freedmen's school in St. Mary's, Georgia, along the Atlantic Coast. She married a man named Garvin, who soon left for Havana. Mary had fifty-five black students, twenty of whom were girls she also taught to sew. She was always short of books and the parents had no money to pay for their kids' education, so Mary used $30 of the $40 the Freedmen's Bureau paid her monthly to operate the school; she kept the remaining $10 for her salary. When she was ill, her pupils gathered around her sickbed for their lessons. She also taught Sunday school to twenty-five youngsters.

The work was hard. The parents were eager for their children to learn. Mary at one point met Harriet Beecher Stowe when the famed author of *Uncle Tom's Cabin* visited St. Mary's. Yet she despaired over whether she was making a difference. Mary wrote her supervisor at the Freedmen's Bureau that she was willing to do what she could to teach these children, but she feared "that in the end it will not prove much."

Van Lew was nearly out of money after the war ended, with no way to replenish her finances—her only assets the Church Hill mansion and her farm outside the city. She could not raise cash with a tell-all spy book. That would put her life and the lives of others from her network in danger, she feared. Her petition to the U.S. government for compensation was only partly successful. The Federals had given her expense money for her spy operation during the war. Afterward, Grant sent her $2,000. But she thought she deserved more. So did Sharpe, who lobbied Congress to pay her $15,000. Van Lew wrote Butler, but he proved to be of no help despite professing earlier that he would do all he could for her. Congress finally approved a $5,000 payment. Van Lew also was paid $100 a month as a Freedmen's Bureau clerk. She would have preferred a position in the bureau with more clout to aid "these poor creatures," she said.

Samuel Ruth, F. W. E. Lohmann, and Charles Carter also asked for remuneration. Sharpe thought they richly deserved $40,000. Stanton refused to pay it. William Rowley, who was wiped out financially after the war, fared a little better. Union soldiers attacking Richmond had destroyed his Henrico County home and seized property they didn't burn. Rowley finally received $1,850 from the War Department's secret service fund—an amount Lafayette Baker, who investigated the case, thought was fair.

Ruth also was destitute after the war, with little of his possessions or home surviving the fire the Confederate Army set when it evacuated Richmond. He managed to hold on to his job as superintendent of the Richmond, Fredericksburg and Potomac Railroad, despite moves to depose him by enemies who suspected him of wartime sabotage. He lobbied Washington to rebuild quickly the rail line's track and bridges that had been destroyed. With his compensation claim rejected, Ruth in November 1869 finally managed to secure a job from the new Grant administration as a revenue collector for the 2nd District of Virginia, based in Petersburg. He resigned from that job on December 2, 1871, after suffering a severe heart attack. He died eight months later from a stroke at age fifty-four.

President Grant took care of his lady in Richmond. On March 17, 1869, he made Van Lew the city's postmaster. It was an important position. The Post Office was the largest and most politicized of federal agencies, with thousands of patronage jobs to dole out. A postmaster for a large city like Richmond held a coveted civil service post, well paid with a $4,000-a-year-salary, whose occupant had political muscle and could use the position as a stepping-stone to higher office. Few women had snared these appointments, although more would under Grant.

Richmond newspapers were predictably outraged; Grant had appointed not only a traitor to the southern cause but also a radical feminist. Even some northern papers condemned Van Lew's selection. Reports about her espionage network now surfaced, fueling even more resentment. Other northern papers, however, praised the selection, as did Union soldiers around the country who had not forgotten her aid to their comrades in Rebel prisons.

Van Lew's financial support of relatives, contributions she made to black charities, plus payments she had to make on a large debt ate up a good deal of her new paycheck. Operating out of offices in the customs house building, she proved a successful postmaster, expanding and modernizing Richmond's mail delivery with a number of reforms. She was also strict with her employees. She refused to back down when mail carriers rebelled against one of her rules and threatened to walk out. Van Lew fired them and Washington backed her up when the carriers appealed. Even more galling for Richmond's elite: Van Lew hired blacks to work in the Post Office and publicly backed African Americans brave enough to protest for civil rights. "We commend Van Lew to somebody's care," fumed a *Petersburg Index* article, "for she is running riot."

Grant was under tremendous pressure in 1873 to fire Van Lew. She took the train to Washington to personally plead her case. Grant appointed her to a second term. A few Richmond papers and one ex–Confederate general grudgingly admitted that she had done a commendable job running the Post Office.

Tragedy struck on September 14, 1875. Van Lew's mother, Eliza, died. At her funeral two days later at Church Hill, her daughter had trouble finding enough pallbearers to carry the casket to the hearse. Those who showed up to pay their respects were ridiculed by neighbors for attending a "nigger funeral."

Her brother, John, moved in with his two daughters. Fewer visitors knocked on the door, save for beggars. For the first time, Van Lew began to feel truly lonely.

During the 1876 presidential campaign, Van Lew knew she was a political liability for Republicans who feared losing Virginia. When Republican Rutherford B. Hayes won (without Virginia in his column), Van Lew lobbied him to keep her job. Opponents pressed just as fiercely, portraying her as too mentally unstable to be postmaster. Hayes in May 1877 replaced her with a former Confederate colonel.

The job loss was a heavy financial blow. Van Lew tried to sell off family property but it brought in little money. She tried to put the mansion on the market but attracted no serious buyers. She lobbied President James Garfield, who succeeded Hayes, to get back her postmaster position, but to no avail. Finally, in 1883, the administration of Chester A. Arthur, who assumed the presidency after Garfield's assassination in 1881, gave her a job as a clerk in the Washington Post Office, which paid just $1,200 a year. Van Lew found life in the capital miserable. Her supervisor was a tyrant, who hated her and eventually cut her small salary. She endured the labor for four years and resigned in 1887.

Nearly seventy years old, nervous and looking worn out, Elizabeth returned to Richmond bitter over the way she felt the federal government had shunned her after the war. She became a constant complainer, irritating her niece Eliza Louise Klapp, who had moved into the mansion to keep house, and began lashing out at others. She became a problem at St. John's Church, arriving late and disrupting the service until congregants finally locked her out. Van Lew wrote in her diary of shouting matches she began having with her niece, claiming that Eliza abused her. The unveiling of Robert E. Lee's statue in Richmond on May 29, 1890, which drew an audience of 100,000, was a breaking point for her. She became increasingly isolated in the city, where residents continued to tell her she would never be forgiven for her betrayal and urged her to leave. "Ever since the Lee unveiling," she wrote in one letter, "I have felt that this was no place for me."

Van Lew was broke. Savings depleted. No income coming in. A for-sale sign remained posted in her front yard. But still no acceptable offers for a property gone to seed and considered tainted because of its owner. Black friends helped and a handful of servants remained on the job, but whites harassed them for coming to her aid. Borrowing money for a stamp, Van Lew wrote to the sister of the late colonel Paul J. Revere, whom she aided when he was a major and an inmate in Libby Prison. She asked for help. The sister had her son, John Phillips Reynolds, organize a fund that Van Lew's Boston friends contributed to. He began sending her annual allotments.

Van Lew soon became close friends with Reynolds, whom she made executor of her estate. On his trips to Richmond, Reynolds frequently told Van Lew it was a shame she had not kept a wartime record. Van Lew finally admitted to him that she had. Reynolds guessed that it was a diary of some sort. She toyed with the idea of publishing it for needed income, but never did. Reynolds assumed she still feared that the diary's revelations would put her in danger. She might have destroyed it, he believed. Reynolds nevertheless kept after Van Lew about the diary.

Her isolation grew. John, who had left the mansion to start a second family, died in 1895. Her sister, Anna, died a short time later and then her niece Eliza passed away five years later. By Christmas of 1899, eighty-one-year-old Elizabeth Van Lew began showing signs of edema, with the swelling beneath her skin becoming painful. Her doctor diagnosed a cancer. She had difficulty moving around her mansion, shorn of many possessions she had sold or donated to the needy over the years. But in the library still sat a bust of Lincoln, on the parlor walls still hung pictures of Grant and prominent Unionists.

Toward the end of September 1900, Van Lew lay in bed at Church Hill drifting in and out of consciousness, "surrounded by a set of hungry, poverty-stricken relations," according to Reynolds. In a lucid moment she told one of her relatives where the diary was hidden. The relative retrieved what appeared to be a manuscript.

Van Lew looked it over and exclaimed: "Why there is nearly twice as much more! What has become of it?" No one knew and Reynolds later said the rest of the manuscript, if it ever existed, was never found. He heard a rumor that some of Van Lew's relations did not want any record preserved and destroyed a large part of her manuscript. Reynolds did not know if that was true. The roughly four hundred pages of journal left behind—a collection of recollections, letters, and mementos—detailed Elizabeth's private battles with Richmond society, her frustrations over slavery, secessionism, and racism in general, and her effort to help Union prisoners. It said little about her spying. Reynolds, who took charge of the manuscript, did find a cipher key Van Lew had used to communicate with Grant.

Elizabeth Van Lew took her last breath at 4:10 a.m. on September 25. Relatives had her body embalmed and placed in a temporary bier in Church Hill's drawing room for a funeral attended by a few family members and friends. Ten pallbearers took her casket to the family plot at Shockoe Hill Cemetery, which was so crowded with graves she had to be buried vertically. No gravestone marked the spot. There was no money for one.

Northern papers like the *New York Times* and *Boston Herald* ran long obituaries with accounts of her aiding prisoners and spying for Grant. The Richmond press did acknowledge her accomplishments and probed the details of the estate she left behind, but otherwise the papers belittled her as something of a flake.

Van Lew's will ordered that her prized rosewood furniture, mahogany secretary, and bookcases be sent to Boston and sold there by her friends to fetch what she thought would be the best price. But the Boston auction brought in only $1,000 from the professional bargain hunters who attended. Her Massachusetts friends sent the proceeds to Richmond to pay the bills she owed. The manuscript Reynolds took control of eventually found its way into a historical archive. She bequeathed Church Hill and the rest of her property to her only niece left alive, Annie Randolph Hall. The items not sent to Boston were auctioned at Church Hill, where curious Richmonders roamed to make their bids. A bureau in her bedroom fetched $10, a safe in her dining room sold for $1.80. Reporters prowling the mansion discovered the attic hideaway behind the washstand, where Van Lew hid Union prisoners.

Cleaned out, the mansion still attracted sightseers. A "Keep Out" sign was eventually put up. Church Hill was later bought and renovated for the Virginia Club. In 1911, the city of Richmond tore it down and built an elementary school on the land.

In 1902, Van Lew's Massachusetts friends delivered a rough-cut, one-ton gray composite stone from the Bay State for her grave at Shockoe Hill Cemetery. On the side of the stone was embedded a heavy metal plaque engraved with the inscription:

ELIZABETH L. VAN LEW

1818–1900

She risked everything that is dear to man—friends-fortune-comfort-health-life itself—all for the one absorbing desire of her heart—that slavery might be abolished and the Union preserved.

—

THIS BOULDER

From the Capitol Hill in Boston is a tribute from Massachusetts friends.

These were fitting words for one of the best of Lincoln's spies.

ACKNOWLEDGMENTS

You cannot write about the Civil War without leaning on the work of many other historians. The number of nonfiction and fiction books written about this conflict is staggering. Type "Civil War" into the Amazon.com search box and it spits out more than 50,000 results. I quickly discovered, however, that credible books on Civil War intelligence are few and far between. But there are good ones out there. Research on the subject must start with Edwin C. Fishel's *The Secret War for the Union*, an encyclopedic account of military intelligence collection primarily in the Eastern Theater through 1863. I read it twice and pored through Fishel's valuable research papers for his massive volume, which are stored at Georgetown University's Special Collections Research Center. For the history of intelligence collection in that theater from 1864 to the end of the war there is no better book than William B. Feis's *Grant's Secret Service*. I can't thank Dr. Feis enough for his encouragement while I labored with my project. I also found Thomas J. Ryan's *Spies, Scouts, and Secrets in the Gettysburg Campaign* extremely useful. Among the military histories on which I relied the most heavily were James M. McPherson's *Battle Cry of Freedom*, Bruce Catton's three-volume *The Centennial History of the Civil War*, David J. Eicher's *The Longest Night*, and the books Stephen W. Sears wrote on the Peninsula campaign and the Battles of Antietam, Chancellorsville, and Gettysburg.

As for my four main characters, Allan Pinkerton and Lafayette Baker wrote memoirs about their Civil War experience, which must be read with caution because they are littered with factual errors, embellishments, and fabrications. Elizabeth Van Lew left behind a journal of recollections, letters, and mementos, which historian David D. Ryan thankfully has edited and published, titled *A Yankee Spy in Richmond*.

George Sharpe wrote no memoir. Numerous biographies have been written on Pinkerton. I found *Allan Pinkerton: The First Private Eye*, by James Mackay, the most useful. Two short biographies were published in the 1960s on Baker. I want to thank Bonnie Mogelever Pollack, who let me look through the research papers of her father, Jacob Mogelever, who wrote one of the Baker biographies, *Death to Traitors*. Elizabeth R. Varon wrote a superb biography of Van Lew titled *Southern Lady, Yankee Spy*. Professor Varon also was generous in helping me hunt for material on Van Lew's spy ring. Historical novelist Lois Leveen helped as well with postwar news clippings she discovered on Van Lew servant Mary Richards. Peter Tsouras has written a biography of George Sharpe, which is also a compilation of unit histories for his combat commands and the Bureau of Military Information.

I want to thank the National Park Service, which does a commendable job maintaining Civil War battlefields. My rides and walks through the Antietam, Chancellorsville, Spotsylvania, Gettysburg, and Wilderness battlefields, armed with brochures and CDs the Park Service provides, gave me an important ground-level education into how intelligence affected the outcomes of these conflicts. At Gettysburg, my guide, John R. Krohn, was particularly helpful in taking me through this complex engagement.

Archivists are the unsung heroes of history books. I had some of the best in the business directing me among the millions of pages of Civil War documents stored in archives and libraries around the country. Michael Musick, who retired as the Subject Area Expert for the U.S. Civil War at the National Archives and Records Administration, spent hours giving me tutorials on what to look for in the Archives' vast collection in Washington, D.C. Trevor Plante, chief of reference at the Archives, directed me to collections where he thought I might find valuable information on my four spies, while archivists DeAnne Blanton, William H. Davis, and Cate Brennan cheerfully retrieved files for me from different Civil War record groups. At the Library of Congress, Michelle Krowl, the Civil War and Reconstruction Specialist in its Manuscript Division, pointed me to important material in the Pinkerton National Detective Agency Records, George B. McClellan Papers, and sixteen other collections. Dr. Krowl also provided me copies of helpful letters and documents she had dug up in her research.

With the aid of American history curator Olga Tsapina, I found important material in the Joseph Hooker Papers, Ward Hill Lamon Collection, and a half-dozen other collections at the Huntington Library in San Marino, California. In Richmond, the staff at the Virginia Historical Society helped me find letters on Van Lew in three collections. The Library of Virginia has a copy of Van Lew's journal (the original is stored at the New York Public Library), a half-dozen collections with material on the Richmond spymaster and her family, as well as her estate appraisal from the Accounts of Fiduciaries for the City of Richmond Chancery Court. My thanks to Edward F. Jewett, Clerk of the Circuit Court of Richmond, for finding documents on Van Lew family civil actions as well as Elizabeth Van Lew's will in the Chancery Court records. I also appreciate American Civil War Museum historian John M. Coski sending me from the museum's collection a copy of Varina Davis's letter denying that Van Lew ever planted Mary Richards in the Confederate White House to spy on them.

Mark McMurray, curator of special collections at St. Lawrence University's library in Canton, New York, helped with my review of its Pryce Lewis Collection. Deana Preston with the Senate House State Historic Site at Kingston, New York, showed me important documents, reports, and letters in its collections for George Sharpe and his family. The staff at the New York State Library's Manuscript and Special Collections Unit in Albany helped with my review of its Kingston Collection and in the main library I found articles on Sharpe and speeches by the spymaster. I want to thank Tammy Kiter, reference librarian at the New-York Historical Society Museum & Library, who found for me documents and reminiscences related to George Sharpe and Lafayette Baker.

In Philadelphia, the staff at the Historical Society of Pennsylvania retrieved items for me from its George G. Meade Collection and several other collections. I want to thank Claudine Catalano-Pipino, records coordinator in Philadelphia's Register of Wills, who found for me Lafayette Baker's will. Scott Taylor, manuscripts archivist at Georgetown University Library's Booth Family Center for Special Collections, pulled out Edwin Fishel's research papers for me to review and found documents related to Lafayette Baker in another collection. The staff at the Special Collections Research Center in the College of William & Mary's Swem Library aided in my review of its Elizabeth Van Lew Collection. I found material in the Southern Historical Collection at the University of North Carolina at Chapel Hill's Wilson Special Collections Library and in Duke University's David M. Rubenstein Rare Book & Manuscript Library. I also want to thank researcher Ginger Frere, who retrieved for me letters from the Allan Pinkerton Papers at the Chicago History Museum, and researcher Susan Burneson, who retrieved for me letters related to Elizabeth Van Lew at the University of Texas at Austin's Dolph Briscoe Center for American History.

Michael Berry sent me from his private collection a copy of an important letter George Bangs wrote his mother in 1863. I can't thank enough Stephen Baker and Ann Baker Cottrell, descendants of Lafayette Baker, who provided me with family letters, genealogies, news clippings, and the memoirs of Joseph Stannard Baker from their private collections. Bart Hall, the great-great-grandson of Elizabeth Van Lew's brother, John, answered numerous questions from me on the Van Lew family and recounted stories that were passed down from generation to generation.

I can't thank enough Elaine Shannon and Dan Morgan, who put me up in their lovely home during the months I spent researching at the National Archives and Library of Congress in Washington. Elaine and Dan were working on their own book projects during my stay, which made my evenings there even more enjoyable as we shared stories about the research or writing we accomplished each day. I also owe a debt of gratitude to Kirk and Evee Jonas, dear friends who let me stay with them during my research in Richmond. Evee also was so kind to lend me history books on Richmond from her collection.

Four Civil War scholars—Michael Musick, Michelle Krowl, William Feis, and Ethan Rafuse—carefully reviewed my first draft, spotting errors that needed correcting and making valuable suggestions for improving the manuscript. I am eternally in their debt. Of course, the conclusions and any errors that remain in the book are all mine.

Kristine Dahl, my literary agent and good friend, became, as she has with all my books, a trusted adviser on *Lincoln's Spies*. I was blessed that Simon & Schuster, which has published some of the best books on Lincoln and the Civil War, enthusiastically backed my addition to their library and that Alice Mayhew, who has edited many of those books, guided me for our second project working together. Alice at the outset helped me shape the concept for the story and encouraged me along the way during my research. After I turned in the manuscript, she made superb suggestions for how to reorganize certain chapters and trim other parts. I followed them all and I'm glad I did. It has been a joy to have her as my editor. My thanks also to editor Stuart Roberts and associate editor Amar Deol, who attended to countless details getting the manuscript ready for publication. Copy editor Tom Pitoniak ably polished my final draft.

Finally, I could not have begun or completed this book without the love and patience of my dear wife, Judy. She endured many months of me being away prowling libraries and archives around the country. Between hours taking care of grandchildren she corrected book chapters as I wrote them and diplomatically pointed out spots where she thought the narrative dragged. It is to the latest two grandchildren to arrive in our family, Cameron and Eva, that this book is dedicated.

SELECTED BIBLIOGRAPHY

MANUSCRIPT COLLECTIONS

In the source notes, abbreviations are used for archives, libraries, museums, and the manuscript collections in them.

ACS: American Colonization Society Records, Library of Congress
ACW: American Civil War Museum, Richmond
AG: Augustus P. Green Collection, New-York Historical Society Museum & Library
AJP: Andrew Johnson Papers, Library of Congress
ALD: Abraham Lincoln Papers, Library of Congress Digital
APP: Allan Pinkerton Papers, Chicago History Museum
BL: Benson Lossing Papers, Huntington Library
CH: Chicago History Museum
CM: Claude M. Monteiro Collection, Library of Virginia
DB: Donald Benham Civil War Collection, Library of Congress
DCP: Daniel S. Curtis Papers, Georgetown University Library
DU: Duke University David M. Rubenstein Rare Book & Manuscript Library
EF: Edwin C. Fishel Papers, Georgetown University Library
ELC: Elizabeth Van Lew Collection, College of William & Mary, Swem Library
EMSP: Edwin M. Stanton Papers, Library of Congress Digital
EVLP: Elizabeth Van Lew Papers, Library of Virginia
FD: Ferdinand J. Deer Collection, 1492–1925, Collection 175, Series LXIV, Generals of the Civil War, Historical Society of Pennsylvania

FP: Felton Family Papers, Historical Society of Pennsylvania

GG: George Kooglar Gilmer Papers, Virginia Historical Society

GMC: George G. Meade Collection, Historical Society of Pennsylvania

GMP: George B. McClellan Papers, Library of Congress

GNMP: Gettysburg National Military Park Library

GSF: American Historical Manuscript Collection, George H. Sharpe File, New-York Historical Society Museum & Library

GU: Georgetown University Library Special Collections Research Center

HF: Hull Family Papers, Virginia Historical Society

HL: The Huntington Library

HO: Henry Threat Owen Papers, Virginia Historical Society

HP: Historical Society of Pennsylvania

HS: Horatio Seymour Letters, New-York Historical Society Museum & Library

IASA: Institute of Aerospace Sciences Archives (Correspondence of T. S. C. Lowe), Library of Congress

JCBP: John C. Babcock Papers, Library of Congress

JDC: Jefferson Davis Correspondence, 1841–62, Duke University David M. Rubenstein Rare Book & Manuscript Library

JDP: John Aldophus Bernard Dahlgren Papers, Library of Congress

JE: James Eldridge Collection, Huntington Library

JHOP: Joseph Holt Papers, Library of Congress

JHP: Joseph Hooker Papers, Huntington Library

JJP: Joseph E. Johnston Papers, Library of Congress

JN: John G. Nicolay Papers, Library of Congress

KS: Kingston Senate House State Historic Site

LC: Library of Congress

LVA: Library of Virginia

M221: Letters Received by the Secretary of War, Main Series, 1801–70, National Archives

M2096: Correspondence and Issuances, Headquarters of the Army of the Potomac, 1861–65, National Archives

M491: Register of Letters Received by the Secretary of War, Irregular Series, 1861–66, National Archives

M492: Letters Received by the Secretary of War, Irregular Series, 1861–66, National Archives

M799: Records of the Superintendent of Education for the State of Georgia Bureau of Refugees, Freedmen, and Abandoned Lands, 1865–70, National Archives

MA: Main Archives, Kingston Senate House State Historic Site

MPD: Marsena Patrick Diaries, Library of Congress

NA: National Archives and Records Administration

NY: New York Public Library, Manuscripts and Archives

NYH: New-York Historical Society Museum & Library

OC: Online Catalogue, Library of Virginia

OR: U.S. War Department, *The War of the Rebellion: A Compilation of the Official Records of the Union and Confederate Armies*, Washington, D.C.: U.S. Government Printing Office, 1880–1900. The volumes are usually divided into separate bound parts. All citations will refer to Series 1 unless otherwise noted. Each citation will begin with the volume number, followed by the part number (if the volume has more than one part) and the page number. So Series 1, Volume 17, of the Official Records, Part 2, page 130, will be cited as OR-17.2:130. For a citation in a series other than Series 1, such as for Series 2, Volume 4, page 168, it will be listed as OR-S2.4:168.

PLC: Pryce Lewis Collection, St. Lawrence University Libraries

PND: Pinkerton National Detective Agency Records, Library of Congress

PPF: P. Phillips Family Papers, Library of Congress

RG107, 976-2206: Office of the Secretary of War, Registered Letters Received, 1873, National Archives

RG107, E: 68: Records of the Secretary of War, Records Concerning the Conduct and Loyalty of Certain Union Army Officers, Civilian Employees of the War Department and U.S. Citizens During the Civil War, National Archives

RG107, M473: Telegrams Collected by the Office of the Secretary of War (bound), 1861–82, National Archives

RG107, M504: Telegrams Collected by the Office of the Secretary of War (unbound), 1860–70, National Archives

RG108: Records of the Headquarters of the Army, Headquarters in the Field, National Archives

RG108, E: 1: Records of the Army, Endorsements Sent by Gen. Grant, March 1864–July 1867, National Archives

RG108, E: 112: Records of the Headquarters of the Army, Reports Containing Military Intelligence Received by Lt. Gen. U.S. Grant, March 1864–March 1865, National Archives

RG109: Union Provost Marshal's File on Papers Relating to Two or More Civilians, National Archives

RG109, M345: Union Provost Marshal's File of Papers Relating to Individual Civilians, National Archives

RG109, M416: Union Provost Marshal's File of Papers Relating to Two or More Civilians, National Archives

RG109, M437: Letters Received by the Confederate Secretary of War, 1861–1865, National Archives

RG109, M474: Letters Received by the Confederate Adjutant and Inspector General, 1861–65, National Archives

RG110: Provost Marshal General's Office, L. C. Baker Papers, 1862–66, National Archives

RG110, E: 31: Records of the Provost Marshal General's Bureau, Correspondence, Reports, Accounts and Related Records of Two or More Scouts, Guides, Spies, and Detectives, 1861–68, National Archives

RG110, E: 36: Records of the Provost Marshal General's Bureau (Civil War), Correspondence, Reports, Appointments and Other Records Relating to Individual Scouts, Guides, Spies, and Detectives, 1861–67, National Archives

RG110, E: 95: Provost Marshal General's Bureau, Secret Service Accounts, National Archives

RG153, M599: Investigation and Trial Papers Relating to the Assassination of President Lincoln, National Archives

RG21: Supreme Court of the District of Columbia Criminal Case, National Archives

RG217: Southern Claims Commission Records, Claims Allowed, National Archives

RG233: Barred and Disallowed Case Files of the Southern Claims Commission, 1871–80, M-1407, National Archives

RG393, E: 3988: Army of the Potomac Intelligence Diary, 1863, Part 1, Volume 113, National Archives

RG46: Records of the U.S. Senate, 44th Congress, Sen. 44A-D1, Committee Report 580, National Archives

RG59, E: 955: General Records of the State Department, Secret Correspondence, Volume 1 (April 12–Nov. 29, 1861), Volume 2 (Sept. 12–Dec. 12, 1861), and Volume 3 (Dec. 12, 1861–Feb. 14, 1863), National Archives

RG59, E: A1-962: General Records of the Department of State, Proceedings of the Commission Relating to State Prisoners, 1862, National Archives

RG59, HMS Entry: General Records of the Department of State, Seized Correspondence of Rose O'Neal Greenhow, National Archives

RG92, E: 1515: Office of Quartermaster General, Office of U.S. Military Railroads, 1860–67, HQ Office of Military Railroads, Washington, D.C., Letters Received, 1860–67

RG94: Office of the Adjutant General, Record and Pension Office Document File, National Archives

RG94, E: 179A: Turner-Baker Papers, National Archives

RG94, M619: Letters Received by the Office of the Adjutant General, 1861–70, National Archives

RG94, M797: Case Files Investigations by Levi C. Turner and Lafayette Baker, 1861–66, National Archives

RGP: Rose O'Neal Greenhow Papers, Duke University David M. Rubenstein Rare Book & Manuscript Library

SB: Samuel Barlow Papers, Huntington Library

SC: Charles Sumner Collection, Huntington Library

SCP: Simon Cameron Papers, Library of Congress

SGF: Sharpe Genealogy File, Kingston Senate House State Historic Site

SHC: Southern Historical Collection, Wilson Special Collections Library, University of North Carolina at Chapel Hill

SLH: Sharpe Letters, Hasbrouck Genealogy File, Kingston Senate House State Historic Site

SLU: St. Lawrence University Libraries, Special Collections and University Archives

TD: Thomas Dudley Papers, Huntington Library

TE: Thomas T. Eckert Papers, Huntington Library

TMR: Thomas McNiven Recollections 1835–1904, Acc. 33664-33683, Library of Virginia

UNC: Wilson Special Collections Library, University of North Carolina at Chapel Hill

USGP: Ulysses S. Grant Papers, Library of Congress

UTA: Dolph Briscoe Center for American History, University of Texas at Austin

VHS: Virginia Historical Society

WBP: William Gilmore Beymer Papers, Dolph Briscoe Center, University of Texas at Austin

WFL: Wise Family Letters, 1862–66, Library of Virginia

WFP: William Fay Papers, 1836–84, Library of Virginia

WL: Ward Hill Lamon Collection, Huntington Library

WM: College of William & Mary, Special Collections Research Center, Earl Gregg Swem Library

WSP: William Seward Papers (microfilm edition), Library of Congress

PERSONAL COLLECTIONS

AC: Ann Baker Cottrell

BP: Bonnie Mogelever Pollack

MB: Michael Berry

SB: Stephen Baker

OTHER ABBREVIATIONS USED

AL: Abraham Lincoln

AP: Allan Pinkerton (also for pseudonym E. J. Allen)

B: Box for a collection

DB: Daniel Butterfield

E: Entry for a record group

EMS: Edwin M. Stanton

EVL: Elizabeth Van Lew

GGM: George G. Meade

GM: George B. McClellan

GS: George Sharpe

GW: Gideon Welles

HH: Henry W. Halleck

JCB: John C. Babcock

JD: Jefferson Davis

JH: Joseph Hooker

JM: John McEntee

LB: Lafayette C. Baker

M: Microfilm

MP: Marsena Patrick

PL: Pryce Lewis

R: Reel of microfilm

REL: Robert E. Lee

RG: Record Group

ROG: Rose O'Neal Greenhow

USG: Ulysses S. Grant

WHS: William H. Seward

WS: Winfield Scott

AUTHOR INTERVIEWS

In the source notes, only the last name of the interviewee will be listed, followed by the date of the interview.

Bart Hall

John R. Krohn

Michelle Krowl
Lois Leveen

BOOKS, PERIODICALS, AND GOVERNMENT REPORTS

A work's full citation is given here. In the source notes it will appear as second reference.

Abbott, Karen. *Liar Temptress Soldier Spy: Four Women Undercover in the Civil War*. New York: Harper Perennial, 2014.

Abraham Lincoln: By Some Men Who Knew Him. Bloomington, Ill.: Pantagraph, 1910.

"Abraham Lincoln at the Willard Hotel." Abraham Lincoln Online. http://www.abrahamlincolnonline.org.

Adams, Charles Francis. *Charles Francis Adams 1835–1915: An Autobiography*. Westport, Conn.: Greenwood Press, 1916.

Agassiz, George R., ed. *Meade's Headquarters 1863–1865: Letters of Colonel Theodore Lyman from the Wilderness to Appomattox*. Boston: Atlantic Monthly Press, 1922.

Alfers, Kenneth G. *Law and Order in the Capital City: A History of the Washington Police 1800–1886*. Washington, D.C.: George Washington University, 1976.

Alford, Terry. *Fortune's Fool: The Life of John Wilkes Booth*. New York: Oxford University Press, 2015.

"The Annals of San Francisco, Third Part: The Vigilance Committee." San Francisco History. http://www.sfgeneology.com, pp. 1–16.

Axelrod, Alan. *The War Between the Spies: A History of Espionage During the American Civil War*. New York: Atlantic Monthly Press, 1992.

Badeau, Adam. *Military History of Ulysses S. Grant*, Vol. 2. New York: Appleton, 1885.

———. *Military History of Ulysses S. Grant*, Vol. 3. New York: Appleton, 1881.

Bakeless, John. *Spies of the Confederacy*. Mineola, N.Y.: Dover, 1970.

Baker, L. B. "An Eyewitness Account of the Death and Burial of J. Wilkes Booth." *Journal of the Illinois State Historical Society* 39, no. 4 (December 1946): 425–46.

Baker, Lafayette C. *History of the United States Secret Service*. Philadelphia: L. C. Baker, 1867.

Baker, Ray Stannard. *American Chronicle: The Autobiography of Ray Stannard Baker*. New York: Scribner, 1945.

———. "The Capture, Death, and Burial of J. Wilkes Booth." *McClure's* 9 (May–October 1897): 574–85.

"The Baltimore Plot to Assassinate Abraham Lincoln." *Harper's New Monthly Magazine* 37 (June–November 1868): 123–28.

Bates, David Homer. *Lincoln in the Telegraph Office: Recollections of the United States Military Telegraph Corps During the Civil War*. New York: Century, 1907.

Benfey, Christopher. "Theater of War: The Real Story Behind Mathew Brady's Civil War Photographs." *Slate*, Oct. 30, 1997, pp. 1–2. http://www.slate.com.

Bergeron, Paul H., ed. *The Papers of Andrew Johnson, Volume 9, September 1865–January 1866, and Volume 11, August 1866–January 1867*. Knoxville: University of Tennessee Press, 1991.

Beymer, William Gilmore. "Miss Van Lew." *Harper's Magazine*, June 1911, pp. 86–99.

———. *On Hazardous Service: Scouts and Spies of the North and South*. New York: Harper, 1912.

Bigelow, John, Jr. *The Campaign of Chancellorsville: A Strategic and Tactical Study*. New Haven, Conn.: Yale University Press, 1910.

Black, Robert C., III. *The Railroads of the Confederacy*. Chapel Hill: University of North Carolina Press, 1998.

Blackman, Ann. *Wild Rose: Rose O'Neale Greenhow, Civil War Spy: A True Story*. New York: Random House, 2005.

Blair, William A. *With Malice Toward Some: Treason and Loyalty in the Civil War Era*. Chapel Hill: University of North Carolina Press, 2014.

Blakeman, A. Noel. *Personal Recollections of the War of the Rebellion*. New York: G. P. Putnam's Sons, 1907.

Blakey, Arch Fredric. *General John H. Winder C.S.A.* Gainesville: University of Florida Press, 1990.

Blanton, DeAnne, and Lauren Cook. *They Fought Like Demons: Women Soldiers in the American Civil War*. Baton Rouge: Louisiana State University Press, 2002.

Bloss, John. "Antietam and the Lost Dispatch," *War Talks in Kansas*, pp. 77–91. Kansas City, Mo.: Franklin Hudson, 1906.

Blumenthal, Sidney. *The Political Life of Abraham Lincoln*, Vol. 1, *A Self-Made Man*. New York: Simon & Schuster, 2016.

———. *The Political Life of Abraham Lincoln*, Vol. 2, *Wrestling with His Angels*. New York: Simon & Schuster, 2017.

Boyd, Belle. *Belle Boyd in Camp and Prison*. New York: Blelock, 1866.

Boykin, Edward M. *The Falling Flag: Evacuation of Richmond, Retreat and Surrender at Appomattox*. New York: E. J. Hale, 1874.

Braden, Charles, ed. *Biographical Register of the Officers and Graduates of the U.S. Military Academy at West Point, New York*. Saginaw, Mich.: Seeman & Peters, 1910.

Brock, Sallie A. *Richmond During the War: Four Years of Personal Observation, Annotated*. Originally published 1867, reprinted 2015 by Lucy Booker Roper.

Brooks, Noah. *Washington in Lincoln's Time*. New York: Century, 1895.

Browne, Edward C., Jr. "Col. George H. Sharpe's 'Soda Water' Scouts." *Gettysburg Magazine*, no. 44 (January 2011): pp. 28–40.

Bryan, George S. *The Great American Myth*. New York: Carrick & Evans, 1940.

Burlingame, Michael. *Abraham Lincoln: A Life, Vol. 1 and 2*. Baltimore: Johns Hopkins University Press, 2013.

———, ed. *With Lincoln in the White House: Letters, Memoranda, and Other Writings of John G. Nicolay, 1860–1865*. Carbondale: Southern Illinois University Press, 2000.

Burrows, J. L. "Recollections of Libby Prison." *Southern Historical Society Papers* 11 (January–December 1883): 83–92.

Burton, Harrison N. "The Capture of Jefferson Davis." *Century* 27, no. 1 (November 1883): 130–45.

Butler, Benjamin. *Butler's Book: Autobiography and Personal Reminiscence of Major-General Benjamin Butler*. Boston: A. M. Thayer, 1892.

Carl, Leo D. *The CIA Insider's Dictionary of U.S. and Foreign Intelligence, Counterintelligence & Tradecraft*. Washington, D.C.: NIBC Press, 1996.

Castel, Albert. "Samuel Ruth: Union Spy." *Civil War Times Illustrated* 14, no. 10 (February 1976): 36–44.

Catton, Bruce. *The Centennial History of the Civil War*. Vol. 1, *The Coming Fury*. New York: Doubleday, 1961.

———. *The Centennial History of the Civil War*. Vol. 2, *Terrible Swift Sword*. New York: Doubleday, 1963.

———. *The Centennial History of the Civil War*. Vol. 3, *Never Call Retreat*. New York: Doubleday, 1965.

Chernow, Ron. *Grant*. New York: Penguin, 2017.

Chittenden, L. E. *Recollections of President Lincoln and His Administration*. New York: Harper, 1904.

Clark, Champ. *The Civil War: The Assassination: Death of the President*. Alexandria, Va.: Time-Life Books, 1987.

Cleaves, Freeman. *Meade of Gettysburg*. Norman: University of Oklahoma Press, 1960.

The Collected Works of Abraham Lincoln. Vols. 4–8. Abraham Lincoln Association, 1953. http://quod.lib.umich.edu/l/lincoln/.

Commemorative Biographical Record of Ulster County, New York. Chicago: J. H. Beers, 1863.

"The Confederate Plan to Abduct President Lincoln." *Surratt Society News* 6, no. 3 (March 1981).

Conroy, James B. *Lincoln's White House: The People's House in Wartime*. New York: Rowman & Littlefield, 2017.

Continental Hotel—Philadelphia, Pa. http://www.restaurantwarecollectors.com.

"The Contumacious State Prisoners in Washington." *Daily Morning News* (Savannah, Georgia), April 18, 1862.

Cook, John. "Military Intelligence During America's Civil War." American Civil War Round Table of Australia (New South Wales Chapter), August 2011.

Corruptions and Frauds of Lincoln's Administration. New York: s.n., 1864.

Corson, William R. *The Armies of Ignorance: The Rise of the American Intelligence Empire.* New York: Dial Press, 1977.

Coski, Ruth Ann. "White House Spy Legend Lives On." *Museum of the Confederacy Newsletter,* Spring/Summer 1999, pp. 6–7.

Cottrell, John. *Anatomy of an Assassination.* London: Frederick Muller, 1966.

Cowley, Robert, ed. *What If? The World's Most Foremost Military Historians Imagine What Might Have Been.* New York: Berkley Books, 2000.

Current, Richard N., ed. *Encyclopedia of the Confederacy.* New York: Simon & Schuster, 1993.

Cuthbert, Norma B., ed. *Lincoln and the Baltimore Plot 1861: From Pinkerton Records and Related Papers.* San Marino, Calif.: Huntington Library, 1949.

Dabney, Virginius. *Richmond: The Story of a City.* Garden City, N.Y.: Doubleday, 1976.

Dahlgren, John A. *Memoir of Ulric Dahlgren.* Philadelphia: Lippincott, 1872.

Dana, Charles A. *Recollections of the Civil War: With the Leaders at Washington and in the Field in the Sixties.* New York: Appleton, 1902.

Davis, Curtis Carroll. "The Civil War's Most Overrated Spy." *West Virginia History* 27, no. 1 (October 1965): 1–9.

———. "Companions of Crisis: The Spy Memoir as a Social Document." *Civil War History* 10, no. 4 (December 1964): 385–400.

———. "'The Pet of the Confederacy' Still? Fresh Findings About Belle Boyd." *Maryland Historical Magazine* 78, no. 1 (Spring 1983): 35–53.

Davis, Jefferson. *The Rise and Fall of the Confederate Government.* Vol. 2. New York: Appleton, 1881.

Davis, Varina. *Jefferson Davis, Ex-President of the Confederate States of America.* Vol. 2. Baltimore: Nautical & Aviation, 1990.

Davis, William C. "Behind the Lines." *Civil War Times Illustrated* 20, no. 7 (November 1981): 26–28.

———. "Behind the Lines: Caveat Emptor." *Civil War Times Illustrated* 16, no. 5 (August 1977): 33–37.

———. "Behind the Lines: 'The Lincoln Conspiracy'—Hoax?" *Civil War Times Illustrated* 16, no. 7 (November 1977): 47–49.

————. *Inventing Loreta Velasquez: Confederate Soldier Impersonator, Media Celebrity and Con Artist.* Carbondale: Southern Illinois University Press, 2016.

Dennett, Tyler, ed. *Lincoln and the Civil War: In the Diaries and Letters of John Hay.* New York: Da Capo Press, 1988.

De Witt, William C. *People's History of Kingston, Rondout and Vicinity.* New Haven, Conn.: Yale University Press, 1943.

Diary of Gideon Welles, Secretary of the Navy Under Lincoln and Johnson. Vols. 1 and 2. New York: Houghton Mifflin, 1910–11.

Diary of Orville Hickman Browning. Vol. 1, *1850–1864.* Springfield: Illinois State Historical Library, 1925.

"Documents: General M. C. Meigs on the Conduct of the Civil War." *American Historical Review* 26 (October 1920–July 1921): 285–303.

Donald, David Herbert, ed. *Inside Lincoln's Cabinet: The Civil War Diaries of Salmon P. Chase.* New York: Longman's, Green, 1954.

————. *Lincoln.* New York: Simon & Schuster, 1995.

Dornbusch, C. E. *Regimental Publications & Personal Narratives of the Civil War: A Checklist.* Vol. 1. New York: New York Public Library, 1961.

Doster, William E. *Lincoln and Episodes of the Civil War.* New York: G. P. Putnam's Sons, 1915.

Durie, Bruce, ed. *The Pinkerton Casebook: Adventures of the Original Private Eye.* Edinburgh: Mercat Press, 2007.

Dykstra, Robert R. "The Continuing War." *Civil War History* 10, no. 4 (December 1964): 434–36.

Eicher, David J. *The Longest Night: A Military History of the Civil War.* New York: Simon & Schuster, 2001.

Eisenschiml, Otto. *Why Was Lincoln Murdered?* Boston: Little, Brown, 1937.

"Elizabeth 'Crazy Bet' Van Lew: Grant's Spy in Richmond." http://www.civilwar home.com.

Ezratty, Harry A. *Baltimore in the Civil War: The Pratt Street Riot and a City Occupied.* Charleston, S.C.: History Press, 2010.

Feis, William B. *Grant's Secret Service: The Intelligence War from Belmont to Appomattox.* Lincoln: University of Nebraska Press, 2002.

————. "Neutralizing the Valley: The Role of Military Intelligence in the Defeat of Jubal Early's Army of the Valley, 1864–1865." *Civil War History* 39, no. 3 (September 1993): 199–215.

————. "A Union Military Intelligence Failure: Jubal Early's Raid, June 12–July 14, 1864." *Civil War History* 36, no. 3 (September 1990): 209–25.

Fishel, Edwin C. "Military Intelligence 1861–63 (Part 1)." CIA Center for the Study of Intelligence. Sept. 18, 1995. https://www.cia.gov/library.

———. "Military Intelligence 1861–63 (Part 2)." CIA Center for the Study of Intelligence. Sept. 18, 1995. https://www.cia.gov/library.

———. "The Mythology of Civil War Intelligence." *Civil War History* 10, no. 4 (December 1964): 344–67.

———. "Pinkerton and McClellan: Who Deceived Whom?" *Civil War History* 34, no. 2 (June 1988): 115–42.

———. *The Secret War for the Union: The Untold Story of Military Intelligence in the Civil War.* New York: Houghton Mifflin, 1996.

Foner, Eric. "Why Reconstruction Matters." *New York Times*, March 29, 2015, pp. 1, 4.

Foote, Shelby. *The Civil War, A Narrative: Fort Sumter to Perryville.* New York: Vintage Books, 1986.

Forbes, Ella. *African American Women During the Civil War.* New York: Garland, 1998.

Forney, John W. *Anecdotes of Public Men.* New York: Harper & Brothers, 1873.

Fowler, O. S. *Phrenological Description of Allan Pinkerton, Esq.* Chicago: Lakeside, 1874.

Fowler, Robert H. "New Evidence in Lincoln Murder Conspiracy." *Civil War Times Illustrated* 3, no. 10 (February 1965): 4–11.

———. "Was Stanton Behind Lincoln's Murder?" *Civil War Times Illustrated* 3, no. 5 (August–September 1961): 5–13.

Fox, William F. *Regimental Losses in the American Civil War 1861–1865.* Albany, N.Y.: Albany Publishing Company, 1889.

Freeman, Douglas Southall. *Lee's Lieutenants: A Study in Command.* Vol. 4, *Part Two of Gettysburg to Appomattox.* New York: Scribner's, 1944.

———. *R. E. Lee: A Biography.* Vol. 4. New York: Scribner's, 1949.

Friedman, Morris. *The Pinkerton Labor Spy.* New York: Wilshire, 1907.

Gates, Theodore B. *The "Ulster Guard" and the War of the Rebellion.* New York: Benjamin H. Tyrrel, 1879.

George, Joseph, Jr. "'Black Flag Warfare': Lincoln and the Raids Against Richmond and Jefferson Davis." *Pennsylvania Magazine of History and Biography* 115, no. 3 (July 1991): 291–318.

Geringer, Joseph. "Allan Pinkerton and His Detective Agency: 'We Never Sleep.'" Crime Library: Criminal Minds & Methods. http://www.crimelibrary.com.

Glantz, Edward J. "Guide to Civil War Intelligence." *Journal of U.S. Intelligence Studies* 18, no. 2 (Winter/Spring 2011): 55–59.

Glassford, W. A. "The Balloon in the Civil War." *Journal of the Military Service Institution of the United States* 18 (1896): 255–66.

Gobright, L. A. *Recollections of Men and Things at Washington, During the Third of a Century.* Philadelphia: Claxton, Remsen & Haffelfinger, 1869.

Goodwin, Doris Kearns. *Team of Rivals: The Political Genius of Abraham Lincoln.* New York: Simon & Schuster, 2005.

Grant, Ulysses S. *Personal Memoirs of U.S. Grant.* Vol. 2. Project Gutenberg EBook, 2004.

Greene, A. Wilson. *A Campaign of Giants: The Battle for Petersburg,* Vol. 1, *From the Crossing of the James to the Crater.* Chapel Hill: University of North Carolina Press, 2018.

Greenhow, Rose O'Neal. *My Imprisonment and the First Year of Abolition Rule at Washington.* London: Richard Bentley, 1863.

"Grenville M. Dodge and George H. Sharpe: Grant's Intelligence Chiefs in West and East." Signal Corps Association 1860–1865. http://www.civilwarsignals.org.

Hageman, Mark. "Lafayette Baker, AKA: Sam Munson." Signal Corps Association. http:www.civilwarsignals.org, pp. 1–13.

Hall, James O. "John Wilkes Booth's Escape Route." *Surratt Society* (2000): 16.

———. "The Spy Harrison." *Civil War Times Illustrated* 24, no. 10 (February 1986): 19–25.

Hammond, Harold Earl, ed. *Diary of a Union Lady 1861–1865: Maria Lydig Daly.* Lincoln: University of Nebraska Press, 1962.

Hanchett, William. "Booth's Diary." *Journal of the Illinois State Historical Society* 72, no. 1 (February 1979): 39–56.

———. "Code Words for Conspiracy." *Civil War Times Illustrated,* October 1988, pp. 33, 45.

———. *The Lincoln Murder Conspiracies.* Urbana: University of Illinois Press, 1983.

Hatch, Frederick. *Protecting President Lincoln: The Security Effort, the Thwarted Plots and the Disaster at Ford's Theatre.* Jefferson, N.C.: McFarland, 2011.

Hay, John. "Life in the White House in the Time of Lincoln." *Century* 41, no. 1 (November 1890): 33–37.

Hazelton, Joseph Powers. *Scouts, Spies, and Heroes of the Great Civil War.* Cincinnati: E. R. Curtis, 1892.

Headley, John W. *Confederate Operations in Canada and New York.* New York: Neale, 1906.

Hebert, Walter H. *Fighting Joe Hooker.* Lincoln: University of Nebraska Press, 1999.

Herndon, William H. *Herndon's Lincoln: The True Story of a Great Life.* Vol. 3. Springfield, Ill.: Herndon's, 1889.

Heron, Louise. *Historic Kingston, New York.* Kingston, N.Y.: Ford Printing, 1967.

Hesseltine, William B. *Civil War Prisons.* Kent, Ohio: Kent State University Press, 1962.

Holzer, Harold. *Lincoln and the Power of the Press*. New York: Simon & Schuster, 2014.

Holzer, Harold, and Craig L. Symonds, ed. *The New York Times Complete Civil War 1861–1865*. New York: Black Dog & Leventhal, 2010.

Hoogenboom, Ari. "Spy & Topdog Duty Has Been . . . Neglected." *Civil War History* 10, no. 4 (December 1964): 368–70.

Horan, James D. *Desperate Men: Revelations from the Sealed Pinkerton Files*. New York: Putnam's, 1949.

———. *The Pinkertons: The Detective Dynasty That Made History*. New York: Bonanza Books, 1967.

Horan, James D., and Howard Swiggett. *The Pinkerton Story*. New York: Putnam's, 1951.

Howard, John. "Assassination and Pathology Case Presentations." PowerPoint presentation at the Surratt Society Conference 2004, James O. Hall Research Center, Surratt House Museum.

Impeachment Investigation. Testimony Taken Before the Judiciary Committee of the House of Representatives in the Investigation of the Charges Against Andrew Johnson. 2nd Session, 39th Congress, and 1st Session, 40th Congress, 1867. Washington, D.C.: U.S. Government Printing Office, 1867.

Impeachment of the President. Nov. 25, 1867, Rep. Com. No. 7. House of Representatives, 40th Congress, 1st Session.

Inglis, William. "A Republic's Gratitude." *Harper's Weekly*, July–December 1911, pp. 23–24.

"Intelligence in the Civil War." Office of Public Affairs. Central Intelligence Agency, Washington, D.C.

Jarman, Rufus. "The Pinkerton Story: Part One." *Saturday Evening Post*, May 15, 1948, pp. 26–27, 167–69.

———. "The Pinkerton Story: Part Two." *Saturday Evening Post*, May 23, 1948, pp. 34–35, 78, 80, 82, 84.

Jeffrey, William H. *Richmond Prisons 1861–1862*. St. Johnsbury, Vt.: Republican Press, 1893.

Johnson, Angus J., II. "Disloyalty on Confederate Railroads in Virginia." *Virginia Magazine of History and Biography* 63, no. 4 (October 1955): 410–26.

Johnson, Byron Berkeley. *Abraham Lincoln and Boston Corbett, with Personal Recollections of Each*. Waltham, Mass.: Byron Berkeley Johnson, 1914.

Johnson, Rossiter. *Campfires and Battlefields: A Pictorial Narrative of the Civil War*. New York: Gallant Books, 1960.

Jones, J. B. *A Rebel War Clerk's Diary at the Confederate States Capital*. Philadelphia: Lippincott, 1866.

Jones, Katharine M. *Ladies of Richmond.* New York: Bobbs-Merrill, 1962.

Jones, Wilmer L. *Behind Enemy Lines: Civil War Spies, Raiders, and Guerrillas.* Dallas: Taylor, 2001.

Joseph Stannard Baker Memoirs from 1838 to 1865. James Stannard Baker, 1980.

Kauffman, Michael W. *American Brutus: John Wilkes Booth and the Lincoln Conspiracies.* New York: Random House, 2004.

———. "Booth's Escape Route: Lincoln's Assassin on the Run." *Blue & Gray Magazine* 7 no. 5 (June 1990): 9–61.

Keegan, John. *Intelligence in War: Knowledge of the Enemy from Napoleon to Al-Qaeda.* New York: Knopf, 2003.

Kennedy, Cramond. "Correspondence." *American Freedman* 2, no. 1 (April 1867): 205.

Kinchen, Oscar A. *Confederate Operations in Canada and the North.* North Quincy, Mass.: Christopher, 1970.

Klement, Frank L. *The Copperheads in the Middle West.* Chicago: University of Chicago Press, 1960.

———. *Dark Lanterns: Secret Political Societies, Conspiracies, and Treason Trials in the Civil War.* Baton Rouge: Louisiana State University Press, 1984.

Kline, Michael J. *The Baltimore Plot: The First Conspiracy to Assassinate Abraham Lincoln.* Yardley, Pa.: Westholme, 2008.

"Lafayette Baker." American Civil War Story. http://www.americancivilwarstory.com.

Lamon, Ward Hill. *The Life of Abraham Lincoln: From His Birth to His Inauguration as President.* Boston: Osgood, 1872.

———. *Recollections of Abraham Lincoln: 1847–1865.* Washington, D.C.: Dorothy Lamon Trillard, 1911.

Lancaster, Robert A., Jr. *Historic Virginia Homes and Churches.* Philadelphia: Lippincott, 1915.

Largent, Kimberly. "Elizabeth Van Lew: 'Crazy Bet' Brings Down Richmond." http://ehistory.osu.edu.

Lavine, Sigmund A. *Allan Pinkerton: America's First Private Eye.* New York: Dodd, Mead, 1963.

Le Fevre, Ralph. *History of New Paltz, New York, and Its Old Families.* Albany: Fort Orange Press, 1909.

Leonard, Elizabeth D. *All the Daring of the Soldier: Women of the Civil War Armies.* New York: Norton, 1999.

Lester, Robert E., and Gary Hoag, eds. *Civil War Unit Histories.* Part 3, *The Union-Mid-Atlantic Regimental Histories and Personal Narratives.* Bethesda, Md.: University Publications of America, 1992.

Letter from the Secretary of War in the case of Joseph H. Maddox, April 8, 1890, Ex. Doc. no. 101, Senate, 51st Congress, 1st Session.

Leveen, Lois. "Mary Richards Bowser (fl. 1846–1867)." *Encyclopedia Virginia,* Virginia Foundation of Humanities, Jan. 8, 2016, web Oct. 3, 2016.

———. "The Spy Photo That Fooled NPR, the U.S. Army Intelligence Center, and Me." *Atlantic,* June 27, 2013. http://www.theatlantic.com.

The Life and Letters of George Gordon Meade. Vols. 1 and 2. New York: Scribner's, 1913.

"Lincoln's Secret Ride on the PRR." *The Pennsy.* February 1953, pp. 6–7.

Lineberry, Cate. "Elizabeth Van Lew: An Unlikely Union Spy." Smithsonian.com Special Report. http://www.smithsonianmag.com.

Livermore, Thomas L. *Numbers and Losses in the Civil War in America 1861–65.* New York: Houghton Mifflin, 1900.

Long, E. B., with Barbara Long. *The Civil War Day by Day: An Almanac 1861–1865.* Garden City, N.Y.: Doubleday, 1971.

Longstreet, James. *From Manassas to Appomattox: Memoirs of the Civil War in America.* Philadelphia: Lippincott, 1896.

Lossing, Benson J. *A History of the Civil War.* New York: War Memorial Association, 1912.

The Loyal Girl of Winchester: Mrs. Rebecca Wright Bonsal. Fremont, Ohio: Birchard Library, 1864.

L. S. H. "Memorandum on the Life of Lincoln." *Century Illustrated Magazine,* June 1890, pp. 305–10.

Luvaas, Jay. "Lee at Gettysburg: A General Without Intelligence." *Intelligence and National Security* 5, no. 2 (April 1990): 116–35.

———. "The Role of Intelligence in the Chancellorsville Campaign, 1863." *Intelligence and National Security* 5, no. 2 (April 1990): 99–115.

Mackay, James. *Allan Pinkerton: The First Private Eye.* New York: Wiley, 1996.

Mahony, D. A. *The Prisoner of State.* New York: Carleton, 1863.

Markle, Donald E. *Spies & Spymasters of the Civil War.* New York: Hippocrene Books, 1994.

Marshall, John A. *American Bastille: A History of the Illegal Arrests and Imprisonment of American Citizens During the Late Civil War.* Philadelphia: Thomas W. Hartley, 1871.

Marvel, William. *Lincoln's Autocrat: The Life of Edwin Stanton.* Chapel Hill: University of North Carolina Press, 2015.

Maslowski, Peter. "Military Intelligence Sources During the American Civil War: A Case Study." *The Intelligence Revolution: A Historical Perspective.* Proceedings of the Thirteenth Military History Symposium, U.S. Air Force Academy, Colorado Springs, Colo., Oct. 12–14, 1988, pp. 39–70.

Massey, Mary Elizabeth. *Bonnet Brigades*. New York: Knopf, 1966.

McClellan, George B. *McClellan's Own Story: The War for the Union*. New York: Charles L. Webster, 1887.

———. *Report on the Organization and Campaigns of the Army of the Potomac*. New York: Sheldon, 1864.

McPherson, James M. *Battle Cry of Freedom: The Civil War Era*. New York: Oxford University Press, 1988.

———. *Embattled Rebel: Jefferson Davis and the Confederate Civil War*. New York: Penguin, 2014.

———. *Tried by War: Abraham Lincoln as Commander in Chief*. New York: Penguin, 2008.

Meade, George Gordon. *With Meade at Gettysburg*. Philadelphia: War Library and Museum of the Military Order of the Loyal Legion of the United States, 1930.

Merrill, Samuel H. *The Campaigns of the First Maine and First District of Columbia Cavalry*. Portland, Maine: Bailey & Noyes, 1866.

Miers, Earl Schenck, ed. *Lincoln Day by Day: A Chronology 1809–1865*. Dayton, Ohio: Morningside, 1991.

Millard, J. J. "The Devil's Errand Boy." *True* 21, no. 122 (July 1947).

Miller, Francis Trevelyan, ed. *The Photographic History of The Civil War: Soldier Life and the Secret Service*. New York: Castle Books, 1957.

Miller, Steven G. "More on Capt. Doherty . . ." *Surratt Courier* 19, no. 9 (September 1990): 5–7.

———. "Roll Call for the Garrett's Farm Patrol." *Surratt Courier* 19, no. 9 (September 1994): 3–5.

———. "A Trooper's Account of the Death of Booth." *Surratt Courier* 20, no. 5 (May 1995): 5–9.

Millican, C. Bowie, Robert M. Gelman, and Thomas A. Stanhope. "Lost Order, Lost Cause." *Studies in Intelligence*, Sept. 22, 1993.

Milton, George Fort. *Abraham Lincoln and the Fifth Column*. Washington, D.C.: Infantry Journal, 1943.

———. *The Age of Hate: Andrew Johnson and the Radicals*. New York: Coward-McCann, 1930.

Moffett, Cleveland. "How Allan Pinkerton Thwarted the First Plot to Assassinate Lincoln." *McClure's Magazine*, November 1894, pp. 519–29.

Mogelever, Jacob. *Death to Traitors: The Story of General Lafayette C. Baker, Lincoln's Forgotten Secret Service Chief.* New York: Doubleday, 1960.

Morn, Frank. *The Eye That Never Sleeps: A History of the Pinkerton Detective Agency.* Bloomington: Indiana University Press, 1982.

Mortimer, Gavin. *Double Death: The True Story of Pryce Lewis, the Civil War's Most Daring Spy.* New York: Walker, 2010.

——. "Super Spy from Wales: Union Agent Pryce Lewis Had His Share of Close Calls." *Civil War Times,* February 2011, pp. 60–67.

Murdock, Eugene C. "New York's Civil War Bounty Brokers." *Journal of American History* 53, no. 2 (1966): 259–62.

——. *Patriotism Limited 1862–1865: The Civil War Draft and the Bounty System.* Kent, Ohio: Kent State University Press, 1967.

"The Name of Kingston and Its Predecessors." *Senate House Journal* 1, no. 2 (Winter 2015–16): 4.

Nevins, Allan. *The War for the Union.* Vol. 1, *The Improvised War 1861–1862.* New York: Scribner's, 1959.

——. *The War for the Union.* Vol. 2, *War Becomes Revolution.* New York: Scribner's, 1960.

——. *The War for the Union.* Vol. 4, *The Organized War to Victory 1864–1865.* New York: Scribner's, 1971.

Nicolay, John G., and John Hay. *Abraham Lincoln: A History.* Vols. 2–10. New York: Century, 1890, 1909.

——. "A History of Abraham Lincoln." *Century* 39, no. 2 (December 1889): 305–13.

Niven, John. *Gideon Welles: Lincoln's Secretary of the Navy.* Baton Rouge: Louisiana State University Press, 1973.

——. *Salmon P. Chase: A Biography.* New York: Oxford University Press, 1995.

Oates, William C. "Gettysburg—The Battle on the Right." *Southern Historical Society Papers* 5 (July–December 1878): 172–82.

"Official Correspondence of Governor Letcher, of Virginia." *Southern Historical Society Papers* 1 (January–June 1867): 455–62.

Old Capitol Prison, 91st PA. http://freepages.military.rootsweb.ancestry.com.

Orrmont, Arthur. *Mr. Lincoln's Master Spy: Lafayette Baker.* New York: Julian Messner, 1966.

"Other Government Buildings: Old Capitol Prison." http://www.mrlincolnswhitehouse.org.

O'Toole, G. J. A. *Honorable Treachery: A History of U.S. Intelligence, Espionage, and*

Covert Action from the American Revolution to the CIA. New York: Atlantic Monthly Press, 1991.

Palfrey, Edward A. "Some of the Secret History of Gettysburg." *Southern Historical Society Papers* 8 (January–December 1880): 521–24.

The Papers of Ulysses S. Grant. Vols. 10–14. Carbondale and Edwardsville: Southern Illinois University Press, 1982, 1984, and 1985.

Parker, Sandra V. *Richmond's Civil War Prisons.* Lynchburg, Va.: H. E. Howard, 1990.

Patten, Zach. "Echoes of an Extravagant Past: The Ben Franklin House's Continental History." June 25, 2013. http://philly.curbed.com.

Peril, Lynn. *Swimming in the Steno Pool: A Retro Guide to Making It in the Office.* New York: Norton, 2011.

Pinkerton, Allan. *Criminal Reminiscences and Detective Sketches.* New York: Dillingham, 1878.

———. *History and Evidence of the Passage of Abraham Lincoln from Harrisburg, Pennsylvania, to Washington, D.C., on February 22–23, 1861 (1907).* Kessinger Legacy Reprints. www.kessinger.net.

———. *The Somnambulist and the Detective: The Murderer and the Fortune Teller.* New York: Carleton, 1874.

———. *The Spy of the Rebellion.* Lexington, Ky.: Forgotten Books, 2015.

———. *Thirty Years a Detective.* Warwick, N.Y.: 1500 Books, 2007.

Poore, Benjamin Perley. *The Conspiracy Trial for the Murder of the President.* Vols. 1 and 3. Boston: J. E. Tilton, 1865 and 1866.

———. *Perley's Reminiscences of the Sixty Years in the National Metropolis.* Vol. 2. Philadelphia: Hubbard Brothers, 1886.

Popchock, Barry. "His Lordship: The Adventures of Union Spy Pryce Lewis." *Civil War Times Illustrated,* September 1988, pp. 22–27, 45.

Porter, Horace. *Campaigning with Grant.* New York: Century, 1897.

Potter, John Mason. *Thirteen Desperate Days.* New York: Ivan Obolensky, 1964.

Private and Official Correspondence of Gen. Benjamin F. Butler During the Period of the Civil War. Vols. 3, 4, and 5. Norwood, Mass.: Plimpton Press, 1917.

Proceedings of the Ulster County Historical Society 1936–1937. Published by the Society at Kingston, New York.

Pryor, Elizabeth Brown. *Six Encounters with Lincoln: A President Confronts Democracy and Its Demons.* New York: Viking, 2017.

Quarles, Benjamin. *The Negro in the Civil War.* Boston: Little, Brown, 1953.

Rafuse, Ethan. *McClellan's War: The Failure of Moderation in the Struggle for the Union.* Bloomington: Indiana University Press, 2005.

Randall, J. G. *Lincoln the President: Midstream*. New York: Dodd, Mead, 1953.

———. *Lincoln the President: Springfield to Gettysburg*. Vol. 1. New York: Dodd, Mead, 1945.

———. "The Newspaper Problems in Its Bearing Upon Military Secrecy During the Civil War." *American Historical Review* 23, no. 2 (January 1918): 303–23.

Recko, Cory. *A Spy for the Union: The Life and Execution of Timothy Webster*. Jefferson, N.C.: McFarland, 2013.

Reid, Brian Holden. "Another Look at Grant's Crossing of the James, 1864." *Civil War History* 39, no. 4 (December 1993): 291–316.

Report of the Joint Committee on the Conduct of the War, in Three Parts. House of Representatives. 37th Congress, 3rd Session. Washington, D.C.: U.S. Government Printing Office, 1863.

"Residence of Van Lew." *Harper's Weekly* 10, no. 498 (July 14, 1866): 444–45.

Rice, Allen Thorndike. *Reminiscences of Abraham Lincoln by Distinguished Men of His Time*. New York: North American, 1886.

Richardson, Albert D. *The Secret Service, the Field, the Dungeon and the Escape*. Philadelphia: American, 1865.

Richardson, James D. *A Compilation of the Messages and Papers of the Confederacy*. Nashville Tenn.: United States Publishing Company, 1905.

Robertson, James I. *Civil War Virginia: Battleground for a Nation*. Charlottesville: University Press of Virginia, 1991.

Roman, Alfred. *The Military Operations of General Beauregard in the War Between the States 1861 to 1865*. New York: Harper & Brothers, 1884.

Roscoe, Theodore. *The Web of Conspiracy: The Complete Story of the Men Who Murdered Abraham Lincoln*. Englewood Cliffs, N.J.: Prentice-Hall, 1959.

Rose, P. K. "Valuable Sources." "The Civil War: Black American Contribution to Union Intelligence—Central Intelligence Agency." https://www.cia.gov/library /center-for-the-study-of-intelligence, pp. 1–8.

Ross, Ishbel. *Rebel Rose: Life of Rose O'Neal Greenhow, Confederate Spy*. St. Simons Island, Ga.: Mockingbird Books, 1954.

Rowan, Richard Wilmer. *The Pinkertons: A Detective Dynasty*. Boston: Little, Brown, 1931.

Rowland, Dunbar. *Jefferson Davis, Constitutionalist: His Letters, Papers and Speeches*. Jackson: Mississippi Department of Archives and History, 1923.

Ryan, David D. *A Yankee Spy in Richmond: The Civil War Diary of "Crazy Bet" Van Lew*. Mechanicsburg, Pa.: Stackpole Books, 1996.

Ryan, Thomas J. "A Battle of Wits: Intelligence Operations During the Gettysburg

Campaign Part 1: Clandestine Preparation for Invasion vs. Quest for Information." *Gettysburg Magazine*, no. 29 (2003): 7–25.

———. "A Battle of Wits: Intelligence Operations During the Gettysburg Campaign Part 4: The Intelligence Factor at Gettysburg." *Gettysburg Magazine*, no. 32 (2005): 7–38.

———. "A Battle of Wits: Intelligence Operations During the Gettysburg Campaign Part 3: Searching for Lee." *Gettysburg Magazine*, no. 31 (2004): 6–38.

———. "A Battle of Wits: Intelligence Operations During the Gettysburg Campaign Part 2: Strategy, Tactics, and Lee's March." *Gettysburg Magazine*, no. 30 (2004): 7–29.

———. "The Intelligence Battle, July 2: Longstreet's Assault." *Gettysburg Magazine* no. 43 (2009): 68–88.

———. "The Intelligence Battle, July 3: A Renewed Offensive." *Gettysburg Magazine* no. 44 (2011): 88–105.

———. *Spies, Scouts, and Secrets in the Gettysburg Campaign*. El Dorado Hills, Calif.: Savas Beatie, 2015.

Schairer, Jack E. *Lee's Bold Plan for Point Lookout: The Rescue of Confederate Prisoners That Never Happened*. Jefferson, N.C.: McFarland, 2008.

Schmidt, C. T. "G-2, Army of the Potomac." *Military Review* 28, no. 4 (July 1948): 45–56.

Schoonmaker, Marius. *The History of Kingston New York: From Its Early Settlement to the Year 1820*. New York: Burr, 1888.

Schuckers, J. W. *The Life and Public Services of Salmon Portland Chase*. New York: Appleton, 1874.

Schultz, Duane. *The Dahlgren Affair: Terror and Conspiracy in the Civil War*. New York: Norton, 1998.

Sears, Stephen W. *Chancellorsville*. New York: Houghton Mifflin, 1996.

———. *George B. McClellan: The Young Napoleon*. New York: Ticknor & Fields, 1988.

———. *Gettysburg*. New York: Houghton Mifflin, 2004.

———. *Landscape Turned Red: The Battle of Antietam*. New York: Houghton Mifflin, 1983.

———. *To the Gates of Richmond: The Peninsula Campaign*. New York: Ticknor & Fields, 1992.

Sears, Stephen W., ed. *The Civil War Papers of George B. McClellan: Selected Correspondence, 1860–1865*. New York: Ticknor & Fields, 1989.

Seward, Frederick W. *Seward at Washington as Senator and Secretary of State: A Memoir of His Life, with Selections from His Letters, 1861–1872.* New York: Derby & Miller, 1891.

Sharpe, George H. "Memorial Address." *Addresses Delivered at Music Hall, Kingston at the Seventh Annual Meeting of the 120th Regimental Union.* Kingston, N.Y.: Daily Freeman Steam Printing House, 1878.

———. "The Old Houses of Kingston." *Journal, City of Kingston,* Dec. 29, 1875.

Shaw, E. R. "The Assassination of Lincoln: The Hitherto Unpublished Account of an Eye-Witness." *McClure's Magazine,* December 1908, pp. 181–85.

Shoen, Harriet H. "Pryce Lewis Spy for the Union." *Davis and Elkins Historical Magazine* 2, no. 1 (March 1949): 22–30.

———. "Pryce Lewis Spy for the Union." *Davis and Elkins Historical Magazine* 2, no. 2 (March 1949): 17–35.

"The Signal Corps in the Confederate States Army." *Southern Historical Society Papers* 16 (1888): 93–107.

Silber, Nina. *Daughters of the Union: Northern Women Fight the Civil War.* Cambridge, Mass.: Harvard University Press, 2005.

Singer, Jane. *The Confederate Dirty War: Arson, Bombings, Assassination and Plots for Chemical and Germ Attacks on the Union.* Jefferson, N.C.: McFarland, 2005.

Singer, Jane, and John Stewart. *Lincoln's Secret Spy: The Civil War Case That Changed the Future of Espionage.* Guilford, Conn.: Lyons Press, 2015.

Smith, Edward M. *Documentary History of Rhinebeck, in Dutchess County, N.Y.* Rhinebeck, N.Y., 1881.

Smith, H. B. *Between the Lines: Secret Service Stories Told After Fifty Years.* New York: Booz Brothers, 1911.

Snyder, Annie Lee. "Lineage of the Abraham Hasbrouck Family." *Olde Ulster: An Historical and Genealogical Magazine* 4 (January–December 1908).

Sparks, David S. "General Patrick's Progress: Intelligence and Security in the Army of the Potomac." *Civil War History* 10, no. 4 (December 1964): 371–84.

———, ed. *Inside Lincoln's Army: The Diary of Marsena Rudolph Patrick, Provost Marshal General, Army of the Potomac.* New York: Thomas Yoseloff, 1964.

Speer, Lonnie R. *Portals to Hell: Military Prisons of the Civil War.* Lincoln: University of Nebraska Press, 1997.

Stahr, Walter. *Seward: Lincoln's Indispensible Man.* New York: Simon & Schuster, 2012.

Starr, Louis M. *Bohemian Brigade.* Madison: University of Wisconsin Press, 1987.

Stashower, Daniel. *The Hour of Peril: The Secret Plot to Murder Lincoln Before the Civil War.* New York: Minotaur Books, 2013.

Steers, Edward, Jr. *Blood on the Moon: The Assassination of Abraham Lincoln.* Lexington: University Press of Kentucky, 2001.

———. *Lincoln Legends: Myths, Hoaxes, and Confabulations Associated with Our Greatest President*. Lexington: University Press of Kentucky, 2007.

Stepp, John W., and I. William Hill, eds. *Mirror of War: The Washington Star Reports the Civil War*. Englewood Cliffs, N.J.: Prentice-Hall, 1961.

Stern, Philip Van Doren. *Secret Missions of the Civil War*. New York: Bonanza Books, 1959.

Stidger, Felix G., ed. *Treason History of the Order of Sons of Liberty, Formerly Circle of Honor Succeeded by Knights of the Golden Circle*. 1903.

Stone, Charles P. "Washington on the Eve of the War." *Century Readings in United States History: The Civil War*. New York: Century, 1920.

Stuart, Meriwether. "Colonel Ulric Dahlgren and Richmond's Union Underground." *Virginia Magazine of History and Biography* 72, no. 2 (April 1964): 152–204.

———. "Dr. Lugo: An Austro-Venetian Adventurer in Union Espionage." *Virginia Magazine of History and Biography* 90, no. 3 (July 1982): 339–58.

———. "Of Spies and Borrowed Names: The Identity of Union Operatives in Richmond Known as 'The Phillipses' Discovered." *Virginia Magazine of History and Biography* 89, no. 3 (July 1981): 308–27.

———. "Operation Sanders: Wherein Old Friends and Ardent Pro-Southerners Prove to Be Union Secret Agents." *Virginia Magazine of History and Biography* 81, no. 2 (April 1973): 157–99.

———. "Samuel Ruth and General R. E. Lee: Disloyalty and the Line of Supply to Fredericksburg, 1862–1863." *Virginia Magazine of History and Biography* 71 (1963): 35–109.

Swanson, James L. *Manhunt: The 12–Day Chase for Lincoln's Killer*. New York: Harper Perennial, 2006.

Temple, Oliver P. *East Tennessee and the Civil War*. Cincinnati: Robert Clarke, 1899.

Thomas, Benjamin P., and Harold M. Hyman. *Stanton: The Life and Times of Lincoln's Secretary of War*. New York: Knopf, 1962.

Thomas, Emory M. *The Confederate State of Richmond: A Biography of the Capital*. Baton Rouge: Louisiana State University Press, 1971.

Tidwell, William A., with James O. Hall and David Winfred Gaddy. *Come Retribution: The Confederate Secret Service and the Assassination of Lincoln*. Jackson: University Press of Mississippi, 1988.

Titone, Nora. *My Thoughts Be Bloody: The Bitter Rivalry Between Edwin and John Wilkes Booth That Led to an American Tragedy*. New York: Free Press, 2010.

Towne, Stephen E. *Surveillance and Spies in the Civil War: Exposing Confederate Conspiracies in America's Heartland*. Athens: Ohio University Press, 2015.

Treasury Department, Report from the Select Committee to Investigate Charges Against the Treasury Department. House of Representatives, 38th Congress, 1st Session, Report no. 140.

The Trial of John H. Surratt in the Criminal Court for the District of Columbia. Vol. 2. Washington, D.C.: French & Richardson, 1867.

Tsouras, Peter G. *Major General George H. Sharpe and the Creation of American Military Intelligence in the Civil War*. Philadelphia: Casemate, 2018.

Tucker, Glenn. *High Tide at Gettysburg: The Campaign in Pennsylvania*. New York: Bobbs-Merrill, 1958.

Turner, George Edgar. *Victory Rode the Rails: The Strategic Place of the Railroads in the Civil War*. New York: Bobbs-Merrill, 1953.

Van Lew, John N. *Natural Force: A New View*. Richmond: Clemmitt & Jones, Book and Job, 1871.

Van Lew, Willard Randolph. "Van Liew, Van Lieu, Van Lew: Genealogical & Historical Record." Upper Montclair, N.J.: Emerio R. Van Lew, 1956.

Van Santvoord, C. *The One Hundred and Twentieth Regiment: New York State Volunteers*. Roundout, N.Y.: Press of the Kingston Freeman, 1894.

Varon, Elizabeth R. *Southern Lady, Yankee Spy: The True Story of Elizabeth Van Lew, a Union Agent in the Heart of the Confederacy*. New York: Oxford University Press, 2003.

———. "True to the Flag: Uncovering the Story of Elizabeth Van Lew and Richmond's Underground." *North & South* 6, no. 6 (September 2003): 68–81.

Velazquez, Loreta Janeta. *The Woman in Battle*. Hartford, Conn.: Belknap, 1876.

Venter, Bruce M. *Kill Jeff Davis: The Union Raid on Richmond, 1864*. Norman: University of Oklahoma Press, 2016.

Weber, Jennifer L. *Copperheads: The Rise and Fall of Lincoln's Opponents in the North*. New York: Oxford University Press, 2006.

Webster, Spencer. *Revenge of the Fugitive Romeo*. New York: Macfadden, 1942.

Weichmann, Louis J. *A True Story of the Assassination of Abraham Lincoln and of the Conspiracy of 1865*. New York: Knopf, 1975.

Wheelan, Joseph. *Libby Prison Breakout: The Daring Escape from the Notorious Civil War Prison*. New York: PublicAffairs, 2010.

"Willard Hotel." Washington, D.C., National Register of Historic Places Travel Itinerary. http://www.nps.gov.

"The Willard Hotel in the 19th Century." http://www.streetsofwashington.com.

Williamson, James J. *Prison Life in the Old Capitol and Reminiscences of the Civil War*. West Orange, N.J.: Reese, 1911.

Wilson, Douglas L., and Rodney O. Davis, eds. *Herndon's Informants: Letters, Interviews About Abraham Lincoln*. Chicago: University of Illinois Press, 1998.

Wilson, James Harrison. "The Pursuit and Capture of Jefferson Davis," *The Century* 39 no. 4 (February 1890): 586–97.

Winkle, Kenneth J. *Lincoln's Citadel: The Civil War in Washington, D.C.* New York: Norton, 2013.

Winkler, H. Donald. *Stealing Secrets: How a Few Daring Women Deceived Generals, Impacted Battles, and Altered the Course of the Civil War.* Naperville, Ill.: Cumberland House, 2010.

Woods, Brett F. "Rise and Fall of a Secret Agent: Lafayette Baker." *Army*, September 1986, pp. 56–64.

Woolseley, Field Marshal Viscount. *The American Civil War: An English View.* Charlottesville: University Press of Virginia, 1964.

Yale University Obituary Record of Graduates Deceased During the Year Ending July 1, 1920. New Haven, Conn.: Yale University, 1921.

SOURCE NOTES

In many instances a source note covers several paragraphs. Unless otherwise indicated, each source note lists material cited up to the previous source note. Some box numbers may have changed as archivists reconfigure their collections.

ONE: ALLAN PINKERTON

3 *working a case:* Rowan, p. 114; Morn, p. 60; Milton, *Abraham Lincoln and the Fifth Column,* p. 33; Kline, pp. 54–57, 233.

4 *"and excitability":* Fowler, *Phrenological Description of Allan Pinkerton Esq.,* pp. 3–10; AP to My Dear Son, Feb. 28, 1883, R: 3, PND, LC.

4 *South Carolina:* Pinkerton, *The Spy of the Rebellion,* pp. 46–47, 50–51, 55–59; Cuthbert, pp. 3–4, 126; Wilson and Davis, pp. 267–68, 317; Stashower, pp. 95–97; Pinkerton, *History and Evidence of the Passage of Abraham Lincoln from Harrisburg, Pennsylvania, to Washington, D.C.,* pp. 7–9, 15.

5 *February 23:* Wilson and Davis, p. 318; Cuthbert, p. 5; Pinkerton, *The Spy of the Rebellion,* p. 54; Pinkerton, *History and Evidence of the Passage of Abraham Lincoln from Harrisburg, Pennsylvania, to Washington, D.C.,* p. 24; Cuthbert, p. xiii.

5 *the killers:* McPherson, *Battle Cry of Freedom,* pp. 284–85; Cuthbert, pp. xii–xiii, 64–68, 127; Ezratty, pp. 29–33, 38, 63; Kline, pp. 32–34; Stepp and Hill, p. 6; Kline, pp. 15–16; Stashower, pp. 101, 103, 105, 183, 190–93; Pinkerton, *The Spy of the Rebellion,* pp. 61–64, 76–79; Potter, pp. 110–14.

6 *Springfield friends:* Cuthbert, pp. xiii, 129–30; Kline, pp. 2, 135; Stashower,

pp. 13, 84; Hatch, pp. 12, 15; "Intelligence in the Civil War," p. 7; Nicolay and Hay, *Abraham Lincoln: A History*, vol. 3, pp. 303–4; Herndon, pp. 480–84; Stone, pp. 30–31; Niven, *Gideon Welles*, p. 317; Hatch, p. 12; Herndon, pp. 492–93.

6   *easily overpowered:* Cuthbert, p. 137; Randall, *Lincoln the President: Springfield to Gettysburg*, pp. 275, 290; Stashower, pp. 90, 111–13; Hatch, p. 12; Winkle, p. 94; Pinkerton, *History and Evidence of the Passage of Abraham Lincoln from Harrisburg, Pennsylvania, to Washington, D.C.*, p. 23.

7   *future president:* Geringer, "Allan Pinkerton and His Detective Agency: We Never Sleep"; Horan, *The Pinkertons*, p. 8; Mackay, pp. 9–10, 20, 230; Rowan, p. 35.

8   *August 25:* Mackay, pp. 15–26; AP to My Dear Son, Feb. 28, 1883, R: 3, PND, LC; Durie, pp. ix–xi; Horan, *The Pinkertons*, pp. 2–4.

8   *because of it:* Mackay, pp. 26–27; Durie, p. x; Horan, *The Pinkertons*, p. 4; AP to Sam, Jan. 25, 1863, Box 4, PND, LC.

9   *musket fire:* Durie, pp. xi–xiii; Mackay, pp. 27–47; Horan, *The Pinkertons*, pp. 4–9; Morn, p. 19; AP to R. W. Dewe, 1862, Box 4, PND, LC.

9   *to Chicago:* Mackay, pp. 8, 48–56; Horan, *The Pinkertons*, pp. 10–12; Durie, p. xiii; Lavine, p. 4; AP to R. W. Dewe, 1862, Box 4, PND, LC; "Obituary: Mrs. Joan Pinkerton, *(Chicago) Daily Inter Ocean*, Jan. 22, 1887.

10   *consulting her:* Mackay, pp. 5, 56–58; Horan, *The Pinkertons*, pp. 11–14; Rowan, p. 7; Pinkerton, *Criminal Reminiscences and Detective Sketches*, pp. 9–12; Morn, p. 20; Durie, p. xiv; Lavine, p. 8.

10   *bogus dimes:* Mackay, pp. 59–62; Pinkerton, *Criminal Reminiscences and Detective Sketches*, pp. 12–18; Horan, *The Pinkertons*, p. 15; Rowan, p. 10; Morn, pp. 20–21.

11   *a case:* Pinkerton, *Criminal Reminiscences and Detective Sketches*, pp. 16–51; Rowan, p. 20.

12   *from envelopes:* Mackay, pp. 62–70; Morn, pp. 21–24; Horan, *The Pinkertons*, pp. 21–24; Stern, p. 54; Irma DuPre, "Dundee Church Record Reveals Pinkerton Trial," *Chicago Daily News*, Nov. 16, 1935; *Daily Democratic Press* story, Sept. 9, 1853, APP, CH; Cyrus Bradley certificate for AP, Jan. 4, 1853, B: 1, PND, LC.

12   *for detectives:* Mackay, pp. 7, 70–71; Horan, *The Pinkertons*, pp. 24–27; Lavine, pp. 20–21; Stashower, pp. 41–42; Rowan, p. 26; Morn, pp. 12–13, 54; Geringer, "Allan Pinkerton and His Detective Agency: We Never Sleep"; O'Toole, p. 120.

13   *the Midwest:* Mackay, pp. 73–76, 92–93; Morn, pp. 14, 37; Horan and Swiggett, pp. 247–48; Jarman, "The Pinkerton Story: Part Two," p. 34; Lavine, pp. 21–22;

Rowan, p. 27; Pinkerton, *The Somnambulist and the Detective*, pp. 6–7; Horan, *The Pinkertons*, pp. 29–30, 50.

14   *an affair:* Mackay, pp. 10, 73–75; Horan, *The Pinkertons*, pp. 27–29; Rowan, pp. 48–49; Pinkerton, *The Somnambulist and the Detective*, pp. 46, 173; Morn, 54–55; photo of George Bangs, Box 27, Assignment of Kate Warne, Superintendent of Female Department, Box 25, PND, LC; "A Remarkable Detective," *New York Times*, Sept. 15, 1883; Cuthbert, p. 19; Recko, p. 75; "The Baltimore Plot to Assassinate Abraham Lincoln," pp. 124–25; Rowan, p. 84; Lavine, p. 52; Stashower, pp. 99–100.

14   *business interests:* Pinkerton's National Detective Agency advertisement, news article on Common Council Meeting, APP, CH; Mackay, p. 11; Pinkerton, *Criminal Reminiscences and Detective Sketches*, pp. 266–67; Jarman, "The Pinkerton Story: Part Two," p. 35; Geringer, "Allan Pinkerton and His Detective Agency: We Never Sleep"; Morn, pp. ix, 25; Horan, *The Pinkertons*, pp. 35–36, 50; Horan and Swiggett, pp. 203–4; Mackay, pp. 77–79, 93.

15   *national one:* Mackay, pp. 77–82, 88–89; Morn, pp. 24–26, 35–37, 211; Geringer, "Allan Pinkerton and His Detective Agency: We Never Sleep"; Pinkerton, *The Spy of the Rebellion*, pp. 459–60; Horan, *The Pinkertons*, pp. 35–37, 44; Lavine, pp. 41–42.

15   *defense fund:* Mackay, p. 74; Geringer, "Allan Pinkerton and His Detective Agency: We Never Sleep"; Pinkerton, *The Somnambulist and the Detective*, p. 6; Lavine, p. 43; Pinkerton, *Thirty Years a Detective*, pp. 18–19; Mackay, pp. 10, 81–85; Stashower, p. 61; Horan, *The Pinkertons*, pp. 37–42; Pinkerton, *The Spy of the Rebellion*, p. xxvi; AP to R. W. Dewe, 1862, Box 4, PND, LC.

15   *"is over":* Kline, p. 264; Gobright, p. 286; Lamon, *Recollections of Abraham Lincoln*, p. 45; Milton, *The Age of Hate*, pp. 3–4; "Lincoln's Secret Ride on the PRR," p. 7.

16   *watching Indians:* Lamon, *Recollections of Abraham Lincoln*, pp. 43–44; Cuthbert, pp. 16, 80–81; Donald, *Lincoln*, p. 259; McPherson, *Battle Cry of Freedom*, pp. 234–36, 312–14, 336; Catton, vol. 1, p. 254; McPherson, *Embattled Rebel*, p. 30; Stone, p. 4; Eicher, p. 58; McPherson, *Tried by War*, p. 11.

17   *political intelligence:* Donald, *Lincoln*, pp. 14, 29–32, 44–46, 52, 90–93, 114–15, 179, 184–85, 211, 228, 236, 245; Goodwin, pp. 27, 51, 89, 152–53, 208–9, 235–36, 239, 247, 265–66, 275; *Abraham Lincoln: By Some Men Who Knew Him*, p. 156; Holzer, pp. xv–xvi, xxii; Catton, vol. 1, 53–54, 62–63; Kline, pp. 211–12; Burlingame, *Abraham Lincoln*, vol. 1, pp. 68–69.

17   *punching him:* AP to Ward Lamon, Dec. 28, 1867, B: 23, WL, HL; Rice, pp. 36–38; Pinkerton, *The Spy of the Rebellion*, pp. 98–99; Lamon, *Recollections of*

Abraham Lincoln, pp. 45–46; Cuthbert, pp. 82–83, 148–49; Rice, pp. 30–35; Kline, pp. 261, 263, 431.

18 *for him:* Rice, pp. 38–39; Kline, pp. 265–66; Milton, *Abraham Lincoln and the Fifth Column*, pp. 34–36; "Willard Hotel," Washington, D.C., National Register of Historic Places Travel Itinerary; "Abraham Lincoln at the Willard Hotel," Abraham Lincoln Online; "The Willard Hotel in the 19th Century"; Milton, *The Age of Hate*, pp. 11–12; Wilson and Davis, p. 287; Kline, p. 266; Stahr, p. 238; Mackay, p. 97.

19 *blackout remained:* Wilson and Davis, pp. 287, 292–93; Cuthbert, pp. 83–84; Kline, p. 275.

20 *left behind:* Wilson and Davis, pp. 293–94, 324; Kline, pp. 283–88; Cuthbert, pp. 17, 133–35; Nicolay and Hay, *Abraham Lincoln: A History*, vol. 3, pp. 315–16; Stashower, p. 298.

20 *the traitors:* Pinkerton, *The Spy of the Rebellion*, p. 99; Cuthbert, pp. 90–96; Wilson and Davis, p. 299.

20 *never existed:* AP letters to S. M. Felton, March 19 and April 13, 1861, Correspondence with Schouler, Lossing, and Pinkerton, B: 1, FP, HP; AP to Ward Lamon, Oct. 31, 1867, B: 23, WL, HL; Wilson and Davis, p. 298; Kline, p. 320; Cuthbert, pp. 114–16; Pinkerton, *History and Evidence of the Passage of Abraham Lincoln from Harrisburg, Pennsylvania, to Washington, D.C.*, pp. 6–7; Winkle, p. 97.

21 *to the job:* Stashower, pp. 262–7; Kline, pp. 292, 306, 310; Nicolay and Hay, *Abraham Lincoln: A History*, vol. 3, p. 315; Foote, pp. 37–38; Randall, *Lincoln the President: Springfield to Gettysburg, vol. 1*, p. 288; Catton, vol. 1, pp. 225–26, 236; Cuthbert, p. xiv.

21 *in jail:* News story, "The Conspiracy to Assassinate Mr. Lincoln at Baltimore," APP CH; Stashower, pp. 319–26; Morn, p. 41; Lamon, *Recollections of Abraham Lincoln*, p. 33; Lamon, *The Life of Abraham Lincoln*, pp. 512–18, 526–27; Cuthbert, pp. xvi–xv; *The Collected Works of Abraham Lincoln*, vol. 4, p. 281; Nevins, vol. 1, pp. 300–301; Ezratty, p. 49; Cuthbert, p. xvii; Mortimer, *Double Death*, pp. 244–45; Stashower, pp. 269, 329; Kline, pp. ix, 337; Lamon, *The Life of Abraham Lincoln*, p. 517.

22 *political grief:* Lamon, *Recollections of Abraham Lincoln*, pp. 46–47; Horan, *The Pinkertons*, p. 60; Cuthbert, pp. xiv, xvii, 114; Winkle, p. 106; Kline, pp. 339–40, 346; Lossing, p. 108; Stashower, pp. 312–13, 329.

22 *threat seriously:* Stashower, pp. 306–10, 329–30; Fishel, *The Secret War for the Union*, pp. 14, 17–18; Hatch, p. 17; Nicolay and Hay, *Abraham Lincoln: A*

History, vol. 3, pp. 303, 306–7, 313; S. M. Felton to Simon Cameron, April 16, 1861, OR-4:577; Burlingame, *With Lincoln in the White House*, pp. 34–36.

22   *of Lincoln:* Pinkerton, *The Spy of the Rebellion*, p. xxvii; Wilson and Davis, p. 319; Stashower, p. 326; AP to S. M. Felton, B: 1, FP, HP; J. Edgar Hoover to Ralph Dudley, Oct. 5, 1943; Robert Pinkerton to Editor, *New York Times*, Nov. 1, 1946, B: 23, PND, LC.

TWO: GEORGE SHARPE

24   *without incident:* Catton, vol. 1, pp. 258–64; Stepp and Hill, p. 27; Gobright, pp. 287–90; Winkle, pp. xiii, 81–85, 108; Stashower, p. 14; Hatch, pp. 20–21, 25; Eicher, p. 79; Nicolay and Hay, *Abraham Lincoln: A History*, vol. 3, pp. 137–38; Fishel, *The Secret War for the Union*, p. 15.

24   *April 13:* McPherson, *Battle Cry of Freedom*, pp. 262–64, 273–74; Eicher, pp. 33–34; Catton, vol. 1, pp. 143, 271–72, 276–77, 279–81, 295–97, 307–9, 311–24; Goodwin, pp. 335–37; McPherson, *Tried by War*, pp. 17, 20–21; Niven, *Gideon Welles*, pp. 352, 354, 359, 402–3; *The Collected Works of Abraham Lincoln*, vol. 4, p. 351.

25   *and Athens:* Catton, vol. 1, p. 327; McPherson, *Battle Cry of Freedom*, p. 274; Van Santvoord, pp. 3–4; Sharpe, "Memorial Address," p. 5; De Witt, pp. 101–45; Gates, pp. 73–74; *Proceedings of the Ulster County Historical Society 1936–1937*, p. 28; "Picture of General Sharpe," *Kingston Weekly Reader*, Nov. 28, 1903.

25   *so loved:* Sharpe, "The Old Houses of Kingston"; Fishel, *The Secret War for the Union*, p. 291; Sharpe, "Memorial Address," pp. 17–18.

25   *in England:* Heron, pp. 2–3, 5; "The Name of Kingston and Its Predecessors," p. 4.

26   *the brew:* Sharpe, "The Old Houses of Kingston"; Heron, p. 3; Schoonmaker, pp. 442, 455.

26   *elm trees:* Sharpe, "The Old Houses of Kingston"; E. M. Smith, "Our Palatine Settlers," June 18, 20, 25, and 27, 1896, written for the *Gazette*, P. G. & H. Sharpe to F. C. Voorhees, Article of Agreement, May 1, 1824, Sharpe family history (5385) 2568, MA, KS; Smith, *Documentary History of Rhinebeck, in Dutchess County, N.Y.*, pp. 211–13; *Proceedings of the Ulster County Historical Society 1936–1937*, p. 26; *Commemorative Biographical Record of Ulster County, New York*, pp. 111–14; Schoonmaker, pp. 435–39, 440–42, 449, 452–56, 465, 470; De Witt, pp. 49, 52–54, 89.

27   *own finances:* Sharpe family history (5385) 2568, GS letters to Mr. Bruyn,

Dec. 21, 1846, Dec. 25, 1848, Jan. 24, Feb. 17, 20, and 23, and July 7, 1849; Abraham Hasbrouck to Iansen Hasbrouck, Feb. 7, 1830, MA, KS; Schoonmaker, pp. 455, 464; *Proceedings of the Ulster County Historical Society 1936–1937*, p. 26.

27 *at Yale:* GS letter to Mr. Bruyn, Oct. 4 and 13, 1848, and Feb. 3 and July 7, 1849, MA, KS; "Gen. G. H. Sharpe Dead," *New York Times*, Jan. 15, 1900, p. 7; "Picture of General Sharpe," *Kingston Weekly Reader*, Nov. 28, 1903; *Proceedings of the Ulster County Historical Society 1936–1937*, pp. 26–27; Sharpe, "Memorial Address," p. 4; Tsouras, p. 15.

27 *learned Italian:* "Picture of General Sharpe," *Kingston Weekly Reader*, Nov. 28, 1903; "General Sharpe," *Journal*, April 7, 1869, MA, KS.

27 *3rd Division:* "Picture of General Sharpe," *Kingston Weekly Reader*, Nov. 28, 1903; GS to Mr. Bruyn, Sept. 17, 1846, MA, KS; Boyd's Kingston & Rondout Directory 1857–8, p. 61, MA, KS; *Proceedings of the Ulster County Historical Society 1936–1937*, pp. 27–28.

28 *wife Carrie:* GS to My Dear Uncle, July 28, 1863, SLH, KS; *Proceedings of the Ulster County Historical Society 1936–1937*, p. 27; James Morice, "Organizational Learning in a Military Environment: George H. Sharpe and the Army of the Potomac," SGF, KS.

28 *were antiques:* Sharpe, "The Old Houses of Kingston"; Gates, pp. 38–40, 51, 57, 59, 62, 70, 75, 77.

28 *preeminent spymaster:* Donald, *Lincoln*, p. 295.

THREE: ELIZABETH VAN LEW

29 *Rebel uniform:* McPherson, *Battle Cry of Freedom*, pp. 282–87, 292–97; Nicolay and Hay, *Abraham Lincoln: A History*, vol. 1, pp. 162, 170; Niven, *Salmon P. Chase*, pp. 252–53; Thomas, *The Confederate State of Richmond*, pp. 4–7; Brock, pp. 9–10; Dabney, p. 161; Catton, vol. 1, p. 325.

30 *being seized:* Elizabeth Van Lew article "To Northern Democrats," Oct. 27, 1876, EVLP NY; Ryan, *A Yankee Spy in Richmond*, pp. 28–30; Varon, *Southern Lady, Yankee Spy*, p. 44.

30 *and flattering:* Bart Hall, Nov. 2, 2016; Personality Sketch of Elizabeth Van Lew, Works Progress Administration of Virginia Historical Inventory, Record 27, OC, LVA; Tuesday, September Richmond news article, EVLP, NY; Ryan, *A Yankee Spy in Richmond*, p. 27.

30 *had accumulated:* Personality Sketch of Elizabeth Van Lew, Works Progress Administration of Virginia Historical Inventory, Record 27, OC, LVA; Bart Hall,

Nov. 8, 2016; Varon, "True to the Flag," p. 68; Ryan, *A Yankee Spy in Richmond*, pp. 25–26.

31 *way up:* Personality Sketch of Elizabeth Van Lew, Works Progress Administration of Virginia Historical Inventory, Record 27, OC, LVA; "Married," *Richmond Enquirer*, Jan. 15, 1818, p. 3; Varon, "True to the Flag," p. 68; Ryan, *A Yankee Spy in Richmond*, p. 27; Varon, *Southern Lady, Yankee Spy*, pp. 9–10, 15; Bart Hall, Nov. 2, 2016; "Grant's Woman Spy," Nov. 11, 1900, Boston news article, EVLP, NY.

31 *Richmond area:* Feb. 27, bill of sale for Van Lew, Smith & Roberts, CM, LVA; eulogy for John Van Lew, *Richmond Compiler*, Sept. 22, 1843, p. 2; Mutual Assurance Society contract with John Van Lew and Thomas M. Smith, April 2, 1842, Record 60, John Van Lew, OC, LVA; Bart Hall, Nov. 2, 2016; Ryan, *A Yankee Spy in Richmond*, pp. 4–5; Thomas, *The Confederate State of Richmond*, p. 22; John Albree speeches on Elizabeth Van Lew, B: 1, ELC, WM.

32 *of Richmond:* "Miss Van Lew's Spies in the Davis Household," *Richmond Evening Journal*, May 2, 1908; Jones, *Behind Enemy Lines*, p. 50; Largent, "Elizabeth Van Lew"; Varon, *Southern Lady, Yankee Spy*, pp. 3, 12–14.

32 *beautiful home:* Ryan, *A Yankee Spy in Richmond*, p. 4; Lancaster, pp. 118–21; "The Van Lew a Nephew Knew," *Richmond Times-Dispatch*, Sept. 23, 1937, p. 10; Beymer, *On Hazardous Service*, p. 66; Beymer, "Miss Van Lew," p. 87; City of Richmond Chancery Court, Accounts of Fiduciaries, no. 12, LVA; pencil note by Miss Van Lew on George Washington's purse, John Albree speeches on Elizabeth Van Lew, B: 1, ELC, WM.

32 *Henry Clay:* Eulogy for John Van Lew, *Richmond Compiler*, Sept. 22, 1843, p. 2; "Union Woman Spy Had Connection in This City," Dec. 13, 1912, B: 1, ELC, WM; Varon, *Southern Lady, Yankee Spy*, pp. 12, 15–17; Beyer, "Miss Van Lew," p. 87; "Many Valuable Autographs" news article, EVLP, NY; "Van Lew Relics Bring $1,000," *Boston Herald*, Nov. 22, 1900; John Albree speeches on Elizabeth Van Lew, B:1, ELC, WM.

33 *strongest willed:* "Van Lew Relics Bring $1,000," *Boston Herald*, Nov. 22, 1900; John Albree speeches on Elizabeth Van Lew, B: 1, ELC, WM; "The Van Lew a Nephew Knew," *Richmond Times-Dispatch*, Sept. 23, 1937, p. 10; Varon, *Southern Lady, Yankee Spy*, pp. 9, 17–18; Largent, "Elizabeth Van Lew."

33 *"the state":* Faxwell letter to Lester, May 29, 1847, Mss2 H 8778 b6–13 Hull, HF, VHS; Varon, *Southern Lady, Yankee Spy*, p. 24; Winkler, p. 52; "Mysteries of the Famous Van Lew Mansion," news article, EVLP, NY; Van Lew, "Van Liew, Van Lieu, Van Lew," p. 1; Ryan, *A Yankee Spy in Richmond*, p. 5.

33 *the reason:* Eulogy for John Van Lew, *Richmond Compiler*, Sept. 22, 1843, p. 2;

"Mysteries of the Famous Van Lew Mansion," Richmond news article on EVL, EVLP, NY; Varon, *Southern Lady, Yankee Spy*, pp. 18–20; Ryan, *A Yankee Spy in Richmond*, p. 6; Abbott, p. 43.

34 Richmond Compiler *eulogized*: Eulogy for John Van Lew, *Richmond Compiler*, Sept. 22, 1843, p. 2; "Residence of Van Lew," p. 444; "Deaths," *Richmond Enquirer*, Sept. 29, 1843, p. 3; Ryan, *A Yankee Spy in Richmond*, pp. 2–3; Varon, *Southern Lady, Yankee Spy*, p. 18.

34 *father's will*: "Marriages," *Richmond Enquirer*, Jan. 20, 1844, p. 3; Van Lew, *Natural Force*; Varon, *Southern Lady, Yankee Spy*, pp. 9, 16, 20–22; Largent, "Elizabeth Van Lew"; Bart Hall, Nov. 2, 2016; Ryan, *A Yankee Spy in Richmond*, p. 5.

35 *her $1,000*: Jan. 1, 1863, receipt for $1,000 from EVL, B: 1, ELC, WM; Varon, *Southern Lady, Yankee Spy*, pp. 24–27, 32; Varon, "True to the Flag," p. 68; Bart Hall, Nov. 2, 2016; Largent, "Elizabeth Van Lew"; Ryan, *A Yankee Spy in Richmond*, p. 3.

35 *Frederick Douglass*: EVL to My Kind Friend, Jan. 16, 1856, Mss 2V3255a, VHS; "A Woman Spy," news article, B: 1, ELC, WM; Varon, *Southern Lady, Yankee Spy*, pp. 22–24, 33–34, 50; Ryan, *A Yankee Spy in Richmond*, p. 6; news article on EVL, EVLP, NY; Beymer, *On Hazardous Service*, p. 67; Van Lew, "Van Liew, Van Lieu, Van Lew," pp. 1–2; Varon, "True to the Flag," p. 70.

35 *"little thing"*: Varon, "True to the Flag," pp. 70–71; Ryan, *A Yankee Spy in Richmond*, p. 50.

36 *"Look out"*: Ryan, *A Yankee Spy in Richmond*, pp. 7, 17; White Caps letter to EVL, EVLP, NY.

36 *sister-in-law*: Bart Hall, Nov. 2, 2016; Abbott, pp. 77–79.

36 *"the people"*: Dabney, p. 159; Varon, "True to the Flag," p. 70; Varon, *Southern Lady, Yankee Spy*, pp. 37–38, 40, 42, 45–47; Thomas, *The Confederate State of Richmond*, pp. 7, 10; Ryan, *A Yankee Spy in Richmond*, pp. 27–35, 49; "To Northern Democrats," letter to the editor by EVL, Oct. 27, 1876, EVLP, NY; Varon, "True to the Flag," p. 70.

37 *"deadly pale"*: Ryan, *A Yankee Spy in Richmond*, pp. 29, 31–32, 35; Varon, *Southern Lady, Yankee Spy*, pp. 43, 51, 54.

37 *Joseph Mayo*: Abbott, p. 42; Varon, *Southern Lady, Yankee Spy*, pp. 6, 34; Ryan, *A Yankee Spy in Richmond*, pp. 32, 34.

38 *"with it"*: Jones, *Ladies of Richmond*, p. 57; Thomas, *The Confederate State of Richmond*, pp. 16–17, 21–22; Parker, p. 1.

38 *manufacture cartridges*: Brock, pp. 28, 34–37, 78, 80–83; Winkler, p. 53; Jones,

Ladies of Richmond, p. 62; Thomas, *The Confederate State of Richmond,* pp. 35–36, 65–68.

38 *the Union:* Beymer, "Miss Van Lew," pp. 87–88; Bart Hall, Nov. 7, 2016; Markle, pp. 180–81.

FOUR: LAFAYETTE BAKER

39 *a spy:* Mogelever, pp. 42–45; Winkle, p. 148; McPherson, *Battle Cry of Freedom,* p. 286; Catton, vol. 1, pp. 345, 349; Milton, *Abraham Lincoln and the Fifth Column,* p. 25; Bakeless, pp. 4–8; Fishel, *The Secret War for the Union,* pp. 10–11, 56; Nicolay and Hay, *Abraham Lincoln: A History,* vol. 4, p. 98; LB to sister, April 28, 1861, B: 3, JE, HL.

40 *in Washington:* LB to sister, April 28, 1861, B: 3, JE, HL; Orrmont, pp. 18–20; Baker, *History of the United States Secret Service,* pp. 19–20.

40 *make money:* LB to sister, April 28, 1861, B: 3, JE, HL; Mogelever, pp. 17, 29, 37; Baker, *History of the United States Secret Service,* p. 20; Corson, p. 530; Millard, "The Devil's Errand Boy"; Robert H. Fowler, "Was Stanton Behind Lincoln's Murder?" p. 13; Baker, pp. 22–34; Corson, p. 531; Morn, p. 10; Mogelever, pp. 18, 39; Hageman, p. 1.

41 *were hunting:* American Ancestors of Ray Stannard Baker, SB; Orrmont, p. 9; *Joseph Stannard Baker Memoirs from 1838 to 1865,* p. 1-1.

42 *a stake:* *Joseph Stannard Baker Memoirs from 1838 to 1865,* pp. 1-2 to 1-4; Baker, *History of the United States Secret Service,* pp. 17–18; Corson, pp. 529–30; Mogelever, pp. 22–25.

42 *the village:* *Joseph Stannard Baker Memoirs from 1838 to 1865,* pp. 1-5 to 1-6, 2-1, 3-1 to 3-4; Mogelever, p. 21; Baker, *History of the United States Secret Service,* p. 18; American Ancestors of Ray Stannard Baker, SB.

42 *an atheist:* Corson, pp. 528–29; Mogelever, pp. 26–29; Orrmont, pp. 9–11.

43 *for gold:* Mogelever, pp. 29–30; Orrmont, pp. 11–12.

44 *unchecked power:* Orrmont, p. 15; Mogelever, pp. 32–36; "The Annals of San Francisco," p. 1; Baker, *History of the United States Secret Service,* p. 19; "The Committee of Vigilance 1851," paper by Brian F. Diaz; Maritime Heritage Project, Vigilance Committee, http://www.maritimeheritage.org/vips/vigilance.html; Vigilance Committee of 1856, Virtual Museum of the City of San Francisco, http//:www.sfmuseum.org; Hageman, p. 1; Treasury Department Report from the Select Committee, p. 183; Corson, p. 530.

44 *Lincoln administration:* Baker, *History of the United States Secret Service,* p. 19; Mogelever, pp. 36–37.

44   *was ensconced:* Baker, *History of the United States Secret Service*, p. 45; Lynette
     Clemetson, "Finding U.S. History in a Washington Hotel," *New York Times*,
     Jan. 4, 2006.

45   *pitched battle:* Eicher, pp. 63, 70, 80–81; Sears, *George B. McClellan*, p. 15;
     Goodwin, p. 313; Foote, p. 102; Stern, p. 30; Nicolay and Hay, *Abraham Lincoln: A History*, vol. 4, p. 126; Scott to George W. Childs, Feb. 14, 1863, B: 137,
     FD, HP; Catton, vol. 1, pp. 118–19, 161, 438–39; McPherson, *Battle Cry of
     Freedom*, p. 333; Jones, *Ladies of Richmond*, p. 57.

46   *for work:* Baker, *History of the United States Secret Service*, pp. 45–46; Orrmont,
     pp. 21–22; Mogelever, pp. 48–50; Morn, p. 42; Corson, pp. 531–32; Millard,
     p. 4.

FIVE: SECRET SERVICE

47   *a paperweight:* Dennett, p. v; Burlingame, *With Lincoln in the White House*,
     p. 36; Winkle, pp. 111–15; Goodwin, pp. 333–35; Donald, *Lincoln*, p. 310.

48   *to Pinkerton:* Pinkerton, *The Spy of the Rebellion*, pp. 56; Corson, p. 525; Recko,
     pp. 5–14, 28, 39, 54, 69.

48   *might encounter:* Package of letters brought by one of Pinkerton's men to Washington, April 23, 1861, Series 1, General Correspondence 1833–1916, ALD,
     LC; Eicher, pp. 53–55; McClellan, *Report on the Organization and Campaigns
     of the Army of the Potomac*, p. 7; Pinkerton, *The Spy of the Rebellion*, pp. 110–13;
     Lavine, pp. 65–68; Rowan, pp. 122–23.

48   *the mail:* Pinkerton, *The Spy of the Rebellion*, pp. 128–30; Beymer, *On Hazardous Service*, pp. 263–66; Brooks, pp. 276–80.

49   *and "rooster":* AP to AL, April 21, 1861; N. B. Judd to AL, April 21, 1861,
     APP, CH.

49   *bombard it:* O'Toole, p. 120; "Intelligence in the Civil War," p. 11; Bakeless,
     p. 2; Goodwin, pp. 357, 366; Marvel, p. 142.

49   *Executive Mansion:* Pinkerton, *The Spy of the Rebellion*, pp. 129–30; Rowan,
     p. 124; Beymer, *On Hazardous Service*, p. 265.

50   *its diplomats:* Pinkerton, *The Spy of the Rebellion*, pp. 136–38; Winkle, pp. xiv,
     121–24, 128–29, 175–77, 217; Roscoe, p. 10; Bryan, p. 51.

50   *of state:* AL to WHS, May 2, 1861, Series 1, General Correspondence 1853–
     1916, ALD, LC; Pinkerton, *The Spy of the Rebellion*, pp. 138–39; Miers, p. 39;
     Nicolay and Hay, *Abraham Lincoln: A History*, vol. 4, pp. 68–69; Milton, *Abraham Lincoln and the Fifth Column*, p. 37; Milton, *The Age of Hate*, p. 13.

51   *for secession:* Niven, *Gideon Welles*, p. 306; Donald, *Lincoln*, pp. 301–4; Milton,

Abraham Lincoln and the Fifth Column, pp. 20, 171; Catton, vol. 3, p. 105; Winkle, p. xiii; Catton, vol. 1, p. 353–57.

51 *were working:* GM to AL, June 10, 1861; W. M. Dickson to AL, June 10, 1861, Series 1 General Correspondence 1853–1916, ALD, LC; Temple, pp. 369–78; Catton, vol. 2, pp. 58, 60, 63–66, 488; Catton, vol. 1, pp. 366–70.

51 *that respect:* Niven, *Salmon P. Chase*, p. 217; Stahr, pp. 201–2; AL to Andrew Johnson, June 9, 1862, vol. 5, pp. 265–66, AL to Joseph Holt, May 23, 1863, vol. 6, p. 227, AL to William S. Rosecrans, May 21, 1863, vol. 6, p. 236, AL to Erastus Corning and others, June 12, 1863, vol. 6, pp. 261–69, *The Collected Works of Abraham Lincoln;* McPherson, *Embattled Rebel*, pp. 73–74.

52 *collect intelligence:* Markle, p. xvi; Jones, *Behind Enemy Lines*, p. 6; Cook, p. 5; Fishel, *The Secret War for the Union*, p. 9.

52 *Service Bureau:* "Intelligence in the Civil War," pp. 4, 13; O'Toole, pp. 119, 128–30; Fishel, "The Mythology of Civil War Intelligence," pp. 345–46, 358; "The Signal Corps in the Confederate States Army," pp. 93–107.

52 *rookie soldiers:* Fishel, *The Secret War for the Union*, p. 8; Fishel, "The Mythology of Civil War Intelligence," pp. 344–45; Feis, *Grant's Secret Service*, pp. 3–4; Axelrod, p. 6; Markle, pp. xvi–xvii, 95–96; Maslowski, pp. 44–46.

52 *Union agents:* Fishel, "The Mythology of Civil War Intelligence," p. 361; Maslowski, p. 41; Markle, p. xvi; John W. Headley, Secret Service, Confederate—Photographic History of the Civil War account (vol. 8, 286–304), B: 5, EF, GU.

53 *"a few days":* Wm. N. Barker, "Captain and Chief of Signal Corps," to Cooper, Aug. 8, 1864, Box 5, EF, GU; Markle, pp. xvii, 1; Bakeless, p. 2; Fishel, *The Secret War for the Union*, p. 570; Pinkerton, *The Spy of the Rebellion*, pp. 139–41; Morn, p. 38.

54 *May 9:* AP to GM, April 28, 1861, GM to AP, April 24, 1861, AP to GM, May 4, 1861, B: 16, EF, GU; Pinkerton, *The Spy of the Rebellion*, pp. 139–41; Mackay, pp. 108–9; Horan, *The Pinkertons*, p. 64.

SIX: BULL RUN

55 *Toutant Beauregard:* Baker, *History of the United States Secret Service*, pp. 45–46; Axelrod, p. 177; Catton, vol. 1, p. 390; Winkle, pp. 150–58; Eicher, p. 78; McPherson, *Tried by War*, p. 36; McPherson, *Battle Cry of Freedom*, p. 335.

56 *to undertake:* McPherson, *Battle Cry of Freedom*, pp. 336–37; Catton, vol. 1, p. 252; Eicher, pp. 36, 74–75; Donald, *Lincoln*, pp. 306–7; McPherson, *Tried by War*, p. 37; Jones, *Ladies of Richmond*, p. 57; Keegan, p. 69.

56   *decidedly lacked:* McPherson, *Battle Cry of Freedom,* pp. 335–36; Catton, vol.
1, pp. 398–39, 438–41; Winkler, p. 7; Eicher, pp. 79–81; McPherson, *Tried by
War,* p. 39; Sears, *To the Gates of Richmond,* pp. 12, 46.

57   *and movements:* Fishel, *The Secret War for the Union,* pp. 29, 37, 40–41; Woods,
p. 56.

57   *"to Dixie":* Hageman, p. 2; Baker, *History of the United States Secret Service,* p. 46.

57   *"try again":* Baker, *History of the United States Secret Service,* pp. 46–48; Orrmont, pp. 22–25; Axelrod, p. 180; Fishel, "The Mythology of Civil War Intelligence," p. 348; Fishel, *The Secret War for the Union,* p. 24; Catton, vol. 1, pp.
441–46.

58   *toward Manassas:* Baker, *History of the United States Secret Service,* pp. 48–49;
Mogelever, p. 52.

59   *five days:* Baker, *History of the United States Secret Service,* pp. 49–55; Corson,
pp. 532–33.

59   *questioned Baker:* Baker, *History of the United States Secret Service,* pp. 57–61;
O'Toole, p. 167; Fishel, *The Secret War for the Union,* pp. 25–26; Maslowski,
p. 41.

60   *the river:* Baker, *History of the United States Secret Service,* pp. 61–69; Fishel, *The
Secret War for the Union,* p. 25; Mogelever, pp. 60–62.

61   *local prostitute:* Fishel, *The Secret War for the Union,* p. 25; Hageman, p. 4.

61   *the city:* Catton, vol. 2, p. 1; Catton, vol. 1, pp. 460–62, 465–68; Winkle, p. 161;
McPherson, *Battle Cry of Freedom,* pp. 335–47; Livermore, p. 77; Eicher, p. 99;
Donald, *Lincoln,* p. 307; Baker, *History of the United States Secret Service,* pp.
70–72.

62   *told him:* Fishel, *The Secret War for the Union,* pp. 26–27, 34–37; Hageman,
p. 4; Baker, *History of the United States Secret Service,* p. 72.

62   *a job:* Sept. 7, 1861, expense vouchers submitted by LB for $803.50, B: 1, E:
95, RG110, NA; Fishel, *The Secret War for the Union,* p. 26; Mogelever, p. 66.

63   *the operation:* Goodwin, pp. 216–17, 290–92, 313; McPherson, *Battle Cry
of Freedom,* pp. 321–22; Niven, *Gideon Welles,* p. 391; Mogelever, pp. 67–72;
Baker, *History of the United States Secret Service,* pp. 72–84; Orrmont, pp. 35–
38; Woods, pp. 56–57.

63   *autumn's frost:* Jones, *A Rebel War Clerk's Diary,* pp. 49–50; Thomas, *The Confederate State of Richmond,* pp. 53–54; Brock, p. 77; Jones, *Ladies of Richmond,*
pp. 69–70.

63   *of casualties:* Thomas, *The Confederate State of Richmond,* pp. 54–55; Brock,
p. 65; Dabney, p. 166; Catton, vol. 1, pp. 471–73.

63   *"to expect":* Varon, p. 55; Ryan, *A Yankee Spy in Richmond,* p. 37.

SEVEN: THE OHIO DEPARTMENT

64 *assassination plot:* Sears, *George B. McClellan*, p. 72; AP to GM, May 4, 1861, GMP, LC.

65 *country's savior:* Brooks, pp. 14–15; Foote, p. 100; McPherson, *Battle Cry of Freedom*, pp. 300–301, 359–60; Sears, *To the Gates of Richmond*, p. 10; Nicolay and Hay, *Abraham Lincoln: A History*, vol. 4, pp. 443–44, 446–48; Sears, *George B. McClellan*, pp. xi, 16; Catton, vol. 1, p. 407; McPherson, *Tried by War*, pp. 44, 47–48; Goodwin, pp. 377–78.

65 *Union uniform:* Sears, *George B. McClellan*, pp. 1, 12–14, 23–32, 35–36, 44–51, 58–59, 66–67; McClellan, *McClellan's Own Story*, p. 162; Rafuse, pp. 40–49.

66 *his force:* Niven, *Salmon P. Chase*, pp. 354–55; McClellan, *Report on the Organization and Campaigns of the Army of the Potomac*, p. 11; Sears, *George B. McClellan*, pp. 69–72; Towne, pp. 61–62; Pinkerton, *The Spy of the Rebellion*, pp. 152–53.

66 *cover expenses:* Pinkerton, *The Spy of the Rebellion*, pp. 153–55; Mackay, p. 110; "Intelligence in the Civil War," p. 17; Fishel, *The Secret War for the Union*, p. 3; Fishel, "The Mythology of Civil War Intelligence," p. 345; Horan, *The Pinkertons*, p. 65; Rowan, p. 129; Horan and Swiggett, pp. 96–97.

66 *Kentucky:* Sears, *George B. McClellan*, pp. 74–76.

67 *intelligence objective:* John Campbell to GM, May 9, 1861, William Musk to GM, R: 5, GMP, LC; Sears, *George McClellan*, pp. 76–77; Horan, *The Pinkertons*, p. 65; Recko, pp. 73–74.

69 *spy mission:* Recko, pp. 74–75; Pinkerton, *The Spy of the Rebellion*, pp. 155–81; Richardson, *The Secret Service, the Field, the Dungeon and the Escape*, p. 32.

69 *"Secretary Cameron":* AP to GM, July 3, 1861, R: 15, Letters Received A2-H39 1861 M2096, NA; Report of T. Webster on Trip to Memphis & Knoxville, Aug. 7, 1861, B: 25, PND; AP letters to AL, July 19 and 26, 1861, Series 1, General Correspondence 1833–1916, ALD; AP to GM, June 26, 1861, R: 7, GMP, LC; Recko, pp. 78–83; Mackay, p. 115; Horan, *The Pinkertons*, pp. 68, 76–78.

71 *to Cincinnati:* Pinkerton, *The Spy of the Rebellion*, pp. 182–202; Pinkerton, *The Somnambulist and the Detective*, pp. 9, 105.

71 *a battleground:* Catton, vol. 1, pp. 405–6; GM Report, Aug. 4, 1863, OR-5:5; Sears, *George B. McClellan*, p. 78.

71 *arm them:* "To the Patriots of Northwestern Virginia!!" R: 16, GMP, LC; GM to AL, June 1, 1861, R: 6, GMP, LC; Sears, *George B. McClellan*, pp. 78–79; McClellan, *Report on the Organization and Campaigns of the Army of the Potomac*, p. 14.

72   *Union victory:* Catton, vol. 1, p. 407; Sears, *George B. McClellan*, p. 80; Eicher, p. 75.

72   *fight Wise:* Sears, *George B. McClellan*, pp. 83–84; Mortimer, *Double Death*, pp. 77–81.

72   *it out:* Intelligence on Kanawha Valley, May 1861, R: 5, GMP, LC; AP to GM, June 24, 1861, B: 16, GU, EF; Mackay, pp. 114–15.

73   *western Virginia:* G. H. Bangs to PL, Feb. 18, 1861, B: 2, Harriet Shoen Notes on the Interpretation of the Pryce Lewis Memoirs, Letters to Harriet Shoen from Mary Lewis, February 1947, B: 3, Memoirs of Pryce Lewis as Told to Major David E. Cronin in 1888, pp. vi, x–xxii, 1–5, B: 4, PLC, SLU; Inglis, p. 23; Mortimer, *Double Death*, pp. 4–13, 17, 20–23.

74   *later wrote:* Photo of Sam Bridgeman, B: 2, Memoirs of Pryce Lewis as Told to Major David E. Cronin in 1888, pp. 6–7, B: 4, PLC, SLU; Popchock, p. 23; Mortimer, *Double Death*, pp. 42–46; "Had an Eventful Life," *Chicago Times*, Dec. 20, 1894.

74   *best of it:* Memoirs of Pryce Lewis as Told to Major David E. Cronin in 1888, pp. 7–9, B: 4, PLC, SLU; Mortimer, *Double Death*, p. 40.

75   *western Virginia:* Memoirs of Pryce Lewis as Told to Major David E. Cronin in 1888, pp. 8–10, 12, B: 4, PLC, SLU; Mortimer, *Double Death*, p. 46; Popchock, p. 23.

76   *in jail:* Memoirs of Pryce Lewis as Told to Major David E. Cronin in 1888, pp. 14–15, B: 4, PLC, SLU; Mortimer, *Double Death*, pp. 51–53.

77   *"day, sir":* Memoirs of Pryce Lewis as Told to Major David E. Cronin in 1888, pp. 12, 15–16, B: 4, PLC, SLU; Mortimer, *Double Death*, pp. 53–55.

77   *their escape:* Memoirs of Pryce Lewis as Told to Major David E. Cronin in 1888, pp. 17–19, Pryce Lewis: Spy for the Union, by Harriet H. Shoen, p. 62, B: 4, PLC, SLU; Mortimer, *Double Death*, pp. 56–58.

77   *troops there:* Memoirs of Pryce Lewis as Told to Major David E. Cronin in 1888, pp. 19–23, B: 4, PLC, SLU; Mortimer, *Double Death*, p. 60.

78   *July 18:* PL receipt, July 11, 1861, for Kanawha House, B: 2, Memoirs of Pryce Lewis as Told to Major David E. Cronin in 1888, pp. 24–36, B: 4, PLC, SLU; Mortimer, *Double Death*, pp. 63–64, 67–69, 75–76.

79   *Union hands:* Memoirs of Pryce Lewis as Told to Major David E. Cronin in 1888, pp. 36–43, B: 4, PLC, SLU; Mortimer, *Double Death*, pp. 77–87; Sears, *George B. McClellan*, pp. 90–92.

79   *Pinkerton's stars:* Sears, *George B. McClellan*, p. 93; Mortimer, *Double Death*, pp. 89–90.

EIGHT: WASHINGTON

80   *"the man"*: Catton, vol. 2, p. 9; McPherson, *Battle Cry of Freedom*, pp. 348, 350; Donald, *Lincoln*, pp. 307–8; Catton, vol. 1, pp. 468–69; GM report on operations of the Army of the Potomac from July 27, 1861, to Nov. 9, 1862, OR-5:6; Sears, *George B. McClellan*, p. 94; AP to GM, July 3, 1861, Roll 15, Letters Received A2-H39, 1861, M2096 NA; AP to GM, July 11, 1861, B: 16, EF, GU.

81   *train east:* GM to AP, B: 2, PND, LOC; AP telegrams to GM, July 26 and 30, 1861, Roll 15, Letters Received A2-H39 1861, M2096, NA; GM to AP, July 30, 1861, B: 16, EF, GU; McClellan, *Report on the Organization and Campaigns of the Army of the Potomac*, p. 37; Sears, *George B. McClellan*, pp. 95–96; Catton, vol. 2, pp. 79–82; Sears, *The Civil War Papers of George B. McClellan*, pp. 70–71; AP to GM, July 30, 1861, OR-4:253-54; Horan, *The Pinkertons*, p. 79.

81   *"a traitor"*: McClellan, *McClellan's Own Story*, pp. 86, 89; Sears, *George B. McClellan*, p. 100; GM to Simon Cameron, OR-5:11; General Orders no. 2, July 30, 1861, OR-2:769; McClellan, *McClellan's Own Story*, pp. 66–68; Pinkerton, *The Spy of the Rebellion*, p. 243; McClellan, *Report on the Organization and Campaigns of the Army of the Potomac*, pp. 41–44; GM report on Operations of the Army of the Potomac from July 27, 1861, to Nov. 9, 1862, OR-5:6; McPherson, *Tried by War*, p. 45; Foote, pp. 99–100; McPherson, *Battle Cry of Freedom*, p. 349; Sears, *George B. McClellan*, pp. 96, 100; Catton, vol. 2, pp. 84–85; Eicher, p. 107.

81   *free moments:* AP to D. C. Clark, Sept. 9, 1861, AP letters to R. H. Laurence, Aug. 22, 25, 28, and 29, 1861, B: 2, AP to Son, April 28, 1883, R: 3, PND, LC; Fishel, *The Secret War for the Union*, pp. 21–22; Lavine, p. 77; Pinkerton, *The Spy of the Rebellion*, p. 245; Horan and Swiggett, p. 10; Morn, p. 37.

82   *plus expenses:* AP to A. Carnegie, Aug. 30, 1861, B: 2, PND, LC; AP expenses for $1,240, Sept. 3, 1861, AP expenses of $3,936 for period ending Aug. 31, 1861, B: 1, E: 95, RG110 NA; Pinkerton, *The Spy of the Rebellion*, pp. xxvii–xxviii; Horan, *The Pinkertons*, pp. 78–79; McClellan, *Report on the Organization and Campaigns of the Army of the Potomac*, pp. 72–74; Ryan, *Spies, Scouts, and Secrets in the Gettysburg Campaign*, p. 2; Winkle, p. 184.

82   *two names:* AP expenses of $3,936 for period ending Aug. 31, 1861, B: 1, E: 95, RG110; AP letters to GM, Dec. 13, 1861, R: 14, GMP, LC; (*Washington*) *Evening Star*, Dec. 11, 1862; AP to P. H. Watson, Oct. 7, 1861, B: 6, E: 95, RG110, NA; Fishel, *The Secret War for the Union*, p. 54; Greenhow, p. 54; Pinkerton, *The Spy of the Rebellion*, pp. 246–49.

83 *them later:* AP letters to George Bangs, Aug. 29 and 30, 1861, AP to R. H. Laurence, Aug. 22, 1861, B: 2, PND, LC; Rowan, p. 145; Geringer, pp. 18–19; Webster, "Editorial: A Remarkable Detective," Memoirs of Pryce Lewis as Told to Major David E. Cronin in 1888, pp. 12, 44–46, B: 4, PLC, SLU; Lavine, p. 84; Jarman, "The Pinkerton Story," Part Two, p. 78.

83 *service operation:* AP to George Bangs, Aug. 29, 1861, AP letters to R. H. Laurence, Aug. 22, 25, and 28, 1861, AP to W. W. Scarloro, Aug. 27, 1861, B: 2, PND, LC; Mackay, p. 120; Horan, *The Pinkertons,* pp. 526–27.

83 *counterintelligence triumph:* AP to W. W. Averell, Aug. 22, 1861, AP to Thomas A. Scott, Aug. 21, 1861, B: 2, PND, LC; Pinkerton, *The Spy of the Rebellion,* pp. 246–48, 301; Mackay, pp. 121–22; Horan, *The Pinkertons,* p. 98; Morn, p. 44; Fishel, "The Mythology of Civil War Intelligence," p. 349.

84 *Gertrude's death:* Winkle, pp. 5, 18, 195–98; Stern, p. 55; Doster, pp. 19, 73; Mackay, pp. 123–24; Ross, p. 87; Fishel, *The Secret War for the Union,* pp. 58–59; Blackman, pp. 36–37; Pinkerton, *The Spy of the Rebellion,* p. 253.

84 *of influence:* Ross, p. 63; ROG on Politics and Washington, D.C., Society, B: 1, HMS Entry, RG59, NA.

84 *powerful woman:* Mackay, p. 124; Markle, p. 159; James Buchanan letters to ROG, March 21, 1853, Nov. 23, 1855, B: 1, HMS Entry, RG59, NA; Bakeless, pp. 9–10; "Intelligence in the Civil War," p. 11; Ross, pp. 63–64, 71; O'Toole, p. 121; Winkler, pp. 1–4.

85 *Confederate spy:* ROG letter discussing the fate of the Union, B: 1, HMS Entry, RG59, NA; ROG letters on behalf of Captain Treadwell S. Moore, James Hamilton's application in relation to the promotion of General William Sherman's Brigade, letter to Simon Cameron concerning recommendation of appointment of A. B. Stockwell, letters from A.C. Whitcomb to ROG concerning Mrs. Allen's position at the Mint, HMS Entry, RG59, NA; Ross, pp. 63–66, 81, 104–5; Fishel, *The Secret War for the Union,* p. 59.

85 *that matter:* Blackman, pp. 36–37; Fishel, *The Secret War for the Union,* p. 59; "Intelligence in the Civil War," p. 11; Horan, *The Pinkertons,* pp. 83–84; Ross, p. 91; Thomas Jordan to J. P. Benjamin, Oct. 29, 1861, OR-5:928–29; Winkler, p. 6; Ross, pp. 105–6, 131.

86 *at Manassas:* Journal in ROG's handwriting, ROG to General Mansfield, Aug. 1, 1861, Pass for ROG, Aug. 3, 1861, William C. Humphrey to ROG, July 26, 1861, B: 1, HMS Entry, RG59, NA; Winkler, p. 197; Blackman, pp. 37–38.

86 *that intelligence:* 1st Bull Run—the Duvall story from Davis, "To His Excellency Jefferson Davis," July 11, 1861, o/a, July 10, evidence that Greenhow sent warning of Federal advance, First Bull Run—Confederate lack of precise

knowledge of Federal plans, B: 6, EF, GU; Bakeless, pp. 18–21; Winkler, p. 8; Markle, p. 19; Leonard, p. 74; Fishel, *The Secret War for the Union*, pp. 59–60.

86 *for battle:* G. T. Beauregard to Augusta Evans, March 26, 1863, B: 6, EF, GU; Jones, *A Rebel War Clerk's Diary at the Confederate States Capital*, p. 47; Bakeless, pp. 22–24; Winkler, p. 9.

87 *and Davis:* First Bull Run—speed with which information leaked from Washington to Manassas, B: 6, EF, GU; "The Movement," "The War for the Union," "The Forward Movement," *New York Daily Tribune*, July 17, 1861, pp. 4–5; "The Latest War News," *New York Daily Tribune*, July 18, 1861, p. 4; Fishel, *The Secret War for the Union*, pp. 58, 60–62; Catton, vol. 1, pp. 442, 504–5; O'Toole, pp. 121–22; Blackman, pp. 44–45, 305.

87 *the enemy:* ROG 9–8–61–Evening letter, Description of defenses and fortifications around Washington, ROG intelligence report, Aug. 21, 1861, Interpretation of torn or ciphered ROG report, July 31, 1861, ROG, Aug. 16, 1861, intelligence report, B: 1, HMS Entry, RG59, NA; Greenhow's surviving reports, B: 6, EF, GU; Winkler, p. 11; Horan, *The Pinkertons*, p. 86; Fishel, *The Secret War for the Union*, p. 63; Blackman, p. 301.

87 *as well:* William Averell transcript, p. 20, DB, LC; Blackman, p. 183; Ross, pp. 112, 117–18; Fishel, *The Secret War for the Union*, pp. 57–58; Bakeless, p. 33; Winkler, p. 12.

89 *arrested them:* Pinkerton, *The Spy of the Rebellion*, pp. 252–59; Mortimer, *Double Death*, pp. 102–3; Memoirs of Pryce Lewis as Told to Major David E. Cronin in 1888, pp. 47–48, B: 4, Louis Sigaud letter to Miss Shoen, Sept. 4, 1945, B: 3, PLC, SLU; Blackman, pp. 52–54; Bakeless, pp. 36, 39; Ross, p. 120.

89 *"under arrest":* Pinkerton, *The Spy of the Rebellion*, pp. 259, 265–68.

90 *of bloodhounds:* Pinkerton, *The Spy of the Rebellion*, pp. 268–69; Rowan, p. 144; Bakeless, pp. 40–44; Axelrod, pp. 62–63; Ross, p. 113; Blackman, pp. 183–87; Greenhow, pp. 18, 52–66, 203–4, 250; Memoirs of Pryce Lewis as Told to Major David E. Cronin in 1888, p. 48, B: 4, PLC, SLU; Horan, *The Pinkertons*, p. 87; Mackay, 125–28; Popchock, p. 25.

90 *her hand:* Greenhow, pp. 18, 53–66; Markle, pp. 19–20; Blackman, p. 187; Bakeless, pp. 47–48; Memoirs of Pryce Lewis as Told to Major David E. Cronin in 1888, p. 49, B: 4, PLC, SLU; Mortimer, *Double Death*, pp. 105–6; Case of Mrs. Greenhow (House Doc. no. 66, 55th Congress, 3rd Session), p. 561, B: 1, HMS Entry, RG59, NA.

91 *plain text:* Case of Mrs. Greenhow (House Doc. no. 66, 55th Congress, 3rd Session), p. 561, General Orders, no. 16, War Department Adjutant General's Office, May 4, 1861, Fragment of note pieced together, Letter from Manassas,

Va., with portions missing, B: 1 Entry HMS, RG59, News clipping found in ROG house, Fragment of cipher message to Beauregard, B: 1, E: 68, RG107, Proceedings of the Commission in the case of ROG, March 29, 1862, Fragments of ROG letters, B: 2, E: A1-962, RG59, NA; Fishel, *The Secret War for the Union*, pp. 62, 68–69, 575–78.

91 *master spy:* Letter from ROG to "Mon Ami," notation explaining contents of nine letters, HMS Entry, RG59, NA; Fishel, *The Secret War for the Union*, pp. 62, 64, 575–78.

92 *the senator:* List of names of persons supposed to be traitors, Letter to Capt. Hamilton, Senator Wilson love notes, Letters to ROG (Private), B: 1, HMS Entry, RG59, NA; Ross, pp. 67–71, 127–28, 135–41; Horan, *The Pinkertons*, pp. 88–90; Mackay, p. 128; Fishel, *The Secret War for the Union*, pp. 63–64; Brooks, pp. 23–24.

92 *"is useless":* Proceedings of the Commission in the case of ROG, March 29, 1862, B: 2, E: A1–962, RG59, NA; Journal of Mrs. Eugenia Phillips, B: 1, PPF, LC; "Secession Women in Custody," news story, B: 146, Section A, RGP, DU; Blackman, pp. 190–97, 218; Winkler, pp. 23–24; Ross, pp. 154–56; Axelrod, pp. 64–65; Greenhow, pp. 63–64, 86–87, 103–4; Winkler, p. 21; Lavine, pp. 98–101; Fishel, *The Secret War for the Union*, pp. 66–67; Thomas Jordan to J. P. Benjamin, Oct. 29, 1861, OR-5:928.

93 *Marie Antoinette:* Journal of Mrs. Eugenia Phillips, B: 1, PPF, LC; "Secession Women in Custody," news story, B: 146, Section A, RGP, DU; "The Cowardly Disposition at Washington," by Rose O. N. Greenhow, *Richmond Whig*, Dec. 3, 1861; Horan, *The Pinkertons*, p. 81; Mackay, pp. 133–34; Blackman, pp. 199–203; Horan, *The Pinkertons*, pp. 94–95; Ross, pp. 141–43, 157–58, 164–65; Greenhow, pp. 202–3; Memoirs of Pryce Lewis as Told to Major David E. Cronin in 1888, p. 49, B: 4, PLC, SLU.

93 *to Richmond:* Greenhow, pp. 213–22, 298–99, 314–17; Blackman, pp. 206–8; Doster, pp. 82–83; Ross, pp. 173, 182, 185–92, 197, 201; Leonard, pp. 41–42; Mackay, pp. 134–35; Horan, *The Pinkertons*, pp. 95–96; Randall, *Lincoln the President: Midstream*, p. 200; Thomas, *Stanton* p. 158; Fishel, *The Secret War for the Union*, pp. 67–68.

93 *in Washington:* Fishel, "The Mythology of Civil War Intelligence," pp. 349–52; Tidwell, p. 73; Fishel, *The Secret War for the Union*, p. 75.

94 *book sales:* ROG to JD, July 16, 1863, B: 2, JDC, ROG to Alexander Boteler, Feb. 17, 1864, B: 2, ROG to A. A. Bates, Dec. 10, 1863, B: 146, RGP, DU; Fishel, *The Secret War for the Union*, p. 68; Blackman, pp. 297–99, 307.

94   *understandable way:* AP $6,805.16 in expenses for September 1861, AP $6,693.22 in expenses for October 1861, AP $6,660.96 in expenses for November 1861, B: 1, E: 95, RG110, NA; Fishel, *The Secret War for the Union*, pp. 3, 54–55; McClellan, *Report on the Organization and Campaigns of the Army of the Potomac*, pp. 119–21.

95   *their value:* Fishel, *The Secret War for the Union*, pp. 115–17, 120–22; Markle, p. 56; Rose, p. 2; Quarles, pp. 80–81.

95   *their uniforms:* AP to GM, Aug. 31, 1861, R: 11, GMP, William Averell transcript, p. 23, DB, LC; Pinkerton, *The Spy of the Rebellion*, p. 343; Fishel, *The Secret War for the Union*, pp. 55, 84–85, 114; Fishel, "The Mythology of Civil War Intelligence," pp. 361–62; McPherson, *Battle Cry of Freedom*, pp. 620–22.

95   *to Pinkerton:* Fishel, *The Secret War for the Union*, pp. 84–86.

96   *and copper:* AP to GM, Dec. 26, 1861, R: 14, GMP, LC; Dabney, pp. 164, 183; Thomas, *The Confederate State of Richmond*, pp. 16, 23–24.

97   *the boat:* Winkler, pp. 89–93; Rowan, p. 154; Pinkerton, *The Spy of the Rebellion*, pp. 395–403.

98   *backed down:* Webster narrative, Aug. 22–23, 1861, B: 25, "The South," Documents seized at this office in Baltimore, Sept. 13, 1861, R: 1, PND, LC; Pinkerton, *The Spy of the Rebellion*, pp. 271–79; Horan, *The Pinkertons*, pp. 98–99; Recko, p. 86; AP report of arrests at Baltimore, Md., Sept. 23, 1861, OR-5:195–96.

98   *of them:* AP letters to McPhail, Sept. 24 and Oct. 19, 1861, R: 1, PND, LC; News item on Webster escape, *Baltimore American and Commercial Advertiser*, Nov. 27, 1861, p. 1; Pinkerton, *The Spy of the Rebellion*, pp. 332–42; Recko, pp. 101–3.

99   *wade through:* Two AP reports to GM, Nov. 15, 1861, R:13, GMP, LC; Pinkerton, *The Spy of the Rebellion*, pp. 308–25; Recko, pp. 92–98; Fishel, *The Secret War for the Union*, pp. 89–91; Fishel, "Pinkerton and McClellan," pp. 121–22.

100   *troop strength:* Fishel, *The Secret War for the Union*, pp. 97–98, 110; Frederick Seward to Andrew Porter, July 14, 1862, p. 124, vol. 3, E: 955, RG59, NA.

100   *to California:* AP to GM, Dec. 27, 1861, R:14, GMP, LC; Jones, *A Rebel War Clerk's Diary at the Confederate States Capital*, pp. 70, 75.

100   *messages south:* AP to GM, Jan. 30, 1861, R: 16, GMP, LC; Pinkerton, *The Spy of the Rebellion*, pp. 468–80; Beymer, *On Hazardous Service*, p. 279.

101   *the Federals:* AP reports to GM, Jan. 30 and 31, 1861, R: 16, GMP, LC; Pinkerton, *The Spy of the Rebellion*, pp. 483–84; Fishel, *The Secret War for the Union*, pp. 98–99; Recko, pp. 105–10.

101   *he thought:* J. E. Johnston to My Dear General, May 28, 1861, B: 1, JJP, LC; Pinkerton, *The Spy of the Rebellion*, pp. 485–92; Mortimer, *Double Death*, p. 254; Recko, p. 111.

NINE: "ENEMIES OF THE STATE"

102   *of intoxication:* Stahr, pp. 5, 90, 204–5, 266, 298, 303, 356; Goodwin, pp. 192–93, 506–7; Brooks, pp. 27–28.

103   *treasonous elements:* Stahr, pp. 7–9, 14, 46–47, 52–59, 93–94, 201, 209, 252–53, 265, 298; Goodwin, pp. 12–15, 29–34, 69–87, 145–46, 250–51, 341–43; Catton, vol. 1, pp. 278, 290–91; Poore, *Perley's Reminiscences of the Sixty Years in the National Metropolis*, pp. 110–11; Milton, p. 26.

103   *of time:* F. W. Leonard to Andrew Porter with enclosure, Nov. 25, 1861, B: 11, EF, GU; Thomas, *Stanton*, p. 157; Randall, *Lincoln the President: Midstream*, p. 194; Stahr, pp. 4, 285–88; WHS to U.S. Marshal Philadelphia, Sept. 24, 1861, p. 114, WHS to John Keyes, Sept. 23, 1861, p. 112, WHS to William Dunn, Sept. 6, 1861, p. 60, WHS to John Kennedy, Aug. 19, 1861, p. 35, WHS to John Kennedy, June 27, 1861, p. 9, WHS to George Ashman, April 12, 1861, p. 1, WHS to GW, Oct. 15, 1861, WHS to John Dix, Oct. 16, 1861, p. 236, WHS to Edward Chase, Sept. 16, 1861, p. 86, F. W. Seward to Justin Dimick, Nov. 27, 1861, p. 507, vol. 1, WHS to Thurlow Weed, Aug. 24, 1861, F. W. Seward to Montgomery Blair, Nov. 21, 1861, p. 421, vol. 2, E: 955, RG59, NA; Randall, *Lincoln the President: Midstream*, pp. 195–98, 201; AL Memorandum: Military Arrests, c. May 17, 1861, *The Collected Works of Abraham Lincoln*, vol. 4, p. 372; Nicolay and Hay, *Abraham Lincoln: A History*, vol. 8, pp. 40–41.

104   *paid him:* Baker's earliest employees from S.S. Accounts, B: 6, EF, GU; LB account, July 9–Sept. 9, 1861, LB account ending Sept. 7, 1861, B: 1, E: 95, RG110, NA; Milton, *Abraham Lincoln and The Fifth Column*, p. 28; WHS to John Kennedy, Nov. 29 1861, p. 539, vol. 1, E: 955, RG59, NA; Mogelever, p. 73; Baker, *History of the United States Secret Service*, pp. 87–88.

104   *United States:* History of the Astor House, BP; WHS to S. W. Morton, Jan. 13, 1862, p. 120, F. W. Seward to LB, Feb. 7, 1862, p. 231, vol. 3, F. W. Seward to Martin Burke, Oct. 28, 1861, p. 317, F. W. Seward to LB, Oct. 22, 1861, p. 290, vol. 1, E: 955, RG59, NA; Baker, *History of the United States Secret Service*, pp. 114–15.

105   *mixed results:* LB to Mrs. L. C. Baker, Sept. 1861, R: 1, M504, RG107, NA; Attorney General Bates to GM, Nov. 12, 1861, B: 6, EF, GU; Patrick Barrett

to Nelson Taylor, Oct. 29, 1861, B: 1, JHP, HL; From HQ 3rd Indiana Cav., Nov. 8, Capt. D. M. Dauglade reports to JH on trip to Patuxent River, B: 6, EF, GU; Tidwell, p. 62; Fishel, *The Secret War for the Union*, pp. 55–56, 73; Hebert, pp. 61–62; Ryan, "A Battle of Wits: Intelligence Operations During the Gettysburg Campaign," Part 2, p. 10; Kauffman, *American Brutus*, p. 144; Baker, *History of the United States Secret Service*, p. 102.

106 *"will flow"*: Baker, *History of the United States Secret Service*, pp. 102–21; LB to JH, Nov. 25, 1861, B: 6, EF, GU.

106 *division escape*: Chapman letters to JH, Dec. 9 and 15, 1861, F. W. Seward to GM, Dec. 16, 1861, B: 2, S. Bodrive to George H. Johnston, Jan. 29, 1862, Letter to Capt. Dickinson, Jan. 31, 1862, B: 3, JHP, HL; LB to JH, Dec. 6, 1861, B: 6, EF, GU.

106 *shown up*: Chapman to Joseph Dickinson, Dec. 24, 1861, B: 2, LB to JH, March 1, 1862, B: 5, JHP, HL; Axelrod, pp. 187–88; Woods, p. 57; Kauffman, *American Brutus*, pp. 144–45.

107 *southern ports*: Tidwell, pp. 171, 174; Markle, pp. 50–54; Jones, *Behind Enemy Lines*, pp. 16–17; WHS to U.S. Dispatch Agent Boston, Oct. 4, 1861, p. 153, WHS to James Rowen, July 8, 1861, vol. 1, WHS to John Wood, Oct. 18, 1861, p. 219, vol. 2, E: 955, RG59, NA.

107 *"that section"*: LB expenses for Jan. 9–Feb. 9, 1862, B: 1, E: 95, RG110, NA; Markle, p. 73; Miller, *The Photographic History of The Civil War*, p. 270; F. W. Seward to John Kennedy, Oct. 9, 1861, p. 178, WHS to Herbert Davis, Sept. 30, 1861, p. 140, vol. 1, E: 955, RG59, NA.

107 *arrested Ashley*: Baker, *History of the United States Secret Service*, pp. 89–92; Orrmont, p. 47; LB to WHS and WHS to LB, October 25, 1861, OR-S2.2:118–19.

108 *to relax*: Marvel, pp. xii–xv, 14, 52; Thomas, *Stanton*, p. 168; Nevins, vol. 2, pp. 34–39; Goodwin, p. 510.

108 *loyal attorney*: Marvel, pp. 3–14, 21–24, 64, 71–73, 84, 117, 121–26, 467–68; Donald, *Lincoln*, pp. 185–86; Goodwin, pp. 173–75, 297; Lamon, *Recollections of Abraham Lincoln*, p. 230; Niven, *Gideon Welles*, p. 398.

109 *days later*: Stahr, pp. 221–22; Goodwin, pp. 298–99, 403–4, 410–12; Marvel, pp. 131–32, 134, 139; *Diary of Gideon Welles*, vol. 1, pp. 12, 58; Nicolay and Hay, *Abraham Lincoln: A History*, vol. 3, p. 252; Catton, vol. 2, pp. 141–44; Sears, *George B. McClellan*, p. 142; Winkle, p. 282.

109 *Department needed*: Marvel, pp. xv–xvi, 153–54, 159, 265–66; Thomas, *Stanton*, p. 162; Goodwin, pp. 414–15, 453–61.

109   *in them:* Thomas, *Stanton,* pp. 157–58; McPherson, *Battle Cry of Freedom,* p. 436; Randall, *Lincoln the President: Midstream,* pp. 198–99, 200–201; Nevins, vol. 4, pp. 129–30; WHS to EMS, Feb. 15, 1862, p. 267, vol. 3, E: 955, RG59, NA.

110   *several bosses:* F. W. Seward to LB, Feb. 7, 1862, p. 231, vol. 3, E: 955, RG59, NA; Mogelever, pp. 17–18, 110, 137; Orrmont, pp. 61–63, 69–70; Baker, *History of the United States Secret Service,* pp. 149–50; Corson, p. 540; *Joseph Stannard Baker Memoirs from 1838 to 1865,* pp. 8-17 to 8-18.

110   *particularly bright:* L. C. Turner to LB, Feb. 16, 1864, B: 4, L. C. Turner to LB, Oct. 24, 1862, vol. 1, Turner Letter Books, E: 179A, RG94, NA; Winkle, pp. 187–88; Thomas, *Stanton,* pp. 152–53; Doster, pp. 73, 126–28; Marvel, pp. 250–55; Milton, *Abraham Lincoln and the Fifth Column,* p. 31; Fishel, *The Secret War for the Union,* p. 27; Fishel, "The Mythology of Civil War Intelligence," p. 347; Axelrod, pp. 188–89.

110   *"War Department":* Fishel, "The Mythology of Civil War Intelligence," p. 347; *Joseph Stannard Baker Memoirs from 1838 to 1865,* p. 7-1; O'Toole, p. 128; Stern, p. 17.

111   *the avenue:* LB expenses for Jan. 9–Feb. 9, 1862, and for the period ending March 31, 1862, LB expense report filed Jan. 9, 1862, for the period from Dec. 9, 1861, to Jan. 9, 1862, LB expense report, March 9, 1862, B: 1, E: 95, RG110, Secret Service Fund, Sept. 3, 1861 to March 6, 1862, B: 6, E: 179A, RG94, NA; Index to Secret Service Payments by Disbursing Clerk, War Dept., 1861–1870, BP; *Joseph Stannard Baker Memoirs from 1838 to 1865,* p. 7-1; Mogelever, pp. 113, 225; Orrmont, p. 64.

111   *and actions:* Henry to Ray Stannard Baker, Oct. 3, 1908, JSB to Alie, 1867, AC; AP to A. Porter, Feb. 19, 1862, with list of prisoners confined in the Old Capitol, Feb. 19, 1862, B: 1, E: A1–962, RG59, NA; Baker, *History of the United States Secret Service,* pp. 34–35; Mogelever, pp. 95, 109–10, 111–16; Corson, p. 553; *Joseph Stannard Baker Memoirs from 1838 to 1865,* pp. 4-1 to 4-4, 4-15, 5-1, 5-5 to 5-7, 6-1 to 6-3, 6-7, 6-17 to 6-18; *Impeachment Investigation,* p. 459.

112   *without him: Joseph Stannard Baker Memoirs from 1838 to 1865,* pp. 7-1 to 7-4; Mogelever, p. 112.

112   *and brothels: Joseph Stannard Baker Memoirs from 1838 to 1865,* pp. 7-4 to 7-6, 7-11 to 7-15; Mogelever, pp. 91–92, 116, 165–69; Swanson, pp. 184–86.

112   *cloak-and-dagger work:* Fishel, *The Secret War for the Union,* p. 27; Fishel, "The Mythology of Civil War Intelligence," pp. 347–48; Morn, pp. 41–42; Miller, *The Photographic History of The Civil War,* p. 274.

113   *the country:* Mogelever, pp. 88–90, 108; Hageman, p. 5; Fishel, "The Mythology of Civil War Intelligence," p. 348; Fishel, *The Secret War for the Union*, p. 27; Fishel, "Military Intelligence," Part 3, p. 2.

113   *her corset:* Milton, *Abraham Lincoln and the Fifth Column*, pp. 46–47; Baker, *History of the United States Secret Service*, pp. 127–29, 168–69; Mogelever, p. 140.

114   *patrolling outside:* "Other Government Buildings: Old Capitol Prison"; Marshall, pp. 323–25; Speer, pp. 41, 82–86, 284; Old Capitol Prison, 91st PA; Mahony, p. 154; Williamson, pp. 26, 28–29, 36, 85.

114   *inmate conversations:* Expense report to EMS, Dec. 8, 1866, on W. P. Wood expenses, B: 6, E: 95, RG110, NA; Doster, 104–5; Williamson, pp. 29–30, 33–34, 75–76; Mackay, pp. 130–31, 322, 326, 348; Stern, p. 103; "The Old Capitol Building and Its Inmates," *New York Times*, April 15, 1862, p. 2; Mahony, pp. 146–47, 151, 239; Mogelever, pp. 117–19; "Other Government Buildings: Old Capitol Prison"; Woods, p. 58.

114   *serious feud:* Axelrod, pp. 165–66; Rowan, pp. 145–46; Fishel, "The Mythology of Civil War Intelligence," pp. 346–47; Fishel, *The Secret War for the Union*, p. 55.

115   *Kerby released:* Axelrod, pp. 165–66; Fishel, *The Secret War for the Union*, p. 56; *Joseph Stannard Baker Memoirs from 1838 to 1865*, pp. 7-17 to 7-18; Benjamin Franklin to LB, May 6, 1862, Case of Frank Lacy Buxton, June 5, 1862, R: 11, M797, RG94, NA; Pinkerton versus Baker, B: 6, EF, GU.

115   *and Pinkerton:* AP to Son, April 28, 1883, R: 3, PND, LC; Doster, pp. 73, 127; Mogelever, pp. 66, 83; Baker, *History of the United States Secret Service*, p. 36; Geringer, p. 21; Hageman, p. 4.

116   *same enemies:* Steer, p. 216; Marshall, p. 357; Mahony, pp. 324–25; Roscoe, pp. 196, 198; Randall, *Lincoln the President: Midstream*, p. 199; Mackay, p. 180; Hageman, p. 5; Milton, *The Age of Hate*, p. 193; Millard, p. 1; Corson, p. 542.

116   *his name:* Chittenden, pp. 345–46, 350; Doster, pp. 73, 127–31; Roscoe, pp. 196–97.

117   *be ignored:* F. Stidger to Joseph Holt, July 15, 1863, vol. 49, JHOP, LC; Mogelever, pp. 121, 126–30, 159–60, 242; Orrmont, pp. 79–80; Stidger, p. 175; Fishel, "The Mythology of Civil War Intelligence," pp. 348–49, 362; Axelrod, p. 188; Mahony, 284–87, 321–24; Millard, p. 12; Chittenden, pp. 346–47; Marshall, pp. 328–29, 356–57.

117   *his camp:* Autobiography of Maj. Augustus P. Green, pp. 41, 193, 242–51, AG, NYH; Mahony, pp. 319–21; Papers relating to claim of Maj. George Blair for horses seized by LB, R: 135, M797, RG94, NA.

118 *treat malaria:* Millard, p. 1; Roscoe, p. 197; Mogelever, pp. 145–50, 248; Baker, *History of the United States Secret Service,* pp. 121–24, 147–48; Cottrell, p. 239; Orrmont, pp. 76–79.

118 *defend himself:* Millard, p. 1; Fishel, "The Mythology of Civil War Intelligence," p. 347; Baker, *History of the United States Secret Service,* pp. 34–37, 169–70, 347.

118 *expensive presents:* L. C. Turner to LB, Nov. 17, 1862, vol. 2, Turner Letter Books, E: 179A, RG94, NA; Millard, p. 13; Baker, *History of the United States Secret Service,* pp. 38, 40–43, 115–16, 153, 256–57, 582–83; Mogelever, p. 111.

119 *disgusted him:* Joseph Stannard Baker Memoirs from 1838 to 1865, pp. 7-2 to 7-4.

TEN: RICHMOND

124 *taunt others:* Ryan, *A Yankee Spy in Richmond,* pp. 35–36; Brock, pp. 91, 97, 108, 147, 212–13; Thomas, *The Confederate State of Richmond,* pp. 46–47, 57–59; McPherson, *Battle Cry of Freedom,* pp. 612–13, 617–19; Jones, *A Rebel War Clerk's Diary at the Confederate States Capital,* pp. 78, 88, 92–93, 104; Jones, *Ladies of Richmond,* pp. xiii, 79–81, 87–88.

124 *of them:* Catton, vol. 2, pp. 118, 171, 359–60; Jones, *A Rebel War Clerk's Diary at the Confederate States Capital,* pp. 49, 78; McPherson, *Embattled Rebel,* pp. 5–9; McPherson, *Battle Cry of Freedom,* pp. 365–66, 434; Blumenthal, vol. 2, p. 228.

124 *building walls:* McPherson, *Battle Cry of Freedom,* pp. 86–87, 235–37; O'Toole, p. 155; Ryan, *A Yankee Spy in Richmond,* pp. 7, 36; Miller, *The Photographic History of The Civil War,* p. 266; Varon, *Southern Lady, Yankee Spy,* p. 47; Brock, pp. 107–8; Markle, pp. 25–27; O'Toole, pp. 155–56.

125 *"Regions lost":* Part 3rd Castle Song, B: 4, PLC, SLU; Blakey, pp. xiv, 1, 59, 132, 141–42, 208; Ryan, *A Yankee Spy in Richmond,* p. 2; Abbott, p. 44; Thomas, *The Confederate State of Richmond,* p. 105.

125 *them to:* Blakey, pp. 45, 47–49, 75, 88, 64–65, 137; Speer, p. 13.

126 *in Richmond:* Blakey, pp. 50–52, 121–24, 128–31, 142, 152, 208; Jones, *A Rebel War Clerk's Diary at the Confederate States Capital,* pp. 71, 123, 127; Markle, p. 4; Tidwell, pp. 117–27; Thomas, *The Confederate State of Richmond,* pp. 81–82, 87, 105–6.

126 *northern facilites:* Davis, *The Rise and Fall of the Confederate Government,* p. 597; Davis, *Jefferson Davis, Ex-President of the Confederate States of America,* pp. 524–25; McPherson, *Battle Cry of Freedom,* pp. 791–92; Speer, pp. xiv, 53–58, 108–13, 323–40; Blakey, p. 212.

126   *at night:* Speer, pp. 10–11, 19–23, 93–95, 124–25, 164; Parker, pp. 1–3; Current, p. 154; Blakey, p. 156.

127   *Van Lew:* Blakey, p. 155; Ryan, *A Yankee Spy in Richmond*, p. 10; Speer, pp. 89–92, 123; Richardson, *The Secret Service, the Field, the Dungeon and the Escape*, pp. 377–78; Hesseltine, p. 60; "The Libby Prison Minstrels!," B: 1, ELC, WM.

127   *the time:* John Albree speech on Van Lew, "Union Woman Spy Had Connection in This City," Dec. 13, 1912, news article, B: 1, ELC, WM; Beymer, *On Hazardous Service*, p. 69; Beymer, "Miss Van Lew," p. 88; Ryan, *A Yankee Spy in Richmond*, pp. 8, 34–35, 139–40; Thomas, *The Confederate State of Richmond*, pp. 37–38.

128   *her library:* Blakey, p. 128; Ryan, *A Yankee Spy in Richmond*, pp. 34–35, 61, 92, 139–40; Miss Revere to TPR, Feb. 10, 1901, R: 14, EVLP, LVA; Varon, *Southern Lady, Yankee Spy*, pp. 56–57, 68–69, 128.

128   *more prisoners:* "The Richmond Spy," *(Richmond) Daily Dispatch*, July 17, 1883, p. 1; Varon, *Southern Lady, Yankee Spy*, p. 59; Winkler, pp. 59–60.

129   *they carved:* Varon, "True to the Flag," p. 71; Beymer, "Miss Van Lew," p. 88; Jeffrey, pp. 29–31; Winkler, pp. 55–56; Varon, *Southern Lady, Yankee Spy*, p. 85; Beymer, *On Hazardous Service*, p. 70.

129   *surgeon's order:* A. T. Bledsoe to EVL and accompanying correspondence, B: 1, ELC, WM; EVL to J. P. Benjamin, Jan. 23, 1862, R: 23, M437, RG109, NA; Varon, *Southern Lady, Yankee Spy*, p. 68; Thomas P. Turner to EVL, Feb. 15, 1862, EVLP, NY; Ryan, *A Yankee Spy in Richmond*, pp. 9, 40–41.

129   *his father:* John N. Van Lew statement, March 14, 1863, on behalf of John Hadon, R: 94 M437, RG109, NA; Report no. 115 on Mrs. Abby Green, July 28, 1866, House of Representatives, 39th Congress, 1st Session; Notes, p. 11, on Charles Palmer, B: 3, EF, GU; Varon, *Southern Lady, Yankee Spy*, p. 94; EVL to USG in William Rowley, EVLP, NY; Stuart, "Of Spies and Borrowed Names," pp. 315–17.

130   *over Virginia:* Footnote on Frederick William Ernest Lohmann, p. 3, B: 3, EF, GU; F. W. E. Lohmann letter, June 20, 1868, 967-2206, RG107, NA; Johnston, p. 422.

130   *way north:* "The Richmond Spy," *(Richmond) Daily Dispatch*, July 17, 1883, p. 1; John Reynolds account of Annie Hall interview, Dec. 9, 1910, B: 2K394, WBP, UTA; "Tell Story of Gen. Grant's Spy in the Civil War," *Newburyport Herald*, May 24, 1912; Varon, *Southern Lady, Yankee Spy*, pp. 89–91, 95; Beymer, "Miss Van Lew," p. 89; Wheelan, p. 46; Varon, "True to the Flag," pp. 71–72; Richardson, *The Secret Service, the Field, the Dungeon and the Escape*, p. 384.

130   *his meal:* Photo of secret door to Church Hill Mansion attic, B: 2, John Albree
      speech on Van Lew, B: 1, ELC, WM; Varon, "True to the Flag," p. 36; Varon,
      Southern Lady, Yankee Spy, pp. 89–91; Beymer, "Miss Van Lew," pp. 93–94.

131   *similar threats:* "Rapped over the Knucks," *(Richmond) Daily Dispatch,* July 31,
      1861, p. 2; "Residence of Miss Van Lew," *Harper's Weekly,* July 14, 1866, p. 444;
      "Elizabeth 'Crazy Bet' Van Lew: Grant's Spy in Richmond"; Van Lew, "Van
      Liew, Van Lieu, Van Lew," p. 2; Thomas, *The Confederate State of Richmond,* pp.
      17–19, 132–33; Ryan, *A Yankee Spy in Richmond,* p. 37; Varon, *Southern Lady,*
      Yankee Spy, pp. 53–54, 59–61; Lineberry, p. 2; Jones, *Ladies of Richmond,* p. 90.

131   *the house:* Varon, *Southern Lady, Yankee Spy,* pp. 63–65, 70–72; Ryan, *A Yankee*
      Spy in Richmond, pp. 36, 39.

131   *the South:* Varon, *Southern Lady, Yankee Spy,* pp. 67–69, 73; Varon, "True to the
      Flag," pp. 71–72.

132   *clandestine agents:* McPherson, *Battle Cry of Freedom,* pp. 33–36, 449; Markle,
      pp. xviii, 96; Lineberry, p. 5.

132   *cover succeeded:* A. J. Whitlock to William Gilmore Beymer, Dec. 12, 1910,
      J. Staunton Moore to William Gilmore Beymer, Dec. 2, 1910, B: 2K394, WBP,
      UTA; Beymer, "Miss Van Lew," p. 89; "Intelligence in the Civil War," p. 19;
      Cook, p. 9; Varon, "True to the Flag," pp. 68, 70–71, 77–78.

133   *effective agents:* AP to GM, Feb. 23, 1862, R: 16, GMP, LC; Varon, *Southern*
      Lady, Yankee Spy, pp. 6–7, 98; Corson, pp. 569–70; Markle, p. 180.

133   *Navy Departments:* 17.108 James H. Sharp Deposition of Clairvoyant, Claim
      of James Sharp, 55.256, RG217, NA; Markle, pp. 182–83; Ryan, *A Yankee Spy*
      in Richmond, pp. 11–12; Varon, *Southern Lady, Yankee Spy,* pp. 92–93, 277.

134   *Van Lew family:* Helen L. Stetson to Mr. Abree, July 9, 1906, B: 1, ELC, WM;
      Varon, *Southern Lady, Yankee Spy,* pp. 49, 177–80; Bart Hall, Nov. 2 and 7, 2016.

135   *to Yankees:* Claim of Sylvanus T. Brown, Claim of William H. Brisby, RG217,
      NA; Fishel, *The Secret War for the Union,* pp. 117–18; Glantz, p. 58; Varon,
      "True to the Flag," p. 68; "Elizabeth 'Crazy Bet' Van Lew: Grant's Spy in Rich-
      mond"; Thomas, *The Confederate State of Richmond,* p. 28.

135   *"foster sister":* John Reynolds to William Gilmore Beymer, Dec. 3, 1910,
      B: 2K394, WBP, UTA; "The Irrepressible Conflict Renewed," *Brooklyn Eagle,*
      Sept. 25, 1865; "Miss Richmond's Lecture," *New York Tribune,* Sept. 12, 1865,
      p. 4; Leveen, "Mary Richards Bowser," pp. 2–3, 25–26; Bart Hall, Nov. 2, 2016;
      Anna Whitehead to John Albree, April 25, 1913, B: 1, ELC, WM.

136   *"by her":* Bart Hall, Nov. 2, 2016; Leveen, "Mary Richards Bowser," p. 4; Varon,
      Southern Lady, Yankee Spy, pp. 27–32; Varon, "True to the Flag," p. 69; "Rich-
      monia Richards," *Anglo-African,* Oct. 7, 1865; Elizabeth Varon, Lois Leveen,

C-SPAN lecture, http://www.c-span.org/video/; EVL letters to Mr. Williamson, Sept. 10 and 22, 1859, R: 87, ACS, LC.

136 *of trouble:* Varon, "True to the Flag," p. 69; Varon, *Southern Lady, Yankee Spy*, pp. 27–32; Leveen, "Mary Richards Bowser," pp. 4–5; "Richmonia Richards," *Anglo-African*, Oct. 7, 1865; Elizabeth Varon, Lois Leveen, C-SPAN lecture, http://www.c-span.org/video/.

136 *Mary Bowser:* Varon, "True to the Flag," pp. 69–70; Varon, *Southern Lady, Yankee Spy*, pp. 27–32; Leveen, "Mary Richards Bowser," pp. 1, 6–7; Bart Hall, Nov. 2, 2016.

137 *evil humans:* "Richmonia Richards," *Anglo-African*, Oct. 7, 1865; Mary Richards to Superintendent Board Ed. Freedmen, Feb. 22 and April 7, 1867, R: 8, M799, NA; Pryor, pp. 217–18.

137 *match it:* Committee of War Claims Report no. 792 on Samuel Ruth, W. F. E. Lohmann, and Charles M. Carter, June 22, 1874, House of Representatives, 43rd Congress, 1st Session; Fishel, "Mythology of Civil War Intelligence," p. 353.

138 *"into war":* McPherson, *Battle Cry of Freedom*, p. 12; O'Toole, pp. 103–10; Turner, pp. ix, 16–18, 36–37; Catton, vol. 2, p. 382; Sears, *The Civil War Papers of George B. McClellan*, p. 73; McClellan, *Report on the Organization and Campaigns of the Army of the Potomac*, pp. 41–42; suggestions as to the most expeditious mode of destroying bridges and locomotive engines, Nov. 1, 1862, report, OR-S3.2:708–10.

138 *the capital:* Black, pp. xi, 3, 294; Turner, pp. 32–33, 37–38; McPherson, *Battle Cry of Freedom*, pp. 514–16; REL to Edmund T. Morris, June 18, 1861, OR-S4.1:394; Catton, vol. 1, pp. 434–35.

138 *him little:* Castel, pp. 36–37; O'Toole, p. 157; Johnston, pp. 418–20.

139 *vital artery:* Stuart, "Samuel Ruth and General R. E. Lee," pp. 35–37; Axelrod, p. 107; O'Toole, pp. 157–58; Castel, 37.

139 *both spymasters:* Southern Claims Commission, Ruth-Lohmann Claim, p. 17, footnote on Charles M. Carter, p. 4, B: 3, EF, GU; P. V. Daniel letter, March 28, 1862, R: 15, M474, RG109, S. Ruth, F. W. E. Lohmann to EMS, Jan. 12, 1866, B: 26, 967-2206, RG107, NA; Johnston, pp. 401–11, 423–26; Stuart, "Samuel Ruth and General R. E. Lee," pp. 90, 103–4.

140 *northern cause:* Stuart, "Samuel Ruth and General R. E. Lee," pp. 79–81; Axelrod, p. 112; Markle, pp. 139–40.

140 *"devour us":* Brock, pp. 79–80; Jones, *A Rebel War Clerk's Diary at the Confederate States Capital*, p. 53; Thomas, *The Confederate State of Richmond*, p. 40; Beymer, "Miss Van Lew," p. 91; "Elizabeth 'Crazy Bet' Van Lew: Grant's Spy in

Richmond," news story on Elizabeth Van Lew, EVLP, NY; Ryan, *A Yankee Spy in Richmond*, pp. 43, 141; Varon, *Southern Lady, Yankee Spy*, p. 78.

ELEVEN: "I HAVE THE HONOR TO REPORT"

141 *over time:* McPherson, *Tried by War*, p. 191; Donald, *Lincoln*, pp. 431–32; Hay, p. 34; Niven, *Gideon Welles*, pp. 364–67; AL to GM, April 6, 1862, p. 182, AL to Isaac R. Diller, Dec. 15, 1862, pp. 3–5, *The Collected Works of Abraham Lincoln*, vol. 5; Eicher, p. 23; *Diary of Gideon Welles*, vol. 1, p. 239.

142 *strung out:* Markle, p. 33; "Intelligence in the Civil War," pp. 4, 33–34; Miller, *The Photographic History of The Civil War*, pp. 312–14, 324, 342; Maslowski, pp. 51–54; "Grenville M. Dodge and George H. Sharpe: Grant's Intelligence Chiefs in West and East," p. 11; O'Toole, p. 137.

142 *phonetic spellings:* Description and key for the cipher McClellan and Pinkerton used, B: 23, PND, LC; letters and cipher key for correspondence to JD, B: 2, JDC, DU; "Intelligence in the Civil War," p. 33; Tidwell, p. 40; Fishel, "The Mythology of Civil War Intelligence," pp. 363–64; Fishel, *The Secret War for the Union*, pp. 4–5; Eicher, pp. 299–302; Maslowski, pp. 55–56; Jones, *Behind Enemy Lines*, pp. 13–15; O'Toole, pp. 138–39; Stern, p. 318; Carl, p. 104.

143 *notoriously unreliable:* Markle, pp. xviii, 151; Jones, *Behind Enemy Lines*, p. 16; Hoogenboom, p. 369; Tidwell, p. 42.

143 *dress shops:* "A Successful and Important Experiment" and "Balloon Enterprise," (*Washington*) *Evening Star*, June 19, 1861, p. 2; "Intelligence in the Civil War," p. 31; Stepp, pp. 51–52; O'Toole, pp. 113–14, 134; Luvaas, "The Role of Intelligence in the Chancellorsville Campaign, 1863," pp. 107–8; Ryan, *Spies, Scouts, and Secrets in the Gettysburg Campaign*, p. 24; Glassford, pp. 255–56, 259–60; Sears, *George B. McClellan*, p. 100; Ryan, *Spies, Scouts, and Secrets in the Gettysburg Campaign*, p. 76; Maslowski, p. 50; Miller, *The Photographic History of The Civil War*, p. 382.

144 *clear photograph:* Glassford, pp. 255–58; Maslwoski, p. 51; Calvin Gardner to GM, Oct. 1, 1861, Letter to Calvin Gardner, Sept. 9, 1861, Letter to GM, Oct. 2, 1861, Letter to "Gentlemen," Sept. 27, 1861, Cover letter comment on Gardner proposal, R: 3, RG109, NA.

144 *of range:* Maslowski, pp. 51, 57; Fishel, *The Secret War for the Union*, p. 5; Glassford, pp. 256, 259; Markle, p. 38; Miller, *The Photographic History of The Civil War*, p. 377.

145 *George McClellan:* McPherson, *Battle Cry of Freedom*, pp. 331, 472–77;

McPherson, *Tried by War*, p. 42; Eicher, pp. 22–23, 68–69, 409; Axelrod, p. 5; Jones, *Behind Enemy Lines*, p. 9; O'Toole, p. 131; Fishel, *The Secret War for the Union*, p. 4.

145 *and manure:* Catton, vol. 2, pp. 126–27; Eicher, p. 157; Milton, *The Age of Hate*, pp. 6–9; Winkle, pp. 173–75.

146 *not moving:* GM to Simon Cameron, R: 7, SCP, LC; G. T. Beauregard to JD, Sept. 13, 1861, J. B. Jones to JD, Oct. 15, 1861, B: 1, JDC, DU; example of correct Confederate intelligence—October 1861, B: 5, EF, GU; Sears, *George B. McClellan*, pp. 96–99, 101, 105–6, 110–11, 115–16; Fishel, *The Secret War for the Union*, pp. 77–81; Chittenden, pp. 316–17; Sears, *The Civil War Papers of George B. McClellan*, pp. 71–75, 98; McPherson, *Battle Cry of Freedom*, p. 365; Stahr, pp. 304–5, 327; Marvel, pp. 165–67, 175–76; Burlingame, *With Lincoln in the White House*, pp. 61–63.

146 *second home:* McPherson, *Tried by War*, pp. 2–4, 8, 52, 137; Goodwin, p. 379; Catton, vol. 2, p. 131; McPherson, *Battle Cry of Freedom*, p. 364; Bigelow, pp. 128–29; Eicher, p. 23; Thomas and Hyman, p. 152; Milton, *The Age of Hate*, pp. 6–7.

147 *good reason:* Pinkerton, *The Spy of the Rebellion*, pp. xxviii, 458–59, 462, 566.

147 *at Manassas:* McPherson, *Tried by War*, p. 52; Sears, *George B. McClellan*, pp. 101–4; GM to WS, Aug. 8, 1861, OR-11.3:3–4; McClellan, *Report on the Organization and Campaigns of the Army of the Potomac*, pp. 50–51; Catton, vol. 2, p. 85; Fishel, *The Secret War for the Union*, pp. 102–3; Fishel, "Pinkerton and McClellan," pp. 116–17; Nicolay and Hay, *Abraham Lincoln: A History*, vol. 4, p. 449.

147 *friend happy:* Markle, p. 5; Horan, *The Pinkertons*, p. 120; Fishel, "Pinkerton and McClellan," p. 140.

148 *with error:* Cook, p. 6; Schmidt, pp. 48–49; Sears, *George B. McClellan*, pp. 107–8; Horan, *The Pinkertons*, pp. 116–17.

148 *jobs well:* Asst. Adj. General to Brig. Gen. A. Porter, Jan. 30, 1862, R: 11, M2096, NA; AP reports to GM, Jan. 27 and 28, 1862, R: 16, GMP, LC; AP to H. F. Clark, March 12, 1862, B: 2, PND, LC; Markle, pp. 5–6, 17–18; Horan, *The Pinkertons*, p. 121.

149 *trash can:* Fishel, *The Secret War for the Union*, p. 104; abstract from return of the Army of the Potomac, General Joseph Johnston, C.S. Army, commanding, for the month of October, 1861, OR-5:932; AP to GM, Oct. 4, 1861, R: 12, GMP, LC.

149 *number, 107,610:* McPherson, *Battle Cry of Freedom*, p. 326; Fishel, "Pinkerton

and McClellan," pp. 118–19; Fishel, *The Secret War for the Union*, pp. 104–5; AP to GM, Oct. 4, 1861, R: 12, AP reports to GM undated and March 5, 1862, R: 17, AP to GM, March 31, 1862, R: 19, GMP, LC.

150 *padding them:* Fishel, *The Secret War for the Union*, pp. 105–6; AP to GM, Nov. 15, 1861, R: 13, GMP, LC; Fishel, "Pinkerton and McClellan," p. 120.

150 *more soldiers:* Fishel, *The Secret War for the Union*, pp. 106, 584–85; Fishel, "Military Intelligence 1861–63 (Part 1)," p. 4; Fishel, "Pinkerton and McClellan," pp. 116, 138; Eicher, p. 58.

150 *and men:* Fishel, *The Secret War for the Union*, pp. 106, 583; Fishel, "Military Intelligence 1861–63 (Part 1)," p. 4; Fishel, "Pinkerton and McClellan," p. 119; Sears, *George B. McClellan*, p. 109.

151 *deceived himself:* Fishel, "Pinkerton and McClellan," pp. 116, 118, 120–21; Fishel, *The Secret War for the Union*, pp. 2, 106–7; McClellan, *Report on the Organization and Campaigns of the Army of the Potomac*, pp. 46–49; McPherson, *Battle Cry of Freedom*, p. 361; Sears, *The Civil War Papers of George B. McClellan*, p. 84; Sears, *George B. McClellan*, pp. 103–4.

151 *"to accuracy":* AP to GM, Nov. 15, 1861, R: 13, GMP, LC; Fishel, *The Secret War for the Union*, pp. 107–9; Fishel, "Military Intelligence 1861–63 (Part 1)," p. 4.

151 *ones before:* Fishel, "Pinkerton and McClellan," pp. 123–24; GM to AL, Dec. 10, 1861, OR-11.3:6.

152 *the report:* Fishel, "Pinkerton and McClellan," pp. 136–37; Morn, p. 45; Fishel, *The Secret War for the Union*, pp. 112–13; Nevins, vol. 1, p. 301; Sears, *Landscape Turned Red*, pp. 23–24.

152 *to him:* AP reports to GM, Dec. 9, 16, 20, 21, and 28, 1861, R: 14, AP reports to GM, Jan. and Feb. 7, 1862, R: 16, GMP, LC; Eicher, pp. 154–55; Sears, *George B. McClellan*, pp. 107, 112, 162; Fishel, "Pinkerton and McClellan," p. 118.

153 *ignored them:* Fishel, *The Secret War for the Union*, pp. 123–27; Fishel, "Pinkerton and McClellan," pp. 141–42.

153 *a secret:* AL to WS, April 1, 1861, *The Collected Works of Abraham Lincoln*, vol. 4, p. 316; Nicolay and Hay, *Abraham Lincoln: A History*, vol. 4, pp. 65–67; Fishel, *The Secret War for the Union*, pp. 1, 23–24; Gobright, pp. 326–27; Richardson, *The Secret Service, the Field, the Dungeon and the Escape*, p. 116; Hay, p. 34; Jones, *Behind Enemy Lines*, p. 6; Grant, p. 309; *Abraham Lincoln: By Some Men Who Knew Him*, pp. 150–53.

154 *"that number":* Fishel, "Pinkerton and McClellan," pp. 134–36; Fishel, *The Secret War for the Union*, p. 582; Woolseley, p. 66.

154 *was ruined:* AP reports to GM, Feb. 15, 1862, R: 16, AP reports to GM, Feb. 17

and 25, 1862, R: 17, AP to GM, March 14, 1862, R: 18, GMP, LC; McPherson, *Battle Cry of Freedom*, pp. 362–63; Catton, vol. 2, pp. 88–90, 188–92; Sears, *George B. McClellan*, pp. 121–22, 144–46; Charles P. Stone to Benjamin F. Wade, March 6, 1863, EMS Order, Jan. 28, 1862, GM to Andrew Porter, Feb. 8, 1862, OR-5:20; Eicher, 125–28.

155   *three weeks:* McPherson, *Tried by War*, pp. 53–54, 136; Fishel, *The Secret War for the Union*, pp. 109–10; Sears, *George B. McClellan*, p. 130; Donald, *Lincoln*, pp. 327, 329; Goodwin, pp. 435–36.

155   *be fought:* McPherson, *Battle Cry of Freedom*, pp. 367–71, 418–20; Catton, vol. 2, pp. 78, 92–106, 117–18, 128–29; Eicher, pp. 136–37; McPherson, *Tried by War*, pp. 37, 84; McPherson, *Embattled Rebel*, p. 35.

155   *rival factions:* Niven, *Gideon Welles*, p. 401; Donald, *Lincoln*, p. 330; "Documents: General M. C. Meigs on the Conduct of the Civil War," pp. 292–93.

156   *the newspapers:* Donald, *Lincoln*, p. 330–31; Catton, vol. 2, pp. 31–33; "Documents: General M. C. Meigs on the Conduct of the Civil War," pp. 292–93; Sears, *George B. McClellan*, pp. 139–42.

156   *much longer:* Donald, *Lincoln*, pp. 330–34; Catton, vol. 2, p. 144; Sears, *George B. McClellan*, pp. 149–50; McClellan, *Report on the Organization and Campaigns of the Army of the Potomac*, pp. 96–97.

TWELVE: THE PENINSULA CAMPAIGN

157   *Virginia defenses:* E. H. Stein's report, April 20, 1862, on return from Richmond, GM to AP, March 30, 1863, B: 7, EF, GU; AP expense reports for January, February, and April 1862, B: 1, E: 95, RG110, NA; Mortimer, *Double Death*, p. 126; Pinkerton, *The Spy of the Rebellion*, pp. 481–83.

158   *two-to-one advantage: Report of the Joint Committee on the Conduct of the War*, p. 425; "George B. McClellan," B: 7, EF, GU; Catton, vol. 2, pp. 144–45, 196–97; Fishel, *The Secret War for the Union*, pp. 135–37; Sears, *George B. McClellan*, p. 130; McClellan, *Report on the Organization and Campaigns of the Army of the Potomac*, pp. 97–98, 103–7; Eicher, pp. 212–13; Nevins, vol. 2, p. 42; Sears, *To the Gates of Richmond*, pp. 5–6, 9.

159   *once pursued:* Memoirs of Pryce Lewis as Told to Major David E. Cronin in 1888, pp. 51–55, B: 4, PLC, SLU; Pinkerton, *The Spy of the Rebellion*, pp. 301–7, 496; Mortimer, *Double Death*, pp. 116–18; Corson, p. 527; Markle, p. 147.

160   *not do:* Memoirs of Pryce Lewis as Told to Major David E. Cronin in 1888, pp. 56–57, B: 4, PLC, SLU; Mortimer, *Double Death*, pp. 118–20; Beymer, *On*

Hazardous Service, p. 280; Pryce Lewis manuscript by Harriet H. Shoen, p. 7, B: 4, PLC, SLU; Recko, p. 111.

161   *McClellan's leadership:* Sears, *To the Gates of Richmond*, p. 8; Catton, vol. 2, pp. 198–99; Sears, *George B. McClellan*, pp. 160–61; Pinkerton, *The Spy of the Rebellion*, pp. 500–501; McClellan, *Report on the Organization and Campaigns of the Army of the Potomac*, pp. 58, 116–17; Winkle, pp. 282–83.

161   *Union lines:* A. Porter pass for P. Lewis, Jan. 29, 1862, B: 2, Memoirs of Pryce Lewis as Told to Major David E. Cronin in 1888, p. 58, B: 4, PLC, SLU; Pinkerton, *The Spy of the Rebellion*, pp. 491–95.

162   *for drinks:* Memoirs of Pryce Lewis as Told to Major David E. Cronin in 1888, pp. 67–68, B: 4, PLC, SLU; Mortimer, *Double Death*, pp. 128–33; Beymer, *On Hazardous Service*, p. 281.

163   *Main Street:* Concerning Lewis and Scully's Guilt in the Apprehension of Timothy Webster, October 1952, B: 3, Memoirs of Pryce Lewis as Told to Major David E. Cronin in 1888, pp. 68–75, B: 4, PLC, SLU; Mortimer, *Double Death*, pp. 125–27, 134–42, 163–64; Pinkerton, *The Spy of the Rebellion*, pp. 501–10.

165   *the night:* Memoirs of Pryce Lewis as Told to Major David E. Cronin in 1888, pp. 75–77, B: 4, PLC, SLU; Mortimer, *Double Death*, pp. 141–42.

165   *the best:* Memoirs of Pryce Lewis as Told to Major David E. Cronin in 1888, pp. 77–79, B: 4, PLC, SLU; Mortimer, *Double Death*, pp. 142–43, 153–54.

166   *of Manassas: Report of the Joint Committee on the Conduct of the War*, p. 426; AP telegram to GM, 1862, R: 24, M504, RG107, NA; Sears, *To the Gates of Richmond*, p. 11; McPherson, *Battle Cry of Freedom*, pp. 423–24; Catton, vol. 2, pp. 199–200; Sears, *George B. McClellan*, pp. 62–64; Fishel, *The Secret War for the Union*, pp. 130–32; W. Stoddert to Joseph E. Johnston, March 26, 1862, OR-11.3:401.

166   *a tip-off:* AP to GM, March 8, 1862, R: 18, GMP, LC; Fishel, *The Secret War for the Union*, pp. 132–34, 139–41; Catton, vol. 2, pp. 199–200; Sears, *To the Gates of Richmond*, p. 14.

166   *the Yankees:* AP to GM, Feb. 1, 1862, R: 16, AP reports to GM, March 9, 10, 12, 13, and 14, 1862, R: 18, AP reports to GM, March 17, 1862, R: 19, GMP, LC.

167   *the locals:* Catton, vol. 2, pp. 200–201; Sears, *George B. McClellan*, pp. 162–64; Donald, *Lincoln*, p. 341; McPherson, *Tried by War*, pp. 79–80; Sears, *To the Gates of Richmond*, pp. 16–17; Fishel, *The Secret War for the Union*, p. 141; Holzer and Symonds, p. 150; Baker, *History of the United States Secret Service*, pp. 141–44; *Report of the Joint Committee on the Conduct of the War*, p. 426.

167   *at Urbanna:* Sears, *To the Gates of Richmond*, pp. 15–18; Davis, *The Rise and*

Fall of the Confederate Government, pp. 81–82; McPherson, *Tried by War,* p. 79; Fishel, *The Secret War for the Union,* pp. 142–44.

167 *his campaign:* Sears, *To the Gates of Richmond,* pp. 18–19, 27; McPherson, *Battle Cry of Freedom,* pp. 423–24; McClellan, *Report on the Organization and Campaigns of the Army of the Potomac,* pp. 132–34; Thomas, *The Confederate State of Richmond,* p. 33; Keegan, p. 69; Catton, vol. 2, pp. 12–15, 210.

168 *wrote later:* EMS to GM, March 13, 1862, OR-11.3:58–59; GM to Lorenzo Thomas, April 1, 1862, OR-11.3:59–60; Catton, vol. 2, pp. 201–3; McClellan, *Report on the Organization and Campaigns of the Army of the Potomac,* p. 124; Pinkerton, *The Spy of the Rebellion,* p. 572.

168 *or incommunicado:* AP to GM, Dec. 2, 1861, R: 14, AP to GM, Feb. 22, 1862, R: 16, GMP, LC; Fishel, *The Secret War for the Union,* p. 147; Sears, *To the Gates of Richmond,* p. 29; Rose, p. 3; AP to Hdqrs. Provost-Marshal General, March 29, 1862, OR-1.1:266.

169 *for weeks:* Memoirs of Pryce Lewis as Told to Major David E. Cronin in 1888, pp. 80–82, B: 4, PLC, SLU; Mortimer, *Double Death,* p. 147.

169 *wrist irons:* Memoirs of Pryce Lewis as Told to Major David E. Cronin in 1888, pp. 82–103, B: 4, PLC, SLU; Mortimer, *Double Death,* pp. 143–48, 155–61.

169 *Union movement:* S. Williams to T. S. C. Lowe, March 23, 1862, B: 7, EF, GU; Letter to J. N. Macomb, April 2, 1862, B: 7, EF, GU; Confederate info on McClellan's intentions, B: 7, EF, GU; Catton, vol. 2, pp. 263, 265, 267; Fishel, *The Secret War for the Union,* pp. 144–47; McPherson, *Battle Cry of Freedom,* pp. 426–27; Eicher, pp. 214–15; Sears, *George B. McClellan,* pp. 167–69; Sears, *To the Gates of Richmond,* pp. xi–xii, 24; "Intelligence in the Civil War," p. 31.

170 *his coming:* AP to Office of the Provost Marshal, March 14, 1862, R: 17, M2096, NA; Horan, *The Pinkertons,* p. 115; E. D. Webster to John A. Dix, March 8, 1862, p. 320, vol. 3, E: 955, RG59, NA.

170 *battle maps:* George Bangs letter to his mother, June 14, 1863, MB; Fishel on Pinkerton and the Peninsula campaign, William Pinkerton to Benjamin Felix, Sept. 30, 1903, B: 7, EF, GU; Fishel, *The Secret War for the Union,* p. 147; Rowan, p. 158; Mackay, p. 155; Horan, *The Pinkertons,* p. 121.

170 *local hotels:* AP to GM, Feb. 2, 1862, R: 16, GMP, LC; "Our Special Washington Dispatches," *New York Times,* July 24, 1862, p. 1; AP expenses for June and August 1862, B: 1, E: 95, RG110, NA; Markle, p. 7.

170 *July 4:* McPherson, *Battle Cry of Freedom,* p. 437; Marvel, pp. 186–87; Jones, *Ladies of Richmond,* p. 93.

171 *her home:* Confederate info on McClellan's intentions, B: 7, EF, GU; Printed

Flyer from Joseph, Mayo, B: 1, ELC, WM; Keegan, p. 72; Thomas, *The Confederate State of Richmond*, pp. 84, 89–90; Sears, *To the Gates of Richmond*, pp. 44–45; "Intelligence in the Civil War," p. 19; Jones, *A Rebel War Clerk's Diary at the Confederate States Capital*, p. 89.

171 *Pinkerton men:* Concerning Lewis and Scully's Guilt in the Apprehension of Timothy Webster, October 1952, B: 3, "The Fate of a Spy," undated *Richmond Dispatch* story, Memoirs of Pryce Lewis as Told to Major David E. Cronin in 1888, pp. 102, 105–7, B: 4, PLC, SLU; Mortimer, *Double Death*, pp. 161–63.

172 *carried out:* Memoirs of Pryce Lewis as Told to Major David E. Cronin in 1888, pp. 109–12, B: 4, PLC, SLU.

172 *said later:* Concerning Lewis and Scully's Guilt in the Apprehension of Timothy Webster, October 1952, B: 3, "News from Rebel Sources," undated news story, Memoirs of Pryce Lewis as Told to Major David E. Cronin in 1888, pp. 112–18, B: 4, PLC, SLU; Recko, pp. 125–28.

173 *Union spies:* Lord Lyons letters to Acting Consul Cridland, April 16 and May 15, 1862, Fred J. Cridland letter, Aug. 19, 1862, B: 3, British Protection by Harriet H. Shoen, Memoirs of Pryce Lewis as Told to Major David E. Cronin in 1888, pp. 112–14, B: 4, PLC, SLU.

173 *no promises:* Lord Lyons letters to Acting Consul Cridland, April 16 and May 15, 1862, Fred J. Cridland letter, Aug. 19, 1862, B: 3, Memoirs of Pryce Lewis as Told to Major David E. Cronin in 1888, pp. 118–21, B: 4, PLC, SLU.

173 *Timothy Webster:* Concerning Lewis and Scully's Guilt in the Apprehension of Timothy Webster, October 1952, B: 3, British Protection by Harriet H. Shoen, Memoirs of Pryce Lewis as Told to Major David E. Cronin in 1888, pp. 121–23, B: 4, PLC, SLU.

174 *More nonsense:* McPherson, *Battle Cry of Freedom*, p. 426; Sears, *To the Gates of Richmond*, pp. 28, 30; Sears, *The Civil War Papers of George B. McClellan*, p. 230; Sears, *George B. McClellan*, pp. 172–73; Sears, *Landscape Turned Red*, p. 32; GM to General Sumner, April 3, 1862, OR-11.3:64; McClellan, *McClellan's Own Story*, pp. 264–65; Catton, vol. 2, pp. 272–74; *Report of the Joint Committee on the Conduct of the War*, p. 428.

174 *near Yorktown: Report of the Joint Committee on the Conduct of the War*, p. 429; Eicher, pp. 215–16; L. Thomas and E. A. Hitchcock letter, April 2, 1862, OR-11.3:61–62; L. Thomas to GM, April 4, 1862, OR-11.3:66; Catton, vol. 2, pp. 268–69; Sears, *The Civil War Papers of George B. McClellan*, pp. 228–29; Sears, *George B. McClellan*, pp. 174–77; McClellan, *McClellan's Own Story*, pp. 281–83; Fishel, "Military Intelligence 1861–63 (Part 2)," pp. 1–2; AP to Hdqrs. Provost Marshal General, March 29, 1862, OR-11.1:264–65; Fishel,

The Secret War for the Union, p. 151; Sears, *To the Gates of Richmond*, pp. 24–26, 37–38, 41–43; Sears, *Landscape Turned Red*, p. 33.

175 *his army:* GM to AL, April 8, 1862, R: 17, GMP, LC; McClellan, *McClellan's Own Story*, p. 274; Eicher, pp. 216–17; Sears, *The Civil War Papers of George B. McClellan*, pp. 243–44; Pinkerton, *The Spy of the Rebellion*, p. 542.

175 *at Yorktown:* Sears, *George B. McClellan*, p. 179; Davis, *The Rise and Fall of the Confederate Government*, pp. 84–85; GM letter, April 7, 1862, OR-11.1:11; Dennett, p. 39; John E. Wool to EMS, April 7, 1862, OR-11.3:76; AL to GM, April 9, 1862, OR-12.1:30–31; EMS to AL, March 30, 1862, Correspondence, March 30–May 4, 1862, EMSP, LC Digital; AL to GM, April 7, 1862, R: 17, GMP, LC.

175 *in Richmond:* AP to GM, April 9, 1862, R: 17, GMP, LC.

176 *he thought:* Memoirs of Pryce Lewis as Told to Major David E. Cronin in 1888, pp. 125–29, B: 4, PLC, SLU.

176 *death sentence:* Memoirs of Pryce Lewis as Told to Major David E. Cronin in 1888, pp. 129–32, B: 4, PLC, SLU; Mortimer, *Double Death*, pp. 181–82.

177 *for blood:* Mortimer, *Double Death*, pp. 178, 248; Jones, *Behind Enemy Lines*, p. 35; Louis Sigaud to Miss Shoen, Aug. 1, 1945, B: 3, PLC, SLU; Concerning Lewis and Scully's Guilt in the Apprehension of Timothy Webster, B: 3, PLC, SLU.

177 *hadn't read:* Memoirs of Pryce Lewis as Told to Major David E. Cronin in 1888, pp. 134–35, B: 4, PLC, SLU; Mortimer, *Double Death*, p. 184; Pinkerton, *The Spy of the Rebellion*, pp. 540–42.

177 *cabinet members:* Pinkerton, *The Spy of the Rebellion*, pp. 544–48; Jones, *A Rebel War Clerk's Diary at the Confederate States Capital*, p. 97; Mortimer, *Double Death*, pp. 185–86; Mackay, pp. 145–47; Fishel, *The Secret War for the Union*, p. 149.

178 *a response:* Fishel, *The Secret War for the Union*, pp. 149, 245; Fishel, "The Mythology of Civil War Intelligence," p. 362; AL order, Oct. 25, 1862, disapproving sentence of Jose Maria Rivas; AL order mitigating death sentence of Sely Lewis, *The Collected Works of Abraham Lincoln*, vol. 5, p. 475.

178 *marshal refused:* Mortimer, *Double Death*, pp. 184–85; Pinkerton, *The Spy of the Rebellion*, pp. 548–52.

178 *to her:* Pinkerton, *The Spy of the Rebellion*, pp. 554–59; Recko, pp. 130–31; Popchock, p. 44; Memoirs of Pryce Lewis as Told to Major David E. Cronin in 1888, pp. 135–39, B: 4, PLC, SLU.

179 *to Illinois:* Ryan, *A Yankee Spy in Richmond*, p. 45; Beymer, *On Hazardous Service*, p. 268; Horan, *The Pinkertons*, pp. 112–14.

179   *112 percent:* Eicher, pp. 268–70; AP to GM, May 3, 1862, OR-11.1:268; Sears, *To the Gates of Richmond,* p. 96.

179   *were leaving:* May 4 chronology entry on Lowe, p. 52, B: 7, EF, GU; Sears, *To the Gates of Richmond,* pp. 60–62; Fishel, *The Secret War for the Union,* pp. 151–53; Eicher, pp. 268–70; Miller, *The Photographic History of The Civil War,* pp. 370–72; McPherson, *Battle Cry of Freedom,* pp. 426–27; Catton, vol. 2, pp. 294–95; Sears, *George B. McClellan,* pp. 182–83.

180   *about it:* McPherson, *Embattled Rebel,* pp. 79–81; McPherson, *Battle Cry of Freedom,* pp. 426–27; GM to EMS, May 4, 1862, OR-11.3:133; GM to EMS, May 6, 1862, OR-11.1:449; Sears, *To the Gates of Richmond,* pp. 95–96.

180   *entertain him:* Catton, vol. 2, pp. 278–86; Wilson and Davis, p. 321; Mackay, p. 155; Niven, *Salmon P. Chase,* pp. 287–90; Donald, *Lincoln,* pp. 350–51.

181   *evacuation under way:* Memo to Confederate Secretary of War from Samuel Ruth, June 9, 1862, R: 68, M437, RG109, NA; Sears, *To the Gates of Richmond,* pp. 87, 89; Thomas, *The Confederate State of Richmond,* pp. 92–99; D. H. Hill to George Randolph, May 10, 1862, OR-11.3:506–7; REL to Joseph Johnston, May 14, 1862, OR-11.3:516; Jones, *A Rebel War Clerk's Diary at the Confederate States Capital,* p. 97; Jones, *Ladies of Richmond,* p. 93; Stuart, "Samuel Ruth and General R. E. Lee," pp. 55–57; O'Toole, p. 157; Axelrod, pp. 109–12; Stuart, "Of Spies and Borrowed Names," pp. 319–20.

181   *to Richmond:* AP expenses for May 1862, B: 1, E: 95, RG110, NA; Sears, *To the Gates of Richmond,* pp. 103–4.

182   *remain unabated:* R. B. Marcy memos to Professor Lowe, and Lowe memo to Marcy, June 1, 1862, IASA, LC; JCB to William Pinkerton, April 9, 1906, JCBP, AP to WHS, May 30 and June 13, 1862, AP to AL, June 2, 1862, AP to EMS, May 28, 1862, R: 70, WSP, LC; GM telegrams, May 10 and 14, 1862, OR-11.1:26–27; Chapter II of GM report, OR-11.1:25–26; Sears, *George B. McClellan,* 186–87; Sears, *To the Gates of Richmond,* pp. 99–100; Fishel, *The Secret War for the Union,* pp. 153–54; McClellan, *McClellan's Own Story,* pp. 264, 289; GM to EMS, May 8, 1862, OR-11.3:151; EMS to GM, May 18, 1862, OR-11.1:27; Catton, vol. 2, pp. 288–90; Eicher, p. 208; Sears, *George B. McClellan,* pp. 190–91; McPherson, *Tried by War,* pp. 91–95; McClellan, *Report on the Organization and Campaigns of the Army of the Potomac,* p. 200.

182   *attack Washington:* Stepp and Hill, p. 121; Thomas, *Stanton,* p. 339; Nicolay and Hay, *Abraham Lincoln: A History,* vol. 9, pp. 158–59; Keegan, pp. 68–74; Catton, vol. 2, p. 296; McPherson, *Battle Cry of Freedom,* pp. 425, 454–55; Sears, *To the Gates of Richmond,* p. 174; Sears, *Chancellorsville,* pp. 45–46;

Catton, vol. 2, pp. 291–92, 300–304; Donald, *Lincoln*, p. 355; Fishel, *The Secret War for the Union*, pp. 165, 171, 173, 180–81; Eicher, pp. 208–12, 257–67.

182   *Confederate commander:* McPherson, *Battle Cry of Freedom*, pp. 425, 457, 460; Horan, *The Pinkertons*, p. 122; Sears, *George B. McClellan*, pp. 190–91; McPherson, *Tried by War*, pp. 91–94; McClellan, *Report on the Organization and Campaigns of the Army of the Potomac*, p. 200; Catton, vol. 2, pp. 300–304; Donald, *Lincoln*, p. 355.

183   *James River:* Fishel, *The Secret War for the Union*, pp. 147–48; Fishel, "Pinkerton and McClellan," p. 126; McPherson, *Battle Cry of Freedom*, p. 487; George Bangs letter to his mother, June 14, 1863, MB; AP to P. Watson, June 23, 1862, R: 203, M221, NA; AP to George Bangs, July 6, 1862, B: 2, PND, LC.

184   *disturb him:* McPherson, *Battle Cry of Freedom*, pp. 461–62; Catton, vol. 2, pp. 311–14; Eicher, pp. 276–79; Fishel, *The Secret War for the Union*, p. 156; Sears, *To the Gates of Richmond*, pp. 110–29, 132–34, 138–40; Sears, *George B. McClellan*, pp. 192–97; Livermore, p. 81; Jones, *A Rebel War Clerk's Diary at the Confederate States Capital*, pp. 98–99; Thomas, *The Confederate State of Richmond*, pp. 96–97; Blakey, pp. 138–39; AP to A. Porter, June 23, 1862, R: 27, GMP, LC.

184   *could imagine:* Varon, *Southern Lady, Yankee Spy*, pp. 77–78; Donald, *Lincoln*, pp. 356–57; Sears, *George B. McClellan*, pp. 195–96; Sears, *To the Gates of Richmond*, p. 145; Catton, vol. 2, pp. 314–15.

184   *lectured them:* Miscellaneous notes of Confederate secret service, Nov. 1, 1995, Milligan in OR card 5, B: 5, Confederate info on McC's intentions, B: 7, EF, GU; Note on newsboys spying for REL, R: 46, M2096, Note on "Colored Boy 10 years old," Part 1, vol. 113, Entry 3988, RG393, NA; Jones, *Behind Enemy Lines*, pp. 12–13; Ryan, "A Battle of Wits: Intelligence Operations During the Gettysburg Campaign, Part 2," p. 14; Tidwell, pp. 10–12; Fishel, "The Mythology of Civil War Intelligence," p. 366.

185   *at all:* Ryan, "A Battle of Wits: Intelligence Operations During the Gettysburg Campaign Part 1," p. 11; Fishel, "The Mythology of Civil War Intelligence," p. 354; Hoogenboom, p. 369; Sears, *To the Gates of Richmond*, p. 167; Fishel, "Military Intelligence 1861–63 (Part 2)," pp. 2–3; Tidwell, p. 135.

186   *superior enemy:* AP to Andrew Porter, June 15, 1862, R: 25, GMP, LOC; R. B. Marcy to GM, June 25, 1862, R: 27, GMP, LC; Associated Press reporter Sidney Deming from McClellan HQ to AP Washington, B: 7, EF, GU; Sears, *The Civil War Papers of George B. McClellan*, pp. 244–45; McPherson, *Battle Cry of Freedom*, p. 462; Thomas, *The Confederate State of Richmond*, p. 98; Sears, *To*

the Gates of Richmond, pp. 152–56, 159–63, 174, 176; Catton, vol. 2, p. 315; Fishel, *The Secret War for the Union*, pp. 157–58, 163–64; Sears, *Landscape Turned Red*, p. 54; Nicolay and Hay, *Abraham Lincoln: A History*, vol. 5, pp. 416–18; Eicher, p. 280; AP to GM, Aug. 14, 1862, OR-11.1:269–70; GM report, June 25, 1862, OR-11.1:51; Pinkerton, *The Spy of the Rebellion*, p. xxix; Sears, *George B. McClellan*, p. 201.

186   *"the East"*: Eicher, p. 280; Fishel, *The Secret War for the Union*, pp. 157, 160; Nicolay and Hay, *Abraham Lincoln: A History*, vol. 5, p. 418; Sears, *To the Gates of Richmond*, pp. 172–73; Fox, p. 540; Statement of the comparative strength of the Army of the Potomac on April 1, 1862, and June 20, 1862, OR-11.3:239; Rowland, pp. 283–84.

187   *fled north:* Mackay, p. 148; Rowan, p. 182; Mortimer, *Double Death*, pp. 191–93, 200, 202; Pinkerton, *The Spy of the Rebellion*, pp. 528–29.

187   *she feared:* AP to Andrew Porter, Aug. 10, 1862, R: 29, GMP, LC; Varon, *Southern Lady, Yankee Spy*, pp. 73–76; Brock, pp. 235–36.

187   *June 25:* AP to A. Porter, June 23, 1862, R: 27, GMP, LC.

188   *supply him:* Donald, *Lincoln*, p. 357; Eicher, pp. 281–96; Sears, *To the Gates of Richmond*, pp. 298, 343–44; McPherson, *Battle Cry of Freedom*, p. 490.

188   *the case:* Ryan, *A Yankee Spy in Richmond*, p. 44; Varon, *Southern Lady, Yankee Spy*, pp. 78–79; Thomas, *The Confederate State of Richmond*, p. 99.

189   *to them:* Livermore, p. 86; McPherson, *Battle Cry of Freedom*, pp. 471–72; Jones, *Ladies of Richmond*, pp. 133–34; Jones, *A Rebel War Clerk's Diary at the Confederate States Capital*, pp. 106–7; Varon, *Southern Lady, Yankee Spy*, pp. 79–83; Ryan, *A Yankee Spy in Richmond*, p. 11; Brock, pp. 165–67, 216; Winkler, pp. 58–59.

189   *"we can":* McClellan, *Report on the Organization and Campaigns of the Army of the Potomac*, pp. 257–58; Sears, *To the Gates of Richmond*, pp. 343–44; Eicher, p. 296; Pinkerton, *The Spy of the Rebellion*, p. 573; McPherson, *Tried by War*, pp. 98–99; Catton, pp. 331–37; Sears, *George B. McClellan*, pp. 212–14; Sears, *To the Gates of Richmond*, pp. 191, 208–11, 220, 225–26, 250, 291, 316–18.

190   *the general:* Movement from Malvern Hill, p. 54, B: 7, EF, GU; Sears, *To the Gates of Richmond*, pp. 345–48; Sears, *George B. McClellan*, p. 235; Eicher, p. 303; Stepp and Hill, p. 129; Marvel, pp. 210–11.

190   *McClellan alone:* Sears, *George B. McClellan*, pp. 223–26; Catton, vol. 2, pp. 338–41; REL to Jefferson Davis, July 6, 1862, OR-11.3:634–35; Sears, *To the Gates of Richmond*, p. 341; James Allen to T. S. C. Lowe, July 25, 1862, B: 7, EF, GU.

190   *intelligence service:* L. C. Turner to EMS, Sept. 21, 1863, pp. 199–203, vol. 2, Turner Letter Books, E: 179A, RG94, NA.

191   *another word:* Catton, vol. 2, pp. 343–48; Donald, *Lincoln*, pp. 359–61;

McPherson, *Tried by War*, pp. 100–101; Goodwin, pp. 450–52; Sears, *George B. McClellan*, pp. 226–29; McClellan, *Report on the Organization and Campaigns of the Army of the Potomac*, pp. 280–82; Horan, *The Pinkertons*, p. 124; Mackay, pp. 152–53.

191   *both sides:* AL's General Order no. 101, Aug. 11, 1862, OR-11.3:371; McPherson, *Tried by War*, pp. 100–101; McPherson, *Battle Cry of Freedom*, p. 394; Catton, vol. 2, p. 88; Fishel, *The Secret War for the Union*, pp. 182–84.

191   *general in chief:* McPherson, *Tried by War*, pp. 111–12; Donald, *Lincoln*, pp. 348–49, 369–70; *Diary of Orville Hickman Browning*, vol. 1, pp. iii, 563; Catton, vol. 2, pp. 371–72; Catton, vol. 3, pp. 14–15.

192   *twenty-four hours:* HH to EMS, July 27, 1862, OR-11.3:337–38; GM to HH, July 26, 1862, OR-11.3:333–34; Fishel, *The Secret War to Save the Union*, p. 162; Fishel, "Pinkerton and McClellan," p. 128; Sears, *George B. McClellan*, pp. 239–41; Sears, *To the Gates of Richmond*, pp. 352–53.

192   *the Peninsula:* McPherson, *Tried by War*, pp. 118–19; Sears, *George B. McClellan*, pp. 241–42; Sears, *To the Gates of Richmond*, p. 353.

193   *order stood:* Sears, *To the Gates of Richmond*, pp. 353–54; GM to HH, Aug. 12, 1862, OR-11.3:372–73; Fishel, *The Secret War for the Union*, pp. 162–63, 584–85; Fishel, "Pinkerton and McClellan," p. 129.

THIRTEEN: SECOND BULL RUN

194   *former home:* GS to Uncle, Oct. 29, 1862, SLH, KS; Van Santvoord, pp. 4, 21; Schmidt, p. 52; De Witt, p. 153.

195   *Company B disbanded:* Proceedings of the Ulster County Historical Society, p. 28; George H. Sharpe, "Memorial Address," p. 6.

195   *for good:* Proceedings of the Ulster County Historical Society, pp. 28–29; Van Santvoord, pp. 4–5, 9–17.

196   *the night:* Lester and Hoag, pp. 14–15; Van Santvoord, pp. 17–21.

196   *was beginning:* McPherson, *Battle Cry of Freedom*, pp. 488, 532–34; Donald, *Lincoln*, pp. 354–55; Goodwin, p. 456; Winkle, pp. xii–xiv, 287–89, 363, 368–69.

197   *the Rebels:* Eicher, pp. 317–18; Donald, *Lincoln*, pp. 357–58, 361; McPherson, *Tried by War*, pp. 95–97; Catton, vol. 2, p. 383; Fishel, *The Secret War for the Union*, pp. 3, 186–87; Fishel, "Military Intelligence 1861–63 (Part 1)," p. 6.

197   *the moment:* Catton, vol. 2, pp. 388–89; McPherson, *Tried by War*, pp. 113–14.

197   *to 55,000:* Catton, vol. 2, pp. 386–88; McClellan, *Report on the Organization and Campaigns of the Army of the Potomac*, pp. 299–301.

198   *southern agents:* AP to A. Porter, Aug. 10, 1862, R: 29, GMP, LC; Pinkerton, *The Spy of the Rebellion*, p. 562.

198   *to Pope:* McPherson, *Battle Cry of Freedom*, pp. 525–28; Catton, vol. 2, pp. 389–91, 416–18; Donald, *Lincoln*, p. 370; Eicher, pp. 319–23; Sears, *George B. McClellan*, pp. 244–50; McClellan, *Report on the Organization and Campaigns of the Army of the Potomac*, pp. 304–6.

198   *own government:* Fishel, *The Secret War for the Union*, pp. 182, 191–94; Stuart, "Of Spies and Borrowed Names," p. 320.

199   *McClellan ousted:* George Bangs letters to AP, Aug. 20 and 23, 1862, AP to George Bangs, Aug. 20, 1862, B: 2, AP to GM, Aug. 25, 1862, B: 4, PND, LC; Catton, vol. 2, p. 440; Horan and Swiggett, pp. 110–14; Mackay, pp. 156–58; Horan, *The Pinkertons*, pp. 123–24; Niven, *Gideon Welles*; Nevins, vol. 2, p. 173.

200   *by defeat:* GS to Uncle, Oct. 29, 1862, SLH, KS; Van Santvoord, pp. 22–25.

200   *toward Maryland:* Second Manassas, CWSAC Battle Summaries, American Battlefield Protection Program, https://www.nps.gov; Sears, *Landscape Turned Red*, pp. 61–62; Catton, vol. 2, pp. 426–36; Fishel, *The Secret War for the Union*, pp. 200–206; Eicher, pp. 326–33; McPherson, *Battle Cry of Freedom*, p. 531.

201   *"of McClellan":* Catton, vol. 2, pp. 440–41; Goodwin, pp. 474–75; Fishel, *The Secret War for the Union*, pp. 206–7; Sears, *George B. McClellan*, pp. 252–59; Pinkerton, *The Spy of the Rebellion*, pp. 563–64.

201   *the government:* LB to Brig. Gen. King, July 24, 1862, R: 25, M504, RG107, LB to EMS, Aug. 19, 1863, with Davis deposition, R: 226, M221, Charles Knox to LB, Oct. 22, 1862, R: 128, M797, RG94, L. C. Turner letters to LB, Nov. 24 and Dec. 27, 1862, vol. 1, Turner Letter Books, E: 179A, RG94, NA.

202   *"British subject":* Messages to LB, July 9, 1862, R: 158, Message to LB, July 26, 1862, R: 159, M473, RG107, NA; L. C. Turner letters to LB, Feb. 4, May 9 and 16, 1863, vol. 1, Turner Letter Books, E: 179A, RG94, Jacob Frick letter, Oct. 5, 1862, C. N. Otis to LB, Oct. 30, 1862, Letter to LB on John L. Kidwell, Nov. 1, 1862, R: 128, Letter to LB from Quarter-Master General's Office, June 10, 1862, M797, RG94, NA.

202   *about unmolested:* Joseph Stannard Baker Memoirs, p. 7-12 to 7-14; Mogelever, pp. 166–69.

203   *officers demanded:* Boyd, pp. 172–74; Davis, "'The Pet of the Confederacy' Still? Fresh Findings About Belle Boyd," pp. 35–39; Davis, "The Civil War's Most Overrated Spy," pp. 4–5; Jones, *Behind Enemy Lines*, pp. 58–62; Winkler, pp. 201–6; Stern, p. 96.

204   *darling overnight:* McPherson, *Battle Cry of Freedom*, p. 456; Davis, "The Civil
      War's Most Overrated Spy," pp. 1–2; Fishel, "Military Intelligence 1861–63
      (Part 1)," pp. 5–6; Davis, "'The Pet of the Confederacy' Still? Fresh Findings
      About Belle Boyd," pp. 37, 39; Winkler, pp. 217–18; Davis, "The Civil War's
      Most Overrated Spy," pp. 2–3; Fishel, *The Secret War for the Union*, p. 176.

204   *local division:* Winkler, p. 218; Tillebrow letter, June 22, 1862, B: 2, E: 36,
      RG110, AP to EMS with attachments, June 25, 1862, R: 106, M797, RG94,
      NA; Comments on Belle Boyd Entry, B: 15, EF, GU; Fishel, *The Secret War
      for the Union*, pp. 174–76; Jones, *Behind Enemy Lines*, p. 63; Davis, "The Civil
      War's Most Overrated Spy," p. 3.

205   *stalked out:* AP expenses for, July 1862, B: 1, E: 95, RG110, NA; brigade sur-
      geon to EMS, July 30, 1862, R: 106, C. P. Wolcott memos, July 18, 1862, Julius
      White memos to C. P. Wolcott, July 29, 1862, R: 25, M797, RG94, NA; com-
      ments on Belle Boyd entry, Belle Boyd references in OR, B; 15, EF, GU; Fishel,
      The Secret War for the Union, p. 176; Boyd, pp. 177, 180–83.

205   *to Richmond:* Belle Boyd to EMS, Aug. 8, 1862, R: 25, M797, RG94, NA;
      Doster, pp. 101–2; Jones, *Behind Enemy Lines*, pp. 64–65; Fishel, *The Secret
      War for the Union*, p. 176; Stern, p. 107; Winkler, pp. 221–22; Davis, "'The Pet
      of the Confederacy' Still? Fresh Findings About Belle Boyd," pp. 42–43.

205   *with them:* Eicher, p. 334; McPherson, *Tried by War*, pp. 119–21; Catton, vol. 3,
      p. 442; Goodwin, pp. 475–79; Marvel, pp. 230–32; McPherson, *Battle Cry of
      Freedom*, pp. 532–34.

206   *around Washington:* Mackay, p. 158; Sears, *George B. McClellan*, pp. 258, 267;
      McPherson, *Battle Cry of Freedom*, p. 534; Catton, vol. 3, p. 439; Fishel, *The
      Secret War for the Union*, pp. 211, 213.

206   *in Virginia:* Van Santvoord, pp. 25–26; Pinkerton, *The Spy of the Rebellion*, pp.
      564–65; Horan, *The Pinkertons*, p. 128; Miller, *The Photographic History of The
      Civil War*, pp. 319, 324; Fishel, *The Secret War for the Union*, pp. 211, 213; A.
      Pleasonton to R. B. Marcy, Sept. 5, 1862, OR-19.2:186; GM to AL, Sept. 10,
      1862, OR-19.2:233; Fishel, "Pinkerton and McClellan," p. 132; Sears, *Land-
      scape Turned Red*, pp. 102–3.

FOURTEEN: ANTIETAM

207   *the North:* McPherson, *Battle Cry of Freedom*, pp. 534–35; Sears, *Landscape
      Turned Red*, p. 68.

208   *the fly:* George Bangs letter to his mother, June 14, 1863, MB; AP expenses
      for Sept. 1862, B: 1, E: 95, RG110, NA; Fishel, *The Secret War for the Union*,

pp. 212–15, 238; Maslowski, p. 51; Fishel, "Pinkerton and McClellan," p. 132; Sears, *Landscape Turned Red*, pp. 103, 108.

208   *menace Washington:* "Grenville M. Dodge and George H. Sharpe: Grant's Intelligence Chiefs in West and East," p. 2; Sears, *George B. McClellan*, pp. 273–74, 277–78; Fishel, *The Secret War for the Union*, pp. 214–18; GM to Gov. Curtin, Sept. 8, 1862, and A. G. Curtin to EMS, Sept, 8, 1862, OR-19.2:216; Thomas Scott to GM, Sept. 9, 1862, OR-19.2:230; John Wool to GM, Sept. 9, 1862, OR-19.2:231; Sears, *Landscape Turned Red*, p. 103; GM to HH, Sept. 9, 1862, OR-19.2:218–19; A. G. Curtin to GM, Sept. 10, 1862, OR-19.2:248; A. G. Curtin to AL, Sept. 12, 1862, OR-19.2:277; Fishel, "Pinkerton and McClellan," p. 132.

209   *the sun:* GM messages to HH, Sept. 9, 1862, OR-19.2:219; Sears, *George B. McClellan*, pp. 276–79, 286–87; Fishel, *The Secret War for the Union*, p. 217; Sears, *Landscape Turned Red*, p. 101; Bloss, p. 83; GM to HH, Sept. 10, 1862, OR-19.2:234; GM to HH, Sept. 11, 1862, Correspondence, Aug. 29–Dec. 19, 1862, EMSP, LC.

209   *an armistice:* Catton, vol. 2, pp. 446–48; McPherson, *Battle Cry of Freedom*, p. 536; Bloss, p. 82; Cowley, pp. 232–38; Millican, pp. 108–11.

210   *and cautiously:* Bloss, pp. 84–85; Sears, *Landscape Turned Red*, pp. 90–91.

210   *got it:* Sears, *Landscape Turned Red*, pp. 91–92; Millican, pp. 105–6.

210   *received it:* Sears, *Landscape Turned Red*, pp. 111–14, 349–50; Bloss, pp. 83, 88–90; Sears, *George B. McClellan*, pp. 280–81.

211   *"you trophies":* Sears, *Landscape Turned Red*, p. 113; Sears, *George B. McClellan*, p. 280.

211   *northern papers:* Eicher, pp. 341–43; Sears, *Landscape Turned Red*, pp. 125, 350–52; Sears, *Chancellorsville*, p. 112; Sears, *Gettysburg*, p. 13.

211   *and conquer:* Sears, *George B. McClellan*, p. 282; Sears, *Landscape Turned Red*, pp. 115–16.

212   *security failure:* Sears, *Landscape Turned Red*, pp. 116–17, 120–21; Bloss, p. 86; Sears, *George B. McClellan*, pp. 283–84; Millican, p. 106; Fishel, *The Secret War for the Union*, pp. 227–28.

212   *Crampton's Gap:* Eicher, pp. 340–41; Sears, *Landscape Turned Red*, pp. 124–26.

213   *Antietam Creek:* Catton, vol. 2, pp. 450–51; Fishel, *The Secret War for the Union*, p. 235; Sears, *Landscape Turned Red*, pp. 119, 140–43, 149, 152–53, 157, 173; Sears, *George B. McClellan*, pp. 287–88, 290–91; Bloss, p. 87.

213   *next day:* Sears, *Landscape Turned Red*, pp. 132, 159, 163, 167, 176; Sears, *George B. McClellan*, pp. 293–95, 296–99, 302; Nicolay and Hay, *Abraham*

Lincoln: A History, vol. 6, p. 134; McPherson, *Tried by War*, pp. 125–26; Eicher, pp. 347–48.

213 *later wrote:* Eicher, p. 349; McPherson, *Battle Cry of Freedom*, pp. 538–39; Pinkerton, *The Spy of the Rebellion*, pp. 568–69.

213 *accomplished nothing:* Mogelever, pp. 137–40, 187.

214 *artillery shell:* Author tour of Antietam National Battlefield at Sharpsburg, Md.; Sears, *Landscape Turned Red*, pp. 185–86, 200, 214, 244, 252, 282, 293–96, 310; McPherson, *Battle Cry of Freedom*, pp. 540–44; Sears, *George B. McClellan*, p. 305; Eicher, p. 363; Catton, vol. 2, pp. 451–57; Livermore, pp. 92–93; Winkle, p. 363; Geringer, p. 19.

215 *"on paper":* McPherson, *Battle Cry of Freedom*, p. 545; Sears, *Landscape Turned Red*, pp. 298–99, 302–3; Sears, *George B. McClellan*, pp. 318–19; Catton, vol. 2, pp. 458–60; McClellan, *Report on the Organization and Campaigns of the Army of the Potomac*, pp. 393–94; Horan, *The Pinkertons*, p. 129; Pinkerton, *The Spy of the Rebellion*, pp. 568–71.

215 *nitpicking complaints:* Eicher, pp. 338, 363; Sears, *Landscape Turned Red*, pp. 303–8; Fishel, *The Secret War for the Union*, p. 237; Sears, *George B. McClellan*, pp. 321–22; Goodwin, pp. 483–85; McClellan, *Report on the Organization and Campaigns of the Army of the Potomac*, pp. 400–401; Sears, *The Civil War Papers of George B. McClellan*, p. 476.

215 *work over:* Goodwin, p. 281; Winkle, p. 113; Conroy, pp. 75–76; Mackay, pp. 159–60; Horan and Swiggett, pp. 115–19; AP to GM, Sept. 22, 1862, B: 4, PND, LC.

216 *antislavery Unionists:* McPherson, *Battle Cry of Freedom*, pp. 186, 504–5, 557–59; Goodwin, pp. 204–7; Donald, *Lincoln*, p. 374; Horan, *The Pinkertons*, p. 134; Baker, *History of the United States Secret Service*, pp. 35, 184–85, 193, 232–34; Varon, *Southern Lady, Yankee Spy*, pp. 98–99; LB to AL, Sept. 30, 1863, Series 1, General Correspondence, 1833–1916, ALD, LC; Burlingame, *Abraham Lincoln*, vol. 2, p. 410.

216 *commander in chief:* Pinkerton, *The Spy of the Rebellion*, p. 571; Conroy, pp. 16–17, 69–70, 94–96.

217 *kept hearing:* Donald, *Lincoln*, pp. 385–86; Sears, *George B. McClellan*, p. 241.

218 *his corner:* AP to GM, Sept. 22, 1862, B: 4, PND, LC.

218 *"another regiment":* AP to GM, Oct. 7, 1862, B: 4, PND, LC; Donald, *Lincoln*, pp. 387–88; Sears, *George B. McClellan*, pp. 330–31; Horan, *The Pinkertons*, p. 135; Mackay, pp. 162–64; Cuthbert, p. 129; McPherson, *Tried by War*, pp. 139, 293.

218 *fire McClellan:* Sears, *George B. McClellan*, pp. 336–38; Fishel, *The Secret War for the Union*, pp. 254–55; McPherson, *Battle Cry of Freedom*, pp. 561–62, 569–70; Goodwin, p. 485; Eicher, pp. 382–83.

219 *general said:* Marvel, pp. 258–59; Sears, *George B. McClellan*, pp. 340–41, 347; Fishel, *The Secret War for the Union*, pp. 255–56; Milton, *Abraham Lincoln and the Fifth Column*, pp. 113–14; Eicher, pp. 199–202; Catton, vol. 2, p. 478; McPherson, *Tried by War*, pp. 140–42; GM to AP, Nov. 28, 1862, B: 2, PND, LC.

219 *the detective:* George Bangs letter to his mother, June 14, 1863, MB; Pinkerton, *The Spy of the Rebellion*, p. 583; Rowan, p. 185; Fishel, *The Secret War for the Union*, p. 255; Horan, *The Pinkertons*, p. 135; Mackay, p. 167.

219 *took command:* AP memos to George Bangs, Oct. 13 and Nov. 10, 1862, R: 24, M504, RG107, Robert Atkinson letter, July 11, 1865, AP certificate Cook County, Ill., John Wilson to EMS, July 28, 1865, memo to T. Eckert, Dec. 1, 1865, T. Eckert letter, Dec. 1, 1864, remibursement for AP, Dec. 21, 1865, B: 6, E: 95, RG110, NA; R. J. Atkinson to GM, July 7, 1863, B: 2, PND, LC; Mackay, p. 172.

220 *intelligence officer:* LB expenses for October and November 1862, B: 2, AP expenses for November and December 1862, January 1863, April–May 1865, B: 1, E: 95, RG110, NA; GM to AP, July 17, 1863, B: 2, PND, LC; AP to GM, March 29, 1863, B: 19, EF, GU; Hageman, p. 5; Cook, p. 6; Fishel, "The Mythology of Civil War Intelligence," p. 351; Mackay, pp. 167–68; Horan and Swiggett, pp. 122–23; Horan, *The Pinkertons*, p. 136; Pinkerton, *The Spy of the Rebellion*, p. 584.

FIFTEEN: FREDERICKSBURG

221 *Jansen Hasbrouck:* Senate House Museum exhibit on George Sharpe memorabilia, KS; GS to Uncle, Oct. 29, 1862, SLH, KS; Van Santvoord, pp. 27–29; Organization of the Union forces at the battle of Fredericksburg, Va., Dec. 11–15, 1862, OR-21:48, 54; Bigelow, pp. 40–43.

222 *the city:* Van Santvoord, p. 30; D. E. Sickles to Lt. Col. Richmond, Nov. 22, 1862, OR-21:789; D. E. Sickles to Chauncey McKeever, Nov. 2, 1862, OR-19.2:533; Hebert, p. 155; Eicher, p. 395; Sears, *Chancellorsville*, pp. 28–31.

222 *Union Army:* McPherson, *Battle Cry of Freedom*, p. 570; McPherson, *Tried by War*, pp. 142–45; Eicher, pp. 396–99; Fishel, "Military Intelligence 1861–63 (Part 1)," p. 7.

223 *John Babcock:* Eicher, pp. 398–99; Fishel, "Military Intelligence 1861–63 (Part 1)," p. 8.

223 *filed there:* JCB letters to Uncle, June 3 and July 3, 1855, George G. Sharpe to Office of Commissary-General, Nov. 8, 1904, JCB letters to Aunt, July 26, 1861, and Sept. 28, 1865, Record of Service of JCB, JCB to William A. Pinkerton, April 9, 1908, JCBP, LC; Comments on Babcock Entry, B: 4, EF, GU; O'Toole, p. 168; Feis, *Grant's Secret Service,* p. 197; Ryan, *Spies, Scouts, and Secrets in the Gettysburg Campaign,* pp. 7–8; Ryan, "A Battle of Wits: Intelligence Operations During the Gettysburg Campaign, Part 1," pp. 10–11; Fishel, *The Secret War for the Union,* pp. 257–59.

223 *their camp:* Comments on Babcock Entry, B: 4, EF, GU; JCB to Maj. Gen. Parke, Dec. 31, 1862, R: 21, M2096, NA; Fishel, *The Secret War for the Union,* p. 262.

224 *the town:* Fishel, *The Secret War for the Union,* pp. 260–63, 267–68; Maslowski, p. 51; Fishel, "Military Intelligence 1861–63 (Part 1)," p. 8.

224 *Marye's Heights:* McPherson, *Battle Cry of Freedom,* pp. 570–74; Eicher, pp. 396–405; Catton, vol. 3, pp. 12–17; Donald, *Lincoln,* pp. 398–99; Fishel, *The Secret War for the Union,* pp. 269–71; Livermore, p. 96.

225 *its commander:* Van Santvoord, pp. 32–34; Report of GS, 120th Infantry, Dec. 17, 1862, OR-21:388–89; Report of Col. George B. Hall, 2nd Brigade, Dec. 18, 1862, OR-21:384–86; Report of Brig. Gen. Daniel E. Sickles, 2nd Division, Dec. 18, 1862, OR-21:377–83; George Sharpe, "Memorial Address," pp. 7–8; *Proceedings of the Ulster County Historical Society 1936–1937,* p. 30; "Picture of General Sharpe," *Kingston Weekly Leader,* Nov. 28, 1903.

225 *proper position:* Proceedings of the Ulster County Historical Society 1936–1937, p. 30.

225 *their muskets:* Report of Brig. Gen. Daniel E. Sickles, 2nd Division, Dec. 18, 1862, OR-21:377–83; Report of Col. George B. Hall, 2nd Brigade, Dec. 18, 1862, OR-21:384–86; Van Santvoord, p. 35; Report of GS, 120th Infantry, Dec. 17, 1862, OR-21:388–89.

226 *"in it":* Catton, vol. 3, p. 25; McPherson, *Battle Cry of Freedom,* pp. 572–74; Report of Brig. Gen. Daniel E. Sickles, 2nd Division, Dec. 18, 1862, OR-21:377–83; Report of GS, 120th Infantry, Dec. 17, 1862, OR-21:388–89; Report of Col. George B. Hall, 2nd Brigade, Dec. 18, 1862, OR-21:384–86; Van Santvoord, p. 36; Hebert, p. 160.

226 *months earlier:* Bigelow, pp. 32–35; Van Santvoord, pp. 37–38.

226 *"early deliverance":* Recko, pp. 132–33; Mortimer, *Double Death,* pp. 204–6.

227   *major general:* Jones, *Ladies of Richmond,* pp. 145–46; Blakey, pp. 140–43, 149; Dabney, p. 178.

227   *be quarantined:* Brock, pp. 296–99, 304–5; Jones, *A Rebel War Clerk's Diary at the Confederate States Capital,* pp. 125–27; Varon, *Southern Lady, Yankee Spy,* pp. 102–5; Thomas, *The Confederate State of Richmond,* p. 114; Jones, *Ladies of Richmond,* pp. 145–46; Dabney, p. 178.

227   *toilet trinkets:* Thomas, *The Confederate State of Richmond,* pp. 108–9, 143.

228   *him down:* Fishel, *The Secret War for the Union,* p. 257; Sears, *Chancellorsville,* pp. 32–33, 110; Castel, pp. 37–39; Stuart, "Samuel Ruth and General R. E. Lee," pp. 46, 65, 68, 72, 74–79; Markle, p. 139; P. V. Daniel to James A. Seddon, Jan. 5, 1862, R: 127, M437, RG109, NA.

228   *against Lee:* Castel, pp. 36, 39; Stuart, "Samuel Ruth and General R. E. Lee," pp. 37–38, 45, 108; James A. Seddon to P. V. Daniel, Jan. 24, 1863, OR-51.2:672–73; P. V. Daniel to REL and REL to P. V. Daniel, April 25, 1861, OR-S4.1:240–41; Axelrod, p. 108; Varon, *Southern Lady, Yankee Spy,* p. 96; "Richmond and Potomac Railroad," *Harper's Weekly* 9, no. 459 (Oct. 14, 1865): 653.

229   *spy chief:* Van Santvoord, pp. 39–40; Fishel, *The Secret War for the Union,* pp. 271–73; Sears, *Chancellorsville,* pp. 19–20; Eicher, pp. 428–29; McPherson, *Battle Cry of Freedom,* pp. 584–85; GS to Uncle, Jan. 26, 1863, SLH, KS.

SIXTEEN: "THE GREAT GAME"

233   *in her:* GS to Uncle, Feb. 3 and 8, 1863, SLH, KS; GS to John Steele, Feb. 27, 1863, R: 198, M504, RG107, NA.

234   *contraband smugglers:* Fishel, *The Secret War for the Union,* pp. 291–92.

234   *his spymaster: Proceedings of the Ulster County Historical Society 1936–1937,* pp. 30–31; Van Santvoord, pp. 40–41; Ryan, "A Battle of Wits: Intelligence Operations During the Gettysburg Campaign, Part 1," p. 10; "Grenville M. Dodge and George H. Sharpe," pp. 4–5; Sears, *Chancellorsville,* pp. 68–70.

235   *him quickly:* General Order no. 32, March 30, 1863, OR-25.2:167; Markle, pp. 6, 15; GS to JH, Jan. 5, 1863, R: 45, M2096, NA.

235   *subpar officer:* Catton, vol. 3, pp. 65–66; Donald, *Lincoln,* p. 411; Brooks, pp. 51–52; McPherson, *Tried by War,* p. 163; Sears, *Chancellorsville,* pp. 11, 54–58; Bigelow, pp. 4–6; Eicher, p. 473; Hebert, pp. vii–viii, 97–98, 122, 142–44, 166–70; *Diary of Gideon Welles,* vol. 1, pp. 229–30; Adams, p. 161; Fishel, *The Secret War for the Union,* p. 276; Dennett, p. 88.

236   *too cocky:* Hearing of the Joint Committee on the Conduct of the War, 1865, vol. 1, pp. 73–74, 112; Catton, vol. 3, pp. 93–96; Hebert, pp. 178–81; Fishel,

The Secret War for the Union, p. 281; Bigelow, pp. 31, 50; McPherson, *Battle Cry of Freedom*, pp. 585–86.

236 *"in China"*: Hearing of the Joint Committee on the Conduct of the War, 1865, vol. 1, pp. 73–74; Hebert, pp. 59–60; Fishel, *The Secret War for the Union*, pp. 277–81; "Grenville M. Dodge and George H. Sharpe," p. 4.

236 *"all-source intelligence"*: General Order no. 40, April 10, 1863, OR-25.2:197; Fishel, *The Secret War for the Union*, pp. 299–300, 571; "Grenville M. Dodge and George H. Sharpe," p. 9; Letter to JH, April 23, 1863, B: 10, C. B. Comstack to DB, Feb. 28, 1863, B: 13, JHP, HL.

237 *provide it*: Hearing of the Joint Committee on the Conduct of the War, 1865, vol. 1, p. 84; Hebert, pp. 122, 183; Ryan, *Spies, Scouts, and Secrets in the Gettysburg Campaign*, p. 97; Sears, *Chancellorsville*, p. 63; Fishel, *The Secret War for the Union*, pp. 282–83; Nevins, *The War for the Union*, vol. 2, pp. 435–36.

237 *his diary*: Ryan, "The Intelligence Battle, July 2," p. 68; James Morice, "Organizational Learning in a Military Environment: George H. Sharpe and the Army of the Potomac," SGF, KS; Fishel, *The Secret War for the Union*, p. 287; Sparks, *Inside Lincoln's Army*, pp. 209, 212, 221; Ryan, "A Battle of Wits: Intelligence Operations During the Gettysburg Campaign, Part 1," p. 10; MP Diary entries, Feb. 11 and 27, 1863, MPD, LC.

237 *marauded noncombatants*: "Obituary, General M. R. Patrick," *Cincinnati Commercial Gazette*, July 28, 1888, p. 2; Gates, pp. 191–95; Sparks, "General Patrick's Progress," pp. 375–76, 381; Sparks, *Inside Lincoln's Army*, pp. 11, 22, 107, 224, 417–19, 423; Morice, "Organizational Learning."

238 *staff work*: "Obituary, General M. R. Patrick," *Cincinnati Commercial Gazette*, July 28, 1888, p. 2; Sparks, "General Patrick's Progress," pp. 373–75; Sparks, *Inside Lincoln's Army*, pp. 12–17, 159; Braden, pp. 43–44; General Order no. 161, Oct. 6, 1862, OR-19.2:389.

238 *brigadier general*: "General Patrick's Progress," pp. 375–78; Sparks, *Inside Lincoln's Army*, pp. 11, 207–8, 250–51; Fishel, *The Secret War for the Union*, pp. 283, 301; abstract from consolidated morning report of the Army of the Potomac for Jan. 31, 1863, Organization of the Army of the Potomac, Jan. 31, 1863, OR-25.2:15–16; Thomas, *Stanton*, pp. 337–38, 378.

239 *their camps*: Negro spies in Sharpe's bureau, B: 7, Manuscript notes, pp. 9–11, B: 3; Captured Rebel mail, B: 14, Gen. Wadsworth letter to Col. Kingsbury, Feb. 15, 1863, B: 5, EF, GU; Fishel, "Military Intelligence 1861–63 (Part 2)," p. 3; Fishel, "The Mythology of Civil War Intelligence," pp. 357, 365; "Grenville M. Dodge and George H. Sharpe," p. 5; Fishel, *The Secret War for the Union*, pp. 5, 296–97, 311–12, 584; Markle, p. 13.

239 *its time:* Examples of Signal Corps reports addressed to BMI, 1863, Signal reports, March 2–15, 1863, evidence of BMI receiving Signal Corps reports, B: 14, EF, GU; Fishel, "The Mythology of Civil War Intelligence," p. 357; Fishel, *The Secret War for the Union*, pp. 3, 298–300; Schmidt, p. 54.

240 *rarely used:* Received from MP, April 27, 1863, 1,751.25 in Confederate money, R: 45, M2096, NA; "Intelligence in the Civil War," p. 23; Fishel, *The Secret War for the Union*, pp. 294–96; Fishel, "The Mythology of Civil War Intelligence," p. 363; Markle, p. 18.

240 *the truth:* Babcock expenses, February 1863, B: 2, E: 95, RG110, D. Shields list of refugees, March 15, 1863, R: 15, M416, RG109, GS list of prisoners and deserters interrogated, April 30, 1863, GS to Gen. Martindale, Dec. 12, 1863, R: 45, M2096, NA; statement of prisoner brought in April 2, 1863, B: 14, JHP, HL; "Famous War Scout Dies at His Home on East Fourth Street," *Mount Vernon Daily Argus*, Nov. 20, 1908, pp. 1, 5; Fishel, *The Secret War for the Union*, pp. 286, 300–302; Cook, p. 6; Ryan, *Spies, Scouts, and Secrets in the Gettysburg Campaign*, p. 9; Maslowski, p. 57; Feis, *Grant's Secret Service*, pp. 199–200; Tsouras, p. 252.

241 *him "McAnty":* Proceedings of the Ulster County Historical Society 1936–1937, p. 31; Fishel, *The Secret War for the Union*, p. 293; Ryan, *Spies, Scouts, and Secrets in the Gettysburg Campaign*, p. 8; Morice, "Organizational Learning"; Feis, *Grant's Secret Service*, p. 197; Ryan, "A Battle of Wits: Intelligence Operations During the Gettysburg Campaign, Part 1," p. 11; Schmidt, p. 54.

241 *been pinpointed:* GS to Col. Parker, Oct. 7, 1863, R: 198, M504, RG107, NA; Morice, "Organizational Learning"; Fishel, *The Secret War for the Union*, pp. 293–94; Fishel, "The Mythology of Civil War Intelligence," pp. 362–63; Sears, *Chancellorsville*, p. 101.

242 *"if possible":* GS to JM, March 2, 1863, GS to A. Yager, March 1863, R: 198, M504, RG107, NA; Statement of A. Yager, JCB to A. Yager 10' am, B: 14, EF, GU; Fishel, *The Secret War for the Union*, pp. 292–93, 303.

242 *without punctuation:* Cline's report and GS notes, March 4 or 9, 1863, B: 14, EF, GU; Ryan, *Spies, Scouts, and Secrets in the Gettysburg Campaign*, p. 8; Fishel, *The Secret War for the Union*, pp. 306–10.

242 *the move:* JCB to DB, March 11, 1863, Joseph Skinker to GS, March 13, 1863, R: 45, M2096, NA; Fishel, *The Secret War for the Union*, pp. 313–15.

243 *spelling corrected:* GS to Gen. Heintzelman, July 10, 1863, R: 198, M504, RG107, NA; Fishel, *The Secret War for the Union*, pp. 315–17; Sears, *Chancellorsville*, p. 101.

243 *Civil War:* Baker to LB, March 4, 1863, LB to Capt. Wescott, March 8, 1863, R: 110, M504, RG107, NA; Baker entry, May 1, 1863, R: 2, M491, LB to EMS,

May 1, 1863, M492, NA; "Grenville M. Dodge and George H. Sharpe," pp. 7–8; Sparks, "General Patrick's Progress," p. 379; Fishel, *The Secret War for the Union*, p. 284; Stuart, "Operation Sanders," pp. 184–87.

244 *be released:* LB letters to MP, Dec. 18, 1862, R: 25, M504, RG107, NA; Fox to Watson, Feb. 28, 1862, R: 129, M797, RG94, S. Williams to LB, May 8, 1863, Lt. Col. Thompson letter to LB, May 10, 1863, Letter to LB, May 10, 1863, B: 2, RG110, NA; Ryan, *Spies, Scouts, and Secrets in the Gettysburg Campaign*, p. 5; Sparks, *Inside Lincoln's Army*, pp. 204–7, 216–18; Mogelever, p. 244; Fishel, *The Secret War for the Union*, p. 285.

244 *up to:* Sparks, *Inside Lincoln's Army*, pp. 114, 248–49, 386; Baker, *History of the United States Secret Service*, pp. 160–61.

244 *sex trafficking:* MP Diary entry, April 24, 1863, MPD, LC; Hebert, p. 180; Mogelever, p. 243; Orrmont, p. 71; MP to Brig. Gen. Williams, May 21, 1863, OR-25.2:512; Stahr, p. 367; Sparks, *Inside Lincoln's Army*, pp. 114–15, 236, 255–56.

245 *warned Washington:* LB to MP, April 22, 1863, R: 110, M504, RG107, LB to EMS, Feb. 8, 1863, R: 129, Papers relating to seizure of Schooner Boscer at Aquia Creek, In the matter of the seizure by Col. Baker of goods of Louis Cohen, R: 130, M797, RG94, MP correspondence, January 1863, on seizures, MP to Assistant Adjutant General, January 23, 1863, R: 23, M2096, Henry Bourdorf to LB, May 6, 1863, J. Brice Smith to LB, May 20, 1863, Louis Shultz to LB, May 19, 1863, B: 2, J. Talbot Pitman to LB, Feb. 20, 1863, B: 4, RG110, NA; Baker, *History of the United States Secret Service*, pp. 155–59, 163, 178–80.

245 *a crook:* "Many citizens" to LB, June 8, 1863, B: 2, F. W. Jones to John Crawford, Feb. 10, 1863, B: 4, RG110, MP to P. H. Watson, April 7, 1863, R: 130, M797, RG94, NA; MP to DB, Jan. 29, 1863, B: 5, EF, GU; Baker, *History of the United States Secret Service*, pp. 164–67; Mogelever, p. 244; Fishel, *The Secret War for the Union*, p. 284.

246 *had access:* Monthly statement showing the amount of government property seized by the provost marshal of the War Department for month ending June 30, 1863, R: 132, M797, RG94, Calvin Baker to LB, May 26, 1863, B: 2, RG110, NA.

246 *fought pillaging:* Fishel, *The Secret War for the Union*, pp. 284–85; Sparks, *Inside Lincoln's Army*, p. 226; Quarter-Master General's Office letter to LB, Feb. 17, 1863, B: 4, RG110, NA.

246 *Green's wife:* Documents, letters, and evidence collected in the case of James L. Green, "a known secessionist and suspected spy and smuggler," and Judge Advocate General report, April 1863, R: 46, M797, RG94, NA.

247   *Confederate resistance:* Fishel, *The Secret War for the Union*, pp. 318–20; Morice, "Organizational Learning"; GS to DB, March 13, 1863, B: 13, JHP, HL.

247   *had accomplished:* Extracts from various reports relative to the position of the Rebel Potomac Army, March 13, 1863, R: 45, M2096, NA.

248   *32,500 infantrymen:* GS monthly report to DB with addendum on Rebel Cavalry and extracts to accompany monthly report, R: 45, M2096, NA.

248   *"best information":* Fishel, *The Secret War for the Union*, pp. 320–22; Sears, *Chancellorsville*, pp. 101–2; Fishel, "Military Intelligence 1861–63 (Part 2)," p. 3; GS to D. McConaughy, June 29, 1863, pp. 4–2, Gettysburg Campaign, Pennsylvania Skirmishes, Folder 1, GNMP.

SEVENTEEN: CHANCELLORSVILLE

250   *Robert E. Lee:* Sears, *Chancellorsville*, pp. 97–100, 178–80, 193–94; Catton, vol. 3, p. 144; Eicher, p. 477; Hebert, p. 197.

250   *on theirs:* John Skinker to William Scott George, April 8, 1863, R: 45, M2096, NA; Fishel, *The Secret War for the Union*, pp. 286, 322–25, 350–51; S. Williams to MP, Feb. 13, 1863, JH to J. C. Kelton, Feb. 13, 1863, OR-25.2:74; DB memo, Feb. 27, 1863, OR-25.2:110; Sears, *Chancellorsville*, p. 126; REL to JD, April 2, 1863, OR-25.2:700; REL to James A. Seddon, Feb. 23, 1863, OR-25.2:646–47; "Grenville M. Dodge and George H. Sharpe," pp. 7, 10.

251   *with information:* John Skinker reports to GS, March 22 and 23, 1863, R: 45, M2096, GS to Capt. Allen, March 22, 1863, R: 198, M504, RG107, NA; Anderson-Tyson report, April 5, 1863, B: 14, EF, GU.

251   *much better:* O'Toole, p. 158; Stuart, "Samuel Ruth and General R. E. Lee," pp. 81, 106; GS to JH, March 21, 1863, R: 45, M2096, NA.

251   *chief wrote: Letter from the Secretary of War in the case of Joseph H. Maddox,* pp. 7, 11.

251   *secret service: Letter from the Secretary of War in the case of Joseph H. Maddox,* pp. 2–10; Fishel, *The Secret War for the Union*, pp. 335–39; LB memos to J. L. McPhail, April 27, March 28, and May 22 (no year), R: 110, M504, RG107, NA.

252   *"at once":* Fishel, *The Secret War for the Union,* p. 97; Recko, p. 104; *Letter from the Secretary of War in the Case of Joseph H. Maddox,* p. 100; Anonymous to EMS, undated, Anonymous to LB, May 11, 1863, AP to EMS, June 23, 1862, J. H. Maddox to the Confederate Secretary of War, Sept. 1862, Joseph Maddox File no. 425928, B: 588–89, RG94, NA; AP to GM, Dec. 19, 1861, R: 14, GMP, LC.

252   *"both sides": Letter from the Secretary of War in the case of Joseph H. Maddox,*

pp. 1, 6, 8; Chairman Committee on Claims to Redfield Proctor, March 31, 1890, Joseph Maddox File no. 425928, B: 588–89, RG94, NA.

252   *his own:* Letter from the Secretary of War in the case of Joseph H. Maddox, pp. 2–3; Varon, *Southern Lady, Yankee Spy,* pp. 97–98; GS to J. McPhail, March 21, 1863, Joseph Maddox File no. 425928, B: 588–89, RG94, NA.

253   *that night:* J. McPhail to GS with attachment on "Wanted," May 2, 1863, Joseph Maddox File no. 425928, B: 588–89, RG94, NA; Fishel, *The Secret War for the Union,* pp. 327–28; Sears, *Chancellorsville,* pp. 83–91; Sparks, *Inside Lincoln's Army,* p. 225.

253   *excellent spymaster:* James Morice, "Organizational Learning in a Military Environment: George H. Sharpe and the Army of the Potomoc," SGF, KS.

254   *"amongst us":* Catton, vol. 3, pp. 138–39; Bigelow, pp. 108, 130–31; McPherson, *Tried by War,* pp. 176–77; Fishel, *The Secret War for the Union,* p. 344.

254   *Rebel capital:* Sears, *Chancellorsville,* pp. 118–20; McPherson, *Battle Cry of Freedom,* p. 639; abstract from return of the Army of Northern Virginia, General Robert E. Lee, March 1863, OR-25.2:696; Eicher, pp. 473–74; Luvaas, "The Role of Intelligence in the Chancellorsville Campaign, 1863," pp. 101–2, 107; George Stoneman to S. Williams, Feb. 28, 1863, OR-25.2:111; Hebert, pp. 187–88.

255   *right flanks:* Luvaas, "The Role of Intelligence in the Chancellorsville Campaign, 1863," pp. 101; Fishel, "Military Intelligence 1861–63 (Part 2)," p. 5; J. H. Skinker to GS, April 2, 1863, R: 45, M2096, NA.

255   *destroy it:* Fishel, *The Secret War for the Union,* p. 345; Sears, *Chancellorsville,* pp. 118–20.

255   *Joseph Maddox:* GS to DB, April 10, 1863, R: 45, M2096, NA.

255   *not Richmond:* Sears, *Chancellorsville,* pp. 119–20; Hebert, pp. 187–88; Catton, vol. 3, pp. 144–45.

256   *real path:* Sears, *Chancellorsville,* pp. 102, 120–26; Fishel, *The Secret War for the Union,* pp. 347–49; REL to JD, April 16, 1863, OR-25.2:724–25; Ryan, *Spies, Scouts, and Secrets in the Gettysburg Campaign,* p. 23.

256   *"another failure":* Sears, *Chancellorsville,* pp. 122–24; Hebert, p. 189; Fishel, *The Secret War for the Union,* p. 346; AL to JH, April 15, 1863, OR-25.1:214.

257   *that intelligence:* Sears, *Chancellorsville,* pp. 128–30, 528.

258   *daring operation:* Sears, *Chancellorsville,* pp. 130–34; Fishel, *The Secret War for the Union,* pp. 360–62, 370.

258   *an exaggeration:* Fishel, *The Secret War for the Union,* pp. 349–50, 371–73; JH to EMS, April 21, 1863, Letter from Medical Director Letterman to JH with EMS cover note, April 23, 1863, W. A. Hammond memo, April 23, 1863, Joseph R. Smith to W. A. Hammond, OR- 25.2:239–41.

259   *Lee had:* GS to Gen. Stoneman, April 24, 1863, R: 198, M504, RG107, NA; Yager to GS, April 24, 1863, JM report on roads, April 28, 1863, B: 14, GS to DB, April 24, 1863, B: 5, EF, GU; GS to DB, April 24, 1863, R: 45, GS to DB, April 28, 1863, R: 23, M2096, NA; organization and strength of force comprising the present Army of Northern Virginia corrected to April 28, 1863, B: 11, JHP, HL; Fishel, *The Secret War for the Union*, p. 362; DB to Commanding Officer, Cavalry Corps, Warrenton Junction, April 28, 1863, OR-25.2:273; MP to S. Williams, April 22, 1863, OR-25.2:219; Fishel, "Military Intelligence 1861–63 (Part 2)," pp. 5, 12.

259   *Union Army:* Sparks, *Inside Lincoln's Army*, p. 237; Sears, *Chancellorsville*, p. 102.

260   *battlefield mistakes:* Fishel, *The Secret War for the Union*, pp. 4, 373–74.

260   *so sure:* Hebert, p. ix; Sears, *Chancellorsville*, pp. 150, 153, 158–60, 168; Eicher, p. 475; Fishel, *The Secret War for the Union*, pp. 377–83; REL report to S. Cooper on Chancellorsville Battle, Sept. 21, 1863, OR-25.1:796.

260   *him immediately:* DB to JH, April 28, 1863, OR-25.2:276; DB to Gen. Sedgwick, April 29, 1863, OR-25.2:292; Sears, *Chancellorsville*, pp. 170–71; Fishel, *The Secret War for the Union*, p. 384; Bigelow, p. 20; T. S. C. Lowe messages to DB, April 29, 1863, OR-25.2:288; P. A. Oliver to Professor Lowe, April 28, 1863, OR-25.2:277; Lowe messages from his aeronauts undated and April 29–May 5, 1863, B: 13, JHP, HL; DB to MP, May 1, 1863, vol. 88 (40B), AP, April 8–May 3, 1863, R: 6, M2096, NA.

261   *his spine:* Author tour of the Chancellorsville Battlefield; Sears, *Chancellorsville*, pp. 197–98, 231, 236; Catton, vol. 3, pp. 146–50; Hebert, pp. 196–98; DB to JH, May 1, 1863, OR-25.2:322–23; Bigelow, pp. 237, 254–55; McPherson, *Battle Cry of Freedom*, pp. 639–40; Eicher, pp. 477–78.

261   *from Fredericksburg:* Fishel, *The Secret War for the Union*, pp. 389–90.

262   *of Fredericksburg:* Sears, *Chancellorsville*, pp. 201, 210–12; Fishel, *The Secret War for the Union*, p. 390; DB to JH, May 1, 1863, OR-25.2:325; Luvaas, "The Role of Intelligence in the Chancellorsville Campaign, 1863," pp. 111–12; organization and strength of force comprising the present Army of Northern Virginia corrected to April 28, 1863, B: 11, JHP, HL.

262   *the battlefield:* Sears, *Chancellorsville*, pp. 212, 226–27; Hebert, p. 202; Fishel, *The Secret War for the Union*, pp. 391–92; Fishel, "Military Intelligence 1861–63 (Part 2)," pp. 5–6; DB to JH, May 1, 1863, OR-25.2:327; DB to J. C. Kelton, May 1, 1863, OR-25.2:332.

263   *"whipped man":* DB messages to JH, May 1, 1863, OR-25.2:329; *Letter from the Secretary of War in the Case of Joseph H. Maddox*, pp. 11–12; Sears,

Chancellorsville, pp. 211–12, 227–278; Fishel, *The Secret War for the Union*, pp. 402–3; DB to John Peck, May 2, 1863, John Peck to DB, May 4, 1863, OR-25.2:371.

263 *"right arm":* McPherson, *Battle Cry of Freedom*, pp. 640–61; Sears, *Chancellorsville*, pp. 238–39, 244–45, 250–51, 268, 293–96, 302, 447–48; Catton, vol. 3, pp. 151–54; Luvaas, "The Role of Intelligence in the Chancellorsville Campaign, 1863," pp. 112–13; T. S. C. Lowe messages to DB, May 2, 1863, OR-25.2:353–54; Fishel, *The Secret War for the Union*, pp. 395–99; Bigelow, pp. 276–77; Hebert, pp. 207–8.

264 *Pickett's division:* GS to JB, May 2, 1863, R: 198, M504, RG107, NA; Fishel, *The Secret War for the Union*, pp. 405–6; Sears, *Chancellorsville*, pp. 391–92.

264 *taken prisoner:* JB to DB, May 3, 1863, Dock Walker (Contraband) report, May 3, 1863, GS to JB, May 2, 1863, Report to DB, May 3, 1863, B: 14, JHP, HL; Eicher, pp. 483–87; Sears, *Chancellorsville*, pp. 335–37, 359, 367–70; Hebert, pp. 212–14.

265 *"is Stoneman":* Report of the Joint Committee on the Conduct of the War, 1865, vol. 1, pp. 85–86; AL to DB, May 3, 1863, B: 13, JHP, HL; Sears, *Chancellorsville*, p. 367; McPherson, *Battle Cry of Freedom*, p. 645.

265 *to do:* JB to GS, May 4, 1863, B: 14, AL to JH, May 6, 1863, B: 13, JHP, HL; McPherson, *Battle Cry of Freedom*, pp. 644–45; Hebert, pp. 216–18; Eicher, pp. 487–88; Fishel, *The Secret War for the Union*, pp. 407–9; Luvaas, "The Role of Intelligence in the Chancellorsville Campaign, 1863," p. 113.

265 *who lagged:* JB to GS, May 5, 1863, OR-25.2:421; Cleaves, pp. 112–13; Sears, *Chancellorsville*, pp. 431–32; Hebert, pp. 220–21.

266 *to complete:* Hebert, p. 221; Sparks, *Inside Lincoln's Army*, p. 243; Santvoord, pp. 222–25; *Proceedings of the Ulster County Historical Society 1936–1937*, pp. 32–33; Fishel, *The Secret War for the Union*, pp. 412–13; DB to Commanding Officer, Cavalry Corps, May 15, 1863, OR-25.2:483; S. Williams to GS, May 13, 1863, OR-25.2:476.

266 *"his throat":* Sears, *Chancellorsville*, pp. 249–50, 309–11, 434–37, 505–6; Hebert, pp. 223–25.

266 *outnumbered him:* McPherson, *Tried by War*, pp. 177–78; Sears, *Gettysburg*, pp. 19–26.

266 *into Pennsylvania:* Hebert, p. 226; Fishel, *The Secret War for the Union*, pp. 413–15; DB to JH, May 13, 1863, OR-25.2:477; JB to DB, May 18, 1863, B: 14, JHP, HL; Organization of the Rebel Army of N. Va., Gen. Robert E. Lee Commanding, Small Collections 145–Z to 167–Z, B: 9, SHC, UNC; Leather-bound

booklet, JB to William Pinkerton, April 9, 1908, JCBP, LC; GS to DB, May 13, 1863, R: 45, M2096, NA.

EIGHTEEN: GETTYSBURG

267 *he concluded:* Van Santvoord, pp. 218, 220–21; McPherson, *Battle Cry of Freedom*, p. 647; Sears, *Gettysburg*, pp. 1, 6, 14; Eicher, p. 490; Catton, vol. 3, pp. 159–61.

268 *for brigades:* McPherson, p. 648; Cleaves, p. 120; Tucker, p. vii; Fishel, *The Secret War for the Union*, pp. 415, 420–21.

268 *march north:* Ryan, *Spies, Scouts, and Secrets in the Gettysburg Campaign*, pp. 44–46, 58–59, 67, 71–72, 79, 213–14; Sears, *Gettysburg*, pp. 59–60.

269 *up to:* Ryan, *Spies, Scouts, and Secrets in the Gettysburg Campaign*, p. 71; Fishel, *The Secret War for the Union*, pp. 418–19; Ryan, "A Battle of Wits: Intelligence Operations During the Gettysburg Campaign, Part 2," p. 26.

269 *his questions:* Ryan, *Spies, Scouts, and Secrets in the Gettysburg Campaign*, pp. xiv–xv, 61–65, 76–79; Ryan, "A Battle of Wits: Intelligence Operations During the Gettysburg Campaign, Part 2," p. 7.

270 *Rebel deserter:* Ryan, *Spies, Scouts, and Secrets in the Gettysburg Campaign*, pp. 81, 100; L. Thomas Prince to EMS, May 20, 1863, Johnson Paenter to HH, May 21, 1863, OR-25.2:509–10; Hebert, pp. 232–33; EMS to HH, May 23, 1863, HH to EMS, May 23, 1863, OR-25.2:514–16; Sears, *Gettysburg*, p. 39; Fishel, *The Secret War for the Union*, pp. 415–16.

270 *right flank:* GS to DB, May 24, 1863, R: 174, M473, RG107, NA.

271 *nineteen days:* W. H. Paine to Brig. Gen. Warren, May 26, 1863, B: 13, JHP, HL; Ryan, *Spies, Scouts, and Secrets in the Gettysburg Campaign*, pp. 82–83, 101–2; GS to Gen. Lockwood, Sept. 11, 1863, R: 198, M504, RG107, NA.

271 *Army commander:* S. Williams to Military Commanders Belonging to the Army of the Potomac, May 26, 1863, B: 6, EF, GU; Sears, *Gettysburg*, pp. 39–40.

271 *"in motion":* JH to EMS, May 27, 1863, p. 176, R: 6, vol. 89 (40c), AP, May 3–June 5, 1863, M2096, NA; GS to Gen. S. Williams forwarded by JH, May 27, 1863, OR-25.2:528; Ryan, *Spies, Scouts, and Secrets in the Gettysburg Campaign*, p. 85.

272 *was outdated:* JH to AL, May 27, 1863, OR-25.2:529; "Grenville M. Dodge and George H. Sharpe," pp. 6–7; Fishel, *The Secret War for the Union*, pp. 416–18, 425–26.

272 *intelligence reports:* Joseph Maddox to Brig. Gen. Winder, B: 588–89, Joseph

Maddox file #425928, RG94, NA; JH to EMS, May 28, 1863, OR-25.2:542–
43; *Letter from the Secretary of War in the case of Joseph H. Maddox*, pp. 6–7, 13.

272   *invisible ink:* Ryan, *Spies, Scouts, and Secrets in the Gettysburg Campaign*, pp. 89,
93; Fishel, *The Secret War for the Union*, pp. 421–23; Ryan, "A Battle of Wits:
Intelligence Operations During the Gettysburg Campaign, Part 1," pp. 16–17.

273   *and ears:* Ryan, *Spies, Scouts, and Secrets in the Gettysburg Campaign*, pp. 46,
92–98.

273   *be ignored:* Sears, *Gettysburg*, p. 33; Ryan, *Spies, Scouts, and Secrets in the Gettysburg Campaign*, pp. xv, 10–19, 99; "A Battle of Wits: Intelligence Operations
During the Gettysburg Campaign, Part 2," p. 24.

274   *grew angry:* Fishel, *The Secret War for the Union*, pp. 435–36; Ryan, *Spies, Scouts,
and Secrets in the Gettysburg Campaign*, pp. 62, 93–94, 115; Sears, *Gettysburg*,
p. 83; Ryan, "A Battle of Wits: Intelligence Operations During the Gettysburg
Campaign, Part 2," p. 16; James Morice, "Organizational Learning in a Military
Environment: George H. Sharpe and the Army of the Potomac," SGF, KS.

275   *was happening:* Fishel, "Military Intelligence 1861–63 (Part 2)," p. 6; Sears,
Gettysburg, pp. 57–59; Fishel, *The Secret War for the Union*, pp. 423–24; Ryan,
Spies, Scouts, and Secrets in the Gettysburg Campaign, pp. 102–4.

275   *Stuart's movements:* DB to GGM, June 4, 1863, OR-27.3:5; Ryan, *Spies, Scouts,
and Secrets in the Gettysburg Campaign*, pp. 99, 105, 121–22; Fishel, *The Secret
War for the Union*, pp. 426–28; Ryan, "A Battle of Wits: Intelligence Operations
During the Gettysburg Campaign Part 1," p. 18.

276   *disinformation agent:* Sears, *Gettysburg*, pp. 60–62; Ryan, *Spies, Scouts, and Secrets in the Gettysburg Campaign*, p. 103; Fishel, *The Secret War for the Union*,
p. 424.

276   *same time:* Sears, *Gettysburg*, p. 61; Hebert, pp. 233–34; Ryan, *Spies, Scouts, and
Secrets in the Gettysburg Campaign*, p. 107; AL to JH, June 5, 1863, HH to JH,
June 5, 1863, OR-27.1:31–32.

277   *days later:* Ryan, *Spies, Scouts, and Secrets in the Gettysburg Campaign*, pp. 115–
18, 121–22; "A Battle of Wits: Intelligence Operations During the Gettysburg
Campaign, Part 1," p. 18.

278   *in place:* GS to DB with JH referral to AL, June 7, 1863, Series 1, General Correspondence 1833–1916, ALD, LC; Fishel, *The Secret War for the Union*, pp.
428–31; GS to JM, June 8, 1863, OR-27.3:35; Ryan, *Spies, Scouts, and Secrets
in the Gettysburg Campaign*, pp. 132, 135, 142.

278   *next day:* Fishel, *The Secret War for the Union*, pp. 431–34; Ryan, "A Battle of
Wits: Intelligence Operations During the Gettysburg Campaign, Part 1," p. 18;

Fishel, "Military Intelligence 1861–63 (Part 2)," p. 7; Ryan, *Spies, Scouts, and Secrets in the Gettysburg Campaign*, pp. 146–49; Sears, *Gettysburg*, p. 72.

278 *their limit:* GS to JH, June 9, 1863, B: 13, JHP, HL.

279 *Brandy Station victory:* DB to GGM, June 10, 1863, A. Pleasonton to JH, June 10, 1863, OR-27.3:48–49; Ryan, *Spies, Scouts, and Secrets in the Gettysburg Campaign*, pp. 134, 152–54, 165.

279 *taking vacations:* Luvaas, "Lee at Gettysburg," p. 122; Ryan, *Spies, Scouts, and Secrets in the Gettysburg Campaign*, pp. 214, 435; McPherson, *Battle Cry of Freedom*, p. 649; Sears, *Gettysburg*, pp. 84–85; Tucker, p. 68; Sparks, *Inside Lincoln's Army*, 253.

280 *and Maryland:* Fishel, *The Secret War for the Union*, pp. 436–37, 440; Ryan, *Spies, Scouts, and Secrets in the Gettysburg Campaign*, pp. 156, 165; JM to GS, June 11, 1863, OR-27.3:67; JM to GS, June 14, 1863, OR-27.3:107; Sears, *Gettysburg*, pp. 78–81, 84; Rose, p. 4; Hebert, pp. 237–38; Ryan, "A Battle of Wits: Intelligence Operations During the Gettysburg Campaign, Part 1," p. 21; Eicher, 493–94.

280 *found later:* MP circular, Oct. 29, 1863, R: 24, M2096, NA; Ryan, *Spies, Scouts, and Secrets in the Gettysburg Campaign*, p. 64; Sears, *Gettysburg*, p. 85; Ryan, "A Battle of Wits: Intelligence Operations During the Gettysburg Campaign, Part 3," p. 18; Tucker, pp. 69–70.

280 *major general:* Sears, *Gettysburg*, p. 85; Ryan, "A Battle of Wits: Intelligence Operations During the Gettysburg Campaign, Part 3," p. 7; Ryan, *Spies, Scouts, and Secrets in the Gettysburg Campaign*, p. 185; Fishel, *The Secret War for the Union*, pp. 458–59; JH to HH, June 18, 1863, GGM to HH, July 10, 1863, HH to GM, July 11, 1863, OR-27.1:51, 90.

281 *Sharpe's bureau:* LB to Watson, March 13, 1863, Edward Mason statement, Jacob Franz statement, R: 130, M797, RG94, John Morrell to Capt. Johnston, Aug. 3, 1863, B: 2, RG110, NA; Fishel, *The Secret War for the Union*, pp. 365, 442–43; "Intelligence in the Civil War," p. 33; Ryan, *Spies, Scouts, and Secrets in the Gettysburg Campaign*, pp. 185–86.

281 *the Potomac:* Luvaas, "Lee at Gettysburg," p. 124; Sears, *Gettysburg*, p. 103; DB to Commanding Officer 11th Corps, June 17, 1863, OR-27.3:173–74; Fishel, *The Secret War for the Union*, p. 457; JH to HH, June 18, 1863, OR-27.1:51.

281 *resounding success:* MP diary entry, June 17, 1863, MPD, LC; Fishel, *The Secret War for the Union*, pp. 459–61; "Grenville M. Dodge and George H. Sharpe," p. 7; Sparks, *Inside Lincoln's Army*, pp. 260–61.

282 *was fought:* MP diary entry, June 19, 1863, MPD, LC; Sparks, *Inside Lincoln's Army*, p. 262.

282   *the transfer:* GS to Uncle, June 20, 1863, SLH, KS; Fishel, *The Secret War for the Union*, pp. 465–66.

282   *in Maryland:* GS to Uncle, June 20, 1863, SLH, KS; Ryan, "A Battle of Wits: Intelligence Operations During the Gettysburg Campaign, Part 3," p. 10; Ryan, *Spies, Scouts, and Secrets in the Gettysburg Campaign*, pp. 61–62.

282   *the rescue:* Ryan, "A Battle of Wits: Intelligence Operations During the Gettysburg Campaign, Part 3," p. 10; Ryan, *Spies, Scouts, and Secrets in the Gettysburg Campaign*, p. 202.

283   *Isaac Moore:* JCB to GS, June 19, 1863, R: 36, JCB to GS, June 20, 1863, R: 46, M2096, NA; Ryan, *Spies, Scouts, and Secrets in the Gettysburg Campaign*, p. 208; Fishel, *The Secret War for the Union*, p. 464; Ryan, "A Battle of Wits: Intelligence Operations During the Gettysburg Campaign, Part 3," p. 14.

283   *being hung:* JCB to GS, June 20, 1863, R: 46, M2096, NA; Ryan, "A Battle of Wits: Intelligence Operations During the Gettysburg Campaign, Part 3," p. 12.

284   *"reliable information":* JH to JCB, June 20, 1863, JCB to JH, June 20, 1863, OR-27.3:225–26; Ryan, *Spies, Scouts, and Secrets in the Gettysburg Campaign*, pp. 204–5; Fishel, *The Secret War for the Union*, pp. 464–65.

284   *miles north:* Ryan, *Spies, Scouts, and Secrets in the Gettysburg Campaign*, p. 208; JCB to JH, June 20, 1863, OR-27.3:227; Ryan, "A Battle of Wits: Intelligence Operations During the Gettysburg Campaign, Part 3," pp. 12, 23.

284   *South Mountain:* JCB to GS, June 21, 1863, R: 36, M2096, NA; Ryan, *Spies, Scouts, and Secrets in the Gettysburg Campaign*, pp. 207–8; Fishel, *The Secret War for the Union*, p. 467; JCB to GS, June 20, 1863, OR-27.3:228; Ryan, "A Battle of Wits: Intelligence Operations During the Gettysburg Campaign, Part 3," p. 14.

285   *to organize:* Fishel, *The Secret War for the Union*, pp. 471–73; Fishel, "The Mythology of Civil War Intelligence," p. 384; Luvaas, "Lee at Gettysburg," p. 128.

285   *moved north:* L. C. Turner letters to LB, June–December 1863, vol. 2, Turner Letter Books, E: 179A, RG94, NA.

285   *Bull Run:* Georgetown student statements, Aug. 25, 1862, in the case of Thomas Conrad, Provost Marshal Office memo on Thomas Conrad, Aug. 7, 1862, Parent complaints about Thomas Conrad, Aug. 20, 1862, Provost Marshal arrest order for Conrad, Conrad written statement, August 1862, R: 57, M345, RG109, NA; Markle, pp. 99–102; Axelrod, pp. 88–92; Bakeless, pp. 66–69, 78–79; Ryan, "A Battle of Wits: Intelligence Operations During the Gettysburg Campaign, Part 1," pp. 12–13.

286   *Baker's office:* Ryan, *Spies, Scouts, and Secrets in the Gettysburg Campaign*, pp.

46, 96–97, 174, 177; Tidwell, pp. 72–73; Bakeless, pp. 2, 69, 85; Markle, pp. 100–101; Axelrod, pp. 93–94.

286 *actually liked:* E. D. Townsend to LB, May 6, 1863, B: 1, DCP, GU; *Joseph Stannard Baker Memoirs from 1838 to 1865*, pp. 10-1 to 10-2; Mogelever, pp. 212–15; Baker, *History of the United States Secret Service*, pp. 196, 202–3; Millard, p. 15; Merrill, pp. 233–34.

286 *"quite unimportant":* Battle Order, Camp Baker, Oct. 29, 1863, LB to Capt. Custis, B: 1, DCP, GY; LB to Capt. Burns, July 10, LB to V. F. Winchester, June 17, LB to EMS, Oct. 26, 1863, R: 110, M504, RG107, Col. Baker letter to Philadelphia relative on horses, B: 2, RG110, NA; Millard, p. 231; Mogelever, pp. 216–17; Baker, *History of the United States Secret Service*, pp. 197–98; *Joseph Stannard Baker Memoirs from 1838 to 1865*, pp. 10-1 to 10-3; War Department commission for Capt. Joseph S. Baker, Sept. 1, 1863, AC.

287 *their battlefields:* "News from Washington: A New Cavalry Battalion," May 11, 1863, *New York Times*; John Faulkner to LB, May 21, 1863, B. Hutcheson letter, May 6, 1863, B: 2, RG110, LB letters to Augusta, Maine, Sept. 20 and Oct. 9, 1863, R: 110, M504, RG107, Capt. Hall to LB, Aug. 21, 1863, R: 179, M473, RG107, NA; LB to Horatio Seymour, July 27, 1863, HS, NYH; LB to Capt. Curtis, B: 1, DCP, GU; Baker, *History of the United States Secret Service*, pp. 195–99; Woods, p. 60; Mackay, p. 180; Merrill, pp. 227–28.

287 *Baker's past:* William B. Butler to EMS, Dec. 12, 1863, undated news clip on LB, LB to Watson, January 21, 1864, R: 242, M221, NA.

288 *of time: Joseph Stannard Baker Memoirs from 1838 to 1865*, pp. 10-5 to 10-8; Mogelever, pp. 219–24; Report of LB, Oct. 22, 1863, OR-29.1:494; Letter to Baker, July 23, 1863, BP.

288 *colonel's rank: Joseph Stannard Baker Memoirs from 1838 to 1865*, pp. 10-20 to 10-22, 11-1 to 11-15; Mogelever, pp. 238–41; Baker, *History of the United States Secret Service*, pp. 199–222; Chronological Record on L. C. Baker Service, BP.

288 *mountaintop observers:* JCB to GS, June 22, 1863, R: 36, M2096, GS to JCB, June 23, 1863, R: 198, M504, RG107, NA; Fishel, *The Secret War for the Union*, p. 471; GS to JCB, June 23, 1863, OR-27.3:271.

288 *on Lee:* GS to JCB, June 23, 1863, R: 198, M504, RG107, NA; Bakeless, p. 313; Sears, *Gettysburg*, p. 117; GS to DB, June 23, 1863, OR-27.3:266; Fishel, *The Secret War for the Union*, pp. 470–71, 477.

289 *Gettysburg:* Ryan, *Spies, Scouts, and Secrets in the Gettysburg Campaign*, pp. 225, 230–31, 236; Fishel, *The Secret War for the Union*, pp. 475–83; JCB to JH, June 24, 1863, R: 46, M2096, NA; JCB to JH, June 24, 1863, OR-27.3:285–56;

Ryan, "A Battle of Wits: Intelligence Operations During the Gettysburg Campaign, Part 3," pp. 36–37; Sears, *Gettysburg*, pp. 118–19.

290 *the Potomac:* Fishel, *The Secret War for the Union*, p. 484; Ryan, *Spies, Scouts, and Secrets in the Gettysburg Campaign*, pp. xv, 244–47, 435; Sears, *Gettysburg*, pp. 104–6.

290 *information blackout:* Ryan, *Spies, Scouts, and Secrets in the Gettysburg Campaign*, p. 239; Catton, vol. 3, pp. 163–64, 167–68; Cleaves, p. 127; Ryan, "A Battle of Wits: Intelligence Operations During the Gettysburg Campaign, Part 1," p. 8.

291 *or resolute:* Fishel, *The Secret War for the Union*, pp. 484–87, 492–93; Sears, *Gettysburg*, p. 129; GS to JM, June 1863, R: 198, M504, RG107, GS to DB, June 20, 1863, R: 46, M2096, NA.

291 *and Sharpe:* Donald, *Lincoln*, 437–39; McPherson, *Battle Cry of Freedom*, p. 652; Goodwin, pp. 531–32; Eicher, pp. 501–2; Cleaves, pp. 123–24; Sparks, "General Patrick's Progress," p. 380.

291 *Potomac Army:* Donald, *Lincoln*, pp. 444–45; Eicher, pp. 501–2; Hebert, pp. 244–46; Tucker, p. 72; Cleaves, pp. 124–25; Meade, pp. 20, 32.

292 *processed reports:* Brooks, p. 86; Tucker, pp. 75–77; Eicher, p. 502; Dana, pp. 226–27; Adams, p. 157; Cleaves, pp. xii, 3–21, 37, 43–44, 66–67, 79–80, 104; Maslowski, p. 49; Ryan, *Spies, Scouts, and Secrets in the Gettysburg Campaign*, p. 31.

292 *his thoughts:* Cleaves, p. 130; Sears, *Gettysburg*, p. 130; Ryan, *Spies, Scouts, and Secrets in the Gettysburg Campaign*, pp. 277–78; Ryan, "A Battle of Wits: Intelligence Operations During the Gettysburg Campaign, Part 4," p. 37; Fishel, *The Secret War for the Union*, p. 495.

293 *at Chancellorsville:* Meade, p. 22; Fishel, *The Secret War for the Union*, pp. 495–96; Sears, *Gettysburg*, p. 129; Ryan, *Spies, Scouts, and Secrets in the Gettysburg Campaign*, p. 257; McPherson, *Battle Cry of Freedom*, p. 653; Bakeless, p. 331; Eicher, pp. 504–6.

293 *Westminster, Maryland:* Sears, *Gettysburg*, p. 131; Fishel, *The Secret War for the Union*, p. 497.

293 *above Gettysburg:* Fishel, *The Secret War for the Union*, pp. 497–502; Eicher, p. 507; Catton, vol. 3, p. 179; Fishel, "Military Intelligence 1861–63 (Part 2)," p. 8; Cleaves, p. 128; Sears, *Gettysburg*, pp. 123–24, 134–36.

294 *either army:* Cleaves, p. 130; Eicher, pp. 507–8; Catton, vol. 3, pp. 180–81; Ryan, *Spies, Scouts, and Secrets in the Gettysburg Campaign*, pp. 8, 269–70; Fishel, *The Secret War for the Union*, pp. 502–3; Ryan, "A Battle of Wits: Intelligence Operations During the Gettysburg Campaign, Part 4," pp. 18–19; DB to GS, June 29, 1863, OR-27.3:399.

295　*the reports:* Sears, *Gettysburg,* pp. 154–55, 159; Eicher, pp. 507–10; Cleaves, pp. 129–30; Luvaas, "Lee at Gettysburg," p. 126; John F. Reynolds to DB, June 29, 1863, OR-27.3:397; Ryan, *Spies, Scouts, and Secrets in the Gettysburg Campaign,* p. 268; Ryan, "A Battle of Wits: Intelligence Operations During the Gettysburg Campaign, Part 4," p. 18; Browne, pp. 28–36; Fishel, *The Secret War for the Union,* pp. 503–4.

295　*his hand:* Fishel, *The Secret War for the Union,* pp. 503–4; GS to D. McConaughy, June 29, 1863, 4–2, Gettysburg Campaign, Pennsylvania Skirmishes, Folder 1, GNMP.

295　*two brigades:* Sears, *Gettysburg,* pp. 143, 155–58; Cleaves, p. 132; Eicher, pp. 508–9.

296　*next morning:* Sears, *Gettysburg,* pp. 136–38, 143–44, 155–58; Fishel, *The Secret War for the Union,* pp. 506–7.

297　*fight Lee:* Tucker, pp. 78–79; Cleaves, pp. 131–34; Sears, *Gettysburg,* pp. 141, 149–52; Fishel, *The Secret War for the Union,* pp. 506–10; Ryan, *Spies, Scouts, and Secrets in the Gettysburg Campaign,* p. 275; Santvoord, p. 221.

297　*occupying Gettysburg:* Sears, *Gettysburg,* pp. 132, 138–39; Luvaas, "Lee at Gettysburg," p. 132; Fishel, *The Secret War for the Union,* p. 510; Ryan, *Spies, Scouts, and Secrets in the Gettysburg Campaign,* p. 277.

298　*his forces:* Author tour of Gettysburg Battlefield; John R. Krohn, Oct. 12, 2016; Cleaves, pp. 134, 139, 140; Sears, *Gettysburg,* pp. 242–44; Santvoord, pp. 223–24; Fishel, *The Secret War for the Union,* p. 524; Catton, vol. 3, pp. 183–84.

299　*he said:* Williams to MP, July 1, 1863, R: 1, vol. 4 (4), M2096, NA; Ryan, "A Battle of Wits: Intelligence Operations During the Gettysburg Campaign, Part 4," p. 30; Fishel, *The Secret War for the Union,* p. 510; Santvoord, pp. 221–22.

299　*with him:* Cleaves, p. 136; Catton, vol. 3, pp. 178, 182; Sears, *Gettysburg,* pp. 160–63, 179, 183–84; McPherson, *Battle Cry of Freedom,* pp. 653–54; Eicher, p. 509; Ryan, *Spies, Scouts, and Secrets in the Gettysburg Campaign,* p. 282; Ryan, "A Battle of Wits: Intelligence Operations During the Gettysburg Campaign, Part 4," p. 27.

300　*at Gettysburg:* Sears, *Gettysburg,* pp. 186–87; Fishel, *The Secret War for the Union,* pp. 520–21.

300　*Cemetery Ridge:* Sears, *Gettysburg,* pp. 164–70, 188, 192–96, 202, 216–19, 221; McPherson, *Battle Cry of Freedom,* pp. 654–56; Eicher, pp. 510–21.

300　*day's battle:* Sears, *Gettysburg,* pp. 223–29, 240–42; Ryan, *Spies, Scouts, and Secrets in the Gettysburg Campaign,* pp. 284–85; Santvoord, p. 223; Catton, vol. 3, pp. 182–83.

301 *darkness fell:* Santvoord, p. 218; Ryan, *Spies, Scouts, and Secrets in the Gettysburg Campaign,* p. 308; Fishel, *The Secret War for the Union,* p. 526; Sears, *Gettysburg,* p. 245; McPherson, *Battle Cry of Freedom,* pp. 656–60.

302 *"the longest":* McPherson, *Battle Cry of Freedom,* pp. 656–60; Eicher, pp. 521–40; Catton, vol. 3, pp. 184–86; Cleaves, pp. 141–44, 152–53; Meade, p. 132; Santvoord, pp. 227–28; Fishel, *The Secret War for the Union,* pp. 525–26; Sears, *Gettysburg,* pp. 272, 276, 305.

302 *the day:* Ryan, *Spies, Scouts, and Secrets in the Gettysburg Campaign,* pp. 299, 314; GS to DB, July 2, 1863, R: 46, M2096, NA; "Famous War Scout Dies at His Home on East Fourth Street," *Mount Vernon Daily Argus,* Nov. 20, 1908, pp. 1, 5.

303 *not know:* Cleaves, p. 154; Eicher, pp. 521–40; Sears, *Gettysburg,* p. 324.

303 *inside it:* Sears, *Gettysburg,* p. 341; Cleaves, pp. 142–43; Ryan, "A Battle of Wits: Intelligence Operations During the Gettysburg Campaign, Part 1," pp. 7–8; Meade, p. 136; Fishel, *The Secret War for the Union,* p. 527.

304 *for duty:* Fishel, *The Secret War for the Union,* pp. 527–28; Cleaves, pp. 155–57; Sears, *Gettysburg,* pp. 342–43; *Proceedings of the Ulster County Historical Society 1936–1937,* pp. 33–34.

304 *than colonel:* Sears, *Gettysburg,* pp. 342–43; *Proceedings of the Ulster County Historical Society 1936–1937,* pp. 33–34; Fishel, "Military Intelligence 1861–63 (Part 2)," p. 9.

304 *charging uphill:* Minutes of council, July 2, 1863, OR-27.1:73–74; Fishel, *The Secret War for the Union,* pp. 528–30; Sears, *Gettysburg,* pp. 343–45.

305 *the dispatches:* JD to REL, June 28, 1863, OR-27.1:76–77; Fishel, *The Secret War for the Union,* pp. 530–32; Sears, *Gettysburg,* p. 354; Ryan, "The Intelligence Battle, July 3: A Renewed Offensive," p. 90; Dahlgren, pp. 160–61; Palfrey, p. 4; P.S. to Lee-to-Davis from near Hagerstown, July 8, 1861, B: 6, EF, GU.

305 *they thought:* Cleaves, pp. 157–59, 161.

306 *"Thank God":* McPherson, *Battle Cry of Freedom,* pp. 660–63; Catton, vol. 3, pp. 186–92; Cleaves, pp. 159–60, 169; Sears, *Gettysburg,* pp. 398–99; Ryan, "A Battle of Wits: Intelligence Operations During the Gettysburg Campaign, Part 1," pp. 36; Ryan, *Spies, Scouts, and Secrets in the Gettysburg Campaign,* pp. 325–27, 333–36; Fishel, *The Secret War for the Union,* pp. 532–34; Sears, *Gettysburg,* pp. 359–60, 394–96, 409, 414–15, 442, 453–57, 467–69.

307 *a thunderstorm:* Fishel, *The Secret War for the Union,* p. 534; Sears, *Gettysburg,* pp. 464–65, 474; Ryan, *Spies, Scouts, and Secrets in the Gettysburg Campaign,* pp. 334, 337, 352; Livermore, pp. 102–3; abstract from the returns of the Army

of the Potomac, June 10–July 31, 1863, OR-27.1:151–52; Meade, p. 189; McPherson, *Battle Cry of Freedom*, p. 663; Cleaves, pp. 168–69; GS to DB, July 3, 1863, R: 46, M2096, NA.

307 *the case:* Goodwin, pp. 532, 540; Donald, *Lincoln*, p. 446; McPherson, *Battle Cry of Freedom*, pp. 663–65; Cleaves, pp. 170–71; Eicher, p. 550; Santvoord, p. 221.

307 *he received:* GS to Gen. Williams, July 11, 1863, R: 35, M2096, NA; Memo to GS, July 6, 1863, R: 1, vol. 4(4), M2096, NA; GGM to Margaret, July 12, 1863, B: 1, GMC, HP; GGM to HH, July 4, 1863, OR-27.1:78; GGM to HH, July 6, 1863, OR-27.1:80–81; Ryan, *Spies, Scouts, and Secrets in the Gettysburg Campaign*, pp. 336, 354, 360–61, 371–73, 381–83, 433, 441; Cleaves, pp. 179–80; Fishel, "The Mythology of Civil War Intelligence," p. 357; Charles E. Livingston to GS, July 5, 1863, OR-27.3:541–42.

308 *lunging boldly:* Fishel, *The Secret War for the Union*, pp. 540–41, 571; Ryan, *Spies, Scouts, and Secrets in the Gettysburg Campaign*, pp. 416–18, 425, 429–30.

308 *replace Meade:* McPherson, *Battle Cry of Freedom*, pp. 666–67; Catton, vol. 3, pp. 210–11; Sears, *Gettysburg*, p. 495; Dennett, p. 67.

308 *it rebuilt:* Fishel, *The Secret War for the Union*, p. 541; Sharpe, "Memorial Address," p. 10; Eicher, pp. 596–97; Sears, *Gettysburg*, pp. 496–99; GS to Uncle, July 18, 1863, SLH, KS.

309 *August 11:* Fishel, *The Secret War for the Union*, pp. 541–42; GS to Uncle, July 28, 1863, SLH, KS; GGM to HH, July 28, 1863, EC9, TE, HL; GS to Gen. Humphries, Nov. 13, 1863, R: 45, M2096, NA; GS to Gen. Humphries, Oct. 31, 1863, R: 45, M2096, NA; news clippings from Richmond papers, Army of the Potomac Intelligence Diary, E: 3988, RG393, NA.

309 *Pennsylvania campaign:* GS listing of regiments of the Army of Northern Virginia, Nov. 12, 1863, AP Intelligence Diary, 1863, vol. 113, Entry 3988, Part 1, RG393, GS memos to Gen. Humphreys, Aug. 24 and Sept. 28, 1863, R: 45, M2096, Michael Graham to GS, Oct. 29, 1863, R: 36, M2096, GS to Michael Graham, Oct. 16, 1863, R: 198, M504, RG107, GS letters to Gen. Humphreys, Aug. 20 and 21, Sept. 11 and 30, Oct. 1, 4, 10, and 15, Nov. 19 and 20, and Dec. 9, 1863, R: 45, M2096, NA; Michael Graham to GS, Oct. 19, 1863, OR-29.2:358; Patrick Cunningham and Michael Graham to GS, Oct. 20, 1863, OR-29.2:360; Michael Graham to GS, Oct. 22, 1863, and J. G. Foster to HH, Oct. 22, 1863, OR-29.2:369–70; Schmidt, p. 55; J. L. McPhail to GS, Oct. 14, 1863, OR-29.2:319; Agassiz, p. 13.

310 *in Kingston:* Fishel, *The Secret War for the Union*, p. 542; "Grenville M. Dodge and George H. Sharpe," p. 10; O'Toole, p. 171; Sparks, *Inside Lincoln's Army*, pp. 318–19; GS letters to Uncle, Aug. 21 and Sept. 18, 1863, SLH, KS; Assistant

Adjutant General to GS, Jan. 16, 1864, p. 50, R:8, vol. 96 (45), M2096, GS to
John Jester, Aug. 6, 1863, R: 198, M504, RG107, NA.

310 *"through timidity"*: GS to Uncle, Aug. 21, 1863, SLH, KS; Sparks, *Inside Lincoln's Army*, pp. 273–75, 288–89, 296–98, 302–3, 306; Sparks, "General Patrick's Progress," p. 381.

310 *openly acknowledge:* GGM to Col. Hardie, February 23, 1864, p. 37, R: 8,
vol. 97(46), M2096, NA; Sparks, *Inside Lincoln's Army*, pp. 333–34; Sparks,
"General Patrick's Progress," p. 381.

NINETEEN: MUCKRAKER

313 *to general:* Corson, pp. 537, 545; Mogelever, p. 241; Baker, *History of the United
States Secret Service*, pp. 39, 40, 153; Winkle, pp. 387–89.

314 *common criminals:* Letter to AL from a cavalry captain, May 18, 1864, Series 1,
ALD, LC; Charles Hallock to AL, Aug. 30, 1863, with LA referral to EMS,
R: 33, M492, W. G. Morris to LB, Aug. 19, 1863, Box 2, RG110, NA; Baker,
History of the United States Secret Service, pp. 375–76; Corson, p. 537.

314 *assignment himself:* Niven, *Salmon P. Chase*, p. 277; Donald, *Inside Lincoln's
Cabinet*, p. 27; Towne, p. 36; Chittenden, p. 345; Mogelever, p. 248.

314 *or corrupt:* Niven, *Salmon P. Chase*, pp. 79, 270, 344–45, 351–53, 363; Goodwin, pp. 435, 509–10; Nicolay and Hay, *Abraham Lincoln: A History*, vol. 9, pp.
81, 83; *Diary of Gideon Welles*, vol. 2, p. 121; Donald, *Inside Lincoln's Cabinet*,
pp. 28, 31–32, 34.

315 *him fired: Treasury Department, Report from the Select Committee*, pp. 13, 20–21,
53; Chittenden, pp. 347–51; Peril, p. 14; Baker, *History of the United States Secret Service*, p. 262; *Joseph Stannard Baker Memoirs from 1838 to 1865*, p. 8-20;
Orrmont, pp. 97–108; Mogelever, pp. 253–54.

315 *of money: Treasury Department, Report from the Select Committee*, pp. 1–4, 20,
65, 117, 121, 124; Corson, pp. 548–51.

315 *currency sheets: Treasury Department, Report from the Select Committee*, pp. 1–2,
5, 395–98.

316 *that amount:* S. M. Clark, shown in photo of fractional currency, BP; *Treasury
Department, Report from the Select Committee*, pp. 7, 46, 52–59, 62–63, 66–67,
115–16, 145, 204–5, 219–20.

316 *by Clark: Treasury Department, Report from the Select Committee*, pp. 8–9, 13,
105, 114–19, 126–27, 131–32, 145, 158, 160–62.

316 *on him: Treasury Department, Report from the Select Committee*, pp. 13, 47, 130,
392; Baker, *History of the United States Secret Service*, p. 263.

317 *from prison: Treasury Department, Report from the Select Committee,* pp. 13, 387–404.

317 *denied it: Treasury Department, Report from the Select Committee,* pp. 13–14, 120–21, 128–29, 179, 181; Millard, p. 19; Baker, *History of the United States Secret Service,* pp. 263–64.

317 *his threat: Treasury Department, Report from the Select Committee,* pp. 14, 47–48; Baker, *History of the United States Secret Service,* pp. 261–62, 277, 328.

318 *a living: Treasury Department, Report from the Select Committee,* pp. 17, 147; Stepp, p. 7; Silber, p. 118; Donald, *Inside Lincoln's Cabinet,* p. 28; "Immorality in the Treasury Department," *New York Herald,* May 3, 1864, p. 4; "The Greatest Magician of Modern Times," *New York Herald,* May 6, 1864, p. 4.

318 *for her: Treasury Department, Report from the Select Committee,* pp. 14, 21, 44, 49–50, 175, 372, 405–14; Massey, p. 137.

319 *"other sex": Treasury Department, Report from the Select Committee,* pp. 14, 17, 178, 184; Massey, p. 137; Silber, p. 118; Peril, p. 14; "High Life in the Treasury Department," *New York Herald,* May 8, 1864, p. 4.

319 *at best: Treasury Department, Report from the Select Committee,* pp. 14–16, 21–22, 147–49, 151–55, 168–71, 202, 207, 220–21, 407–8, 414–15.

319 *of tuberculosis: Treasury Department, Report from the Select Committee,* p. 16; Massey, pp. 137–38.

320 *Lincoln administration: Treasury Department, Report from the Select Committee,* pp. 1, 17–19, 32; Baker, *History of the United States Secret Service,* pp. 287–89, 308–9, 313–19.

320 *Union prisoners:* Mortimer, *Double Death,* pp. 207–8, 211–12, 214–17; Inglis, p. 2; Memoirs of Pryce Lewis as Told to Major David E. Cronin in 1888, pp. 140–43, 147–49, 156–63, B: 4, Notes on Castle Thunder, B: 3, Seth Paine to PL, Dec. 12, 1862, T. H. Hutcheson to PL, March 23, 1863, B: 2, PLC, SLU; AP to AL, June 5, 1863, Series 1, General Correspondence, 1833–1916, ALD, LC; Mackay, pp. 171–72; Horan, *The Pinkertons,* pp. 138–40.

320 *the capital:* S. E. Chamberlain pass for PL, Sept. 30, 1863, B: 2, Memoirs of Pryce Lewis as Told to Major David E. Cronin in 1888, pp. 158–63, B: 4, PLC, SLU; Mackay, pp. 171–72; Horan, *The Pinkertons,* pp. 138–40; Mortimer, *Double Death,* pp. 214–17.

321 *his telegram:* Memoirs of Pryce Lewis as Told to Major David E. Cronin in 1888, p. 162, B: 4, AP to Wood, Oct. 1, 1863, B: 2, PLC, SLU; Mackay, pp. 171–72; Horan, *The Pinkertons,* pp. 138–40; Mortimer, *Double Death,* pp. 214–17.

321 *son William:* Memoirs of Pryce Lewis as Told to Major David E. Cronin in

1888, p. 163, B: 4, William Pinkerton to PL, Jan. 15, 1864, B: 2, Pryce Lewis chronology for 1863 and 1864, B: 3, PLC, SLU; Mortimer, *Double Death*, pp. 222–23; Popchock, p. 44; Mackay, pp. 171–72.

321   *picture, too:* Pryce Lewis chronology for 1863 and 1864, B: 3, Wood to whom it may concern, Nov. 26, 1863, Correspondence on PL work at Old Capitol Prison, November 1863–May 1864, Analysis of the "L.B." letter by Harriet H. Shoen, L. B. to PL, Aug. 17, Could not be from Belle Boyd, To My Dear Major, Feb. 19, 1905, B: 2, Concerning Lewis and Scully's guilt in the apprehension of Timothy Webster, B: 3, Memoirs of Pryce Lewis as Told to Major David E. Cronin in 1888, pp. 163–64, B: 4, PLC, SLU; Popchock, p. 44; Mortimer, *Double Death*, p. 223.

321   *in August:* Pryce Lewis chronology for 1863 and 1864, B: 3, LB to whom it may concern, June 20, 1864, B: 2, Memoirs of Pryce Lewis as Told to Major David E. Cronin in 1888, p. 166, B: 4, PLC, SLU; Mortimer, *Double Death*, pp. 224–25.

TWENTY: THE RICHMOND RING

322   *Van Lew wrote:* Brock, pp. 272–73, 283–84, 395; Eicher, pp. 569, 571; Blakey, p. 120; Thomas, *The Confederate State of Richmond*, pp. 163–67; Jones, *Ladies of Richmond*, pp. 219, 221; McPherson, *Battle Cry of Freedom*, p. 691; Ryan, *A Yankee Spy in Richmond*, pp. 54, 86–87.

323   *raise cash:* Jones, *Behind Enemy Lines*, p. 49; *Richmond News* clipping on EVL, EVLP, NY; Ryan, *A Yankee Spy in Richmond*, pp. 17, 49.

323   *before him:* J. McPhail to GS, Dec. 1, 1863, R: 35, M2096, NA; Message to Major Eckert, February 14, 1864, and McPhail to GS, Feb. 14, 1864, vol. 40. p. 124, R: 17, USGP, LC; *Letter from the Secretary of War in the case of Joseph H. Maddox*, pp. 13–15; Fishel, p. 555–56.

323   *Radical Republicans:* Jones, *Ladies of Richmond*, pp. 331, 333; McPherson, *Embattled Rebel*, p. 120; Dennett, p. 183; Adams, p. 159; Stahr, p. 404; Varon, *Southern Lady, Yankee Spy*, pp. 107–8.

324   *Van Lew:* Fishel notes p. 2 on Butler spending $11,250, B: 3, EF, GU; Eicher, pp. 75–77, 237–42, 385; Catton, vol. 1, pp. 394–96, 436–37; Wheelan, p. 80; Butler, pp. 415–19, 617; Niven, *Salmon P. Chase*, pp. 316–18; *Private and Official Correspondence of Gen. Benjamin F. Butler*, vol. 3, p. 330; Varon, *Southern Lady, Yankee Spy*, p. 106.

324   *in danger:* VL letter on Rowley, Jan. 9, 1866, B: 6, E: 95, RG110, NA; "A 'Dead' Yankee Turns up Alive in the North," *Richmond Daily Examiner*, Jan. 23, 1864,

p. 1; H. S. Howard statement, Jan. 23, 1866, William Rowley to EMS, B: 6, E: 95, RG110, NA; Varon, *Southern Lady, Yankee Spy*, pp. 109–11; Lineberry, p. 5; Winkler, pp. 62–63.

324   *Boutelle did:* Varon, "True to the Flag," p. 72; Ryan, *A Yankee Spy in Richmond,* p. 51; Varon, *Southern Lady, Yankee Spy*, pp. 111–12; *Private and Official Correspondence of Gen. Benjamin F. Butler,* vol. 3, pp. 228–29.

325   *her watch case:* H. S. Howard statement, Jan. 23, 1866, B: 6, E: 95, RG110, NA; Varon, *Southern Lady, Yankee Spy*, pp. 112–13; *Private and Official Correspondence of Gen. Benjamin F. Butler,* vol. 3, p. 319; Ryan, *A Yankee Spy in Richmond,* pp. 53–54, 143; Winkler, pp. 63–65; "Sale of Historic Relics," *Richmond News* clipping, Sept. 26, 1900, copy of the cipher EVL used, EVLP, NY.

325   *Union lines:* H. S. Howard statement, Jan. 23, 1866, Rowley to EMS, B: 6, E: 95, RG110, NA; Varon, *Southern Lady, Yankee Spy,* p. 114.

325   *"in Richmond":* Ryan, *A Yankee Spy in Richmond,* pp. 3, 12, 58; Varon, "True to the Flag," p. 72; Varon, *Southern Lady, Yankee Spy*, pp. 113–14; Bart Hall, Nov. 7, 2016; Maslowski, p. 43.

326   *along information:* Schultz, p. 55; Ryan, *A Yankee Spy in Richmond,* pp. 16–17, 128; "Intelligence in the Civil War," p. 20; Axelrod, p. 143; Blakey, pp. 2, 143; Stuart, "Colonel Ulric Dahlgren and Richmond's Union Underground," p. 193; *Private and Official Correspondence of Gen. Benjamin F. Butler,* vol. 3, p. 564.

326   *Fort Monroe:* Ryan, *A Yankee Spy in Richmond,* pp. 7, 25; Varon, *Southern Lady, Yankee Spy*, pp. 168–69; John Reynolds biographical sketch of EVL, p. 6, EVLP, LVA; news clipping on EVL, EVLP, NY; Beymer, *On Hazardous Service,* pp. 85–86; Jones, *Behind Enemy Lines,* p. 50; "Intelligence in the Civil War," p. 20; Varon, *Southern Lady, Yankee Spy*, pp. 162–64.

327   *that year:* "Intelligence in the Civil War," p. 20; Varon, "True to the Flag," pp. 73–76; Fishel, "The Mythology of Civil War Intelligence," p. 353; *Private and Official Correspondence of Gen. Benjamin F. Butler,* vol. 3, pp. 485, 564–65; GM to HH, March 16, 1864, OR-33:681–82.

328   *the west: Private and Official Correspondence of Gen. Benjamin F. Butler,* vol. 3, pp. 331–32, 382–83; Varon, *Southern Lady, Yankee Spy*, pp. 114–15; Ryan, *A Yankee Spy in Richmond,* pp. 55–56, 143; McPherson, *Battle Cry of Freedom,* p. 802.

328   *eventually perished:* Varon, *Southern Lady, Yankee Spy*, pp. 100–101; Speer, pp. 204–7; Hesseltine, p. 68; Blakey, p. 175.

328   *rescue attempt: Private and Official Correspondence of Gen. Benjamin F. Butler,* vol. 3, pp. 380–83; Varon, *Southern Lady, Yankee Spy*, pp. 115–17, 142; Schultz, pp. 64–67; McPherson, *Battle Cry of Freedom,* pp. 796–98.

329   *the city:* LB messages to Gen. Butler, Jan. 8 and 29, 1865, R: 227, M504, RG107,

NA; LB to Gen. Butler, Jan. 30, 1864, Correspondence 1831–70, EMSP, LC; *Private and Official Correspondence of Gen. Benjamin F. Butler*, vol. 3, pp. 337–38, 340–46, 351, 360, 365, 373–74; *Private and Official Correspondence of Gen. Benjamin F. Butler*, vol. 4, p. 39; Butler, pp. 619–21.

329 *Wistar's cavalry: Private and Official Correspondence of Gen. Benjamin F. Butler*, vol. 3, pp. 375, 384, 396–97, 400, 409–10; Butler, p. 621; Joseph, pp. 297–98; Schultz, p. 66; I. J. Wistar messages to Gen. Butler, Feb. 6, 7, 8, and 9, 1864, Eppa Hunton report, Feb. 7, 1863, OR-3:145–49.

330 *planned raid:* Joseph, pp. 295–97, 299–302; *Private and Official Correspondence of Gen. Benjamin F. Butler*, vol. 3, pp. 399, 401, 408.

330 *45,000 troops:* Fishel notes p. 2 on Wistar raid, B: 3, EF, GU; *Private and Official Correspondence of Gen. Benjamin F. Butler*, vol. 3, p. 421.

330 *Libby escapees:* Varon, *Southern Lady, Yankee Spy*, pp. 117–18, 132; Varon, "True to the Flag," p. 72; Wheelan, pp. 89, 171, 183; "Mrs. Abby Green," Report no. 115, July 28, 1866, Committee of Claims, House of Representatives, 39th Congress, 1st Session.

330 *Richmond's underground:* Varon, *Southern Lady, Yankee Spy*, pp. 118–25; "Mrs. Abby Green," Report no. 115, July 28, 1866, Committee of Claims, House of Representatives, 39th Congress, 1st Session.

331 *federal prisoners:* Varon, *Southern Lady, Yankee Spy*, pp. 126–28; Ryan, *A Yankee Spy in Richmond*, pp. 58–60; Wheelan, p. 171; "Address by a Colored Lady and Henry Ward Beecher," *Brooklyn Eagle*, Sept. 25, 1865; Dr. Taliaferro notes on John Van Lew, March 14, 1864, Mss 10w25a 142–136, HO, VHS; P. T. Browne message, March 1, 1864, Anto Bilisvly notes on John Van Lew, B: 1, ELC, WM; Memo on John Van Lew, June 11, 1864, John Van Lew Oath of Allegiance, June 12, 1864, R: 273, M345, RG109, NA.

332 *"of them":* "Mrs. Abby Green," Report no. 115, July 28, 1866, Committee of Claims, House of Representatives, 39th Congress, 1st Session; "The Richmond Spy," (Richmond) *Daily Dispatch*, July 17, 1883, p. 1; Varon, *Southern Lady, Yankee Spy*, pp. 125–31; Wheelan, pp. 183–84; Richardson, *The Secret Service, the Field, the Dungeon and the Escape*, pp. 367, 370, 403–4; Ryan, *A Yankee Spy in Richmond*, pp. 62–64, 144–45.

332 *another escape:* Blakey, p. 173; Jones, *A Rebel War Clerk's Diary at the Confederate States Capital*, p. 164; Speer, p. 206.

332 *other prisons:* John Albree speeches on Elizabeth Van Lew, B: 1, ELC, WM; Varon, *Southern Lady, Yankee Spy*, p. 133; Speer, pp. 260–61.

333 *the presidency:* Stepp, p. 311; Axelrod, p. 253; Schultz, pp. 68–73; Leonard, p. 245.

333 *believed them:* Fishel, *The Secret War for the Union,* p. 543; Cleaves, p. 222; A.
     Pleasonton to Maj. Gen. Humphreys, Feb. 17, 1864, OR-33:171–72; J. Kilpat-
     rick to E. B. Parsons, Feb. 16, 1864, OR-33:172–73; Joseph, p. 307; Schultz,
     pp. 62–64, 73–74, 77; GGM report, April 8, 1864, OR-33:170–71; McPhail
     messages to GS, Feb. 14, 1864, JCB to McPhail, Feb. 14, 1864, OR-33:559.

334 *sea stories:* GS to Maj. Gen. Pleasonton, Feb. 29, 1864, R: 503, M504, RG107,
     NA; Tidwell, p. 244; Schultz, p. 78; Varon, *Southern Lady, Yankee Spy,* pp. 136–
     38; A. A. Humphries to J. Kilpatrick, Feb. 27, 1864, OR-33:173–74; GGM
     report, April 8, 1864, OR-33:170; Cleaves, p. 222; Schultz, p. 117; Winkler,
     p. 70; Axelrod, pp. 254–55; Niven, *Gideon Welles,* pp. 402–3; Hay, "Life in the
     White House in the Time of Lincoln," p. 34.

334 *their trustworthiness:* GS to Col. U. Dahlgren, Feb. 28, 1864, R: 303, M504,
     RG107, NA; JM to GS, March 4, 1863, R: 46, M2096, NA; GS to JM,
     March 11, 1864, OR-33:666.

334 *Dahlgren stranded:* JM to GS, March 4, 1863, R: 46, M2096, NA; GGM report,
     April 8, 1864, OR-33:170–71; Schultz, pp. 105–6, 121, 123, 127–28, 131–34.

334 *being captured:* JM to GS, March 4, 1863, R: 46, M2096, NA; GGM report,
     April 8, 1864, OR-33:171; Edward Fox report, April 1, 1864, OR-33:206;
     Stuart, "Colonel Ulric Dahlgren and Richmond's Union Underground," pp.
     152–53; Schultz, pp. 124–30, 134–35.

335 *Confederate officials:* Davis, *The Rise and Fall of the Confederate Government,*
     p. 507; Winkler, pp. 72–73; Axelrod, pp. 260–63.

335 *the Confederacy:* Axelrod, pp. 258–63; Headley, p. 175; Varon, *Southern Lady,*
     Yankee Spy, pp. 138–42; Tidwell, pp. 18, 245–46; Braxton Bragg to J. A. Sed-
     don, March 4, 1864, James Seddon to REL, March 5, 1864, OR-33:217–18;
     REL to James Seddon, March 6, 1864, OR-33:222; Stuart, "Colonel Ulric
     Dahlgren and Richmond's Union Underground," p. 153; Schultz, p. 183.

335 *name misspelled:* Joseph, pp. 305–7; Varon, *Southern Lady, Yankee Spy,* pp. 138–
     42; Axelrod, pp. 260–63; Schultz, pp. 186–87, 199–200; documents found on
     Ulric Dahlgren's body, OV-1, JDP, LC.

336 *such orders:* Assistant adjutant general letters on Col. Dahlgren, March 19 and
     20, 1864, pp. 144, 147, R: 8, vol. 97(46), Assistant Adjutant general message
     on Col. Dahlgren, p. 47, R: 6, vol. 91(47), M2096, NA; A. A. Humphreys to
     Maj. Gen. Pleasonton, March 14, 1864, E. B. Parsons to J. Kilpatrick, March
     14, 1864, OR-33:175; Axelrod, pp. 260–63; J. Kilpatrick to F. C. Newhall,
     March 16, 1864, OR-33:176; J. Kilpatrick to S. Williams, April 16, 1864,
     OR-33:180; Schultz, pp. 184–85.

336 *"be clear":* REL to GGM, April 1, 1864, OR-33:178; S. Cooper to REL,

March 30, 1864, OR-33:223; GGM to REL, April 17, 1864, OR-33:180; Joseph, pp. 291, 312, 316; Cleaves, pp. 223–24; *The Life and Letters of George Gordon Meade*, vol. 2, pp. 190–91; Sparks, *Inside Lincoln's Army*, p. 347.

336   *proper burial:* Ryan, *A Yankee Spy in Richmond*, pp. 72–73, 78–80, 82, 148; Varon, *Southern Lady, Yankee Spy*, pp. 142–43; Schultz, p. 173; William Rowley statement, Jan. 5, 1866, B: 26, 976–2206, RG107, NA.

337   *the danger:* Stuart, "Colonel Ulric Dahlgren and Richmond's Union Underground," pp. 162, 202; Varon, *Southern Lady, Yankee Spy*, pp. 136, 143, 145–46, 151–52; F. W. E. Lohmann statement, Oct. 7, 1865, Box 26, 976–2206, RG107, NA.

338   *two days:* William Rowley statement, Jan. 5, 1866, F. W. E. Lohmann statement, Oct. 7, 1865, B: 26, 976–2206, RG107, F. W. E. Lohmann deposition, Jan. 6, 1866, Rowley statement, Dec. 8, 1863, B: 6, E: 95, RG110, NA; Schultz, pp. 173–74; Varon, *Southern Lady, Yankee Spy*, pp. 143–49; Stuart, "Colonel Ulric Dahlgren and Richmond's Union Underground," pp. 195–97; Ryan, *A Yankee Spy in Richmond*, pp. 67–72, 146–47.

339   *so far:* Beymer, "Miss Van Lew," pp. 97–98; Schultz, pp. 190–91, 198; Stuart, "Colonel Ulric Dahlgren and Richmond's Union Underground," p. 158; "Miss Van Lew's Spies in the Davis Household," *Richmond Evening Journal*, May 2, 1908, p. 8; *Private and Official Correspondence of Gen. Benjamin F. Butler*, vol. 3, pp. 504–5, 509.

339   *Van Lew ring:* *Private and Official Correspondence of Gen. Benjamin F. Butler*, vol. 4, pp. 5–6, 83, 102, 113; Schultz, pp. 192–94; Stuart, "Colonel Ulric Dahlgren and Richmond's Union Underground," pp. 156, 201–2; Van Lew, "Van Liew, Van Lieu, Van Lew," p. 3.

339   *no clues:* Varon, *Southern Lady, Yankee Spy*, pp. 151–52; Varon, "True to the Flag," p. 74; Winkler, pp. 74–75; Schultz, p. 193.

TWENTY-ONE: ULYSSES S. GRANT

340   *meet others:* Goodwin, pp. 614–16; Catton, vol. 3, pp. 297–300; Brooks, pp. 144–46; Chittenden, pp. 317–19; *Diary of Gideon Welles*, vol. 1, pp. 538–39.

341   *the reverse:* Eicher, pp. 112–13, 659; McPherson, *Battle Cry of Freedom*, pp. 296, 396–402, 408–15, 586–88, 631–38; Marvel, p. 277; Catton, vol. 2, pp. 42, 163–64; Feis, *Grant's Secret Service*, pp. 21–24, 29, 43–44, 49–51, 72–75, 91, 189; Catton, vol. 3, p. 261.

341   *bothered with:* McPherson, *Battle Cry of Freedom*, pp. 414, 588; Donald, *Lincoln*, pp. 488–90; Eicher, p. 624; Badeau, *Military History of Ulysses S. Grant*,

vol. 2, p. 3; Gobright, p. 339; McPherson, *Tried by War*, p. 212; *The Papers of Ulysses S. Grant*, vol. 10, p. xii; Cleaves, p. 225; Chernow, p. 211.

342 *"the machine":* Catton, vol. 3, pp. 300–301; *The Life and Letters of George Gordon Meade*, vol. 2, p. 185; McPherson, *Battle Cry of Freedom*, p. 718; Cleaves, pp. 228–29, 232; *Personal Memoirs of U.S. Grant*, pp. 306–7; GS to Uncle, March 16, 1864, SLH, KS.

342 *force stood: Personal Memoirs of U.S. Grant*, p. 309; *The Life and Letters of George Gordon Meade*, vol. 2, pp. 177–78, 182–85; Eicher, pp. 624–25; Badeau, *Military History of Ulysses S. Grant*, vol. 2, pp. 3, 5, 11.

343 *vital region:* McPherson, *Battle Cry of Freedom*, pp. 721–72; Catton, vol. 3, p. 304.

343 *rankled Meade:* GS to Uncle, March 16, 1864, SLH, KS; Cleaves, pp. 226, 233–34, 248.

343 *George Meade:* GS to Uncle, March 16, 1864, SLH, KS.

344 *army level:* Catton, vol. 3, p. 303; Feis, *Grant's Secret Service*, pp. 15–16, 56, 185, 189.

344 *John McEntee:* GS to Gen. Williams, June 10, 1864, R: 26, M2096, NA; Sparks, "General Patrick's Progress," pp. 381–82; Miller, *The Photographic History of The Civil War*, p. 279; Sparks, *Inside Lincoln's Army*, pp. 349–50; Porter, p. 232; Fishel, *The Secret War for the Union*, pp. 543–44.

345 *the valley:* Fishel, *The Secret War for the Union*, pp. 543–44; JM reports to GS, April 17 and 28, May 3, 4, 7, 11, and 20, 1864, R: 46, M2096, NA.

345 *"to say":* McPherson, *Battle Cry of Freedom*, p. 724; Feis, *Grant's Secret Service*, p. 196; GS to JM, May 4, 1864, R: 303, M504, RG107; GS to Gen. Humphreys, March 31, 1864, B: 1, E: 112, RG108, NA.

346 *Court House headquarters:* Fishel, *The Secret War for the Union*, p. 544; Feis, *Grant's Secret Service*, pp. 204–5; GS to JM, April 27, 1864, OR-33:999; GS to Gen. Humphreys, April 3, 1864, MP reports to Gen. Humphreys, March 28 and 30, 1862, GS to Gen. Humphreys, April 22, 1864, B: 1, E: 112, RG108, JM messages to GS, April 22, 28, and 29, 1864, R: 46, M2096, GS reports to Gen. Butler, April 23 and 27, 1864, R: 303, M504, RG107, NA.

346 *as well:* MP to Gen. Humphreys, March 30, 1864, GS reports to Gen. Humphreys, April 18, 22, and 25, 1864, B: 1, E: 112, RG108, GS to Gen. Butler, April 23, R: 303, M504, RG107, JM to GS, April 19, 1864, R: 46, M2096, NA.

347 *wrote home:* MP to Gen. Humphreys, March 30, 1864, GS reports to Gen. Humphreys, April 14 and 18, 1864, B: 1, E: 112, RG108, NA; "Last Hours of the Confederacy," *New York Times*, Jan. 21, 1876.

347   *his sources:* GS letters to McPhail, April 16 and June 21, 1864, Maddox in-
        telligence report, April 1864, B: 588–89, Joseph Maddox File no. 425928,
        RG94, NA.

347   *forces were:* GS to Gen. Humphreys, April 22, 1864, B: 1, E: 112, RG108, NA;
        Feis, *Grant's Secret Service,* pp. 204–6; Fox, p. 540; Badeau, *Military History
        of Ulysses S. Grant,* vol. 2, pp. 93–95; GS to Gen. Humphreys, May 4, 1864,
        OR-36.2:372; GS to General, May 4, 1864, OR-36.2:405; GS to Gen. Han-
        cock, May 2, 1864, OR-36.2:334.

348   *both sides:* Author tour of the Wilderness and Spotsylvania Battlefields; Feis,
        Grant's Secret Service, pp. 206–9; Eicher, pp. 600–601, 664–67, 676–78;
        McPherson, *Tried by War,* p. 218; McPherson, *Battle Cry of Freedom,* pp. 725–
        28; Catton, vol. 3, pp. 354–59.

349   *warned Meade:* GS to Gen. Humphreys, May 20, 1864, OR-36.3:5–6; GS to
        Gen. Humphreys, May 10, 1864, OR-36.2:597; GS messages to Gen. Hum-
        phreys, May 13, 1864, and Cline to GS, May 13, 1864, OR-36.2:699–700; GS
        to Gen. Humphreys, May 17, 1864, OR-36.2:842; GS to Gen. Humphreys,
        May 18, 1864, OR-36.2:865; GS to Gen. Humphreys, May 19, 1864, OR-
        36.2:907–8; Cline to General, May 16, 1864, OR-35.2:814; Sparks, *Inside
        Lincoln's Army,* pp. 371–72; GS to Gen. Humphreys, May 16, 1864, OR-
        36.2:813–14; Fishel, *The Secret War for the Union,* pp. 544–45.

349   *Rebel deserters:* JM to GS, May 7, 1864, R: 46, Dr. W. J. Bunnell flyer, R: 25,
        M2096, NA; Eicher, pp. 661–62; Winkle, p. 361.

349   *drive refreshing:* McPherson, *Battle Cry of Freedom,* pp. 722–24, 728–31;
        Eicher, pp. 680–81; Fishel, *The Secret War for the Union,* p. 545; Catton, vol. 3,
        pp. 345–47, 351–54; Donald, *Lincoln,* pp. 500–501.

350   *she realized:* J. H. Carrington pass for EVL, July 6, 1864, B: 1, ELC, WM; Ryan,
        A Yankee Spy in Richmond, pp. 93–94, 150; Varon, *Southern Lady, Yankee Spy,*
        pp. 154–56.

350   *ten days:* GS to Uncle, June 7, 1864, SLH, KS; McPherson, *Battle Cry of Free-
        dom,* pp. 733–35; Feis, *Grant's Secret Service,* pp. 213–14; Eicher, pp. 683–86.

351   *their report:* GS messages to JM, June 2 and 6, 1864, R: 303, M504, RG107,
        NA; *The Life and Letters of George Gordon Meade,* vol. 2, pp. 199–200.

351   *their home:* Fishel, *The Secret War for the Union,* p. 545; GS to Gen. Humphreys,
        May 22, 1864, OR-36.3:79; H. G. Wright to MP, June 7, 1864, OR-36.3:680;
        Statement of Miss Jane Bowles, June 8, 1864, GS to Gen. Humphreys, June 8,
        1864, OR-36.3:695–97; GS to Gen. Humphreys, May 22, 1864, OR-36.2:80;
        GS to Gen. Humphreys, May 29, 1864, OR-36.3:293.

351 *be beaten:* Feis, *Grant's Secret Service,* pp. 211–12; GS to Gen. Humphreys, June 10, 1864, OR-36.3:725–26; C. A. Dana to EMS with GS communication, June 9, 1864, OR-36.1:93; GS to Gen. Humphreys, June 3, 1864, OR-36.3:527–28.

352 *to admire:* Lohmann note, March 15, 1864, R: 45, M2096, GS endorsement of claims by Ruth and Lohmann, no. 1, 976–2206, B: 26, RG107, NA; "Last Hours of the Confederacy," *New York Times,* Jan. 21, 1876; S. Williams to Commanding Officer, Cavalry Corps, March 16, 1864, OR-33:682; GGM to HH, March 16, 1864, OR-33:681–82; *Private and Official Correspondence of Gen. Benjamin F. Butler During the Period of the Civil War,* vol. 4, p. 94; Ryan, *A Yankee Spy in Richmond,* p. 17; A. A. Humphreys to Gen. Rawlins, June 11, 1864, OR-36.3:746; Varon, *Southern Lady, Yankee Spy,* pp. 156–57; Fishel, "Military Intelligence 1861–63 (Part 2)," p. 4.

352 *Rivers met:* Commissioner of Claims file no. 14990 for James Duke, Commissioner of Claims file no. 17108 for James Sharp, RG217, Petition of Major Marable Microfiche no. 2696, Commission no. 7728, Sept. 27, 1871, RG233, NA; Varon, *Southern Lady, Yankee Spy,* pp. 33, 157–64; Bart Hall, Nov. 2, 2016; Winkler, pp. 76–77; Leonard, pp. 53–54.

353 *"of Richmond":* Varon, *Southern Lady, Yankee Spy,* p. 169; Ryan, *A Yankee Spy in Richmond,* pp. 114–19; Winkler, pp. 75–76.

TWENTY-TWO: THE RICHMOND-PETERSBURG CAMPAIGN

355 *southern states:* Thomas, *The Confederate State of Richmond,* p. 177; Badeau, *Military History of Ulysses S. Grant,* vol. 2, pp. 243–45; McPherson, *Battle Cry of Freedom,* p. 737; Feis, *Grant's Secret Service,* p. 214; Eicher, pp. 686–87; Fishel, *The Secret War for the Union,* pp. 545–46; Reid, pp. 304, 308–9; Feis, "A Union Military Intelligence Failure," p. 213.

355 *Confederate corps:* McPherson, *Battle Cry of Freedom,* pp. 737–42; Catton, vol. 3, pp. 366–68; Feis, *Grant's Secret Service,* pp. 215–16; Eicher, pp. 689–90; "Grenville M. Dodge and George H. Sharpe," pp. 8–9; Greene, pp. xi, 55–65, 76–77, 114–15.

356 *"good results":* Feis, *Grant's Secret Service,* pp. 222–23; Sears, *Landscape Turned Red,* p. 219; Sears, *To the Gates of Richmond,* pp. 79–80; Feis, "A Union Military Intelligence Failure," pp. 213–14; REL to JD, June 29, 1864, B: 3, JDC, DU.

356 *away unnoticed:* Feis, *Grant's Secret Service,* pp. 221–23; Badeau, *Military History of Ulysses S. Grant,* vol. 3, p. 141; Chernow, pp. 50–51.

357 *Richmond defenses:* Feis, *Grant's Secret Service,* pp. 223–27; Fishel, *The Secret*

War for the Union, pp. 546–47; Feis, "A Union Military Intelligence Failure," pp. 216, 218; Sparks, *Inside Lincoln's Army*, pp. 381, 385–86, 391; JCB to Gen. Humphreys, July 3, 1864, OR-40.2:601; Robertson, p. 158; GS to Gen. Humphreys, June 17, 1864, OR-40.2:119; GS memos to Gen. Humphreys, June 18, 1864, OR-40.2:158–61; GS to MP, July 3, 1864, R: 303, M504, RG107, NA.

357 *for Grant:* GS to Gen. Humphreys, June 20, 1864, OR-40.2:235; GS to Gen. Humphreys, June 21, 1864, OR-40.2:271; GS to Gen. Humphreys, June 22, 1864, OR-40.2:306; Feis, "A Union Military Intelligence Failure," p. 220.

357 *the valley:* Feis, *Grant's Secret Service*, pp. 219, 228–29; JM to GS, June 28, 1864, OR-37.1:684.

358 *at Richmond:* Feis, *Grant's Secret Service*, pp. 229–30; Feis, "A Union Military Intelligence Failure," pp. 221–22.

358 *around Washington:* Feis, *Grant's Secret Service*, pp. 221, 231; USG to GGM, July 3, 1864, OR-40.2:599; GGM to USG, July 3, 1864, OR-40.2:600; Feis, "A Union Military Intelligence Failure," p. 222; GS to Gen. Humphreys, July 4, 1864, OR-40.2:620; *The Papers of Ulysses S. Grant*, vol. 11, p. 169; USG to HH, July 3, 1864, USG to GGM, July 3, 1864, 1864–1865 General Records, Letters sent by General Grant, March 1864–December 1865, vol. 1, pp. 236–37, RG108, NA.

359 *capturing Washington:* Chittenden, pp. 386–90; Brooks, pp. 173–80; Nicolay and Hay, *Abraham Lincoln: A History*, vol. 9, pp. 163–66, 169; *The Papers of Ulysses S. Grant*, vol. 11, p. 170; McPherson, *Tried by War*, p. 231; Badeau, *Military History of Ulysses S. Grant*, vol. 2, p. 442.

359 *the capital:* Feis, *Grant's Secret Service*, p. 232; Feis, "A Union Military Intelligence Failure," pp. 209–10, 223–24; *The Papers of Ulysses S. Grant*, vol. 11, pp. 170–72, 178–79, 202–4; GGM to USG, July 5, 1864, OR-40.3:5–6; GS to Gen. Humphreys, July 6, 1864, OR-40.2:37–38; USG to HH, July 9, 1864, General Records, Letters sent by General Grant, March 1864–December 1865, vol. 1, p. 251, RG108, NA.

359 *slip away:* Feis, *Grant's Secret Service*, p. 232; Eicher, p. 717; Winkle, pp. 392–94; Dennett, pp. 208–9; McPherson, *Battle Cry of Freedom*, p. 757.

359 *three weeks:* Sparks, *Inside Lincoln's Army*, p. 396; James Morice, "Organizational Learning in a Military Environment: George H. Sharpe and the Army of the Potomac," SGF, KS.

360 *intelligence failure:* Badeau, *Military History of Ulysses S. Grant*, vol. 2, pp. 441–44; Winkle, pp. xii, 163; Nicolay and Hay, *Abraham Lincoln: A History*, vol. 9, pp. 163–64; *Diary of Gideon Welles*, vol. 2, pp. 77–78; Feis, "A Union Military Intelligence Failure," p. 211.

360   *intelligence service:* Feis, *Grant's Secret Service,* pp. 233–34; Feis, "A Union Military Intelligence Failure," p. 224.

361   *something wrong:* "Gen. G. H. Sharpe Dead," *New York Times,* Jan. 15, 1900, p. 7; GGM to USG, July 6, 1864, R: 2, vol. 5 (5), M2096, NA; Morice, "Organizational Learning"; Feis, *Grant's Secret Service,* pp. 234–35; Sparks, *Inside Lincoln's Army,* pp. 385, 387, 392–95; Fishel, *The Secret War for the Union,* pp. 546–47; *The Papers of Ulysses S. Grant,* vol. 11, p. 180; Sparks, "General Patrick's Progress," p. 382; Greene, pp. 368–69.

361   *his absence:* Sparks, *Inside Lincoln's Army,* pp. 420, 422, 425, 436; Morice, "Organizational Learning."

361   *to Washington:* Fishel, *The Secret War for the Union,* p. 548; *The Papers of Ulysses S. Grant,* vol. 13, p. 469; Morice, "Organizational Learning"; Badeau, *Military History of Ulysses S. Grant,* vol. 3, p. 135; Robertson, p. 164; Porter, p. 233; Nicolay and Hay, *Abraham Lincoln: A History,* vol. 10, p. 214.

362   *the vessel:* Badeau, *Military History of Ulysses S. Grant,* vol. 3, pp. 142, 145; Brooks, p. 147; Varon, *Southern Lady, Yankee Spy,* pp. 174–75; Porter, pp. 273–75; *Private and Official Correspondence of Gen. Benjamin F. Butler,* vol. 5, p. 22; Eicher, pp. 723–24; *The Papers of Ulysses S. Grant,* vol. 11, p. 384.

362   *each other:* *The Papers of Ulysses S. Grant,* vol. 11, p. 388–89; Eicher, pp. 719–20; GS to Uncle, June 25, 1864, SLH, KS.

363   *refugee added:* McPherson, *Battle Cry of Freedom,* pp. 758–60; Catton, vol. 3, p. 380; Feis, *Grant's Secret Service,* pp. 254, 256; JCB to Gen. Humphreys, July 17, 1864, OR-40.3:293–94; *The Papers of Ulysses S. Grant,* vol. 11, pp. 272, 369; JM to Gen. Humphreys, Aug. 1, 1864, OR-42.2:4–5; GS to JCB, Aug. 16, 1864, OR-42.2:213; Committee on Claims report for the petition of F. W. E. Lohmann, Walter H. Ruth and Charles M. Carter, B: 23, RG46, NA; F. W. E. Lohmann, Samuel Ruth, Deceased, and Charles M. Carter petition before the Committee on War Claims, Aug. 11, 1876, Report no. 823, U.S. House of Representatives, 44th Congress, 1st Session; Greene, pp. 399, 415–16.

363   *the idea:* *The Papers of Ulysses S. Grant,* vol. 11, pp. 97–98; McPherson, *Tried by War,* p. 228; Dana, p. 225; GS letters to Uncle, July 14 and Aug. 15, 1864, SLH, KS.

364   *ventured across:* Fishel, *The Secret War for the Union,* p. 550; Badeau, *Military History of Ulysses S. Grant,* vol. 3, p. 352; GS to Gen. Humphreys, June 23, 1864, OR-40.2:337; Fred Manning to GS, Sept. 5, 1864, R: 36, M2096, GS to JM and Lt. Manning, Sept. 4, 1864, R: 303, M504, RG107, NA.

364   *or Atlanta:* Fishel, *The Secret War for the Union,* pp. 550–51; *The Papers of*

Ulysses S. Grant, vol. 11, pp. 228, 387–88; *The Papers of Ulysses S. Grant*, vol. 12, pp. 278–79; Feis, *Grant's Secret Service*, p. 253.

365 *with them:* GS messages to JM, Aug. 28 and Sept. 5, 1864, R: 303, M504, RG107, Letter to GS, Oct. 20, 1864, R: 34, M2096, NA; *Private and Official Correspondence of Gen. Benjamin F. Butler*, vol. 5, pp. 354–55; Sparks, *Inside Lincoln's Army*, p. 412; Van Santvoord, pp. 153–54.

365 *"Confederate service":* The Papers of Ulysses S. Grant*, vol. 11, p. 173; GS to Gen. Humphreys, July 18, 1864, OR-40.3:315; GS to Gen. Humphreys, July 20, 1864, OR-40.3:345–46; GS to Gen. Rawlins, July 29, 1864, OR-40.3:593.

366 *July 11:* REL to JD, B: 3, JD, DU; GS to Capt. Parker, July 31, 1864, E: 112, RG108, GS to MP, July 30, 1864, R: 303, M504, RG107, NA; Schairer, pp. 5–7, 168, 224; Greene, pp. 342–43.

366 *"twenty-four hours":* JM to GS, Aug. 31, 1864, R: 36, M2096, NA.

367 *a week:* Feis, *Grant's Secret Service*, pp. 235–36, 241; Feis, "A Union Military Intelligence Failure," pp. 224–25; *The Papers of Ulysses S. Grant*, vol. 11, p. 395; Feis, "Neutralizing the Valley," pp. 203–5; Fishel, *The Secret War for the Union*, p. 549; GS to JM, Aug. 20, 1864, OR-42.2:330; GS to Gen. Humphreys, Aug. 25, 1864, OR-42.2:473–74; GS to JCB, July 25, 1864, GS to JM, Aug. 29, 1864, R: 303, M504, RG107, GS to JCB, Aug. 13, 1864, R: 36, M2096, NA; "Fighting Them Over," *(Washington) National Tribune*, May 4, 1893, p. 5.

367 *papers contained:* GS to Lt. Col. Bowers, Dec. 25, 1864, B: 1, E: 112, RG108, NA; GS to Gen. Ord, Jan. 17, 1865, B: 575, War of 1861–65, NYH; "The Richmond Spy," *(Richmond) Daily Dispatch*, July 17, 1883, p. 1.

367 *was working:* "The Richmond Spy," *(Richmond) Daily Dispatch*, July 17, 1883, p. 1; Lineberry, pp. 5–6; Varon, *Southern Lady, Yankee Spy*, pp. 169–70, 173; Fishel, *The Secret War for the Union*, p. 553; Ryan, *A Yankee Spy in Richmond*, p. 17; *The Papers of Ulysses S. Grant*, vol. 14, p. 160; Maslowski, p. 48; Biographical sketch of EVL by John Reynolds, EVLP, LVA; Feis, "Neutralizing the Valley," pp. 205–6.

368 *the Shenandoah:* GS reports to Lt. Col. Bowers, Nov. 20 and 23, 1864, B: 575, War of 1861–65, NYH; GS to JCB, Aug. 25, 1864, JCBP, LC; Varon, "True to the Flag," pp. 78–79; GS to Gen. Hmphreys, Nov. 26, 1864, OR-42.3:710; "Grenville M. Dodge and George H. Sharpe," p. 9; Varon, *Southern Lady, Yankee Spy*, pp. 173–74; Robertson, pp. 160–61.

368 *he said:* Feis, *Grant's Secret Service*, pp. 237–38; John Van Lew to William Fay, Oct. 31, Nov. 20, Dec. 11, 20, and 31, 1864, WFP, LVA.

368 *the wash:* Bart Hall, Nov. 2, 2016; Varon, "True to the Flag," p. 77; Leveen,

"Mary Richards Bowser," pp. 8–9; Varon, *Southern Lady, Yankee Spy*, p. 173; "Miss Richmonia Richards's Lecture," *New York Tribune*, Sept. 12, 1865, p. 4; Richmonia Richards, *Anglo-African*, Oct. 7, 1865.

369   *jail again:* Varina Davis, pp. 198–200; Thomas, *The Confederate State of Richmond*, pp. 44–45, 155; Jones, *Ladies of Richmond*, pp. 194–95, 197; "Miss Richmonia Richards's Lecture," *New York Tribune*, Sept. 12, 1865, p. 4; Richmonia Richards, *Anglo-African*, Oct. 7, 1865; Elizabeth Varon, Lois Leveen, C-SPAN lecture, http://www.c-span.org/video/. (For footnote); Bart Hall, Nov. 2, 2016; *Richmond News* article, undated, EVLP, NY; Forbes, p. 41; Leonard, pp. 54–55; Largent, p. 2; Markle, p. 58; Rose, p. 5; Winkler, p. 78; Abbott, pp. 82, 124–25, 232, 252, 256; Varon, *Southern Lady, Yankee Spy*, pp. 165–68; "Grenville M. Dodge and George H. Sharpe," p. 12; Leveen, "Mary Richards Bowser," p. 8; "True to the Flag," pp. 76–77; Kennedy, p. 205; "Intelligence in the Civil War," pp. 27–28; John Reynolds letters to William Beymer, Dec. 3, 6, and 9, 1910, B: 2K394, WBP, UTA; Varina Davis to Miss Maury, ACW; website for the Military Intelligence Corps Hall of Fame, citation for Mary Bowser, https://www.ikn.army.mil/apps/MIHOF/Home.

370   *did Grant:* REL to JD, April 12, 1864, OR-33:1275; *The Papers of Ulysses S. Grant*, vol. 12, pp. 437–38; postwar claims of Samuel Ruth, W. F. E. Lohmann, and Charles Carter, Samuel Ruth to EMS, Jan. 12, 1866, B: 26, 976–2206, RG107, USG endorsement on petition of S. Ruth and F. W. E. Lohmann, p. 216, vol. 1, E: 1, RG108, NA; Committee on War-Claims Report for Samuel Ruth, F. W. E. Lohmann, and Charles M. Carter, Report no. 792, House of Representatives, 43rd Congress, 1st Session.

370   *dinner table:* GM to AP, Feb. 22, 1864, B: 4, GM letters to AP, Feb. 3 and May 10, 1864, B: 2, PND, LC; Donald, *Lincoln*, p. 529; McPherson, *Battle Cry of Freedom*, pp. 713–17, 771–73, 803; Goodwin, pp. 563–65; Mackay, p. 168; Horan, *The Pinkertons*, p. ix.

371   *as nonsense:* GM to AP, Oct. 20, 1863, B: 2, PND, LC; GM to AP, March 30, 1863, B: 7, EF, GU; GM to Samuel Barlow with enclosure, Oct. 27, 1864, B: 53, SB, HL; Horan, *The Pinkertons*, p. 143; Sears, *George B. McClellan*, pp. 382–83; Mackay, pp. 168–69.

371   *or illegally:* Goodwin, pp. 663–66; Winkle, pp. 401–2; C. A. Dana to MP, Oct. 30, 1864, OR-42.3:435–36; Sparks, *Inside Lincoln's Army*, p. 440; LB to C. A. Dana, Oct. 29, 1864, R: 116, M473, RG107, NA.

371   *everyone involved:* LB to C. A. Dana, July 28, 1864, OR-41.2:435; Corson, pp. 554–55; Baker, *History of the United States Secret Service*, 335–40, 350–54, 358–60.

372   *of him: The Papers of Ulysses S. Grant*, vol. 11, pp. 84–86; Benfey, p. 2.

372   *even contemplated:* LB to Charles A. Dana, Oct. 25, 1864, R: 136, M797, RG94, NA.

372   *in Chicago:* Goodwin, p. 603; Donald, *Lincoln*, pp. 530–31; McPherson, *Tried by War*, pp. 242–44; McPherson, *Battle Cry of Freedom*, pp. 775–76, 805–6; Catton, vol. 3, pp. 382–83; Eicher, pp. 714–15, 735; Horan, *The Pinkertons*, p. 146.

372   *defeat looming:* Varon, *Southern Lady, Yankee Spy*, p. 174; McPherson, *Embattled Rebel*, p. 220; Dabney, p. 187; Thomas, *The Confederate State of Richmond*, p. 186; Badeau, *Military History of Ulysses S. Grant*, vol. 3, pp. 353–54; McPherson, *Battle Cry of Freedom*, pp. 778, 780, 844; JM to Lt. Col. Bowers, Nov. 12, 1864, B: 1, E: 112, RG108, NA.

373   *be evacuated:* JCB to Gen. Humphreys, Aug. 7, 1864, OR-42.2:75–76; GS to Gen. Humphreys, Sept. 17, 1864, OR-42.1:34; GS to JCB, Sept. 22, 1864, OR-42.2:964; GS to Gen. Humphreys, Sept. 27, 1864, OR-42.2:1050; GS to Gen. S. Williams, Dec. 31, 1864, OR-42.3:1107–8.

374   *to "Romona":* Claim no. 44695 for L. E. Babcock, Oct. 14, 1876, RG217, To whom it may concern from J. B. Sare, March 12, 1866, Testimonial of J. M. Humphreys, March 12, 1866, Nance Williams testimony on L. E. Babcock, Smith testimony on L. E. Babcock, Letter to EMS on L. E. Babcock, Aug. 13, 1878, George Thomas statement on Pole, L. E. Babcock letter to EMS, March 15, 1866, B: 6, E: 95, RG110, NA; Ryan, *A Yankee Spy in Richmond*, pp. 17–18, 101–3, 151–53; Varon, *Southern Lady, Yankee Spy*, p. 187.

374   *feeble mother:* Varon, *Southern Lady, Yankee Spy*, pp. 175–77; Ryan, *A Yankee Spy in Richmond*, pp. 95–96, 151.

374   *and "offensive":* Testimony of L. M. Bullifont, Nov. 3, 1864, Testimony of A. B. Montcastle, Nov. 8, 1864, Testimony of George Mott, Aug. 1, 1864, R: 148, M474, RG109, NA.

375   *"that government":* Testimony of Mary C. Van Lew, Sept. 27, 1864, R: 148, M474, RG109, NA; Bart Hall, Nov. 2, 2016; Varon, "True to the Flag," p. 77.

375   *"on her":* Submission of Charles Blackford, R: 148, M747, RG109, NA; Varon, *Southern Lady, Yankee Spy*, p. 180.

375   *to Sharpe:* Varon, *Southern Lady, Yankee Spy*, pp. 180–82; Ryan, *A Yankee Spy in Richmond*, pp. 97, 151.

376   *poison himself: The Papers of Ulysses S. Grant*, vol. 13, p. xiii; JCB to GS, Nov. 19, 1864, R: 37, M2096, USG to Ould, Dec. 24, 1864, pp. 606–7, letters sent to Grant, March 1864–Dec. 1865, vol. 1, RG108, JM to JCB, Dec. 22, 1864, R: 37, M2096, NA; JM to Gen. Sheridan, Dec. 19, 1864, OR-43.2:804–5; Feis, *Grant's Secret Service*, pp. 258–59.

376 *for this: The Papers of Ulysses S. Grant*, vol. 13, pp. 487–88; Morice, "Organizational Learning"; Sparks, *Inside Lincoln's Army*, pp. 442–44; GS to Gen. Ingalls, Dec. 15, 1864, GS messages to MP, Nov. 11 and Dec. 15, 1864, R: 303, M504, RG107, MP to Gen. S. Williams, Nov. 29, 1864, R: 37, M2096, NA; GS to Uncle, Feb. 24, 1865, SLH, KS.

TWENTY-THREE: RICHMOND'S FALL

380 *"are in":* Brooks, pp. 235–40; Goodwin, pp. 697–98; "Last Hours of the Confederacy," *New York Times*, Jan. 21, 1876; GS letters to Uncle, Feb. 24 and March 7, 1865, SLH, KS.

380 *the scuffle:* Donald, *Lincoln*, pp. 568–69; Gobright, pp. 341–44; Stepp, pp. 327–28; *Diary of Gideon Welles*, vol. 2, p. 251; Swanson, pp. 1–2; Lamon, *Recollections of Abraham Lincoln*, pp. 271–73; Hatch, p. 40.

380 *and Navy:* Milton, *Abraham Lincoln and the Fifth Column*, pp. 93, 97, 101–5; Murdock, "New York's Civil War Bounty Brokers," pp. 259–62; Morn, p. 42; Smith, *Between the Lines*, pp. 178–79, 182.

382 *"promptly furnished":* Baker, *History of the United States Secret Service*, pp. 396–99; Corson, p. 555; Murdock, *Patriotism Limited 1862–1865*, p. 132; James Fry to LB, Jan. 16, 1865, B: 4, A. Lyons advertisement, B3, RG110, NA.

382 *the military:* Murdock, *Patriotism Limited 1862–1865*, pp. 110–11, 114, 120; letter to LB, Feb. 20, 1865, Edward H. Dingley affidavit, Jan. 28, 1865, John Parnale to LB, March 2, 1865, Max Stein to LB, March 1, 1865, Edward Bourke to LB, March 21, 1865, with enclosure by Mary Tighe, B: 1, RG110, NA; Weber, pp. 51, 56.

382 *enlistment quota:* Baker, *History of the United States Secret Service*, pp. 399–400; Chittenden, p. 350; Murdock, *Patriotism Limited 1862–1865*, pp. 133–36.

383 *con men:* Baker, *History of the United States Secret Service*, pp. 400–401, 405; Murdock, *Patriotism Limited 1862–1865*, p. 134.

383 *it away:* Murdock, *Patriotism Limited 1862–1865*, pp. 134–35; Baker, *History of the United States Secret Service*, pp. 404–5.

384 *the idea:* Baker, *History of the United States Secret Service*, pp. 400, 431–33, 438–41; letter to LB on Hoboken Station, B: 1, RG110, NA; Murdock, *Patriotism Limited 1862–1865*, pp. 134, 139–44; James B. Fry to LB, March 11, 1865, OR-S3.4:1232.

384 *the reward:* Murdock, *Patriotism Limited 1862–1865*, pp. 147–48; James B. Fry to LB, March 11, 1865, OR-S3.4:1231; Baker, *History of the United States Secret Service*, pp. 425–26, 433, 436.

384 *in Washington:* Lists of arrests made by LB "Authorized by the president or Secretary of War," B: 4, RG110, NA; War Department Report to the president, Nov. 22, 1865, Part VII Bounty, OR-S3.5:675; Baker, *History of the United States Secret Service,* pp. 436–37; Murdock, *Patriotism Limited 1862–1865,* p. 148.

385 *surrender terms:* Brooks, pp. 242–43; McPherson, *Tried by War,* pp. 336–38; Paul A. Oliver to J. G. Parke, Jan. 29, 1865, OR-46.2:286–87; JCB to J. G. Parke, Jan. 7, 1865, OR-46.2:61; *The Papers of Ulysses S. Grant,* vol. 13, p. 391; JCB to GGM, Feb. 9, 1865, OR-46.2:499; Paul A. Oliver to J. G. Parke, Jan. 30, 1865, OR-46.2:299.

385 *Van Lew reported:* C. A. Dana to EMS, April 5, 1865, OR-46.3:574; Jones, *A Rebel War Clerk's Diary at the Confederate States Capital,* pp. 441, 443, 446; GS to GGM, Jan. 18, 1865, OR-46.2:171; GS to Lt. Col. Bowers, Feb. 8, 1865, B: 1, E: 112, RG108, NA.

386 *than Richmond:* Fishel, *The Secret War for the Union,* p. 554; Feis, *Grant's Secret Service,* pp. 259–60; GS to GGM, Jan. 13, 1865, OR-46.2:114–15; Varon, *Southern Lady, Yankee Spy,* p. 189; Stuart, "Samuel Ruth and General R. E. Lee," pp. 85–89; GS reports to Lt. Col. Bowers, Feb. 23 and 26, 1865, B: 1, E: 112, RG108, NA.

386 *long time:* Feis, *Grant's Secret Service,* pp. 259–60; GS to Lt. Col. Bowers, Feb. 23, 1865, news story titled "Richmond—General Lee About to 'Astonish the World,'" B: 1, E: 112, RG108, NA; GS to Uncle, Feb. 24, 1865, SLH, KS.

387 *"ridiculous affair":* Feis, *Grant's Secret Service,* pp. 260–61; Jones, *A Rebel War Clerk's Diary at the Confederate States Capital,* p. 457; GS reports to Lt. Col. Bowers, Feb. 23 and March 26, 1865, B: 1, E: 112, RG108, NA.

387 *"Richmond friends":* Catton, vol. 3, p. 436; McPherson, *Battle Cry of Freedom,* pp. 825–30; GS to Lt. Col. Manning and Manning's reply, Feb. 17, 1865, OR-46.2:580–81; Bart Hall, Nov. 7, 2016; W. Randolph Van Lew, p. 3; Paul A. Oliver to Col. Bowers, March 31, 1865, Series 1, General Correspondence, 1833–1916, ALD, LC; "Last Hours of the Confederacy," *New York Times,* Jan. 21, 1876.

388 *Libby Prison:* GS reports to Lt. Col. Bowers, Jan. 3, 21, and Feb. 23, 1865, GS to Lt. Col. Parker, Jan. 21, 1865, B: 1, E: 112, RG108, EVL to "Dear Sir," Jan. 20, 1865, R: 46, M2096, NA; Page 13 of Fishel notes on Paul Oliver, B: 3, EF, GU.

388 *to send:* GS to GGM, Feb. 11, 1865, OR-46.2:525; Maslowski, p. 48; Feis, *Grant's Secret Service,* p. 239; GS to GGM, Jan. 9, 1865, OR-46.2:75–76; *The Papers of Ulysses S. Grant,* vol. 13, pp. 361–62; GS to Lt. Col. Bowers, Feb. 26, 1865, B: 1, E: 112, RG108, NA.

388   *a spy:* Varon, *Southern Lady, Yankee Spy,* pp. 185–88; Stuart, "Samuel Ruth and General R. E. Lee," pp. 90–96, 99, 101; Committee on Claims report for the petition of F. W. E. Lohmann, Walter H. Ruth, and Charles M. Carter, B: 23, RG46, William Rowley statement, Jan. 5, 1866, Ruth expenses for last year of the war filed June 23, 1865, B: 26, 976–2206, RG107, Note on Lohmann and Hancock still in Castle Thunder, R: 35, M2096, NA; F. W. E. Lohmann, Samuel Ruth, Deceased, and Charles M. Carter petition before the Committee on War Claims, Aug. 11, 1876, Report no. 823, U.S. House of Representatives, 44th Congress, 1st Session; "City Intelligence," *Richmond Examiner,* Jan. 25, 1865; page 20 of Fishel notes Lohmann arrest, B: 3, EF, GU.

389   *be made:* F. W. E. Lohmann, Samuel Ruth, Deceased, and Charles M. Carter petition before the Committee on War Claims, Aug. 11, 1876, Report no. 823, U.S. House of Representatives, 44th Congress, 1st Session; Committee on Claims report for the petition of F. W. E. Lohmann, Walter H. Ruth, and Charles M. Carter, B: 23, RG46, William Rowley statement, Jan. 5, 1866, Postwar claims of Samuel Ruth, F. W. E. Lohmann, and Charles Carter, B: 26, 976–2206, RG107, GS to Lt. Col. Bowers, Jan. 21, 1865, B: 1, E: 112, RG108, P. Daniel statement, May 21, 1867, Samuel Ruth letter, Jan. 20, 1866, Joseph Maddox File no. 425928, B: 588–89, RG94, NA.

389   *Fort Monroe:* USG telegram to EMS, March 8, 1865, Joseph Maddox File no. 425928, B: 588–89, RG94, NA; US to GS, March 3, 1865, vol. 46, p. 188, USGP, LC; Report of Col. Samuel H. Roberts, March 9, 1865, OR-44.1:442–44; *The Papers of Ulysses S. Grant,* vol. 14, pp. 87, 93, 100–102; Stuart, "Samuel Ruth and General R. E. Lee," pp. 102–3; Stuart, "Of Spies and Borrowed Names," p. 320.

389   *to smoke:* Inspector general report in the matter of the claim of J. Maddox, Jan. 25, 1868, Joseph Maddox File no. 425928, B: 588–89, RG94, NA; *The Papers of Ulysses S. Grant,* vol. 14, pp. 121–22; *Letter from the Secretary of War in the Case of Joseph H. Maddox,* pp. 18, 45.

390   *sent south:* GS to GGM, March 2, 1865, OR-46.2:786–87; GS to GGM, March 18, 1865, OR-46.2:29; USG to GGM, March 14, 1865, OR-46.2:963; Jones, *A Rebel War Clerk's Diary at the Confederate States Capital,* pp. 458, 461; *The Papers of Ulysses S. Grant,* vol. 14, pp. 478–80; Fishel notes p. 3 on GS report, March 22, 1865, B: 3, EF, GU.

390   *matters were:* John Albree speeches on Elizabeth Van Lew, B: 1, ELC, WM; GS to Lt. Col. Manning, March 11, 1865, OR-46.2:928–29; Sparks, *Inside Lincoln's Army,* pp. 470, 477, 479.

391   *dangerously thinned:* F. W. E. Lohmann, Samuel Ruth, Deceased, and Charles M.

Carter petition before the Committee on War Claims, Aug. 11, 1876, Report no. 823, U.S. House of Representatives, 44th Congress, 1st Session; McPherson, *Battle Cry of Freedom*, pp. 844–45; Catton, vol. 3, pp. 435, 437–39; Feis, *Grant's Secret Service*, pp. 261–62; Eicher, p. 804; Stuart, "Samuel Ruth and General R. E. Lee," p. 81.

391   *of Richmond:* Catton, vol. 3, pp. 439–41; Donald, *Lincoln*, p. 571; Niven, *Gideon Welles*, pp. 490–91; Eicher, p. 804; Nicolay and Hay, "A History of Abraham Lincoln," p. 309.

391   *his president:* Feis, *Grant's Secret Service*, p. 262; McPherson, *Battle Cry of Freedom*, pp. 845–46; Catton, vol. 3, pp. 442–47; Eicher, pp. 806–9; Sparks, *Inside Lincoln's Army*, pp. 484–85; Varina Davis, p. 582; Thomas, *The Confederate State of Richmond*, p. 194; Freeman, *R. E. Lee*, vol. 4, p. 153.

392   *pillaging mobs:* Catton, vol. 3, pp. 444–47; Badeau, *Military History of Ulysses S. Grant*, vol. 3, pp. 529–30, 539–41; Goodwin, p. 716; Johnson, *Campfires and Battlefields*, pp. 453–54; Eicher, pp. 811–13; Speer, p. 286; Jones, *Ladies of Richmond*, pp. 271–72; Brock, pp. 419–29; Stepp, p. 336; Boykin, p. 13; Blakeman, pp. 479–80.

392   *Main Street:* W. Randolph Van Lew, pp. 5–6; Dabney, p. 190; Ryan, *A Yankee Spy in Richmond*, pp. 103–6; Varon, *Southern Lady, Yankee Spy*, pp. 192–94; Nicolay and Hay, *Abraham Lincoln: A History*, vol. 10, p. 207; "Sale of Historic Relics," news article, "Van Lew Relics Bring $1,000," *Boston Herald*, Nov. 22, 1900, EVLP, NY; John P. Reynolds biographical sketch of EVL, p. 6, EVLP, LVA.

392   *mob dispersed:* John Albree speeches on Elizabeth Van Lew, B: 1, ELC, WM; W. Randolph Van Lew, p. 1; "The Richmond Spy," *(Richmond) Daily Dispatch*, July 17, 1883, p. 1.

393   *had seized:* John Albree speeches on Elizabeth Van Lew, B: 1, ELC, WM; Varon, *Southern Lady, Yankee Spy*, p. 197; EMS to HH, May 16, 1865, HH to Maj. Gen. Schofield, May 16 and 17, 1865, J. M. Schofield to HH, May 17, 1865, OR-47.3:510–11, 519.

393   *Georgia Room:* Catton, vol. 3, pp. 73, 444–47; Blakeman, pp. 480, 483–85; Jones, *Ladies of Richmond*, p. 280; Boykin, pp. 11–12; Badeau, *Military History of Ulysses S. Grant*, vol. 3, pp. 534–35; Goodwin, pp. 715, 718–20; McPherson, *Battle Cry of Freedom*, pp. 846–47; Eicher, pp. 813–15; Donald, *Lincoln*, pp. 576–77; Nicolay and Hay, "A History of Abraham Lincoln," p. 310; L. S. H. "Memorandum on the Life of Lincoln," pp. 306–7; "The Confederate Museum: In the Capital of the Confederacy," B: 1, ELC, WM; Charles Sumner to Salmon P. Chase, 1865, SC, HL.

393   *him greatly:* "The Richmond Spy," *(Richmond) Daily Dispatch*, July 17, 1883,

p. 1; Varon, *Southern Lady, Yankee Spy*, p. 196; Fishel, *The Secret War for the Union*, p. 552; Sparks, *Inside Lincoln's Army*, p. 488; Ryan, *A Yankee Spy in Richmond*, p. 107; Fishel notes p. 12 on Sharpe in Richmond, B: 3, EF, GU; Committee of War Claims Report no. 792 on Samuel Ruth, F. W. E Lohmann, and Charles M. Carter, June 22, 1874, House of Representatives, 43rd Congress, 1st Session.

393   *the body:* F. W. E. Lohmann deposition, Oct. 17, 1865, B: 26, 976–2206, RG107, NA; Schultz, pp. 258–59; EMS to Gen. Weitzel, April 11, 1865, OR-46.3:712.

394   *White House:* Cleaves, pp. 328–29; *Personal Memoirs of U.S. Grant*, pp. 466–67; GS to Gen. Rawlins, April 6, 1865, Series 1, General Correspondence 1833–1916, ALD, LC.

394   *surrender terms:* McPherson, *Battle Cry of Freedom*, p. 848; Eicher, pp. 818–20; Freeman, *R. E. Lee: A Biography*, vol. 4, pp. 121–23.

395   *Lee had:* "At Appomattox: Incidents of Lee's Surrender," *Philadelphia Weekly Times*, June 1877, MA, James Morice, "Organizational Learning in a Military Environment: George H. Sharpe and the Army of the Potomac," SGF, KS; Badeau, *Military History of Ulysses S. Grant*, vol. 3, pp. 602–9; *Proceedings of the Ulster County Historical Society 1936–1937*, pp. 36–37; McPherson, *Battle Cry of Freedom*, p. 849.

395   *"their parole":* Porter, *Campaigning with Grant*, p. 487; Schmidt, p. 56; *The Papers of Ulysses S. Grant*, vol. 14, pp. 373–74; *Proceedings of the Ulster County Historical Society 1936–1937*, p. 38; text of GS's parole for REL and staff, OR-46.3:667.

396   *no different:* Freeman, *Lee's Lieutenants*, pp. 160–61; Fishel, *The Secret War for the Union*, p. 557; *Diary of Gideon Welles*, vol. 2, p. 276; Stepp, p. 349; Eicher, p. 844; Badeau, *Military History of Ulysses S. Grant*, vol. 3, p. 538; Chernow, pp. 550–53.

396   *to end:* Badeau, *Military History of Ulysses S. Grant*, vol. 3, pp. 594–95, 598–99, 601, 622–23; McPherson, *Battle Cry of Freedom*, p. 848; *Personal Memoirs of U.S. Grant*, p. 467; *The Papers of Ulysses S. Grant*, vol. 14, pp. 391–92; E. O. C. Ord to USG, April 29, 1865, OR-46.3:1013.

396   *indictment quashed:* USG to REL, June 20, 1865, OR-46.3:1286–87; *Proceedings of the Ulster County Historical Society 1936–1937*, p. 39; USG endorsements of communication of REL, June 13, 1865, General Records, Endorsements sent by General Grant, March 1864–July 1867, vol. 1, pp. 168–69, RG108, NA.

397   *colonel said:* GS to Col. T. S. Bowers, April 20, 1865, OR-46.3:851–53; *Proceedings of the Ulster County Historical Society 1936–1937*, p. 38; Feis, *Grant's Secret*

Service, p. 264; GS to MP, April 1865, R: 415, M504, RG107, NA; REL pass for GS, April 11, 1865, MA, KS.

397 *"the regiment"*: GS to Uncle, April 28, 1865, SLH, KS.

397 *their arms*: Eicher, pp. 821–22, 831, 834–46; Jones, *A Rebel War Clerk's Diary at the Confederate States Capital*, p. 473.

397 *husband executed*: The Papers of Ulysses S. Grant, vol. 14, pp. 385–86; Blakeman, p. 499; "Richmonia Richards," *Anglo-African*, Oct. 7, 1865.

398 *a companion*: Brooks, pp. 250–55; Goodwin, pp. 726–28; McPherson, *Battle Cry of Freedom*, p. 851; Titone, pp. 13–14.

398 *Surratt house*: Hatch, pp. 85–89; Swanson, p. 19; Hanchett, *The Lincoln Murder Conspiracies*, p. 48; Eicher, p. 823; Hageman, pp. 5–6; Statements of Mary E. Surratt, R: 6, M599, RG153, NA.

398 *practically nil*: Lamon, *Recollections of Abraham Lincoln*, p. 277; Orrmont, pp. 139–41; Mogelever, pp. 328, 330–31; Baker, *History of the United States Secret Service*, pp. 419–21; LB to James Polhemus, April 12, 1865, M504, RG107, NA.

TWENTY-FOUR: ASSASSINATION

399 *he landed*: Donald, *Lincoln*, pp. 592–97; Brooks, p. 257; Catton, vol. 3, pp. 457–58, 462; Goodwin, pp. 728–39; Hatch, pp. 111–13, 116–17.

400 *for Georgetown*: Stahr, pp. 435–37; Brooks, pp. 268–71; Hatch, pp. 77–83; Poore, *The Conspiracy Trial for the Murder of the President*, vol. 1, pp. 12–13; Swanson, pp. 153–54.

400 *in Maryland*: Swanson, pp. 63–67, 79–82, 86–88; Kauffman, "Booth's Escape Route," pp. 12–13, 52.

400 *of innocence*: Jones, *A Rebel War Clerk's Diary at the Confederate States Capital*, p. 479; Swanson, pp. 174–75.

400 *"our midst"*: Jedediah Paine to William Beymer, Feb. 12, 1912, with enclosed column by EVL, "To the Federal Army," B: 2K396, WBP, UTA.

401 *the assassination*: LB to EMS, May 26, 1865, R: 455, M619, RG94, NA; Orrmont, pp. 141–42; Baker, *History of the United States Secret Service*, p. 524; EMS to LB, April 15, 1865, EMS to John Kennedy, April 15, 1865, OR-46.3:783; Swanson, pp. 146–47.

401 *his people*: Mogelever, p. 332; Donald, *Lincoln*, pp. 547–49; Roscoe, p. 5; Hatch, pp. 4, 27, 30, 34; Winkle, pp. 124–25, 412; Baker, *History of the United States Secret Service*, p. 525.

401 *who failed*: AP to EMS, April 19, 1865, B: 4, PND, LC; Markle, p. 7; Hageman, p. 5; Roscoe, pp. 4, 198; Mogelever, pp. 332–33.

402   *Baker's part:* Hatch, pp. 75–76; Mogelever, p. 282; Baker, *History of the United States Secret Service*, pp. 465, 475; LB to C. A. Dana, April 24, 1865, R: 2, M599, RG153, NA; Roscoe, pp. 17–18, 198; Dykstra, p. 434.

402   *their property:* Hatch, pp. 83–84; Swanson, pp. 95, 103, 106, 122–32, 155–58, 160–79, 184–85, 204–5, 208–10, 224–33, 246–67, 270–79, 287–88, 296; Voluntary Statement of David E. Herold, R: 4, M599, RG153, NA; Alford, p. 295.

403   *massive operation:* Swanson, pp. 112–13, 147–48, 186; Baker, *History of the United States Secret Service*, pp. 525–26; Mogelever, pp. 335–36; Jones, *Behind Enemy Lines*, p. 88; Axelrod, p. 280; Kauffman, "Booth's Escape Route," p. 10; Marvel, pp. 369–74; Thomas, *Stanton*, p. 401; Tidwell, pp. 441–42.

403   *the assassins:* Swanson, pp. 101–2, 110–12, 116, 119–20, 133–35; T. S. Bowers to A. H. Markland, April 17, 1865, OR-46.3:810; Tidwell, p. 440; Hatch, pp. 85–87; *Impeachment Investigation*, p. 675; Gen. Augur to Gen. Townsend, Aug. 16, 1865, R: 455, M619, RG94, NA.

404   *miles away:* Swanson, pp. 89–90, 132, 153; Tidwell, p. 441; John Wilkes Booth cipher inventory of articles found in Room no. 136, Kirkwood House, R: 2, M599, RG153, NA.

404   *Philadelphia forces:* Chittenden, p. 350; Baker, *History of the United States Secret Service*, p. 529; Roscoe, pp. 204–5; Mogelever, p. 336; Orrmont, pp. 144–45; LB to Gen. Holt, Aug. 26, 1865, LB to EMS, May 26, 1865, R: 455, M619, RG94, Brown to EMS, July 25, 1865, R: 279, M221, LB to B. Franklin, April 17, 1865, R: 337, M504, RG107, NA; "Lincoln and Booth: The Inner Story of the Great Tragedy of Fifty Years Ago," *Washington Herald*, April 28, 1915, p. 2.

404   *the assassin:* Baker, *History of the United States Secret Service*, p. 526; Kauffman, *American Brutus*, pp. 257–58; Baker, "The Capture, Death, and Burial of J. Wilkes Booth," p. 575; LB to EMS, May 26, 1865, R: 455, M619, RG94, Burnett to LB, April 27, 1865, Burnett to Col. Foster, April 25, 1865, R: 1, M599, RG153, LB to Provost Marshal Frederick, Md., April 17, 1865, R: 377, M504, RG107, LB's $30,000 reward poster for John Wilkes Booth, R: 455, M619, RG94, NA.

405   *"defy detection":* Roscoe, p. 307; Kauffman, *American Brutus*, p. 263; Swanson, p. 205; LB to C. A. Dana, April 24, 1865, R: 2, April 27, 1865, statement taken by LB, LB interview with Blanche Booth, April 22, 1865, anonymous letter, April 24, 1865, A. Fisher to Burnett, April 19, 1865, Col. Olcott note, April 25, 1865, R: 1, note from Booth imposter to Gen. Augur, April 17, 1865, R: 3, M599, RG153, Garrett to LB, April 25, 1865, R: 225, M473, RG107, NA.

405   *gone cold:* LB to EMS, May 26, 1865, R: 455, M619, RG94, NA; Baker, *History*

of the United States Secret Service, pp. 526, 530, 533; Baker, "An Eyewitness Account of the Death and Burial of J. Wilkes Booth," pp. 426–27; Swanson, pp. 156, 176, 189–93, 197–98, 219–21, 272; Kauffman, *American Brutus*, p. 263.

405 *it rich:* Swanson, pp. 213–14, 221–23; Baker, "The Capture, Death, and Burial of J. Wilkes Booth," p. 576; Roscoe, p. 33.

406 *"get him":* AP to EMS, April 19, 1865, EMS to AP, April 24, 1865, B: 4, PND, LC; Mackay, p. 176; Horan, *The Pinkertons*, p. 253.

406 *in Virginia:* Swanson, pp. 281–83; Tidwell, pp. 468–69; Hanchett, *The Lincoln Murder Conspiracies*, pp. 176–77; Report upon the distribution of the Rewards for the arrest of Davis, Booth & Co., R: 457, M619, RG94, NA.

406 *the Rappahannock:* Millard, "The Devil's Errand Boy"; Axelrod, pp. 281–82, 284; Baker, *History of the United States Secret Service*, pp. 494–507, 526–28, 533; LB to EMS, May 26, 1865, R: 455, Report upon the distribution of the Rewards for the arrest of Davis, Booth & Co., R: 457, M619, RG94, NA; "Lincoln and Booth: The Inner Story of the Great Tragedy of Fifty Years Ago," *Washington Herald*, April 28, 1915, p. 2.

407 *Wild-goose chase:* LB to EMS, May 26, 1865, R: 455, M619, RG94, NA; Statement of E. J. Conger before Gen. Holt, April 27, 1865, R: 455, M619, RG94, NA; Luther Baker publicity on Booth capture, AC; Doherty statements, April 29 and May 9, 1865, R: 456, M619, RG94, NA; Mogelever, pp. 345–47; Merrill, pp. 252, 270; *Joseph Stannard Baker Memoirs from 1838 to 1865*, pp. 11-9; Roscoe, p. 368; Baker, *History of the United States Secret Service*, pp. 527, 533–34; Swanson, pp. 283–85; Baker, "An Eyewitness Account of the Death and Burial of J. Wilkes Booth," p. 428; "More on Capt. Doherty . . . ," *Surratt Courier* 19, no. 9 (September 1990): 5–7; Roscoe, p. 368; Kauffman, *American Brutus*, p. 306; Millard, p. 22; "Lincoln and Booth: The Inner Story of the Great Tragedy of Fifty Years Ago," *Washington Herald*, April 28, 1915, p. 2.

408 *to Washington:* Statement of E. J. Conger before Gen. Holt, April 27, 1865, E. J. Conger to EMS, Dec. 24, 1865, statement of Luther B. Baker, April 27, 1865, R: 455, M619, RG94, NA; Baker, *History of the United States Secret Service*, pp. 528, 531; Kauffman, *American Brutus*, pp. 310–11; Swanson, p. 289.

408 *April 25:* Baker, *History of the United States Secret Service*, p. 534; Baker, "An Eyewitness Account of the Death and Burial of J. Wilkes Booth," pp. 428–29; *The Trial of John H. Surratt in the Criminal Court for the District of Columbia*, vol. 2, pp. 315–17; Statement of E. J. Conger before Gen. Holt, April 27, 1865, R: 455, Lt. Doherty statement on Booth capture, R: 456, M619, RG94, NA.

408 *Garrett farm:* Swanson, pp. 298–303; Kauffman, *American Brutus*, p. 312;

Baker, *History of the United States Secret Service*, pp. 534–35; Baker, "An Eye-witness Account of the Death and Burial of J. Wilkes Booth," pp. 429–30; "Lincoln and Booth: The Inner Story of the Great Tragedy of Fifty Years Ago," *Washington Herald*, April 28, 1915, p. 2.

409   *about 2 a.m.:* Statement of Willie Jett, May 6, 1865, R: 5, M599, RG153, NA; *The Trial of John H. Surratt in the Criminal Court for the District of Columbia*, vol. 2, p. 317; Poore, *The Conspiracy Trial for the Murder of the President*, vol. 1, pp. 312–18; Swanson, pp. 311–14; Baker, "An Eyewitness Account of the Death and Burial of J. Wilkes Booth," p. 431; Baker, *History of the United States Secret Service*, pp. 535–38; Kauffman, *American Brutus*, pp. 312–20; Hatch, pp. 125–26.

410   *of value:* "Lincoln and Booth: The Inner Story of the Great Tragedy of Fifty Years Ago," *Washington Herald*, April 28, 1915, p. 2; E. J. Conger statement, April 27, 1865, R: 455, Affidavits for John M. and William H. Garrett, May 20, 1865, R: 457, Statement of Sgt. Boston Corbett, R: 456, M619, RG94, LB report, May 5, 1865, R: 1, M599, RG153, NA; Howard, "Assassination and Pathology Case Presentations"; Kauffman, "Booth's Escape Route," pp. 48–49; Swanson, pp. 316–43; Hatch, pp. 125–29, 150–51; *The Trial of John H. Surratt in the Criminal Court for the District of Columbia*, vol. 2, pp. 305–8, 317–20; Tidwell, p. 477; Roach, p. 387; "John Wilkes Booth's Escape Route," James O. Hall, Clinton, Md., *Surratt Society*, 2000, p. 16; Baker, "An Eyewitness Account of the Death and Burial of J. Wilkes Booth," pp. 432–39, 441; Poore, *The Conspiracy Trial for the Murder of the President*, vol. 1, pp. 322–25; Hanchett, *The Lincoln Murder Conspiracies*, p. 178; *Impeachment Investigation*, p. 327.

411   *the capital:* "John Wilkes Booth's Escape Route," James O. Hall, Clinton, Md., *Surratt Society*, 2000, p. 16; Swanson, pp. 346–50; *Impeachment Investigation*, pp. 327, 485; Baker, "An Eyewitness Account of the Death and Burial of J. Wilkes Booth," p. 441; Kauffman, *American Brutus*, p. 320.

411   *so hated:* Steers, *Lincoln Legends*, pp. 180–81; Baker, "The Capture, Death, and Burial of J. Wilkes Booth," p. 583; Hatch, p. 129; Baker, "An Eyewitness Account of the Death and Burial of J. Wilkes Booth," p. 443.

412   *with Stanton:* LB to Maj. Eckert, April 26, 1865, R: 337, M540, RG106, NA; Baker, *History of the United States Secret Service*, pp. 508, 528, 540–41; *Impeachment Investigation*, pp. 330, 451.

412   *cell floor:* Baker, *History of the United States Secret Service*, pp. 507–8, 528, 541–42, 703–4; Swanson, pp. 350–56, 362; Howard, "Assassination and Pathology Case Presentations"; Hatch, p. 129; *Impeachment Investigation*, p. 455;

Baker, "An Eyewitness Account of the Death and Burial of J. Wilkes Booth," pp. 445–46.

413 *reward money:* Baker, *History of the United States Secret Service,* p. 563; *Impeachment Investigation,* p. 450; Mogelever, pp. 378–80; Swanson, pp. 364–65; Burnett to LB, April 26, 1865, LB report, May 11, 1865, R: 1, LB certificate, June 1, 1865, R: 3, M599, RG153, NA.

413 *behind it:* LB to EMS, May 26, 1865, R: 455, M619, RG94, NA; Chronological Record on L. C. Baker Service, BP; Poore, *The Conspiracy Trial for the Murder of the President,* vol. 1, p. 4; Orrmont, pp. 159–60; Holzer and Symonds, p. 434; Baker, *History of the United States Secret Service,* pp. 539, 563–64.

413 *on May 10:* Edward Doherty to EMS, March 24, 1866, R: 456, M619, RG95, NA; "Capt. Doherty's Story," *New York Times,* Aug. 22, 1879, p. 3; Luther Baker publicity on Booth capture, AC; Mogelever, p. 383; "More on Capt. Doherty . . . ," *Surratt Courier,* 19, no. 9 (September 1990): 5–7; Swanson, pp. 347–49; Kauffman, *American Brutus,* p. 381.

414 *get even:* Report upon the distribution of the Rewards for the arrest of Davis, Booth, R: 457, M619, RG94, NA; "The Lincoln Assassination Rewards," Legislative Reference Services Report, Library of Congress, BP; Mogelever, pp. 381, 383–85; Eicher, p. 842; Baker, *History of the United States Secret Service,* pp. 564–66.

TWENTY-FIVE: PEACE

416 *of pounding:* Brooks, pp. 307–21; Fox, p. 542; McPherson, *Battle Cry of Freedom,* pp. 854–57; Eicher, pp. 22, 41, 848–49.

417 *lessons learned:* Fishel, "Military Intelligence 1861–63 (Part 2)," p. 1; Fishel, *The Secret War for the Union,* pp. 563–68, 571; Cook, p. 18; Maslowski, p. 41; "Intelligence in the Civil War"; O'Toole, p. 173.

418 *international culprits:* Morn, pp. 45–47, 52; Durie, p. 74; Geringer, pp. 23–26; Lavine, pp. 139–40, 147; Mackay, pp. 11, 182–83, 187, 201; Horan, *The Pinkertons,* pp. x, 181, 189–93, 196–202, 323–26, 247, 254–55; Horan and Swiggett, pp. 14, 18–29, 34–41, 53, 63–64; Stashower, p. 5.

418 *in 1869:* AP to WHS, June 7, 1870, R: 108, AP to WHS, March 7, 1872, R: 110; WSP, LC; "Timothy Webster's Grave," *(Chicago) Inter Ocean,* Dec. 1, 1901; "The Fate of a Spy," news article, B: 4, PLC, SLU; AP letters to Salmon Chase, Feb. 3 and June 7, 1872, APP, CH; Horan, *The Pinkertons,* pp. 181, 192–93, 326–27; Pinkerton, *The Spy of the Rebellion,* p. 560; Mackay, pp. 200, 233.

418 *multimillionaire industrialist:* AP to son, April 28, 1883, R: 3, PND, LC;

"Chalmers—Pinkerton," *Chicago Tribune*, Oct. 22, 1878; Horan, *The Pinkertons*, p. 180; Mackay, pp. 184–85, 201, 229–32, 237–38.

418 *could speak:* AP to WHS, June 7, 1870, R: 108, WSP, LC; Mackay, pp. 199, 201–2; Horan, *The Pinkertons*, p. 159.

419 *the Army:* Pinkerton historical events, APP, CH; Pinkerton, *The Spy of the Rebellion*, p. xxxi; Mackay, pp. 205–6; Horan, *The Pinkertons*, p. 187.

419 *that conflict:* Horan, *The Pinkertons*, pp. 238–39; Mackay, pp. 208–9; Durie, p. 153; Lavine, p. 185; Morn, p. 83; Recko, p. 1; Markle, p. 6.

419 *"not confess":* William Pinkerton to PL, Jan. 15, 1869, B: 24, PND, LC; PL letters to William Pinkerton, Feb. 29 and March 21, 1884, B: 2, PLC, SLU; Mortimer, *Double Death*, pp. 232, 236; Memoirs of Pryce Lewis as Told to Major David E. Cronin in 1888, pp. vii–viii, 167, B: 4, PLC, SLU.

419 *his daughter:* Concerning Lewis and Scully's Guilt in the Apprehension of Timothy Webster, October 1952, Pryce Lewis—Chronology for 1863 and 1864, B: 3, Memorandum of agreement between PL and David E. Cronin, Jan. 31, 1889, B: 2, PLC, SLU; Mortimer, "Super Spy from Wales," p. 67; Inglis, p. 3; Mortimer, *Double Death*, p. 233; Popchock, p. 44; "Plunges 365 Feet from World Dome," *New York Times*, Dec. 9, 1911, p. 10; "World Dome Suicide a Famous Spy," *New York Times*, Dec. 10, 1911, p. 1.

420 *touring car:* "Plunges 365 Feet from World Dome," *New York Times*, Dec. 9, 1911, p. 10; "World Dome Suicide a Famous Spy," *New York Times*, Dec. 10, 1911, p. 1; Photo of PL in his last days, B: 3, PLC, SLU; Inglis, p. 4; Mortimer, "Super Spy of Wales," p. 67; Mortimer, *Double Death*, pp. 1–3.

420 *and Chase:* "Historic American Buildings in Illinois," news article, B: 4, PND, LC; Horan, *The Pinkertons*, pp. 182–87; Morn, p. 66; Mackay, pp. 202–5.

420 *July 1:* "Death Comes at Last," *Chicago Herald*, July 2, 1884; "Allan Pinkerton's Death," *New York Times*, July 2, 1884; Horan, *The Pinkertons*, pp. 323, 327; Mackay, pp. 233–37; Lavine, pp. 207–8.

421 *the world:* Mackay, pp. 11, 237–39; Horan, *The Pinkertons*, p. 327; Morn, p. vii; "Allan Pinkerton's Death," *New York Times*, July 2, 1884; "In Memory of Allan Pinkerton," eulogy at funeral, B: 4, PND, LC; Company Fact Sheet, www.pinkerton.com.

421 *impeachment growing:* Marvel, pp. 392, 426–29, 432–33, 445–50; Eicher, p. 828; Goodwin, pp. 751–52; Milton, *The Age of Hate*, pp. 335, 401–4; Butler, p. 926; Hanchett, *The Lincoln Murder Conspiracies*, p. 83; LB to Mrs. John Butler, Sept. 27, 1865, LB to Stidpole, Oct. 9, 1865, LB to Mrs. Baker, Oct. 16, 1865, M504, RG107, Secret Service fund, quarters ending June 2, June 26,

June 30, Aug. 2, and Nov. 3, 1865, B: 6, E: 179A, RG94, Secret Service expenditures, April 25–Sept. 4, 1865, B: 5, E: 95, RG110, NA.

421   *to Stanton:* Orrmont, p. 164; Baker, *History of the United States Secret Service,* pp. 565–67, 583–87; Mogelever, p. 388; *Impeachment Investigation,* p. 462.

422   *the case:* Mogelever, pp. 385–86, 389; Baker, *History of the United States Secret Service,* p. 582.

422   *serious trouble:* Mogelever, pp. 386–87; Orrmont, p. 164; Fishel, *The Secret War for the Union,* pp. 27–28; "Intelligence in the Civil War," p. 47.

422   *the president:* Bergeron, vol. 9, pp. 370–72; Milton, *The Age of Hate,* p. 407; Poore, *Perley's Reminiscences of the Sixty Years in the National Metropolis,* p. 200; *Impeachment Investigation,* pp. 8, 12–13.

422   *sting operation:* Bergeron, vol. 9, pp. 370–72; *Impeachment Investigation,* p. 8; Baker, *History of the United States Secret Service,* pp. 592–93; Mogelever, pp. 390–93.

423   *Old Capitol Prison:* Baker, *History of the United States Secret Service,* pp. 589–90; Bergeron, vol. 9, pp. 370–72; Bergeron, vol. 11, pp. 269–70; George Alfred Townsend on Lucy Cobb, BP; Michelle Krowl, Sept. 18, 2016; Joseph Cobb to Andrew Johnson, R: 25, Joseph Cobb to Andrew Johnson, May 11, 1867, AJP, LC; "City News," *National Daily Intelligencer,* Jan. 25, 1866, p. 3; "Local News: The Case of Gen. L. C. Baker," *Washington Star,* Jan. 25, 1866; "City News," *National Daily Intelligencer,* Jan. 26, 1866, p. 3; "Local News: The Pardon Brokerage Case," *Washington Star,* Jan. 26, 1866.

423   *his boss:* Baker, *History of the United States Secret Service,* p. 593; *Impeachment Investigation,* p. 352; Milton, *The Age of Hate,* p. 407; Bergeron, vol. 9, pp. 370–72; "City News," *National Daily Intelligencer,* Jan. 27, 1866, p. 3; "Local News: The Pardon Brokerage Case," *Washington Star,* Jan. 27, 1866.

424   *given her:* Baker, *History of the United States Secret Service,* pp. 595–96; Mogelever, pp. 393–96; Bergeron, vol. 9, pp. 370–72; "City News," *National Daily Intelligencer,* Jan. 25, 1866, p. 3; *Washington Star,* Jan. 25, 1866; Bergeron, vol. 9, pp. 370–72; Baker, *History of the United States Secret Service,* pp. 593–95, 612–17; "City News," *National Daily Intelligencer,* Jan. 25, 1866, p. 3; *Washington Star,* Jan. 25, 1866.

424   *Mrs. Cobb:* Baker, *History of the United States Secret Service,* pp. 596–98; *Impeachment Investigation,* p. 10.

424   *her entry:* Mogelever, pp. 396–97; Baker, *History of the United States Secret Service,* pp. 599, 603–4; *Impeachment Investigation,* p. 11.

424   *virtuous woman: Impeachment Investigation,* pp. 10–11; Baker, *History of the*

United States Secret Service, pp. 605–6; Mogelever, pp. 397–98; Bergeron, vol. 9, pp. 370–72.

424   *from her:* Baker, *History of the United States Secret Service*, pp. 599, 684; Mogelever, pp. 399–400; "City News: Trial of Baker, the Detective," *National Daily Intelligencer*, Feb. 2, 1866, p. 3; District of Columbia grand jury indictment documents for LB, B: 9 Files 1863–1934 and B: 10 Files 2925–29, RG21, LB note on his bail of $5,000, 1866, R: 237, M473, RG107, NA.

425   *thirty dollars:* Baker, *History of the United States Secret Service*, pp. 611, 627, 630, 690–91; *Impeachment Investigation*, p. 355; Bergeron, vol. 9, pp. 370–72; "City News: Trial of Baker, the Detective," *National Daily Intelligencer*, Feb. 2, 1866, p. 3; "City News," *National Daily Intelligencer*, Jan. 25, 1866, p. 3; "The Case of Gen. L. C. Baker," *Washington Star*, Jan. 25, 1866; "City News," *National Daily Intelligencer*, Jan. 27, 1866, p. 3; "Local News: The Pardon Brokerage Case," *Washington Star*, Jan. 27, 1866; "City News," *National Daily Intelligencer*, Jan. 26, 1866, p. 3; "Local News: The Pardon Brokerage Case," *Washington Star*, Jan. 26, 1866; "Local News: The Trial of Gen. L. C. Baker," *Washington Star*, Jan. 29, 1866; "City News: Trial of L. C. Baker, the Detective," *National Daily Intelligencer*, Jan. 30, 1866, p. 3; "The Trial of Gen. Baker," *Washington Star*, Jan. 30, 1866; "City News: Trial of L. C. Baker, the Detective," *National Daily Intelligencer*, Jan. 31, 1866, p. 3; "Local News: The Case of Gen. Baker," *Washington Star*, Jan. 31, 1866; "City News: Trial of L. C. Baker, the Detective," *National Daily Intelligencer*, Feb. 1, 1866, p. 3; "Local News: The Pardon Brokerage Case," *Washington Star*, Feb. 1, 1866; Criminal Docket, vol. 3, 2261–3463, Baker Trial Entry Case no. 2925.6, Entry 37, RG21, NA.

426   *Pennsylvania Avenue shuttered:* Memo to EMS on general officers mustered out of service, Dec. 14, 1865, pp. 574–76, vol. 2, RG108, NA; Chronological Record on L. C. Baker Service, BP; Baker, *History of the United States Secret Service*, pp. 607–8, 684–85; Mogelever, pp. 414–15.

426   *his savings:* Notes to J. M., July 6, 1959, BP; Baker, *History of the United States Secret Service*, p. 609; Mogelever notes on LB building a hotel, BP; *Washington Star* report on LB wealth after leaving Washington, BP; Mogelever, p. 416; *Impeachment Investigation*, pp. 469, 479.

426   *had reneged:* Corson, p. 581; Orrmont, pp. 181–83; *Impeachment Investigation*, p. 452; Fishel, *The Secret War for the Union*, p. 25; Davis, "Companions of Crisis," p. 387; Stern, p. 65.

426   *first day:* Horan, *The Pinkertons*, pp. 156–57; Milton, *The Age of Hate*, pp. 411, 732.

427   *final bombshell: Impeachment Investigation*, pp. iii–vi, 1–4, 6–9, 13–14, 32,

1191; Cottrell, p. 199; Kauffman, *American Brutus*, p. 380; Hanchett, "Booth's Diary," p. 44; Milton, *The Age of Hate*, pp. 406–7.

427 *assassination conspirators:* Hanchett, "Booth's Diary," p. 59; Davis, "Behind the Lines: Caveat Emptor," p. 34; Bryan, p. 302; *Impeachment Investigation*, pp. 32–33, 458–59; Hanchett, *The Lincoln Murder Conspiracies*, pp. 83–84.

428 *him up: Congressional Globe*, 40th Congress, 1st Session, pp. 18–19, 262–64; Hanchett, "Booth's Diary," p. 44; Milton, *The Age of Hate*, pp. 410–11; Steers, *Lincoln Legends*, pp. 185–86; Fowler, "Was Stanton Behind Lincoln's Murder?," p. 7; Hanchett, *The Lincoln Murder Conspiracies*, p. 245; Hageman, pp. 7, 9, 17, 19; Axelrod, p. 282; Hatch, pp. 163–64.

428 *Baker's book:* Bureau of Investigation director letter, Jan. 10, 1923, Irving C. Root letter, Nov. 2, 1948, Report of the FBI Laboratory RE: John Wilkes Booth, Nov. 30, 1948, William D. Ruckelshaus letter, May 30, 1973, Letter to Clarence Kelly, May 19, 1977, photocopy of Booth diary cover, Memo to Robert T. Keyy on Lincoln assassination, Aug. 3, 1977, FBI FOIA on John Wilkes Booth; *Impeachment Investigation*, pp. 2–4, 6–8, 371–72, 449–52, 678–79; Steers, *Lincoln Legends*, pp. 186–88; Hanchett, "Booth's Diary," pp. 40–41, 43.

428 *"dog" afterward: Impeachment Investigation*, pp. 285–87, 308–12, 323–25, 330, 408, 484–85, 761–62; Hanchett, "Booth's Diary," pp. 53, 56.

429 *"American people":* Eicher, p. 829; *Impeachment of the President*, pp. 1, 59, 104–5, 110–11.

429 *Lincoln assassination:* Orrmont, pp. 183–84; Mogelever, pp. 416, 418; *American Brutus*, p. 382; Millard, p. 1; Hageman, pp. 11, 19–20; "Lafayette Baker," *American Civil War Story*, p. 4; Millard, p. 1; Davis, "Behind the Lines," pp. 26, 28; "Obituary: General Lafayette C. Baker," *(Philadelphia) Daily Evening Telegraph*, July 3, 1868, p. 4; *(New York) World*, obituary on LB, July 4, 1868, BP.

429 *wife, Jennie:* Will for Lafayette Baker, Philadelphia Register of Wills, 1868, no. 400; Mogelever, pp. 418–19; Mackay, p. 180.

430 *"the rogues":* "Death of a Remarkable Character," *(New York) Evening Post*, July 6, 1868.

430 *war secretary:* Sparks, *Inside Lincoln's Army*, pp. 498, 507–8; James Morice, "Organizational Learning in a Military Environment: George H. Sharpe and the Army of the Potomac," SGF, KS.

430 *escaped convicts:* JCB to MP, June 5, 1865, Memo to Capt. Babcock, June 13, 1865, Memo to JCB, Aug. 14, 1865, JCB to Maj. Gen. Turner, June 14, 1865, B: 6, E: 31, RG110, Albert Ordway telegram to JCB, Oct. 28, 1865, William Beckwith telegram to JCB, Aug. 1, 1865, B: 1, E: 36, RG110, NA; Sparks, "General Patrick's Progress," p. 383; Sparks, *Inside Lincoln's Army*, p. 489; JM

memos to Lt. Col. Ordway, June 23, 24, and July 15, 1865, OR-S2.8:667, 671–72, 706–7.

430   *his diary:* Sparks, "General Patrick's Progress," p. 383; Sparks, *Inside Lincoln's Army,* pp. 498–99, 507.

431   *provost marshal post:* Sparks, *Inside Lincoln's Army,* pp. 12, 19, 489, 512–13.

431   *the volunteers:* Headquarters of the Army, Adjutant General's Office, Special Order no. 276, June 3, 1865, OR-46.3:1250; Van Santvoord, p. 235.

431   *the funeral:* Exhibit of GS sword in Kingston Senate House Museum, KS; Van Santvoord, pp. 194–98; *Proceedings of the Ulster County Historical Society 1936–1937,* p. 36.

432   *as prisoners:* "Gen. Sharpe Dead," news article, SGF, KS; Van Santvoord, pp. 202–6, 215–19; Sharpe, "Memorial Address," pp. 2–3; Lester and Hoag, p. 16; Markle, p. 15; Fishel, "The Mythology of Civil War Intelligence," p. 357; Sparks, "General Patrick's Progress," p. 384.

432   *a history:* George Sharpe's son to JCB, July 7, 1904, JCBP, LC; "Last Hours of the Confederacy," *New York Times,* Jan. 21, 1876; *Proceedings of the Ulster County Historical Society 1936–1937,* pp. 45–46.

432   *Kingston society:* "Gen. Sharpe Dead," news article, SGF, KS; GS to Benson Lossing, Aug. 2, 1877, B: 3, BL, HL; *Proceedings of the Ulster County Historical Society 1936–1937,* p. 45; Tsouras, p. 5.

433   *for trial:* GS report to WHS on the assassination of the president, Dec. 17, 1867, 40th Congress, 2nd Session, Exec. Doc. 68; GS letters to Thomas H. Dudley, March 18 and April 7, 1867, B: 33, TD, HL; Hatch, p. 159; *Impeachment Investigation,* pp. 375–76; *Proceedings of the Ulster County Historical Society 1936–1937,* p. 40.

433   *"have succeeded":* GS report to WHS on the assassination of the president, Dec. 17, 1867, 40th Congress, 2nd Session, Exec. Doc. 68; GS to Uncle, May 15, 1867, SLH, KS.

433   *diplomatic posting:* GS report to WHS on the assassination of the president, Dec. 17, 1867, 40th Congress, 2nd Session, Exec. Doc. 68; Fishel notes on Sharpe trip to Vermont, B: 3, EF, GU; "General Sharpe," *Journal,* April 7, 1869, MA, KS.

434   *scientific farming:* Levi P. Luckey to GS, Oct. 22, 1875, and O. E. Babcock to GS, Oct. 27, 1875, vol. 3, pp. 20 and 23, R: 14, GS to James McKean, Oct. 6, 1870, vol. 5, p. 26, R: 4, USGP, LC; *Proceedings of the Ulster County Historical Society 1936–1937,* pp. 40–41, 46; Sparks, *Inside Lincoln's Army,* p. 518; Tsouras, p. 391.

434   *in 1899:* Fishel, *The Secret War for the Union,* pp. 557–58; "About General

Sharpe," *Weekly Leader*, March 25, 1887, "A Republican Attack on Gen. Sharpe," *(New York) Sun* undated news article, "Tribute to Gen. Sharpe," *Kingston Daily Freeman*, Feb. 12, 1900, "Sharpe Resigns at Appraiser," February 1899 article, MA, KS; GS letter, March 9, 1889, GSF, NYH; GS to James Eldridge, July 7, 1894, B: 54, JE, HL; "Gen. G. H. Sharpe Dead," *New York Times*, Jan. 15, 1900; *Proceedings of the Ulster County Historical Society 1936–1937*, pp. 41–45.

434   *of her:* "In memory of General George H. Sharpe," *Christian Intelligencer*, March 14, 1900, MA, KS; news clip on George Sharpe presentation of bronze statue for his wife, SGF, KS; Tsouras, p. 442.

434   *years later:* "Obituary: General M. R. Patrick," *Cincinnati Commercial Gazette*, July 28, 1888, p. 2; Gates, pp. 196–97; Sparks, *Inside Lincoln's Army*, p. 518.

435   *an architect:* Theodore Lyman to JCB, March 24, 1876, William Pinkerton to JCB, Sept. 10, 1903, GS letters to JCB, Aug. 21, Nov. 8, and Nov. 11, 1905, B: 4, EF, GU.

435   *in 1908:* GS letters to JCB, June 10, Nov. 14, 1905, B: 4, EF, GU; "Famous War Scout Dies at His Home on East Fourth Street," *Mount Vernon Daily Argus*, Nov. 20, 1908, p. 1; Fishel, *The Secret War for the Union*, p. 558.

435   *his bedside:* "Death of General George H. Sharpe," *Kingston Daily Leader*, Jan. 15, 1900; Tsouras, p. 442.

435   *"his heart":* "Funeral of Gen. Sharpe," *Daily Freeman*, Jan. 16, 1900, MA, KS.

435   *still alive:* "Funeral of Gen. Sharpe," *Daily Freeman*, Jan. 16, 1900, MA, KS; Lester and Hoag, pp. 5, 7–8, 21; "Sharpe Memorial Site Selected," Kingston news article, MA, KS; "Picture of General Sharpe," *Kingston Weekly Leader*, Nov. 28, 1903; Tsouras, p. 444.

436   *"Witch, witch!":* John P. Reynolds biographical sketch of EVL, Letter to E. J. Carpenter, April 2, 1901, R: 14, EVLP, LVA; Ryan, *A Yankee Spy in Richmond*, pp. 20–21; "To Northern Democrats: An Appeal, Which Should Not Go Unheeded," news article, EVLP, NY; Varon, *Southern Lady, Yankee Spy*, p. 209; W. Randolph Van Lew, p. 4; Benjamin Butler to EVL, Jan. 14, 1867, EVL album, VHS; Wise letter Accession #25648, WFL, LVA; J. Staunton Moore to William Beymer, Dec. 2, 1910, B: 2K394, WBP, UTA; "The Van Lew a Nephew Knew," *Richmond Times-Dispatch*, Sept. 23, 1937, p. 10.

436   *totaled $5,000:* Lancaster, p. 122; Varon, *Southern Lady, Yankee Spy*, pp. 200–202; "Miss Van Lew's Spies in the Davis Household," *Richmond Evening Journal*, May 2, 1908, p. 8; W. Randolph Van Lew, p. 4; Ryan, *A Yankee Spy in Richmond*, pp. 21–22.

436   *Oliver Wendell Holmes Jr.:* John Albree speeches on Elizabeth Van Lew,

B: 1, ELC, WM; "The Van Lew a Nephew Knew," *Richmond Times-Dispatch*, Sept. 23, 1937, p. 10; "Van Lew Relics Bring $1,000," *Boston Herald*, Nov. 22, 1900.

437 *federal inmates:* "The Van Lew a Nephew Knew," *Richmond Times-Dispatch*, Sept. 23, 1937, p. 10; Smith, *Between the Lines*, pp. 324–26; *Elizabeth and John Van Lew v. James Duke*, Richmond Chancery Court case ending file 15, 1869, Richmond Clerk of Circuit Court.

437 *burned them:* Ryan, *A Yankee Spy in Richmond*, p. 133; Varon, *Southern Lady, Yankee Spy*, pp. 204–6; Record and Pension Office note to Edmund J. Carpenter, March 21, 1901, R: 14, EVLP, LVA.

438 *"prove much":* Leveen, "Mary Richards Bowser (fl. 1846–1867)"; Leveen, "The Spy Photo That Fooled NPR, the U.S. Army Intelligence Center, and Me"; "Miss Richmonia Richards's Lecture," *New York Tribune*, Sept. 12, 1865, p. 2; Mary Richards to Superintendent Board of Education Freedmen, Feb. 22, 1867, Mary Richards letters to Eberhart, March 10, April 1 and 7, and June 1, 1867, R: 8, M799, NA; "The Irrepressible Conflict Renewed: Addresses by a Colored Lady and Henry Ward Beecher," *Brooklyn Eagle*, Sept. 25, 1865.

438 *she said:* Fishel notes on GS and EVL, pp. 5–15, B: 3, EF, GU; Benjamin Butler to EVL, April 8, 1883, B: 1, ELC, WM; Varon, *Southern Lady, Yankee Spy*, pp. 206–9; Ryan, *A Yankee Spy in Richmond*, p. 19.

438 *was fair:* Fishel notes on GS and EVL, pp. 5–15, B: 3, EF, GU; F. W. E. Lohmann postwar payment claim for $15,975, F. W. E. Lohmann letter, June 20, 1868, Acting Assistant Secretary of War Kellogg letter, March 30, 1866, B: 26, 976–2206, RG107, T. E. Foster to LB, Dec. 13, 1865, LB to EMS, Dec. 18, 1865, JM statement on William Rowley, Jan. 6, 1866, William Rowley petition for $1,850, B: 6, E: 95, RG110, Secret Service fund quarter ending March 31, 1866, B: 6, E: 179A, RG94, NA; Varon, *Southern Lady, Yankee Spy*, p. 204.

439 *age fifty-four:* Fishel notes on GS and EVL, pp. 5–15, 20, B: 3, EF, GU; Committee on Claims report for the petition of F. W. E. Lohmann, Walter H. Ruth, and Charles M. Carter, B: 23, RG46, F. W. E. Lohmann and Samuel Ruth statement to EMS, Jan. 12, 1866, B: 26, 976–2206, RG107, Samuel Ruth letter, April 25, 1865, B: 6, E: 1515, RG92, NA; Johnston, pp. 423–24; Castel, pp. 43–44; Stuart, "Of Spies and Borrowed Names," p. 319.

439 *Rebel prisons:* Varon, *Southern Lady, Yankee Spy*, pp. 216–19; Chernow, p. 751.

439 *"running riot":* John Reynolds to William Beymer, Dec. 26, 1910, B: 2K394, WBP, UTA; Alexander Rives to Dr. Gilmer, Jan. 31, 1870, MSSIG4215a 59–62, GG, VJS; "Miss Van Lew and Post Office Troubles," *Petersburg Index*,

June 5, 1869, p. 2; Beymer, *On Hazardous Service*, p. 97; Varon, *Southern Lady, Yankee Spy*, pp. 219–22, 225–27; "Miss Van Lew at Richmond," news article, EVLP, NY.

440 *Post Office:* Varon, *Southern Lady, Yankee Spy*, p. 224; W. C. Wickham to EVL, Feb. 24, 1877, R: 14, EVLP, NY.

440 *"nigger funeral":* "Deaths," *(Richmond) Daily Dispatch*, Sept. 15, 1875; "To Northern Democrats: An Appeal, Which Should Not Go Unheeded," news article, EVLP, NY; Varon, *Southern Lady, Yankee Spy*, p. 230.

440 *Confederate colonel:* "Miss Van Lew's Spies in the Davis Household," *Richmond Evening Journal*, May 2, 1908, p. 8; Varon, *Southern Lady, Yankee Spy*, pp. 229, 231, 235–37; Ryan, *A Yankee Spy in Richmond*, pp. 122–23.

440 *in 1887:* Chief Clerk to John Albree, April 17, 1905, B: 1, ELC, WM; "The Richmond Spy," *(Richmond) Daily Dispatch*, July 17, 1883, p. 1; Varon, *Southern Lady, Yankee Spy*, pp. 238–41.

441 *"for me":* Ryan, *A Yankee Spy in Richmond*, pp. 21, 131–32; Varon, *Southern Lady, Yankee Spy*, p. 244.

441 *annual allotments:* "Funeral of Miss Van Lew," Sept. 25, 1900, news article, "Miss Van Lew Dead," Richmond news article, "Crazy Bet," news article, EVLP, NY; Varon, *Southern Lady, Yankee Spy*, pp. 246–48; Ryan, *A Yankee Spy in Richmond*, pp. 21, 130–31; "The Story of 'Crazy Van Lew,'" *Boston Evening Transcript*, Sept. 26, 1900; John Reynolds to William Beymer, Dec. 6, 1910, B: 2K394, WBP, UTA.

441 *the diary:* Ryan, *A Yankee Spy in Richmond*, pp. 21; John Reynolds letters to William Beymer, Dec. 6 and 14, 1910, B: 2K394, WBP, UTA; Varon, *Southern Lady, Yankee Spy*, p. 3.

441 *prominent Unionists:* Postwar photo of an elderly EVL, B: 2, ELC, WM; note by Henrietta R. Winfrey, June 18, 1864, Elizabeth Louisa Van Lew, MSS7: 1V3255:1, VHS; Varon, *Southern Lady, Yankee Spy*, pp. 4, 242, 250–51; Bart Hall, Nov. 2, 2016; "Miss Van Lew's Spies in the Davis Household," *Richmond Evening Journal*, May 2, 1908, p. 8; "Miss Van Lew Dead," Richmond news article, EVLP, NY.

442 *a manuscript:* John Reynolds to William Beymer, Dec. 14, 1910, B: 2K394, WBP, UTA.

442 *with Grant:* John Reynolds to William Beymer, Dec. 14, 1910, B: 2K394, WBP, UTA; John Albree speeches on Elizabeth Van Lew, B: 1, ELC, WM; Ryan, *A Yankee Spy in Richmond*, p. 22; Varon, *Southern Lady, Yankee Spy*, pp. 250–51.

442 *a flake:* "Miss Van Lew Dead," Richmond news article, EVLP, NY; Varon,

Southern Lady, Yankee Spy, pp. 251–53; "Miss Van Lew's Spies in the Davis Household," *Richmond Evening Journal,* May 2, 1908, p. 8; Ryan, *A Yankee Spy in Richmond,* pp. 3, 22.

443   *Union prisoners:* John Albree speeches on Elizabeth Van Lew, B: 1, ELC, WM; EVL will, Will Book 7, pp. 419–21, Chancery Court of the City of Richmond; Estate appraisal for EVL after her death, Accounts of Fiduciaries, No. 104, City of Richmond Chancery Court, LVA; note by Henrietta R. Winfrey, June 18, 1864, Elizabeth Louisa Van Lew, MSS7: 1V3255:1, VHS; "Van Lew Relics Bring $1,000," *Boston Herald,* Nov. 22, 1900.

443   *Lincoln's spies:* "Miss Van Lew's Spies in the Davis Household," *Richmond Evening Journal,* May 2, 1908, p. 8; Ryan, *A Yankee Spy in Richmond,* p. 22; "Honors Miss Van Lew," *Richmond Dispatch,* July 29, 1920, EVLP, NY; EVL gravestone from her Massachusetts friends, B: 2, ELC, WM.

INDEX

PHOTO CREDITS

ABOUT THE AUTHOR

A former correspondent for *Newsweek* and *Time*, Douglas Waller reported on the CIA for six years. Waller also covered the Pentagon, State Department, White House, and Congress. Before reporting for *Newsweek* and *Time*, he served eight years as a legislative assistant on the staffs of Representative Edward J. Markey and Senator William Proxmire. Waller is the author of the bestsellers *Wild Bill Donovan: The Spymaster Who Created the OSS and Modern American Espionage*; *Big Red: The Three-Month Voyage of a Trident Nuclear Submarine*; and *The Commandos: The Inside Story of America's Secret Soldiers*. He is also the author of the critically acclaimed *Disciples: The World War II Missions of the CIA Directors Who Fought for Wild Bill Donovan* and *A Question of Loyalty: Gen. Billy Mitchell and the Court-Martial That Gripped the Nation*. He lives in Raleigh, North Carolina, with his wife, Judy.